JUVENILE JUSTICE
Policies, Practices, and Programs

By
H. Ted Rubin, J.D., M.S.W.

CRI
Civic Research Institute
4478 U.S. Route 27 • P.O. Box 585 • Kingston, NJ 08528

Printed in the United States of America

Library of Congress Cataloging in Publication Data
Juvenile Justice: Policies, Practices, and Programs/H. Ted Rubin, J.D., M.S.W.

ISBN 1-887554-33-5
Library of Congress Control Number 2003103107

Dedication

To my love, Bunny, and our countless chapters
And to our progeny …
Marjorie, with Art
Steven, with Dana
And our eternal Jefferson.
Also to our grandchildren …
Ariana, Shoshana, and Anjelica

And to all those who have helped me
illuminate what is just and possible

About the Author

H. Ted Rubin became a private consultant to juvenile/family court and justice agencies in August 1992. As a consultant, he is employed by governmental and private associations to conduct research studies, provide direction on policy issues, help implement organizational or programmatic changes, assist with demonstration projects, and make presentations to conferences. His clients include state and local court systems, national and state juvenile delinquency agencies, legal organizations seeking to improve court handling of child abuse and neglect proceedings, foundations, and national court and Native American organizations.

From January 1971 until August 1992, Mr. Rubin served as Director for Juvenile/Criminal Justice and then Senior Staff Attorney for the Institute for Court Management (ICM) of the National Center for State Courts, Denver. There, he directed ICM's juvenile justice training program (89 national workshops) and participated in a wide variety of court and justice agency studies (more than 150). He served as director for the Civil Jurisdiction of Tribal Courts and State Courts: The Prevention and Resolution of Jurisdictional Disputes Project, 1989-1992, and as Co-Director for the Integration of Child and Family Legal Proceedings Project, 1990-1992. He was a principal in the national Restitution Education, Specialized Training, and Technical Assistance Project (RESTTA) (1984-1992), and a member of the Board of Directors of the Colorado Children's Trust Fund (1990-1997, and chair, 1995-1997). Mr. Rubin was honored in 1990 with the National Center for State Courts' Award of Excellence. He served as reporter for the volume on Court Organization and Administration, IJA-ABA Joint Commission on Juvenile Justice Standards.

Mr. Rubin was Judge of the Denver Juvenile Court (1965-1971), a Colorado state legislator (1961-1965), a lawyer in private practice in Denver (1957-1965), and earlier held social service positions in Denver and Chicago. He obtained his law degree from DePaul University, a master's degree in social work from Case Western Reserve University, and an A.B. degree (Phi Beta Kappa) from Pennsylvania State University. He served as Visiting Professor, School of Criminal Justice, State University of New York at Albany (1978), and primary American instructor for the American University Institute on Juvenile Justice in Great Britain and the United States, London (1982).

Mr. Rubin has written more than 250 articles and research reports concerned with juvenile justice and corrections, along with three books: *The Courts: Fulcrum of the Justice System* (Second Edition, Random House, 1984), *Juvenile Justice: Policy, Practice, and Law* (Second Edition, Random House, 1985), and *Behind the Black Robes: Juvenile Court Judges and the Court* (Sage, 1985). He was editor of *Juveniles in Justice: A Book of Readings* (Goodyear, 1980). Currently, he is an editorial board member and columnist for *Juvenile Justice Update*, and has served for 26 years as a board member of the Denver Area Youth Services. He served, recently, as a member of the Boulder County Jail Use Commission.

Introduction

The juvenile court was born in what historians term the Progressive Era, roughly the first two decades of the 20th Century. This was a time of reform when visionaries sought to reinvent government and make it work honestly, responsibly, and well. They provided strong support for clean elections, women's suffrage, public health protections, expanded welfare programs, more and better schools, controls on business, constraints on the labor of women and children, workplace safety and compensation for worker injuries, and juvenile courts. Adult courts and penal systems destroyed children, the visionaries proclaimed, and they were right. Children needed their own specialized consideration, they contended, and they were right.

EVOLUTION OF THE JUVENILE COURT

The founding of the first juvenile court, in Chicago in 1899, sent a revolutionary message that children were different and their needs, rather than what they had done, would become the spotlight of judicial attention. This event resounded across the United States. Within a little more than two decades, every state had legislated some form of a juvenile court and juvenile code. Other nations embraced this format.

However, there was a questioning of the efficacy of this enterprise, initiated in the 1920s by social workers and psychiatrists who contended juvenile courts failed to understand and treat the needs of the individual child. This was followed in the 1950s by law enforcement officials who used strongly deriding references to what they perceived as a court that was overly solicitous in understanding and treating children, and overly gentle with the sanctions it used. Attorneys, rarely welcomed in this setting, also questioned the juvenile court, because they found when they did participate that the court's informality and absence of legal regimen were disturbing, if not confounding.

Another development was the constitutionalization of this court, pronounced by the U.S. Supreme Court in 1967 **Gault (In re**, 387 U.S. 1 (1967)), which ushered legal safeguards, legal procedures, and lawyers into these halls, and forever changed the nature of juvenile court proceedings. The Court ruling responded to the earlier concerns of attorneys.

This was later followed by the exponentially increased removal of more serious or chronic juvenile offenders from juvenile to criminal courts that preceded, accompanied, and followed the grave juvenile violence wave that had rough bookends of 1987-1994. The expanded criminalization of juveniles was a response to the earlier concerns of law enforcement officials.

A recent trend, now transcending into a movement, combines juvenile cases with other family-related case types such as divorce and domestic violence, into some form of a "family court." The formats are varied, the technologies of case coordination are experimental, and the numbers of families and family members who might benefit from one family/one judge consistent case handling are now small, but definitely growing. Juvenile delinquency proceedings will be handled as before except more juveniles will be heard in tandem with other cases that involve family members, There will be greater continuity of ongoing hearings with the same judge, and judges will be informed of other proceedings that involve this family and, accordingly, make better informed dispositions. An improved judicial understanding and treatment of the needs of the child and family members is one form of response to the earlier concerns expressed by social workers and psychiatrists.

BENEFITS OF THE JUVENILE COURT

Early judges trumpeted the benefits of the new juvenile court: that the issue was not guilt or innocence but how the child had become this way and what might be done in his interest—which is in the state's interest—to enable a constructive and law abiding future. This court was not without sanctions, but its heavier duty, indeed its spirit, was to treat and rehabilitate. Successful cases were highlighted. Children were not only being helped, they were being "saved."

The juvenile court was born in optimism. There is strong reason to retain this optimism. There are very legitimate criticisms that can and should be leveled at deficiencies in juvenile court efficacy. Yet, most of its progressions should be seen as its pathway toward better meeting the needs of young people and of communities as times have changed and new eras have evolved.

Here are reasons that justify feelings of confidence about today's juvenile courts and the juvenile justice system of which the court is the centerpiece:

- There are very well trained professionals in this field—judges, probation officers and detention officials, prosecutors and defense counsel, court administrators and clerks, and those who work in community corrections and residential institutions. Training is ongoing.

- Alternatives to detention, substitutes for the pretrial lock-up of offending juveniles, are much more commonplace, and objective risk assessment instruments now lead to more skilled determinations of who must be locked up prior to court hearings.

- There is greater awareness that it is better to reserve costly residential programs for more serious and chronic offenders, and that working with juveniles in the community, and within their communities, is supportive of the ongoing expansion of community correctional dispositions and programming.

- Evaluation of the effectiveness of intervention programs is now much more common, and research findings increasingly find their way into policies, practices, and programs. Research-based risk screening instruments determine levels of supervision intensity so that resources can be differentially applied to meet the different risk levels of offenders.

- The principles of balanced and restorative justice—victim restoration, victim participation in the justice system, public safety protection, juvenile restoration of victims and the communities they injured, community participation in justice, and juvenile competency development—are in day-to-day use in countless juvenile courts and are embodied as objectives in numerous juvenile codes.

- There are barriers to juvenile court assertion of jurisdiction and significant limitations on judicial use of secure custody for status offenders (those who are truant, beyond the control of parents, run away, and demonstrate other conduct that is illegal only for children). These constraints allow the juvenile justice system to better allocate its resources to its two primary workloads: (1) juvenile delinquency and (2) child abuse and neglect.

- State juvenile correctional departments better classify and treat deeper-end juveniles. They have expanded their partnerships with local juvenile correctional entities to enable more juveniles to be held accountable and assisted at a pre-institutional, community level. Further, investment in more and better-targeted programming for those who reenter the community following institutional life is now evident.

- More states and communities are grappling with the problem of minority overrepresentation in the juvenile justice system.

CURRENT JUVENILE COURT ISSUES AND TRENDS

The juvenile court originated as a confidential entity. Enabling legislation protected those who came to court from public scrutiny. Their names and identities were kept secret, as disclosure was thought to negatively affect their welfare. Only very recently has this begun to change. It is changing because some offense or abuse situations are very serious and the public has, or particular members of the public have, an interest in knowing what is transpiring there. It is changing because, in not knowing what is happening, there is a certain distrust of private proceedings that take place in this courtroom.

The pages of this book reveal much of what is transpiring inside as well as next door to the court. They describe varied developments and diverse efforts to hone or at least improve the instruments of intervention with juvenile justice clients. They provide numerous profiles of how youths are handled and might better be handled in your town and mine, in your state and mine.

This book consists of 44 chapters, most originally published as articles in *Juvenile Justice Update* and *Community Corrections Report*, written by the author over a 10-year time span. They represent both focused observations on a facet of this world as well as descriptive commentaries of happenings in a state where the author was otherwise engaged in study and research. The chapters are complemented by commentaries that expand on their content and prescriptions. Numerous chapters have been updated by or with the assistance of professionals from the settings that have been profiled, or otherwise brought forward by the author. Chapters and commentaries concentrate on the juvenile delinquency workload of juvenile courts, though the other major workload, abused and neglected children, does receive consideration.

I have lived in the juvenile court world for most of the past four decades. I continue to state my positions on what is good, bad, or indifferent. My perspectives and standards derive from my work as a Colorado state legislator, as a Denver juvenile court judge, from research and consulting with countless juvenile and family courts and justice systems, as a participant in national juvenile justice reform endeavors, and through service on youth agency boards.

The positions I take have been impacted by graduate school insights in both social work and law, and my affection for the U.S. Bill of Rights, for the movements that have furthered civil rights and liberties for all, and with efforts to eliminate poverty and equalize justice and citizenship.

We do not now live in as progressive an era as a century ago, and punishment of juvenile offenders has greater currency. But there remains prominent today a rather vast interest in assisting young people. The world they experience is far more complex than that of a century ago, and juvenile courts must contend with the effects of what our young people are contending with and with what they do that is not positive. The juvenile court workload was never an easy one.

There should be a pervasive feeling of hopefulness about this creation, this complex entity that is constantly being more finely tuned. There are many positive indicators, certain forward momentum, and extensive public confirmation of the vital need for it to succeed with its mission. Rehabilitation of young people is preferred; it is better to redirect offenders while they are young.

In 1909 the English author G. K. Chesterton described a court scene through the eyes of a layman:

> And the horrible thing about all legal officials, even the best, about all judges, magistrates, barristers, detectives, and policemen, is not that they are wicked (some of them are good), not that they are stupid (some of them are quite intelligent); it is simply that they have gotten used to it. Strictly they do not see the prisoner in the dock; all they see is the usual man in the usual place. They do not see the awful court of judgement; they see only their own workshop.[1]

This remains one of my concerns as to juvenile courts and the juvenile justice system today. We have ever better trained judges and lawyers and probation officers and juvenile agency personnel who want to do a good job. But yes, even good people are subject to seeing only the usual person in their own workshop.

Let us not let them get too used to it.

—H. Ted Rubin

Endnotes

[1] Chesterton, G. K. (1909). *Tremendous trifles*. London: Methuen, p. 68.

Table of Contents

About the Author v
Introduction vii

Part 1: The Doorway of the Juvenile Court P1-1

Chapter 1: The Pioneering Vision of Judge Ben B. Lindsey,
Denver's Juvenile Court Judge, 1901–27 1-1

Chapter 2: The Constitutionalization of the Juvenile Court
Adjudicatory Process: The Case of Gerald Gault 2-1

Chapter 3: Keep Them in Juvenile Court 3-1

Chapter 4: Juvenile and Family Courts' Increasing Role in
Child Abuse and Neglect Cases 4-1

Chapter 5: The Other World of the Juvenile Court:
Reforming Child Abuse and Neglect Proceedings 5-1

Chapter 6: Collaboration to Speed Court Process and
Curb Foster Care Drift in California 6-1

Chapter 7: Revisiting Status Offenders 7-1

Chapter 8: What Is a Juvenile Court? On the Function of the
Court as Disciplinarian for Non-Dangerous School Offenses 8-1

Chapter 9: A Community Imperative: Curbing Minority
Overrepresentation in the Juvenile Justice System 9-1

Chapter 10: Judges Encourage Greater Role for
Crime Victims in Juvenile Court 10-1

Part 2: The Handling of Offenders: The Legal Side P2-1

Chapter 11: New Mexico's Revised Children's Code 11-1

Chapter 12: North Carolina Enacts Major Juvenile Code
Revisions: All Delinquency Cases Continue to Be
Initiated in Juvenile Court 12-1

Chapter 13: The Juvenile Court Judge's Role: Planting Good Seeds 13-1

Chapter 14: Prosecutors in Juvenile Court 14-1

Chapter 15: The Role of Defense Attorneys in
Juvenile Justice Proceedings 15-1

Chapter 16: Judges and Probation Officers:
Improving the Working Relationship 16-1

Part 3: The Handling of Offenders:
Apprehension Through Disposition P3-1

Chapter 17: Dejailing and Rejailing Juveniles 17-1

Chapter 18: Reflections on Pretrial Detention 18-1

Chapter 19: The Ins and Outs of Detention: Sacramento
        Addresses Detention Center Overcrowding 19-1

Chapter 20: Diversion to the Community: Neighborhood Accountability
        Boards in Santa Clara County, California 20-1

Chapter 21: Improving Juvenile Delinquent Case Flow 21-1

Chapter 22: Thoughts on Improving Juvenile Court Dispositions 22-1

Part 4: Community Intervention Programs P4-1

Chapter 23: Transformation: A New Start for Juvenile Probation in Atlanta 23-1

Chapter 24: School-Based Probation Officers in Pittsburgh:
        A New and Different School-Juvenile Court Partnership 24-1

Chapter 25: A New Probation Opry in Nashville:
        Decentralization Strikes a Positive Chord 25-1

Chapter 26: Dakota County, Minnesota: Repairing Harm
        and Holding Juveniles Accountable 26-1

Chapter 27: Let's Do More With Monetary Restitution and
        Community Work Service 27-1

Chapter 28: Youth Restitution Program Achieving Juvenile
        Accountability in Madison, Wisconsin 28-1

Chapter 29: Work Crews Working: Montana Project
        Uses Community Service to Build Skills 29-1

Chapter 30: Youth Passages: Enriched Community-Based
        Intervention With High-Risk, Mid-Range Offenders 30-1

Chapter 31: How Santa Cruz County's GROW Program
        Uses Interdisciplinary Teams to Curb Out-of-Home Placements 31-1

Chapter 32: IMPACTing Detention and Commitment: Multi-Agency
        Collaboration Serves Juveniles With Multi-System Needs in
        Boulder County, Colorado 32-1

Chapter 33: Zero Commitments to the State: The Commitment to
        Community-Based Intervention in Delaware County, Ohio 33-1

Part 5: Beyond the Community: State Institutions and Aftercare......................... P5-1

Chapter 34: Teen Quest: Female-Specific Program Services for
    Colorado's Delinquent Girls 34-1

Chapter 35: Tallulah: Lessons From Louisiana 35-1

Chapter 36: Georgia Department of Juvenile Justice Moves
    Forward by Moving Back to the Community 36-1

Chapter 37: RECLAIM Ohio: Funding Formula Bolsters
    Development of Community-Based Alternatives While
    Reducing Commitments to the State 37-1

Chapter 38: Taking More Care With Juvenile Aftercare 38-1

Part 6: The Juvenile Court of the Future P6-1

Chapter 39: Should Juvenile Courts Become Family Courts? 39-1

Chapter 40: The Future of the Juvenile Court 40-1

Chapter 41: Getting Serious about the Coordination of
    Family-Related Cases: Family Court Operation in Bend, Oregon 41-1

Part 7: Juvenile Justice in Other Worlds P7-1

Chapter 42: Visiting Native American Juvenile Justice 42-1

Chapter 43: Peacemaking: From Conflict to Harmony in the
    Navajo Tradition 43-1

Chapter 44: El Salvador Initiates a Juvenile Court 44-1

Postscript PS-1

Index I-1

Part 1

The Doorway of the Juvenile Court

Who *may* enter the doorway of the juvenile court is one concept. Who *does* enter the doorway is another. State legislatures define who is eligible for juvenile court handling. Officials who work in the probation office or with key collaborative agencies such as the prosecutor's office or the public child protection agency determine whether eligible cases shall be brought through this doorway.

For example, an 11-year-old apprehended for a first, minor law violation is eligible for formal court handling, but officials likely will prefer to send him home with only a warning, or require only that he or a parent provide restitution to any victim of the offense. The public child protection agency, in evaluating a case of child neglect, may conclude that though neglect can be lawfully established, prospects for voluntary cooperation by the parents are promising and there is sufficient relative and community support to allow the agency to avert filing a court petition at this time.

The two types of case situations just described, which involve juvenile delinquency and child neglect (a category which itself includes cases of child abuse or dependency), have been the primary workloads of the juvenile court since its founding in 1899 in Chicago. It needs to be kept in mind, however, that many juveniles commit offenses and are not caught, and that numerous juveniles who are apprehended are not processed formally before the court. Similarly, far more children are abused, neglected, or dependent than come to official attention, and many less severe cases that do come to this attention are handled other than by formal court process.

JURISDICTIONAL AGE FOR DELINQUENT ACTS

Many who become interested in juvenile justice or in working with a juvenile court are dumbfounded when they learn there is no single maximum age for juvenile courts that applies uniformly in all 50 states. It is the 50 state legislatures, not the U.S. Congress, that define age maximums for the purpose of determining juvenile court (as opposed to adult criminal court) jurisdictional authority. Since legislative thinking is idiosyncratic and influenced by particular legislative or political or in-state cultures or history, states do vary in this and other guidelines for a juvenile court.

The initial Illinois Act listed age in several contexts. The first juvenile court's delinquency jurisdiction was restricted to children under the age of 16 (later amended to allow jurisdiction for those under age 17, the current standard). Boys less than 10-years-old could not be committed to the state reformatory, and girls under 10-years-old could not be committed to the "State Home for Juvenile Female Offenders." Further, children under 12 could not be committed to a jail.[1] This founding act sought to govern not only who might be subject to this court's authority but also the particular authority the court might exercise.

Today the most prevalent maximum age for delinquency violations is one's 18th birthday. This maximum has been the common denominator of various model juvenile court acts and commissions that have promoted national juvenile justice standards.[2] However, 10 states—Georgia, Illinois, Louisiana, Massachusetts, Michigan, Missouri, New Hampshire, South Carolina, Texas, and Wisconsin—draw this line at one's 17th birthday, and Connecticut, New York, and North Carolina end one's childhood for this purpose on one's 16th birthday. Several states provide minimum ages for the juvenile court's exercise of its delinquency jurisdiction (e.g., such as Colorado and Wisconsin, 10-years-old; New York, 7-years-old; and North Carolina, 6-years-old).

However, the legislatively set maximum age is no longer relevant to a significant number of more serious offenses that are committed today by juveniles under the maximum age. All but a few legislatures have redirected particularized youthful offenders to criminal court handling and authorize, for many, very lengthy incarceration terms. While few would argue that a juvenile justice system should exclusively handle all serious or violent juvenile offenders, I, along with many others, object to the sweep of these criminalization laws and believe that the juvenile justice system could handle many of these juveniles more effectively and achieve better results than the criminal justice system. Research evidence to this effect is cited in the following sections.

DELINQUENCY JURISDICTION AND USE OF WAIVERS

Juvenile delinquency is generally defined as the violation of a state, municipal, or federal law, which, if committed by an adult, would constitute a crime. The juvenile court's delinquency jurisdiction operates in some form of combination with local criminal courts. Until a decade or so ago, the primary route for transfer of a juvenile to a criminal court was through and following a specialized juvenile court hearing known variously as waiver, transfer, amenability, or decline. State statutes that were enacted following the U.S. Supreme Court's decision in **Kent v. United States**, 383 U.S. 541 (1966), the High Court's first formal opinion in review of a delinquency proceeding, provided guidelines for conducting this hearing and criteria for measuring amenability. This procedure offered the advantage of a determination by a juvenile court judge as to whether the juvenile appeared capable of achieving rehabilitation within the facilities, services, and institutional time frame available to the court.

The juvenile court judge had the benefit of a report on an investigation of the youth prepared by a probation officer, and, often, a psychological evaluation. The particular judge also may have heard earlier cases that involved this youth and previously ordered stratagems to help assist the youth's rehabilitation within the community. The waiver or transfer hearing was the "escape valve" for the juvenile court. As a quasi-guardian for all juveniles, the juvenile court could defray criticism that it was too soft on juvenile offenders by using its authority to shift certain offenders to criminal courts

Nonetheless, the offense records of numerous juveniles transferred by juvenile court judges were not always serious ones. Many records reflected a series of offenses, but often only repetitive property offenses. These juvenile court judges had given up on these youths. Their interventions and warnings had not led to conformity with the law. I and others were critical that more imaginative and holistic interventions were not used to curb many of these transfers. Nonviolent offenders comprised 66% of juveniles waived from a juvenile court to a criminal court in 1992.[3] Further, many transferred juveniles received only a probation sanction following a criminal court adjudication. Juvenile court transfers to criminal court handling peaked nationally in 1994 with the transfer of 12,100 cases of the 1,000,300 cases filed formally in juvenile courts that year.[4]

Increased authorizations for criminal court handling of juveniles actually began in the late 1970s and accelerated during the following two decades. The juvenile violent crime arrest rate jumped dramatically beginning in 1989, and surged annually until 1994. Juvenile homicide arrest rates doubled between 1987 and 1993 and juveniles experienced comparable increases with aggravated assaults.[5] The media continuously and graphically depicted and described juvenile violence. Prosecutors and police officials called juvenile courts the incorrect forum for handling juvenile violence. Political officials and candidates made juvenile justice reform a hot-button item and enacted a wave of new laws that criminalized juveniles who allegedly committed serious and violent offenses.

This criminalization stratagem, of course, was meant to enlarge juvenile accountability, expand punishments, and protect public safety through longer-term incapacitation of offenders. Some of this was necessary; some was not. Clearly the stratagem more greatly empowered prosecution and police officials. It retained the juvenile court's transfer authority, but only for less serious offenders.

Far too many young people, influenced by gang membership, drug use or sale, poverty, anomie, family breakdown, and other causative factors, have victimized each other or others with heinous crimes. Indeed, minors every day, somewhere, commit offenses that are major. The newly accepted conventional wisdom was to place these juveniles in adult courts and prisons. I, and many others, believe these measures went too far. One-dimensional decision making replaced individualization. The focus was on the offense, not the offender.

Studies that have compared reoffense rates of juveniles handled in criminal courts with similar juveniles retained in juvenile courts have found a greater number of reoffenses committed by the criminalized juveniles. There have been findings of more serious rearrest offenses and shorter time spans until rearrest. While the methodology for assessing comparative rearrest data continues to be refined, those who were handled in the criminal justice system appear, with a limited exception, to have fared less well, and have not attained the restorative goals set forth by advocates of the harder line.[6]

ABUSE/NEGLECT/DEPENDENCY JURISDICTION

In the abuse/neglect/dependency jurisdiction, the child is a victim, not an offender. Abuse refers to the physical, sexual, and/or emotional abuse of a child. Neglect is based on an absence of proper care due to the actions or omissions of the parents; this absence of proper care extends to a failure to provide education or medical care. Dependency refers to an absence of proper care through no fault of the parents. State statutes define these types of child cases in much greater detail than is encapsulated above.

The 1899 Illinois Act's definition was:

> ...dependent child and neglected child shall mean any child who for any reason is destitute or homeless or abandoned; or dependent upon the public for

support; or has not proper parental care or guardianship; or who habitually begs or receives alms; or who is found living in any house of ill fame or with any vicious or disreputable person; or whose home by reason of neglect, cruelty or depravity on the part of its parents, guardian or other person in whose care it may be, is an unfit place for such a child; and any child under the age of 8 years who is found peddling or selling any article or singing or playing any musical instrument upon the streets or giving any public entertainment. [7]

Absent from present-day statutes are references to begging and alms, living in a house of ill fame, and peddling or playing a musical instrument on the streets. Additions to today's statutes include provisions that specifically describe the different forms of abuse; incorporate a very broad provision such as "the child's environment is injurious to his or her welfare," an allegation frequently admitted to by parents in a bargained-down plea that they see as preferable to more stigmatizing allegations; and a child subject to sexual exploitation or prostitution.

The Wisconsin statute defines this child as a child in need of protection or services (CHIPS), but adds to the definition such juvenile misbehaviors as habitual truant or "habitually truant from home," matters more often included today in a separate status offense classification. A child under age 10 who commits a delinquent act is a CHIPS, as well. [8]

STATUS OFFENDERS

A status offense is a type of misbehavior best described as conduct illegal only for children. It has had a very interesting history in juvenile codes and juvenile court doorways. There are juvenile courts today that hold their doors wide open for this type of matter, while other juvenile court doorways allow little space for entry.

The three primary types of status offense have been running away, being incorrigible or beyond parental control, and habitual truancy. Other status offenses are curfew violation, tobacco use, and alcohol use. Adults who perform these same acts or have similar problems are not subject to court sanction. It is the status of childhood in combination with this misbehavior that may subject a child to court review.

The 1899 Illinois Act did not describe this type of youth, but status offense misbehaviors were added two years later and incorporated into the definition of a delinquent youth. Other states then proceeded to include and classify this misconduct as a delinquent offense.

Juvenile courts did little to differentiate the two types of delinquent youth—those who broke a law versus those who performed non-criminal misbehaviors—for 60 years or so. But status offenders became a passionate issue during the juvenile court legal evolution/revolution of the 1960s and 1970s. A consensus developed that status offenders should be separated out from the delinquency category. No consensus developed to the call by child advocates that juvenile courts should not intervene at all with these young people, that this just was not the law's business. In time, aided and abetted by the U.S. Juvenile Justice and Delinquency Prevention Act of 1974 (JJDPA), [9] a consensus developed that status offenders should not be locked up at the state institutional level, or at the local secure pretrial detention level except for perhaps 24 hours. State laws were enacted to parallel the federal provisions.

Everyone was well aware that irreverent juveniles would continue to violate society's norms and that some would endanger themselves when courts could not restrain their liberty. But many knew that court interventions and restraints of this liberty often had been ineffectual and many had gotten worse in our care.

Available data show a very real decline in the use of secure detention with status offenders. The estimated total detained in 1975 was 143,000, while the 1996 estimate was 39,100. In 1975 status offense cases were twice as likely as delinquency cases to involve secure detention between the time of referral to court and case disposition. By 1992 the likelihood that a status case would involve detention was less than half that for delinquency.[10]

The offense profile of detained status offenders for 1997[11] shows:

- Runaway, 40%;

- Incorrigibility, 22%;

- Truancy, 9%;

- Underage drinking, 8%;

- Curfew violation, 6%;

- Other, 15%.

Decriminalization and deinstitutionalization have gained large-scale acceptance and implementation, though one remains apprehensive that significant amendment to or repeal of the JJDPA could flip-flop some states back to harsher court handling of status offenders. The restraints remain the better policy. I strongly favor limiting the court's role with these youngsters and expanding community prevention and non-court-based intervention programs and services.

THE WORKLOAD OF JUVENILE COURTS

Case filings in state juvenile courts reached an historic high in 1998 of nearly 2.1 million cases, and then declined by 4.4% to just over 2 million in the year 2000. Causes for this decline have been attributed to a falling off in juvenile crime rates and to criminal court rather than juvenile court filings for certain more serious juvenile offenses. A 27-state tabulation of 2000 juvenile caseload composition shows that delinquency matters comprise 61% of this court's workload, abuse and neglect matters 19%, status offenders 16%, and other 3%.[12]

In 1998, 2.8 million children were reported to authorities as possible victims of abuse, neglect, or dependency. Nearly one million of these children, following investigation, were confirmed as victims of some form of maltreatment. They often become case filings and a very significant part of the juvenile court workload. These cases typically involve a significant number of judicial hearings.[13]

The "other" category includes a variety of child or juvenile related matters depending on a statute and the particular organizational structure of the court. For example:

- The North Carolina statute[14] authorizes proceedings to determine whether a juvenile should be emancipated, to allow judicial consent for emergency surgical or medical treatment when a parent refuses to consent to the treatment, or similarly to allow court authorization for an abortion on an unemancipated minor, which is a legally necessary alternative to parent rejection of an abortion request or when there may be need to skirt a parental request requirement, as with an incest matter.

- The Colorado statute[15] allows juvenile court proceedings for judicial consent to an underage marriage, in regard to the treatment or commitment of a possibly mentally ill or developmentally disabled child, to terminate parental rights, for the adoption of a person of any age that may in rare cases include adoption of an adult, and determinations of paternity and for support of children together with support enforcement. The paternity and support jurisdiction, in whatever court these cases are handled, is a substantial workload.

- California juvenile courts hear juvenile traffic offenses, matters that are more commonly considered in municipal courts.

While juvenile court workloads are variable, their preoccupation is with delinquency and abuse and neglect cases.

MINORITY OVERREPRESENTATION

Juvenile Delinquency Proceedings

A look at the waiting room population of any urban juvenile court, except on adoption day, finds those on the chairs to be largely people of color and of apparent low income. While suburban juvenile courts maintain a somewhat more middle class clientele, they also experience an overrepresentation of less affluent members of their districts.

A look at virtually any community's geographic map of low-income neighborhoods and then its comparison with a mapping of the court's workload of delinquency and abuse and neglect cases invariably finds major overrepresentation in the court from the low-income census tracts. The white poor and not so poor do come to juvenile court, but in so many settings there is minority overrepresentation, African American or Hispanic, and often of low income. Asian youth, where there is a significant Asian American population, are visible court clients as well. Native Americans are also over represented when they reside off-reservation.[16]

The states, required by the JJDPA to gather data on juvenile representation,[17] have reported disproportionate minority confinement in all but one state (Vermont) and that state lacks a sufficient minority population to allow for a statistically significant finding.

The states have made only slow progress with this concern. A federal initiative is now assisting a handful of states, and communities within those states, to address overrepresentation. Private organizations such as the Youth Law Center, Annie E. Casey Foundation, Justice Policy Institute, and W. Haywood Burns Institute are effectively assisting a number of community efforts. The issue is a live one, but overrepresentation, or what is often referred to as disproportionate minority confinement or DMC, is not readily corrected and remains a very serious problem.

Yet it is the juvenile justice system, not the adult criminal justice system, that has employed a state-by-state effort to convene individuals, organizations, and justice system agencies to search out and work at implementing a range of improvement efforts. There is a general belief that it is not deliberate racial or ethnic prejudice on the part of officials that prompts overrepresentation. Rather, though with exceptions, it is the nature of how the juvenile justice system itself operates. Further, studies have shown unequal treatments of equals; majority youths are receiving less severe sanctions than minority youths with similar offenses and offense backgrounds.

A Utah juvenile court judge once told me that he always considered himself bias free, but after participating in an out-of-state training program that brought him into direct contact with neighborhoods of poverty he went back to his court and asked his research director to review his case dispositions. The research director reported that the judge had been disproportionately more severe with Hispanic youths. He had not known this and proceeded to correct this imbalance.

Child Welfare Cases

Minority overrepresentation has been well documented with delinquent case handling. Overrepresentation haunts the abuse-and-neglect child protective service approach as well. Minority children far too often are removed from their parents, placed in foster care, moved to other foster care arrangements, and experience life without an adoptive family or other stable family life grounding. However, systematic state-by-state measurements have not been undertaken and there is as yet no consensus that this problem must be prioritized among the plethora of concerns these agencies must address

Both far better staffing for child protection agencies and greater cultural awareness of alternate life styles by those who work in this field appear critical here. Impoverished parents sometimes lose their children due to misperceptions and, perhaps, middle class biases on the part of the child welfare and juvenile court systems. Of course, children must be protected from harm and many have suffered very real harms and require removal, on a short-term basis if not for a longer term.[18]

Child protection agencies often are insufficiently appreciated. Their workloads require staff members to labor with overwhelmingly difficult family situations: often sexual abuse, sometimes severe physical abuse and injury, dreadful neglect, chronic drug using parents, domestic violence that may even orphan the children, and more. The pressures produce great emotional strain and result in high staff turnover rates. Courts complain they all too frequently find new caseworkers appearing who have just received the case and are insufficiently aware of what is happening with the treatment plan earlier ordered by the court.

Yet I have seen notable progress in the child welfare field in recent years as the federal-state Court Improvement Project has focused key actors on developing approaches to improve case management in the states. More judges now devote more time to these matters. Expedited case processing timelines now lead to earlier permanent plans for children removed from their homes (though not all courts meet these standards). Adoption of removed children has increased and been expedited. Children's rights are now better protected by lawyer or guardian representation. State laws now fit better with the needs of these children and expand the court's role as overseer of intervention effectiveness with these children.[19] Nonetheless, shortcomings remain prominent and in numerous child welfare systems overwhelming.

A DIFFERENT JUVENILE COURT

Roscoe Pound, a former Harvard Law School dean and one of the most highly regarded American legal scholars once proclaimed the juvenile court one of the greatest inventions in the history of jurisprudence. But later he was to complain, in 1937, that "the powers of the Star Chamber were a trifle in comparison with those of our juvenile courts ... too often the placing of a child in a home or even in an institution is done casually or perfunctorily or even arbitrarily. ... Even with the most superior personnel, these tribunals call for legal checks."[20] He was referring, in particular, to delinquency proceedings.

Legal checks came in 1966 and 1967 with **Kent v. United States**, 383 U.S. 541 (1966) and **In re Gault**, 387 U.S. 1 (1967). These opinions served as the foundation for the Court's later decision in **In re Winship**, 397 U.S. 358 (1970), which held that a juvenile's loss of liberty—in this case as long as the six-year confinement of a 12-year-old boy charged with stealing $112 from a woman's pocketbook—required proof beyond a reasonable doubt. The New York statutory measure of a preponderance of the evidence, said the Court, failed to comport with due process of law.

These holdings then led to other protective reforms. One was the universalization of judicial detention hearings, held shortly after a youth's admission to a secure pretrial facility, to ascertain the safety need for holding the youth. Another was the provision to expedite adjudication and disposition of detained youth. Further, the duration of a probation, institutional, or parole experience was often curtailed by statute, rather than simply being open ended until one's 21st birthday.

Dramatic changes in the handling of juvenile offenders along with major Supreme Court decisions that extended the Constitutional rights of adult offenders were to trigger a counterbalancing national effort to promote a recognition that victims, too, merited prominent consideration in courts of law. A heightened consciousness of victimization promoted, in turn, the movement for harsher sanctions for both juvenile and adult offenders.

A victims' movement has grown exponentially and has led to officials notifying victims of court hearings, restitution, use of victim impact statements by the courts, and a requirement of victim approval of plea-bargain offers. Victims do come to juvenile court dispositional hearings today, though infrequently, to offer an oral statement for judicial consideration. Far more often they file impact of offense statements and restitution requests.

Judicial system notifications to victims and the objectives of restoration of victims and the protection of public safety have been incorporated into the principles of Balanced and Restorative Justice (BARJ) that gained numerous advocates, including the author, during the 1990s. BARJ's forward-looking precepts and guidelines now hallmark juvenile justice systems in a growing number of states and communities. Its principles emphasize juvenile accountability and include the development of a juvenile's competencies and community participation in justice system activities to facilitate achievement of BARJ goals. I support these principles.

THE CHAPTERS THAT FOLLOW

The 10 chapters in Part 1 will help the reader understand the juvenile court both as it was yesterday and as it is today. Historical sketches initiate this section (Chapters 1 and 2), followed by a strenuous plea to restrict the criminalization of juveniles (Chapter 3). Chapters 4, 5, and 6 bring to consciousness the expanding juvenile court occupation with abused and neglected children, neglected by the court for many years due to its preoccupation with delinquency matters and, also, to a *laissez faire* attitude of allowing the public child welfare agency to do its work without significant court oversight.

The status offender issue is then presented (Chapters 7 and 8), making clear my view that the community, rather than the court, should maximally resolve these troublesome concerns of youths and families. Further, it is urged that schools, not the juvenile court, manage limited offense matters that occur on school grounds. School sponsored anti-bullying programs, now mandated in some states, represent perhaps the newest of numerous stratagems schools can apply to enhance juvenile collegiality and avert harmful scenarios that might otherwise lead youngsters to enter the juvenile court.

Chapter 9 centers on disproportionate minority confinement across the juvenile justice system. Last, Chapter 10 highlights the need to usher victims through the juvenile court doorway.

Endnotes

[1] Ill. Laws 1899, 131-137.

[2] National Council on Crime and Delinquency (1959). *Standard Juvenile Court Act, §8.1. Sixth edition.* New York: National Council on Crime and Delinquency; National Advisory Committee for Juvenile Justice and Delinquency Prevention (1980). *Standards for the administration of juvenile justice, Standard 3.115.* Washington, DC: Office of Juvenile Justice and Delinquency Prevention (which also recommended a minimum age of 10).

[3] U.S. General Accounting Office (1995). *Report to congressional requesters. Juvenile justice: Juveniles processed in criminal court and case dispositions).* Washington, DC: Government Printing Office.

[4] See Puzzanchera et al. (2001). *Juvenile court statistics 1998.* Washington, DC: Office of Juvenile Justice and Delinquency Prevention.

[5] Snyder, H. N. & Sickmund, M. (1999). *Juvenile offenders and victims: 1999 National report.* Washington, DC: Office of Juvenile Justice and Delinquency Prevention, pp. 120-123.

[6] Bishop, D., Frazier, C., Lanza-Kaduce, L., & Winner, L. (1996). The transfer of juveniles to criminal court: Does it make a difference? *Crime & Delinquency* 42, 171-191; Fagan, J. (1996). The comparative advantage of juvenile vs. criminal court sanctions on recidivism among adolescent felony offenders. *Law and Policy* 18, 77-112; Bishop, D. (2000). Juvenile offenders in the criminal justice system. In Tonry, M. (Ed.), *Crime and Justice* 27, (pp. 81-168). Chicago: University of Chicago Press.

[7] Ill. Laws 1899, 131 §1.

[8] Wis. Stat. Ann. §938.13.

[9] Public Law 93-415, Section 223(a) (12).

[10] Snyder, H. N. & Sickmund, M. (1999), supra n. 5, p. 207.

[11] Id.

[12] Ostrom, B., Kauder, N. & LaFountain, R. (Eds.) (2001), *Examining the work of state courts, 2001.* Williamsburg, VA: National Center for State Courts), 44-45.

[13] Id., pp. 47, 52.

[14] NC Gen. Stat. §7B-200.

[15] Colo. Rev. Stat. §19-1-104.

[16] Leonardson, G. R., Mountain Plains Research. Report on disproportionate minority confinement in Montana, Presentation to Montana Board of Crime Control, January 30, 2001.

[17] Public Law 93-415, section 223(a)(23).

[18] Roberts, D. (2001). *Shattered bonds: The color of child welfare.* New York: Basic Books.

[19] See American Bar Association Center on Children and the Law (2000). *Court improvement progress report 2000.* Washington, DC: American Bar Association.

[20] Pound, R. (1952). Foreword to Young, P. V. *Social treatment in probation and delinquency.* 2d. ed. New York: McGraw-Hill, p. xv.

Chapter 1

The Pioneering Vision of Judge Ben B. Lindsey, Denver's Juvenile Court Judge, 1901-27

In the centennial year of the juvenile court, judicial, legal, and social services personnel celebrate the groundbreaking Illinois Juvenile Court Act of 1899, the nation's first such act. Early Cook County judges will be unearthed—Richard S. Tuthill and Julian W. Mack—and their contributions will be extolled. Denver's Ben Lindsey, however, richly deserves significant attention during the centennial for his singular and visionary contributions. Lindsey rightly has been credited with having the greatest impact on juvenile court developments, not because of his very lengthy tenure, but because of his positive conceptualization that the court's role was to enhance the life prospects of youth; his activist stance that required the court to apply an array of helping services while punishing adults who contribute to delinquency or dependency; his vigorous and tireless advocacy and travels; and the charisma he demonstrated as juvenile court salesman. Further, he germinated the seeds of a broader family court.[1]

DENVER COURT DIFFERED SIGNIFICANTLY FROM EARLY CHICAGO JUVENILE COURT

Lindsey created a different kind of court, one that differed significantly from the Chicago juvenile court. While the Chicago juvenile court was created as a division of the general trial (circuit) court, the Denver juvenile court became a stand-alone court. While the Chicago court was founded on the principle of modifying the criminal law and applying it to youth, the Denver court established an informal approach to handling cases that was unencumbered by tradition or precedent. Indeed, Lindsey wanted nothing to do with the punitive criminal justice system. Finally, the courts differed in the degree to which they relied on institutional placements. Data compiled by the Cook County chief probation officer in a comparative juvenile court data survey of 1904, indicates a rate of institutional placements in 44% of cases at a time when the Denver court was institutionalizing just 6% of court youth. The Chicago court also relied on transfers to the criminal court, while the Denver court emphasized informal resolution, and probation (double the Chicago percentage).[2]

This chapter originally appeared in Juvenile Justice Update*, Vol. 5, No. 1, February/March 1999.*

LINDSEY TOOK HIS MODEL TO THE NATION

Interestingly, Lindsey's "juvenile court" preceded Colorado's enactment of juvenile court legislation. Appointed Denver's probate court judge in 1901, Lindsey interpreted a school truancy statute so broadly that he was able to arrange for the district attorney to transfer all delinquent offenders to his de facto juvenile court. Two years later, in 1903, he engineered Colorado's juvenile court act, then considered the most extensive and comprehensive law in the land, and, in 1907, obtained passage of a law that established a separate independent court, the Juvenile and Family Relations Court of Denver. The 1903 juvenile court act's preamble embraced Lindsey's operating ideology that "as far as practicable any delinquent child shall be treated, not as a criminal, but as misdirected and misguided, and needing aid, encouragement, help and assistance."

In 1904, Lindsey published a 200-page booklet, *The Problems of the Children and How the State of Colorado Cares for Them*. This how-to publication, which featured his model statute, operational guidelines, court forms, and a comparison of its costs versus the costs of the criminal system, went out across the nation. He appeared before legislature after legislature in this country as well as before parliaments in other countries, stimulating widespread adoption of juvenile court acts. He became a close friend and advisor to President Theodore Roosevelt and to many of the nation's governors and mayors. In 1914, a national magazine poll named him one of the 10 "greatest living Americans."

COURT FAVORING PROFESSIONALS OTHER THAN LAWYERS ENVISIONED

Lindsey maintained that the best juvenile court would consist of an independent court with a full-time specialist judge and probation staff, and with medical and vocational experts. It would have sweeping and exclusive jurisdiction over every matter pertaining to children's behavior, care, and support, including all criminal offenses against children. He believed that legal procedures and lawyers obstructed the court's rehabilitative mission and interfered with his quite singular ability to communicate informally and effectively with youth and bring out their best. He held that there were no "bad kids," but there were "bad" conditions and environments which resulted in "bad" conduct.

Lindsey saw institutions as a very last resort. But upon a commitment, he frequently used an honor system and provided trolley tokens or bus tickets to these juveniles and instructed them to take themselves to the "reform school." He claimed that during 24 years of this practice, he had "lost" only five boys.

Lindsey tried to make his vision a reality. Following enactment of the 1903 statute, the Lindsey court began operations with three salaried probation officers. This was in contrast to Cook County and other early juvenile courts whose probation officers were citizen volunteers or assignees from other agencies such as a police department. Later, a Colorado enactment transferred the appointing authority for these officers and for court clerks from the patronage of the elected county commissioners to the judge. Lindsey wanted a judicial-branch probation department.

There were four doorways to Lindsey's court:

1. Walk-ins by juveniles wanting to talk with the judge or a court official;

2. Non-court youth wanting to access the court's youth employment service or medical clinic;

3. Agency, law enforcement, or parent referrals handled informally; and

4. Referrals handled formally.

Informal resolution was very frequent, expanding from about 52% of all complaints in 1909 to nearly 88% in 1924. Complaints of a sexual nature against girls were handled at least half of the time on an informal basis.[3]

ADDRESSING SEXUALITY OF YOUTHS

Lindsey's court became known as a place where Denver's young people could come to talk about matters, particularly sexual concerns, which they were unable to discuss with their parents or teachers. Lindsey had a knack of making young people feel comfortable, and of letting them know he was supportive and not judgmental. From his informal talks with countless young people and from his readings of the works of the English sexologist, Havelock Ellis, he deepened his perception of the normality of sexuality and its occurrence across economic classes. Similarly, he noted that "all children are delinquent at some time or other," i.e., children of all economic classes. Lindsey did not stereotype youthful sexual experiences or delinquent acts as the province of the poor.

Lindsey wrote and spoke of sexual exploration as natural and often not delayed until marriage. He was in no way critical of youthful "indiscretions," which he viewed as common. Rather, he was critical of those who scorned the "indiscreet." This view, likely, was atypical of juvenile courts of the day. That the Lindsey court served as the site for relinquishing children, generally by unwed mothers of all economic classes, for the purpose of adoption, provided a further foundation for Lindsey's view of the naturalness of sex.

Walk-ins by Adolescent Girls

In his book, *The Revolt of Modern Youth*, Lindsey records that in 1920 and 1921, the court dealt with 769 girls of high school age, though 465 of this number were no longer in school. Three-fourths of the girls, he states, came to the court on their own accord.

He writes of one 17-year-old and two 16-year-old girls from "good, middle class homes" coming together to seek advice from him. The oldest feared she might be pregnant and was informed she could consult a male or female physician who assisted the court (the court's medical clinic disbursed contraceptives) and, if she was pregnant, the court would help her in a "legal and proper way." The second girl was worried she might yield completely to a boy. The judge suggested she tell the boy Judge Lindsey would not tolerate "further improper liberties"; also, she should continue to seek support from Lindsey. The third girl was contemplating an elopement, but abandoned this plan on accepting Lindsey's argument that neither party was able to support a child.

The judge unabashedly proclaimed the inherent goodness of young people and his successful interventions, for example: "Years ago I had in my charge a girl of 17 who, when I became acquainted with her five years before, had already had relations with several school boys. Immoral? Bad? Poppycock! She was ignorant. One talk with me ended it; she became one of the finest young women in Denver. No casual male would dare cross her path. She is very beautiful, has a remarkable mind, and some time ago was married to a youth who, I trust, deserves her."[4]

Sexual Activity Not Viewed as Moral Failing

While acknowledging some of his best friends and heartiest sympathizers were ministers, Lindsey reported, without revealing names, case examples of sexually active girls whose own minister fathers had publicly attacked Lindsey's work and views as warped, and who trumpeted against sexually active young people as moral lepers—not knowing of their daughters' experiences and believing only that their daughters were "pure." He found a way to survey and talk with about 100 non-court boys from Denver high schools, more than half of whom had engaged in sexual relations—mostly in the Red Light District; and he seemed to delight on finding that two were sons of Sunday school superintendents in two of the city's largest churches.

DENVER APPROACH REFLECTED LINDSEY'S BACKGROUND

Lindsey experienced severe poverty in his childhood, forgoing high school due to his father's job loss, deep indebtedness, and subsequent ill health and suicide. He became the prime support of his mother and three siblings. He has written of subsisting, often, on only gingerbread and molasses, and of frequently holding three poorly paying jobs all at one time. But one job, clerking in a lawyer's office, opened his career into law and the courts. Likely, his own youth, growing up on the other side of the tracks, impacted his ability to relate, as a judge, with impoverished youth, and his easy rapport with youth furthered his embrace of informal court proceedings.

Lindsey took pains to confer with court youth in a way which he underlined was both private and public. He did this in his chambers behind a closed door, which officials, reporters, and others knew they could open and walk through—and he had his co-worker and wife stationed at a desk in the next room, connected by a door that she or another could open at any time. Further, a woman referee, Ida Gregory, was employed beginning in 1903, to serve as an assistant judge in girls' cases; she headed the girls' probation section when it was initiated in 1909.

Traditional Criminal Court Trappings Eliminated

The wearing of a judicial robe and the hearing of cases from a three-step-up judicial bench were, to Lindsey, "absurdities of police or criminal court procedures." He took pride in facilitating the retitling of legal documents in juvenile cases. Instead of the criminal court caption of "the people of the state" versus the "defendant," juvenile cases became titled the "people of the state in the interest of" the child and "concerning the parents" or other involved adult.[5]

Lindsey Institutes "Snitching" and "Ditching"

Lindsey has described his "snitching bees," where he persuaded several youths to tell, not what a co-offender did, such as stealing newspapers, but what they themselves had done. With the promise of a non-punitive disposition upon a confession, these boys succeeded in getting other co-offenders to come voluntarily before the judge and snitch only on themselves.

Lindsey's Saturday morning "ditching" sessions with 200-300 law-violators and status offenders are described by Lindsey's biographer, with the help of a 1906 *McClure's* magazine article, written by the noted journalist Lincoln Steffens:

> The boys appear "as clean as possible, and happy." The judge leans against a table or sits on a chair and talks of a former court youth who has "made good." He reads the boy's letter from Oregon, where he now lives. Since the previous Saturday Lindsey talked about snitching, this Saturday he talks about "ditching"—ditch your bad habits and get strong. He calls groups of boys up front by the school they attend. He calls them by name or nickname (e.g., Skinny, Mumps) as he opens their school report, announces how they have improved or failed to improve at school, banters with them, supports them, encourages them.[6]

"Kids' Judge" Implements Creative Dispositions

The statutory sweep of what constituted delinquency in the early years of the century was enormously broad. The law explicated such offenses as: entering railroad cars; incorrigibility; "growing up in idleness or crime"; using "vulgar" or "indecent language"; visiting saloons, gambling settings, or houses of ill-repute; and knowingly associating with "thieves, vicious or immoral persons." Any law violation, of course, was subject to a petition.

In his dispositions, Lindsey differentiated between more serious offenses or offenders who violated his trust, and the great bulk of court youth who needed only his support and direction. There are reports of Lindsey's taking court youths to shows, going on weekend outings with them, and talking sports with them. He corresponded with youths he committed to a training school, and helped them find jobs upon release. He organized youth sports and assigned a probation officer to lead these activities. He mediated between adolescents and their parents, police and provocative youths, and Catholic and Protestant gangs. He used his influence to shut down certain child labor exploitation, to obtain public baths, and to facilitate an array of youth recreation resources.

Lindsey was referred to in Denver and across the nation as the "kids' judge."

EXERCISING JURISDICTION OVER ADULTS WHO HARM OR FAIL TO SUPPORT CHILDREN

Lindsey was briefly able to exercise criminal jurisdiction over adults who offended against minors, as provided by a law he obtained. Reports indicate the court tried adults for incest, statutory rape, and indecent liberties. This statutory grant was later rejected by the state supreme court as insufficiently clear, was then amended to provide a concurrent jurisdiction for the juvenile court, and was ultimately rejected by the supreme court post-Lindsey. In 1909, Lindsey did obtain a civil non-support statute, the forerunner of today's paternity and child support proceeding, and a well-regarded Lindsey invention. With this mechanism he could enforce an unjustified support default by a civil contempt sanction, jail, or a suspended jail sentence that did not brand the delinquent father as a criminal.

LINDSEY'S BROAD VIEW OF THE JUVENILE COURT'S ROLE

Lindsey writes in his autobiography, *The Dangerous Life*:

In the juvenile court—probably miscalled a court—the state employed experienced persons called judges and probation officers to understand the child and to deal with him in a way to help, and not to hurt, him (just the reverse of the theory of the criminal court, which was only to hurt him) and to bring him into a course of conduct that was social, not anti-social, and that meant respect, and not contempt, for the law.[7]

He believed that a similar holistic approach would become the standard of the criminal court, in time, toward "most of the conduct and behavior of adults."

Lindsey lauded the statutes he had facilitated which could bring to court adults who had contributed to the delinquency or dependency of children. These proceedings, he contended, placed the "moral and human rights" of children on the same plane as the judicial system's long-held ability to protect the property rights of children. Lindsey noted that few children, in fact, experienced the need for any safeguarding of property, but far more required protection of the "human right to be well-bred, well-cared for, trained and directed as to [their] health and morals."[8]

Beyond the Bench

Lindsey often was embroiled in controversy during his tenure. Diminutive and fiery, he made his voice heard on many social justice concerns. His first book, *The Beast*,[9] took on the Colorado and American political and economic establishment as inhumane, causing poverty, and, therefore, responsible for crime, delinquency, and child dependency. He blamed the economic system for work-related injuries and deaths and for blocking a suitable social welfare net. He was a muckraker. Always on the side of working people, Lindsey lobbied the Colorado governor and, in 1914, led a delegation to meet with President Wilson in Washington to seek an end to the bitter labor dispute, known as the Ludlow Massacre, which had resulted in 20 deaths of coal miners, their wives, and children.

Lindsey was a public advocate of sex education for all teenagers, to include information on birth control and venereal disease. His series, "Marriage of," published in *Redbook Magazine*, and expanded into a book, *The Companionate Marriage*,[10] provoked a firestorm of media-generated misinformation. Lindsey did not advocate free love or a "barnyard marriage," as the public came to believe. Rather, he believed in the premise of divorce by mutual consent if there were no children, to be preceded by significant counseling attempts; with children, the parties would need to prove to the court they had considered their children's interests.

Lindsey Burned Juvenile Court Records After Being Forced From the Bench

When an angry Ben Lindsey was removed from the Denver bench in 1927—a victim of the Ku Klux Klan with whom he had feuded for years and which was then dominating Colorado government—he responded with a highly-publicized record-burning bonfire, and destroyed most of the court records of the young people his court had served. "I was happy in the knowledge that the secrets of thousands of humans whom I had helped were safe forever from the public gaze or blackmail use by agents of the Ku Klux Klan."[11]

Colorado Loses Lindsey to California

After leaving the Denver bench, Lindsey shifted his venue. He was elected a judge of the superior court in Los Angeles in 1934, and reelected in 1940. His main accomplishment there was to obtain the legislation and then preside over the "Children's Court of Conciliation." This divorce-related court provided mandatory counseling and reconciliation efforts if a divorce was filed and the parties had children. This was to be done within a 30-day cooling off period and could be provided by court staff, through arrangements with physicians and mental health personnel, or by clergy. Lindsey, while still a judge, died in Los Angeles in 1943, at age 73. The conciliation court survived for decades after his death.

A BIOGRAPHER'S CRITIQUE

Lindsey's biographer constructs a critical last chapter analysis of the judge:

[He] invariably portrays himself as the embodiment of wisdom and virtue....[He] continually conveyed the impression that he had done it all by himself.... His greatest vice was his need to boast.... One of his greatest strengths was his showmanship," which helped him win political support, spread the juvenile court idea, and achieve legislative victories. His combativeness, a weakness and a strength, embroiled him with machine politicians, moralists, and the Klan, but won for him many creditable social action and political victories.[12]

Not too bad for one who never graduated from high school.

A MESSAGE FROM JUDGE LINDSEY

Were Judge Ben Lindsey alive today, he likely would get on his soapbox and tell today's judges to attack aggressively the social and economic conditions that impact and exacerbate juvenile delinquency and child neglect. Likely, too, he would urge them to campaign to decriminalize drug use and make treatment available to all users. He would have judges striding legislative halls to insist on humane laws, discretion in case handling and disposition, and resources to keep virtually all juveniles within the juvenile court system. He would admonish judges that it is not enough just to do a good job with the case one is handling; the "change agent" role and opportunity for the juvenile court judge should allow a judge few relaxed evenings at home.

Lindsey likely would downplay an adversarial juvenile court. Probably he would want plea and sentence bargaining to be a very open affair, with the youth and family present and the judge taking the lead role in the discussion—but actively obtaining the participation and involvement of the youth and family. He would want the defense attorney to serve also as a social worker and counselor, and he would want both prosecutor and defense attorneys actively scouting out alternative dispositions and monitoring the quality of service delivery by agencies and individuals.

Of course, Lindsey would want the criminal justice system to be like the juvenile justice system at its best. And he would want to combine the juvenile court with the array of domestic relations jurisdictions into a family court, and create what he called a House of Human Welfare. His key to each of these court systems would be an interdisciplinary professional staff, collaborative community-based organizations, an actively engaged citizenry, and a judge who was a great communicator with court clients.

Much of his life, Lindsey was in trouble with political and economic interests and with public mores. He would say that today's judges should be as challenging and feisty as he was. They should work tirelessly to create a society which allows a judge to truly say to court kids "this land was made for you and me"—even if this results in job loss and a new career as a judge in another state.

Endnotes

[1] Colomy, P. & Kretzman, M. (1995). Projects and institution building: Judge Ben B. Lindsey and the juvenile court movement. *Social Problems, 42*(2), 191-215; Fox, S.J. (1996). The early history of the court. In Behrman, R.E. (Ed.), *The juvenile court*. Los Altos, CA: Center for the Future of Children, The David and Lucile Packard Foundation, pp. 29-39.

[2] Colomy & Kretzman, note 1 supra; Platt, A.M. (1969). *The child savers*. Chicago: University of Chicago Press.

[3] Colomy, P. & Kretzman, M. (1996). The gendering of social control: Sex delinquency and progressive juvenile justice in Denver, 1901-1927. In McGillivray, A. (Ed.), *Governing childhood*. Aldershot, UK: Dartmouth Publishing Co.

[4] Lindsey, B.B. & Evans, W. (1925). *The revolt of modern youth*. New York: Boni & Liveright, pp. 76, 80, 115, 116.

[5] Lindsey, B.B. & Borough, R. (1931). *The dangerous life*. New York: Horace Liveright, Inc. pp. 113, 115, 118.

[6] Larsen, C. (1972). *The good fight: The life and times of Ben B. Lindsey*. Chicago: Quadrangle Books, pp. 39, 47-49.

[7] Lindsey & Borough, note 5 supra, p. 113.

[8] Id., p. 115.

[9] Lindsey, B.B. & O'Higgins, H. (1970 reissue of 1910 publication). *The beast*. Seattle: University of Washington Press.

[10] Lindsey, B.B. & Evans, W. (1927). *The companionate marriage*. Garden City, NY: Garden City Publishing Co., Inc.

[11] Larsen, note 6 supra, p. 205. See also Rogers, F.B. (1976). Judge Ben B. Lindsey and the Colorado Ku Klux Klan. *Colorado Lawyer, 5*(11), 1632-1649.

[12] Larsen, note 6 supra, p. 248-267.

Chapter 2

The Constitutionalization of the Juvenile Court Adjudicatory Process: The Case of Gerald Gault

Recently I asked a distinguished professor of constitutional law at a noteworthy law school whether he taught **In re Gault,** 387 U.S. 1 (1967). He was not familiar with the case. Soon after, I asked a juvenile prosecutor whether all principles of the **Gault** case were applied in her juvenile court and justice system. In reply, she asked me what the case held. I recalled a talk by Studs Terkel, chronicler of American life, who was concerned with what he termed the National Alzheimer's Disease. He lamented that important historical events of his time were unknown to the next generations.

This chapter describes the most critical development in juvenile court history, other than the statutory enactments that created juvenile courts in each of our states. I hope that this description will help us avoid an Alzheimer's diagnosis for juvenile justice practitioners.

ADVOCATES WELCOMED THE *GAULT* DECISION

The U.S. Supreme Court published the **Gault** decision on May 15, 1967. It was both hailed and scorned by those who then worked in this field. It was hailed by law-oriented professionals, juvenile advocates, social science researchers, and progressive citizen and correctional groups. They had been critical of arbitrary procedures in the court, the overall absence of law and lawyers, deficiencies in rehabilitative intervention efficacy and availability, the broad definition of delinquency that included status offenses and allowed the court to institutionalize runaways as readily as repeat burglars, and much more.

JUVENILE COURT JUDGES OPPOSED THE *GAULT* DECISION

The decision was scorned by traditional juvenile court judges and their national organization. My judicial colleague, then in his 27th year as a Denver juvenile court judge, proclaimed that May 15, 1967, was the day the U.S. Supreme Court hung black crepe paper on the juvenile court door. The Blue Ridge Institute for Southern Juvenile Court Judges prefaced a resolution it approved with, "Whereas, there are those who

This chapter originally appeared in Juvenile Justice Update, *Vol. 5, No. 2, April/May 1999.*

would seek to destroy the basic principles of the juvenile court and convert that court into a criminal court for children...." It urged the national organization "[t]o be alert as to the magnitude and potential potency of any attack on the juvenile courts of our land" and to become informed of "every instance where any juvenile court is attacked on constitutional grounds."[1] Further, the basic law enforcement response was that since juveniles now had the same rights as adults, they should be treated as adult criminals.

Gault Underscores Need for Due Process

The Supreme Court's decision had four basic holdings. All underscored a requirement that due process of law must accompany the good intentions of the juvenile court:

1. A juvenile must be provided with notice of the specific charges that brought him or her to court.

2. A juvenile must be provided with notice of his or her right to counsel and to free counsel if indigent.

3. A juvenile must be advised of the privilege against self-incrimination and the right to say nothing during any questioning.

4. A juvenile has the right to confront witnesses who testified against him or her, and normal rules that exclude hearsay testimony are to be followed.

GAULT FOUND GUILTY OF MAKING OBSCENE PHONE CALL

The **Gault** case arose in Gila County (Globe), Arizona in 1964. At that time, Gerald Gault, age 15, was serving six-months probation for "having been in the company of another boy who had stolen a wallet from a lady's purse." The theft occurred at the Globe theater. (The **Gault** case was, indeed, very Shakespearean.)

Subsequently, Gerald and a friend, Ronald Lewis, were taken into custody by the sheriff's office based on the verbal complaint of Mrs. Cook, a woman of reportedly questionable reputation, who was a neighbor in the trailer colony where the Gault and Lewis families lived. Cook complained that the boys had phoned her and made lewd or indecent remarks. The Supreme Court later characterized the remarks or questions put to her as being of the "irritatingly offensive, adolescent, sex variety."

Gault Questioned by Probation Officer

Gerald's probation officer, who was also the detention center superintendent, questioned him about the alleged offense. Gerald's parents were not present during the questioning, and the probation officer never suggested that Gault might want to remain silent or talk with an attorney.

Informal Hearings Formed Basis of Conviction

Later two informal hearings were held by Judge McGhee. No rights were enunciated. The court petition, which included no statement of facts but only a general recital that Gerald was a delinquent minor, was never served on Gerald or his family. Mrs. Cook did not attend the hearing. No record was made. There was great ambiguity as to what Gerald denied or admitted. His mother and father suggested only that Gerald acknowledged dialing the number and handing the phone to the Lewis boy. A law school dean later described it as the "immortal phone call." It was the phone call that changed forever the nature of juvenile court proceedings.

Gault Committed Until He Reaches 21

Seven days after being picked up by the sheriff, Gerald was committed by Judge McGhee to the Arizona State Industrial School for Boys until his 21st birthday, unless sooner discharged. (The fate of the Lewis boy is unknown.) Had Gerald been an adult, his maximum sentence would have been incarceration in a local jail for up to two months and a fine of $5-$50.

Gault's Rescue Begins

Amelia Lewis, an attorney, had moved from New York City to the retirement community of Sun City, Arizona. There she maintained a small law office and served as a volunteer attorney for the Arizona branch of the American Civil Liberties Union (ACLU). Previously, Amelia had worked as a defense attorney for the New York City Legal Aid Society, regularly representing criminal defendants in a court system known for its rigorous legal procedures and due process. She told me the following story:

One day I received a call from the office of the Attorney General, in Phoenix, asking if he could send a man out to my office. The man believed something was wrong about his son being in the state boys' school, and I had told him I couldn't help him as our office represented the state. A few hours later, a man knocked on my door and said he was Mr. Gault. He was wearing washed out overalls, had teeth that needed much care, and worked in the copper mines. He told me, "My son Gerald is no angel, but when he tells me he is speaking the truth, I have learned to believe him. He said he did not talk to that lady."

Arizona Code Permits No Appeal

Amelia Lewis had never handled a juvenile case in her life, but she was appalled at the tale Mr. Gault related and believed he was speaking the truth. She took the case, but discovered quickly that the state juvenile code had no provision for an appeal. She called a justice on the state supreme court for advice on how to proceed and was told she could initiate a habeas corpus proceeding. This was filed in the state supreme court and then referred to the superior court in Phoenix. These efforts failed to obtain Gerald's freedom.

Amelia Lewis pondered placing Gerald on the witness stand at the superior court hearing, to contradict what Judge McGhee might say, but relied instead on Mrs. Gault. In the words of one legal commentator, Judge McGhee

testified in such a manner as to suggest that he had no real notion of what law it was that Gerald was supposed to have violated. At one point he stated it consisted of disturbing the peace and at another point he indicated that he thought it consisted of using lewd language in the presence of another person, and finally he thought it might have been that the boy had been habitually involved in immoral matters."[2]

Arizona Supreme Court Sees No Process Problems

Amelia Lewis prepared her briefs and argued Gerald's case in the state supreme court. She lost again. The judge who wrote the opinion, **Application of Gault**, 407 P. 2d 760 (Ariz. 1965), was a former juvenile court judge in Phoenix. The opinion validated the juvenile court and indicated that Gerald Gault received as much process as was his due in this court. The opinion defended the juvenile court's summary proceedings as a useful way to hide "youthful errors from the full gaze of the public and bury them in the graveyard of the forgotten past." Notice of the specific charges or basis for taking a juvenile into custody and for the hearing were necessary, held the court, though this could be given at the time of the initial hearing before the judge.

Further, since the juvenile code required the probation officer to look after the interests of juveniles and represent their interests in court, there was no need for a lawyer even though the probation officer was authorized to be an arresting officer and to initiate proceedings against a youth. Also, it was sufficient that the code required sworn testimony from court-related officials such as the police and probation officers, but did not require sworn testimony from outside witnesses. According to the opinion, any privilege against self-incrimination would hamper the juvenile court's therapeutic opportunities, since confession is good for a youth and leads to trust and confidence in court officials.

Gault Heads for the United States Supreme Court

Amelia Lewis picks up the story at this point:

I thought this case was extremely important and might well be accepted by the Supreme Court, but I didn't have the experience or skills to take it there. Then I remembered that my son used to play basketball in New York City with the son of Norman Dorsen, the New York University law professor who was a general counsel to the national ACLU. So I called Norman, and I made sure he got all the **Gault** materials that were needed. The ACLU took the case, and Norman Dorsen became lead counsel. The Court granted certiorari!

SUPREME COURT REVERSES *GAULT* BECAUSE OF DUE PROCESS VIOLATIONS

The Supreme Court reversed the Arizona Supreme Court on the four due process issues it chose to decide. A better understanding of the Supreme Court's decision emerges from an examination of prior decisions that created the context in which **Gault** was decided.

Earlier Case Required Counsel in Capital Cases

In 1932, the Supreme Court established the principle of a constitutional right to counsel, including free counsel, in a state capital case, the celebrated decision relating to the death sentences meted out to the seven Scottsboro Boys. **Powell v. Alabama**, 287 U.S. 45 (1932). There the Court recognized that a defendant "requires the guiding hand of counsel at every step in the proceedings against him. Without it, though he be not guilty, he faces the danger of conviction because he does not know how to establish his innocence." The due process clause of the 14th Amendment requires a hearing, and for a meaningful hearing, counsel is "fundamental."

Court Extends Right to Counsel to Other Criminal Proceedings

The Court later ruled that the Sixth Amendment mandated the necessity for, and the right to, counsel, including free counsel, in any federal criminal proceeding. **Johnson v. Zerbst**, 304 U.S. 458 (1938). The Court declined to compel states to provide counsel in all felony cases but allowed the individual defendant, on a case-by-case basis, to secure a reversal on the ground that denial of this right had, in his or her particular case, caused a denial of fundamental fairness. **Betts v. Brady**, 316 U.S. 455 (1942). In the aftermath of **Betts**, federal courts overturned a number of denials of counsel. Already, some Supreme Court justices were questioning the validity of the case-by-case approach when a handwritten, penciled petition by a Florida prisoner was brought into the Court's Friday conference of justices on June 1, 1961. Penitentiary inmate Clarence Earl Gideon complained in his petition that when the Florida court denied his request for a free attorney, it denied him due process. He had been forced to represent himself and was subsequently convicted of an after-hours burglary of a poolroom.

Court Decides to Hear Gideon's Case, Naming Abe Fortas as His Counsel

The Court decided to hear Gideon's case and, significantly, appointed Abe Fortas, a prominent Washington, D.C. corporate attorney, to present the case to the nine justices. The decision that followed overturned **Betts** and established the principle that the due process clause of the 14th Amendment guarantees the right to counsel in felony proceedings. **Gideon v. Wainwright**, 372 U.S. 335 (1963). One too poor to hire a lawyer "cannot be assured a fair trial unless counsel is provided for him."

Following the Supreme Court decision, Gideon was retried, this time with a lawyer, and found innocent by a jury. He was released from the penitentiary after two years of incarceration.[3]

Kent v. United States

Not long after he argued Gideon's case, Abe Fortas was appointed by President Lyndon B. Johnson to the Supreme Court. Fourteen months before the **Gault** ruling, a ruling which Fortas was to author, Fortas wrote the Court's opinion in another juvenile case, one not based on the U.S. Constitution—**Kent v. United States**, 383 U.S. 541 (1966).

Morris A. Kent, Jr., 16-years-old and on probation to the District of Columbia juvenile court, was charged anew with three counts each of housebreaking and robbery and two counts of rape. His mother obtained a lawyer who arranged for psychiatric and psychological examinations of Morris. The procedural issue in the case was whether the judge should waive or transfer Morris to a criminal court for trial. Opposing the waiver, Kent's lawyer filed a psychiatrist's affidavit that certified that Kent suffered from "severe psychopathology" and recommended psychiatric hospitalization. Counsel offered to prove that providing psychiatric treatment would make Morris a suitable subject for juvenile court rehabilitation. Also, he moved to examine probation department records regarding Morris.

Court Finds Juvenile Court Proceedings In *Kent* Defective

The judge did not rule on these motions. He held no hearing. He did not confer with Morris, his mother, or his lawyer. He entered an order reciting that after full investigation he was transferring jurisdiction to the criminal court. The judge made no findings and entered no reasons for the transfer.

The Supreme Court found the juvenile court proceedings were defective. There should have been a hearing. Counsel should have been granted access to probation agency records. The judge should have recorded a statement of reasons for the transfer. The juvenile court hearing "must measure up to the essentials of due process and fair treatment." Justice Fortas, in words often quoted, wrote, "There is evidence, in fact, that there may be grounds for concern that the child [in juvenile court] receives the worst of both worlds: that he gets neither the protections accorded to adults, nor the solicitous care and regenerative treatment postulated for children." The decision and the words were signals of the direction the Court would take in its forthcoming **Gault** opinion.

Mr. Justice Fortas for the *Gault* majority

In its opinion in **Gault**, the Court rejected Arizona's defense that, a *parens patriae*, informal juvenile court justified significant denials of due process. The Court held:

- Regarding notice, the alleged misconduct must be set forth with "particularity" and be given sufficiently in advance of court proceedings to afford reasonable opportunity to prepare.

- In a delinquency proceeding which may result in commitment to an institution, the youth and parents must be notified of the juvenile's right to be represented by court-appointed counsel if they cannot afford private counsel.

- The constitutional privilege against self-incrimination applies to juveniles as well as adults.

- Juveniles, like adults, have the right to confront their accusers.

The most often repeated Fortas words from this memorable opinion are: "Neither the 14th Amendment nor the Bill of Rights is for adults alone."

Fortas's opinion drew on social research findings to buttress its conclusions. At the time, a quarter of juvenile court judges had not attended law school; in New York where most juveniles had counsel, 22% of petitions were dismissed for failure of proof at the fact-finding hearing; juveniles were often waived to criminal courts, yet in over half of the states, there was no assurance that juveniles would be kept separate from adult criminals; juvenile recidivism was high despite the services the juvenile system was supposed to be offering youth; and dispositional services that might have helped were often lacking, overloaded, or inadequate.

The historic juvenile court trade-off had to end, Fortas indicated, but he suggested the court could function well, indeed better, with legal safeguards and with lawyers. If it was, as it claimed, a civil court, the "civil label of convenience" still allowed for incarceration and, therefore, the Constitution must apply to juveniles. "Unbridled discretion" must be replaced by principle and procedure.

SOME STATES INTRODUCED DUE PROCESS PROTECTIONS PRIOR TO *GAULT*

While the practices the Court found defective were commonplace, some states had already enacted legislation to initiate due process reforms. Notable among them were California, New York, and the District of Columbia. Others like Illinois and Utah were in the process of doing so when **Gault** was decided.

After **Gault**, legislatures went into high gear to alter their juvenile codes to comply with its requirements and to build in procedures and criteria to guide the transfer process.

GAULT GENERATED TRAINING, RESEARCH, AND LITIGATION

The **Gault** decision became the focal point of juvenile justice conferences, training programs, and research projects across the country. Studies tracked and compared different juvenile courts and found varying degrees of adversarial advocacy either encouraged or discouraged.

A flurry of court suits challenged how far the basic principles of **Gault** should extend. What should be the standard of proof in juvenile cases? In 1970, the Supreme Court resolved this in favor of the beyond-reasonable-doubt measure. **In re Winship,** 397 U.S. 358 (1970). Were juveniles entitled to jury trials? The Supreme Court resolved that issue in 1971, concluding there was no federal constitutional requirement. **McKeiver v. Pennsylvania,** 402 U.S. 528 (1971). If a juvenile court purpose was to rehabilitate youth, and if an institution failed to provide a suitable intervention program and staffing, shouldn't the institution be forced by law to provide such a program? Yes, said several federal courts. See, e.g., **Martarella v. Kelley,** 349 F. Supp. 575 (S.D.N.Y. 1972).

Other issues were litigated: Is a status offense charge like "habitually disobedient" or "ungovernable" too vague to meet constitutional standards of notice and due process? Can status offenders, who have violated no criminal law, be institutionalized in delinquency facilities? Must parents be present before police advise a youngster of rights and obtain permission to interrogate? Is there a right to counsel at a detention hearing? Can school officials search a youth's locker without permission? And many more.

ATTORNEYS NOW PLAY SIGNIFICANT ROLES IN JUVENILE PROCEEDINGS

For a while, defense counsel, particularly where there were organized public defender services, were on top of the power heap in juvenile court. They made judges and probation officers very nervous, worried state youth agencies and institutions, and challenged juvenile justice system procedures from top to bottom. For them it was a golden age. America was still positive about its young people, and juvenile law breaking and violence were not page one stories.

Juvenile prosecutors were rare. Probation intake officers had full control of intake decisions. But in the early to mid-1970s, district attorneys began assigning significantly more prosecutors to this court as crime overall became a greater national concern, and prosecutors were perceived as protectors of the community. Over time, prosecutors became intake decisionmakers in many states, controlled plea and sentence bargaining, and became very influential at dispositional hearings. Today, state legislators look to them first in developing new and harder-line juvenile legislation.

At the same time defense influence waned. In many areas, effective defense representation is curtailed: Significant numbers of juveniles appear in court without lawyers. Juvenile defenders carry staggering caseloads and may rotate to another court in a relatively brief period of time. Defenders rarely take appeals, have insufficient investigative staff, and lack training funds. Still, good defenders carry forward the thrust of the **Gault** decision.

GERALD GAULT: A POSTSCRIPT

Gerald Gault served about six months in the Arizona institution, the norm at the time for institutional stays. Amelia Lewis told me that early in the Vietnam War, while serving there in the Army, Gerald complained to her that he was only doing kitchen duty and wanted to get into the fighting. She replied she had not fought for his freedom so that he could die in battle. Gerald Gault survived Vietnam and made a career of the Army. He served with distinction and ultimately retired as a master sergeant.

In 1987, the Army flew him to Washington to watch his lawyer, Amelia Lewis, receive the coveted American Bar Association's Livingston Hall award for her contribution to juvenile justice. It was the 20th anniversary of the decision. Lewis died in 1994 at age 91. Gault now lives in California, has a business, and has been married for many years. One son has graduated from college. Another son presently attends college.

The **Gault** opinion questioned why Gerald had not been kept at home with his two working parents and older brother. Because his parents questioned the same thing and because they believed in their son, they fought, along with Amelia Lewis, for justice. Their fight benefited millions of American youth. It was a very good fight.

Endnotes

[1] Juvenile Court Judges Journal 143 (Winter 1968); Lemert, E.M. (1970). *Social action and legal change: Revolution within the juvenile court.* Chicago: Aldine; American Bar Association, Youth Law Center, Juvenile Law Center (1995). *A call for justice.* Chicago: American Bar Association.

[2] Clark, H.H., Jr. (1968). Why *Gault*: Juvenile court theory and impact in historical perspective. In V.D. Nordin (Ed.), Gault*: What now for the juvenile court?* Ann Arbor, MI: Institute of Continuing Legal Education.

[3] Lewis, A. (1964). *Gideon's trumpet.* New York: Vintage Books.

Chapter 3

Keep Them in Juvenile Court

Way back in 1966, as a consultant to President Johnson's Commission on Law Enforcement and Administration of Justice, I wrote the following: "We should move to abolish waiver (transfer); every youth charged with violating the law should be handled in the juvenile court and in the juvenile justice system."[1] Years later, in the early 1980s, I said: "In 1966, I wrote we should move to abolish waiver. But today, I say 'thank heavens for waiver. Without that safety valve, legislators would move to abolish the juvenile court.'"[2]

Current trends in juvenile justice lead me to continue to embrace the latter stance.

SOCIETY'S RESPONSE TO JUVENILE VIOLENCE

Year after year, in state after state, we have witnessed changes to the juvenile code. Most of these amendments harden juvenile court sanctions or curb the court's authority over more serious or more repetitive juvenile offenders. Fortunately, to date, no legislative body has abolished its juvenile court nor lowered the maximum age of eligibility for juvenile court handling.

Nevertheless, the lethality of recent juvenile violence has prompted exasperated calls to action. Typically, that action has not been to enrich the juvenile justice system's capabilities so as to deal better with very difficult juveniles.

What has gone wrong with this great invention we call the juvenile court? What has happened to what noted legal scholar Roscoe Pound once termed the most significant advance in Anglo-Saxon administration of justice since the Magna Carta in 1215? Is it that the emphasis of the question should be changed? Should we now ask what has gone wrong with American society? Should we be concerned with why the responding battle cry has been such mean-spirited revenge and retaliation? Why has the long-deferred counterattack on the causes of crime and violence been excluded—yet again—from the proposed "solutions"?

PUNISHMENT OF JUVENILES

Some juveniles do terrible things and, yes, punishments need to be ordered. We must respond to these offenses with serious sanctions (but with more than sanctions).

It used to be that the most common serious sanction was state commitment. Now it is waiver to criminal court or direct filing in criminal court. Research findings on

---

This chapter originally appeared in Community Corrections Report, *Vol. 1, No. 5, May/June 1994.*

cases transferred 15-20 years ago found that criminal courts often did not incarcerate waived juveniles following conviction.[3] This has now changed.[4]

The most common denominator for judicial waivers used to be, and still might be, chronic property offenders. Juvenile courts in a growing number of states see fewer, rather than more, violent offenders since these juveniles now increasingly receive direct adult processing.

There is very little that is wonderful about how adults are handled in the criminal justice system. Of course, legislative policy makers do not decide to feed juveniles into adult facilities because they think they will be helped. Juvenile justice systems may fail to maximize the rehabilitative potential, may be bureaucratic and impersonal, and may let antagonistic or nonverbal kids fall through the cracks. But their failures pale when one looks at the adult jails and prisons and assesses the dreadful environments and consequences of these incapacitations.

In general, we can do it better. We should endeavor to hang onto every youth we can, though we know that right now the battle is uphill.

SOME COMMON LEGISLATIVE APPROACHES

Legislative Waiver

One prominent legislative approach—sometimes termed "legislative waiver"—removes certain offenses or chronic offenders above a specified age, such as 16 years, from the juvenile court. This youth is now an adult. Sooner or later, a legislature will tinker with this law so that additional offenses or offenders (three strikes and you're in criminal court) or certain 14-year-olds will bypass the juvenile court.

Prosecutorial Waiver

Some states allow this bypass to happen at the discretion of the prosecutor. This is known as "prosecutorial waiver." Prosecutors, who I believe have become the most powerful actors in the justice system—more powerful even than judges—really like this approach. They say it gives them another tool with which to protect the community. Prosecutors decide which qualifying juveniles will remain in juvenile court and which will go to criminal court.

Judicial Waiver

The third and very long-standing method, "judicial waiver," lets the juvenile court judge make this decision. The decision is made in the courtroom, not in the prosecutor's cubicle, and not by a legislature's sweeping generalization. It is made according to time-hewn legal standards that reflect a clear body of law that has been tested over and over again in state appellate courts. This is the superior approach, but it is being de-emphasized as prosecutors stalk legislative halls and influence passage of simpler, more efficient, basically unreviewable waiver approaches.

"Proving Up"

Another frequent legislative tactic has been to switch who is the "proving up" party with judicial waivers. Now, in a number of states, instead of the prosecutor having to show that a juvenile is not amenable to rehabilitation within the juvenile justice system, it is the juvenile who must convince the court that he or she can become rehabilitated through juvenile justice resources and within the time the juvenile justice system can retain its jurisdiction. The result, of course, is the grant of more waivers for criminal processing.

IMPACT OF WAIVERS

The former president of the American Society of Criminology, Professor Delbert S. Elliott of the University of Colorado, has written that the effects of increased waivers to adult court have been:

> 1) longer processing time and longer pretrial detention, 2) higher conviction rates and longer sentences, 3) disproportionate use of waivers for minority youth, and 4) a substantially lower probability of treatment while in custody. There is no clear evidence that increases in sentence length or confinement in adult institutions have any significant deterrent effect over shorter sentences and confinement in juvenile institutions.[5]

YOUTH SURVEY POINTS OUT SOME INTERESTING TRENDS

Professor Elliott also heads the Center for the Study and Prevention of Violence and directs the National Youth Survey, which has conducted more than 15,000 interviews and obtained and examined national self-report data since 1976. From his data and data provided from other research sources, Elliott has reached conclusions regarding youth violence:

1. The adolescent homicide rate has more than doubled since 1988.

2. There has been a relatively small increase (8%-10%) in the proportion of adolescents involved in some type of serious violent offending.

3. There is an increase in the rate of violent victimization of adolescents, particularly of 12- to 15-years-olds.

4. The "dramatic increase in the lethality of adolescent violence is explained almost entirely by the increased use of handguns in these violent exchanges."

5. Once social class is taken into account, there is little evidence of differences in predisposition to violence by race.

He adds that youth violence is very widespread in our society. It is not just a problem for the poor, or minorities, or those in our large cities. It crosses all class, race, gender, and residential boundaries.

Among violent offenders, racial, ethnic, and social class differences are small during adolescence but become substantially greater during the adult years. Approximately 80% of interviewees who self-reported violence during their adolescent years stopped their violence by age 21. By age 18, the cumulative proportion of blacks involved in serious violent offending was only 18% greater than that of whites. However, nearly twice as many black as white youth continued committing offenses after age 21.

Elliott notes that growing up in poor minority families and disorganized neighborhoods increases violent offending in two ways:

1. There are limited opportunities for employment, which, in turn, reduces the chances of marriage. These are two important definers of adult status.

2. Youths from these settings have lower levels of personal competence, self-efficacy, social skills, and self-discipline, all of which hamper entry into the labor market.

In some ways, people in this category are trapped in an extended adolescence, so they fail to give up the more violent ways associated with adolescent behavior.[6]

FEDERAL OFFICIALS ARE URGING HARSHER TREATMENT OF ADOLESCENTS

Meanwhile, President Clinton rants about the need for life-long sanctions, and Attorney General Reno urges a "toughened" juvenile justice system where "we have got to let youngsters know there is no excuse for putting a gun up to someone's head and hurting them."[7]

JUVENILE COURTS HAVE RESPONDED TO SERIOUS CRIME

The swept-under-the-table truth is that juvenile courts responded long ago to more serious juvenile crime. At least 20 years ago the legal facts of age, seriousness of offense, prior record, and status on probation or parole began to dominate decision making in the court. Social factors such as family, neighborhood, school, and psychological dynamics that may have impacted juveniles' violations of law became secondary influences.

Similarly, prosecutors became dominant actors in many of these courts.[8] Numerous statutes disallowed informal adjustment of more significant offenses; others compelled admission into pretrial detention centers until a judge could hold a detention review 48 hours later; still others mandated juvenile court dispositions of secure confinement for two years, five years, or even 30 years (Texas). Also, many states authorized dispositions that included time in the "pretrial" detention center prior to placement or replacement onto probation. Here are some techniques that have become popular:

- In-home detention programs became common, with returns to secure detention applied for those who failed to adhere to house arrest or violated the condition of only approved departures from home.

- Electronic monitoring became a part of many juvenile probation programs, as an alternative to secure pretrial detention or as part of a plan to avoid institutional incarceration.

- Intensive probation programs became more intensive, using surveillance officers or trackers to augment intensified supervision by probation officers.

- Foster or mentor homes became available to delinquent youth in more communities and a variety of adventure programs—in the mountains or on the rivers or seas—have become programmatic options.

- Community service hours became a common sanction, as did monetary restitution. There are more day treatment programs and late afternoon–all evening projects that compel juvenile participation throughout this time.

- Urinalysis became a frequent feature of the probation experience.

- Community corrections expanded sharply under probation department or state auspices, and, with it, more day treatment and residential options (often run by private for-profit or non-profit organizations). Even boot camps, the favorite of simplistic politicians, became available to juveniles.

STATE BUDGETS

Presently, every state's budget is held hostage by the exorbitant and ever expanding costs of its prison system. Education has suffered, mental health and developmental disability services have suffered, state parks and recreation budgets have suffered, and likely all state government programs have suffered because of the number and duration of adult prison sentences. Still, the prison population grows every year, and so does the number of juveniles in it. Yet, the results of imprisonment fail to show dividends—the crime rate continues at record or near record levels and prison releasees continue to recidivate at very high levels.

Unlike the astronomic growth industry of adult corrections, juvenile correctional systems remain relatively small, relatively workable, and comparatively cheap. This, indeed, is another major strength. We still individualize. We are not, in general, sausage factories.

And numerous juvenile courts and state youth agencies continue to defy the screamers and the headliners. They take their mission seriously, continue to expand dispositional options, and take pride in saving juveniles—even serious juvenile offenders—from criminal careers. Further, some states still prefer to curb costly state juvenile institutional commitments by providing subsidy or financial incentives to local juvenile courts or correctional agencies to keep kids in the community by means of extending the local continuum of care.

A MODEL PROGRAM

Here's an example. I visited the Kent County Juvenile Court, Grand Rapids, Michigan, in February, 1994. This court, which serves a population of about 500,000 persons, committed 26 juveniles to the state in 1992. In 1993, the court committed just four juveniles! The major reason cited for this abrupt reduction was the start up of the "Day Treatment/Night Watch Program," funded by the state youth agency at an annual cost of $344,000. (Note: In 1992, Michigan training school costs for one resident for a full resident year were reported at $62,970.) This alternative to institutionalization program extends for about one year and consists of three phases:

1. Thirty days in secure detention that includes the day treatment school.

2. Approximately four months of transported attendance to the day treatment school in the detention center, with surveillance commencing immediately following drop off at home. The portal-to-portal 12-hour weekday is filled with classroom instruction, recreation, structured group activities, group therapy and individual counseling, family therapy and parent training sessions, drug testing, educational and vocational plan development, the provision of three meals, and much more. Saturday and Sunday programming of six hours each day is outside the center and emphasizes adventure experiences, cultural enrichment, and family outings. Tracking surveillance occurs constantly during non-programmed weekend hours, also, and electronic monitoring is used with juveniles who require still more control.

3. Six to eight months' participation at a regular school or an alternative education or job program, augmented by counseling, care management, surveillance, family support, and tri-monthly judicial review hearings.

The program phased in the enrollment of 24 youths in 1993; three failed the program. Twenty youths were from ethnic minorities. Court data show that 20 of the juveniles had committed three or more offenses and 17 had committed five or more offenses prior to program entry. Forty percent of their offenses were crimes against persons, weapons charges, or drug-related offenses. A total of 19,081 staff contacts were made, including 8,664 personal contacts, 3,079 random phone contacts, 4,446 answering machine or beeper contacts, and 1,798 family contacts. Juveniles are given financial incentives for acceptable performance and behavior in the program (a total of $6,500 in 1993, and an anticipated $15,000 in 1994).[9]

PROVISIONS OF MICHIGAN'S LAW

Michigan juvenile courts stop initial jurisdictional eligibility on one's 17th birthday rather than the 18th birthday, as occurs in 37 states and the District of Columbia. Also, Michigan legislators recently authorized prosecutorial waivers for more violent juvenile offenses, thus reducing the use of judicial waiver there (although the day/night program could well become accepted by prosecutors as an alternative to their waiver decision).

Yes, there are programs elsewhere that use secure detention, provide day treatment, and/or use lots of tracking and surveillance. But the Grand Rapids program has usefully combined a significant number of program elements. Risks to the community are minimized, juvenile violations of rule or law are better detected and responded to, all kinds of individualized help are offered, families are strengthened, and juveniles' futures have become brighter. Program graduates are better able to make the transition to adulthood that Professor Elliott has described as so vital.

Author's Note

I obtained updating information regarding the Kent County Day Treatment/Night Watch program from Jack Roedema, Administrator, Court Services, in a conversation in July 2002. The program continues with certain modifications. The phase one secure detention requirement is no longer an automatic 30 days. Juveniles are evaluated on a case-by-case basis. A juvenile may be held anywhere up to 30 days and often for much less time. Bedspace available in the detention center may factor into the duration of stay. Overall, the detention stay is not seen as critical as before since phase two programming and controls are perceived as sufficient and satisfactory.

Phase two typically requires six months of transported attendance at the day treatment school in the detention center. Tracking surveillance remains extensive and surveillance officers are present in school classes and around the clock otherwise.

Phase three often extends just three months. Juveniles are then transferred to a regular probation officer and various intensities of supervision are made available.

One probation officer serves the overall program full-time. Six surveillance officers dedicate their time exclusively to monitoring juveniles during phases two and three. A typical population count finds five juveniles in phase one, about 15 in phase two, and perhaps five in phase three.

Roedema indicates few program juveniles reoffend. Technical violations and any non-serious offenses are handled within the community. A more serious reoffense may result in significant time spent in a different, regional detention center. Just nine juveniles were committed to the state during the past year. The state pays 50% of the costs of the program.

A local issue is the schools-court interface. The school system wants to place mandatory expulsion students into the program. The court resists this as the program is reserved for juveniles who commit serious offenses and the state subsidizes the program to reduce the flow of serious offenders to more costly state institutions. Numerous school expulsion cases do not meet the offense criteria.

Endnotes

[1] Rubin, H. T. (1966). *Improving juvenile justice.* Unpublished manuscript. Denver, CO.

[2] Rubin, H. T. (1982). Presentation to juvenile justice management program. Institute for Court Management, July 12, 1982. Snowmass, CO.

[3] Hamparian, D. (1982). *Youth in adult courts.* Columbus, OH: Academy for Contemporary Problems.

[4] Fagan, J., Forst, M, & Vivona, S. (1987). *Separating the men from the boys: The criminalization of youth violence through judicial waiver.* San Francisco: Ursa Institute.

[5] Elliott, D. S. (1994). Youth violence: An overview. Prepared for Children's Policy Forum (Children and Violence Conference), February 18-21, 1994.

[6] Ibid. Also see Elliott, D. S. (1994). Serious violent offenders: Onset, developmental course, and termination. *Criminology 32,* 1-21.

[7] Presentation by Attorney General Janet Reno to Colorado Juvenile Crime Conference, reported in Boulder (Colorado) *Daily Camera*, March 5, 1994, pp. 1-2.

[8] Rubin, H. T. (1980). The emerging prosecutor dominance of the juvenile court intake process. *Crime & Delinquency 26.* 299-318.

[9] Kent County (Michigan) Juvenile Court Annual Report 1992, Day Treatment/Night Watch Program description materials, and reports to the Michigan Department of Social Services, January and February 1994.

Chapter 4

Juvenile and Family Courts' Increasing Role in Child Abuse and Neglect Cases

Abused and neglected children constitute one of the major areas dealt with by juvenile courts and juvenile departments of family courts. Prompted by federal and state legislation that pushes courts into more active monitoring of children's welfare and by the intervention efforts of child protection agencies, juvenile and family court judges now allocate more time to these matters. The trends in child welfare described in this chapter could be adapted by probation agencies and others who seek to work more effectively with delinquent children. Coordinating intervention strategies with the flow of cases through the judicial system can further juvenile justice system accomplishments.

JUDICIAL INVOLVEMENT WITH CHILD ABUSE AND NEGLECT CASES

Juvenile court judges no longer focus predominantly on juvenile delinquency matters. Their new focal point is child abuse and neglect, and that means many judges have joined forces with social workers and management staff from state or local departments of social services. (These child protection agencies have different names in different states. For the sake of convenience, this chapter will refer to them as "DSS agencies.")

Before this trend began, juvenile court personnel across the country looked down on social workers from these agencies as a soft-edged staff serving young, neglected children on behalf of a bureaucratic entity. Probation officers saw themselves as harder-edged personnel who dealt with older youth who threatened the community's welfare. Because they served—and often were employed by—the court, they looked at themselves as "officers" who had a certain amount of authority that derived from the center of the power (i.e., the judges). These officers exercised a great deal of power over the youth they supervised.

Around 1970, while I was a juvenile court judge, I estimated that 20% of my case hearing time was allocated to the child abuse and neglect workload. Today, full-time juvenile court judges who hear both delinquency and child abuse and neglect cases estimate that they spend 50%-60% of their time dealing with child abuse and neglect cases and advocacy. Further, there are some multi-judge courts (e.g., in Chicago, San Jose, and Denver) where some judges spend all of their time with an abuse and neglect calendar while other judges specialize in delinquency matters. These changes are noteworthy.

This chapter originally appeared in Community Corrections Report, *Vol. 2, No. 1, November/ December 1994.*

Even the terminology has changed. The term "child abuse and neglect" has replaced "dependency" or "dependency and neglect" as the more common statutory reference to this type of case. The change explains a lot about the workload change. Early juvenile codes defined dependency and neglect, but not abuse. The concept of child abuse became more recognized partway through the 1970s. It came to be used to describe certain forms of mistreatment of children. For example, the courts and the media used it to refer to children who had been sexually abused by their parents, step-parents, a parent's live-in lover, other adults in authority (e.g., boy scout leaders, foster parents, and priests), or older children.

In addition to these abuse cases, DSS agencies and juvenile courts became inundated with babies born of drug-addicted mothers. Further, the number of children living in poverty increased significantly. These factors, too, prompted state intervention into more lives under various rationales.

ABUSE AND NEGLECT ISSUES CONFRONTING JUDGES

Legal Issues

All of this has meant that an array of complicated, time-consuming abuse and neglect legal issues confront judges. Here are just a few of them:

- Does the child need to testify in front of the person he or she is accusing?

- Can a child's hearsay statements be admitted?

- Does the frequent striking of one's own child with a belt constitute abuse?

- Should the attending media be allowed to print the name of the child victim?

- Is the risk of harm to a third daughter great enough for the court to take jurisdiction when the father has already sexually abused two other daughters?

- Is a father who is incarcerated for sexually abusing his children entitled to be transported from prison to be present at a hearing to terminate his parental rights?

Some Statistics

Annual juvenile court reports indicate vast jumps in abuse and neglect case filings. For example, the 1991 Annual Report issued by the Philadelphia Court of Common Pleas, Family Court Division, reported 41,934 case filings in 1991 compared with 22,767 case filings in 1987. Another source reports that about 460,000 children currently are in foster care across the country,[1] and most of these children are subject to ongoing court hearings and reviews.

In addition, a significant number of legal issues like these are appealed. I counted 42 child abuse and neglect-related appellate court decisions, compared with 41 delinquency-related appellate court decisions, in the annual index of cases published in the 1993 Juvenile and Family Law Digest. The appeal process puts disposition of the case on hold.

Federal and State Legislation

The Adoption Assistance and Child Welfare Act of 1980 (P.L. 96-272) increased court activity in this area.[2] P.L. 96-272 had two main purposes:

1. Removing children who are at risk from unhealthy home environments; and

2. Preventing children from being placed in foster care for long periods or being "bounced" from one foster home to another.[3]

Many state legislatures passed parallel legislation. The result was that juvenile courts were cast into an active oversight role that required them to monitor DSS agency practices.

Neither the courts nor the DSS agencies performed the way Congress wanted them to, however. Congress tried to remedy this in the Omnibus Revenue Reconciliation Act of 1993 (P.L. 103-66). Sections 13711(d)(2) and 13712 of that Act awarded $35 million to state court systems for (1) an assessment of their handling of abuse and neglect cases, including an evaluation of their compliance (or noncompliance) with federal and state mandates, and (2) the design and implementation of a court improvement plan. Undoubtedly, this evaluation/planning process will lead to more judicial time directed toward abuse and neglect cases—and less judicial time for delinquency cases. Perhaps all of this will result in the belated authorization of additional judges or referees/masters/ commissioners for juvenile courts.

Oversight Requirements

Although compliance with both federal and state legislation has been erratic, juvenile courts are required to do the following:

1. Hold speedy, detention-like hearings for children who are removed from their homes. These hearings are supposed to determine whether the DSS agency (1) made "reasonable efforts" to avoid removal and (2) is making reasonable post-removal efforts to "reunify" the family.

2. Approve all voluntary placements of children with the DSS agency within 180 days of placement.

3. Review each foster child's status at least every six months. This function may be conducted by the court, a court-delegated DSS agency, or a foster care review board comprised of citizens appointed by a court or the state's governor. Many juvenile courts refuse (properly, I believe) to delegate these review hearings even though they impinge on the time a judge could otherwise allow for delinquency matters.

4. Hold a "permanency planning hearing" within 18 months of the initial out-of-home placement. At this hearing, a decision is to be reached about a permanent plan for the child. The determination might result in a projected date for return home or to a relative, a guardianship, an adoption, long-term foster care, or independent living. Regrettably, some courts have delegated this task to the DSS agency, thereby asking the agency to review itself.

FRONT-END FAMILY PRESERVATION

There is a widespread perception—and considerable evidence—of major "foster care drift." That is, children are moved from one foster care setting to another and countless children are held in foster care for as long as 18-24 months (and sometimes longer). This time frame reduces the likelihood that the child ever will return home. Until recently, federal and matching state/local dollars were substantially over-allocated to the back end of the system, that is, the costs of servicing long-term foster care. Prevention and early intervention approaches were slighted. But this has begun to change.

Many have heard of the Homebuilders program, initiated in Tacoma, Washington, which combines a small caseload (just two families) and a short working time (four to six weeks). Unless actual harm or the clear risk of significant harm dictates that the children should be removed from the home, the family worker's goal is to do everything possible to avoid removal and facilitate family competency.

This method worked so well in Tacoma, it was picked up as a model and funded at numerous sites by the Edna McConnell Clark Foundation. In addition, it was absorbed into P.L. 103-66 under the rubric of "family preservation."[4] P.L. 103-66 allocated $1 billion over five years for the expansion of the states' use of this and other models of intensive family preservation, as well as "family support" services such as home visitations to new parents and family service centers.

USE OF INTENSIVE PROBATION INTERVENTION WITH DELINQUENT OFFENDERS

The Homebuilders approach has an analog with intensive probation intervention with delinquent offenders that has become common with probation agencies. But have you ever heard of an intensive and front-end probation caseload of just several cases? At least two states (Arizona and Colorado) are adapting Homebuilders to families of delinquent youth.

Arizona's RAFT Program

Arizona calls its program Renewing Arizona Family Traditions (RAFT). The Arizona Supreme Court has contracted with an array of private sector agencies to provide RAFT services in both metropolitan and rural areas. The state describes the RAFT program as

> an in-home, psychoeducational, skills-oriented model of intervention. Timely and intense interventions involve diffusal of the immediate crisis, engaging the family, assessing the problem and developing goals with the family, teaching specific family members skills to help them solve their problems, function more effectively, avoid future crises, and reduce the amount of involvement with the juvenile and related courts.

Arizona officials do not hide the fact that motivation for RAFT includes a goal of reducing numerous and very costly placements into private and state residential care.

Early Intervention in Michigan

On visiting the Kent County (Grand Rapids, Michigan) Juvenile Court in February, 1994, I learned of the following abuse and neglect intervention model: a caseload of two for four to six weeks that yields to a caseload of 10 that, in time, yields to a caseload of 25. This model is different from, but related to, delinquency intervention where juveniles are reclassified from time to time from more to less intensive supervision.

I visited Grand Rapids to find out how its juvenile court did such a remarkable job handling its abuse and neglect workload. The key was the construction of an ideological common ground between the court and the child protective and child placement agencies. The plan was supported by intensive cross-communication, training, and management data review. The common belief was that several layers of intensive intervention could rebuild a number of families.

Consequently, the parties work under the following guidelines:

- Court filings occur only when there is significant harm (or its very real threat), or when a family fails to make necessary progress as a result of the preservation strategies;

- Court cases move quickly toward termination of parental rights (TPR) unless an alternate permanent plan becomes workable (the average TPR is just 15 months from petition);

- The court moves still more swiftly to adoption (85% of children who have been freed for adoption are placed with adoptive parents within six months of the TPR);

- Judicial case reviews occur every three months (rather than every six);

- The permanency planning hearing takes place at 12 rather than 18 months following placement; and

- Every child (and perhaps 50% of the parents) has a lawyer who accepts the court-community philosophy that children must have quality care, preferably at home, but otherwise in a sound, loving, long-term alternative home.

As a result of this program, Grand Rapids has comparatively few of the long-term cases that clog other court calendars and burden public budgets with unnecessary and prolonged social work and legal services costs.

STAFF CONTINUITY RATHER THAN STAFF SPECIALIZATION

Another Michigan-based program that may eventually impact on the probation field involves grants from the Kellogg Foundation to a handful of abuse and neglect intervention programs. The Foundation has several requirements that must be met before the grants will be considered.

One such requirement is that the child have only one "temporary" foster care placement following removal from a parent. Relocation is permitted only to a necessary long-term placement, such as an adoptive home. This requirement would change the practice of DSS agencies that keep children in an emergency shelter before placing them in a foster home. The goal is minimum dislocation for the child, rather than convenience for the agency. Such a strategy, applied in the delinquency field, would favor release to parents, home detention tracking, house arrest, and home-based electronic monitoring, in contrast to reliance on secure pretrial detention.

Another Kellogg Foundation requirement is that of one family/one social worker. In its purest form, this means that one social worker would be responsible for performing all functions related to intervention with a particular family and child, from the case investigation to the resolution of the case, whether that means family reunification or completion of the adoption process.

The one family/one social worker model is akin to the current trend of restructuring separate juvenile and domestic relations courts into a single family court featuring a one family/one judge approach to court docketing—that is, assigning one judge to handle all cases involving members of the same family. It is very difficult to achieve this model, although the concept of judicial hearing officer continuity is very attractive, and some courts are pursuing its implementation.

If more courts think that they should no longer further fragment an already fragmented family, isn't there reason for probation to consider a one juvenile or one family/one probation officer model? There are good reasons why probation agencies developed staff specializations (e.g., intake evaluations, prepare and present predisposition investigations, and supervision). Still, I'm beginning to think that it may be time to reconsider this approach.

Author's Note

This 1994 article focused on the increased court role with abuse and neglect cases. The 1998 article that follows (Chapter 5) focuses on the reforming of juvenile/family court proceedings and procedures with this type of matter, a process that is ongoing and positive. But severe family dysfunctions, as daily newspaper and television news accounts report, take place in all communities. Many of these situations enter the doorways of DSS agencies and, in turn, juvenile and family courts. The agencies and courts have a rather overwhelming task to confront, while needing to institute ways to better function in this difficult context.

Endnotes

Endnotes

[1] Statement by Carol Williams, Associate Commissioner, U.S. Children's Bureau, Court Improvement Conference, Washington, D.C., August 22, 1994. pp. 2-4.

[2] U.S.C. Sec. 670 et seq. (1989). Also see Hardin, M. (1990). *Ten years later: Implementation of Public Law 96-272 by the courts*. Chicago: American Bar Association; Edwards, L.P. (1994). Improving implementation of the Federal Adoption Assistance and Child Welfare Act of 1980. *Juvenile and Family Court Journal, 45*(3), 3-28.

[3] See Hardin, note 2 supra.

[4] See Katz, M. (1993). New legislation pours $1 billion into family preservation. *Youth Law News, 14*(5), 8-10.

Chapter 5

The Other World of the Juvenile Court: Reforming Child Abuse and Neglect Proceedings

COURT IMPROVEMENT PROJECT BRINGS CHANGES TO HANDLING OF CHILD ABUSE AND NEGLECT CASES

A small amount of federal dollars ($35 million annually) is triggering significant reworking in state juvenile courts of the handling of child abuse and neglect matters. The early results hold promise of major improvements in how the judicial system and the social service system address the needs of these children. Court decisions are being made more promptly. Children are returning to a parent or moving into adoption or other long-term care more quickly. More courts of appeal are expediting reviews of juvenile court decisions, particularly terminations of parental rights. There is an excitement in the air. Waves are being made.

The initiative is titled the Court Improvement Project (CIP). It was inspired by the huge problems associated with foster care drift—that is, children spending long blocks of their childhoods, sometimes their entire childhoods, in one foster home or other foster care facility after another. Many of these children have gotten worse in our care. We have, indeed, substituted governmental neglect for parental neglect.

COURT AND CHILD WELFARE AGENCY SHORTCOMINGS

Earlier federal legislation and implementing state laws had moved juvenile courts into active oversight of the work of public child welfare agencies. The courts were to make sure children were not unnecessarily removed from their parents, were reunited with their parents as soon as risks could be minimized, or were freed from their parents and placed in stable, fulfilling, long-term care settings when necessary. But much had not been done well by either courts or social agencies.

Numerous parents and children manifested severe problems. Helping resources often were in short supply or were unable to effectuate solid gains. Really good alternative home settings were difficult to obtain and maintain. The workload was

This chapter originally appeared in Juvenile Justice Update, *Vol. 3, No. 6, December/January 1998.*

extremely difficult, often crushing for the agency and the court. And courts frequently sputtered in executing their legal responsibilities. So, enter the CIP.

REPRESENTATIVE STATE STUDY/ACTION COMMITTEES

Currently, states are in Year Three of a change process. The process is a typical one of (1) assessing current statewide practices against normative standards, (2) designing a plan to significantly improve practices, and (3) implementing the recommended plan over the final two years. Surveys have been conducted, court case files reviewed to see how long it takes to complete different mandated hearings, on-site interviews held, barriers to timely permanency identified, funding issues considered, practices and laws from other states examined, and national guidelines reviewed.

State advisory committees required for the CIP are very multi-disciplinary. They recognize the range of functions and organizations involved with these case types and typically include judges and public child welfare agency managers, attorneys for children, for parents, and for the child welfare agency, officials of the Court Appointed Special Advocate (CASA) agency, and citizen foster care review board members, court administrators, state and county legislators, foster and adoptive parents, private agency representatives, and citizen advocates. These committees, using their findings, have become coalitions pressing for reform.

COURT PROCEEDINGS

There are similarities and differences in abuse and neglect and juvenile delinquency proceedings. Both involve early court hearings to determine whether removal of a child from the family is warranted under the law and the facts. Both involve adjudicatory and dispositional hearings. Lawyers represent both types of children, but parents frequently have their own attorneys only in abuse and neglect cases.

Post-dispositional review hearings are mandated with abuse and neglect cases, but are not, with exceptions, routinely scheduled following delinquency dispositions. Review hearings for abuse and neglect cases evaluate the child's adjustment, whether the parents have complied with and benefited from the array of requirements the agency and court have imposed, and the prospect for a return home.

A court may, but does not always, conduct this review. It may be conducted by a citizen review board and/or the child welfare agency. The court must, however, conduct a particularized review hearing that is to be held within 18 months following the child's removal. This is termed the permanency planning hearing. Informally, it is known as the "fish or cut bait" hearing. Unless it is found likely that reunification of the child into the family a short time down the road is very probable, the next step is to petition the court to either terminate parental rights—a severe, irrevocable action—or approve a long-term care plan in a foster or relative home or other setting.

CIP FINDINGS—PROBLEMS FROM START OF PROCESS TO FINISH

State CIP assessments have revealed that the entire court process may be very slow; that a hearing may constitute a "three minute children's hour"; that lawyers may be appointed late in the process, lack specialized training, or be compensated by a payment so low it may act as a disincentive; that agency workers are overburdened and turn over rapidly; that agency reports arrive late and prompt rescheduling of hearings; that there are not nearly enough CASAs for all the children who need this special support; that the 18-month permanency hearings, if held, resolve little but to continue the matter and hope things get better; and, yes, there is vast foster care drift.

The Iowa Year One CIP report published its judicial survey of average estimated case processing times from stage to stage. When termination of parental rights occurs, it is 632 days from the filing of the petition. If adoption follows, it occurs 340 days later. Actual time to adoption placement in Texas was found to be 928 days (30.5 months). The numbers are depressing. No child should be in limbo for so long a time.

STATES MOVE TO EARLIER PERMANENCY HEARINGS

An examination of state CIP reports finds fundamental consistency that a permanent home for a child needs to be found earlier than has been the practice. State after state has now speeded up this process. State CIP groups often obtained legislative changes to promote this even before they had fully formulated their overall revision plans.

The 18-month review had been federally mandated. Michigan, nearly a decade ago, decided this was too long a span and shortened its time line to 12 months. The Michigan model, in turn, influenced numerous other states. A pending federal re-enactment would adopt this time frame.

New Mexico is now among the speediest. Its new law allows no more than 11 months from removal to permanency hearing, but in most cases this will not exceed 10 months. Virginia expedited its permanency hearing to 12 months from removal.

A second permanency hearing is required three months later in New Mexico and six months later in Virginia to reconsider those cases where return to family had been seen as a feasible strategy at the first hearing, but where more experience was needed to determine whether what had appeared feasible was in fact viable. The second hearing is slanted toward moving the child away from the family unless reuinification is succeeding.

PARENTAL REHABILITATION MUST BE EXPEDITED

Expediting permanency hearings aims at increasing adoption opportunities for children where the prospect for reunification with the family is scant and the adoption time clock is ticking. Speedier determinations place a burden on the parents to "get their houses in order" more promptly or risk severance of parental rights. Lawyers who represent parents oppose accelerating these hearings. For example, their clients may have trouble obtaining substance abuse treatment, may fall off the abstinence wagon, or may need more time to emerge from an abusive relationship.

State laws are, however, placing priority on a child's safety rather than reunification with the family. And fast track parental rights terminations are being enacted with cases involving such things as abandonment, severe physical abuse, and chronic parental drug abuse. The needs of children for permanence are resonating in legislative halls.

PERMANENT HOMES FOR CHILDREN

Adoption, of course, is the favored long-term care plan for children who cannot be returned to parental care. However, not all children available for adoption attract adoptive parents. Some children have been so scarred by parental abuse or neglect and, perhaps, by problems in foster care arrangements, that they have been seen as outside the loop of adoption.

Many children removed from their parents will grow up with relatives (i.e., "kinship care"). Others will remain in foster homes throughout their childhoods, possibly with periodic stints in residential group home care. For older youth, the plan may be emancipation and the provision of supports to enable a suitable transition. A positive development has been the significant number of adoptions by foster parents.

There is state consensus to achieve far more adoptions or other permanent homes and to accomplish these more readily. Federal funding of state efforts to obtain such placements was increased in 1997. An additional stimulant is the executive action initiated by President Clinton in concert with the Department of Health and Human Services.

Adoption 2002

The President wants to accomplish a doubling of the number of children who are adopted or permanently placed by the year 2002. He has noted that returning home is not an option for about 100,000 of the more than 450,000 children in the foster care system, that 20,000 are adopted annually, and another 7,000 are permanently placed in legal guardianships.

He wants to reach this goal "by working with states to identify and break down barriers to permanent placements, setting annual numerical targets, rewarding successful performance, and raising public awareness."

All states are developing baseline data and incremental targets, and several states have received federal awards of excellence for their accomplishments to date. Congressional funding action will enable states to earn financial bonuses that reward increased adoption levels. The President noted that increased adoption levels and expedited adoptions should result in savings in foster care costs.

Children With Special Needs

"Children with special needs" is the term of art that describes children who have characteristics that make them harder to place in permanent homes. These are children with significant physical, mental, and emotional handicaps. Since children of minority heritage remain in care longer and are over-represented among the children seeking permanency, they are classified as children with special needs. So are sibling groups that merit a unified home care plan.

Nationally, children who have been freed for adoption but await adoption have a median age of almost 9-years-old. Slightly over half of these children are of minority heritage. The pool of permanent families for special needs children is insufficient. This is a barrier that needs to be overcome.

One direction to take to do this is the award of a second, supplementary bonus to states which exceed a baseline in finding permanent homes targeted for special needs children. Another is an aggressive implementation of the Multiethnic Placement Act, which bans discrimination in the placement of children on the basis of race, color, or national origin. Further, the Act requires diligent recruitment of adoptive and foster care families that reflect the ethnic and racial diversity of children needing out-of-home care.

The President has proposed, also, the incentive of a tax credit for adopting parents.

State Actions to Further Permanent Placements

South Carolina, aware that more than 60% of children in its child welfare system are African American, has created an African-American Adoption Center through a partnership between the One Church One Child organization and the Reid House of Charleston. Its three goals are to offer statewide adoption and foster care recruitment, adoptive applicant review, and community and church support services to adoptive and foster parents. Follow-up assistance, crucial to the success of the transition following adoption, is now being provided.

This effort is part of what South Carolina officials call their "backlog blitz." A new statute calls for a permanent plan within 12 months of removal. Adoptions have increased from 200 (1995) to 300 (1996), and are projected at 400 (1997), and 700 (1998). The child welfare agency, accordingly, can now redeploy certain foster care workers as adoption workers.

Utah is down to a 12-month permanent plan standard, but just six months for children less than two years of age. Private agencies have been employed in Salt Lake County to conduct adoptive home studies and, thus, expedite placements. Montana and North Dakota now use the 12-month guideline and also have contracted with private agencies to find and approve adoptive homes and convert foster parents to adoptive parents.

FIXING THE FRONT END OF THE SYSTEM

The same legislation that enabled the CIP also directed more funds to public child welfare agencies to intensify services to families and, thereby, reduce the removal of children from home in the first place. It is too early to know how effective this strategy, known as family preservation, has been, but it makes good sense.

Provision of services to avoid or shorten children's placement, however, remains often inadequate, as Arkansas found. There, high priority unmet service needs consist of emergency cash assistance, housing, transportation, homemaker services, medical and psychiatric services, in-patient substance abuse treatment, job training, and parent education.

Further, no matter what, children do reenter the system. Texas has found that 27% of children have been repetitioned back into court following an earlier successful completion of family preservation services.

Need for Attorney Representation

Often three and sometimes four different attorneys are engaged in a case — for the child welfare agency, for the child, and for at least one parent. Courts in some states have sought to limit the public costs of lawyer representation. Arkansas reports "few parents are represented at all stages of these cases." Numerous jurisdictions appoint a CASA but no attorney for the child.

Better practice mandates attorneys for children and parents and ensures their presence at the initial hearing. It is more than a matter of advocacy for a child or a parent. It leads to a better prepared hearing or agreed-to court determination. In the court's own interest, it means fewer hearings are postponed to a later date. In the public interest, it means a more fair procedure.

Colorado's report found fault with lawyers for children who had "minimal contact" with these children, who exhibited minimal levels of performance, and who "rubber-stamped" social services by failing to perform an independent investigation.

Contributing Factors to Poor Representation

The Colorado report found that court system contracts with lawyers or law firms to represent parties brought knowledgeable attorneys into play as well as high caseloads and certain minimum performance levels. These lawyers are paid $40 per hour for out-of-court preparation and $50 per hour in court. These sums are $45 and $65 per hour respectively for lawyers in Virginia who serve as guardians ad litem for children, but court-appointed attorneys for parents there have been capped at $100 per case— which curbs this advocacy and obviously needs to be raised. The hourly rate paid attorneys in Wyandotte County (Kansas City), Kansas, was found to be just $16 an hour.

Requiring better qualified attorneys, preliminary and ongoing specialized training for them, and suitable attorney compensation schemes are universal recommendations. New Arkansas legislation heals certain negative CIP findings by compelling clear notice of a parent's right to counsel, if indigent, and by creating a statewide office to standardize and improve attorney compensation and coordinate training provisions across the state.

Lawyers for child welfare agencies also took their lumps in several reports. These offices often assign neophyte lawyers to juvenile court work, rotate them frequently, assign them case overloads, believe other workloads have greater priority, or simply provide insufficient lawyer time. The public agency even lacked representation in some Virginia counties.

Additional Strategies

State reports and newly enacted laws also direct:

- *More rapidly completed adjudication, disposition, and review hearings:* New Mexico has shaved 30 days off its adjudication requirement and four months off its first judicial review hearing. Arkansas has accelerated a disposition hearing to follow within no more than 14 days of adjudication.

- *More one family/one judge scheduling:* This allows judges or judicial hearing officers to spend longer terms in the juvenile court and to take individual responsibility for a child from the beginning to the end of the court experience (and, preferably, matters involving other family members). Judges would hold review hearings three or six months after terminating parental rights in order to oversee placement progress and cajole the agency to move ahead.

- *More mediation services:* These are being mandated or offered when there is disagreement between the parties. More courts will avoid going to trial unless there has been a prior formal mediation attempt, at least in larger jurisdictions.

- *Expanded CASA programs:* The screening, training, assignment, and supervision of volunteers to assist court children is very popular. The investigations and advocacy by outside people who genuinely care for children, who often facilitate additional resources for them, and who spend more time with the children than the social workers or attorneys, are appreciated quite universally.

- *Establishment of improved management information systems (MIS):* Not only better systems, but MISs that cross over between the court and the child welfare agency are needed. The courts need better management data on their case flow, and agencies need immediately available information about court schedules and orders.

MUCH MORE TO DO

Expediting permanency for foster children is not a new concept, but it is today's national agenda. The ability of the judicial and social service systems to arrange their houses into order and compel excellence in the quality of the actors and actions to be taken in these matters, however, requires no little attention and no pause in oversight.

The two systems have now begun to talk to each other in earnest. The fit needs much tailoring, but judges, social workers, and their collaborators in this responsibility are finding substantial common ground as they focus on children's needs and interests and look at their practices and results through children's eyes. The spark of change is visible. Yet there are miles to go before they, we, and enmeshed children and families can sleep.

Author's Note

The Court Improvement Project (CIP) was extended by the Congress beyond its original four-year authorization and continues in 2002.

Congressional enactment of the Adoption and Safe Families Act (ASFA; P.L. 105-89) has boosted child welfare reforms in the states. It mandates that states hold an initial permanency hearing within 12 months rather than 18 months, and establishes that the safety of children must be the paramount consideration in decision making regarding service provision, placement, and permanency planning. It provides for expedited services to help families in crisis, while encouraging development of an early concurrent plan for implementation if reunification fails. The law promotes terminations of parental rights for children who had been in extended foster care and establishes adoption incentive payments for states to increase adoptions of children in foster care.

A General Accounting Office study (02-585) reports that adoptions of children in foster care have grown annually and reached a total of 48,680 in FY 2000. This total includes 36,947 children with special needs. ASFA requirements and adoption incentive payments were credited with stimulating this growth. Illinois, as one example, finalized an average of 2,200 annual adoptions during FY 1995-1997, compared to an average of 5,786 annual adoptions during FY 1998-2000.

Particular progress in reforming practices and procedures with child abuse and neglect cases has occurred with the ongoing federally funded Model Courts Project conducted by the National Council of Juvenile and Family Court Judges and currently in place in 23 courts. An assessment of the El Paso, Texas, model court found earlier case planning had been achieved and the average number of months to achieve case closure had been reduced from 21 in 1995 to 10 in 2000. Appointment of counsel was now accomplished early in the court process. The cases of parents subject to criminal prosecution were assigned to the judge who handled the child protection case, which facilitated consistency in judicial orders. Foster parents were included in all phases of the planning and court process. [1]

Endnotes

[1] See Gatowski, S. et al. (2002). *The El Paso, Texas 65th Judicial District Court: Evaluation of model court activities* [1999-2001]. Reno: National Council of Juvenile and Family Court Judges.

Chapter 6

Collaboration to Speed Court Process and Curb Foster Care Drift in California

The numbers are ugly. The numbers are shorthand for the children who drift into and out of California child protection agencies and juvenile courts, with less than 4% of the children placed in adoptive homes. For fiscal 1996, California's court filings in abuse and neglect increased from 32,215 to 38,629. On June 1, 1997, 104,097 children were in foster care—one-fifth of the nation's count—and one-third of these children had experienced three or more placements.

As the nation's most populous state, California should have the largest numbers. But this is an area where more is not better. Many, perhaps all, states lack pride in their own numbers. Fortunately for the children, the states have been evaluating their shortcomings in their care of these children, and staking out an array of remediation strategies.

GETTING THE PLAYERS TO "BUY IN" TO REMEDIES

Effective collaboration and coordination are critical to an effective court process. There is need for careful preparation and timely reports and testimony. All of the lawyers and everyone else have to be in the right place at the right time, and there has to be reserved, ready-to-go space on the judicial calendar. Far too often, something goes wrong and a hearing must be rescheduled. Far too often, a plan approved for a child goes awry.

California has held public hearings to listen to statements on problems and remedies. The National Center for State Courts (NCSC) conducted a California assessment. NCSC surveyed 600 professionals, performed case file reviews of stage-to-stage case processing times in six counties, and conducted extensive on-site interviews in those counties. The study revealed numerous strengths, but a wasteland of needs.

State judicial system officials then embarked on a major effort to obtain local buy-in and improvement planning. Interdisciplinary teams from the 58 California counties, each co-led by the presiding judge of the juvenile court and the director of the department of social services, gathered in San Francisco in December 1997 for the Beyond the Bench IX Conference. More than 400 officials came to review the NCSC findings, hear national presenters and in-state leaders speak to approaches found effective or

This chapter originally appeared in Report on At-Risk Children & Families, *Vol. 1, No. 1, March/April 1998.*

which held promise, and schematize how they would collaborate on progressive advancements.

In a field which until a few years ago was separated by yawning chasms and fingerpointing between the courts and the public child welfare agencies, the representative teams heard twin keynotes from the director of the state Department of Social Services (DSS) and the Chief Justice of the California Supreme Court.

Integrated and Comprehensive Case Management Needed

The DSS director, Eloise Anderson, stressed the need to accomplish integrated and comprehensive case management intervention that meets families' needs for child protection, child support, delinquency rehabilitation, and mental health and substance abuse services. She noted, correctly, that the conference would promote expedited terminations of parental rights to free more children for speedier adoptions, but warned that nine months later mothers might well give birth again unless improved outcomes were facilitated for these mothers.

Anderson commented that child protection is a police function, and that DSS agencies are like military organizations designed to go to war—but the war has held more benefits for staff than children. She urged improved social worker skills, and stressed that "... we must engage the community in our work. Courts can't keep kids safe, but communities can. We should transfer more care and treatment to communities."

Interagency Cooperation Demanded

Chief Justice Ronald George picked up the collaboration baton, stating that courts cannot work alone, but must work with the other agencies in the system. As Chief Justice and chair of the Judicial Council, the state's judicial system supervisory and oversight body, he declared that the Council has designated improved court handling of child abuse and neglect matters (known in California as dependency cases) as one of its top priorities.

He highlighted several themes which would become prominent conference concerns:

- Timeliness is especially important, and a special sense of urgency must affect this work;

- Completion of court hearings must be expedited;

- More resources are needed to decrease judicial workloads and increase the time which judicial hearing officers can allocate to case hearings;

- Unnecessary delays in determining permanent plans for children must be eliminated;

- More CASAs need to be recruited and supervised; and

- More specialized and interdisciplinary training must be conducted.

Chief Justice George, having earlier visited an array of local courthouses, proclaimed that the two worst facilities he had visited were both juvenile courts. He wants to do something about this. Others at the conference wanted to create separate, supervised children's waiting rooms in all courthouses, as supported by Judicial Council Standards of Judicial Administration. The NCSC study had observed another facility shortcoming, the all-too-common absence of court waiting area interview rooms which attorneys and social workers could use in preparation for a hearing.

SLOW CASE MOVEMENT TARGETED

California has long had very fast statutory case processing guidelines, perhaps as fast as any in the nation. An adjudication hearing for a child removed from a family is to occur within 18 court days of removal, and a judicial disposition within 10 additional court days. Petitions that do not involve removals have 60 calendar days to complete this overall process.

The NCSC case reviews, focused essentially on fast-track removal cases, revealed that the timelines are not being complied with (this phenomenon is certainly not unique to California). Just two of the six counties got to disposition within 60 days in 50% of cases. The slowest 10% of cases in the four slowest counties required from six to 12 months to reach disposition.

The permanency hearing, where a permanent plan is to be approved for a child, by law is to be conducted no later than 18 months from removal. But the median six-county time was 23 months, and the 75th percentile of these hearings occurred at 27 months.

Time guidelines always allow for good cause exceptions to the rules, but these courts and their collaborative agencies much too readily accept exceptions and allow significant patterns of delay. California officials expressed determination to better meet the time guidelines. Further, the completion of a permanent plan within 12 months of removal was targeted.

Avoiding Rescheduling of Cases

A prominent court management principle is that judges should insist on universal readiness and maintain a "strict continuance policy." The lawyers, social workers, parties, and witnesses are to be present in court, prepared to proceed at the appointed hour, and the court shall start on time.

But NCSC case file reviews found that 47% of adjudication hearings, 45% of disposition hearings, and 62% of permanency planning hearings had to be rescheduled, and that two and even three continuances were quite common. The failure to notify or locate a parent, to have sufficient court time available to proceed with a scheduled case, or to file a timely report were frequent reasons stated for deferring hearings. Another reason is a late attorney appointment, particularly for a parent.

Further, many of these courts do "block," rather than "time-certain" scheduling. With block scheduling, many if not all cases are scheduled for 8:30 a.m. or 9:00 a.m., court waiting rooms appear more like zoos, and cases may not be heard until 11 a.m., later, or carried over to another day. There was considerable conference interest in breaking down a judicial calendar and reorganizing it so that most cases could be heard within 30-60 minutes of a scheduled time.

Scheduling Approaches

Another calendaring aid would be to have juvenile courts hear these cases in a concentrated schedule, not integrated with delinquency cases. Then, agency social workers could complete their different hearings *seriatim*. This efficiency concept applies to legal professionals, as well, who increasingly specialize either in abuse and neglect cases or delinquency matters.

Another specialization practice, used in several large, multi-judge California courts, is to have the same team of an agency attorney, child's attorney, and parent's attorney assigned to one courtroom only. This concept, which attracted conference interest, avoids the problem of a judge having to wait to begin a hearing until one lawyer completes a hearing in a different courtroom or courthouse.

Speeding Paperwork

The length of time, often six weeks, which is presently required to clear channels and get a parent to court from a state or federal prison was another cited concern. This problem causes both a slowed-down process and case rescheduling when the parent is not transported in time for the hearing. There was interest in both local-level and state-level efforts to improve procedures and timeliness.

Deficiencies in accomplishing early notifications to out-of-custody parents was another problem addressed. Still another was late-filed social worker reports, a shortcoming complained about across the nation. While the Los Angeles County DSS director urged conference participants to "love" social workers and appreciate the incredibly difficult tasks they perform and decisions they must make, judges generally would find it easier to love the social workers if their case reports have gotten to court on time. Some judges lack awareness, however, that poor court case flow management renders social work witnesses less efficient and contributes to the lateness of these reports. Nonetheless, the different disciplines are talking more with each other, and more efficient practices should result.

THE LAWYERS' ROLE: QUESTIONS OF FAIRNESS, TIME, AND COST

Although federal law mandates a guardian ad litem for every child, and this can be interpreted to require either an attorney, a court appointed special advocate (CASA), or a responsible individual who can represent and present the child's best interests, at least several counties admitted they do not comply with this law. They prefer to limit the public funds they expend on attorneys, and, likely, the judicial officer believes that fewer attorneys enable more settlements and require fewer trials.

Many California courts disagree, and insist there be a lawyer for every child, for every parent who has lost custody of a child, for every out-of-custody parent who requests one, and a government lawyer for the agency. Whether the agency lawyer can serve, also, as the child's lawyer, is arguable. Los Angeles County judges have taken a firm stand and will not appoint the county counsel as the child's attorney. They see dual representation as a conflict of interest, and an appellate court has approved the court's insistence on singular representation. Numerous California courts permit dual representation, however.

Other attorney issues are the heavy public costs, deficiencies in representation due to certain ultraheavy caseloads, deficits in the quality of representation by some attorneys, stronger specialized training needs, and better compliance with the recommended state standard that attorneys serve at least two years and, preferably, three to five years in this setting. Also, attorneys too often complete their interviews and enter into negotiations on the day of a hearing, rather than on an earlier date. Accordingly, they are not "ready-to-go" when the judge is.

WORKLOAD STANDARDS FOR ATTORNEYS AND JUDGES

How many cases, summed up from the different types of abuse and neglect cases and stages of proceedings that take varying time investments, can a judge—or an attorney—handle effectively? This concept, lacking here and elsewhere, is referred to as "weighted caseloads."

Behind the NCSC recommendation that the Judicial Council should promote the designation of an adequate number of judicial officers is the implication that weighted caseload measures should be developed for these courts. But this is no easy task. There is no national empirically-based workload measure, and even if there were one, it would require considerable adaptation to guide any state's measured determination of need.

Officials who were interviewed in Los Angeles stated unequivocally that there needed to be more judicial personpower. In low population counties such as Humboldt and Butte, interviewees indicated that the resources and time devoted to this caseload were not adequate, but were within tolerable ranges. The broad statewide mail-in survey of officials found that the amount of time allotted for different types of hearings was seriously below what *Resource Guidelines*, the product of national judicial and legal organizations working in this field, has recommended.

A rationale for more judges is the overall slow pace of case movement. Further, more than a third of surveyed judges acknowledged that when they held a contested hearing, sometimes, often, or most of the time they began the hearing one day but had to continue the hearing to another date, frequently 10 to 30 days later, in order to complete the trial.

GOAL: ONE FAMILY/ONE JUDGE

California juvenile courts are always divisions or units of the superior court, that state's general trial court. The juvenile courts have long relied on referees or commissioners to supplement the judge(s) assigned to this court. It is easier to appoint a lawyer as a referee or commissioner than to obtain legislative approval for another judgeship.

Observation suggests there is growing judicial interest in California in obtaining an assignment to juvenile court, and in remaining there for a lengthier term. The NCSC study found that referees and commissioners had a median time on this bench of just under seven years, and that judges reported a median time of 3.5 years. Pre-bench legal experience with abuse and neglect cases was reported by 77% of referees and commissioners and 39% of judges. These are positive findings.

Less positive was the finding that court clients far too often face a different judicial officer when they return for another hearing. Clients experienced at least three judicial officers in 30% of case file reviews, and 13% of the cases reported more than three such officers. Conference participants expressed considerable interest in curbing this practice, and in seeking to maximize the likelihood that court clients would experience just one judicial officer during the lifetime of their case.

There are pilot courts in this state that are merging certain family-related matters and all juvenile matters to form family court divisions—seeking to stretch the one family/one judge model to a broader array of cases and allow for a more focused judicial concentration on wider family concerns.

REDUCING THE NEED FOR CASE FILINGS

There is hope that a federally assisted DSS effort with intensive family preservation will bear fruit. The theory is sound, that pouring in resources and a social worker who only has two to three at-risk families to assist should be able to prevent some removals and some court petitions.

Another trickier petition-reduction measure involves voluntary placements. Federal law permits voluntary placements for up to six months, and a California-acquired waiver will allow this for up to 12 months. Voluntary placement means that a family consents to a removal and, if all works well, a petition and lawyers and court hearings can be avoided. But parents' attorneys doubt there can be a true, knowledged, willful consent. They believe coercion will occur, or that parents will not know their rights or have the ability and strength to exercise these rights. A high-up DSS official is wary, too, but believes this can work suitably with placements with relatives.

DSS is designing a grander prevention strategy which will greatly expand and, it is hoped, over time universalize home visitations for newborns in at-risk families. This is a prevention direction which research has found to be effective.

USING FAMILY GROUP CONFERENCES

Another approach which can reduce formal court intervention is family group conferencing, the New Zealand import now in place in Santa Clara and several other California counties. The conference gathers the extended family as far as it can extend, so long as the mother or father can accept these family members. Children age 12 and older may attend, and a non-attorney guardian, designated by the legal agency which represents children, is present. Primary purposes of a conference are to engage participants' assistance with the child and parent(s), determine whether a relative can take temporary custody of a child, and inform and link participants with useful community resources.

Santa Clara County DSS has trained more than 50 staff member facilitators, as well as 16 staff members of community-based organizations. About 130 conferences had been held through mid-December 1997, 53% of them at pre-petition stages. The results to date have been very encouraging.

The Santa Clara court commissioner, who has served in this position since 1983, states: "Nothing that I've ever seen gives me so much hope as family group conferencing. The power stays with those who know the most about the problems; families are trusted to solve their own problems with assistance. The process does not look to a judge for a decision."

WORKING TOGETHER

The December 1997 conference participants generally favored an expansion of mediation services, which are offered in a number of these courts to facilitate informal, non-adversarial resolutions. Court after court called for improved automation to enable the production of instant court orders, to track cases and time frames, and to produce management reports that allow a system to really know where it is and to plan how to get to where it wants to go.

The vision of this California conference was that each county develop and implement a local action plan, with support, such as on-site technical assistance and technology advancements, provided by the Judicial Council and the State DSS. County-by-county progress is to be reviewed at "Beyond the Bench X," to be held in late 1998.

But beyond all the improvement tasks that are to be put into place was the stated imperative that there must be close, regularized, ongoing collaboration across the spectrum; the actualization of interdisciplinary ownership of both problems and solutions; an openness which builds trust. The fulcrum of the collaborative effort is the juvenile court judge, and every judge who attended this conference is likely to have returned home pledged to do his or her best to provide leadership to local efforts to bring far more hope to court children.

Author's Note

California court filings fell from 38,629 in FY 1999 to 35,787 in FY 2001. As of July 1, 2001, 97,024 California children were in foster care, a reduction of approximately 7,000 from the 1997 total. Seventy-two percent of these children were children of color, who otherwise constituted 50% of the state's population of children. Thirty-eight percent of children of color were placed in kinship care. Of all children in foster care, just 4% were less than 1-year-old while 72% were age 6 or older.[1]

Endnotes

[1] Judicial Council of California (2002). *Statistical report.* San Francisco: Author; Needell, B. et al. (2002). *Child welfare services reports for California.* Berkeley: University of California Center for Social Services Research.

Chapter 7

Revisiting Status Offenders

Historically, juvenile delinquency included what we now term status offenses. As such, these offenders were subject to any of the dispositions allowed for delinquents. An ungovernable child, for example, could be dispatched to a state institution as readily as a chronic or severe juvenile law violator, and many were.

DECRIMINALIZATION OF STATUS OFFENDERS BEGINS

This situtation began to change in 1961 when California legislators, concerned about unbridled discretion and due-process-deficient juvenile proceedings, enacted sweeping statutory revisions. One such change separated non-criminal conduct from the delinquency definition and differentiated the status offender from the delinquent child. Another change made the commitment of status offenders to the state's youth authority more difficult.

New York made similar changes a year later, creating the status offender term of person in need of supervision (PINS). Illinois (MINS), Colorado (CHINS), New Jersey (JINS), Montana (YINS), and Ohio (Unruly), among numerous other states, then took similar action. Pennsylvania and Florida, taking a somewhat different tack, placed status offenders within their definitions of child dependency or neglect and, along with at least three other states, shifted service responsibility from probation officers to state social services agencies. Thus, decriminalization of status offenders progressed.

ADVOCATES MOBILIZE TO CHANGE TREATMENT OF STATUS OFFENDERS

In the years that followed, numerous national organizations urged repeal of court jurisdiction over victimless crimes committed by juveniles. They argued that the judicial system was not designed to handle children in conflict with their parents or the rebelliousness and resistance to authority that characterize adolescence. They urged that this should be a community, not a court, responsibility.

Defense lawyers, who radically strengthened their juvenile court presence following the U.S. Supreme Court decision in **In re Gault**, 387 U.S. 1(1967), made much of the legal difference between status offending and law offending. They challenged, though usually unsuccessfully, vagueness in state definitions of "habitual truancy," "habitual disobedience," and "beyond the control of one's parents." There followed challenges as to whether status offenders, like delinquents, must be afforded notice of a right to counsel and free counsel, whether court sanctioning for non-criminal mis-

This chapter originally appeared in Juvenile Justice Update, *Vol. 5, No. 6, December/January 2000.*

behavior constituted cruel and unusual punishment, whether a beyond a reasonable doubt proof standard applied, whether one act of disobedience constituted incorrigibility, and whether extending jurisdiction over girls to an older age than for boys was constitutional (it was not).

Researchers made much of findings that 40% of juveniles detained in certain adult jails and 48% of those held in 10 pretrial juvenile detention centers were status offenders, that 45%-55% of residents committed to juvenile correctional institutions were status offenders, and that 60%-70% of girls ordered into correctional facilities had not committed criminal acts.

PASSAGE OF JUVENILE JUSTICE AND DELINQUENCY PREVENTION ACT LEADS TO FUNDAMENTAL CHANGES

In 1974, Congress responded by enacting the Juvenile Justice and Delinquency Prevention Act (JJDPA). States that accepted funding under the Act were prohibited, following a grace period, from institutionalizing status offenders in delinquency facilities and locking them up in secure pretrial detention facilities, except for brief periods under limited circumstances. States bought in, and the result was a sea change in court handling of status offenders. Due to curbs on court sanctioning, law enforcement apprehension of status offenders dropped markedly after passage of the JJDPA, and police, school, and parent referrals to juvenile courts dropped as well. Close to 200,000 non-delinquent children had been held annually in secure confinement when the JJDPA was passed in 1974; by 1981, this number had been reduced by 82%. Thus, the ban on the use of secure detention and institutionalization has largely succeeded.

Violation of Valid Court Order Permits Judges to Sanction Status Offenders

Some judges who continued to accept status offense cases were stymied in their efforts to compel conformity from nonconforming youths. Predictably, states failed to invest significant money in alternatives to court intervention. Pressured to take these cases by schools, parents, and law enforcement and social agencies, judges were hamstrung when their rules were violated, as inevitably some were. Consequently, more than a few courts "bootstrapped" repeat status offenders into delinquents in order to gain access to delinquency sanctions.

This practice, while scorned by many, found its way into a 1980 amendment to the JJDPA that allowed courts to place a reoffending status offender in secure detention. The JJDPA required only that an offender initially be provided clear judicial warning that the consequences of violating judicially imposed conditions could include secure detention. The second violation was not a bootstrapped delinquency, but a civil contempt of a court order.

Some Courts Continue to Intervene Extensively With Status Offenders

Some juvenile courts, particularly suburban and rural ones, define themselves as receptive to status offense referrals. One suburban Louisiana county I examined a

Handling Status Offenders in a Large Urban Environment

"I don't want to be a paper tiger," said a judge of a large urban juvenile court that I recently evaluated. "I believe status offenders will become delinquents unless we get them the right kinds of help, and I must back this up with 'therapeutic incarceration.' They fail to comply with my orders or they walk away from shelter facilities, so I must use the secure detention center for up to 20 days. I must assert the court's authority when they have 'oppositional defiance.'"

I found an annual average of 1,783 status offenders processed by this court's intake or beyond during the past five years—18% of the combined status offender-delinquency caseload. (The annual average of delinquency cases was 8,034.) The status offender total included 263 youths brought to court attention for truancy.

The extent of this court and this judge's engagement with status offenses piqued my interest and curiosity. My perception had long been that large urban courts pretty well ignored status offenders since the decriminalization movement and its accompanying curbs on locking up these youths. But no, this court went against this premise. My observations follow.

Extensive Involvement With Status Offenders Generally Disliked

This urban judge mandates family mediation or counseling, anger management classes, and includes out-of-home placements in the sanctions status offenders receive. When the judge orders reoffending status offenders into the secure detention center, the center's administration gets many sleepless nights. The judge also imposes up to a 90-day commitment to a state boot camp which also houses delinquent offenders. The other judges hinted displeasure with the extent of the status offense judge's specialized workload in the face of what they viewed as more pressing workloads for judicial officers. A court public defender also complained. With just three-plus defenders to handle the entire court, one defender is tied up day-in/day-out in the status offense division. The public defender observed: "We are required to represent all kids in this judicial division. Hearings typically take an hour each, and this is not our priority."

Prosecutors do not attend status offender hearings. The judge has mandated an attorney for all status offense youth, which is good practice, but also requires a guardian ad litem (GAL). GALs in this jurisdiction are court-paid private attorneys, pro bono attorneys, or, questionably, probation officers.

Detention and Crisis Counselors Used

Probation staff at this court control admission to the executive-administered secure detention facility. Runaways may be locked up initially for 24

Continued on next page

Continued from previous page

hours if no parent is available to take them home. After 24 hours, if parents refuse or fail to appear to pick up their children, the child protection agency is given temporary custody of the child. Curfew violators are not detained unless the violator is on probation status.

To its credit, the court inserts crisis counselors at the front end of the system. Their post-complaint, pre-petition intervention shortstops numerous filings and is a prerequisite to a petition. Nonetheless, status offenses comprise 90% of the case hearing/management time of the one status offense judge.

Significant Probation Officer Attention Given

Nine probation officers work exclusively with status offenders. The total workload ranges between 211-236 youth and averages 23-26 per officer. This contrasts with the delinquency workload where 16 probation officers are responsible for approximately 1,475 adjudicated offenders, an average of about 92 per officer. This court, at present, seems to find it more expedient to seek to address non-criminal misbehaviors than to further public safety by focusing its efforts on offenders who injure others.

decade ago received more status offense referrals in a year than all the juvenile courts in California combined. A paucity of intervention services in rural areas often convinces judges that their engagement with status offenders meets a real community need. Surprisingly, some urban courts also elect to intervene with status offenders despite the high demands of their delinquency dockets (See boxed report).

Does Intervention With Status Offenders Reduce Delinquency?

Conventional wisdom states that assisting status offenders thwarts future delinquencies. This may seem reasonable, but it is not confirmed by research findings. Different studies of status offender careers contain little evidence to support the escalation hypothesis. Status offenders, like delinquents, reoffend frequently, but usually commit new status offenses. One study found that when escalation occurred, it was more often to a misdemeanor, and less often to a felony.[1] Another study found that 62% of status offenders never returned to court again.[2] A Chicago study found that 68% did not escalate to delinquent acts.[3]

Also, an eight-site follow-up survey of 3,017 status offenders found that 69% had no subsequent offense of any type. When they did recidivate, reoffenses occurred less often than with a comparison delinquency group. Further, 55% of the status offenders who recidivated committed another status offense.[4] Other studies have found status offender reoffenses carried low seriousness scores and that escalation by male reoffenders was more likely to be a property offense. Runaway girls often run from abusive homes; only very infrequently do they escalate into serious delinquency.[5]

Certainly, many delinquents have truancy backgrounds, and truants commit numerous delinquencies during the hours they should be in school. But again, there is no clear line of escalation from truancy to delinquency to serious delinquency.

NATIONALLY, JUVENILE COURTS HANDLE MORE STATUS OFFENDERS

The National Center for Juvenile Justice data archive reports significant increases in both numbers and rates of status offense petitions over the 10-year span from 1987-1996 in each of the four specific offense categories that are counted (runaway, truancy, ungovernability, and liquor law violation) and in a miscellaneous category as well. Much of the increase took place from 1992 through 1996. The NCJJ report did not cover the number of status offenders referred to a court, just those petitioned.

During the 10-year period, the number of all types of status offense petitions jumped from 80,600 to 162,000, a 101% increase, and the petition rate for every 1,000 youth at risk of referral rose from 3.2 to 5.7 (an 81% increase). Miscellaneous offenses, apparently led by curfew violations, showed the largest growth.

In 1996, male juveniles were involved in 59% of the cases, bolstered by liquor law violations that involved males in nearly 7 of 10 petitions. About 6 in 10 runaways involved girls. Boys were engaged in 53% of truancy and 57% of ungovernability cases. Detention was used in 10% of runaway cases, 7% of ungovernability cases, 6% of liquor law violations, and 2% of truancy cases, but declined over the 10-year span.[6]

A final note on court processing: Just 52% of petitioned status offenders were adjudicated. Of these, 59% received probation, 14% were placed in residential facilities, and the balance received "other" sanctions such as counseling or treatment, community service, restitution, or fines.[7]

COURTS CAN EXPECT MORE STATUS OFFENDER REFERRALS

Outbursts of Juvenile Violence Prompt Community Prevention Interventions

Juvenile courts should prepare for more status offense referrals for several reasons. First, both during and after the violent offense rampages by juveniles in recent years, interest in preventing juvenile crime of all sorts expanded. More, but of course not enough, money and energy are flowing into prevention. Prevention includes focusing on school truancy and child-family conflict. But when these prevention efforts fail, and many will fail, there will likely be a greater turn to court.

Second, in the aftermath of the Columbine High School slayings in Littleton, Colorado, many communities did extensive soul-searching and resolved to increase services to children and youth who exhibited unusual behaviors that raised the specter of psychological difficulties. In addition, parents, concerned about their children, are more likely to seek child or family counseling, and some will turn to the juvenile court for its reinforcing authority.

Third, truancy is now of great concern, not only because truancy is sometimes connected to delinquent offenses during school time, but also because it both interferes with preparation for lifelong achievement and impedes students' ability to achieve the test scores they need to earn their diplomas and that schools require for accreditation.

Curfews Add to Status Offender Docket

In recent years, significantly more community curfew ordinances have been enacted. These statutes are, increasingly, withstanding constitutional challenges. Further, tighter enforcement of these ordinances is viewed as preventative.

Stricter Liquor Law Enforcement Leads to More Referrals

A large federal initiative is underway to help the 50 states develop comprehensive and coordinated approaches to enforce laws that prohibit sales to and consumption of alcohol by minors. Educational and community strategies accompany this effort. While all this has merit, it is likely to result in more documented liquor law violations and subsequent court referrals.

Community Assessment Centers May Result in Greater Court Involvement

Community assessment centers (CACs) are being established to provide a one-stop shop for "at-risk" and law-violating juveniles. They can be places for police to take apprehended truants or curfew violators and, with other referral sources, seek improved parental engagement, along with professional assessment and case management. CACs prompt worries about stigmatizing and labeling youth, widening the juvenile justice net, and due process deprivations, but they are part of the expanding effort to intervene early with services—and will lead to court referrals when youths or their families fail to cooperate.

WHERE DO WE GO FROM HERE?

Among the legislative provisions before Congress are efforts to relieve states of the deinstitutionalization mandates of the JJDPA. If these go, many states could be expected to give judges the authority to lock up these youth. This would be unfortunate. While judges should not be left powerless to deal with status offenders, permitting judges to institutionalize them as was done in the past would be even more unsatisfactory. Overall, it is better to "just say no" and for the court to stay away from general intervention.

Liquor law and curfew violations can be appropriately handled by summary processing punishable by fine and/or community service, or the use of a one-shot educational program. Certain runaways and ungovernable children may appropriately be handled as dependent or neglected. Tobacco violations should be ignored.

Courts should avoid filing truancy petitions. Court leadership in the development of sound community resources and court alternatives for status offense youth is an easy recommendation to urge.

The prime sponsor of the JJDPA, Senator Birch Bayh, once urged juvenile justice professionals to consider the

> ...sensible words of Carl Van Doren, who wrote: "Affection, indulgence, and humor alike are powerless against the instincts of children to rebel. It is as essential to their minds and wills as exercise is to their bodies. If they have no reasons for it, they will invent them, like nations bound on war. It is hard to imagine families limp enough to always be at peace. Wherever there is character there will be conflict. The best that parents and children can hope for is that the wounds of their conflict may not be too deep or too lasting."[8]

So let us tread softly and do the least harm.

Author's Note

The proposed amendment to the U.S. Juvenile Justice and Delinquency Prevention Act was not approved by Congress.

Endnotes

[1] Murray, J.P., (Ed.) (1983). *Status offenders: A sourcebook.* Boys Town, NE: Boys Town Center, at pp. 16–17.

[2] Thomas, C.W. (1976). Are status offenders really so different? A comparative and longitudinal assessment. *Crime & Delinquency, 22,* 438-455.

[3] Rankin, J.H. & Wells, L.E. (1985). From status to delinquent offenders: Escalation? *Journal of Criminal Justice, 13,* 171-180.

[4] Kobrin, S. & Klein, M.W. (1982). *National evaluation of the deinstitutionalization of status offenders programs, Vol. 2.* Washington, DC: Office of Juvenile Justice and Delinquency Prevention.

[5] Shelden, R.G. et al. (1989). Do status offenders get worse? Some clarification on the question of escalation. *Crime & Delinquency, 35*(2), 202-216.

[6] Snyder, H.N. & Sickmund, M. (1999). *Juvenile offenders and victims: 1999 national report.* Washington, DC: Office of Juvenile Justice and Delinquency Prevention, pp. 166-169.

[7] Id.

[8] Bayh, B. (1975). Juvenile justice. Des Moines: Iowa Civil Liberties Union, p. 38.

Chapter 8

What Is a Juvenile Court? On the Function of the Court as Disciplinarian for Non-Dangerous School Offenses

RELIANCE ON JUVENILE COURT TO SOLVE TRUANCY AND MINOR SCHOOL DELINQUENCY ON THE RISE

Statistics show, and informal reports support, that schools increasingly turn to juvenile courts to solve problems presented by errant juveniles. Nationally, from 1988-1997, truancy referrals to juvenile courts increased by 96%. Washington State, for example, reported 2,203 truancy filings for 1995 but 16,607 for 1998. In the states, 59% of all truancy petitions result in adjudication, while 41% are either dismissed or handled informally. Probation, with an array of conditions, is by far the most common sanction.[1]

While there are no data available on trends of referrals for minor school offenses, my ongoing studies of juvenile courts have found regular and unequivocal staff reports, indeed complaints, of such increased referrals. It appears that more schools are turning to juvenile courts to handle minor school-related offenses, matters earlier handled informally by school officials without court intervention.

There should be no disagreement that significant crimes committed in school settings should be referred to the court. Whether minor school offenses and truancies should be referred, however, is debatable. This is not to suggest that they should be ignored. They are disruptive to teaching and learning and require interventions. The debate should be about how and by whom they are addressed.

Children Need Education to Succeed

There are many reasons schools turn to the courts to solve problems that arise with students on their campuses. Some motivation is altruistic. A child requires a solid education to "make it" in this complex world. Chronic absences impede the learning enterprise. As children fall behind, the likelihood they will graduate from high school and enter college evaporates. Most schools turn first to the family. Some

This chapter originally appeared in Juvenile Justice Update, *Vol. 7, No. 5, October/November 2001.*

use a school counselor or social worker to assist a family in obtaining a child's reliable attendance. Some test to determine whether undiagnosed disabilities are contributing to truancy or behavior problems. Some refer families to community agencies to address intrafamily issues that have an impact on attendance. Others provide cultural competency training to their educators and support staff. But truancies often continue. Then what? Judicial authority will be invoked to buttress school and community efforts. This may be invoked earlier in some communities than in others.

Cases Referred to Court May Add to School Funding

In other instances, motivation stems from self-interest. That motivation may result from funding considerations. For example, in Colorado, one day each October is known as "count day." Based on that day, public schools must submit their pupil enrollments to the state department of education for funding purposes. The more students enrolled on "count day," the more state dollars the schools will receive. Because chronic truants do not count in the enrollment total on "count day," school districts send out social workers or counselors or truant officers prior to "count day" to foster attendance. They also file truancy petitions, because a chronic truant for whom a petition has been filed in the court does count. This enables the school to get state funding for this child. Hence, the school has a financial incentive to refer to the court.

Truants May Commit Crimes

Police officers are aware that considerable juvenile crime takes place during school hours in mid-afternoon. They may, acting preventively and positively, scoop up a truant and return him or her to school or to an assessment center if there is one in the community. The center may invoke parental assistance or seek to connect the youth and family to a community intervention agency, which may arrange for a mentor or placement in an alternative school. They may even seek the filing of a juvenile court petition based on dependency in lieu of truancy.

However, while many delinquent youth have truancy backgrounds, there is no clear line of escalation from truancy to delinquency to serious delinquency. Nonetheless, fear that delinquencies may flow from truancy may well lead to the intake door of the juvenile court.

Fear of Violence in School

School officials, justifiably, are worried about violence at school. All know the name Columbine. They know of recent suburban and rural killings of school children by other school children. They also work within a framework of legislatively imposed zero-tolerance policies that compel a sharp punitive reaction to any weapon, any hint of violence, or any kind of drug possession. While provable serious offenses need to go to court, schools should distinguish between those and minor offenses that should not require court intervention. But there are ubiquitous reports of students sent home, suspended, or expelled for modest or innocent mistakes and for exercising poor though harmless judgment. There are large, perhaps vast, numbers of suspensions or expulsions; many include the second punishment of a referral to court. In still other areas, schools suspend or expel children from school for offenses that take them to juvenile court, even if committed off school grounds. The American Bar Association now opposes zero tolerance policies and mandatory punishments.

Presence of Police Officers in Schools

Then there is the matter of police officers in schools. There are more police officers in more schools today than ever before, in large part because federal money for local policing has resulted in a far greater police presence in educational settings. They are there for different reasons—to teach about the harms of drugs, to help maintain order, to take charge when weapons or drugs are discovered or when significant assaultive behavior occurs, and to handle disruptions large or small. They can make major contributions to school safety. But too often they refer minor matters to the court. Just because they are there, matters that might have been handled informally are more likely to go to court. Additionally, law enforcement agencies count how many arrests their officers make. They are not likely to give the same kind of credit for offense prevention that they give to higher arrest totals.

Moreover, naming an offense for court purposes often makes it look more serious than it is. A minor shoving incident becomes a battery. Slamming a door represents school disruption. Snatching a peer's lunch money is a robbery. Ignoring a police officer's questions and then leaving school grounds constitutes evading arrest. An exploratory touching of another person may become attempted sexual assault. In fact, one youth's playground experiment to focus the sun's rays through a magnifying glass to ignite a small piece of paper became arson when referred to a California juvenile court.

Required Communication Between Courts and Schools Changes Traditional Confidentiality

Another policy change, reflected in statutes in a number of states such as North Carolina and Virginia, abandons the traditional confidentiality of juvenile court records and proceedings to require probation officers or court clerks to inform schools of some of the delinquent acts committed by their students. North Carolina requires probation officers to notify schools before the beginning of the next school day of a felony offense, juvenile court dispositional orders, or transfer to criminal court. Virginia requires intake officers to notify school superintendents when students are charged with certain enumerated felonies. Court clerks must notify the superintendents when youths are adjudicated for these offenses. While schools can use this information to better understand the problems their students are experiencing and to provide services, both academic and personal, they can also use it to label them as troublemakers and exclude them from school.

Losing Teachable Moments

There are reasons why the number of referrals to court should be minimized. There are many lessons that students can learn when truancy or lesser delinquent behavior is handled informally by the schools. Bernadine Dohrn, who directs the Children and Family Justice Center of the Northwestern University Legal Clinic that serves the Cook County Juvenile Court in Chicago, notes that school-based offenses such as fighting, theft, and vandalism used to be handled by school officials—by referring to the vice principal, requiring after-school tasks, holding parent conferences, prompting apologies, or other informal measures. It would have been difficult to imagine police being called, arrests and handcuffs employed, court filings and incarceration being options. However,

> Rather than insisting on the teaching potential in adolescent misbehavior for both the miscreant and the other students, rather than seizing the 'teachable moment,' rather than keeping an educational perspective on sanctioning and social accountability, principals and teachers—admittedly under pressure from frightened parents—have ceded their authority to law enforcement personnel, particularly to police and prosecutors, and willingly participated in excluding troublemakers, difficult kids, disabled youth, and children in trouble from the very education that is their primary hope.[2]

SCHOOL AND COMMUNITY-BASED MEASURES BENEFIT BOTH THE COMMUNITY AND MISCREANT YOUTH

Some schools use trained peer mediators to resolve problems. Other schools use circling, gathering peers into a circle with the participants suggesting reasons for the problem and approaches to resolution. Such programs engage non-offending youth in problem resolution, thus teaching skills to a wide range of students.

In addition, some schools arrange for trained adult mediators to work with conflicts involving children, parents, and teachers. Schools can also tap service agencies that exist in most communities to work with child and family issues. Youth recreation agencies provide opportunities for troubled and troublesome juveniles to work off steam in the presence of friendly and interested staff members. There are growing numbers of ethnic minority service programs with staff who may understand ethnic minority youngsters and families better than school staff. Other measures can be taken or undertaken without a turn to the court.

Let's look now to a few of the many positive approaches to dealing with truancy and lesser school-related offenses that exist in several communities across the country.

Delaware County, Ohio

The schools and the court jointly fund two school liaisons who facilitate interorganizational communication, provide informal interventions that prevent formal court involvement, participate in developing individualized education plans, provide crisis interventions in the school, intervene informally with youth who have truancy charges pending, and develop school/court behavior plans or advocate at school for youth who are court-involved. A court mediator is available to conduct school-based mediation when that is needed.

Santa Cruz County, California

The probation agency supplies a staff member to serve as a hearing officer for truancy and other school matters that are not resolved by the county School Attendance Review Board. The policy of the local court probation agency directs the hearing officer to avert formal handling of these matters. Instead, the hearing officer regularly directs the school to change a juvenile's curriculum, or be more culturally sensitive, or reach out further to the family, or transfer the youth to an alternative school. And when these measures fail? They still divert these children from court filing. Negligent parents who make no effort to get their children to school, however, have been referred to the district attorney for prosecution.

Fresno County, California

Probation department leadership obtained state and local funding to purchase an array of services that target more than 1,100 elementary and middle school youths who have had the most absences and tardiness. "Keep Kids in School" (KIDS) inserts community-based organization services such as tutoring, mentoring, family counseling, mental health services, anger management classes, and after-school recreation programs. Prevention of delinquency is a program goal. Working with the "whole family" is a project objective. A Fresno newspaper (Fresno Bee, April 23, 2000) reports that the increased attendance resulting from the interventions has enabled the school district to obtain an additional $216,000 in state average daily attendance money, more than the amount the district contributed to the program.

Court-Related Special Programs

While I prefer community-based interventions to court referrals, a number of juvenile courts gear up specialized efforts for these juveniles once they have been to court. For example, Cobb County, Georgia, next door to Atlanta, assigns up to 70 such youths to a specialized probation officer whose job is to maintain consistent contact with these juveniles, their families, and school officials. Further, all parents must attend Common Sense Parenting classes provided by the court.

The Fulton County Juvenile Court (Atlanta), Georgia, has maintained a Truancy Intervention Project (TIP) in collaboration with the Atlanta Bar Association since 1991. Volunteer lawyers, more than 500 in the past decade, accompany truancy youth to court hearings and provide ongoing mentorship, while another entity coordinates the provision of additional resources needed by these youths and families. TIP served 60% of the 225 truancy cases referred in 2000 and reported high success rates with return to school and avoidance of additional truancy referrals.

Across the country, there are countless other special court-related efforts for truants. And there are countless truants and minor school offenders. The question comes down to: Why court?

Court Truancy and Minor School Delinquency Interventions Can Be Expensive

In 2000, I studied an urban court that served a population slightly in excess of 500,000 persons. An enormous array of resources was mobilized to deal with 947 truancy filings, which entailed 1,796 truancy hearings. Personal service of legal process was first made on the family in each case, at a cost of $20-$30 per service. The private attorney employed by the school board was paid $66,173 during the year to bring truants to justice. Those appointed as attorneys or guardians *ad litem* for the truants were compensated $26,161. Also involved were sheriff deputies guarding courtrooms, interpreters who were appointed and paid in numerous cases, and a part-time court magistrate who conducted the hearings which typically required at least one-full day a week and involved, toward the end of the school year, as many as 60 scheduled hearings in a day.

The court division clerk's time cost $9,598 for these cases. A school social worker attended at least the first hearing of all children who appeared. A child protective services agency worker also attended all hearings to determine if the case appeared to have child abuse/neglect/dependency correlates (and made 83 referrals as a result). A school department employee prepared all petitions for court filing. Several community agencies had staff members in attendance as they might be asked to accept referral of a youth into their reeducation programs.

Some Courts Lock-Up Truants

Schools turn to courts because of their powers. But these powers are not always exercised in ways that rehabilitate youngsters. The batting average does not win most valuable player awards. For example, it is not uncommon for a judicial officer to lock up a repeat truant in a secure detention facility. It is not uncommon for a judicial officer to lock up a truant, earlier placed on probation for a minor delinquency, in a secure detention facility, sometimes for as long as 45 days. In this way the truant or minor offender may have his or her first intensive interaction with youths accused of serious crimes. The detention center takes the place of school and the lessons taught may well be those we would rather not have these children learn.

Youths Are Drawn Further Into the System

Truants and lesser school offenders who are placed on probation are required to comply with many probation conditions (in one court, 29 specific conditions). And if one opens the door to the court, the court has to be prepared to take action when a youth returns with a new violation. Thus the youth may be drawn into the juvenile delinquency system for minor acting out behavior, and probation violations draw him or her further into the system, with penalties increasing in severity.

For example, in 2000, the Ohio General Assembly added "chronic truancy" to its code.[3] Chronic truants are absent more days than "habitual truants" and fit within the Ohio status offense grouping known as "unruly child." One cannot be found unruly twice for habitual truancy. The second time around, the youth is classified as a delinquent child! Further, if the first petition was based on a chronic rather than habitual truancy, then the court petition is in delinquency. This deviates from the national norm that requires a youth to commit an act that would be a crime if committed by an adult in order for the youth to be charged with delinquency. Delinquency based on school absences is a throwback to the early *parens patriae* juvenile code days.

Juvenile Court Has Limited Resources

The juvenile court should be seen as a setting with limited resources. Its limited resources should be applied to best ensure public safety with those who are significant offenders—to prevent reoccurrences. The community should assume the responsibility for the basic prevention job with this population, with the court facilitating this community enterprise.

Should Court Involvement Be Promoted?

So, the question remains: Is this the best way to run a railroad? Or a school-court connection? What is clear is that any court that sharply discourages court referrals will experience substantial hostility from educators, who are likely to accuse the court of wrist-slapping. Nonetheless, it is wise practice for these and all juvenile courts to assert a proactive role in assisting school districts and communities to structure and mobilize alternative-to-court resolutions for both truancy and minor misbehaviors on school campuses.

Endnotes

[1] National Center for Juvenile Justice (2000). *Juvenile court statistics 1997*. Washington, DC: Office of Juvenile Justice and Delinquency Prevention.

[2] Dohrn, B. (2001). Look out kid, it's something you did: The criminalization of children. In Polakov, V. (Ed.), *The public assault on America's children: Poverty, violence, and juvenile justice*. (157–187, at p. 162).New York: Teachers College Press, Columbia University.

[3] Ohio Rev Code Ann. § 2152.02 (F)(4) and (5).

Chapter 9

A Community Imperative: Curbing Minority Overrepresentation in the Juvenile Justice System

JUVENILE JUSTICE APARTHEID: MINORITY OVERREPRESENTATION

The research demonstrates overwhelmingly that minority youth are treated more harshly than their white peers at every stage of the juvenile justice system. This is referred to as "minority overrepresentation." Minority overrepresentation is different from, and broader than, "disproportionate minority confinement." Disproportionate minority confinement (DMC) refers only to those locked up in secure facilities at pretrial or post-dispositional stages. Minority overrepresentation, in contrast, also looks at police arrests, decisions whether or not to file petitions, and dispositions to probation or other non-incarcerative programs. It can refer to aftercare revocations, as well.

James Bell of the Youth Law Center and a critic of minority overrepresentation recommends that chief probation officers and other justice system officials receive no pay raises until they have accomplished significant progress toward reducing minority overrepresentation. He refers to a growing apartheid where youth of color constitute two-thirds of many states' juvenile institutional populations, and where greater efforts may be made to avoid institutionalization for white youth than are made on behalf of minority youth. Bell adds that the direct filing procedure that waives juvenile court proceedings and places juveniles directly into criminal courts is the "most pernicious" of all overrepresentation practices. Minority juveniles, 34% of the 10-17 year old population, currently represent 75% of juvenile admissions to adult prisons.[1]

This chapter looks at data on minority overrepresentation, details one community's successful approach to addressing the issues, and summarizes areas communities can explore to reduce overrepresentation locally.

A LOOK AT THE DATA

While African-American youth constitute 15% of their age group, 1996 data indicate they account for 26% of juvenile arrests, 32% of referrals to juvenile courts, 41% of those held in secure pretrial detention, 46% of those committed to correctional

This chapter originally appeared in Juvenile Justice Update, *Vol. 7, No. 2, April/May 2001.*

institutions, and 52% of those transferred to criminal courts following juvenile court transfer hearings.[2] Longitudinal self-report studies have not shown significant differences in the rate of less serious offending by African-American youths compared with white youths in their social class, though the African-American youths are more often arrested. While comparatively more violent offenses are committed by African-American youths, the ratio is not comparable to the disparate handling of these youths in the justice system.

Howard Snyder, data guru of the National Center for Juvenile Justice, notes that victims report a higher rate of serious/violent offenses committed by African-American versus white (Hispanics included) juveniles, but this overrepresentation rate has shrunken sizably in the last six years from a 5.1 overrepresentation to a 2.4 overrepresentation. The serious/violent offense arrest rate for African-American juveniles 10 - 17 years old, other than for aggravated assault offenses, is now lower than at any time since 1980, when statistics were first collected. According to Snyder, white youths who commit serious/violent offenses are arrested at the same rate as similarly offending African-American youths; he suggests this occurs because police exercise little discretion in apprehending serious or violent offenders.[3]

But, Snyder notes, greater police latitude is allowed with minor offenses, with the result that African-American youths are arrested more often for minor offenses than are similarly offending white youths. Drug crimes illustrate this. Curfew and truancy may, as well. Consequently, how law enforcement treats minority youths apprehended for minor offenses, compared to those in the majority, is one useful focus for efforts to address minority overrepresentation.[4]

IMPACT OF DIFFERENTIAL HANDLING ON MINORITY OVERREPRESENTATION

A Florida study concluded that minority youth had a higher probability of receiving the harshest disposition available at each processing stage.[5] A statewide California assessment found that disproportion occurred at all stages of proceedings and became worse the further youths penetrated into the system. In Los Angeles County, African-American and Hispanic juveniles were much more likely than white youth to be transferred to adult court and then sentenced to the California Youth Authority.[6]

These studies support the national consensus that differences in offending rates between minority and white youths cannot explain the extent of minority overrepresentation in the juvenile justice process.

ADDRESSING DMC BY STATES IS A CORE REQUIREMENT OF JJDPA

Since 1988, under the Juvenile Justice and Delinquency Prevention Act, each state has been required to identify whether disproportionate minority confinement (DMC, in this context, refers only to overrepresentation with detained or confined juveniles) exists, assess reasons for it, and design and implement a plan to reduce it. Beginning in 1992, unless a state makes specific efforts to reduce overrepresentation, it may forfeit 25% of its formula grant. To date, while several states have had funding withheld for noncompliance, no state yet has had to forfeit that money. OJJDP has also prepared a technical assistance manual to help states and localities address the problem.[7] Its approach goes well beyound confinement only and deals with all processing stages.

MEASURES NEEDED AT ALL STAGES OF PROCESSING

Significant progress in reducing overrepresentation does not come readily. As a starting point, communities need to monitor decisions made at each stage of the juvenile justice system to assess the impact of race as a factor in and on the decision that is made.

Most juvenile justice professionals know intuitively that there is overrepresentation in their systems. A look at juvenile court waiting rooms, especially in urban centers but in myriad other communities as well, provides a snapshot of a disproportionate minority presence. The public knows that white kids commit delinquent offenses, but, aided hugely by media crime coverage and photographs, does not perceive them as the problem. Rather, the public sees juveniles of color as the problem, and many support harsh court handling, preferably in adult criminal courts, as the preferred response. Policy makers have heard and contributed to this drumbeat.

This perception also seeps into the modus operandi of juvenile justice professionals. This is not to say intentional discrimination against youth of color is frequent. Rather, juvenile justice professionals live and work in a society that holds certain biases, and justice professionals are not immune. As a result, the biases are reflected in court reports and decisions. They impact arrests and offense accusations, which, even when not sustained, may remain in a juvenile's record and haunt later charges.

SANTA CRUZ COUNTY, CALIFORNIA'S APPROACH

Statewide leadership and coordination to contend with DMC are vital, can facilitate funding for reduction initiatives, and can have an impact on how state agencies address or fail to address overrepresentation. Yet much of the nitty gritty work needs to occur at the local level. What follows is an account of how Santa Cruz County, California, attacked overrepresentation.

Probation Department Took the Initiative

To begin the process, the Santa Cruz County Chief Probation Officer, the county's Latino Strategic Planning Collaborative, and the Latino Affairs Commission convened a task force of juvenile justice stakeholders to survey the multi-systemic aspect of overrepresentation of Latino youngsters and to make agency by agency recommendations. Regularized monitoring of representation data and of approaches undertaken to deal with this concern became a critical community effort component.

The largest stakeholder, the probation department that also administers detention and other juvenile justice programs, embarked on its own concerted effort to curb DMC. The following account of its progress is drawn from a paper prepared by Judith Cox, Assistant Chief Probation Officer, and from a telephone discussion with her.[8]

Santa Cruz County: Demographics and Overrepresentation

Santa Cruz County, with a population of approximately 250,000, begins 85 miles south of San Francisco. Latino youth constitute 33% of the juvenile population between 10- and 17-years-old. During the 1990s, Santa Cruz youths referred to the juvenile justice system experienced a high rate of gang involvement and heroin use compared to youths in other California counties of similar size. In 1998, Latino youths represented 64% of juveniles detained in the department's pretrial secure detention facility and 46% of the juvenile probation caseload. Concerted efforts have reduced the detention ratio to 53% for 1999 and to 50% for 2000. From 1997 to 1999, police arrests of Latino youths dropped 5% while this population increased by 1%.

Identifying Factors That Contribute to Overrepresentation

To achieve this reduction, the probation department had to shift to an activist posture. This was not easy. An earlier but limited study by the probation department had concluded that minority youths were held in detention more than white youths because they were charged with more serious offenses and had more serious offense histories than did their white cohorts. Staff had been satisfied that these juveniles experienced greater risk factors in their daily lives and that solutions lay in improved economic and social conditions, matters essentially outside the control of staff members. This view, though not entirely inaccurate, prevented the department from surveying a broader landscape to identify the policies, procedures, practices, and programs over which the department had control that did contribute to overrepresentation.

Judith Cox encourages other juvenile justice agencies to follow Santa Cruz County into this broader landscape:

> When we looked for clients who experienced barriers to service or lack of service, we found them. When we looked for points of subjective rather than objective decision making, we found them. When we looked for examples of cultural insensitivity, we found them. When we looked for unnecessary delays, which contributed to longer lengths of stay in detention, we found them.[9]

The department also found that justice agencies and their agents might exacerbate disparity at each decision point.

Step-by-Step Approach Required Altering Objectives

As a first step, the Santa Cruz County Probation Department adopted reducing DMC as a key organizational objective. This enabled allocation of departmental resources to the objective. Personnel practices, including recruiting, hiring, and training were examined and adjusted, outcome indicators were redesigned, and service and program strategies were altered to support the effort. The agency developed a cultural competence plan and appointed a cultural competency coordinator to oversee progress.

As a crucial part of the process, decision points as well as the decision makers at each of these points were identified. Then data were collected about the outcomes at each decision point, by ethnicity. Santa Cruz County now collects information on ethnicity with respect to arrest, booking, detention, length of detention, use of alternatives to detention, and dispositional placement and programs. As a result, the county can track any progress made on its overrepresentation reduction objective.

Risk Assessment Instruments Were Scrutinized for Bias

Countless juvenile justice agencies use risk assessment scales to objectify detention or release decisions and to classify probation supervision intensity. Risk assessments curb discretion, which is often the enemy of equal treatment. Santa Cruz County not only reviewed its risk assessment criteria for unintended ethnic bias, it also involved all major stakeholders in redesigning the criteria.

The agency noted that adding extra risk points for gang involvement and/or lack of employment might have caused higher detention rates for minority youth accused of the same offenses for which other youth were released. A gang member label also placed a youth on intensive supervision even when his offense history was comparable to others not assigned to such a high level of scrutiny. Since more intense supervision often results in technical violations and longer periods of incarceration, the gang member label that was often applied had a detrimental effect for numerous youths.

Staff Hiring and Training Practices Were Changed

Santa Clara County established guidelines to ensure staff had the skills and abilities to provide services to a diverse client population. The probation department inventoried caseloads to determine cultural and language profiles. It determined that bilingual staff members were needed in key positions. All staff were trained in cultural sensitivity, cultural competency, and the dynamics of DMC. As a result of these changes, in this community, where Latinos comprised 46% of the juvenile probation caseload, 44% of juvenile probation officers are now bilingual and 34% are bicultural.

Additionally, the department developed client/customer surveys that provided insights into the barriers that parents experienced with the justice system process. It learned parents needed more help to comprehend the role of the intake officer at detention and court intake. It also learned that parents' failure to understand the process or to participate in it, or a staff member's discomfort with people who spoke a different language, might contribute to a tendency to detain or to file a petition. Parents were encouraged to take a more active role supervising their children and seeking or facilitating services or programs.

The department also learned that other agencies needed to reorganize their approaches to minorities, adopt a multicultural orientation, and enroll more minority youth so that barriers to services other than detention and institutionalization could be eliminated. Enhanced family conferencing and parental involvement at all levels were found to be vital to this effort.

Alternatives to Detention Were Essential

The Annie E. Casey Foundation Detention Initiative provided assistance to Santa Cruz County to develop an array of detention alternatives to help reduce its detention populations. As a result, Santa Cruz County now holds to the belief that when no significant public safety risk is posed, and when simple release to a family is not sufficient, detention alternatives such as crisis intervention, tracking, informal supervision, and shelter care must enroll minority youngsters on an equal basis and without barriers.

Santa Cruz County moved to shorten detention stays by expediting youth into placements of post-detention programs. The county, with involvement of stakeholders, developed a local continuum of services that were culturally sensitive and made them available on an equal basis to all youths. They created more than one level of probation supervision so that youths who committed technical probation violations could be sanctioned without necessarily being returned to a detention center. Year 2000 data show Latino youths remained an average of 11 days in detention pending placement, compared to 12 days for African-American youths, and 14 days for white youths.

The addition of a family preservation program, school-based day treatment, and a culturally competent residential drug treatment program also helped limit DMC by reducing gaps in the service continuum. Finally, the probation department's small residential ranch program has seen a decline of Latino admissions from 18 in 1988 to 12 in 2000. Meanwhile, the court's commitments to the California Youth Authority, which totaled 13 in 1998 and included 11 Latino youths, were only 11 in 2000 with just 2 Latino youths.

SUGGESTIONS FOR REDUCING OVERREPRESENTATION

To reduce overrepresentation, communities must assess what is done at every step in the process.

1. **Minority overrepresentation can be tackled with interventions prior to arrest.** Delinquency prevention strategies that improve education, strengthen families, offer job training and job opportunities, build and strengthen communities, and otherwise reduce law violations by juveniles are desirable. These should include multi-agency efforts that involve citizens, not just agency professionals. Schools, community-based organizations, youth-serving agencies, governmental entities, and churches are integral to such an effort. Pennsylvania, for example, has received noteworthy attention for prevention and youth-building efforts that have reduced overrepresentation in certain counties.

2. **Law enforcement involvement is critical to reducing overrepresentation at arrest.** Law enforcement must assess the impact of its policies and practices on overrepresentation and take steps to ensure the diversity and cultural competency of its personnel. Community policing may help as officers who know their neighborhoods and residents are more likely to take low-level offenders home or to a relative or neighbor instead of to detention. They are more likely to divert a youth to a YMCA or community center instead of referring to court. Further, alternative handling of minor offenders needs to be viewed as important as apprehending major offenders.

3. **Revamping the detention intake process can have an impact on overrepresentation.** Not only must communities scrutinize how detention decisions are made, they must also consider how detention alternatives are used. The impor-

tance of informed and bias-free decisions at this juncture cannot be overemphasized. Length of detention stays needs examination as well.

4. **Changes in intake or prosecutor diversion and formal petitioning practices can curb overrepresentation.** This is a particularly fertile place to assess bias. Lane County (Eugene), Oregon, e.g., inserted a Latina and two African-American advocates to provide culturally sensitive diversion with 86 minority first-time offenders and their families. It then compared outcome measures with 78 similar offenders who had received traditional case handling prior to this innovation. The experimental group reflected 5% less recidivism over 12 months, a 27% reduction in secure detention days, and a 63% reduction in commitments to the state training school.[10]

   Prosecutor decision making requires systematic evaluation, from charging through plea bargaining, including decisions to seek transfer to adult criminal court.

5. **Probation practices and expectations can have a significant impact on overrepresentation.** Probation agencies need to examine their practices, staff diversity, cultural competencies, and expectations for minority youth and their families. Traditional office-based counseling can profitably yield to neighborhood offices where staff better know the lives their probationers lead and can better call on neighborhood agencies and citizens to help redirect these young people.

6. **Practices in community correctional programs, institutions, and aftercare demand scrutiny.** More effective, diversified, and culturally friendly community correctional programs can reduce deep-end DMC by keeping minority youths out of juvenile institutions. However even in training schools, more effective programming that reduces reoffending is needed. Cultural sensitivity is needed; bias is not. And then there is aftercare. Another Oregon program, e.g., provides minority transition specialists to link new parolees with neighborhood and community services, and with agencies for a five-month intensive stint. It is proving to reduce reoffenses and curb minority youth returns to the institution.[11]

7. **Defense and judicial practices can have an impact on overrepresentation.** Although not a focus in Santa Cruz County, defense counsel practices as well as judicial decisions should be examined for impact on minority overrepresentation.

DO IT

Overrepresentation and DMC are national concerns that have an impact on many communities. The data are not pretty. The effect on young people's lives is tragic.

Thousands of our youths are not handled neutrally in what we have wanted to believe is a race-neutral juvenile justice system. There is little doubt but that the criminal justice system is far worse. But we in juvenile justice have a greater consciousness of the problem, and hundreds of good people are at work to curb this injustice. Let's do more. Let's do better. Let's do it.

Author's Note

Judith Cox, now Chief Probation Officer, Probation Department, Santa Cruz County, California, prepared the following update and added commentary on disproportionate minority confinement for us:

Santa Cruz County continues to monitor and measure disproportionate minority confinement on an ongoing basis as part of its efforts in detention reform sponsored by the Annie E. Casey Foundation's Juvenile Detention Alternative Initiative. (See the Pathways to Juvenile Detention Reform at *www.aecf.org*.) In the year 2001, the Latino detention rate was 53.3% (this compares to a detention rate of 64% for Latino youths in 1997 prior to the initiation of the effort). The booking rate for Latinos was 49.7%. The percentage of Latino youths in the general population for 2001 was 35.2%, ages 10 through 17.

In 2001, a group of advocates attempted to get the City of Watsonville to work with Attorney James Bell, from the Youth Law Center, San Francisco, on a community effort to evaluate juvenile arrests and citations in conjunction with mapping community assets and concerns (parks, liquor stores, empty lots, broken street lights, youth centers, etc.). By comparing the two, policy makers can get an idea about how and where to invest in community improvements. Although council members elected not to participate, a group of Latino leaders, youth advocates, and county personnel are going to proceed with the work independently. James Bell has launched the Haywood Burns Institute (*www.burnsinstitute.org*) and is offering technical assistance and/or providing information to a number of new jurisdictions nationwide and in California that are interested in doing this work.

In March of 2002 the *California Judicial Council's Journal of the Center for Families, Children and the Courts* published an article on DMC co-authored by James Bell and Judy Cox based on the Santa Cruz experience, with Mr. Bell providing a context and historical perspective (available at *www.courtinfo.ca.gov/programs/cfcc*).

The goal of the probation department is to ensure that its policies, procedures, practices and programs do not unintentionally contribute to DMC. The percentage of Latino youths in detention has remained approximately the same since the department experienced the initial impact of its efforts. Although these efforts take constant work just to maintain the current level of achievement, and there are always new strategies on the work plan, there is a limit to what one department can do. It is felt that all juvenile justice agency partners, including local law enforcement, prosecutors, defense counsel, and courts, must also join in the effort in order to further reduce DMC.

The probation department has also developed materials such as a work plan for addressing DMC, a document which delineates the issues to consider relating to DMC at each decision point, and a cultural competency assessment tool, all of which may be helpful to other probation departments wishing to address the issue of DMC. As a model site for the Annie E. Casey Juvenile Detention Alternative Initiative, the department has frequent opportunities to share this information to jurisdictions throughout the United States and contributed to the Pathways document published by the Foundation on the topic of DMC.

Endnotes

[1] Bell, J. (2000, December 12-14). Juvenile justice policies and their impact on minority youth (Panelist). Presentation at Office of Juvenile Justice and Delinquency Prevention Conference, Washington, DC.

[2] Hamparian, D. & Leiber, M. (1997). *Disproportionate confinement of minority juveniles in secure facilities: 1996 national report.* Champaign, IL: Community Research Associates.

[3] Snyder, H. (2000, December 12-14). Very young offenders and preventing and responding to child delinquency. Presentation at Office of Juvenile Justice and Delinquency Prevention Conference, Washington, DC.

[4] Id.

[5] Bishop, D. & Frazier, C. E. (1990). *A study of race and juvenile processing in Florida: A report to the Florida Supreme Court race and ethnic bias study commission.*

[6] Males, M. & Macallair, D. (2000). *The color of justice: An analysis of juvenile court transfers in California.* Washington, DC: Justice Policy Institute.

[7] Office of Juvenile Justice and Delinquency Prevention (2000). *Disproportionate minority confinement technical assistance manual.* Washington, DC: Office of Juvenile Justice and Delinquency Prevention.

[8] Cox, J. A. (2000). *Addressing disproportionate minority representation within the juvenile justice system.* Santa Cruz, CA: Santa Cruz County Probation Department.

[9] Id., p. 3.

[10] Jackson, L. (2000, December 12-14). Juvenile justice policies and their impact on minority youth (Panelist). Office of Juvenile Justice and Delinquency Prevention Conference, Washington, DC.

[11] Id.

Chapter 10

Judges Encourage Greater Role for Crime Victims in Juvenile Court

During the six years I served as Denver juvenile court judge (1965 to 1971), I didn't want to have anything to do with victims of juvenile offenders. Today, my file cabinet still retains a folder titled "Nasty Letters" filled with complaints, often from victims who charged I was interested only in the offender and ignored the victim's injury or loss.

Today, juvenile courts are far more aware of crime victims and recognize that someone should pay attention to their plight. However, victims are not often adequately perceived as critical players in the juvenile justice system.

JUDGE-VICTIM FOCUS GROUPS

Recently, I had the opportunity to co-conduct a series of focus groups in California, Florida, Minnesota, and Pennsylvania with juvenile court judges and victims of juvenile offenses. The judges, when face-to-face with victims, became far more aware of victim concerns about juvenile justice. With virtual unanimity, the 20 judges involved stated they would work to improve their courts' interfaces with victims.

Arranging a local or in-state dialogue between judges/juvenile justice officials and victims is an exercise that should be replicated across the country. Such forums provide an unusual opportunity to assess a juvenile justice system's practices or lack of practices in this context.

What follows is a summary that highlights the views of the judges involved in the four focus groups.

IS THE VICTIM A CLIENT OF THE COURT?

A prominent management theory preaches that organizations should determine who their clients or customers are, and then vigorously address their interests and needs. A starting point for our focus group discussion was to discuss whether the victim should be seen as a client or customer of the court. Juveniles and their families, unequivocally, fit this definition in the context of the juvenile court. But do the victims?

This chapter originally appeared in Juvenile Justice Update, *Vol. 4, No. 11, February/March 1998.*

In general, California and Pennsylvania judges said "yes." Florida and Minnesota judges, however, preferred to view victims as clients of the broader juvenile justice system. In effect, this latter brace of judges placed victim responsibility on law enforcement, prosecutors, probation officers, and other officials.

Perhaps it is academic to argue whether victims are clients or customers of the juvenile court or of the juvenile justice system. What is important, acknowledged all judges, is that each juvenile court/justice system take a hard look at victim concerns and interests, and at the opportunities that victims have to impact decision making within the system.

SHOULD THE VICTIM BE IN COURT?

Should victims be able to observe any juvenile court hearing, from the detention hearing through disposition and beyond? Virtually all judges said "yes." But what about the laws of confidentiality? Confidentiality constraints are weakening in many states, ignored in some courts, and strictly adhered to in others. Several Pennsylvania judges stated that they warn attending victims not to disclose what they learn about the juvenile or family at any hearing they attend. When discussing whether the juvenile and/or family could waive confidentiality, one California judge stated it is easy to finesse having the juvenile/family waive their privilege of confidentiality.

Should victims be entitled to speak at a juvenile court hearing? "Emphatically yes," exclaimed a California judge. "It's been magical when there is a last minute plea bargain and the victim proceeds to speak at the dispositional hearing. Having a live victim is so superior to reading a victim impact statement that has been folded into the predisposition report. I would like many more victims in court."

Minnesota judges, in general, accept victims coming to dispositional hearings but want them to make their statements, be excused, and be called back later to be told by the judge what the disposition was and why it was made. These judges do not want victims to learn certain personal information about a juvenile and/or family. One Minnesota victim was unimpressed with this view, however. She related that juvenile burglars invaded her home, looked into her chests and drawers, and learned lots of personal information about her family. The Pennsylvania approach of warning victims not to disclose what they learn should be more satisfying to victims than not getting access to the information.

One Florida judge expressed discomfort about victims testifying other than at trial, saying, "I feel like I'm in the heating, ventilating, and air conditioning business." He believes that certain victims seem to ask for sympathy, others need a forum where they can "vent" their feelings, and some, believing they have been oppressed by the system and thus doubly victimized, may have outbursts.

WHAT VICTIM NOTIFICATION PROCEDURES ARE IN PLACE?

Several judges said they would conduct a systematic review or audit of victim notification procedures to look at (1) whose job it is to notify victims of different hearings, hearing outcomes, and of the right to file restitution claims and impact statements, and (2) how effective notification procedures are in each of these areas.

Judges in the four states wanted their systems to provide regular, timely notifications to all victims. But this is easier said than done. Many courts have a vast number of victims but limited staff resources and funds. In addition, many courts are still focused on the offender and have not yet embraced paying serious attention to victims.

Several judges urged law enforcement officers to do a better job of informing victims about the juvenile process, victims' rights, and when detention hearings take place. (But does a court instruct law enforcement officers of its schedule for these hearings?) These judges also want law enforcement to describe to victims the role and responsibility of a court and the due process rights of juveniles. However, some judges suspect that police officers might be insufficiently informed of what the Constitution requires of the court and justice process.

Prosecutors' offices and victim advocates frequently have responsibility for notifying victims of court dates. Victim advocates frequently are employees of the prosecutor, but they often concentrate largely on victims of adult offenders. As a result, there are often notification shortcomings in the juvenile sphere. Notifications may not go out or may go out only to felony victims, or they may go out late. Staff may even give up on contacting a victim who does not respond to a single phone call or letter—without ascertaining whether the victim had simply made a choice not to attend a particular hearing. Numerous victims in these four states repeated time and again, "We want to be notified of a court date, but want to choose whether or not to appear."

Several victims noted they wanted to be informed when a juvenile is being considered for discretionary release from a state institution. Some states mandate such notice. In any case, a victim's communication that the youth should remain institutionalized is only a recommendation.

DOES SPEEDY CASE RESOLUTION PROMOTE VICTIM INTERESTS?

Case processing-time guidelines are prominent, now, in most statutes and in the juvenile court rules of many states. Their origins are found in the protections provided by the Constitution for due process and speedy trial. The contemporary focus on court management and judicial administration is allied with these protections. The courts want to process cases quickly and consistently in order to efficiently utilize court personnel and resources.

There is the belief that crime control and rehabilitative intervention work best when judicial system action is expeditious. Speedy case conclusion is, generally, seen to be in the victim's interest. Several victims in each state reported strong fears that they would be re-victimized by the same offenders, but their fears were lessened when they knew the justice system was engaging the juvenile quickly, thoroughly, and accountably. Victims want restitution paid, and the quicker the better. Above all, they want "peace of mind." Slow court proceedings for detained or non-detained juveniles may deter the ability of victims to resolve these injuries as well as they might.

There are exceptions to the principle that delay is an enemy of justice and of victims. Some victims indicated additional time is needed to absorb the effects of their victimization experience before they want to participate in the court process. In some cases, expedited proceedings do not allow sufficient time to obtain victim impact statements or to document restitution claims.

ARE VICTIMS TREATED WITH DIGNITY OR ABUSED BY THE JUSTICE SYSTEM?

Victims in all four states emphasized that what they wanted most of all was to be treated with respect and dignity. Each judge group echoed that this is of paramount importance. For this to happen, all agreed that there is a need for a better information flow to and from victims.

The provision of full and timely explanations of procedures and rights as they affect both victims and offenders is an important part of this. Having a court begin at the scheduled time is another. The judges were critical of their own deficiencies here. A number of Minnesota judges, for example, tend to schedule a block of cases at the same time and want everyone present when court begins. This facilitates judicial efficiency but inconveniences everyone whose case is not the first one called.

Prosecutors also took their lumps from victims. Several victims contended some prosecutors preferred not to have to deal with them, dealt poorly with some victims, might be inaccessible, or were just terribly busy and not receptive to victim questions or concerns.

A Florida victim complained he took off work to attend a hearing to determine restitution, then never received any restitution payment or any explanation of why. This was hardly treatment with dignity.

Many victims repeated they were intimidated by the justice system and needed far more help in understanding it. A Florida victim described:

I testified, but when the judge found the juvenile innocent, I believed he thought I had lied on the witness stand. No one explained to me that the juvenile hadn't really been found innocent, just that the charge had not been proven beyond a reasonable doubt.

ARE VICTIM IMPACT STATEMENTS USED IN JUVENILE COURT?

Victim impact statements are important ingredients of good juvenile justice practice. But unless victims appear at dispositional hearings, judges as well as prosecutors, defense counsel, and probation officers must make do with reviewing impact statements that have been incorporated into predisposition reports and with any victim commentaries set forth in a police report.

Injured victims of juvenile offenders do not always prepare and submit these statements. Numerous victims are never notified of the opportunity to do so. More than a few victims need encouragement, if not help, in preparing a statement, and this help may not be readily available.

Further, some probation departments do not prepare predisposition reports for the court on many juvenile offense cases—reports that should include a victim impact statement. Others do, but may "boil down" the impact statement to two or three lines.

Minnesota judges chorused that they read these statements and that the statements impact their decisions. Several California judges believed the statements often received only limited attention; however, when a prosecutor or probation officer stressed the impact on a victim in open court or when the victim made a personal statement at a dispositional hearing, they paid more attention. A Pennsylvania judge commented that these statements are vital for judicial use but are also useful for probation officers and youth counselors to review with delinquent juveniles.

Victim impact statements came onto the scene two decades or so ago. They were quickly incorporated as standard operating procedure in many courts. Now is a good time to take a hard look at how they are used in your system and whether their use can be made more effective.

WHAT ROLE SHOULD THE VICTIM HAVE IN DECISION MAKING?

Judges in all four states were basically consistent in their support for giving victims an opportunity to provide input before decisions are made at any stage of the process; but they also stressed that all decisions should be made by justice professionals.

In practice, victims are often ignored at the initial stage where intake officers or prosecutors determine whether to proceed informally or formally with an offense referral. When Florida enacted legislation[1] more than 20 years ago to require an intake officer to notify a victim that the officer was recommending a no-file decision by the prosecutor and giving the victim a right to appeal this recommendation, the procedure was viewed as unnecessary and costly. Today, this practice can be seen as fulfilling a victim's interest in having an opportunity to impact decisions.

The judges appeared to agree that it is good practice for prosecutors to discuss potential bargains with victims and respectfully solicit their input and assessment (although national juvenile prosecutor standards are silent on this matter). If a victim says no to a particular bargain, the prosecutor can still say yes. But prosecutors should explain their decisions, especially when they differ from a victim's wishes.

Similarly, at detention or dispositional hearings, victims who speak may urge ongoing detention or sanctioning of a particular kind, but the judge remains the decisionmaker. Like the prosecutor, the judge should explain the reasons for the decision.

IS THERE A SEPARATE WAITING AREA FOR VICTIMS?

Good courthouse standards and a few state statutes direct that there should be safe and separate waiting areas for victims. This is a dignity, an anxiety, and a safety issue. A California victim of violent crime, who suffered severe injuries, related how difficult it was for her to sit near the offender in the court waiting room and to see and be seen by the offender in the court hallway. One California judge responded he had to threaten county government with contempt before he was able to obtain a separate victim and witness waiting area.

Specialized waiting areas are hard to come by in many courthouses. Space is at a premium and there are competing demands for any available space. Nonetheless, a proactive coalition of judges, prosecutors, and victim rights advocates can be an effective lobby. In the meantime, it is essential that someone, whether victim advocate or prosecutor, arrange waiting space and dependable child care for victims who come to court.

ARE RESTITUTION PRACTICES EFFECTIVE FOR VICTIMS?

Florida judges place expanded and expedited restitution payments high on their agendas for reform. They want county governments to provide funds with which to pay juveniles to do community service tasks, with payments going to victims automatically. Arranging private or governmental contracts for juveniles' work was another approach they favored. Only a few judges in the four states, however, appeared to assert a leadership role in promoting restitution by going to the community for money or for help in finding jobs for juveniles so they could repay their victims.

Judges, overall, acknowledged they were passive regarding restitution oversight. They order restitution, but do not monitor payments. They are not usually informed of delinquencies in payments—which are legion. Typically, they do not know how much restitution they and their colleagues have ordered, nor how much has been collected. Several judges vowed to take a much harder overall look at deficiencies in their restitution systems as the result of the focus group discussions.

ARE THERE OPPORTUNITIES FOR VICTIM-OFFENDER DIALOGUES?

Victim-offender dialogue is a component of restorative justice.Typically, the focus group judges believed victims should have opportunities to describe their experiences and express their concerns about victimization in the presence of the offender. Many of the victims who participated commented positively about having an opportunity to confront the offender in a controlled setting, though few had actually engaged in such a dialogue.

Judges and victims saw carefully crafted meetings between willing victims and offenders as an unalloyed good, but noted, with one exception, that this takes place far less often than is desirable. The exception was a California county where a government mediation office, which mediates many forms of conflict, was readily available whenever the judge indicated a victim-offender dialogue should be accomplished.

ARE THERE VICTIM IMPACT PANELS?

Another restorative justice practice also captured judicial attention—victim impact panels. These panels were first used in California Youth Authority (CYA) institutions in 1984. Three or four crime victims speak before an assembly of residents. They share their victimization experience—its traumatization, accompanying emotions, pains, and fears that occurred then and exist now. The rationale for the program is that youth-serving agencies should address what an offender has done as vigorously as it should address what an offender needs.

Today, panel presentations are incorporated in a larger CYA scheme to expand offender empathy and teach positive decision making. Called the "Impact of Crime on Victims Program," it is now offered at all CYA institutions. It involves 60 hours of classroom instruction along with panels, small group discussions, case studies, role playing, written exercises, and homework. Nine crime-specific modules, such as sexual assault and crimes against the elderly, are part of the curriculum.

Judges, in general, were in support of victim presentations at institutions and at other locations such as pretrial detention facilities, day treatment or reporting centers, and residential programs. One judge reported that a few panels have begun to speak to junior and senior high school assemblies.

ARE THERE COMMUNITY ACCOUNTABILITY BOARDS?

Judges expressed both interest in and concern regarding still another restorative justice concept—neighborhood or community accountability or reparations boards. This concept, not a new one, is taking on renewed life in a growing number of states. Boards may be used for diversion or they may propose recommendations to the court in formal cases.

The basic concept is that a group of citizens will determine or recommend appropriate sanctions for an offender who lives near them. Board members may take over functions traditionally provided by probation officers. They may arrange and directly supervise community service work assignments or mentor juveniles. The participation of the victim in board deliberations fulfills restorative justice principles, although boards can operate in the absence of victim involvement.

Several Minnesota judges expressed serious concern over "abdicating judicial authority to a community group which does not have the responsibility which courts possess to safeguard due process rights." Unquestionably, justice system officials should prescribe and proscribe what community panels can do with diverted or formal cases. Due process must be applied outside as well as inside the court, and court-related officials should oversee these programs.

CONCLUSION

Juvenile court judges in four states decided that victims' needs are extremely important, but are often poorly addressed by today's juvenile justice system. There was general consensus that it is extremely important to hold dialogue with victims and victim advocates and to evaluate and reevaluate their own justice systems' practices in this context.

Endnote

---

[1] Fla. Stat. Ann. Sec. 39.047(4)(d).

Part 2

The Handling of Offenders: The Legal Side

Juvenile courts operate within a legal framework that is outlined by state legislatures and state supreme court and local court rules. Also, the U.S. Juvenile Justice and Delinquency Prevention Act of 1974 imposes certain mandates on the states relating to the deinstitutionalization of status offenders and the dejailing of juveniles. Pertinent U.S. Supreme Court rulings have been incorporated into state statutes.

Early juvenile codes were simple and provided enormous flexibility and discretion to judges and probation officers. These courts operated as informal non-legalistic settings. Codes were largely silent as to prosecutors and defense attorneys. Probation was a prominent recourse. Statutes provided some guidance to administrators of state delinquency institutions. There were no state juvenile correctional departments, just delinquent institutions and reformatories.

Following the Chicago juvenile court establishment in 1899, state legislators in all but two states authorized juvenile courts by 1923. These courts were a spirited reform that united socially minded citizens, social workers, judges, lawyers, and media officials in promoting laws that would separate juveniles from the criminal law process and facilitate "child saving." This was a movement, a significant social development.

The structure of the court within a state's family of courts varied significantly. As examples, legislators provided for separately organized juvenile courts in the more populous counties of a state, along with juvenile jurisdiction in either a lower or upper trial court in less populous districts; or for juvenile jurisdiction within the lower trial court throughout a state; or placing this jurisdiction within the upper trial court throughout a state; or for a mixture of this jurisdiction among upper and lower trial courts in a state. Over time, structural revisions were authorized, such as the creation of separately organized statewide juvenile (Utah), family (Rhode Island), or juvenile and domestic relations (Virginia) courts, or the shifting of the juvenile jurisdiction from the lower to the upper trial court (Colorado, except for the separate juvenile court in Denver).[1]

FORMALIZING THE JUVENILE JUSTICE SYSTEM

The juvenile court is the centerpiece of what is now termed the juvenile justice system. One might say this term was born in 1967, during the Johnson Administration, when the President's Commission on Law Enforcement and Administration of Justice issued its influential report, *The Challenge of Crime in a Free Society*.[2] This was the year, as well, of **In re Gault**, 387 U.S. 1 (1967) (see Chapter 2 for a description of this seminal decision).

A consequence was a flurry of legislative activity relating to juvenile courts and an updating and modernizing of juvenile codes that began to explicate the roles of other actors and the interface of the court with law enforcement, detention, prosecution and defense counsel, juvenile institutions, and parole. At state and local levels, the various actors increased their intercommunication and consultations and began laying an infrastructure for a juvenile justice system. At first, the term "juvenile justice system" brought laughs to the various actors. They perceived the "system" as a disjointed and clumsy arrangement still dominated by judges and probation officers. Over time, roles became better defined, and the different agencies established and maintained their different responsibilities and functions in making a reasonably coherent whole.

Probation officers grudgingly accepted defense attorneys as they entered this arena following the **Gault** decision. The cozy and extremely influential relationship probation officers had with their judges was now diluted as defense counsel asked to see the reports on juveniles they had prepared for the judge, to question these officers as to why they recommended a certain disposition, and to advance alternative dispositions to the court. Probation officers were dismayed, and remain dismayed today, with adversarial practices that defense counsel may employ.

Prosecutors entered later into this setting, holding off representation due to other perceived priorities until juvenile crime concerns received greater attention beginning in the 1970s. At first their most common representation occurred when defense counsel requested a trial. With greater familiarity with this court and expanded staff allocations, prosecutors moved more up to the front end of the process, often participating at the initial hearing to influence or approve pleas, plea bargains, and sentence bargains.

In some jurisdictions they moved further up front to take over the historic probation intake function of determining whether an offense should be handled informally or formally, and with the latter, the specific charges that would be filed.

The new paradigm, common to many juvenile courts today, is for the legal actors to dominate the in-court proceedings, with probation staff managing diversion cases authorized by their own functionaries or by prosecutors, preparing predisposition reports for the court's sentencing hearing, and then supervising juveniles on probation and monitoring other juveniles placed in community-level residential care.

There remain numerous courts, however, where prosecution staff and the prosecutor role are modest, where defense counsel only infrequently represent juveniles, and where the early paradigm of the probation officer domination of the juvenile justice process and product remains prominent.

CRIMINALIZATION OF JUVENILE OFFENSES

Juvenile codes have received ongoing legislative interest and activity since 1967. Prominent for nearly two decades now has been the concern that some juvenile offenses, indeed more juvenile offenses and juvenile offenders, should be placed under criminal court jurisdiction and sanctioning. (The several approaches to transferring jurisdiction over juveniles to a criminal court are discussed in Chapter 3.) North Carolina is one exception to this trend, but its initial jurisdiction is limited to those under age 16.

However, because of the sweep of the offenses that were criminalized, and the harshness of the potential criminal court sanction, states such as New York, Maryland, and Pennsylvania enacted a "reverse waiver" process where juveniles could ask a criminal court judge to transfer them back to the juvenile court's case processing procedures if the jurist found this to be in the public interest or perceived the juvenile as likely to be rehabilitatable within the juvenile justice system. Also, states such as Kentucky authorize a criminal court judge, following a guilty plea or adjudication, to redirect a criminalized juvenile back to a juvenile court judge for a juvenile disposition.

Several concerns are pertinent to the criminalization drive in addition to the lengthier processing time required in criminal courts:

- *Where should juveniles be held prior to criminal court decision-making?* Some jurisdictions retain these youths in a juvenile pretrial detention center (e.g., California; Cook County, Illinois) where they can continue their education. Others remand the juvenile to an adult jail where there is no schooling (e.g., Florida). Hopefully there is separation from adult offenders. While juveniles in criminal court do have a right to bail—except for a non-bailable offense such as murder—many are unable to post a bond and thus wait a very long time in jail, as long as six months or more, until their criminal case is resolved.

- *Where should a juvenile, once sentenced to incarceration by a criminal court, be incarcerated?* Some states, e.g., Montana, retain such youths in a juvenile institution until their 18th birthday, with a transfer at that time to an adult prison. Other states, e.g., Ohio, have created segregated juvenile institutions at adult correctional facilities for this type offender. Numerous juvenile offenders, however, enter state prisons prior to their 18th birthdays.

- *Who should hear matters involving criminalized juveniles?* At the criminal court level, a New York City court designated a specialist judge to hear matters that involved criminalized juveniles. So instead of a specialist juvenile judge hearing a juvenile in a New York family court, this specialization moved upstairs to enable one criminal court judge to develop broad knowledge about adolescent criminality and alternative sanctioning resources. But generally elsewhere, a judge serving a rotation as a criminal court judge will hear this case without specialized knowledge of this type of offender.

JUVENILES IN ADULT PRISONS

The numbers of juveniles in adult prisons have increased dramatically. The most recent tabulation goes only through 1997,[3] but the U.S. Bureau of Justice Statistics (BJS) reveals that from 1985 through 1997 the number of juveniles sentenced to adult prisons has more than doubled—from 3,400 to 7,400. The data count is based on juveniles under age 18, and therefore includes juveniles from the 13 states whose juvenile court jurisdiction ends on a 16th or 17th birthday, as well as the other 37 states and the District of Columbia where the jurisdiction may extend to one's 18th birthday. But in 1997, 26% of juveniles sentenced longer than one year were between 13 and 16 years old. Further, 58% of juveniles were African American while 15% were of Hispanic background.

The BJS survey estimated 61% of these juveniles were incarcerated for a violent offense such as murder (7%) or aggravated assault (14%). Another 22% were incarcerated for property crimes such as burglary (13%) or motor vehicle theft (2%). Eleven percent were imprisoned for drug offenses and 5% for public order offenses.

The average maximum sentence for those convicted of a violent offense approximated eight years, while the minimum time expected to be served was almost five years. The year-end count of those under than age 18 in prisons increased from an estimated 2,300 in 1985 to 5,400 in 1997.

There is concern about what happens with youthful state prisoners. One commentary notes

> ... the adult corrections system is on the precipice of disaster. The violent youthful offender presents some tremendous burdens to the system. Their housing, special program needs, individualized attention, impulsivity, erratic behavior, and unpredictable situational reactions certainly compromise security. However, more critically, each represents potential hazards to the orderly operation of the entire system.... If we do not take the time and care to develop appropriate, adolescent-relevant programs and services, then we certainly will provide this youthful offender population an environment with which to fill their vast reservoirs with what currently happens in prison. That will allow these young felons to use their own resources and develop into a more vicious hybrid of street youth and experienced inmate.[4]

Some state prison systems are adapting programs for youthful residents.[5] Emphasis should be placed on well-directed treatment and vocational skill development programs for these youths during their incarceration and during aftercare, in seeking to monitor their health and welfare during their incarceration, and on working to avert their entry in the first place.

A Juvenile Court Reformulation: The New Mexico Children's Code of 1993

New Mexico's unique statutory revision[6] provided an intriguing middle ground for the handling of serious and violent juvenile offenders. Except for 16- to 17-year-olds (amended in 1996 to 15- 17-year-olds) charged with first-degree murder, New Mexico retained all juveniles in its juvenile courts but empowered the juvenile court judge to serve in a criminal court judge capacity with "youthful offenders" for whom the prosecutor had filed a notice of intent to seek criminal sanctions and who met statutory requirements as to offense severity or chronicity. The defendant was provided the right to a 12-person jury in such a case. This juvenile court judge, when presiding over a criminal trial where guilt was established, still needed to make a series of non-amenability findings before a criminal sanction could be invoked. If not found, the sanction would revert to a juvenile rather than a criminal justice disposition. If found, sentences other than prison, such as an adult probation stretch or probation with a suspended sentence to prison, could be ordered.

A follow-up study of youthful offenders who were sentenced by a juvenile court to a prison experience examined offender profiles three years after the new law took effect. The typical offender was an Hispanic male who was not in school, and the typical offense committed by these 34 youthful offenders was robbery or aggravated assault that involved a firearm, was done with accomplices, and had one victim, usually of the same ethnicity and gender as the offender. Their law violation histories typically included both violent and extensive offenses. Their average sentence was six years.[7]

The Minnesota Blended Sentencing Reform of 1994

A second middle ground reformulation of the legislative criminalization drive occurred in Minnesota.[8] Rather than expand its legislative waiver net, the state improvised a blended sentence that authorized a juvenile court judge, in selected serious offense case situations of juvenile offenders 14- through 17-years-old, to simultaneously issue two sentences, one within the juvenile justice system and another to the criminal justice system. Accordingly, the right to a jury trial was provided. A youth began his post-sentence experience within the juvenile system. The judge could later invoke the criminal sentence following a violation of the juvenile system conditions—such as behavioral requirements with probation, or institutionalization, or even treatment in an out-of-state residential facility followed by a parole experience—that were ordered.

The juvenile court's jurisdiction was extended to age 21 under this Extended Jurisdiction Juvenile Prosecutions Act (EJJ). Certain additional funding was appropriated to expand juvenile intervention services. Numerous juveniles successfully met their requirements, possibly motivated in part by the criminal sanction they would otherwise experience. Others failed. During the first 21 months of EJJ implementation, just 14% of designees had their juvenile dispositions revoked and adult sentences executed.[9]

Montana[10] and Kansas[11] subsequently enacted EJJ laws, as well.

JUVENILE CODES IN ACTION

Juvenile court and collaborative agency officials memorize their state juvenile delinquency codes. The codes are not static; statutory policies and procedural provisions are changed from time to time. Code analysis begins with who is a juvenile, that is, any minimum age set forth, the maximum age, and legislative, prosecutorial, or judicial waiver provisions or reverse waiver provisions that are prescribed.

One looks at provisions that direct each stage of the process and how different actors are keyed to participate in the actions. There are significant variances among the states, but differentiating provisions often can be classified and grouped.

Role of Intake Officer vs. Prosecutor

The role of an intake officer in comparison with the role of the prosecutor at front-end decison making is one grouping. A statute may ignore the prosecutor and empower probation officers to divert lesser cases or initiate the formal petition process (Pennsylvania). A statute may authorize probation staff to adjust or divert certain lesser offenses but compel these officers to notify a prosecutor when a more serious or repetitive offense occurs (New Mexico, California). A statute may direct initial offense and offender screening by a probation officer who then recommends for a prosecutor's final decision whether an action should proceed formally or not (Florida). A statute may ignore any probation officer screening role and send all police charges to the prosecutor (Washington).

Case Processing Time

Case processing time lines are another variance. A statutory time line may direct expedited adjudications and dispositions for juveniles who are detained prior to court action. For example, in California detained juveniles must be adjudicated within 15 judicial days from the detention hearing and a disposition entered within 10 judicial days thereafter; Colorado requires an adjudicatory trial within 60 days of the entry of a plea of not guilty. A statute may provide simply that the adjudicatory hearing shall be held "without unnecessary delay" (Kansas).

Standard of Proof Applied

There are universals, such as the quantum or standard of proof, beyond a reasonable doubt, established for all states by the Supreme Court in **In re Winship**, 397 U.S. 358 (1970). Another universal is the right to have notice of having the assistance of defense counsel and of free counsel if indigent, established by **In re Gault**, 387 U.S. 1 (1967), but there are variances in applying the right to counsel. The right may be waived in many if not most states. A parent may waive this when there is no conflict of interest between parent and child, as in Pennsylvania. The right cannot be waived in New Mexico. Myriad juveniles proceed without counsel in American juvenile courts.

Other Provisions

Numerous other provisions are important such as an authorization for law-trained hearing officers other than judges to conduct certain hearings (Delaware). The extent of the confidentiality of juvenile records and court proceedings, weakened in recent years, is another. Whether there is a right to a jury trial (Michigan) is another, though the Supreme Court in **McKeiver v. Pennsylvania**, 403 U.S. 528 (1971), held that the U.S. Constitution did not require that state juvenile courts provide this option. A state constitution or statute may permit this, though an overwhelming number of states do not allow a jury trial for juveniles, and it is infrequently obtained in those states that allow it.

The maximum term lengths for probation, state institutionalization, and aftercare are other important provisions. Some codes state that the duration of a juvenile institutional requirement shall not exceed that required of an adult who commits a similar offense (California) while others are silent on this issue. The ongoing registration of juvenile sex offenders now characterizes a growing number of statutes (North Carolina).

THE JUDGES

Statutes that authorize judges of the juvenile court are normally contained in laws other than juvenile code sections. Several approaches are taken, among them:

- Judges are appointed to serve a separately structured juvenile court for the duration of their term (Utah statewide, Denver);

- Judges are elected to a numerically designated court intended as a juvenile court judgeship (Texas);

- Judges are appointed or elected to the general trial court bench, from where the judge may be assigned to a juvenile division of this court or otherwise to hear juvenile cases (Indiana, Washington);

- Judges are appointed or elected to the lower trial court bench, where the judge may be assigned to hear juvenile cases (Maine); and

- Judges are appointed by the judges of the general trial court to serve as judge of an independent juvenile court (Georgia).

Some judges, then, serve this court exclusively; others are subject to rotation to a trial court's criminal, civil, domestic relations, or probate division.

Unified Court Systems

The conventional wisdom of court organization is to eliminate structurally separate courts and combine all courts at the local level into a unified trial court. This approach seeks to improve judicial system efficiency and is increasingly evident across the country (e.g., Washington, DC; Minnesota, Oregon). With this approach, all judges and non-judicial personnel are functionaries of a single court with a chief judge, assisted by court administration, responsible for administering the single court's workload and responsibilities. There is one overall budget, one central purchasing system, one personnel system, sometimes one courthouse, and one level of judge. Judges in unified trial courts are to be judicial generalists assignable to any court workload. This is true, as well, with two-level trial court systems where judges of the upper general trial court and the lower court are judicial generalists. They rotate assignments, often annually. They bring experience with other court workloads to the juvenile court assignment, though some judges are able to avoid this assignment.

Judicial generalists may be criticized by juvenile justice officials as entering a juvenile court assignment without specialized understanding of juvenile justice law or resources and of departing this assignment before expertise has been developed and demonstrated. However, a growing number of trial courts prefer to normalize assignment to the juvenile court as a two- or three-year rotation. Some judges assigned to juvenile court, however, truly enjoy this arena, provide important leadership, and continue this assignment for years.

Separate Juvenile Court Structure

The separate juvenile court structure offers the advantage of judicial specialization. All of these judges have requested appointment or election to this bench, indicative of their interest in working with young people. Note should be made of the separately structured family courts in Rhode Island, Delaware, and South Carolina that combine juvenile and domestic relations workloads and where the judges have sought this specialized long-term task.

Appointments to a judgeship, as contrasted with popular elections to a judgeship, are made by a state's governor—e.g., from among three recommendations submitted by a judicial nominating commission (Colorado) or with the consent of the senate (Delaware). The most common background denominator of trial court judges is that of a former prosecutor. But judges selected for juvenile and family courts often possess backgrounds as practicing lawyers in these courts and some earlier served there as hearing officers.

However, it must be noted that not all long-term juvenile or family court judges are noteworthy. I have observed that some project particular values onto their work that are counterproductive and damaging to the morale or effectiveness of other judges, of probation staffs, and of juveniles. Some make all agency representatives comport with their singular perspective of procedures and practices. Some may be said to be prima donnas. Some are not particularly competent. But many are outstanding. This holds true for the rotating judges as well.

On-Bench and Off-Bench Roles of the Juvenile Court Judge

The public best understands the "on-bench" role of a juvenile court judge—a judge hears and enters judgments on juvenile cases. The legalization of the juvenile court has made it more difficult for judges to communicate meaningfully with juvenile defendants. Typically, lawyers on both sides present or discuss the case situation with the judge in a formal courtroom. A probation officer may present a report. The juvenile and the family are then asked by the judge whether they understand and agree to what has been described by these officials. It is too easy for a judge to become a rubber stamp to the assessments of other officials.

But some judges who really care about young people find ways to individualize a youth and communicate personal interest in his or her well being, particularly at the dispositional hearing. They look to and talk to the juvenile and encourage responses that are much more than head nods or yes sir/yes ma'am. They may seek to make the youth comfortable by asking questions about school activity or sports interest. They may ask whether they have learned of the content of the report prepared for the court, what they think of the findings, and what dispositions may be more fruitful than those listed. They may ask the family for comments on what might be done to help their youngster. They show positive interest in the juvenile while suggesting the benefits of a non-delinquent lifestyle. They explain the sanctions they will enter and ask if they can be followed. They say goodbye and good luck. Offenders can be personalized without compromising the authority of the robe.

The "off-bench" role is less well known—here the judge works actively to stimulate ways to improve the juvenile justice system and to expand or improve intervention resources. This judge consults with system officials and seeks remedies on finding slow moving cases, late filed police reports, delays with case petitioning by intake officers or prosecutors, excessive public defender turnover, poorly prepared predisposition reports, or difficulty in obtaining a prompt psychological report. Some do this systematically, conducting monthly "brown bag luncheons" with officials to review shortcomings, seek remedies, and also review resource needs of all sorts.

Interested judges sit down with probation leadership to search for ways to better fulfill objectives, improve methods of working with youth, and provide the judiciary with the information it needs, including feedback on the utility of various resources and placements that are invoked.

These judges work actively with the consortia of agencies and community groups and with legislative entities in seeing expanded resources for youth and families, both preventive and rehabilitative in nature. They meet with the media, and ask them to observe court hearings. They make presentations to all kinds of citizen groups to explain the work of the court and the needs of young people. Some may follow what one wise judge urges: don't make any presentation without asking the audience to do something on behalf of court youth. Another notes that one should not become a juvenile court judge if one wants only a 9 to 5 job.[12]

THE LAWYERS IN COURT

Roles of Attorneys

Prosecutors are public officials. They have a special opportunity to effectuate change and improvement in the juvenile justice system. By definition, their position is a powerful one. Prosecutors can influence much more than the decisions that are made at the different processing stages. They can make suggestions that improve the professionalism of court and related agency staff. They can accomplish procedures that support the predictability of case processing and case decision-making. They can influence judges to use or not use particular community-level intervention resources depending on rehabilitation outcomes. They can find ways to expedite case processing.

Defense counsel may or may not be public officials. Defense attorneys may be public defenders whose office represents indigent youth. They may be private attorneys appointed by the court for this purpose, or even a law firm that has a contract to provide representation. Private attorneys paid for and retained by parents provide a comparatively small percentage of representation.

Large urban or suburban juvenile courts often use public defender representation. Here, staffing of this and the prosecutor office are of significant size. What works best in a busy juvenile court is to have very experienced prosecutors and defense counsel making case handling decisions at the front end of the system. Case processing responds to this approach so that lesser offenses are diverted away from court, cases that are quite well founded are filed, plea and sentence bargaining occurs early, relatively few trials are held, and lawyer advocacy turns to the disposition or sentencing disposition where, often, prosecutors seek more severe dispositions and defense attorneys argue for less restrictive decisions.

Smaller jurisdictions may use these attorneys more sparingly. Some states have statewide public defense organizations and provide defenders to all juvenile courts. Elsewhere court appointment of private attorneys is common.

Juvenile court judges will deny they discourage adversarial representation, but many juvenile courts are not seriously adversarial. The culture of many courts prefers to simply hold law-violating youth accountable and negotiate rehabilitative requirements rather than deal with frequent legal challenges to evidentiary sufficiency or processing and dispositional decisions.

Appeals Work

The enormously influential juvenile delinquency decisions of the Supreme Court were proclaimed, essentially, during the period 1966-1978. Since then, it has largely been state appellate courts as the appellate entity that determined rulings on delinquency matters, their decisions having state rather than national importance and application. The Court did rule on several death penalty cases relating to juvenile offenders in 1988 and 1989, cases that arose in adult courts rather than juvenile courts. It held, first, that the Eighth and Fourteenth Amendments to the Constitution prohibited the execution of a youth who committed first-degree murder when he was 15-years-old. **Thompson v. Oklahoma**, 487 U.S. 815 (1988). The Court next held that the Eighth Amendment did not prohibit capital punishment of persons who committed murder at age 16 or 17, four justices dissenting from this holding. **Stanford v. Kentucky**, 492 U.S. 361 (1989).

Still, the application of international treaties to this issue retains pertinence. True, the U.S. Senate has never ratified the 1989 United Nations Convention on the Rights of the Child that provides "nations shall ensure that no child shall be subjected to torture or other cruel, inhuman or degrading treatment or punishment," though more than 100 nations have agreed to be bound by this convention. The Senate did ratify the International Covenant on Civil and Political Rights in 1992, which among other provisions prohibits imposition of the death penalty for crimes committed by persons below 18 years of age at the time of commission. However, in its ratification, the Senate reserved the right, "subject to its constitutional constraints," to impose this penalty on any person including persons below age 18.

The Nevada Supreme Court accepted the Senate's reservation but overturned a trial court's order of capital punishment directed at one who was 16-years-old at the time the murder was committed. **Servin v. State**, 117 Nev. Adv. Op. No. 65 (October 17, 2001). This imposition was "excessive," wrote the court. One justice concurred the sentence was excessive, but cited an additional rationale, that "customary international law," the acceptance of a proposition by a great many nations such as to become binding on all nations, banned executions of juveniles who committed murder in this country.[13]

It is, of course, defense attorneys who generally initiate appeals of juvenile court decisions. State appellate court decisions have covered important turf such as approving dispositions that combine public safety protection or punitive purposes so long as rehabilitative aims are provided, and to compel individualized dispositions. Decisions were reviewed and decided as to the validity of an array of probation conditions such as non-association with gangs and wearing of gang clothing, revocation of a drivers license, payment of a monthly probation supervision fee, curfew hours, possession of weapons, and barring contact with a victim. Numerous decisions have reviewed restitution requirements and determinations.[14]

Lawyers vis-à-vis the Predisposition Report

Almost forever, probation officers have prepared reports on juveniles to aid judges in making informed dispositions. These reports describe any past offense history and expand on the police incident report with any offense-related information obtained from the youth. They provide extensive information on a juvenile's school, social, medical, psychological, drug use, gang membership, and family history. A report is best done, from a due process perspective, following the entry of a plea or a finding of guilt at trial, though as many as four or five or weeks or more may elapse until disposition in some juvenile courts. The reports are prepared in many courts prior to adjudication, however, on obtaining the consent of a youth and parent or counsel, so that the disposition can follow immediately after adjudication.

Typically, these reports were processed from the report writer to the judge, similar to a confidential report. In 1966 the Supreme Court ruled in **Kent v. United States**, 383 U.S. 541 (1966), that a defense attorney must be furnished the report in order to provide zealous advocacy, as is the lawyer's required ethic. Still, my study of a Georgia juvenile court in 2001 found there was no provision of this report to defense counsel. Nor did the attorney receive a copy of any psychological or sex offender examination that may have been conducted. Further, my study that year of a Midwestern court found an old practice still evident, a probation officer speaking privately to a jurist about a youth or family situation prior to the initiation of the hearing and outside the presence of the youth's attorney.

It is true that some reports may include and need to include personal information as to the youth's or a parent's psychological or sexual issues. Defense attorneys need to review report contents with the youth and family members for accuracy and response. With very few exceptions, defense counsel should provide the actual report to the youth and family. With exceptions, little of this personal information is unknown to the juvenile. Prosecutors need to be informed, as well.

The point is that information communicated only to the judge that impacts a disposition constitutes a due process denial.

Non-Judicial Hearing Officers

Another lawyer in many juvenile courts is a hearing officer who hears cases in place of a judge. This official is known, depending upon the state, as a referee, a master, a commissioner, or a magistrate. Increasingly this official is acquiring greater authority and acceptance, though this is a subordinate position often serving at "the pleasure of the court"—thus, if a judge or judges are displeased with this official's performance, the official can be terminated without recourse. In general, this hearing officer is expected to enter decisions that are "politically correct," that is, consistent with the practices of the appointive judge or judges.

Still, except for the hearing of preliminary matters, a juvenile or attorney may reject this official and request that a judge hear the matter. Further, even if the conduct of a trial by the hearing officer is accepted, the hearing officer's decision may nonetheless be appealed to a judge. However, some juvenile courts, as allowed by rule as in California, authorize parties to stipulate this official may serve as a temporary judge with the same powers as a judge of the court.[15]

There are many excellent non-judicial hearing officers. Many take the major day-by-day workload off of judicial shoulders. Ideally, legislatures should authorize a sufficient number of judges for all juvenile courts, as judges provide the court with independence and higher status. Juvenile courts merit recognition as judge courts, not as a court with one or two judges and six or seven referees or masters, as occurs in some urban juvenile courts. The hearing officers are paid less than judges and usually are provided smaller courtrooms and less staff support than judges obtain.

PROBATION OFFICERS

Probation officers are not lawyers though they function on the legal side. Law frames their duties, like those of judges, and their function is to fulfill the purposes of a law-directed juvenile justice system. Like judges and attorneys, they are officers of the court. Probation officers have long functioned as their judges' right arm, doing as their judges direct them to facilitate court objectives. But some probation agencies like to orient newly assigned judges as to how the probation agency likes to work and obtain judicial acceptance of its ways of operating.

These officers perform three primary tasks:

1. The intake function determines whether a referral to the court from law enforcement or another source such as a school should be handled formally or informally, diverted to an external agency, or dismissed without further consideration. (But in some states prosecutors have taken over this screening function either as a unilateral duty or in some form of tandem combination with probation staff.) Also, the intake function often includes determination as to whether a referred juvenile should be admitted to the secure pretrial detention facility.

2. Probation officers prepare reports on juveniles and families for court use at dispositional hearings. Earlier known as social studies or social histories, they are more often referred to today as predisposition reports, presentence reports, or court reports.

3. Probation officers handle the supervision of a juvenile offender in the "field" or community, perhaps the function best associated with the position. This supervision combines control and monitoring of behavior and activities along with personal counseling and the task of helping arrange beneficial interventions from other community agencies. Supervision intensity varies with the perceived need. The duration of supervision is variable, as well.

There are courts where each of these three functions is performed separately by an intake officer, a predisposition report writer, and a field supervision officer. There are courts where the intake officer is also responsible for predisposition investigation and report. There are courts where the predisposition report responsibility is that of the field supervision officer. Normally, this officer is responsible for an updated report when a probationer reoffends or commits a technical violation of probation conditions.

Historically, probation was usually organized within the judicial branch, with appointments made by the judiciary and funding derived from local government. For the past three decades, however, there has been a decided shift to state executive organization and state funding. There are other organizational and funding arrangements and even some changes of name for these officials, but in all jurisdictions they serve court juveniles.

There are juvenile justice entities, some attached to a juvenile court and others attached to an executive agency, that provide the probation function as well as the parole or aftercare function for one released following institutional commitment.

FAMILY AND JUVENILE DRUG COURTS

Some juvenile courts in recent years have added a component that is termed a family drug court. Some have added a juvenile drug court. Both are derivatives of adult drug courts, which were developed earlier. Juvenile court judges or their hearing officers govern these proceedings.

Family drug courts tend to focus on the parents of children brought to court as abused, neglected, or dependent. This represents a useful effort to promote, indeed compel, drug treatment for the parents who are at risk of losing their child through termination of their rights. A further benefit is that the drug evaluation and treatment are made quite readily available, without a need to go onto a lengthy waiting list for these services.

Requirements of law now mandate an expedited court declaration of a permanent plan for such children. Accordingly, drug treatment must be expedited so that an addicted parent can quickly enroll and proceed to deal with the addiction. It is well known that one or more relapses often accompany treatment participation. A family drug court understands this as it continues to both support and cajole a parent toward health and regaining custody of a child. Typically it holds frequent review hearings to further a parent's wish to report favorably to a judicial officer and for the court to be informed of treatment progress and of other needs of the parent to obtain rehabilitation.

Juvenile drug courts are less common than family drug courts and both are less common than adult drug courts. A juvenile drug court follows the adult drug court model as it brings juvenile drug offenders into specialized court proceedings that blend accountability for one's law violation with the provision of treatment services and ongoing monitoring. Probation officers may be engaged with this enterprise. There are combination drug courts whose dockets include drug-related abuse and neglect or delinquency cases.

Federal funds have played a major role in drug court development. Family and juvenile drug courts are add-ons to juvenile courts, not newly structured court entities.

THE CHAPTERS THAT FOLLOW

This section begins with an examination of two juvenile codes enacted during the 1990s. Chapter 11 looks at the expansion of the New Mexico juvenile court's authority with youthful offenders, which was mentioned earlier. Other unique provisions interrelate the state's juvenile court with its 22 pueblo and tribal entities. Probation staff are to consult and reportedly do consult with pueblo/tribal officials in obtaining information for a predisposition report in regard to Indian Country youth who are apprehended or reside off-reservation. Further, cultural ties and cultural awareness are to be maintained when residential/institutional placements are made by the state.

Chapter 12 discusses North Carolina code provisions that reflect transfer of the probation function from the local judiciary to a state executive agency, a continuing trend. But this enactment, which took effect in 1999, retains a juvenile court waiver hearing as the only route for a juvenile to be transferred to a criminal court.

In Chapter 13, a Florida judge describes the atmosphere he creates and the values he communicates. Role functions and commentaries on juvenile court prosecutors and defense lawyers are then presented in Chapters 14 and 15.

Last, chapter 16, actually the first article the author prepared in writing for *Community Corrections Report* and *Juvenile Justice Update*, is directed to probation officers and is, in effect, a conversation with these officers about their relationships with their judges.

Endnotes

[1] Rubin, H. T. (1985). *Juvenile justice: Policy, practice, and law,* 2d. ed. (Chapter 11). New York: Random House.

[2] President's Commission on Law Enforcement and Administration of Justice (1967). *The challenge of crime in a free society.* Washington, DC: U.S. Government Printing Office.

[3] U.S. Department of Justice, Bureau of Justice Statistics (2000). *Profile of state prisoners under age 18, 1985-97.* Washington, DC: U.S. Department of Justice.

[4] Glick, B. & Sturgeon, W. (1998). *No time to play: Youthful offenders in adult correctional systems.* Lanham, MD: American Correctional Association, p. 133.

[5] Glick, B. B. & Rhine, E. E. (Eds.) (2001). *The Journal of Corrections Best Practices: Juveniles in Adult Correctional Systems.* Lanham, MD: American Correctional Association.

[6] N. M. Stat. Ann. §32A-3.

[7] Hanke, P. J. (1996). Working paper no. 20: Profile of youthful offenders and serious youthful offenders in New Mexico's prisons. Albuquerque: Institute for Social Research, University of New Mexico, cited in Torbet P. et al. (2000). *Juveniles facing criminal sanction: Three states that changed the rules.* Washington, DC: Office of Juvenile Justice and Delinquency Prevention, p. 21.

[8] Minn. Stat. Ann. §260B.130.

[9] Hanke, note 7 supra, pp. 27-39.

[10] Mont. Code Ann. §41-5-203.

[11] Kan. Stat. Ann. 38-1636.

[12] Rubin, H. T. (1985). *Behind the black robes: Juvenile court judges and the court.* Beverly Hills, CA: Sage.

[13] Morgan D. K. II (2000). International covenant on civil and political rights: New challenge to the legality of the juvenile death penalty in the United States. *Catholic University Law Review, 50,* 143-174.

[14] See Arthur, L. G. (2000). The case law of possible dispositions. *Juvenile and Family Court Journal, 51,* 31-57.

[15] California Rules of Court, Rule 1415

Chapter 11

New Mexico's Revised Children's Code

Let's take a close look at the 1993 reenactment of the Children's Code of New Mexico (Code).[1] The Code seeks a balanced, non-hysterical response to today's juvenile offending concerns. The Code won't please either pro-kid or lock 'em up advocates, but the Code's main features represent some reasonably enlightened and interesting concepts.

The Code authorizes criminal sentences for certain more serious and repetitive juvenile offenses, but does so in a more thoughtful manner than most state rewrite provisions have done lately. At the same time, the Code affirms and extends the historic juvenile justice interest in rehabilitation and community corrections.

CATEGORIES OF JUVENILE LAW VIOLATORS

Prior to the enactment of the Code, all juvenile offenders in New Mexico were initially processed in a juvenile court, although older youth were subject to waiver or transfer to a criminal court. The Code changed that by creating three categories of juvenile law violators: serious youthful offenders, youthful offenders, and delinquent offenders. Each of these categories is discussed below.

Charges on "Serious Youthful Offenders" Filed Directly in Criminal Court

The serious youthful offender category comprises 16- or 17-year-olds charged with first degree murder. The charge is filed directly in criminal court. The juvenile court (termed "children's court" in New Mexico) has lost jurisdiction over this youth. If the youth is convicted of the murder charge, the criminal court judge has discretion to impose a sentence less than, but not to exceed, the mandatory term for an adult. (A minor may be sentenced to life imprisonment, but not to death.). Reportedly, only a few such cases occur annually in New Mexico. If conviction on a lesser charge occurs, the criminal court judge may sentence the youth as either a youthful or a delinquent offender, as described below.

"Youthful Offenders" May Be Sentenced Using Either Juvenile or Criminal Sanctions

Youthful offenders are 15- to 18-year-olds faced with any of the following charges:

• First degree murder by a 15-year-old;

This chapter originally appeared in Community Corrections Report, *Vol. 1, No. 6, July/August 1994.*

- A felony combined with three prior felony adjudications over a two-year period; or

- Second degree murder, assault with intent to commit a felony, kidnapping, aggravated battery, dangerous use of explosives, criminal sexual penetration, robbery, aggravated burglary, or aggravated arson.

Youthful offenders are handled exclusively by juvenile courts and are not subject to waiver. However, they may be "sentenced" by the juvenile court judge using either juvenile sanctions or criminal sanctions. This is an unusual provision among juvenile codes. Youthful offenders, if detained prior to trial, must be held in a juvenile pretrial facility. Even serious youthful offenders can be detained either in a juvenile or adult facility. If it is the latter, the director must "presume that the child is vulnerable to victimization by detainees within the adult population because of his age, and shall take measures to provide protection ... [without] diminishing a child's civil rights to less than those existing for an incarcerated adult."

A juvenile disposition may be to age 18 or two years, whichever is longer, unless discharged sooner. Institutional commitments may be judicially extended one year at a time to age 21. The sentence may be less (but not more) than the sentence an adult could receive for the same offense. The defendant has a right to a 12-person jury trial. The law mandates that a juvenile probation officer prepare a predisposition report. In addition, a prosecutor must file a motion 10 days subsequent to the filing of the petition to ask the juvenile court judge to apply adult sentencing provisions. A juvenile parole board participates in the determination of a committed juvenile's institutional release date.

The court determines whether a juvenile disposition or an adult sentence should be applied following a prosecutor's request. The primary criterion is an assessment of amenability to treatment within the juvenile system. The relevant factors that must be be weighed are similar to those typically used with waiver proceedings. Nonetheless, much depends on the particular judge, prosecutor, or culture of a local court.

This is a concern. Allowing a juvenile court judge to issue a lengthy adult sentence to a juvenile is personally troublesome. In 1987, when the Texas legislature passed House Bill 682 authorizing a juvenile court to sentence a child aged 10-17 to a determinate sentence of up to 30 years following the commission of one of six violent offenses, my outcry reverberated across the Colorado mountains into the Lone Star State. Do we get numb from everything in the media about today's violent world, including the cries for retribution and calls for long-term incarceration? Do we lose our sense of outrage, and feel only that the changes could have been a lot worse?

"Delinquent Offenders"—The Catch-All Category for All Other Juvenile Offenders

The final category in the New Mexico Code is that of "delinquent offender." This category is a catch-everything-else category. This class of offenders may receive only juvenile sanctions. A six-person jury trial is available to this class.

State commitment may be for (1) up to two years in a "long-term (i.e., secure) facility," (2) up to one year, of which no more than six months may be in a long-term facility, or (3) up to six months in a state-managed or state-arranged facility for alcohol or substance abuse offenders if the court determines the treatment is "likely to be beneficial."

In addition, alternatives to institutionalization, or add-ons to probation are spelled out. Fines, a disposition of up to 15 days in a "pretrial" detention center, revocation of a driver's license following an alcohol or substance abuse offense, monetary restitution, and "paid" community-work service programs where partial earnings are paid over to victims. Not all dispositional options are specified in the Code. Creative judges can and should work within the considerable leverage they have in fashioning conditions.

INTAKE PROBATION OFFICER HAS CONSIDERABLE AUTHORITY

New Mexico opted to retain considerable authority in the intake probation officer, retaining a first-level screening role. This official can adjust up to three misdemeanor offenses for a youngster over a two-year period without informing a prosecutor. However, notification is a must with a fourth such offense, and an "appropriate disposition" will be recommended. The intake officer must submit any felony complaint to the prosecutor together with a recommendation on how the case might best be handled.

A TASK FORCE CREATED BY A PRIVATE, NON-PROFIT ENTITY DRAFTED CODE

Let me once again say that juvenile offenders merit sanctions, but that we should want fair punishments that teach accountability, uphold a community's sense of an appropriate minimum sanction, and provide opportunities for youth to strengthen their competencies and capabilities for constructive citizenship. In particularly severe cases, an adult sanction is indicated, although no juvenile should be housed in an adult jail until he or she becomes 19 years of age. New Mexico fails this housing standard, and only future research will tell us whether less than severe cases receive adult incarceration.

Still, this statute is "better" than most of those I've reviewed over the last five years or so. A major reason is that this Act was not put together by a legislative committee. Instead, the law was drafted by a task force created by the New Mexico Council on Crime and Delinquency, a private non-profit entity and long-term advocate for progressive legislation and quality justice system practices. Before having friendly legislators submit this comprehensive bill, the Council obtained agreement between key prosecutors and defense counsel on the above provisions (and the entire package). Remarkably, the bill became law without significant amendment.

CODE'S PROGRESSIVE PROVISIONS PROVIDE A CONTINUUM OF SERVICES THAT STRESS PREVENTION AND TREATMENT

The law contains a number of progressive or reasonably balanced provisions. Some of these provisions are discussed below.

The general purpose clause of the Code contains desirable objectives, including: providing a continuum of services from prevention to treatment and, whenever possible, "prevention, diversion, and early intervention"; providing children with services "that are sensitive to their cultural needs"; minimizing interagency conflicts and enhancing the coordinated response of all agencies; and providing, whenever possible, a single judge to hear all successive cases or proceedings involving a child or family.

A further purpose clause, specific to the delinquency provisions of the Code, holds juveniles accountable for their actions to the extent of their age and other relevant factors, but provides for supervision, care, and rehabilitation, including "rehabilitative restitution" to victims. Further, in seeking "effective deterrents" to law violations, the legislature urged that emphasis should be placed on "community-based alternatives."

Comment: Purpose clause provisions represent guidelines of legislative intent. Judges, probation personnel, prosecutors, defense counsel, and other juvenile system representatives are to follow these policy statements.

The state youth agency must publish standards for the facilities and operations of the county-administered (and for Santa Fe County, the privately administered) pretrial detention centers. At least annual inspections and certification are mandated; negative findings may be appealed to the court in the county in which the facility is located.

Comment: State standards and certification should become the handle for precipitating improvements in substandard and/or dangerous centers where local governments have deferred improvements or failed to conduct careful audits.

Another provision prohibits a detention center from holding juveniles sentenced by a federal court unless the facility meets state standards. One of these standards is that juveniles may not serve more than a 15-day disposition to a pretrial facility.

Comment : This condition is aimed at confronting the U.S. Bureau of Prisons' recent practice of purchasing long-term beds, up to two years or even longer for some youth, in a local short-term pretrial detention center.

A judge or other judicial officer must determine within 48 hours of arrest, including Saturdays, Sundays, and legal holidays, whether there is probable cause for the arrest. This nonadversarial determination may be made by telephone and in the absence of the juvenile and counsel. Within 24 hours of the filing of a petition in conjunction with an admission to detention, excluding Saturdays, Sundays, and legal holidays, a detention hearing shall be held to determine whether continuing detention is required "pursuant to the criteria established by the Code." Juvenile probation officers are expressly disallowed from serving as hearing officers in these matters.

Comment : In **JV-111701 v. Superior Court**, 786 P.2d 998 (Ariz. App. 1980), an Arizona appellate court ruled in 1980 that juveniles should receive the same legal protection afforded jailed adults. That is, an initial hearing must be held within 24 hours, not excluding weekends or holidays. The New Mexico statute is directed at this issue. For some years, New Jersey and Michigan have required Saturday detention hearings. However, this requirement is rare, and juvenile justice officials in other states are not likely to adopt this procedure until they are forced to do so. You might review your own state's law and practice in this regard and perhaps anticipate a successful legal challenge.

Confessions, statements, or admissions concerning the allegations of the petition made by a youth aged under 13 to a "person in a position of authority" may not be accepted into evidence. When made by 13- and 14-year-olds, there is a rebuttable presumption of inadmissibility. Corroboration by other evidence is necessary for admissions or confessions made outside of court.

Comment : These provisions give some protection to youth who have been intimidated by law enforcement interrogation methods. The statute does not require parental presence at questioning of those under 18, specific criteria guide the courts in weighing whether a prosecutor has met the "totality of the circumstances" test for admissibility of a knowing, intelligent, and voluntary waiver of constitutional rights.

Just as probation, residential care, institutionalization, and parole may be extended annually, for cause, until one's 21st birthday, so may the court terminate jurisdiction early when the youth is "no longer in need of care, supervision, or rehabilitation."

Comment : While any number of juvenile courts effectively stop supervising countless juveniles, but keep them officially on probation until their official term ends, an approved judicial procedure to officially accomplish early termination is an efficient incentive for juvenile probationers and for efficient caseload management. The procedure can be made available by statute, as in New Mexico, or by local practice. It is best done by bringing a juvenile back before the judge for a small ceremony that makes everyone feel good.

Holding onto juveniles until their 21st birthdays sounds like—and in fact is—a very long time. Hopefully, this power will be exercised sparingly. There is an important, potential advantage to this authorization. A judge, facing a juvenile versus a criminal sentencing determination with a difficult 16- or 17-year-old is more likely to fall back on the juvenile justice system since it would not necessarily have to cast him/her out on an 18th or 19th birthday, and more time could be made available to vindicate a severe offense and to accomplish rehabilitation.

The New Mexico Code also provides positive connections between the state juvenile justice system and Native American youth who are caught in its web. Juvenile probation officers "shall contact an Indian child's tribe to consult and exchange information for the purpose of preparing a predisposition report when commitment or placement of an Indian child is contemplated or has been ordered." With disposition, cultural needs are to be considered, and "reasonable access to cultural practices and traditional treatment shall be provided." Finally, if placed in a secure facility, the youth's cultural ties are to be maintained and representatives of the youth's culture to be allowed access "to provide activities that strengthen cultural awareness."

Comment : The above provisions break new ground for juvenile codes in states with significant Indian populations. The Council on Crime and Delinquency created a task force of Native American attorneys and juvenile justice officials to draft the language in the last item listed above. At least six New Mexico legislators are Native Americans, and according to one, Senator Leonard Tsosie, a watchful eye was maintained to ensure retention of these provisions.

While there are 19 pueblo and three tribal courts in New Mexico, Native American youth who are apprehended off-reservation are handled in the state juvenile court/justice system where the above provisions are to be applied.

The written law is one thing; implementation may be something else entirely. Numerous, though not exhaustive, inquiries made by the author to pueblo/tribal and state juvenile justice authorities this spring, as part of a New Mexico Indian juvenile justice planning study, failed to locate experience or familiarity with implementation of these cross-cultural connections.

Author's Note

David Schmidt, Executive Director, New Mexico Council on Crime and Delinquency, provided the following updated information to the author:

- The "serious youthful offender" classification, cases that are filed directly in a criminal court, which had originally been restricted to juveniles 16- and 17-years-old charged with first degree murder, now also allows for this type of handling for 15-year-olds charged with this offense.

- A "youthful offender," the classification that may be proceeded against in children's court either as a juvenile or as an adult, now qualifies juveniles for this handling at age 14 rather than age 15. Several additional offense charges that qualify one for youthful offender handling have been added: aggravated battery on a police officer, shooting at a dwelling or occupied building, and abuse or neglect of a child that results in great bodily harm or death.

- A juvenile sentence may now extend to age 21 (rather than to age 18) or two years, whichever is longer. If sentenced as an adult, the offense will become part of a potential future habitual offender/three strikes and you're out sentence basis.

- For the regular juvenile delinquent offender, a community service requirement is now mandatory on proof of a graffiti charge.

This state code is viewed as the most culturally friendly to Native American youth of any juvenile code in the country. Tribes are indeed notified when a juvenile with tribal ties is in custody. Other provisions remain intact, and a Full Faith and Credit provision has been added to allow tribal courts to access New Mexico juvenile facilities without a similar charge having to be first proven and the disposition made by a state children's court. Recognition by state courts under the Full Faith and Credit provision requires, however, that a tribe and the state enter into an inter-governmental agreement that considers payment sources for the use of state juvenile facilities. Schmidt indicates the tribes are very willing to enter into such agreements but that the state youth agency has not signaled it is ready to address this matter.

Endnotes

[1] N. M. Stat. Ann. §32-2.

Chapter 12

North Carolina Enacts Major Juvenile Code Revisions: All Delinquency Cases Continue to Be Initiated in Juvenile Court

NORTH CAROLINA JUVENILE CODE GETS MIXED REVIEWS

It is newsworthy and praiseworthy today when a state legislature goes to work on its juvenile code and decides to continue its policy of starting all cases in a juvenile court, rather than allowing prosecutors to originate some in criminal court. Despite that, however, the new North Carolina juvenile code[1] that took effect July 1, 1999, still inserts a significant number of harder line provisions. Reactions to the code vary. One North Carolina jurist commented that "the changes could have been far worse." A child advocate countered that the code reflects "the politically popular concept that harsher punishment—no matter how short-sighted or ineffectual the result—is preferable to preventing crime."

The new code is an outgrowth of a 1998 report by the Governor's Commission on Juvenile Crime and Justice.[2] The report contained 61 recommendations for change that led to an extensive review and rewrite during that year's legislative session. Like other new codes around the country, the North Carolina code reflects how political and public perceptions of delinquent youth have shifted toward punishment and away from rehabilitation. The first purpose of the new code, like that of many states', is to protect the public safety.

SINGLE STATEWIDE JUVENILE JUSTICE ENTITY

In the new code, North Carolina decided that intake probation officers should keep their control of the decision to file a petition. In this regard, North Carolina has chosen not to follow the lead of numerous states that have empowered prosecutors with the trump card at this critical stage of a case. The law transfers judicial ownership of probation departments to the state executive, thereby creating a single

This chapter originally appeared in Juvenile Justice Update, *Vol. 6, No. 2, July/August 2000.*

statewide juvenile justice entity that is expected to provide more coherent and integrated services. The new law launches juvenile crime prevention councils to strengthen delinquency and drug prevention efforts at local and state levels. It acts to curb institutional commitments of misdemeanor offenders. And, for the first time, it provides statutory criteria to guide judicial transfer decisions.

Yet, on balance, the new code tips far more toward sterner juvenile handling than toward balanced and restorative justice. The array of more punitive approaches outweighs the hope that more funding and more program services will in fact be made available to prevent juvenile crime or to successfully intervene with juvenile offenders. Still, the new law could have been worse. And, indeed, many states have done far worse.

JURISDICTIONAL AGE AND TRANSFER PROVISIONS

North Carolina has long had a low jurisdictional age. It is important to note that all juveniles in North Carolina become adults on their 16th birthdays, a dubious distinction shared only with Connecticut and New York. The state's minimum delinquency age of six years, likely the lowest in the nation and one that defies both legal precedent and gravity, was maintained, along with the maximum age of 15.

Transfer Eligibility Age Remains 13

The state's last major code revision, in 1979, allowed for discretionary transfer of 14- and 15-year-old felons by a juvenile court judge. Amendments in 1994 reduced the transfer eligible age to 13 and mandated transfer for 13- to 15-year-old youths charged with a Class A felony (first degree murder), where the juvenile court judge finds probable cause. These two provisions went unchanged in the latest revision. In this context, also, many states have been more draconian.

Youths Can Be Held Past Their 18th Birthday

New, tougher juvenile court sanctioning authority, which will be described later, may, however, result in a reduction of the number of transferred juveniles. Certain 13- to 15-year-olds, charged with serious felonies that are not automatically transferable following a probable cause finding may now be committed to a training school until their 21st or 19th birthdays, depending on the offense. Previously, youths could be held only until their 18th birthdays. It is quite possible that the potential for a more extended stay may head off transfers to criminal court, as prosecutors and judges may be satisfied to retain juvenile court jurisdiction when longer sentences are available.

Reverse Transfer Permitted in Limited Cases

A modest reverse transfer/waiver provision was added, which should be applauded. However, it applies only to juveniles transferred to criminal court following a discretionary finding that the protection of the public and needs of the juvenile are best served by transfer, and is available only if there was an abuse of discretion by the juvenile court judge. This option has the potential to lead to better-founded decisions when transfer is ruled on in juvenile court.

Criteria to Guide Transfer Decision Are Added

Eight statutory factors that are to guide a transfer hearing determination of "whether the protection of the public and the needs of the juvenile will be served by transfer" have been added to the code. While this is a positive step, such factors should have been added long ago.

Status Offender Jurisdictional Age Extended Two Years Beyond Delinquency Age

In North Carolina, status offenders are called "undisciplined juveniles" and, as with delinquents, the court can exert jurisdiction over these children when they reach age six. Under the new code, however, the court can now continue to exercise jurisdiction over these youth until they reach 18. North Carolina may be the only state whose status offense jurisdiction extends two years beyond its delinquency jurisdiction.

Sanctions have been enhanced for status offenders. While undisciplined youths cannot be placed in secure confinement as a disposition, they may be held in contempt for violation of a court order. Sanctions for contempt include one day in secure detention on a first status reoffense, three days on a second reoffense, and five days on a third. A juvenile may not "be confined for more than 14 days in one 12-month period." The code does not, however, spell out the due process prerequisites to invoking such sanctions.

While an under 16-year-old undisciplined juvenile must be beyond control of his or her parents, or a runaway regularly found in places unlawful for juveniles to be, or a truant, an undisciplined juvenile who is 16 or 17, is subject only to the first two grounds because these youths are no longer subject to compulsory school attendance laws.

Fingerprints and Photographs Required for 10-Year-Olds Adjudicated for Any Felony Offense

Under the old code, only juveniles ordered transferred to a North Carolina criminal court were to be fingerprinted. Now, juveniles 10 years and older, adjudicated for any felony offense, must be both fingerprinted and photographed by law enforcement.

YOUTH STILL PROTECTED AS TO ADMISSIONS AND CONFESSIONS

Not changed in the code revision is the directive that juveniles are to be advised by law enforcement that they have a right to consult an attorney, that one will be appointed upon request, and that admissions or confessions made by juveniles under age 14 shall not be admissible unless a parent is present and advised of a juvenile's rights, or an attorney is present. Not all states are this protective.

NEW CODE INCREASES INTAKE'S POWER TO STRUCTURE PLAN

Probation officers, here called court counselors, remain the decision-makers in determining whether a referral will be dropped, handled informally, or filed. The prosecutor holds no veto power over an intake decision other than in the rare case when a complainant appeals intake's rejection of a petition to a prosecutor.

Intake's power is emphasized, constructively and probably uniquely, in a new purpose clause objective: "To provide an effective system of intake services for the screening and evaluation of complaints and, in appropriate cases, where court intervention is not necessary to ensure public safety, to refer juveniles to community-based resources." However, the new code, like the old, prohibits diversion of youths charged with any of a specified list of serious offenses.

Also new is a provision that authorizes intake staff to formalize a diversion plan into a diversion contract that requires satisfactory program participation for up to six months, with the filing of the petition the consequence for failure to complete the contract.

"Least Restrictive Interference" Is Abandoned

Regretfully, the new code abandons the prior command that a judge, at a detention hearing, shall impose the "least restrictive interference with the liberty of a juvenile who is released from secure custody." Instead a judge may impose "appropriate restrictions" on the "liberty of this juvenile."

Burden on State to Prove Detention Need

The new code does retain the earlier code's directive that the state bear the burden of proving by clear and convincing evidence that restraints on the juvenile's liberty are necessary and that "no less intrusive alternative will suffice." This progressive and beneficial provision supports the historic principle that law should favor freedom. Also, defense counsel is now mandated to be present at this hearing; prior law required only advisement of the right to counsel.

Review detention hearings, for those earlier ordered into continuing detention, are maintained. This is a valuable provision that can expedite release from detention in appropriate circumstances.

LIMITED USE OF DETENTION FOR PUNISHMENT

In North Carolina, a secure detention facility holds both those youths awaiting trial or disposition and those juveniles "sentenced" there as a punishment. The old law limited a sentence to five 24-hour periods during the probation period. New law permits Level 2 offenders (described below) as well as status reoffenders to be sentenced for up to 14 24-hour periods during probation.

NEW CODE RADICALLY ALTERS DISPOSITIONS AND ESTABLISHES POINT SYSTEM FOR CLASSIFYING JUVENILE OFFENDERS

The new code makes radical changes in disposition proceedings. Changes begin with the purpose clause. The rehabilitative principle that "[i]f possible, the initial approach should involve working with the juvenile and his family in their own home, so that the appropriate community resources may be involved in care, supervision, and treatment according to the needs of the juvenile," is now history. Gone also are the mandates that (1) "the judge shall select the least restrictive disposition both in terms of kind and duration, that is appropriate to the seriousness of the offense, the degree of culpability indicated by the circumstances of the particular case and the age and prior record of the juvenile," and (2) "a juvenile should not be committed to training school or to any other institution if he can be helped through community-level resources."

New Classification System Establishes Levels for Dispositions

The new code launches a formulaic classification of offending juveniles based on: (1) prior offense adjudications; (2) probation status, if any; and (3) present offense severity. Points are allocated for delinquency history and class of present offense, as provided by statutory directives and then totaled to arrive at one of three levels.

- *Level 1: Community Disposition.* The judge is to retain the youth in the community (though community includes group home or wilderness camp placements); consider a newly mandated risk and needs assessment that must be prepared for the dispositional hearing; select one or more from the first 13 of 23 authorized dispositions, which are typically less stringent than the dispositions in categories 14 through 23, while considering the youth's needs, appropriate resources, and protection of the public.

- *Level 2: Intermediate Disposition.* This youth is also to be retained in the community, with community defined as anything short of a training school. The judge is to select one or more of 23 types of authorized dispositions, at least one of which must be from the more stringent disposition types listed in categories 14 through 23 in the statute. Alternatives include boot camp, residential placement, an intensive substance abuse program, day treatment or reporting center, house arrest, intensive probation, sentence to detention of up to 14 24-hour periods, restitution of $500 or more, and/or community service of 100-200 hours.

- *Level 3: Commitment.* A point score at this level results in commitment to a training school, but an exception is allowed with a reduction to Level 2 "if the court submits written findings on the record that substantiate extraordinary needs on the part of the offending juvenile." Conversely, a Level 2 juvenile may be dispatched to a training school if the juvenile had earlier received a Level 3 disposition.

Commitments for 10-Year-Olds

A youth age 10 and older can be committed to a training school, possibly until his or her 18th, 19th, or 21st birthday, depending upon the offense and offense history. Although any commitment must be for at least six months, no juvenile commitment can exceed the duration for which an adult may be imprisoned.

Dispositional Changes Pose Potential for Good

Regrettably, the need to justify dispositions other than the least restrictive alternative is gone, although there is nothing inherently wrong in the new dispositional approach. A predictable disposition should have benefits in terms of equal justice. A judge should now have similar classifications presented for disposition for similar offenders by different court counselors. Judicial discretion that could otherwise result in different judges treating similar offenders unequally is discouraged. The new code approach is akin to having sentencing guidelines. But guidelines, like any approach to judicial dispositions, can be subject to bias and, ultimately, manipulation. As a result, whether the points accorded different offenses and delinquency histories are soundly based or not should be a target for future evaluation.

CODE ADDRESSES MINORITY OVER-REPRESENTATION

The code creates a new state Office of Juvenile Justice and prescribes that:

where Office statistics indicate the presence of minority youth in juvenile facilities disproportionate to their presence in the general population, the Office shall develop and recommend appropriate strategies designed to ensure fair and equal treatment in the juvenile justice system.

The states, having been directed by federal law to examine the question of minority over-confinement, invariably find it occurs. Law enforcement targets minority neighborhoods. Proportionately, more minority youth are detained, and detained youth are more often charged. Consequently, minority youth appear more often before the judge. Further, predisposition reports may reflect media suggestions and community biases that minority youth require greater punishments and state control. Therefore it is likely that this Office will have much work to do.

RESTITUTION AND COMMUNITY SERVICE PROVISIONS STILL LAG BEHIND NEED

The old law provided for full or partial restitution, payable within a 12-month period, with a judge authorized to excuse restitution upon a finding that a juvenile lacked the means to make restitution and cannot reasonably acquire them. Further, the number and nature of community service hours were to be related to the seriousness of the offense as well as to the age, skill, and ability of the youth.

The new statute specifies and authorizes up to $500 restitution for a Level 1 offender, more than $500 for a Level 2 offender, and incorporates the other provisos of the earlier law, including judicial modification of a victim's claim. Maximum community service hours are now specified as up to 100 hours for a Level 1 offender and not less than 100 or more than 200 hours for a Level 2 offender, again with the inclusion of the constraints of the earlier Act.

Currently, practical implementation of restitution and community service options lag behind need. Generally speaking, communities in North Carolina, as in other states, need to develop programs that allow youth to earn money so they can make restitution—opportunities that should include paid community service. Such programs facilitate a higher ratio of payments to victim damage or loss. In addition, community service opportunities should provide solid work training and supervision for involved youth.

AFTERCARE PROVISIONS CAN AFFECT LENGTH OF COMMITMENT

Post-release supervision, commonly known as aftercare or parole, is to be imposed for not less than 90 days or more than one year, and will be provided by court counselors. Except for juveniles charged with certain specific offenses, juveniles committed to training schools may be furloughed into post-release supervision 90 or more days prior to the end of a sentence. In addition, the Office of Juvenile Justice is obligated to inform all victims of Class A or B1 felonies in advance of the juvenile perpetrator's scheduled release date, if the victim wants this information.

OPEN HEARINGS, SEX OFFENDER REGISTRIES, AND SCHOOL NOTIFICATION REFLECT THE CHANGING TIMES

Delinquency hearings are now open to the public unless closed by a judge for good cause. Formerly, hearings were closed unless the juvenile asked that they be open. Juveniles age 11 and older, adjudicated for specified sex offenses and deemed by a judge to be "a danger to the community," will need to comply with sex offender registration requirements.

Greater communication with schools is now mandated. When a youth is charged with a felony, a court counselor is now required to notify the youth's school principal, public or private, before the next school day. Probation orders compelling school attendance must also be communicated.

ROLE OF OFFICE OF JUVENILE JUSTICE EXPANDS

The Office of Juvenile Justice takes over management of the court counselor function, as well as the institutional and related responsibilities of the state's former Division of Youth Services. Its director is appointed by the governor and it is located within the Office of the Governor. It is charged with prevention as well as post-release supervision, and subsidizes county operated detention centers that it does not itself administer.

Interesting statutory provisions direct the Office to provide leadership to implement "state policy which requires that training schools be phased out as populations diminish," and to transfer savings when a training school is closed to community-based programs. Everyone from taxpayers to juvenile justice professionals will be surprised if these eventualities occur, since lengthier sentences and state population growth typically mitigate against institutional closures.

FINAL COMMENTARY

North Carolina juvenile courts have not suffered an attrition of jurisdiction, as the revisions have not resulted in any direct criminal court filing provision or eased transfer procedures. These courts have acquired additional jurisdiction over 16- and 17-year-old undisciplined juveniles—a strange gain. New code provisions, termed medieval by one official, could result in benefits if alternative sanction authorizations such as victim-offender mediation, wilderness programs, intensive probation, day treatment programs, and residential treatment are in fact funded and made broadly available across the state.

Another official pessimistically stated that "one would have hoped for a better and more realistic balance between increased accountability for juveniles and their therapeutic needs." Juveniles are likely to be held more accountable than are state legislators.

Endnotes

[1] N.C. Gen. Stat. Chapter 7B.
Governor's Commission on Juvenile Crime and Justice (1998). *Final Report*. Raleigh, NC: Author.

Chapter 13

The Juvenile Court Judge's Role: Planting Good Seeds

*[**Editor's Note:** This chapter presents an interview with Judge James H. Seals, Circuit Court Juvenile Division, Fort Myers, Florida.]*

THE ROAD TO JUDGESHIP

Rubin: Please talk about your background—from childhood on, and the values you bring to the juvenile court bench.

Seals: I grew up in a conservative Southern home where my parents taught me to be respectful, to have faith in God, and to realize that we are placed on this earth to serve—not to consume. I developed a passion for the underdog from my mother. My folks were racially tolerant and taught me to treat everyone in the community with equal dignity, including African Americans, which I discovered early on was not the norm in the place and time of my childhood.

I committed my share of minor mischief as a child, but never went to juvenile court. That's why I believe it is in the nature of children to be a little mischievous, and I guess that is why I give some latitude to minor offenders in my court. I grew out of it and moved on to become a moderately high achiever.

After four relatively calm years at Georgia Tech I attended law school at the University of Florida during the campus tumults of the late 1960s. Those years honed my idealism and I decided to do public interest law. I went to work for the Legal Aid Society in Orlando (1970-1972). There I defended juvenile offenders, represented parents in dependency proceedings, tenants in landlord-tenant matters, and handled domestic relations cases for those who could not afford attorneys. Our mission was to help individual people with their particular problems and not to turn the world upside down with class action lawsuits. It was there I learned that justice is individualized and case specific.

Later I moved to Fort Myers and practiced for 11 years doing mostly civil law work for individuals. In the early 1980s all these influences on my life converged into a great hunger to become a judge.

Rubin: I'd like to hear about your different judgeships.

Seals: In 1984 I ran in a nonpartisan election for county court judge and won. A year and a half later I was appointed to the circuit court, our court of general jurisdiction. There I initially sat in the civil division, but after five years I began to tire of

---

This chapter originally appeared in Juvenile Justice Update, *Vol. 4, No. 4, August/September 1998.*

those proceedings. I then moved to the criminal division, but became bored with routine trials and upset over the erosion of judicial discretion in criminal court. Next came family court and the domestic relations cases. In family court judges have wide discretion and can still be quite creative. I really enjoyed tailoring my rulings and decisions to meet each family's individual needs. Our family court emphasizes a kinder, gentler approach with heavy stress on mediation and reaching resolutions amicably. The dependent children's docket was also added to my family court duties.

In February, 1997, I dropped my family court docket and took the entire dependency and delinquency dockets for my county (population 400,000). Before that juvenile court was the domain of nine judges (three in dependency and six in delinquency) all working part time on this workload. Now there is one full time juvenile court judge—me. I like to believe I evolved from the "balls and strikes" civil and criminal courts through the high-impact family court to the most important court of all—the juvenile court.

SETTING THE COURT ATMOSPHERE

Rubin: Talk about the environment you create in your court. How do you control the nature of the proceedings in the court?

Seals: I run a low key court. I always try to remain calm. I tell everybody that we're going to conduct business with respect and dignity, and everyone is to be courteous. I try to conduct proceedings in a manner that shows I'm interested in each person's case. I want them to believe that this is not only a court of sanctions and consequences, but also a court that cares and wants to help.

The atmosphere I want my court to present is one of control—where the judge is in control of the courtroom and his temperament is also under control; that all adults in the courtroom are under control as well; and the process itself is under control. I strive to impress upon children and families that this is a competent court—that this is not a joke.

Rubin: Every child has a lawyer in court. Lawyers often speak for the child or prosecute the child—but to what degree do you seek to individualize the child and to speak to the child?

Seals: As much as I can, but naturally it depends upon where we are in the proceedings. At disposition hearings I let the child know I have read and considered the predisposition report—that I did my homework in other words. I usually ask questions of the child to bring him or her out and dialogue with the court. Sometimes it takes no effort, but most of the time it takes some doing.

Often, when I notice a child is showing no improvement, I encourage the child to speak candidly to me or anyone so we can better identify problems needing solutions. When there has been improvement, I praise the child. If parents or counselors compliment a child in open court, I'll ask how it feels to be complimented instead of bashed or blamed. Children seem to really enjoy that question. I feel it is my duty to offer hope and encouragement every chance I get.

Rubin: Do you ever ask the child what do you think the consequences should be?

Seals (laughing): No, I don't do it that particular way. I do ask all parties and lawyers for comments on the recommended disposition. A child's response will sometimes lead to "What do you think?" as a follow-up question.

Rubin: What do you ask the child after you've announced your disposition? Whether he or she understands this? Whether he or she has any feelings about this? Whether there is agreement or disagreement?

Seals: I usually don't, but I probably should since the standard colloquy covers that. If children or parents want to speak after my pronouncement, I don't cut them off. Most of time these children have gone over their predisposition reports, talked to their lawyers, and pretty well know what the situation is.

However, I often vary somewhat from the menu of recommended sanctions so they know I am putting my own imprint on the disposition and not mindlessly parroting our juvenile justice agency, the Department of Juvenile Justice (DJJ). I'll ask the child if he or she understands the new twist I am putting on the disposition order.

COMMUNITY SERVICE ASSIGNMENTS

Rubin: What about community service assignment? Doesn't DJJ decide the actual assignment?

Seals: Yes, but when possible I will recommend a community service that matches with the child's interests. Community service should be more than an accountability issue—it should also be about competency development. Of course that cannot be done in many cases, but it should, whenever possible, serve both objectives.

PERSONAL SATISFACTIONS

Rubin: What are the satisfactions in being a juvenile court judge?

Seals: From a purely personal point of view, I like the broad discretion, being creative, and the endless opportunities to make a difference. Juvenile court is the greatest challenge in the judicial system, and the handful of successes make up for all the tragedy and heartbreak you see in so many children's lives.

Rubin: How do you know if you're getting ahead?

Seals: Sometimes you get feedback from the parents, DJJ counselors, and other related sources. Sometimes you can read it in faces of the children when they stand in front of you. Please understand—every case is not a success. I'm not a miracle maker, but I can't help but think a caring court will get further ahead with children than one that doesn't care.

Rubin: Do you get satisfaction just from the conduct of the hearing—when a hearing is going well?

Seals: Yes. A juvenile court judge is just like a parent, and what good parents do is plant as many good seeds in a child as they can, cultivate them, and then hope and pray the child grows into something good. What I do at some particular moment may have no immediate impact, but I may have planted a seed that will germinate later on. So I look at each contact with a child as an opportunity to plant seeds. Whether I succeed or fail is something I may never know.

HANDLING DISPOSITIONS

Rubin: How long do dispositional hearings average?

Seals: They will vary. Some may take five minutes or less, as when a child knows he or she is heading to a high-level commitment program and there isn't much to do but preach a short sermon and pronounce the disposition. Sometimes my mind fails to come up with something to say, and I can't find any seeds to plant.

Dispositions heading toward community control, which is Florida's term for probation, usually take longer because the child is staying in the community and that brings up many issues. The longest, and usually the most unpleasant, dispositions involve contentious parents arguing for a disposition furthering their own self interests and not the best interests of the child. Disposition hearings average perhaps 10 minutes, but I've had some last 45 minutes to an hour.

Rubin: Early juvenile court judges wanted to be on the same floor level as the child. Some juvenile court benches today are one step up from the floor. Your bench looks about two steps up. Will you comment on the advantages and disadvantages of the height of your bench and the structure of your courtroom.

Seals: I generally like the raised bench, but I don't like it when I have a small child in front of me. Sometimes I hold dispositions back in the conference room where we're all at the same level. I don't mind being eye to eye, but I do not want to have to look up at a child.

Often I have 40-50 people waiting in my large courtroom while personal, sensitive business is going on at the bench. I wish I could change the architecture to a small courtroom and have more waiting and private conferencing spaces outside the courtroom.

PARENTS AS PART OF THE PROBLEM

Rubin: We've talked somewhat of the satisfactions of your judgeship. What about the dissatisfactions? The hardships?

Seals: I don't like stereotyping children—they're individuals with their very own set of characteristics, strengths and weaknesses. I'm bothered when law enforcement, prosecutors, public defenders, juvenile justice boards, or DJJ place their organizational agenda above the mission of the court. Our mission is too important. I'm disappointed by some people's pettiness and by many parents who insist on continuing to be a part of the problem and do not want to be part of the solution. I'm disappointed when a child misses out on the opportunities that have been provided.

The major hardship is stress. So much work—so little time.

Rubin: Do we work enough with parents?

Seals: We order a lot of family counseling, but, no, we don't work enough with parents. It is very hard to get parents to buy into problem solving when they are telling me that it is the court's duty, and only the court's duty, to fix their child. Better strategies for improving parental involvement is one of my high priorities.

NEED TO SPEED COURT PROCESS

Rubin: Will you speak to the impact of the slow court process on sanctioning and intervention with a juvenile?

Seals: I accept the findings of many studies that swiftness and certitude count more than severity, that courts are most effective when the consequence comes quickly and as advertised. I am very concerned about kids who spend a lot of time waiting for their cases to be adjudicated. There's a lot of wasted time and, when that happens, the seeds lose their potency.

THE ROLE OF THE PROSECUTOR

Rubin: Will you speak to the authority and influence of the prosecutor on today's juvenile court?

Seals: In my judgment, the prosecuting agency is the second most powerful entity in the system. Because of their expansive direct filing authority, prosecutors, not the judges, are the gatekeepers to the adult criminal court. Although many children are going to our adult court, none have gotten there through me.

In the courtroom, a thoughtful prosecutor who charges fairly, prosecutes competently, and recommends wisely—knowing when to be stern or merciful—can have a tremendous impact on children. Juvenile court is no place for Rambo prosecutors. Children do not respect an adversary with that kind of attitude, and respect for authority is one of the most important values we can teach. They already see enough "hard asses" at home or out on the streets where they are picking up all their bad habits and attitudes.

Rubin: Do you feel that direct files into criminal court could be reduced if there were more resources within the juvenile system?

Seals: I think we send too many kids to the adult system. Most of them could be better served in juvenile court. I don't think it is so much a question of resources as it is of attitude. Too many adults want to give up on too many children too soon. I once heard someone say that if all governments resolved never to build another jail or prison we would solve our juvenile delinquency problem. There is some truth to that.

Rubin: Is there strong prosecutor advocacy for hard-line dispositions in your court?

Seals: It is moderately strong. We don't get much of that "hard ass" advocacy. Usually our prosecutors bring necessary concerns to my attention and do it in a thoughtful, rational manner.

Rubin: Many juvenile court judges complain about the inexperience of prosecutors assigned to juvenile court and the short duration of their rotation. Do you?

Seals: Yes. I have already had three different generations of prosecutors in my court this past year. The juvenile court should not be a transitory, entry level position for prosecutors, or for judges, for that matter. The position requires experience, wisdom, and plenty of discretion delegated to them so they can be flexible and act swiftly and appropriately. I anxiously await the day when the prosecutorial culture recognizes and embraces this. I am beginning to see hopeful signs.

FOLLOWING UP ON DISPOSITIONS

Rubin: Do you set further hearings a few weeks or a month after a disposition as some judges do?

Seals: I don't call many back after I make my disposition. My calendar is too full and I just don't have time. I can't review every case, and I'm not sure how to select those which might benefit from a review hearing. I would like to have citizen boards reviewing juveniles on community control. Citizen panels currently review our dependent children in foster care and it has worked well. Juveniles need a timely pat on the back or kick in the pants from the court and I would like to have citizen assistance in bringing them to me.

I am a strong advocate for citizen participation in juvenile court. I believe it would really help spread the message that juvenile courts can and do work pretty effectively.

Rubin: Have you visited the facilities where you place children?

Seals: I have visited some of them, but not enough. I plan to visit as many as time allows.

Rubin: Recently you helped develop a victim-offender mediation program. Can you speak to your motivation for this development?

Seals: My initial motivation was selfish. I wanted to reduce the number of restitution hearings. But I had a secondary motivation, as I believed mediation could help provide closure and healing to victims and have a beneficial impact on children. I'm quite surprised and very pleased at how well victims have responded to this process, not only in terms of their own self healing, but also in how eloquently and constructively they express to the child their anger, pain, and loss. I still believe that people, including victims, love and care about children, even the difficult ones.

BENEFITS OF A ONE-JUDGE JUVENILE COURT

Rubin: What about political influences on your decision making?

Seals: I feel virtually none. If there are political forces out there who do not like what I am doing, I am pleased to say they are keeping silent.

Rubin: Please discuss your relationships with other judges since you became the juvenile court judge.

Seals: I have an excellent, almost fraternal, relationship with my chief judge. A juvenile court judge could not ask for a better boss. He has designated himself as my back-up judge, he's knowledgeable and concerned, and understands the juvenile court extremely well.

My colleagues are glad that I am handling all of juvenile court because that means they are handling none of it—just kidding.

Rubin: Six judges used to combine to do the delinquency docket. You handle that docket as well as the dependency docket exclusively. Everyone I have interviewed in your justice system clearly prefers a one-judge court. Is it a better court when there is one judge, or when this responsibility is divided among six judges?

Seals: A one-judge court provides the consistency and coordination which a six-judge court cannot provide. Moreover, not all of the six judges wanted or preferred this assignment. I did. Furthermore, I have only juvenile court to worry about. The six-judge group had many other dockets to handle.

The only problem I have that they did not is burnout. The daily court calendars are long and there are seemingly endless difficult decisions to make each day with little time for consideration. In addition, the juvenile court judge, if he is worth his salt, must find time to be a leader for continual systemic improvements in juvenile justice, both in his community and across the state. The latter work is usually more enjoyable, but the children coming before you today are always your first and most important responsibility. That's your opportunity to plant seeds.

Author's Note

Judge Seals, in July 2002, prepared the updating commentary that follows.

I've been out of juvenile court for over two years now, so there isn't too much to add. We have begun a drug court, however, which I think is great and which I support, but regrettably I have no personal experience with it.

The main thing that concerns me is the political-legal-judicial-community culture toward juvenile courts and juvenile justice throughout Florida. I believe juvenile courts should be, for the most part, therapeutic courts. I still believe most juvenile crime is the result of bad relationships and the losses and deficits this generates. Yet there is no strong systemic effort anywhere to repair those relationships and point children back into the right direction. Florida is currently committed to deep-end institutional financing (along with mass direct filing into adult court). Prevention and community empowerment will have to come from other sources. However, Florida is so state government dependent that there is no one to fill the voids left behind.

The political culture for the most part uses fear and toughness tactics to get votes, but not help at-risk children. Children's issues remain among the first and hardest hit by budget downsizing when fiscal pressures face lawmakers. Most of the legal culture—green prosecutors and public defenders—sees juvenile court as a practice field for the bigger courts, and through ignorance, inexperience, or neglect sends too many wrong messages to children and the parents. The judicial culture and our constitutional structure are designed to prevent, discourage, and even make sport of a judge who seriously wants to be a long-tenured, highly trained, effective juvenile court judge. The community continues to be on the outside, depending on, God forbid, the media and politicians for information. I'm not totally cynical, but I don't see Florida, which has both an outstanding bench and bar, as one of the leading states in juvenile justice reform and effectiveness.

I'm still keeping the faith and continue to believe more than ever in planting good seeds, whether the sower is a judge, prosecutor, public defender, probation officer, legislator, journalist, victim, parent, teacher, neighbor, or whatever. I'm still praying for a good harvest. The future of our nation depends on it.

Chapter 14

Prosecutors in Juvenile Court

In different states, prosecutors in juvenile court are known as assistant district attorneys, state's attorneys, commonwealth attorneys, attorneys general, or county prosecutors. Some stay in juvenile court for four months; others stay for a year or more.

Where there is speedy turnover, the juvenile court is viewed as a training ground. Newly recruited assistant prosecutors may be assigned to the juvenile court for training. Some longer-term assistant prosecutors have been, in effect, dumped on the juvenile court because they have not been effective in other courts. Other juvenile court prosecutors demonstrate great capabilities and aim at a rapid move to the felony court. Chief juvenile court prosecutors in larger jurisdictions may make a career out of this assignment. Juvenile court judges tend to complain about rapid prosecutor rotation and seek more extended prosecutor tenure.

This chapter examines several standards that guide prosecutors in juvenile court, comments on their increased presence and authority in this setting, describes prosecutor activities at different processing stages, notes organizational problems that confront one large-city juvenile prosecution office, and provides tips on working with prosecutors.

JUVENILE PROSECUTION STANDARDS OF THE NATIONAL DISTRICT ATTORNEYS ASSOCIATION

The juvenile prosecution standards of the National District Attorneys Association (NDAA) take an overall positive and balanced direction. Standard 19.2 (A.2) provides:

> The primary duty of the prosecutor is to seek justice while fully and faithfully representing the interests of the state. While the safety and welfare of the community, including the victim, is their primary concern, prosecutors should consider the special interests and needs of the juvenile to the extent they can do so without compromising that concern.

The commentary to this standard adds that attention to the special interests and needs of juveniles "reflects the philosophy that the safety and welfare of the community is enhanced when juveniles, through counseling, restitution, or more extensive rehabilitative efforts and sanctions, are dissuaded from further criminal activity." Juvenile probation and community correctional agency personnel share common ground with this vision.

This chapter originally appeared in Community Corrections Report, *Vol. 2, No. 5, July/August 1995.*

DEVELOPMENT OF THE PROSECUTOR'S ROLE

Prosecutors essentially ignored juvenile courts until the late 1960s. Until then, juvenile courts had not been user-friendly to prosecutors (nor to defense counsel), and judges and their probation departments ran the show. Two major developments changed this.

The first development was the U.S. Supreme Court's decision in **In re Gault**, 387 U.S. 1 (1967), which announced that constitutional safeguards surrounded alleged juvenile offenders. One such constitutional right was notice of the right to counsel and, if indigent, to free counsel. The decision ushered defense counsel into the court. (See Chapter 2 for a fuller discussion of **Gault**.)

The second development was an intensified national examination of adult and juvenile crime that began in the early 1970s, and sought improvements in police, court, and corrections efficacy. As a consequence, numerous prosecution offices quickly decided to assert a much stronger presence and influence in the juvenile justice system. Emphasizing the "safety and welfare of the community" as a primary concern, prosecutors ushered themselves into court, and more than re-balanced the brief defense counsel advantage.

For example, Chicago's chief juvenile prosecutor, Maurice M. Dore, simply and unceremoniously usurped the "file-no file" decision-making function of the probation department's intake unit. My notes from a 1977 interview with this official reveal balance, as well as humor, in his commentaries: "I'm critical of public defenders who file motions by the ton. You could replace them with parrots or with dictaphones, their motions and arguments are so routine." He was critical, also, of prosecutors "who just want to lock kids up." He wanted his assistants to "develop into decent human beings, to think about what they are doing, and to think about the kids and their families." Further, while he faulted the court's "poor standards" in returning certain serious and violent juvenile offenders to the community at detention and dispositional hearings, he took satisfaction from playing a major role in developing a needed diversion program. He expressed pride, also, in the working relationships he had established with many community agencies and the court's judges, while retaining an independent identity.

PROSECUTORS AND THE DECISION TO FILE A CASE

Initially, the prosecutor's role in juvenile court was to present the evidence at the adjudication stage. This function remains the primary prosecutor activity in a number of states, particularly the less populous ones. Elsewhere, this office has taken on, or taken over, the up-front screening function, deciding whether felony offenses (and, in some jurisdictions, misdemeanor offenses) should be formally petitioned. Legislators have been receptive to prosecutor requests that statutes be amended to transfer intake control from probation departments to prosecutor offices. There are several models for this:

- First-level prosecutor screening provides for a "paper flow" from police to prosecutor. The prosecutor determines whether an offense will be handled formally. Colorado, Idaho, Oklahoma, and Washington are among the states using this approach.

- There are several forms of second-level prosecutor screening. One, best illustrated by Florida (and subsequently adopted by the 1980 American Bar Association Standards), has probation intake officers conduct the first screen. All referrals are then transferred to the prosecutor with either a file or no-file recommendation. The prosecutor can accept or reject a recommendation.

- A variation of this second-level prosecutor screening approach occurs in Arizona. There, the probation agency is the sole decision maker with misdemeanors. Probation officers cannot adjust a felony without a prosecutor's review and concurrence. Maryland has a similar procedure, except that the prosecutor also must ratify the diversion handling of a gun-related misdemeanor offense. New Mexico intake officers may adjust up to three misdemeanors, but a fourth, as well as all felony offenses, must be forwarded to the prosecutor for a filing decision. (Recommendations are made for or against filing.)

- Prosecutors remain outside the basic filing decision loop in a number of states. One is North Dakota, where a reported 90%-95% of cases are handled informally. The juvenile code there authorizes an informal adjustment time frame of up to nine months, which a judge may extend for an additional six months.

The NDAA standards unequivocally prefer first-level prosecutor screening. NDAA Standard 19.2 (B.1) proclaims that only prosecutors should screen the legal facts from the police, determine whether the facts are legally sufficient for prosecution, and decide whether a juvenile should be transferred to adult court, charged in juvenile court, or diverted from formal adjudication.

I concur. This is a job for prosecutors, not for probation officers. The commentary to the NDAA standards on point appropriately emphasizes that "juveniles are abused when they are charged by non-lawyers in cases where there is insufficient evidence that they committed a crime." They are abused, also, when intake probation officers divert them with requirements, or place them on informal probation when there is insufficient evidence.

IMPACT OF *BREED V. JONES* ON FRONT-END DECISION MAKING

The greater prosecutor influence in juvenile courts has been due also to the impact of **Breed v. Jones**, 421 U.S. 519 (1975), the U.S. Supreme Court decision that overturned a California juvenile court judge's action. The judge, following trial, had adjudicated a 17-year-old boy as delinquent. At the subsequently scheduled dispositional hearing, the judge announced that, instead, he would hold a transfer hearing one week later. He did, and the juvenile was transferred to criminal court. There, charged with the same offense, he was again found guilty of robbery in the first degree.

The issues on appeal included: (1) Was the transfer proceeding barred because of the prior juvenile court adjudication? and (2) Was the juvenile court a true court, so that Jones was twice placed in jeopardy?

The Court unanimously held that Jones had been denied the protection of the Double Jeopardy Clause of the Fifth Amendment, as applied to states through the Fourteenth Amendment. Further, he had been "subjected to the burden of two trials for the same offense; he was twice put to the task of marshalling his resources against those of the State, twice subjected to the 'heavy personal strain' which such an experience represents."

How did **Breed v. Jones** change front-end decision making? Prosecutors had to get into the act early with transferable offenses. Prosecutors had to implement a protocol that ensured their review of all juvenile offenses that met statutory criteria for transfer. They did not want a transfer-eligible juvenile to enter a quick admission/plea without their concurrence, as this would retain the juvenile in juvenile court and eliminate consideration of the youth's transfer to a criminal court.

Intake officers had to accept this prosecutor's mandate, even in states that did not provide for a prosecutor's front-end review of all or certain felonies.

PROSECUTORS AT DETENTION HEARINGS

Probation officers did lose power when the juvenile court became subject to constitutional protections. Initially, they did not welcome either defense attorneys or prosecutors. Many, today, seem to prefer that lawyers come into court only when there is a contested adjudication or transfer hearing. What follows is a stage-by-stage description of what prosecutors actually do or might do in juvenile courts today.

Detention Hearings

Lead juvenile prosecutors in Cleveland, Ohio, and Wilmington, Delaware, recently told me their offices are represented at detention hearings only when there are very serious offenses. Many prosecutors (and defenders) skip detention hearings for one or more of the following reasons: (1) they accept the capabilities of detention screeners and screening instruments to make suitable judgments; (2) they are not displeased to see a significant number of lesser offenders released following several nights of being locked up; (3) they believe the judge or referee does not particularly want or need their input; (4) they prefer not to be present because these hearings are often delayed or their timing is unpredictable; or (5) they contend their staffing complement precludes this representation.

Preparation of the Petition for Court

I place the task of preparing the court petition in the lawyer's (prosecutor's) domain regardless of the decision-making authority granted the prosecutor at the intake stage, but not everyone agrees. Key Chicago prosecutors, despite their first-level prosecutor screening role, rejected my recommendation, three years ago, to take over this responsibility from the probation department. They did not want to add a new task or a new budget item. Some years earlier, it took the intervention of the Chief Justice of Colorado to convince Denver's district attorney to assume this function following a statutory change which gave that office a first-level prosecutor screening authority.

It is good practice, where probation departments exclusively control intake and still prepare petitions, to have prosecutors provide clear formats and language for probation staff use in petitioning the various offenses. It is desirable, also, to have prosecutors review and approve these petitions, as to form, within a 24-hour turnaround time.

Plea Bargaining and Dispositional Hearings

NDAA standards ratify the practice of plea bargaining. They urge, for example, that a burglary be reduced only to a lesser scale burglary and not to theft, and that a bargained sexual offense reflect a lesser sexual offense rather than only a simple assault. Further, if three burglaries are reduced to one, prosecutors are to obtain the juvenile's approval, as part of the bargain, to include restitution for all three offenses, and recite this into the court record as the basis for full financial liability (NDAA Standard 19.2 (D. Commentary)).

It is common for prosecutors to appear at dispositional hearings and state their agreement or disagreement with key recommendations of the predisposition report. If they disagree, it is usually to urge a more serious sanction. They may question the probation officer who did the study. They may warn the juvenile of more serious consequences if there is another offense. Often, their opinions are influential with the judge.

Many prosecutors avoid these hearings. This may be due to a limited staff complement, or because a judge sends a clear message that the probation department and the judge are to handle this proceeding. Some years ago, I observed the juvenile prosecutor in Atlanta routinely exit the courtroom following adjudication. "Why don't you participate in the dispositional hearing that follows?" I asked. "Because the judge relies on the probation officer's study and doesn't want attorney input at this hearing," he answered.

Currently, Cleveland prosecutors avoid dispositional hearings, except with serious felony offenses. They sometimes use another strategy. They may announce at the conclusion of an adjudicatory hearing that they do not plan to attend the disposition, then place into the court record a recommendation that the judge commit this offender to the state.

There are juvenile courts where the probation agency sends only the predisposition report, not a probation officer, to the dispositional hearing. Prosecutors and defense attorneys can dominate these hearings.

Finally, there are juvenile courts where plea/sentence bargains are put together by the prosecutor and defense counsel, without probation department input or a predisposition report, and the judge simply ratifies the agreement.

PROSECUTORS' ORGANIZATIONAL PROBLEMS

Last year, I consulted with a large-city juvenile prosecution office. Some of the office's problems have kinship with those of probation or community correctional agencies. Many assistant prosecutors complained that:

- They were cast into their jobs with no specialized training and with grossly insufficient supervision.

- They worked much harder than numerous co-workers, but received no rewards.

- There were significant inefficiencies. They reported, among others, considerable "goofing off" by colleagues who performed the off-hours petition preparation task.

- Cases were handled by a different prosecutor at each of three processing stages—arraignment, adjudication, and disposition. Instead, they favored instituting "vertical prosecution" (i.e., one assistant prosecutor carrying a case throughout these three stages).

- Another specialized unit had the status in the office, but assistant prosecutors there were no better than other experienced assistants. Also, the specialized unit had greater plea bargaining authority than other trial attorneys.

- Case records were often misplaced.

- They were overworked. They didn't have enough out-of-courtroom time to review and prepare for upcoming cases, catch up with phone messages from law enforcement, victims, the police, etc.

- They were bored with their jobs and wanted to move on to more challenging roles.

TIPS ON WORKING WITH JUVENILE PROSECUTORS

Prosecutors are trained in the law; they are not schooled in how professionals work with offenders. They are trained to search for facts, not feelings. They look at the world differently than you (probation officers) do. But many will be interested in learning what you do and how you do it. They will be interested in ways you might make their task easier rather than harder. So, here are a few suggestions for strengthening your relationships with prosecutors:

- Go to coffee, lunch, or happy hour with juvenile prosecutors. Talk about your work, their work, how the court might be improved. Ask a prosecutor to give your staff a seminar on juvenile law.

- Take prosecutors on visits to the pretrial detention facility, a branch probation office (walk nearby streets together), day treatment and residential programs, community service sites, state institutions, and other public and private services that work with court juveniles. Help prosecutors understand what resources work best with what types of youth. Arrange for prosecutors to interact with the boys/girls.

- Learn prosecutors' language. Know what's in the Fifth, Sixth, Fourteenth, and other pertinent amendments to the U.S. Constitution. Read or reread **In re Gault**. Be able to converse on the different measures or quanta of proof: beyond reasonable doubt, clear and convincing, preponderance. Know some of the key statutory citations in your state, so you can talk shorthand about 48-13-5 (b) or 48-21-2. (Prosecutors will be wowed, unless you've used the wrong citation!)

- Get your predisposition and other court reports done on time. Make your findings and recommendations concrete. Avoid terms like "I feel," or "passive aggressive-personality."

- Be candid about the juveniles you work with. Let prosecutors know if probationers are not making restitution payments or performing community service, and suggest what might be done about this. If you receive a negative report about a juvenile's adjustment in a residential facility, share this. Knowing about problems does not mean a prosecutor will move in to "bust" a kid. Rather, the prosecutor will have greater trust in you and want to rely on your judgment for a course of action.

- Discuss your differences openly, but review the common ground. The prosecutor's most prominent goal, community protection, does overlap with your purpose to facilitate rehabilitation. Prosecutors have the power to pursue legal actions; your power is the information you have about a juvenile that the prosecutor needs.

- If you find a particular prosecutor is unworkable and truly a pain, remember that it won't be long until the prosecutor leaves for another court. Then you can start all over again with the replacement.

Chapter 15

The Role of Defense Attorneys in Juvenile Justice Proceedings

The 30th anniversary of the U.S. Supreme Court's decision in **In re Gault**, 387 U.S. 1 (1967), will be celebrated next year. The decision energized juvenile courts and ushered defense attorneys into the forum. Prior to **Gault** there were few defense attorneys in juvenile court. (For a more detailed discussion of **Gault**, see Chapter 2.) A 1963 survey of 73 urban and metropolitan juvenile court judges found that the frequency of representation was 10% or less in 81% of these courts.[1]

In penning the **Gault** ruling, Justice Fortas noted that neither probation officers nor judges adequately represent a child's interests at adjudicatory hearings. He stated that a juvenile who was facing the loss of liberty needed the assistance of a lawyer "to cope with problems of law, to make skilled inquiry into the facts, to insist upon regularity of the proceedings, and to ascertain whether he has a defense and to prepare and submit it." Accordingly, the child and parent must be notified of their right to representation, and told that counsel will be appointed at public expense if they are unable to afford an attorney.

WAIVER OF RIGHT TO COUNSEL

Note that the Supreme Court did not mandate counsel, only notice of the right to counsel. This right could be waived knowingly and intelligently. Such waivers occur regularly in many states. However, there are jurisdictions that either do not permit waiver or require the youth to consult with an attorney prior to making a valid waiver.

National standards promulgated by the Institute of Judicial Administration (IJA)-American Bar Association (ABA) Juvenile Justice Standards Project recommend that waivers should not be permitted.[2] Related standards prepared by the National Advisory Committee on Criminal Justice Standards and Goals authorize waiver, but only after the juvenile and his or her parent consult with an attorney about whether such waiver is wise.[3]

A 1995 publication by the U.S. General Accounting Office (GAO) reported to Congress on right to counsel provisions in the statutes, case law decisions, and practices in 15 states. Of the 15 states surveyed, only New Mexico prohibits waiver at any stage of the process. Texas prohibits waiver at any adjudicatory, dispositional, or transfer hearing. New York bars waiver, except when an attorney appears for a youth at a court hearing and the court permits the waiver. The remaining 12 states (Arizona, California, Florida, Idaho, Kansas, Louisiana, Maryland, Missouri, Nebraska, Pennsylvania, South Carolina, and Utah) allow broad waiver provisions.[4]

This chapter originally appeared in Juvenile Justice Update, *Vol. 2, No. 2, April/May 1996.*

The American Bar Association, the Juvenile Law Center of Philadelphia, and the Youth Law Center of San Francisco also collaborated to assess the issue. After surveying hundreds of public defenders and private counsel representing juveniles, the study found that approximately 34% of each group reported juveniles waived their right to counsel at the detention hearing stage. Often, there was no "colloquy" or advisory discussion between the judge/referee and juvenile/parents before the waiver was entered. The authors concluded that there is the "possibility—perhaps the likelihood—that a substantial number of juvenile waivers are not 'knowing and intelligent.'"[5]

EXTENT OF REPRESENTATION

The GAO study examined frequency of representation in three states (California, Nebraska, and Pennsylvania), though unfortunately the data are incomplete:

- The data for California only pertain to five counties. Juveniles had attorneys in 97% of the cases examined.

- Nebraska data were statewide, but information from one of the largest counties failed consistently to indicate whether counsel was present at adjudicatory hearings. The data collected showed that attorneys were present at 65% of the adjudications. Juveniles went unrepresented in 12% of hearings in metropolitan jurisdictions and 55% in nonmetropolitan counties.

- Pennsylvania had statewide data, but none from Philadelphia. The data indicated that 91% of youths had representation at adjudication. The rate of unrepresented youth was 8% in metropolitan counties and 19% in other areas.

- Property offenders in California and Pennsylvania, but not Nebraska, were as likely to be represented as other offenders.

Predictably, representation was substantially more common in metropolitan jurisdictions.

The most often cited study on this issue is that of University of Minnesota law professor Barry Feld. Feld's study, which examined six states, found higher representation rates in larger, more urban states (85%-95%) than in more rural states (38%-53%). Representation also varied within a state; in Minnesota, for example, there was a variance from 10%-90% in different counties.[6] Other studies from the 1980s reported representation in less than half of cases.[7]

TYPES OF LAWYER REPRESENTATION

There are three basic types of lawyer representation for juveniles; the lawyers may be public defenders, court-appointed private attorneys, or family-retained private attorneys. The GAO study also conducted a multi-state survey of juvenile prosecutors, juvenile court judges, and other juvenile justice system officials, and found an overall favorable response to the quality of lawyers for juveniles. Public defenders were seen to be at least as capable as private attorneys, and were perceived by some as more knowledgeable and experienced with juvenile proceedings. There were concerns that the quality of their practice was impaired by very high caseloads and limited resources.

The study does not tell us much detail about lawyer effectiveness. However, it found that California juveniles represented by private-appointed lawyers were more likely to be adjudicated for certain offenses than those represented by other attorney types, but less likely to be adjudicated for serious violent crimes. It also found that California and Nebraska juveniles represented by privately retained attorneys were less likely to be removed from home for certain offenses than those represented by other attorney types; the opposite was true in Pennsylvania.

PRESENCE OF COUNSEL MAY HAVE NEGATIVE EFFECT

One study of two populous North Carolina jurisdictions found that juveniles without lawyers were substantially less likely to be committed to an institution even when the nature and seriousness of the offense were held constant. If there was a defense attorney, a prosecutor had to appear, and the prosecutor "may have counteracted the [positive] effects of the child's lawyer." When there was no defense attorney, a prosecutor did not appear.[8]

Feld's six-state study came to a similar conclusion. Whether controlling for offense seriousness, offense seriousness and detention status, or offense seriousness together with prior referrals, unrepresented juveniles fared better than those with lawyers.[9]

There are several possible explanations for this:

- *Attorney incompetence:* This may be due to work overloads, neophyte attorneys, or appointed counsel who might opt to comport with court expectations rather than furnish vigorous advocacy. The findings of the earlier-cited ABA/JLC/YLC Study seem to agree with this.

- *Attorneys and clients do not have time to develop a relationship:* The ABA/JLC/YLC Study notes that many juveniles first meet their lawyers when they sit down at counsel table for a detention hearing; lawyers often lack information to answer a judge's questions at a pretrial hearing; they do not have time to file a pretrial motion; workloads and courthouse culture deter aggressive pursuit of defenses at trial; many lawyers fail to present alternative recommendations at disposition; and lawyers rarely take appeals to a higher court.

- *Early identification of chronic or serious offenders:* Judges may identify chronic or serious offenders at detention or arraignment hearings and ensure representation.

- *Leniency toward unrepresented youth:* Judges may be inclined to be lenient toward offenders who appear without counsel.[10]

ABA/JLC/YLC RECOMMENDATIONS

The ABA/JLC/YLC Study has few surprising recommendations. The list of "shoulds" would have been much the same had the study been conducted 25 years ago. Pessimists might say that the results would also be the same if the same study were conducted 25 years from now. The following are suggestions from this study:

1. Increase the number of defense attorneys and expand non-lawyer support from social workers, investigators, and graduate students.

2. Obtain funding equity between juvenile defenders and prosecutors, and between juvenile and adult defenders. The hourly or maximum fee allowed appointed attorneys should be commensurate with that provided for comparable legal work. The rate should not serve as a disincentive for full, vigorous representation.

3. All lawyers, including those in more remote communities, should receive training prior to initial representation of juveniles in court and regularly thereafter. Training should focus on legal issues, and on an array of subject matters and resources available to young clients.

4. Defense attorneys should be permitted to refuse a case if they feel they cannot effectively represent a client due to an excessive caseload.

5. Juvenile court should not be used simply as a training ground for new attorneys. Defender offices should allow attorneys to specialize and remain in juvenile courts. Promotion should not be conditioned on rotation out of juvenile court.

6. Minimum standards should guarantee that every juvenile has counsel from the earliest to the final stages of proceedings, and that counsel may not be waived. In addition, standards should address caseload limitations; adequate law libraries and computer systems; secretarial support; and access to paralegals, social workers, interpreters, and investigators.

7. Local and statewide data on defense attorney representation, caseloads, compensation, and cost-per-juvenile should be gathered, published, and compared.

8. The U.S. Congress should fund a training academy for juvenile defense attorneys that is equivalent to the federally funded training currently available to juvenile court judges and prosecutors.

COMMENTARIES FROM DEFENSE ATTORNEYS

The juvenile and family court studies I conduct include interviews with defense attorneys. Their input is very instructive. For instance, one Midwestern court pays private attorneys an hourly amount to represent juveniles in court. Since they are not paid for out-of-court time, the lawyers, naturally, avoid case investigation and witness interviews until they arrive in court and their meter can begin to tick.

A defense attorney in a large southeastern juvenile court said his jurisdiction has only 15 public defenders to handle its extensive delinquency workload. Unlike the prosecutors in the jurisdiction, the defenders do not move to other courts very quickly. Unlike the prosecutors, individual defenders are empowered to make case decisions without getting their chief's approval. The office employs two social workers, one to promote the use of detention alternatives and the other to prepare different alternative dispositions for presentation to a judge or referee.

Defense attorneys who were interviewed also made more personal observations:

"Our workloads are at a comfortable level. We do plea bargain most cases. That makes it easy for us. We tend to meet our client for the first time at the pretrial. There we talk with the client and the prosecutor, and then we generally have a deal."

"Some public defenders are co-opted by the system, think kids should be punished, and don't question deficiencies in training school treatment. Still, defenders are far better than court-appointed counsel who largely provide token defense of children."

"Defender budgets are bare bones and barely pay for the modest attorney and investigator staffing levels and possibly a social worker. Public defenders are incredibly under-balanced in comparison with prosecution offices. Defender salaries tend to be lower than prosecution salaries, and you see a number of defenders switching to become prosecutors."

"The maintenance of an independent posture by defense lawyers is imperative, though difficult. Judges and probation officers constantly want you to serve instead as a guardian of the child and as a collaborator with the court."

One public defender made a stinging statement about his view of his role:

No one in the system understands my role. The prosecutors are always yanking on my shoulders not to obstruct what they say is in the best interests of the kid. But the best interests of my kids are to keep them out of detention and institutions. They have a right to good treatment, but they don't get this.

Parents generally work against their own kid. They take their kid to the cops and tell him to tell everything that happened. The cops soft-soap the parents, the kid tells everything, and then no one understands why I should defend a confessor, even if the police acted unconstitutionally.

I'd like to treat each client as if he were a millionaire, but I can't. In juvenile court you want to scream: doesn't anyone care? And they will all say they care. But 20 minutes after the hearing the judge has forgotten the kid's name. Clearly the system discriminates against minorities, poverty, and not-together families. And the police scare the s___ out of the parents.

Prosecutors pretty well own the juvenile court. If a prosecutor opposes something, the court goes along with him. At detention hearings we're just a wall decoration. We could change the system if I could get three great defenders from the felony court. We would get them so angry that they would change things. We would declare a world war with every case, because juvenile court is the worst of both worlds. It is the worst of criminal justice and the worst of juvenile justice. They have introduced the adversary system and then softened the rules so you can't be an adversary.

FORCEFUL DEFENSE OF JUVENILES IS IN EVERYONE'S BEST INTERESTS

I sense that quite a few juvenile justice professionals, including judges, presume juveniles to be guilty, rather than innocent, and are bothered when defense lawyers vigorously challenge legal procedures and the apparent good intentions of law enforcement, probation, and community correctional officials. However, juveniles must have independent counsel whose primary goal is ensuring that the law and the Constitution are fully adhered to. The courts must require such advocacy, and attorneys should zealously apply these standards.

I also see a preference among court and state agency professionals to use intervention and control methods without legal checks. In the belief that they know what is best, they often move youths back and forth between secure and non-secure resources without legal review. Similar practices are what brought us the **Gault** decision 29 years ago. The best check on uncertain intervention and legal accomplishments is judicial oversight and the forceful exercise of legal defense for juveniles. This is in everyone's best interest.

Endnotes

[1] Skoler, D. L. & Tenney, C. W. (1964). Attorney representation in juvenile court. *Journal of Family Law, 4,* 77–98.

[2] Institute of Judicial Administration-American Bar Association Juvenile Justice Standards Project (1980). *Standards relating to pretrial court proceedings, Standard 6.1 and commentary.* Cambridge, MA: Ballinger.

[3] National Advisory Committee on Criminal Justice Standards and Goals (1976). *Juvenile Justice and Delinquency Prevention, Standard 16.8 and Commentary*: Washington, DC: U.S. Government Printing Office.

[4] Government Accounting Office (1995). *Juvenile justice: Representation rates varied as did counsel's impact on court outcomes.* Washington, DC: U.S. Government Printing Office.

[5] American Bar Association Juvenile Justice Center, Juvenile Law Center, & Youth Law Center. (1995). *A call for justice: An assessment of access to counsel and quality of representation in delinquency proceedings, executive summary.* Washington, DC: American Bar Association Juvenile Justice Center.

[6] Feld, B. C. (1988). *In re Gault* revisited: A cross-state comparison of the right to counsel in juvenile court. *Crime & Delinquency, 34,* 393-424; Feld, B. C. (1989). The right to counsel in juvenile court: An empirical study of when lawyers appear and the difference they make. *Journal of Criminal Law & Criminology, 79,* 1185-1346.

[7] Clarke, S. H. & Koch, G. G. (1980). Juvenile court: Therapy or crime control, and do lawyers make a difference? *Law & Society Review, 14,* 263-307; Aday, D. (1986). Court structure, defense attorney use, and juvenile court decisions. *Sociological Quarterly, 27,* 107—119.

[8] Clarke & Koch, note 7 supra.

[9] Feld, The right to counsel in juvenile court, note 6 supra.

[10] Feld, *In re Gault* revisited, note 6 supra.

Chapter 16

Judges and Probation Officers: Improving the Working Relationship

For probation officers (POs), achieving and maintaining an effective working relationship with a juvenile court judge—who is your employer or who can inform your executive agency employer that you're no longer welcome in the judge's court—is a high-priority goal, but not always an easy task. Some judges are strange, or authoritarian, or need you to laugh at their dumb or off-color jokes, or harangue you in open court in front of your probationer and his mother, or parade prejudices, or prescribe peculiar remedies for kids that make little sense, or come late to court while you waste your time waiting for them. But stop a minute to reflect on the similarities between the judge-PO relationship and the PO-probationer relationship. In the latter connection, you have the authority, a youth has to smile as you try to be friendly or as you try to get him to talk, and the youth has to play your game or risk the equivalent of being fired, i.e., your recommendation to the judge that he be committed to the state or experience another serious sanction.

This chapter describes certain of the problems or pitfalls in the judge-PO relationship, explores the common ground these professionals share or should share, and suggests approaches that can be taken to further effective collaboration.

The independence of the judiciary is a widely broadcast precept. Have you ever broadcast the principle of the independence of the probation function? If you do, you might need for look for a new job. But there are smart ways you can, or your department can, achieve a relative independence that can obtain judicial acceptance and respect. More on this later.

PITFALLS: THE THINGS JUDGES DO

I've watched scores of juvenile court judges in action and have talked with countless POs about judges. Here are some of the "downers" that have taken place. Recognize any?

- Judge *A* wants a two-page predisposition report (PDR); Judge *B* wants far more social history, lots of detail regarding school problems, careful analysis of the applicability of various dispositional alternatives, an explicit treatment plan, and at least seven or eight pages.

This chapter originally appeared in Community Corrections Report, *Vol. 1, No. 1, November/December 1993.*

- Judge *C* commits all drug offense cases to the state, but gives speeches to the "zoological societies" (i.e., the Elks, the Lions, the Moose) about the juvenile court's administration of individualized justice.

- Judge *D* rejects a carefully crafted PDR that recommends an array of non-residential sanctions and orders the youth into a costly private placement administered by an agency director who took the judge to lunch the day before.

- Judge *E* fires a good Chief PO/director of juvenile court services—without recourse—and provides no reason since this official serves at the judge's pleasure.

- Judge *F* makes seductive remarks to a PO.

- Judge *G* ignores the PO at the dispositional hearing and listens only to the arguments and recommendations of the attorneys.

- Judge *H* puts you on trial. You're supposed to keep this kid out of trouble. Why have you let him reoffend?

- Judge *I* again refuses to lock up Johnny even though you've warned Johnny repeatedly that he can't keep getting away with reoffending.

- Judge *J* likes to talk with you informally, before the dispositional hearing, about the next kid up, even though the lawyers in court have told you it is wrong for you to give information to the judge when they are not present.

We could fill up the rest of the judicial alphabet and more, and we could go through the alphabet again with how Probation Officer *A* forgot to obtain a victim impact statement, how Probation Officer *B* wants a psychological on every middle-class white kid, how Probation Officer *C* totally spaced out a scheduled hearing, etc.

DESPITE GROWING PRESSURES THERE ARE STRONG BONDS

Judges, like POs, have blemishes and blind spots. Most judges and POs have solid capabilities and a commitment to a better world for young people. In recent years, statutory juvenile court purpose clauses have been altered in a number of states to go beyond the best interests of the child and a least restrictive alternative directive to add protection of the public's interest and safety or a proviso for a juvenile's accountability. Judges, like POs, vary as to whether they emphasize deprivations of freedom or more expansive rehabilitation efforts, and differ as to how many bites of the apple can be tolerated. In recent years, also, POs have seen their often-symbiotic relationship with their judges dissipated as lawyers have moved, necessarily, into this court—lawyers who speak the same language as and share a common background with the judge. The great growth in the child abuse and neglect caseload during the past decade has, also necessarily, absorbed vast judicial energy and further diluted the judge-PO bond. But strong common ground exists between judges and PO:

- Judges and POs (whether attached to the judicial or the executive branch) are officers of the court, and officers of the same court.

- For both sets of officials, law is the guiding principle and they are guided by the same law. **In re Gault**, 387 U.S. 1 (1967), resolved this. Judges' procedures and findings must meet legal standards. Actions undertaken by POs must be consistent with law.

- Further statutory guidance for both judges and POs is provided by the usual juvenile court purpose clause, such as "each child shall remain in his/her home whenever possible," "removal from family only where necessary," and "if removed, to provide that quality of care, guidance, discipline and control the child otherwise should have received."

- There must be an assumption that judges taking this bench and POs who accept appointment to their positions hold an affection for youth, and jointly possess at least a tempered optimism that young people, with assistance, can become constructive, productive citizens.

- Both sets of officials live in a community, often the same community, which looks to them to intervene positively into the lives of young people.

- Both are part of a historic movement, a tradition, that advocates legislation, funding, and community activities that can assist young people as they contend with the conflicts, concerns, confusions, and changes that accompany adolescence.

- Each set of officials has a complementary role to play in the effective administration of juvenile justice. There can be no POs without judges, nor judges without POs to facilitate judicial responsibilities and the execution of judicial orders. Probation was born into and grew up with the courts.

WAYS TO EXPAND THE COMMON GROUND

Following are some ideas for expanding the judge-PO common ground:

1. *Get judges to approve policies and procedures.* Develop or revise departmental policies and procedures and give your judge(s) 30 days to review, amend, approve. Then, when a judge faults the way a PO has done something, and you can show the judge you were only following the court-approved procedure, a smile will erase the frown from the judge's face. Where judges rotate through the court annually, or frequently, run the policies and procedures through the new judge for approval. While judges will not usually review the entire contents, you've given them the opportunity and they've signed off.

2. *Try to get the approval of a standard PDR.* Ask the judiciary for a meeting to discuss PDR content, format, and use. Crank up your Chief PO to meet with a multi-judge court to review the PDR, but also to boost the department's interest in providing a similar PDR for all judges, rather than tuning a report for a particular judge.

3. *Educate judiciary as to what PO staff can and cannot do.* Probation manage-ment needs to educate the judiciary as to what it can and cannot do with its staff capabilities and use of available community resources. For example, "intensive probation can only be as intensive as presently budgeted staff will allow. To make this more intensive, judge, we'll have to stop making home visits with our PDRs, or shorten them, or hire two paraprofessionals to replace the next PO who resigns, or you'll have to go to bat with our funding source for more money for more intensive coverage." Judges see probation failures regularly. You want judges to know, ahead of time, why failures may occur.

4. *Get judges to give and allow you to give seminars.* Invite your judiciary to give you legal seminars. Invite your judiciary to invite you to put on probation sem-inars for the judiciary. Most judges want to relate to probation staff, but may not know how to do it. They're often uncomfortable with their status-caused dif-ference, but do okay in educational or problem-solving environments. Don't be too deferential. Learn the rudiments of legal language. Judges will try to talk your language, too. Jointly share concerns; jointly seek a plan for constructive action. Seek to meet again to review your progress.

5. *Get the judges to visit.* Arrange for the judiciary to visit the branch probation office, and the community service sites you use, and the residential programs you tap, and the other resources that work with probationers.

6. *Give judges feedback.* Have probation management gather the data and evalu-ate what happens with different dispositional alternatives. Judges need to receive this feedback on what happens with what they do. Help clarify what program works best with what kind of kid.

7. *Share information and data.* Develop, use, and share management information with the judiciary. Your sole judge or your chief judge needs data reports on what and how the court, the department, and the youth are doing. Aggregate useful data. Get accurate data. Go over the data with the judges. Get their informed direction.

8. *Find out what's happening elsewhere.* Judges attend national training pro-grams and conferences, and you should, too. They and you need the stimulation of promising concepts, procedures, and programs developed elsewhere. Arrange joint meetings to share what you've all learned and how this might change and impact what you do.

The judge-PO relationship, obviously, will never be perfect. Judges have to dance to many different drummers, and they have an array of interests or pressures to which they need to respond. You can help your judiciary do its job well when you do your job well, and when the judges understand the value and methodologies of the probation enterprise. Then judges can stop micromanagement and provide greater respect for your (relative) independence.

Part 3

The Handling of Offenders: Apprehension Through Disposition

FACTORS IN THE USE OF A PRETRIAL DETENTION CENTER

Law Enforcement/Juvenile Justice Agency Perspectives

In the realm of juvenile justice, law enforcement officers greatly influence the decision whether an alleged juvenile law violator shall be initially locked into a secure pretrial juvenile detention center, at least until a detention hearing takes place 24 to 72 hours following admission.

Technically, admission authority belongs not to the police officer but, rather, to a probation department intake officer, a designated detention center official, or another juvenile justice agency screener. While some offenders unequivocally require secure pretrial detention and will be immediately accepted into any American detention facility, other case situations are less clear. With these cases law enforcement personnel can prompt a decision to admit because they know how the system works and know how they can influence the system to detain a youth. This statement is not intended to be critical of law enforcement. It is to say, rather, that admissions officials often have not sufficiently clarified their standards for admission and that they sometimes do not wish to challenge a police prescription.

Detention officials want good working relationships with law enforcement. They want to avoid rejecting a request for admission that is followed shortly after by the commission of an offense by the youth in question, which in turn is followed by a law enforcement testimonial, sometimes to the media, that an admission official overruled its recommendation.

One might suggest these several sets of officials hold different perspectives on the need to detain a youth. Law enforcement more generally prefers detention; juvenile court and detention officials opt less for its use. However, another precept may apply to the latter set of officials: "There is risk associated with rejecting admission so, when in doubt, admit a juvenile on a short-term basis and allow the more powerful decision maker, the judge or the magistrate/judicial surrogate, to retain or release the youth at the follow-on detention hearing." Yet worrying too much about risk may lead to an overcrowded facility and management problems in maintaining a positive institutional environment.

Victims', Juveniles', and Families' Perspectives

There are other interested parties who may want to and sometimes do impact an admissions decision. One is the victim who may express an opinion to the arresting police officer. A victim of a more significant offense may more strongly urge detention compared with a victim of a more routine matter. But victims of lesser offenses may vocally urge detention, as well.

The juvenile's family is a very interested party. Many families want to do the disciplining themselves, to take their youngster home and do this directly and immediately. Then there are families who believe some time in detention is needed, and can be a teaching moment for their youngster.

The juvenile is rarely ambivalent. The only time a juvenile may want to be detained is for fear of his/her safety upon release or where home conditions are particularly dysfunctional, abusive, or punitive.

Detention Alternatives

Still, it is very hard to get into some detention facilities unless a very serious or repetitive offense is committed or the juvenile is already on probation or parole status. It is very easy to get into others. Different communities have different "cultures" as to the use or non-use of secure pretrial holding.

Another variable is known as detention alternatives. It used to be that all we had available was the detention center or the parents. Today we may have electronic monitoring, human trackers to monitor juveniles' whereabouts, reporting or calling in to a probation officer, house arrest requirements, curfew restrictions, short-term foster homes, non-secure shelters (Fairfax, Virginia), day reporting centers (Sacramento), or evening reporting centers (Chicago). Some communities offer more alternatives than others.

The Problem of Minority Overrepresentation

Detention center usage has a direct connection to minority overrepresentation as juveniles wend their way through the juvenile justice system. It has been found that when white youths and African-American youths with no prior admissions to public facilities were charged with the same offenses, African-American youths were six times more likely to be held in secure detention than white youths. Latino youths were three times more likely than white youths to be held in secure detention.[1]

Multnomah County (Portland), Oregon, has reported sharp reductions in detention of minority as well as majority children with no subsequent increase in crime. Its juvenile justice system took several actions, one that few communities have undertaken. It diversified its service delivery system by deliberately contracting with organizations located in communities of color and managed by people of color. Contracts centered on shelter care, foster homes, home detention, and a day reporting center. These facilities were established both as alternatives to detention and to divert youth from being returned to custody for violating terms of their release.[2]

And, yes, there is the geographic factor. Busy police officers are more likely to bring a juvenile to detention when the arrest location is relatively near the detention center than when the center is more distant. This impacts minority youngsters in some communities, where their neighborhoods and the detention center are both located in the same general vicinity. Conversely, suburban youths are less likely to be driven to a center 20 miles distant from an offense location.

PURPOSES SERVED BY DETENTION CENTERS

The term detention center is sometimes misapplied by the media or misunderstood by the public as referring to a secure state institution that receives juveniles at the back end of the juvenile justice system, following a court commitment. Rather, a detention center is a secure *pre-institutional* facility whose primary purposes are to hold a youth until release is approved (1) at a detention hearing held within a few days, or (2) if not released then, until a judicial officer orders release following an arraignment, an adjudicatory hearing, or a dispositional hearing. Release may be deferred following a disposition that involves placement in a private or public residential facility until a space becomes available to allow the juvenile to enter the placement. Such a placement constitutes a custodial transfer rather than a release.

In some states a detention facility serves an additional purpose when authorized by statute. Then it may be used as a sentence prerogative, typically to confine a repeat offender, for example up to 45 days. Likely, these reoffenders have been held in the detention facility prior to the disposition, and the sanction is an "add on," one that reinforces the court's authority to teach a youth that freedom can be maintained only if one abides by the law and does not commit a further offense. Florida judges are authorized to use another vehicle, a contempt of court finding, as a basis for directing a repeat violator to do detention time.

LEGAL PARAMETERS OF DETENTION

Statutory Detention Admission Provisions

Who may be detained is founded on state statutory admissions criteria. The constellation of factors described above surrounds and influences this decision, but the language that most heavily supports the use of detention is the provision, common to many states with only slight wording variation, that there is "reasonable necessity for [detention for] the protection of the person or property of another,"[3] or that if the youth is not held, "he or she will commit injury to the person or property of others."[4]

Other provisions supporting detention may be spelled out, e.g., when "the juvenile will run away or be taken away so as to be unavailable for proceedings of the court,"[5] or when detention is of "immediate and urgent necessity for the protection of the minor."[6]

Danger to the person or property of others is an enormously broad provision that is to be based on a prediction of renewed law violations. Use of a risk assessment instrument (RAI) provides a reasonably objective measure of the reoffense potential, but where this instrument is not in use, the decision to detain reflects less a prediction and more a concern about the severity of the present offense. If the present offense is not severe, a juvenile may still be held if there is staff perception of weakness in a parent's ability to control the youth if released. And this perception may be based on valid or sometimes erroneous or even prejudicial factors. A working parent in a single parent family may be viewed as less able to control a youth if released than parents in an intact family. Minority parents may be seen as less able to control their juveniles than majority parents. (Few officials will admit to this latter observation.)

Supreme Court Decision on Detention

The U.S. Supreme Court, in **Schall v. Martin**, 104 S. Ct. 2403 (1984), upheld the constitutionality of the New York detention admission law and its accompanying procedures. It rejected the premises that secure pretrial detention is a form of punishment, that punishment is to follow and not precede adjudication, and that the prediction that detention is necessary because release may result in injury to others is based on a most inexact estimate of probabilities. Instead the Court held the possibility that detention may deter future crimes serves a legitimate state objective, is protective and regulatory rather than punitive, and does not violate fundamental fairness requirements. It determined that erroneous detention admissions could be corrected through available review mechanisms. Thus, the Court accepted what has been referred to as preventive detention.

No General Right to Bail

Adults, as a rule, except for a limitation concerning capital offenses, have a constitutional right to bail pending trial and disposition. Whether juveniles have a constitutional right to bail has never been determined by the U.S. Supreme Court. Laws in some states do permit the posting of bail by or on behalf of a minor but most states do not make this provision. They view the juvenile justice system as different in purpose and practice and consider that juvenile code procedures, when applied in a manner consistent with due process, are an adequate substitute for bail.

Georgia and Louisiana are among the states that provide for bail for juveniles. The actual posting of monetary or property bail is not utilized widely in those states, however. Bail, or bond, can be accepted on personal recognizance, based on a promise to appear at future court proceedings. A judge may approve such a bond arrangement but attach a range of behavioral conditions pending next hearings.

More universally, court-directed restraints on apprehended juveniles who are not held in detention custody prior to adjudication are illustrative of the tightened controls on juvenile behaviors that have taken place in juvenile justice in more recent years. Judicial approval of electronic monitoring during this interim is another widespread example of control features applied before a juvenile has been found to have committed an offense.

RISK AND HEALTH ASSESSMENTS

Risk Assessment Instruments

Numerous juvenile justice systems now utilize RAIs to help screening staff make more objective and consistent determinations of (1) who must be admitted, (2) who may be released but with conditions and controls, and (3) who may be released to parents with only a promise to appear at the next court hearing. An RAI lists factors that can be readily measured. The factors are given points. Some factors merit more or fewer points. Common factors are seriousness of present offense, prior adjudications, current legal status (e.g., currently on probation or other cases are pending), and prior failures when on release status rather than having been held in detention.

RAIs differ in different court systems as the point scores used reflect local experience, concerns about various offenses or juvenile characteristics, and interest in maintaining a particular detention population. Multnomah County (Portland), Oregon, uses a maximum 20-point score for its determinations. Attempted murder or a Class A felony involving violence or use or threatened use of a weapon counts 12 points while a Class C felony involving violence or use or threatened use of a weapon counts 6 points. Prior sustained offenses count from 1 to 3 points. Aggravating factors such as no verifiable local community ties can add up to 3 points while mitigating factors such as a first law violation reduces the count by 1 to 2 points. A total score of 12 or more is presumptive detention; 7-11, a conditional release; and 0-6, an unconditional release. There is provision for an "override," i.e., the screener can find certain factors that should overturn the presumptive measure. A supervising official needs to agree to such an override recommendation. Other communities have similar scoring instruments that may use a different maximum total such as a 10- or 15 - point score.[7]

A Multnomah County reevaluation of its RAI use concluded it resulted unnecessarily in the confinement of minority youth and required amendment. Instead of a mitigating factor such as "good family structure," which could be biased for an intact family and biased against minority youth, it now asks whether there is an adult willing to be responsible for assuring the youth's supervision and appearance in court. It dropped its measure of "gang affiliation" as something that is biased against where a youth lives. Instead of just using "regular school attendance or employed" as a mitigating factor, this concept was expanded to include engaged in "productive activity."[8]

Mental Health Assessment

Recent research indicates that a substantial number of juveniles taken into juvenile justice custody have significant mental health concerns that need immediate attention.[9] A relatively simple measure to administer, the Massachusetts Youth Screening Instrument (MAYSI)[10] is now being used at a growing number of detention sites at the admissions stage. Some case situations call out for immediate secure custody and comprehensive psychological evaluation, e.g., the case of one 13-year-old boy apprehended with five small homemade bombs and bomb-making materials, and who talked of blowing up his junior high school.

Ascertaining mental health service need and the speedy delivery of this service are two different concepts. It is very well known that mental health service provision to almost all populations in need is in very short supply. It is also very well known that as a consequence of this shortage, both the juvenile and adult criminal justice systems receive and must work with large populations that would be better served in the underfunded mental health agencies and institutions.[11]

Physical Health Assessment

At least superficial physical examinations are conducted reasonably quickly in most detention facilities. Detention center personnel have training in making an initial oral inquiry and surface viewing of a referred juvenile. Nursing staff are available to further this inquiry in larger centers, and it is common practice for a center to have a working relationship with a hospital where a juvenile can be taken immediately, either by law enforcement or detention center officials.

Drug/Alcohol Screening

Drug/alcohol screening is, likely, a universal practice at detention centers. As with juvenile offenders manifesting severe and obvious mental or physical health problems, juveniles showing obvious drug/alcohol symptoms are best initially taken by law enforcement to hospital care before being transferred to detention center intake.

WHY THE DETENTION DECISION IS SO IMPORTANT

More than a few detention centers are seriously overcrowded, and overcrowding presents dangers to residents and to staff. Very careful management of admissions, expediting court case processing, and stratagems to move juveniles out of detention more quickly can control populations and curb new construction or expansion need. The old adage is too often true: If you build or enlarge a detention facility you will fill up the beds. I and many others consider it better policy to divert the costs of the perceived need to expand a facility to instead expand reliable detention alternatives and intervention services for juveniles and families.

Nonetheless, a recent boom in detention center construction has been underway, fueled in part by federal dollars that were authorized during the 1994 peak year of violent juvenile crime and continue to be appropriated and used. Some of this construction or expansion is necessary, but this should not take place without careful planning and a comprehensive development of detention alternatives so that fewer beds are necessary and certain construction money can, instead, be used with detention and intervention alternatives.

It is important to note that those who are admitted into detention have a higher probability of becoming a formal case. Conversely, those juveniles not admitted into detention have a higher probability of informal handling. This is the way it should be if the right decisions are made as to who should or should not be admitted. But the right decisions are not always made.

Juvenile codes typically state that a petition shall be filed within 24 to 48 hours of entry into a detention facility.[12] The petition is the gateway for formal processing into a judge's courtroom. A juvenile who is still held in detention at the time of judicial disposition is more likely to receive a harsher sanction than another juvenile, of like record and offense, who has not been detained or was released from detention at an early detention hearing.

The detention admission decision can be mechanized and lose individuation. It can easily fail to consider the feelings of a juvenile who is far more comfortable emotionally on return to his/her family than on remaining in a lock-up behind closed, secure doors, even if released at a detention hearing 24 to 72 hours later. A detention center can become a place of business for the staff. It is a strange and impersonal setting for a first offending youth.

LAW ENFORCEMENT OFFICERS CHOOSE WHETHER TO REQUEST DETENTION

Law enforcement agencies typically have a policy and procedures manual that provides guidelines as to when an officer should request detention. Still, as throughout juvenile justice, a large amount of discretion is vested in officials to make one decision or another. For example, the author has observed police officers bring to the detention intake office juveniles whose offenses are only small dollar amount shoplifts. Police officers in other communities would seek instead to return these youth to their families and either close out the matter with a warning or forward a written complaint to the court intake officer or prosecutor without seeking detention entry.

Police department record keeping can provide a database that influences police officer decisions. Record checks are made to ascertain if a youth has a prior record of one or more arrests. A previous arrest, even for a non-serious matter, even if no formal action had been taken earlier, more likely results in taking the youth to detention intake.

JUVENILE COURT INTAKE

As noted earlier, different states authorize different personnel to make the decision whether or not to file a charge, i.e., probation or court intake staff, prosecutors, or some combination of these officials.

Prosecutors, in particular, may dismiss a charge or charges for failing to reach a level of case provability. A decision to not file a provable charge also may result in a complete dismissal of the charge, sometimes with a warning that any next offense will be brought before a judge. Alternatively, a provable charge can be held in abeyance while certain conditions are to be met such as no further law violations, payment of restitution or performance of community service hours, improved school attendance and achievement, or progress in acceptance of parental requirements and curfew hours. There may be an informal probation status of three to six months with or without much contact with a probation officer or diversion to an external community agency to obtain services such as family counseling or a mentor. In some communities the charge may be transferred to a neighborhood accountability board or peer court for an accountability sanction. The juvenile justice system should obtain a written waiver of a speedy trial processing deadline when formal action is deferred.

Some juveniles fail to adhere to one or more conditions. Good practice suggests an individualized review of particular conditions that are violated and the reasons for violation. Deliberate violations should result in a formal petition of the offense, though it needs to be reported that some inexcusable violations fall through the cracks and these juveniles are not held accountable.

SOURCES OF REFERRALS

Law enforcement agencies refer 85% of delinquency cases. Such others as schools, parents, victims, or probation officers make referrals. Approximately one out of four juveniles who are arrested are dismissed by police officers without referral to a juvenile court.[13]

Some juvenile courts serve judicial districts that have just one or two law enforcement agencies. Other districts may be served by as many as 8-12 agencies, though normally it is the police agency of the largest city in the district and the county sheriff's office that are the main referral sources.

Numerous law enforcement agencies are slow in moving on to court the referral of youths for whom detention is not sought, and courts are often slow in processing these youths. Two to five months may elapse between these offenses, the court's disposition, and the intervention directed by a judge.

Preferably, 100% of law violation referrals should be made by law enforcement. Intake units in some courts are wrongly given the responsibility to conduct police-like investigations of law violation complaints that have come directly to them from schools, businesses, and other sources. Police investigations better assure a sound legal basis for moving a case forward. The police are better trained in evaluating criminal evidence than are intake officers.

A small but growing number of police agencies now handle lesser delinquency matters, even lesser felony cases, within the agency using restorative justice practices such as education as to the impact of crime and restitution. The Woodbury, Minnesota, Public Safety Department reports, e.g., that its diversion approach, initiated with shoplifting offenses only, now handles 50% of juvenile cases. The department quickly assembles the offender and family members, the victim and support representatives, other support and community people, and the agency's community justice officer to examine incidents and their impacts more deeply. Repairing the harm done is a key objective, and restitution is reported to be paid at a very high rate. Conference agreements may include drug rehabilitation, family counseling, educational or job assistance, and cognitive restructuring classes.[14]

ALTERNATIVES TO COURT

I, along with many others, takes the position that community agencies rather than the court should handle and manage minor offense matters, that intake or prosecution officials should also shortstop the penetration of next level up violations, and that considerable non-court interventions should be arranged or applied by probation units, often in concert with community agencies.

Avoiding a Juvenile Record

An adage in juvenile justice is that we should seek to avoid a record for a juvenile. Having a record has meant being the subject of a formal proceeding brought before a judge and having been subjected to a judicial disposition that could include probation, restitution or community service, residential or state institutional placement, or other sanctions. The record was seen as handicapping someone on applying for a job, college, the military, financial loans, and other applications. Many youth may see this as an affront to their self-esteem or feeling of worth.

The record concern influences the tradition to handle cases informally and then have the case dismissed without having a "record." One can then state honestly that there is no record. A similarity occurs with juvenile code provisions that refer to "take into custody" rather than an "arrest" by a police officer. A taken into custody juvenile can then forthrightly answer he or she has had no arrests.

Another rationale for diversion or informal handling is that numerous juveniles never repeat an offense but have found this alternative handling educational and salutary, or otherwise a good influence for future conformity.

Informal Strategies

There are informal strategies other than the basic stock in trade of counseling services for the juvenile and family that probation officers or external services, public or private, provide. I strongly support the provision of monetary restitution to victims as a diversion strategy. This is not done often enough. Some juvenile system processing officials prefer not to deal with restitution at an informal handling level or on noting that a poor juvenile and family cannot make a single speedy payment of the total amount of the damage. Instead they proceed to file a formal petition. While a small percentage of juveniles may cause property damage in the thousands of dollars and formal processing should take place because of the severity of the damage caused, most victim loss or damage is in amounts that juveniles or their families can arrange to repay, or could repay if a court or community program provided opportunities to earn this amount and pay it back to a victim. Of course, a serious or repetitive offender whose offense causes victim loss or damage should be proceeded upon formally.

Community service may be and should be used as a diversion from court stratagem. Again, some officials do not use this as an option at this processing stage.

Ensuring Equal Protection of the Law

I have long had a favorite case on the issue of equal protection: Laurence and two other juveniles, who were brothers, broke into a home, took $12, and ransacked the house, causing $1,200 in damage. The father of the brothers pledged to pay for two-thirds of the damage; Laurence's mother made no firm promise to pay her son's share. There was no distinction in the prior records of the three youths, but only Laurence was formally petitioned. The intake supervisor acknowledged that the mother's refusal or inability to pay restitution played an important part in the decision to file. The Maryland Court of Appeals overturned the single petition as discriminatory. **In re Laurence T.**, 403 A. 2d 1256 (Md. 1979). The court held that while officials may proceed against one law-breaker and not another for the same unlawful act, the equal protection clause of the Constitution prohibits selective enforcement based on an arbitrary classification. A parent's inability or unwillingness to promise restitution is not a justifiable standard and is distinct from a youth's need for state rehabilitative intervention.

I once asked a Miami juvenile prosecutor about equal handling of equals as cases came across his desk for filing decisions. He recalled that once he had approved diversion of a defendant, but had decided to file the case of a co-defendant that had been delayed and had come to his attention a week later. He had not connected the two decisions. The prosecutor, when the attorney for the second youth brought the divergent decisions on the two boys, both lacking any prior record, to his attention, reversed the second decision.

Few equal protection matters are brought to appellate court scrutiny. The best way to apply this principle is to prepare and promulgate written guidelines that direct file or no-file decisions based on present offense, prior offense record, and age, as modified by a may-file provision grounded on certain stated case characteristics such as the time that has elapsed since a prior offense, or family matters that can be assisted by a community agency and for which there is strong family motivation to counsel.

Diversion to Community Hearing Panels

A New Jersey statute,[15] in 1948, authorized the invention of juvenile conference committees to hear family, neighborhood, and school concerns regarding children. Professionals were prominent panelists in this effort to help children in their adjustment. Over time, juvenile and family courts in that state diverted lesser juvenile offenders for panel assistance. King County (Seattle), Washington, initiated community accountability boards in suburban Renton in 1959 as an in lieu of court procedure.[16] Twenty-five such citizen boards are now active in the county and consider an estimated 3,000 lesser offenders annually.

Growth in the development of citizen hearing boards, very limited for years, accomplished a quantum leap in the mid 1990s, as Balanced and Restorative Justice concepts, including community participation in juvenile justice, became better understood. Teen courts, another form of citizen hearing panel and a diversion practice that will be discussed later, developed from a different foundation and have achieved more widespread replication, in part due to a substantial allocation of federal funds for this purpose.

Community boards take different names but most include accountability or reparations within their title. Often they comprise a panel of four to five adult citizens, but a community may have several panels of trained and screened citizen volunteers, each panel hearing cases on a weekly basis. Panels convene in different locations. The seven panels in San Bernardino County, California, e.g., meet at a family restaurant, a fire station, two police stations, and two sheriff's sub-offices. Elsewhere, panels may meet at a church, a community center, a school, or another public building.

The probation department is the most common program coordinator and case referral source. A prosecutor's office may fulfill both functions, but this is less common. Police and schools may refer cases, as well. It is good practice for a probation officer or another agency staff member to interview juveniles and present a short-form social history for the panel, and for staff to follow up with these youth to help them fulfill the behavioral contract agreed to with the panel. Juveniles, characteristically, are first- or second-time lesser offenders.

A review of several juveniles brought before the Santa Clara County, California, board that is described in Chapter 20 found such offenses as shoplifting (a 15-year-old girl suspended from school for not attending and with 12 runaways from home in the last six months); a threat to a teacher in the form of a picture drawn of a devil with the caption, "you're going to die" (a 13-year-old boy, a special education student living with a sole parent father who had a long unemployment history); and shoplifting (a 15-year-old boy failing most school subjects who, when not in school, was "primary caretaker" of a younger brother confined to a wheel chair).

Panel meetings are informal and cordial. Admission to the offense is a prerequisite for a panel case. Panel members often ask the youth how the offense was committed, what damage resulted, how reparations might be made, and how offense repetition might be avoided. I favor a practice of victim participation at the hearing, but this appears to be arranged irregularly.

Panels seek a juvenile's agreement to the sanctions and requirements they are considering. These may include community service, restitution, improving school attendance and achievement, obtaining a drug or alcohol evaluation, entering or continuing a mentoring or tutoring program, attending a gang awareness class or a life skills class, or preparing an apology letter to a victim. Many panels direct a youth to report back to them at a later date as to progress made in meeting required conditions.

Neighborhood or community accountability boards move the justice system response closer to the life experienced by the juvenile and allow board members, as fellow community dwellers, to take a direct interest in neighborhood youth. They can add important contributions to a diversion experience that might otherwise be without any intervention.

Diversion to Peer Courts

Another diversion strategy is known variously as peer court, teen court, or youth court. It involves youths determining sanctions for youthful defendants, the proceedings assisted by and supervised by adults. A judge, attorney, or adult staff person or volunteer may oversee the hearings, which require a prior admission to the offense that is charged. Juvenile volunteers, usually ages 15 through 17, may fulfill such roles as judge, prosecutor, defense attorney, juror, bailiff, or clerk. Juvenile prosecutors and defense attorneys present arguments to the teen jury to influence its sanctioning decisions. The juvenile offender may testify.

The number of teen courts nationwide is reported to have grown from 50 programs in 1991 to between 400 and 500 programs in 1998. A national survey found that these courts handled approximately 65,000 cases in 1998, or 163 cases per court.[17] Very likely, peer courts hear significantly more cases than community accountability boards at this time. Their proceedings are more formal than those of the community accountability boards. They combine the application of system-approved alternative sanctions for a juvenile offense with an educational experience for teens who serve in the various peer court roles.

Sanctions often consist of having the youth perform community service hours and then return at a later date to serve as a juror in the peer court. This subsequent service as a juror has been a popular feature of these courts. Other sanctions may be apologies to victims, written essays on an assigned subject related to the offense, participation in drug/alcohol, anger management, or conflict resolution classes, improved driver-training workshops, and restitution. Here, too, first-time offenses, such as petty theft, vandalism, simple assault, disorderly conduct, and alcohol or marijuana possession, are the basic workload.

There is substantial value in both the community accountability board and peer court approaches. If choosing, I would prefer the former as it engages adults who can facilitate and arrange resources for juvenile defendants, maintain a mentoring contact with them, and further a community's "ownership" of its youth. It would be advantageous if a community panel also included youthful members.

DIVERSION DATA

National statistical estimates indicate that 57% of delinquency referrals to intake or prosecutor are formally petitioned, and 43% are handled informally or dismissed at the intake stage. Those not petitioned are modest offenses committed by younger children, first-time non-serious matters, or occasionally a second offense that is not especially serious. One frequent decisional criterion used is whether the offense is a misdemeanor or a felony. In general, but with exceptions, misdemeanors are handled informally and felonies handled formally.

The author has studied intake decision-making in numerous juvenile courts and has found varying percentages of formal case decision-making. One court was found to formally petition 95% of referrals but then schedule a hearing before a judicial officer where 69% of those reviewed were disposed with just 29% of all referrals formally petitioned. That court preferred that a judicial officer make the fundamental intake decision, believing an appearance before this official was salutary.

Low filing ratios tend to occur in less populous jurisdictions, as offenses are less often serious, informal handling has been traditionally used, and this judiciary prefers to tend to other types of case filings due at least in part to the limited number of judges in rural America. A chief probation officer in an urban Montana juvenile court suggested to me in 2002 that the filing ratio in this court was no more than 20% of referrals. The court had five judges, but none specialized in juvenile court work and the clerk assigned each judge every fifth formal petition.

Nationally aggregated data show that 58% of person offenses were formally petitioned, as were 53% of property offenses, 63% of drug offenses, and 61% of public order offenses.[18] Analysis would question why a person offense does not have the highest percentage of case filings.

PREPARATION OF A CASE

There is now greater awareness of the value of expeditious handling of juvenile offenses. There remain myriad courts, however, where obtaining justice, accountability, and intervention come all too slowly. Juveniles held in detention must be processed more speedily than those not detained. I would prefer there be but one track, a speedy track, but for now detained juveniles should be the priority.

The juvenile justice system is a complex entity. It is not just the court, though the court is its focal point. There are the different actors and many different tasks to be performed to bring a youth to court and arrange post-court or even pre-court intervention.

To focus just on the paper work and notification approaches needed with a detained juvenile case, there is need for:

- Police documentation of the offense and delivery of this report;

- Risk assessment instrument documentation or other written documentation of reasons for detaining a youth along with detention center entry of the youth into its population database;

- Providing written notice to the family and, ideally, the victim, to attend a detention hearing;

- Getting the case onto the docket of the judicial officer within 24-72 hours;

- Obtaining a formal court petition prepared by an intake officer or prosecutor;

- Notification to a public defender and prosecutor of this hearing;

- Recording the result of this hearing;

- Placing the juvenile on a forthcoming arraignment docket; assembling the actors for this hearing and recording its outcome;

- Setting a trial date when the charge is contested, with the accompanying need to have subpoenas prepared and served on the victim and witnesses;

- Making an official record of the adjudicatory hearing and entering its outcome into official court records;

- Docketing this case on the judicial officer's calendar for a disposition, notifying probation to prepare a predisposition report; and making a record of this hearing;

- Providing notice to a probation officer to intervene with this youth if placed on probation and have the judge sign the probation conditions and enter any specialized conditions that appear necessary; and

- Setting a next court action date if, for example, restitution has yet to be determined.

And then there are probation department records of contacts with the juvenile and court clerk records of restitution paid and disbursed and the need to go over most of this process again if the juvenile reoffends. There is, also, the need to arrange for court interpreters, skilled in one of the many different languages that come to court.

An unsung actor in certain of this process, a court clerk, is a critical performer in any juvenile court, but receives no attention in books or articles that deal with juvenile justice. Herewith I announce my high regard for the vital importance, competencies, and contributions of this office.

CASE-FLOW MANAGEMENT

Need to Monitor Case Flow

Some juvenile courts employ court administrators and case managers whose duties include obtaining an efficient flow of cases into the court. But they have other responsibilities and too little monitoring is done in a systematic way that enables a court to clearly ascertain how long it takes to move a case between steps 1, 2, 3, 4, and more.

A practical assignment is to go into court record files and randomly select, for example, 150-200 cases of juveniles who were handled formally through court disposition. Separate tabulations can be made for those detained until adjudication and those who were not so detained. Then tabulate, for example for those not detained, the amount of time that has elapsed for each case from receipt of police documentation to petition filing, from petition filing to first court hearing and then the times to adjudication and disposition. The time lapse from offense to court receipt of police documentation should be recorded, as well. Related case markings should be made for detained juveniles.

Medians and means should be calculated. The time-lapse data should then be assessed for any processing delays so the court can initiate actions to improve case movement.

I recorded in one juvenile court study,

> Comments were made that a police citation might arrive at the probation department intake door two-three months post-offense. There were reports of prosecutor delay in preparing petitions regarding non-detained offenders. One interviewee suggested some continuances are granted by the court following an attorney's request even though the real cause of the request is attorney negligence in case preparation. Further, consultant was informed that victim offender mediations are conducted six-to-eight weeks from request, that referrals often are not timely made, and that a mediation session sometimes takes place as late as one year after a judge's disposition of a case.[19]

Juvenile justice system officials spend considerable time in meetings with each other, with community agencies, with citizen groups, with the media, and others. These officials should take on another meeting, to be held regularly, to use case-flow data to root out where processing delays take place and to have these agencies and the court curb delay so as to better maximize impacts on offenders and benefits to victims and the community.

The Court as Manager of the Court's Environment

When a judge calls a meeting, officials of the system show up. The judge is an enormously powerful figure and influence. A judge who asks a prosecutor to speed up case handling in the interest of justice will obtain a response. The response may be only an excuse that the agency is short handed, but a response will be given. Or the judge might ask this prosecutor to carefully examine the office's case handling procedures and inform the judge in a few weeks of any shortcomings and how these might be improved. An activist judge may need to meet with the chief prosecutor to stimulate the assignment of an additional prosecutor to juvenile court.

A prosecutor may need to slow down the prosecution of a contested hearing that requires police laboratory analysis of a drug found on a juvenile defendant, or a DNA, bullet match-up, or other investigation. The backlog at the state bureau of investigation or local police laboratory is the likely culprit here, which has in several jurisdictions resulted in a judicial mandate that unless the evidence is present by a particular date it will have to be excluded.

When a judge is concerned that too long a time transpires between adjudication and disposition, the jurist should sit down with probation officials and review the format and content of the predisposition report—what must be, might be, and need not be included? The judge explores a reduced preparation time while also reviewing the staffing complement and role assignments. The judge may need to seek funding for another probation officer.

The point is that the court should not only manage how well it processes cases but also ensure that collaborative agencies participate with the same objective of efficient case handling.

Juvenile court judge bench time has had to be increased, in recent years, with cases of child dependency/abuse/neglect. Law and policy, very properly and wisely, have promoted earlier permanent plans for these children and an increased number of judicial review hearings on the status of these children. Delinquency case scheduling must compete for judicial time with these cases. Glitches in case processing need to be removed with both sets of case types, and the court and its management staff are in the best position to proactively obtain the collaboration that is so necessary.

It should not happen, as happened, e.g., in a Colorado juvenile court in 2002, that parties and their attorney and witnesses arrived for a dependency case hearing at 8 a.m. and were told, finally, at 1 p.m. that the court would have to postpone the hearing to another date. For five hours the privately employed lawyer's meter was ticking. Excessive delay is not, of course, limited to this court.

JUVENILE COURT DISPOSITIONS

Nationally, probation is the most severe sanction used in 54% of dispositions. Residential placement is used in 28% of dispositions. The residential placement category includes state training schools, private placement and drug treatment facilities, ranches, camps, and group homes. Further, white juveniles are less likely to be ordered into some form of residential placement, particularly a state training school, than minority juveniles.[20]

Five Juvenile Court Dispositional Models

Several simplified court dispositional structures might be etched. One can sketch out a strong judge model, a strong prosecutor model, a strong probation department model, or hybrid models:

1. In the *strong judge model*, the judge sets the tone of how juveniles should be handled. This may be hard-line, medium-line, or soft-line, but it is the judge's line and the system responds to this direction. Probation department predisposition reports and prosecutor advocacy will respond to and cater to the judicial stance.

2. A *strong prosecutor model* will insist that more offenders be handled formally and that adjudicated juveniles serve more residential time. In former years this prosecutor would have called for more hearings to transfer more juveniles to a criminal court, but today in most states waiver statutes now allow for direct filing of more serious offenders and obviate any juvenile court process.

3. A *strong probation department model* dominates court processes and decision-making with its influence and recommendations. Judges and prosecutors respond and accept these practices and directions. Defense attorneys are very much in tune with a department that emphasizes community correctional alternatives.

4. One can sketch, as well, a *combined strong judge-strong probation department model* where these two entities are in fundamental agreement and the prosecutor and defense counsel accede to this arrangement or are largely absent from court proceedings.

5. Another hybrid model places the power in a *combination of prosecutor and defense counsel joint decision-making* with the court offered the plea and sen-

tence bargain the attorneys derive. Probation department perspectives may or may not be a part of the bargain tendered.

Expanded Add-Ons to the Probation Experience

Historically, juvenile court dispositions have consisted of a probation directive (sometimes enhanced by local public or private counseling or assisting agencies) or, otherwise, placement in a private non-profit residential program or sometimes state institutionalization. Risk and needs instruments had not been invented. The nature of probation officer intervention was to see a new probationer several times within a month or so and then let the case drift until a parent complained of problems or a reoffense occurred.

Judges today can direct a probation disposition that includes intensive supervision. Overall caseloads, though, may be excessive, which may result in too many cases receiving a lower level of supervision or no supervision in order to maintain a small intensive supervision caseload. Today's probation officers must oversee far more behavioral contracts, control elements or conditions, and monitor random or periodic urinalysis checks for drugs.

In different jurisdictions there may be electronic monitoring, human trackers to check whether a juvenile is really at school or home, day treatment, gang intervention, cognitive retraining programs, community service, restitution earning programs, mentoring, tutoring, alternative schools, and more.

Other Dispositional Influences

Private for-profit corporations have invaded juvenile justice in recent years, eager to do good along with doing well for their investors. They have made their presence felt in non-residential programming but more often with residential care. Judicial dispositions can be influenced by the seductions of the private enterprise engineers. I acknowledge that certain of these programs appear beneficial, but decry that profit making has entered the public interest field of juvenile justice. Large-scale private non-profit program services are increasingly evident, as well, particularly in residential treatment offerings.

Judicial dispositions are influenced, also, by whose dollars are being spent. When county government funds much of a juvenile court operation there is an unstated preference to place juveniles in state-operated or state-subsidized facilities. Accordingly, some states seek to curb the expensive costs of state institutionalization by subsidizing, in some form, community-based dispositions.

THE CHAPTERS THAT FOLLOW

Chapters 17, 18, and 19 focus on detention, a processing stage that I see as critical in shaping what happens to juveniles in this court. Clearly, I prefer to limit detention to those who reveal a strong likelihood of injuring public safety if released and those who have previously demonstrated or clearly indicate an inability to appear at required court hearings.

A significant number of detained juveniles are released at 24-72 hour detention hearings, many of them not needing to have been admitted to detention in the first place. Admitting officials often are conservative and do not appreciate the trauma many youth experience from being away from home for several nights. Alternatives to detention are now well accepted across juvenile courts though many lag in developing an expansive array that could seriously curb detention numbers. Chapter 19 reports on a populous jurisdiction, Sacramento, which has made numerous efforts to curb detention usage. One stratagem is to accelerate judicial case decisions with detained juveniles, a direction that is pertinent to Chapter 21, on improving court case flow.

Chapter 20 describes one community's initiatives in establishing neighborhood accountability boards as a diversion stratagem. In Chapter 21 I make suggestions, macro and micro, for enhancing juvenile case flow. In Chapter 22 I analyze practices and issues related to the dispositional hearing, its process and its decision making.

Endnotes

[1] Jones, M. & Poe-Yamagata, E. (2000). *And justice for some.* Washington, DC: Building Blocks for Youth.

[2] Schiraldi, V. & Ziedenberg, J. (2002). *Reducing disproportionate minority confinement: The Multnomah County, Oregon, success story.* Washington, DC: Justice Policy Institute.

[3] Cal. W & I Code § 628 (a)(4).

[4] Wis. Stat. §938.205 (1)(a).

[5] Wis. Stat. §938.205 (1)(c),

[6] Cal. W & I Code §628 (a)(4).

[7] Orlando, F. (2000). *Controlling the front gates: Effective admissions policies and practices. Volume 3, Pathways to juvenile detention reform.* Baltimore, MD: Annie E. Casey Foundation.

[8] Schiraldi & Ziedenberg, supra note 2.

[9] Teplin, L., Abram, K. & McClelland, G. (1998, July). Psychiatric disorders among juvenile detainees. Paper presented at Annual Conference on Criminal Justice Research and Evaluation, Office of Juvenile Justice and Delinquency Prevention, Washington, DC.

[10] Grisso, T. & Barnum, R. (2000). *Massachusetts Youth Screening Instrument—Second Versioin: User's manual and technical report.* Worcester, MA: University of Massachusetts Medical School.

[11] See Redding, R. E. (2001, Jan-Feb). Barriers to meeting the mental health needs of offenders in the juvenile justice system. *Juvenile Correctional Mental Health Report 1(2),* 17-18, 26-30.

[12] Wis. Stat. §938.21; Cal. W & I Code §626.5.

[13] Snyder, H. N. & Sickmund, M. (1999). *Juvenile offenders and victims: 1999 national report.* Washington, DC: Office of Juvenile Justice and Delinquency Prevention, p. 97.

[14] Hines, D. (2002 Winter). Shoplifting, criminal justice and community restorative approaches. *Beyond Just Us, 6,* 6–7.

[15] N.J. Stat. Ann. 2A: 4A.75 and R. 5:25.

[16] King County Superior Court, Partnership for Youth Justice (2002). Seattle, WA.

[17] Butts, J. et al (1999), *Teen courts in the United States: A profile of current programs.* Office of Juvenile Justice and Delinquency Prevention Fact Sheet #119. Also see Fisher, M. (2002). *Youth courts: Young people delivering justice.* Chicago: American Bar Association.

[18] Puzzanchera, C. et al. (2000). *Juvenile court statistics 1997.* Washington DC: Office of Juvenile Justice and Delinquency Prevention, pp. 10-11.

[19] Rubin, H.T. (2000). Evaluation of juvenile court organization and case processing. Boulder, CO: Unpublished manuscript.

[20] Snyder & Sickmund, supra note 13, p.159.

Chapter 17

Dejailing and Rejailing Juveniles

Believe it or not, we really were making vast progress in reducing the number of juvenile court youths held in adult jails, and real advances in curbing lengthy holding of juveniles in police- and sheriff-station lockups. Generally, these young people were being detained just because that is how it had always been done. Most of them were not serious offenders; they were run-of-the-mill delinquency suspects, status offenders, or abandoned, abused, or neglected children.

Dejailing constituted a bright spot in the juvenile justice picture, until 1989. Since then, however, the state-by-state legislative and judicial trend has centered on transferring youths from juvenile court to criminal court. This has resulted in substantially increased pretrial jailing of juveniles. In addition, where we used to keep youths like these in pretrial juvenile facilities, they are now being relabeled as adults and are held in jails until the slower criminal court process has been concluded. While these youths are of juvenile court age, they are no longer juvenile court youths.

The dejailing achievements we saw over the past two decades owe much to the U.S. Juvenile Justice and Delinquency Prevention Act (JJDPA) of 1974, which established the Office of Juvenile Justice and Delinquency Prevention (OJJDP). The OJJDP handed out some (not much) money to the states if juveniles who were held in adult jails were sight-and-sound separated from adult prisoners. Juvenile advocates were hopeful.

The current trend toward rejailing is based on a retributive justice model that has its roots in the victim rights movement ("a victim of a violent crime suffers as much whether the offender was a juvenile or an adult"). The 1994 election campaigns did not contain any debate about how to prevent serious juvenile crime; instead, candidates vied with rejailing proposals to strike out juveniles with one, two, or three strikes.

DEJAILING JUVENILES

In 1974, the number of jailed juveniles was estimated at about 500,000 per year.[1] Ugly things were happening to youth in jails. They committed suicide five times more often than juveniles in the general population, and almost eight times more often than juveniles in juvenile detention centers (JDCs).[2] Many were victimized, sexually or physically, by adults who shared a cell with them or by jail staff. There was no education provided to them. Frequently, medical care, food, and recreation were substandard.[3] These scary, depressive settings exacted a psychological toll.

This chapter originally appeared in Community Corrections Report, *Vol. 2, No. 2, January/February 1995.*

Many states used the money they got from the OJJDP to keep kids out of jail or, alternatively, to reorganize their facilities to keep juveniles fully segregated from adult prisoners. These states then proceeded to set up schemes to visit and accredit jails as either sight-and-sound separated or not.

Costly lawsuits began popping up that resulted in liability for local governments when jailed juveniles were abused or injured, or when the conditions of a jail were found inhumane or endangering. Cities and counties were very displeased as the cost of liability insurance began to skyrocket.

A CONGRESSIONAL BAN ON JAILING

Congress revisited the jailing issue in 1980. It amended the JJDPA to require that states remove all juveniles from jails and police lockups by the end of 1985, or lose their federal juvenile justice funds. But Congress was practical. It knew that telling local officials what they could not do would meet with resistance. It knew that even with good intentions and strong effort, 100% compliance would be very difficult in many states. It also preferred that states not opt out of the JJDPA and go their own ways.

So Congress legislated that 75% compliance by 1985 would be acceptable, and a December 1988 deadline would apply to those 75% compliance states which had made an "unequivocal commitment" to accomplish full compliance. However, an exception permitted delinquent juveniles to be held for up to 24 hours in rural jails under certain restrictions such as sight-and-sound separation and the absence of an acceptable alternative placement, or to be held for up to six hours in urban police lockups for purposes of identification, processing, or transfer to other facilities. Subsequent federal amendments have replaced either the full compliance or "de minimus" exceptions, the latter being quantified as a very limited allowance.

The OJJDP focused a major effort on rural areas where JDCs were scarce and, when youths were detained, they were almost invariably detained in jails. These areas were characterized by small and spread out populations, a limited delinquent universe, great distances for transportation to any specialized facility, no specialist juvenile court judges to ascend the soap box and, frequently, low tax bases.

What worked at many of these sites was the engagement of juvenile justice and community leaders in problem assessment and remediation planning, establishment of 24-hour intake staff review of/control over law enforcement requests to hold, the design of written detention criteria, implementation of alternatives to jailing, and legislation that had parallels to the federal initiative.[4] The process was helped along by a series of successful jail conditions lawsuits that began in the early 1970s.

Most states made significant headway. For example, Idaho cut back juvenile jailings from 7,469 in 1980 to 1,744 in 1986 (aided by the governor's jail removal executive order), and Ohio reduced its confinements from more than 3,500 in 1981 to just 245 in 1987.[5] The National Jail Census found a 38% reduction in juvenile admissions to adult jails in 1988 compared with 1983.[6] Nonetheless, the *Federal Register* reported in August 1987 that at least 40 states had failed to achieve full compliance with the jail removal mandate.[7]

The difficulties in achieving compliance and the resistance to dejailing should not be understated. They were philosophical, practical, or both.

STRONG PROGRESS IN NORTH DAKOTA DUE TO FACTORS THAT INCLUDE JDC FACILITIES AND AN ATTENDANT CARE NETWORK

North Dakota (overall population about 635,000) has come a long way in dejailing its youth. I consulted with state and Ward County (Minot) officials there in July 1994.

The North Dakota state youth agency currently reports a 96% reduction in jailing since 1981, as well as compliance (but not yet 100% compliance) since 1992. This state's accomplishments were grounded on several detention support system models that had been pioneered in the Upper Peninsula of Michigan. The rural exception of up-to-24-hour jailing, under certain conditions, is allowed for North Dakota.

Here are some of the factors that have aided dejailing there:

- The attorney general's office employs a jail inspector. All jails send this office carbon copies of identification characteristics of all admissions. The inspector actively monitors the reports for juvenile admissions, and also inspects all jails annually.

- Only 12 of the 38 county or multi-county jails are now approved for up-to-24-hour juvenile beds that are separate and removed from adults.

- All city jails have been closed since the establishment of jail standards in 1981, thus shutting down a previous major venue of juvenile jailing.

- Just four city police departments have been approved for the up-to-six hour secure lock-up; for them also, the jail inspector's policies discourage use for juveniles and prohibit violation of JJDPA requirements.

JDC Facilities

There are now a total of 38 secure beds at the five licensed JDC facilities in North Dakota (about 12 of these beds were added during the past several years). Four JDCs are administered by counties. These four programs may "sell" space to other counties that have no JDC. The state delinquency institution created a fifth JDC, and sells up to six detention beds for county use and purchase. Juvenile detention here is a county responsibility. Counties have an incentive if they will transport juveniles to a licensed JDC. They will receive 50% reimbursement (all from OJJDP funds) for the first four days of detention use when quite strict intake criteria are met (essentially felonies, and when non-secure alternatives are not considered satisfactory). Another incentive is that a county sheriff is reimbursed mileage and meals (but not staff costs) for the transport of juveniles to and from a JDC.

Attendant Care Network

An "attendant care" network of 24 sites was developed to provide constant and direct supervision in a non-secure setting for lesser delinquents and status offenders who cannot be immediately returned to parental custody. Previously, many of these youngsters had been held in jails, police lock-ups, or in a JDC. A typical site is a sin-

gle room in a public or private social service agency building or law enforcement center. A typical placement averages six to eight hours, though some may extend to 24
hours or more. Typical attendant care workers are people having a sincere interest in
working with youth, who pass a criminal record check, and who undergo initial and
ongoing training. The array of approved workers stands by, to provide their services on
call. When working, they are paid $6.00-$7.00 per hour. Typically, there are one or two
youths to be attended to; attendants must be of the same sex as the juveniles supervised. Both private agencies and counties administer attendant care. One hundred
percent of program, staffing, and transportation costs are reimbursed by the state youth
agency, again, fully using OJJDP funds.

Annually, the overall alternatives program provides non-secure supervision for
over 800 youths and the subsidized secure juvenile detention for approximately 100
delinquent offenders.

Juveniles in Police Lock-ups

In some jurisdictions, juveniles taken into law enforcement custody are brought
initially to central or decentralized processing centers in jails, rather than to JDCs.
Following booking and efforts to contact parents or juvenile authorities, youth may
well be logged into a jail cell pending transfer or release to wherever or whomever they
may be going. This might be a long, terrifying wait.

Consider this: A report on the Detroit police department's holding practices discovered 3,087 violations of the six-hour rule in 1988. The next year a social worker
was employed by the department to do something about this. Violations dropped to
2,833 that year; 2,164 in 1990; and 762 in 1991. A three-pronged program was credited for the progress: (1) strong, broadly based, ongoing training regarding handling of
juveniles; (2) renovation of existing space in the 13 precinct stations to create juvenile
holding areas that were nonsecure or staff secure, and segregated from adult prisoners;
and (3) staffing these with police cadets, also provided training, and paid $6 per hour.[8]

Anyone who works in the juvenile justice field should check into police/sheriff
holding practices in their community to inquire about procedures and compliance.

REJAILING JUVENILES

Table 17.1 provides the latest juveniles in jail data I could acquire:[9] This chart tells
us a lot. It doesn't repudiate the claims of the jail removal effort we have known. It
does tell us what juveniles are now doing, and that more juveniles are now handled as
adults. One can only expect that 1993 or 1994 statistics will cross the 3,000 mark for
the number of juveniles who are in jail on the day in late June when this census is
taken, and for the average daily number of youth held in jails. It is no consolation that
the one-day counts for jailed adults jumped from 221,815 in 1983 to 441,781 in 1992,
or the average daily adult population soared from 225,781 to 439,362 during those
years.[10]

Table 17.1
Juveniles in Jail

Year	1 Day Counts	Average Daily Population
1983	1,736	1,760
1984	1,482	1,697
1985	1,629	1,467
1986	1,708	1,405
1987	1,781	1,575
1988	1,676	1,451
1989	2,250	1,891
1990	2,301	2,140
1991	2,350	2,333
1992	2,804	2,527

Author's Note

The *Sourcebook of Criminal Justice Statistics* (2002) provides an update of one-day counts of juveniles under age 18 in jail. The data reported are 4,300 for 1993, 6,700 for 1994, 7,800 for 1995, 8,100 for 1996, 9,105 for 1997, 8,090 for 1998, 9,458 for 1999, 7,615 for 2000 and 7,613 for 2001.[11]

North Dakota (and 38 other states) accomplished "full compliance with de minimus exceptions" in regard to the JJDPA jail and lockup removal requirement based on 1998 reporting. Eleven states were in "full compliance."[12]

Endnotes

[1] Sarri, R. (1974). *Under lock and key: Juveniles in jails and detention*. Ann Arbor: University of Michigan, National Assessment of Juvenile Corrections.

[2] Community Research Center (1980). *Incidence of juvenile suicide*. Champaign, IL: Community Research Center.

[3] Children's Defense Fund (1976). *Children in adult jails*. Washington, DC: Author.

[4] Office of Juvenile Justice and Delinquency Prevention Bulletin No. 220, May/June 1990.

[5] Soler, M. (1988). Litigation on behalf of children. *Crime & Delinquency*, 34, 190-208.

[6] Office of Juvenile Justice and Delinquency Prevention Bulletin, supra note 4.

[7] Frazier, C. E. & Bishop, D. M. (1990). Jailing juveniles in Florida: The dynamics of compliance. *Crime & Delinquency*, 36, 427-442.

[8] Bureau of Justice Statistics (1984). *National Jail Census* 1983. Washington, DC: U.S. Department of Justice; Bureau of Justice Statistics (1989). *National Jail Census* 1988. Washington, DC: U.S. Department of Justice.

[9] Community Research Associates (1992, September). *Profile*. Champaign, IL: Author.

[10] Hindelang Criminal Justice Research Center (1993). *Sourcebook of criminal justice statistics*. Albany, NY: State University of New York, School of Criminal Justice.

[11] Hindelang Criminal Justice Research Center (2002). *Sourcebook of criminal justice statistics*. Albany, NY: State University of New York, School of Criminal Justice.

[12] Office of Juvenile Justice and Delinquency Prevention (2000). *Annual report* 2000. Washington, DC: Author, p. 31.

Chapter 18

Reflections on Pretrial Detention

The world of pretrial detention is changing. This is what I heard as I observed a recent detention hearing in the juvenile court in New Haven, Connecticut,

Judge: "Son, I need to keep you in the detention center."

Fifteen-year-old boy: "Judge, I would like to be visited by the mother of my child."

In telling this story one month later to the assistant director of detention in Palm Beach County, Florida, I was told that "the same thing happens here all the time."

This is but one sign of the changes in pretrial detention. Another, as many readers know, is the use of risk-screening instruments that facilitate the decision as to whether a law enforcement referred juvenile should be locked up in detention pending a detention hearing.

TO DETAIN OR NOT TO DETAIN

Risk-screening instruments replace, in part, the subjective professional judgments that have been used historically. More weight is given to the "legal facts" (i.e., offense seriousness, prior record, age, whether other offenses are pending, and whether one is on probation or aftercare status), which are scored along with perceived parental ability to control a released juvenile, and several "social facts," such as peer or gang associations and previous runaways, than to professional judgment. However, professional judgment is built into the assessment in the form of an "override" provision. The screener may override the total score and reach a contrary decision.

WHAT HAPPENED TO THE PRESUMPTION OF INNOCENCE?

Let's say that the risk-screening instruments in use today are promising. Many are, and all should be, research-based and validated as to their predictive capabilities. They regularize decision making, so that all screeners reach similar conclusions.

But let me share with you one assessment format that I believe to be enormously invasive, which contains questions that should not be asked in reaching the hold–no hold judgment, or which are irrelevant to that decision. This technique is used by screening staff at a pretrial facility in a western state.

The staff asks and records information on very personal questions that go beyond stereotypical social facts. Keep in mind that this questioning takes place about an hour

---

This chapter originally appeared in Community Corrections Report, *Vol. 3, No. 6, September/October 1996.*

after a juvenile is booked in, that no prosecutor has ascertained whether the police charge is sufficiently grounded, and that there has been no consultation between the juvenile and an attorney. Detention screening staff are required to obtain information such as:

- The psychiatric history of father, mother, and siblings;

- The criminal history of father, mother, and siblings;

- Whether family violence has been witnessed;

- Whether the family is receiving welfare assistance;

- Whether the juvenile has been sexually abused;

- Whether the juvenile is promiscuous;

- Whether the juvenile has had sexual experience and, if so, whether it is more important to have one steady partner or many different partners;

- The "age of onset" of any sexual experience;

- Whether the juvenile is "unconcerned" with birth control;

- Whether the juvenile has a history of psychological intervention;

- Whether the juvenile has tattoos; and

- Whether there has been a fire-setting pattern, bedwetting, or "animal cruelty."

Take a look at the questions you ask juveniles and parents at this processing stage. It would be legally cleaner to make broad-based inquiries after adjudication, as with a predisposition report (PDR) investigation. But even at that stage, it might be better if we forgot about some of the above inquiries.

THREE CHOICES FOR DETAINED JUVENILES: JAIL, BOND, OR JUVENILE DETENTION

We all know that more juveniles face the criminal court process because they have been made into premature adults. But where do these juveniles sit, if locked up, to wait for their cases to be disposed?

In some jurisdictions, they are shifted to adult jail. (Some jail settings do segregate these juveniles from adult inmates; the U.S. Juvenile Justice and Delinquency Prevention Act does not require segregation when a criminal information or indictment has been filed.) But most are eligible to be bonded out since the criminal justice system retains some belief in the Eighth Amendment's provision that "excessive bail shall not be required." Someone should study how many and what types of such offenders do bond out, versus those who sit, as well as how long the sitters sit.

In other jurisdictions, such as Chicago, New York City, Sacramento, and Portland, Oregon, criminalized juveniles are held in juvenile detention centers pending the adult proceedings. There are advantages for these juveniles: they can continue their education in these settings, and their prospects for being raped or committing suicide are substantially lowered. Nonetheless, some would prefer adult handling, either because they take pride in a rite of passage symbolized by being held in a real jail, or because they may be able to bond out to conditional freedom.

Time Needed for Case Processing

Here is the big rub. Criminal court case processing requires substantially more time than juvenile court processing. Commonly, criminal case speedy trial requirements allow six months to trial or plea for in-custody adults. The time allowed for adjudication of juveniles is much shorter. For instance, Florida's statute requires adjudication of detained juveniles in 21 calendar days from the detention hearing, while California mandates this within 15 judicial days. Even Michigan, which has the very slow requirement of adjudication of a juvenile within 63 days of detention admission, is a lot swifter with case resolutions than adult processing requirements.

So, criminalized juveniles, held in juvenile detention, occupy space for quite a long time. Juvenile court officials who seek to speed up juvenile processing in order to move on and out those who have been detained, need to persuade their adult court colleagues to speed criminal court case processing in order to more readily close out the detention of criminalized juveniles. It is time to trot out solid, comprehensive programs for these types of juveniles and seek to persuade prosecutors to use the juvenile court, not the criminal court, as a forum for them.

Tough Job for Detention Centers

Detention center administrators are likely to feel ambivalent about holding criminalized juveniles at their facilities. Some of these juveniles are quite difficult to manage, and administrators probably would not mind giving up some of their altruism for a good night's sleep. Some disrupt classrooms and other activities. Others may want the mothers of their several children to be able to visit them at the center.

Also, there are juvenile detention facilities, such as Chicago's, that have to hold and program a difficult triple mix of (1) criminalized juveniles awaiting the adult court process, (2) juveniles ordered into detention as a juvenile court disposition (this can be for up to 30 days in Illinois, or six months in Virginia), and (3) regular pretrial detainees.

OTHER APPROACHES TO CURBING OVERCROWDING

Besides speeding up case processing in juvenile court (and as applicable in criminal court), and better calibrating detention risk-screening instruments and practices, juvenile justice system officials can take other steps to limit detention populations. Some of these steps are outlined here:

- *Screening procedures:* Allowing screening staff to screen appropriate juveniles away from any night or two in detention and substituting home detention in conjunction with an appearance at a detention hearing held within 48 hours.

- *Electronic monitoring:* Expanding pre-adjudicatory/pre-disposition home detention, augmented by electronic monitoring in appropriate cases. (But do not widen this net just because the information age is here.)

- *Early case resolution:* Getting the lawyers in better sync with early case resolution. This may mean ensuring defense attorney presence at the detention hearing or arraignment (if not detained); expediting procedures for the prosecutor to open the case file to the defense attorney; having both attorneys complete witness interviews at an early date; obtaining a court practice that mandates, with contested cases, that the two sides confer promptly and agree to a plea settlement or, otherwise, be fully prepared for trial within a one- or two-week time span (and that the court will really back up this scheme and hear the trial on the first scheduled date).

- *Swift PDRs for detained juveniles:* A number of juvenile courts, particularly larger urban juvenile courts, bifurcate the adjudicatory hearing from the dispositional hearing by a four-to-five week time span. This is the clean due process model (i.e., PDR investigations are deferred until there has been an adjudication). It is not the swift, expedited case-flow management approach where the PDR is prepared following an early informal admission, and the disposition is ready to go 30 seconds after the plea is entered.

Florida law compels a dispositional hearing for detained juveniles to be held within 15 calendar days of adjudication (extendible another 15 days for "good cause"), while California law mandates this hearing within 10 judicial days (extendible another 15 calendar days).

I once tried to push a southern-state probation director, working in a true bifurcation court, to speed up the PDR process span for detained juveniles from five or six weeks to three. He all but had a heart attack. Yet I am familiar with larger probation shops that set aside several probation officers whose job is to do speedy PDRs for detained juveniles and get them done quickly. The "system" will find a way to meet a two-to-three week PDR guideline if the juvenile court statute/rule or cultural norm requires it (a minority of cases will necessitate a good cause extension, as when seeking a private residential placement).

Speeding Release After a Disposition

I asked a simple question, in 1971, while conducting my first study of a juvenile court, in Atlanta: "How long do detained juveniles wait, following commitment to the state, until they are admitted to a state facility?" The answer was "about one month." When I expressed chagrin about this long dead-time waiting period (committed juveniles were locked into that center's unadorned maximum security, jail-type unit awaiting transportation), staff reassured me that it used to be three or four months.[1]

I've asked the same question a lot, since then. I like to get the answer: "In all cases they go the same day, or the next day." Not so in Montgomery, Alabama, in 1989. Complaints on this issue in Montgomery and across that state led to an interesting new statute:

After October, 1991, the Department of Youth Services shall accept all children committed to it within seven days of notice of disposition.[2]

Florida statutes also have dealt with this matter. The law has mandated removal from detention within five days of a commitment order. Most commitment resources in that state are local or regional. The state court of appeals has ruled that this law meant what it said. **R.P. v. State**, 550 So.2d 543 (Fla. 1989). But a subsequent amendment allows for a 15-day extension of the five-day removal deadline, and removes any deadline if the commitment is to a "high-risk residential program," that is, the most secure facilities.[3] However, detention center release to home detention with electronic monitoring is expressly authorized when a time limit expires, and commitment has been to other than the most secure facilities.

Waiting Following Disposition to a Non-Secure Placement

Juvenile justice administrators are beginning to come to grips with bed space limitations in another way. Juveniles committed to non-secure placements, private residential facilities, for example, often have waited in the secure pretrial facility until a placement has opened up. This may take a month or more. In two communities that I know of, and with the cooperation and funding of the public child welfare agency (which will pick up the tab for the ultimate residential placement, anyway), some juveniles awaiting placement are being placed in (1) foster homes that hold up to four youth, or (2) special hospital units staffed by houseparents.

And then, there is the New Jersey statute which states:

When a juvenile has been adjudicated delinquent and is awaiting transfer to a dispositional alternative that does not involve a secure residential or {secure} out-of-home placement and continued detention is necessary, the juvenile shall not be detained in a secure facility but shall be transferred to a non-secure facility.[4]

So look at your practices, and look into alternatives to secure post-disposition detention for juveniles awaiting non-secure placements.

HOW ABOUT WEEKEND AND HOLIDAY DETENTION HEARINGS?

Scheduling detention hearings on weekends and holidays may prove beneficial. While this suggestion will gain me no friends among judges, referees, prosecutors, or defense counsel, detention center staff should appreciate it, since they work weekends and around the clock.

I believe we should hold detention hearings on Saturdays and on holidays that fall on a Friday or Monday. Some juveniles who are locked up should never have been locked up; others, who may rightfully have been detained, may have had their parents come forth in the interim and should not have to wait for the weekend to pass before being released.

Will anyone out there implement this concept? Some states have addressed this issue.

- *Arizona:* JV, an Arizona youth (same state, but not Gerald Gault whose 1967 U.S. Supreme Court decision brought the U.S. Constitution into state juvenile courts) did not think it was fair for arrested adults to obtain a first judicial appearance on Saturdays, Sundays, and holidays, while detained juveniles had to wait for a detention hearing until the weekend or holiday had ended. JV convinced an appellate court that since Rule 4 of the Arizona Rules of Criminal Procedure stipulated that adults must have their first hearing within 24 hours (no exceptions) or be released immediately, so must juveniles. However, Juvenile Rule 3(d) excluded weekends and holidays from the time interval before the detention hearing must be held. JV successfully argued that this difference violated the U.S. Constitution's requirement of equal protection of the laws. The court held that both juveniles and adults should be promptly told of the charges against them and of the constitutional protections available to them. "Detention may be harmful to a juvenile when detention is subsequently found to have been unnecessary." **JV-111701 v. Superior Court**, 786 P.2d 998 (Ariz. App. 1980).

- *New Jersey:* The New Jersey Supreme Court Rule 5:21-3 is explicit: "A detention hearing shall be held no later than the morning following the juvenile's placement in custody, including holidays and weekends."

- *Michigan:* Michigan Court Rule 5.935 states the detention hearing "must commence no later than 24 hours after the juvenile has been taken into court custody, excluding Sundays and holidays, or the juvenile must be released." Actually, juvenile court judges and juvenile court referees (or however these quasi-judicial hearing officers are referred to in a particular jurisdiction) need not necessarily give up their R & R time to hold weekend/holiday hearings, although these latter officials conduct Michigan hearings. Juvenile courts are a part of the state court system. Local magistrates, or weekend duty judges from the larger trial court can hear these matters. The official who hears these cases must be an independent decision maker, and without question should be an attorney.

JUDICIAL DISCRETION IN SENTENCING

Florida: Follow Legislative Guidelines

A number of detention-related cases have arisen in Florida. (Even though public defenders are elected—not appointed—in Florida, the defenders there are litigious.) One such case, **State v. R.F.**, 648 So.2d 292 (Fla. 1995), dealt with the application of new legislative measures intended to control juvenile weapon possession. The Florida statute mandates five days in secure detention and 100 community service hours, in addition to other court sanctions, for firearm possession. In this case, there was an early plea to carrying a concealed firearm, and release from detention occurred after two days. At disposition, a sensitive judge directed that R.F. also serve three eight-hour days at the secure facility.

But the state appealed, and overturned the trial judge. "We think the legislature intended the term 'day' to refer to a 24-hour period of time, not to an eight-hour work day," wrote the appellate court. It added that the trial judge can use discretion in deciding when the mandatory term is served, that is, school and work can be considered in determining when the remaining three days x 24 hours shall be implemented.

Arizona: Unconstitutional Delegation of Judicial Authority

I've written before, in the restitution context, that it is an unconstitutional delegation of judicial authority for a judge to let a probation officer decide how much restitution shall be required. An Arizona case applies the same reasoning with a sentence to a detention center case. **Juvenile Action No. 92-J-040**, 885 P.2d 1127 (Ariz. 1994). In this case, a juvenile violated his probation. The judge reinstated intensive supervision, and ordered that the juvenile serve 30 days in detention at the probation officer's discretion. The probation officer could impose or suspend the 30 days based on the juvenile's compliance with intensive probation conditions. Wrong, said the appellate court—this was impermissible delegation.

PROBATION OFFICERS AND OTHER COMMUNITY CORRECTIONAL OFFICIALS MUST STAND UP AND SAY NO IF JUDGES ASK THEM TO STEP BEYOND THEIR JOB BOUNDARIES

Cleveland's Reputation in Disrepute

About 20 years ago, a juvenile court judge in Cleveland, Ohio, drew headlines when he tossed a probation officer who was late for a hearing into jail for contempt. The *Cleveland Plain Dealer* reported a similar incident—same court, different judge—on March 8, 1996.

The new headlines concerned the incarceration of Thomas Foster, director of juvenile detention services for the Cuyahoga County Juvenile Court, by Judge Robert A. Ferreri. His crime: giving "unsatisfactory answers" to the judge's questions about how two boys had broken out of the facility. Foster was ordered jailed for 30 days and fined $250 for contempt of the judge.

One day later, Foster was released on the order of the court's administrative judge, who also filed a complaint about his colleague, Judge Ferreri, with the Ohio Supreme Court. The complaint charged harassment and intimidation of court employees, and called for appropriate disciplinary action. Administrative Judge Sikora urged Ferreri to resign "in the best interests of the court."

Cleveland's Judges Strike Again

Not only detention officials but, also, enterprising juvenile prosecutors should pause before accepting an offer to serve in this court. The *Plain Dealer's* companion editorial [of March 8] noted, in addition, that Judge Betty Willis Ruben (no relative of the author) had that same day fined two prosecutors and sent one of them to jail for contempt. An appellate court stayed Judge Ruben's order pending a further hearing.

The editorial, titled "*Court Jesters*," had a subtitle: "The people most in need of adult supervision may be the ones who judge juvenile cases." It referred to this juvenile court as a circus, noted that Judge Ferreri had a "long history of shameless self-promotion and troubling conduct," urged a close examination of the judge's conduct, and found Ruben's action "vindictive and mean-spirited."

Probation officers and community correctional officials, or for that matter prosecutors or defense attorneys, may be asked by judges to do something that is outside the law. Consider the Arizona case cited above, where the judge essentially asked a probation officer to determine a juvenile's sentence.

It is hard to stand up to a judge who is clearly erroneous. But it must be done—and done in a nice way. If you lose your job over it, and have lost your innocence as well, look favorably on Ohio, as you may be very well qualified for the next opening in Cleveland.

Endnotes

[1] Rubin, H.T. (1972). *Three juvenile courts: A comparative study.* Denver, CO: Institute for Court Management, p. 256.

[2] Ala. Code § 12-15-16(b).

[3] Fla. Stat. Ann. § 39.044(10).

[4] N. J. Rev Stat. § C.2A: 4A-48-19.k.

Chapter 19

The Ins and Outs of Detention: Sacramento Addresses Detention Center Overcrowding

The juvenile justice system has developed a number of approaches to curb pretrial detention use over the last 30 years. One often-used strategy is detention intake screening: the assignment of probation officers or detention center staff to review whether a juvenile referred for secure detention by law enforcement really needs to be locked up. Today, risk-assessment instruments, with numerical score categories, are often used in reaching this decision.

Another review measure, detention hearings conducted by a judicial officer, is part of the juvenile justice process in every state. A juvenile admitted to detention is not to be retained unless the judicial officer finds that there is probable cause to believe the youth has committed a crime and, further, that a statutory requirement, such as a serious threat of danger to others following release, has been shown.

Intensive "tracking" of juveniles as a detention substitute was an exciting development integral to the home supervision movement of the 1970s and, perhaps, a forerunner to post-dispositional intensive supervision models in frequent use today with higher-risk probationers. Certainly, "human tracking" was a forerunner to the current use of electronic monitoring instruments to keep track of the whereabouts of released offenders.

Finally, policy and statutory changes have led to a general ban on the admission of status offenders to these settings.

WHO MAY BE HELD AND FOR HOW LONG?

Although a secure detention center was long seen as a facility that should hold juveniles awaiting adjudication, disposition, or implementation of a judicial placement order, this precept has changed in a significant number of states. Statutes in California, Colorado, Illinois, Virginia, Washington, and other jurisdictions now authorize judges to "sentence" youth to local detention facilities as a disposition. Sentences may extend for 30, 45, 60, or more days.

Another factor in the makeup of a detention center population is whether juveniles transferred to criminal court and awaiting processing there are held in the juvenile

This chapter originally appeared in Juvenile Justice Update, *Vol. 4, No. 2, April/May 1998.*

facility or in a local jail. The preferred policy of juvenile advocates, which is reflected in some laws, is to use the former setting.

Also factored into the population mix is the case-processing time required by statute or court rule. These provide that detained juveniles be court-processed more rapidly than non-detained youth. For example, in California detained youth are to be adjudicated within 18 court days, with a judicial disposition to occur within another 10 court days. Non-detained juveniles are to be adjudicated within 30 days of first appearance, with a disposition required within an additional 30 days.

SACRAMENTO JUVENILE JUSTICE INITIATIVE ADDRESSES COSTS OF OVERCROWDING

Governmental entities that have embarked on new or expanded detention center construction know the enormous cost involved. While the application of certain of the above-described methods has helped hold down unnecessary detentions and their costs, many juveniles are still held in significantly overcrowded facilities. One of these overcrowded facilities has been the Sacramento juvenile hall (the statutory name for a detention center in California.[1]

The Sacramento City/County population is approximately, 1,500,000 and the juvenile hall is designed to hold 254 youth. This chapter describes a band of strategies instituted to control the population confined there. These measures sought to reduce admissions (the "ins") and expedite releases of the detained (the "outs"). Emphasis is placed on the more innovative, ground-breaking approaches used to avoid or defer breaking ground for an expanded Sacramento facility.

The Annie E. Casey Foundation invited Sacramento officials to organize a multi-pronged detention-control initiative. The Foundation was actively searching for communities interested in and willing to commit themselves to an anti-business-as-usual approach of continuous detention center expansion. A Foundation award to Sacramento provided rather massive multi-year technical assistance by Casey staff and consultants and funded several new positions and a significantly expanded management information system (MIS) capability. Local leadership emerged to concertedly tackle the overcrowding.

Admission Criteria and Risk Assessment Instruments Developed

Up front, the probation department led a multi-agency effort which designed detention admission criteria and spelled out the types of offenses, offenders, and legal and social situations that merited secure confinement. Next up was a detention risk-assessment instrument which was developed with the necessary consultations and pretested, modified, and validated. It provides point scores that identify the release-risk of assessed juveniles.

Expanded Home Supervision

Home supervision is usually accomplished in two ways, either using a human contact model or an electronic monitoring model. In Sacramento, detention intake screeners can release juveniles onto daily human-contact home supervision, but electronic monitoring can only be authorized by a judicial officer, typically at a detention hearing. Those who are placed initially on home supervision in lieu of detention are required to appear within a day or two at a formal detention hearing to ascertain whether home supervision is a suitable requirement or whether, for example, release status without supervision is appropriate.

Currently, an average of 220 youth are placed on home supervision or electronic monitoring each month. One-third of these youth are on monitors. While this required the purchase of additional electronic bracelets, the overall daily supervision cost is $11.40 per youth.

Accelerated Citation Program

Several juvenile case types, earlier admitted to juvenile hall on law enforcement request, have now been excluded by the criteria or risk instrument. Still the Sacramento Initiative had to address the question of how the juvenile justice system could accommodate police concerns over abandoning practices they were used to. Enter the Accelerated Citation Program.

For the now-excluded juveniles, the probation agency offers an expedited intake conference. When law enforcement stamps "Accelerated Citation" on a citation, interview notices are phoned or mailed out within 72 hours of its receipt, allowing the conference to be held within five court days of notice. The police move these reports to intake more quickly than their other citations. Informal handling decisions by probation intake frequently result in six months of informal supervision, often accompanied by an 8-, 16-, or 24-hour assignment to a work crew project that can begin the following weekend.

Program data reflect that police have placed the "Accelerated Citation" stamp on 10% of citations, increased their use of citations by 8%, and reduced by 8% the percent of juveniles they drive over to juvenile hall. This amounts to about 800 fewer trips annually. Thus they have significantly reduced their professional time and travel costs incident to the transportation of lower-risk juveniles who would most likely have been released within hours of arrival.

DETENTION RELEASE EXPEDITER

Dedicated Staff Position

To help shorten stays of detained juveniles, Sacramento created an unusual staff position. According to the job description, the release expediter, a senior and highly regarded probation officer, is responsible "for monitoring the juvenile hall population on a daily basis and the movement of minors between institutions." The job's primary goal is to "reduce the unnecessary use of juvenile hall by advocating alternative release programs for both pre- and post-dispositional detainees."

The expediter, in practice, works proactively to:

- Facilitate alternative considerations of juveniles who may be eligible for release to home supervision or another alternative;

- Bang on doors and get the "paper" moved to expeditiously shift detained youth who have been ordered into residential placement or state institution into placement and out of juvenile hall;

- Encourage prompt transfer hearings and criminal court resolutions for transferred youth (who are held in juvenile hall unless they are over 18-years-old); and

- Speed up the return of out-of-county youth apprehended in Sacramento County to their home counties for case handling.

Database Support

The expediter maintains a database on all detained minors; tracks their status, characteristics, and timelines, and uses these materials to initiate contacts with probation officers, court staff, and attorneys in order to illuminate a decision that a removal from juvenile hall is appropriate. Following such a decision, he then makes sure detention staff release the juvenile at the earliest moment.

The court referees and judge regularly seek out the expediter to conduct specialized investigations, obtain particularized information, or otherwise provide information to facilitate decisions.

The expediter also obtains predisposition investigation reports prior to the court hearing. If the report recommends probation, he will seek approvals to release a detained juvenile, for example on electronic monitoring, pending the scheduled court hearing. The Sacramento expediter is aggressive, and this is what the system wants.

Sacramento data show the expediter is engaged with 20%-25% of cases admitted into detention, and his recommendations are followed in 80%-90% of cases. Further, since the position was initiated, the detained pre-disposition population has been reduced by an average of 37 youths, from 178 to 141.

SPEEDING UP COURT HEARINGS FOR DETAINED JUVENILES

A major plank in the Sacramento Initiative was the acceleration of judicial hearings involving detained juveniles. This is an obvious strategy, but as far as I know Sacramento is the only community to embrace it in such a systematized way. Many communities should.

The chief juvenile prosecutor was the point person for what became known as the Detention Early Resolution (DER) program. He states:

I was struck by the problems in the office ... our attorneys each trying to cope with 70-90 felony cases ... and the time frames within which we had to be ready. We were working up the case of every detained juvenile as if it were going to trial, since pretrials were held on court day 13, and trials on day 15. Witnesses had to be subpoenaed, lab reports obtained, and investigations made on all cases, so that if no settlement occurred at pretrial, we were ready for trial two days later.[2]

He adds that there was system-wide concern with overcrowding, and that he had professional concerns that "juveniles were locked up longer than they should be in a non-treatment facility. So I thought...let's advance the pretrial hearing date." [3] Other officials agreed to structure an early resolution procedure which was piloted with non-detained youth. When that proved successful, it was then applied to detained youth.

Short-Form Predisposition Report

Instead of holding a pretrial on day 13 and any trial that was needed two days later, DER scheduled an arraignment five court days from the detention hearing. If resolution was not reached at that time, trial would be set within 10 court days, or a pretrial held within eight court days followed by a trial date two days later.

DER success hinged on a high percentage of plea/sentence bargain agreements. Effective attorney negotiations require information about a juvenile/family, not just the offense/offense history. And this is where the probation department, which also administers juvenile hall, eagerly joined the bandwagon. The probation department created the short-form report. This is to be completed within three to four days of detention admission and consists of three to four pages of categorized information, a face sheet, and attachments. The report seeks to provide the attorneys and judge with the fundamental information they need to reach settlement, if settlement can be reached.

The short report requires 4.5 hours of staff time to complete, compared with seven hours for a regular report, and 12 hours for a transfer-to-criminal-court-proceeding report. Unlike some juvenile justice systems, probation investigators here conduct their case studies prior to, rather than post-adjudication. Sacramento officials rely very heavily on report findings and recommendations.

Benefits of DER and the Short-Form Report

Not every detained juvenile meets the criteria for DER (12 more serious felonies were exempted). Not every eligible case is viewed as suitable for the short report. Certainly, not every DER/short form case reaches settlement. During its first eight and a half months, DER resolved 576 cases; 509 cases were not resolved on day five although some of these were resolved at the pretrial on day 13 or prior to trial on day 15.

Sacramento officials stress that the key to having such a high resolution frequency is experienced prosecutors and public defenders who are able to weigh realistically the nature of a case and the advantages or disadvantages of going to trial. To spur additional early resolutions, each courtroom team of prosecution and defense counsel and a judge or referee meets daily at 8:15 a.m. to review settlement options for the day's cases.

The short report has become embedded in Sacramento practice. Indeed, data show that 77% of all court cases—including DER, the early resolution program for non-detained juveniles known as ER, and all other case types—use the short report. One positive benefit is that two probation officer investigators and two probation department secretaries are now no longer needed and have been transferred to other responsibilities.

What we have here is a "front ending" of the system. Characteristically, officials are used to the rhythm of their present pattern of functioning. But the Sacramento Initiative demonstrates that expediting court resolutions saves officials' time and money, and reduces detention costs. Data analysis reveals that DER has reduced the detention length of stay by 3.3 days compared with non-DER detained cases.

DIVERTING GIRLS FROM DETENTION TO EMERGENCY SHELTER

To reduce the female detention population, the Initiative contracted with a community organization to accept and assist delinquent girls who otherwise would be held in juvenile hall—some just because their families would not accept their return home. A girls' shelter was established by the Good Samaritan agency to house six girls, and the population diverted to the shelter has averaged five to six on a daily basis. As might be expected, runaways from the open shelter do take place,

Prior to the opening of the shelter, the juvenile hall housed an average of 32 girls daily. With the opening, the daily average dropped to five, and the average length of stay has declined by three days.

Another program was designed to assist pregnant girls and those who were mothers who were detained in secure detention or held at the shelter. The Sacramento Birthing Project provides intensive case management services to an average of three pregnant or parenting teens each month. Program goals are to reduce average length of stay, connect clients to helpful health and community services, and facilitate sound futures for mother and child.

DEALING WITH TRANSFER CASES

Transferred juveniles and those undergoing the transfer process are also held in juvenile hall. During several months in 1996, more than 60 of these juveniles were held at one time in juvenile hall pending hearings in one or both courts. Two changes resulted in a significant reduction of this population and in the average length of stay.

Better Targeting for Transfer

It had become clear that (1) a significant number of juveniles were not, in fact, transferred at this hearing; and (2) a significant number of transferred juveniles were receiving probation sentences in adult court. With encouragement from the presiding judge, a new lead prosecutor obtained approval to selectively petition, rather than mandatorily petition, an offense that was legally eligible for transfer. The changed policy resulted in far fewer transfer hearings. Only those cases which were extremely likely to be transferred and in which the accused was likely to receive an adult court sentence of incarceration were petitioned.

More carefully targeted transfer cases also resulted in early resolution of cases which were no longer subject to transfer consideration. Because only juvenile court sanctions were available, fewer trials were held in these matters and earlier exits from juvenile hall were a consequence.

Settling Criminal Court Transfers in Juvenile Court

A second very unusual procedure, blessed by the judiciary, initiated by the prosecutor, and agreed to by defense counsel in appropriate transfer cases, resulted in adult court sentencing agreements that were reached in juvenile court. In these cases, the legal evidence needed to be absolutely compelling, and the prosecution's sentencing offer advantageous to the defendant. Prosecution and defense counsel could then appear in criminal court to enter the negotiated plea and sentence offer within two weeks of the juvenile court transaction. As a result, juveniles who otherwise might have spent 300 to 400 days in juvenile hall prior to imposition of a criminal court sentence relinquished their beds after just a short period.

DETENTION AS A DISPOSITION

Sacramento judicial officers sentence 350 to 500 juveniles annually to secure detention as a disposition. Fewer than 100 juveniles are committed annually by this court to the state youth authority. Judicial officers also enter dispositions to three non-secure residential programs operated by the probation department: a 100-bed boys' ranch, a 50-bed facility which targets 13- to 15-year-olds, and a 27-bed center that works at reunifying residents with their families. Dispositions to juvenile hall are particularly used with reoffenders who run from an open facility and with older juveniles in an attempt to capture their attention prior to their turning age-eligible for adult handling. These dispositions are for specific durations, such as 30, 60, or 90 days.

As a population control device, a three-person board of highest-level probation officials holds a formal case review half way through the time to be served, except when a judicial officer has specified that the full sentence must be served. As a result of these reviews, some juveniles are released early.

HOLDING SITE FOR HARD TO PLACE YOUTH

A final scheme employs two community placement coordinators to expedite judicial orders for placement of "hard to place" minors, who tend to be quite severely emotionally disturbed, demonstrate behavioral problems, and/or are chronic placement failures. The youth are held in juvenile hall pending difficult-to-arrange placements. Concentrated efforts by the coordinators have reduced both the average number of these juveniles in detention and their lengths of stay.

REFLECTIONS

The Sacramento initiative is a broadly conceived strategy to arrest detention center overcrowding. Since 1988, the facility has always operated at more than 100% of capacity; it averaged 126% of capacity when this Initiative went into gear. As a result of the Initiative, gone are the days of 347 residents (March 1996). In the first five months of 1997, the hall averaged only 280 youth (still 110% of capacity). Overall, fewer juveniles are being admitted and average lengths of stay have declined.

Nonetheless, the October 1997 Sacramento County Comprehensive Juvenile Detention Plan recommends a 30-bed expansion for construction within three years, to be followed by a 60-bed expansion. This commentator's analysis is that without Initiative programs, expansion numbers would be substantially larger. Further, expansion recommendations are not yet cast into concrete. They are not yet funded and they may not be found necessary within a few years.

Numerous components of the Sacramento Initiative involve low- or no-cost features, and some involve savings. An upgraded MIS data capability was a more costly but critical feature. The Sacramento Criminal Justice Cabinet and its Juvenile Institutions and Programs Committee have been vital to bringing the system together to find common ground and to work on the high ground of effective collaboration.

The methods and technologies used in Sacramento are not copyrighted. It would be right to copy them in numerous communities.

Author's Note

The detention center (juvenile hall) population does continue to increase despite the application of an ever-expanding array of stratagems to constrain the number of residents. Fewer juveniles are now sentenced to juvenile hall, however. The court commits an amazingly low figure of juveniles to the California Youth Authority for a county of this size, relying instead on its residential programs, those administered by other entities, and community-based non-residential programming.

The information below was prepared on July 30, 2002 by Yvette Woolfolk, Court Analyst, Superior Court of California, County of Sacramento, and Fred Campbell, Consultant, Criminal Justice Research Foundation, Sacramento.

- Proposition 21, was implemented on March 8, 2000, and prompted important changes, among them the two discussed in Table 19.1.

- Juvenile hall admission criteria and risk assessment instruments are still in place.

- The accelerated citation program was expanded to target all citations with the goal of trying to see all minors two to four weeks from the citation date. Also, the district attorney "prescreens" citations and lets the probation department know if they are going to pursue the matter if the department cannot resolve this at the citation hearing. This new process allows the probation officer to serve the minor/parents personally with a date-certain to appear in court when the matter does not resolve informally. This saves the court from having to send a notice of hearing and allows the minor to be seen in court 15 days after the citation hearing.

- The detention release expediter position continues.

- As to speeding up court hearings for detained juveniles, the early resolution programs continue and have been expanded to include two new target populations: (1) For complex cases or cases with serious charges, a "Serious Case Review" (SCR) hearing is scheduled 10 days from the date of the detention hearing. The probation officer prepares the pre-sentencing report, but does not include dispositional recommendations If the matter resolves, a disposition hearing is scheduled 10 days later. (2) Violations of probation have been streamlined. When a minor violates and is arrested, the court attempts to resolve the matter at the detention hearing through an "ER-VOP" hearing. The probation department does not prepare a report, but relies on the probation field officer's adjustment summary report for a summary of the incident and dispositional recommendation(s). The parties usually stipulate to modify the "previous" court order (i.e., add 10 additional days of work project, etc.). If modified, the court then dismisses the violation.

Table 19.1
Proposition 21 Changes

Change	Comments
1. Requires more juvenile offenders to be tried in adult court.	Our District Attorney developed internal filing policies so that every youth that qualifies for adult court is not automatically transferred. In 2000, 37 and in 2001, 45 youths were automatically referred to adult court. For the first six months of 2002, 11 youths have been referred.
2. Requires that certain juvenile offenders be held in local or state correctional facilities.	This provision has impacted juvenile hall, since certain offenses now require automatic detention.

Facilities

Sacramento still has:

- Boys' ranch (100 beds).

- Thornton Youth Center (50 beds). Sixty beds are being added to this facility next year (2003); funding and construction have been approved.

- The Morgan Alternative Center (21 beds) was turned into an assessment center for placement-bound youth. Extensive assessment is completed to better match youth with placement services and/or refer back home with wraparound services.

- Juvenile Hall (261 rated capacity). Despite all efforts, the facility remains overcrowded. There are plans to expand by 90 beds in the future (probably three to four years out). Juvenile hall average daily population (ADP) numbers are as follows:

    1999: 289

    2000: 304

    2001: 320

    2002 (first six months): 323.

There is one all-new facility: the Larson Youth Center (74 beds) came on-line September 2001. The program is similar to that of the Thornton Youth Center.

Commitments to the California Youth Authority (CYA) in the past two years were:

- 2000: 50

- 2001: 49

Youth Profile

The profile of juveniles detained in juvenile hall has dramatically changed. About one out of every five youths booked into juvenile hall has an extensive history of chronic delinquency, which can include as many as four or more bookings in a 20-month period. These detained youths have negatively impacted all available county resources and programs. On any given day, 45 to 50 detained minors are awaiting out-of-home placement. Minors awaiting placement frequently demonstrate five common characteristics:

1. Family history of neglect, inconsistent discipline, and high degree of criticism;

2. Physical and/or sexual abuse;

3. Gang involvement;

4. Illicit drug usage; and

5. Poor academic achievement.

While detained in juvenile hall, a large percentage of these minors receive psychotropic medication. The majority participate in mental health counseling and/or report some type of suicidal ideation. Given the complexity of their needs, minors awaiting placement demand more staff attention than any other group of minors housed in the facility.

What's on the Horizon?

Planning is currently underway in the following areas:

- *Health and mental health issues of detained youth:* Sacramento is looking at a need for a locked mental health facility (not the juvenile hall) and a mental health court.

- *Truancy Court:* Juvenile justice officials are working with the district attorney's office on a program designed to keep probationers in school, utilizing the court as "the hammer."

- *Drug Court:* A collaborative planning effort is underway to determine the need for a delinquency drug court.

Endnotes

[1] See Cal. W & I Code § 50.

[2] Author interview with Marvin Stern, Supervising Deputy District Attorney, Office of the District Attorney for Sacramento County, November 20, 1996.

[3] Id.

Chapter 20

Diversion to the Community: Neighborhood Accountability Boards in Santa Clara County, California

A NEIGHBORHOOD ACCOUNTABILITY SANCTION

These are the words 15-year-old Eloy (not his real name) used to write to his Neighborhood Accountability Board (NAB), a Santa Clara County Juvenile Diversion Program, about his assigned day with an attorney mentor:

Being an attorney is alot of work. You have to really know what your doing.... The first court we went to was for felony charges. Stacie, the attorney, told me not to talk.... I don't know what most of the people were charged for.... No one was really talking but the judge. There wasn't much to see, just the judge discussing his dicisions. Some people got to go, some didn't. One girl had to pay a fine and then her case was closed.

The next courtroom was the mistiminor courtroom. There wasn't really anything interesting, just the judge asking them do you understand. Most people said yes.

Then we went back to Stacie's office and talked about what went on in the courtrooms. Then we ended up talking about what she does all day. That day she didn't really do anything, just sit there and talk about once or twice. Most of the time she just filled out paper work.

Then we talked about my school and how I'm doing and if I'm in sports or other things. We talked about how you have to have good grades to be a successful attorney.

So being an attorney isn't so bad. After the day I had, it's made me realize if I don't get my act together, what am I going to turn out to be. I am looking forward to be an attorney. I also want to thank Stacie and Rafael [project community coordinator] for helping me set my goals for the future. THANKS!!

This chapter originally appeared in Juvenile Justice Update, *Vol. 4, No. 5, October/November 1998.*

Eloy's Offense Was Petty Theft

Maybe Eloy will not become a lawyer. Maybe he liked his lawyer more than the law. Maybe a family member helped him phrase his report. Certainly, juveniles can be attached to a mentor other than by a NAB. But the day had meaning for Eloy (and, further, he has given us a wonderfully incorrect spelling of misdemeanor).

Eloy's offense was petty theft. He and another 15-year-old walked out of a K-Mart with a CD player, but did not walk far. The diversion report, prepared by an intake worker with the Santa Clara County, California, Probation Department (San Jose is the county seat), indicates walking is part of Eloy's problem. Eloy walks tardily to school, often walks elsewhere than to school on school days, and walks out of school with overall failing grades. Eloy comes from an intact family with five children, "mostly stays at home," and says he has no special learning problems. "I just don't do my work."

Eloy's NAB Hearing

The paper flow for non-detained juveniles, from police contact to probation intake to referral and appearance at a diversion program, in this case a NAB, is slow in Santa Clara County as it is in many justice systems. Two months and 13 days elapsed between Eloy's offense and his NAB hearing.

At the hearing, which is confidential, a citizen NAB member begins by explaining the agenda. This includes an explanation of Eloy's rights, questioning of Eloy and his family, review of the police report, additional questioning, a 10-minute break for panel members to discuss observations and preliminary recommendations, presentation of a proposed agreement following the return of the youth and family to the hearing room, discussion, and the signing or rejection of the proposed agreement. Provisions of a NAB agreement may extend up to six months.

Eloy and his parents signed on. In addition to the day with a mentor and a required written report, Eloy had to prepare a letter of apology to K-Mart within eight days, and continue with a tutoring program to improve his grades to average. He also had to submit his grades "from counseling office on March 31" (33 days from date of hearing).

His apology letter, dated five days after the hearing, states in part:

I'm very sorry and I do apologize for what I did wrong.... Please except this letter as an apology for my mistakes, and please except me back at your store without any recongnization or questions. Sometimes teens don't understand the wrong things in life until they face the consequences and as a teen I understand now what is right and what is wrong.... I have learned it is a commandment not to shoplift, and I understand it was wrong to blame the fact that it was a temptation. I'm sorry.

THE MOVEMENT TO COMMUNITY-BASED JUSTICE IN SANTA CLARA COUNTY

Implementation of four NAB boards in four communities within Santa Clara County represents the probation department's opening thrust into restorative justice.

Funding for three additional NABs has been granted. The project has sparked great excitement across this county. The active, not token, engagement of citizens in the justice system is observable. Delivery of justice is being decentralized into the community. This is evidenced in many ways.

This project effectively began January 2, 1998. Each of seven either existing or in-the-planning-stage NABs created here was formed as a completely new entity. None were created, as could be done alternatively, by asking an existing community organization to add a NAB as an additional program interest.

The San Jose Police Department has made major moves into community policing. A deputy district attorney has moved into one of these neighborhoods as a community prosecutor. He works from his car and from a Burger King, with a laptop, helping the community deal with crime. He handles complaints about code enforcement, about vandalism and graffiti, about family disputes. He wants to refer certain case situations to a NAB. He is opening a neighborhood office.

Community Coordinator Organizes Project

A project community coordinator organizes and trains a NAB. He recruits NAB members from the neighborhoods. Mostly they are working-class people who care about children and community; they are rank-and-file citizens, not agency professionals. NAB members are provided a stipend of $25 per evening of hearings. Some members decline the stipend. Potential members must undergo a criminal background check, but conviction of a crime is not necessarily a bar to becoming a volunteer. Potential members undergo six hours of training, with six follow-up hours of training every three months. They are asked to commit to one year of service. Depending on the extent of case referrals, a board may divide into panels of three to five members so that several hearing evenings can be scheduled in a week. Up to three cases are scheduled an evening. A translator may be required at a hearing, which can prolong the normal one-hour time allocation considerably.

Another role of the community coordinator is to locate resources which NABs draw on to assist youth (the lawyer, Stacie, is an example of such a resource). The community coordinator also organizes citizens and law enforcement officials to discuss and take actions which will lead to a safer community. He works to create neighborhood watch programs, and works on safety issues with community associations. Enhancing public safety is an additional restorative justice tenet. The result is that NAB hearings and follow-up assistance provide more than a band aid.

Youth Intervention Workers Staff the NAB

A youth intervention worker is the basic staff for a NAB. These workers are attached to community-based organizations which have contracts with the county. A worker gets the case from diversion intake, which has interviewed the juvenile and parents, recommended NAB handling, and obtained a release form for the worker to obtain school records. Only non-adjudicated juveniles are diverted to a NAB at this time.

The worker completes a home visit prior to presenting the juvenile's case at a NAB hearing. Post-hearing, the worker goes over the agreed-upon sanctions with the juvenile and parents, oversees compliance, and provides or facilitates direct helping services as may be needed. Workers' active "caseloads" vary from 25 to 37 youths. Facilitating improved educational accomplishments is an important worker agenda with a youth, as this is equated with competency development.

Victim Involvement Encouraged

Victims, now, are contacted by diversion intake to obtain restitution claims and a victim impact statement and are advised of the NAB hearing date and of their right to attend and speak. Only infrequently do victims attend these hearings, but a new emphasis more strongly encourages their participation or that of a victim surrogate who has spoken with the victim, to make a victim-oriented presentation at the hearing.

Numerous NAB members, youth intervention workers, and community coordinators have undertaken specialized training to serve as victim-offender mediators. Victims will be offered an opportunity to experience neighborhood-based victim-offender meetings.

NABs Offer Neighborhood-Focused Sanctions

Accountability is a priority of NAB sanctions and of restorative justice. This is done differently in the neighborhood. One youth joined a NAB member in painting signs that advertised a neighborhood block sale where they both lived. Several youths did their community service at a member's home, which was a foster home for babies born with an addiction to crack cocaine. Others, joined by NAB members or their youth workers, participated in community health fairs and community clean-up days.

Some youths have been assigned to feeding the homeless at nearby soup kitchens or shelters, or to join in a police department project to paint over graffiti. One youth enrolled in a 15-session leadership development program at a family resource center, and earned a stipend of $150 to be paid into his restitution account. A NAB member obtained a part-time job at a radio station for a youth who had interest in this type of career. Another NAB member took on a tutoring role with a youth. Competency development is a further by-product of efforts such as these.

A NAB CELEBRATES RESTORATIVE JUSTICE

Restorative Justice Principles Drive NAB

I sat in on a celebration of one young NAB project on June 30, 1998. It was held at a Lutheran church in the Burbank neighborhood. The probation department's restorative justice project coordinator opened the gathering and described project principles:

- Crime is an offense against human relationships.

- Victims and the community are central to justice processes.

- The first priority of justice processes is to assist victims.

- The second priority is to restore the community to the degree possible.

- The offender has personal responsibility to victims and to the community for crimes committed.

- Stakeholders share responsibilities for restorative justice through partnerships for action.

- The offender will develop improved competency and understanding as a result of the restorative justice experience.

Youth Intervention Worker Lauds Benefit of Accountability

A project youth intervention worker told the audience he receives great satisfaction from working with youth, families, and community. He is convinced it is the way to go to make a juvenile accountable the first time he does something wrong. Further, parents are grateful that "someone is giving my child a hand."

Community Members Endorse NABs

The school principal wanted to "talk from my heart. It is an honor and a blessing to play a small part in this project which presents renewal and hope. The quality of life in our neighborhood can only get better."

A mother then movingly described that she had never expected to have to deal with problems with her 13-year-old, straight-A-student son. She sobbed as she related attending a detention hearing and learning of the assault charge lodged against him. She continued, "I was told we could go to a NAB hearing, and I was shocked. Is the neighborhood coming to life? We agreed to his doing community service, to home visits and counseling by the project youth worker, and obtaining weekly school attendance and grade reports."

She added,

I've been blessed. I have a message. When we pull together as a community, we're helping our children. Later, my son said he might get into a fight. I didn't know what to do. So I called the principal, and I called the youth worker and the community coordinator, and they met with my son and the other boys. I have never seen such community support in my life. They saved and changed our lives. I only know that God was there and had sent them.

A NAB board member then addressed the audience. He had volunteered because he wanted to do something for his community. "Kids need a little bit of love and need some guidance." He likes the involvement with the family as well as the youth, and stated that his NAB recently varied its procedures to conduct deliberations in the presence of the youth and family. This was positive and is to become standard procedure with all NABs, he said. He invited "any and all of you" in the audience to become NAB board members.

Strong Support from County Officials

A member of the board of supervisors, the elected entity which governs the county, stated his pride in granting the funds to enable a NAB in four communities. He had listened during the last election when Burbank people expressed concern about juvenile crime and said they didn't think the county was listening to them. He added:

> It makes a lot of difference when I see a lot of people involved. And we've now added a public health nurse and a department of social services branch office and a community prosecutor. And we've improved street lighting, and we did lots of street and road repairs [the evening's largest applause followed this remark]. And we're going to keep doing these things.

The presiding judge of the juvenile court emphasized that our future is our children. "Hopefully," he said, "100 years from now, reaching out and helping your neighbors will be commonplace." The city councilman who represents Burbank then spoke of his support for the project.

An array of officials were introduced: The presiding judge of the family court, members and staff to the Burbank NAB and other NABs, aides to other city and county elected officials, police and sheriff's officers, the chief probation officer and a lead juvenile probation official, city and county executive department directors, the community prosecutor, the director of the neighborhood health center, members of the county juvenile justice council and the county juvenile justice commission, and a Kiwanis representative who announced a financial contribution to a different youth project in this community.

ADDITIONAL NAB PROJECTS

An intriguing idea under discussion in Santa Clara County is to have NAB members visit with neighborhood youth who are temporarily residing in the pretrial detention center or at a ranch or residential facility operated by the probation department. The approach would represent community interest and assistance to youth, communicate that neighbors care, and facilitate reintegration into the community. The purpose is not directly connected with the NAB hearing procedure, though some detained juveniles might show up at a NAB hearing.

Broadening case referral criteria to include adjudicated youth referred for a neighborhood disposition within justice system-approved guidelines is another future consideration. The NAB disposition could then lead to a ratifying court order. There is no reason this could not be accomplished within due process requirements.

There are plans, also, to implement victim panels, as are used in Norfolk, Virginia. (See Exhibit 20.1.)

WILL RESTORATIVE JUSTICE LEAD TO A SEA CHANGE?

Yes and no. Yes, in the sense that the very real beginnings of meaningful community engagement in the justice system are in evidence in many states. Yes, in the sense that implementation of restorative justice principles is changing how we look

Exhibit 20.1
Restorative Justice in Norfolk, Virginia

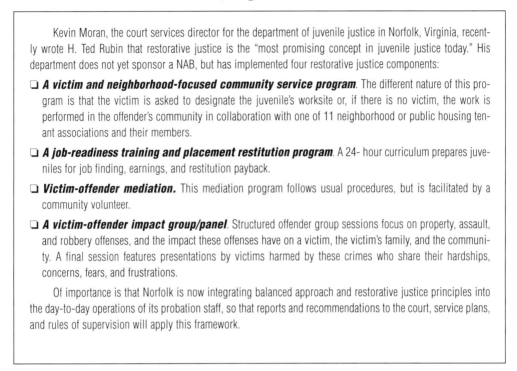

Kevin Moran, the court services director for the department of juvenile justice in Norfolk, Virginia, recently wrote H. Ted Rubin that restorative justice is the "most promising concept in juvenile justice today." His department does not yet sponsor a NAB, but has implemented four restorative justice components:

❏ *A victim and neighborhood-focused community service program.* The different nature of this program is that the victim is asked to designate the juvenile's worksite or, if there is no victim, the work is performed in the offender's community in collaboration with one of 11 neighborhood or public housing tenant associations and their members.

❏ *A job-readiness training and placement restitution program.* A 24- hour curriculum prepares juveniles for job finding, earnings, and restitution payback.

❏ *Victim-offender mediation.* This mediation program follows usual procedures, but is facilitated by a community volunteer.

❏ *A victim-offender impact group/panel.* Structured offender group sessions focus on property, assault, and robbery offenses, and the impact these offenses have on a victim, the victim's family, and the community. A final session features presentations by victims harmed by these crimes who share their hardships, concerns, fears, and frustrations.

Of importance is that Norfolk is now integrating balanced approach and restorative justice principles into the day-to-day operations of its probation staff, so that reports and recommendations to the court, service plans, and rules of supervision will apply this framework.

at the world of justice and is resulting in an enlarging consensus of different bedfellows who have begun to share a broadened and positive common ground. Yes, restorative justice has begun to take hold. Yes, there are new citizen constituencies which will seek to expand and maintain these changes.

No, in the sense that juvenile courts will not regain jurisdiction over the youth who have been swept into criminal courts as part of the ocean change of the decade of juvenile violence. No, in the sense that business as usual will still be widespread.

RESTORATIVE JUSTICE AT WORK

NABs are just one approach to restorative justice. They are being initiated in a number of California counties and in other states, but take different names. They have similarities with "juvenile conference committees," which New Jersey has used for at least 30 years. They are similar in purpose and method, also, to the "community reparations boards" of Vermont, where citizen panels in more than 20 communities enter and oversee dispositions with adult misdemeanants.

Santa Clara County's restorative justice logo contains two triangles which we know well by now. One is the public safety, juvenile accountability, and competency development triad of the earlier balanced approach to probation prototype. The second is the victim, offender, and community triad conceived more recently as an exposition of restorative justice purposes.

Different organizations and world views can embrace one, two, three, or more prongs of these two triads, and their overlaps, as well. When a community creates jobs or provides work crew contracts for delinquent youth, public safety is protected during the work experience, earnings can be applied to restore victims' losses or damage, the juvenile is held accountable, competencies are developed, and the community is an active participant in justice and in seeing that justice is done.

A NAB, in helping a youth fulfill a community service hours requirement, and in some communities working side-by-side with the youth on a community project, is taking an active part in assisting with the restoration of the community as victim, and in applying accountability and competency development precepts.

The administrative assistant to the chair of the Santa Clara County board of supervisors exclaimed to the author that, "The board is so excited there is a politically feasible way to change the juvenile justice system ... it's so politically viable it's unbelievable!" This embrace of restorative justice exemplifies the fit and wholeness of the two triangles.

Author's Note

Karen Berlin, Supervising Probation Officer, Probation Department, Santa Clara County, California, prepared the following program update.

NABS IN SANTA CLARA COUNTY, CALIFORNIA

Building Strong Relationships

Following are just a few examples of how the Restorative Justice Program (RJP) of Santa Clara County, California, continues to build stronger relationships within the community:

- "If I hadn't gone through the Restorative Justice Program (RJP), I wouldn't have achieved the success I have at my age. I thank RJP for being there." These are the words of 18-year-old Mario Garcia*, an aspiring musician and RJP graduate. Mario is in the process of completing his education and now wants to become a Neighborhood Accountability Board (NAB) member. He wants to give back to his community, after benefiting from his participation in Santa Clara County's Restorative Justice Program.

- Stewart Jones* was a victim of repeated vandalism to his vehicle. He attended the NAB conferences of the two neighborhood high school students who were caught "egging" his car, and also decided to become a NAB member.

- A NAB member was quoted in the Third Year Evaluation Report of the Program as saying, "The Program youth are our kids. It is our responsibility to assist them to live in peace with their neighbors. These kids are not Juvenile Hall, Ranch or CYA (California Youth Authority) kids, they're our kids."

---

*Mario and Stewart's names have been changed to protect their confidentiality.

The RJP began in January 1998, in response to the California Board of Corrections' challenge to each county to address and reduce juvenile crime and violence through community partnerships. The state awarded the grant to fund three areas within Santa Clara County and the Board of Supervisors quickly funded a fourth. During the next two years, expansion continued with the support of the County Board of Supervisors, who funded an additional seven areas. The funding available through the Crime Prevention Act of 2000 allowed the program to expand to encompass the entire county, having grown from the original four sites to 15 in just five years. The RJP has engaged over 500 people as NAB members, making a tremendous difference in the lives of the youth and the NAB members in the community.

The Structure of the Program Remains Relatively the Same

Youth Intervention Workers (YIWs) are hired by community-based organizations contracted by the Probation Department to provide case management throughout the 90-day contract period and to conduct competency development classes. The eight-week competency development classes focus on the themes of harm and empathy, relationships, and risk avoidance and resiliency. The YIWs also implement weekly community service projects performed by the youth.

Deputy Probation Officers (referenced as intake workers in the original article) continue to interview the youth and family to assess the youth's strengths and identify concerns for the NAB prior to the conference. They also serve as the consultants to the YIWs in casework issues.

Community Coordinators recruit the NAB members within their assigned community and assist with training. They identify community service projects for the youth to perform in their neighborhood, based upon community input. They also team up with Community Prosecutors from the District Attorney's Office to address quality of life issues, blight and code enforcement complaints, and safety programs.

The RJP, at the request of the NAB members, institutionalized the practice of having youths appear before the same NAB with whom they negotiated their contract for a closure conference. The NAB members feel a great sense of satisfaction seeing a youth's transformation at the end of the contract. NAB members also participate with the youth in the weekly community service projects and the competency development classes, and make other follow-up contacts with youths who appeared before them at the conferences.

Maintaining a Balanced and Restorative Approach

The inclusion of the victim's presence and/or voice in the NAB conference has been a challenge to the RJP since its inception. In recognition of this and the broader concern for victim services throughout the juvenile justice system, in July 2001, the Probation Department Administration created the necessary infrastructure for these services through the establishment of a Victim Services Coordinator Probation Officer and two Probation Community Worker positions. These positions support the following goals within both the NAB and formal court processes:

1. Victim participation in youth accountability;

2. Expansion of victim offender meetings;

3. Expansion of victim awareness classes; and

4. Staff training in victim awareness and restorative justice principles.

Improvements in each of these areas have already been realized within the first nine months of the existence of Victim Services.

To encourage consistency in the RJP's focus on the harm to the victim and the community, the NAB members and staff are offered continuous skill enhancement training in victim awareness, bias awareness, conflict resolution, facilitation, and communication by contracted trainers who have an expertise in these areas. In order to reinforce the principles of restorative justice, staff and community members have participated in training from both the Balanced and Restorative Justice Project (BARJ) of Florida Atlantic University and the National Institute of Corrections.

The RJP is presently in the process of forming a Victim Advisory Council, a NAB Advisory Council, and a Youth Advisory Council. These Councils will serve as a forum for these groups to share their perspectives and recommendations to the Probation Department for Program improvement. The RJP is also developing its partnership with the Cornerstone Project, a countywide collaborative whose goal is to connect youth and adults through the promotion of the 40 "Developmental Assets."[1] The Search Institute of Minneapolis identified these assets to be the experiences and values youth need to be successful.

Santa Clara County's RJP has been identified as one of the largest restorative justice programs in the United States. After just five years and rapid expansion, the RJP's accomplishments are substantial. As one NAB member stated, "The NAB is the first step towards community healing."

Endnote

[1] Search Institute (2000). *Forty developmental assets for adolescents*. Minneaplois, MN: Author.

Chapter 21

Improving Juvenile Delinquent Case Flow

EFFECTIVE CASE FLOW REQUIRES COLLABORATION

All juvenile courts want to do a good job, but many are overly content with the jobs they are doing, accept that business as usual is quite okay, and perceive that the politics of their systems prefer things as they are. However, any juvenile court that looks hard at itself and listens to its staff, members of collaborative agencies, or court clientele will discover that everything is not okay.

This chapter focuses on one element of the juvenile justice system that is often not "okay"—the flow of delinquency cases from the beginning through the end of the system—"case flow." Court management of case flow affects the work of collaborative agencies just as case flow within collaborative agencies affects the court's work and its case flow. The court and collaborative agencies, such as law enforcement, need to assess how they can individually and collectively improve delinquency case flow, and thereby better fulfill the purposes of the juvenile justice system. The beneficiaries of improved case flow are juveniles and their families, victims of juvenile offenders, the community and its public safety, and the juvenile courts themselves, as evidenced by the trust extended to them by the wider community.

WHAT IS CASE FLOW MANAGEMENT?

Case flow management is the coordination of court processes and resources to move cases in timely fashion from filing through disposition. The time between case events should be long enough to allow for preparation but short enough for juveniles to understand the connection between their behavior and the sanction for it. The court should supervise case progress and, moreover, should ensure prompt completion of work by collaborative agencies.

Early court intervention and speedy dispositions are fundamental elements of good case flow management. Minimal postponement of scheduled court hearings is another. Adhering to case processing time standards and official time lines for accomplishing court processing events is a necessary quality. A proficient monitoring and information system is an additional fundamental.

This chapter originally appeared in Juvenile Justice Update, *Vol. 7, No. 3, June/July 2001.*

My assessment of several hundred juvenile courts forms the basis for the discussion that follows. The intent of the chapter is to be practical. It calls on each juvenile justice agency to look at how its case movement might be improved in order to make the system as a whole work better. It calls attention to macroelements, such as whether law enforcement can divert lesser cases away from the court in the first place, and to microelements, such as how many days a prosecutor takes to prepare a petition or how long a probation officer takes to prepare a predisposition report.

THE VERY FRONT END: REGULATING INFORMAL AND FORMAL HANDLING OF CASES

The number of complaints or cases brought to the front door of the juvenile court has a substantial impact on case processing times. This varies by court. Rural juvenile courts often define themselves as the place to come with status and lesser offenses; rural courts frequently open their doors very wide, as alternative services may be scant. Not so with urban juvenile courts that generally want to focus on more serious and repetitive juvenile offenders.

Observations indicate more juvenile courts of all sizes have opened up in recent years to holding habitual truancy case hearings. Community protection meetings between school and juvenile justice system officials seem to have created a symbiosis in which courts agree to try to stem illegal acts by juveniles who should be in school by bringing these youth before the court. Many of these courts have become courts of early, not last, resort. Allowing this to happen has an impact on the resources available to offenders who have committed real harms. It also affects case processing time.

The School Offense Nexus

Three adjoining suburban counties in one state that the author evaluated in 2000 reflected a common front-end problem. The schools had hired school resource officers who chose to refer lesser school incidents to court. Shoving incidents were labeled batteries and other mildly disruptive behaviors were similarly given criminal labels. One county's overworked intake unit took 45 to 70 days to arrange an initial interview with these juveniles and their parents. Typically these juveniles were then placed on "informal supervision," which meant three telephone calls to the juvenile over the following three months, together with a $100 supervision fee charge.

These school matters need to be handled, but is court handling necessary? Compare this community's "culture" with others that use peer mediation, circling, school attendance review boards, or other alternative methods to solve school problems internally. These school-based programs protect the court and its limited resources from being overloaded with minor offenses and at the same time address problem behaviors directly and in a timely fashion.

The Police Referral Nexus

Like referrals from schools, police policies have a significant impact on case flow, since the police typically determine which cases will be referred to the juvenile courts for intervention and which youth will be referred for secure detention. They also control the promptness with which referrals of non-detained youth are delivered to court intake or prosecutor.

Some law enforcement agencies send almost every incident to the next processing stage, while others handle a significant number of incidents on an informal basis such as "warn and release." Some agencies overload the secure detention center with pretrial referrals, while others work with the juvenile justice system to request admission only for those who meet stringent criteria that consider offense, prior record, and risk score.

The point is that police practices are adjustable. They can be shaped or reshaped to fit better with a smart juvenile justice system. For example, police paper referrals for non-detained juveniles frequently take 10 to 12 days to reach the court. This delays and thus harms a court's accountability efforts. Regularized collaboration between key agencies of a system, preferably invoked by the lead judge, is a prerequisite to achieving model practices.

The Detention Nexus

The cases of children in detention take case flow priority. Because a juvenile's freedom has been taken away, state laws and rules allow less time between processing events for detained juveniles. A slower time frame is permitted to process the cases of juveniles who are not detained, including those released at detention hearings. When detention is overloaded, more cases must be processed in the fastest manner and this can overtax resources.

While processing times for non-detained youth are frequently absent from statute or rule, courts should delineate their own guidelines for these cases and then collect data to measure compliance with them. Should juveniles who are placed on electronic monitoring or home detention/supervision be positioned on the fast processing track or the slower one? Practice varies. I prefer the former. Since both involve a partial deprivation of freedom, quick resolution is valuable for both the youth and the system. Similarly, detained youth from out of the area should be placed on a fast track for arraignment and adjudication, then quickly transferred to the home community for disposition.

The Intake Nexus

Intake, which used to be the sole preserve of juvenile court intake officers, is often now shared with or transferred to prosecutors. In some states, intake officers retain sole control over diversion and informal and formal handling of all cases. Elsewhere they retain this authority only over lesser offenses, or are limited to screening cases and providing the prosecutor with a file/no file recommendation in all cases. In a significant number of states, intake is bypassed completely, and the prosecutor has sole control over the decision to file a case.

However organized, the intake process should be expeditious. However organized, it should maximize diversion and informal handling. This should permit more prompt handling of the reduced number of formal cases that will then proceed to a judge or magistrate. Prosecutors with enhanced intake powers need to examine the nature and extent of diversion and informal handling in their systems. Prosecutors often do not want to add professional intake staff to their operation, yet are not typically linked to community agencies, as traditional intake staffs have been. Although prosecutors may divert or elect not to file charges in cases that lack prosecutorial merit or which are *de minimus*, they too often appear to opt for formal process. They should approve increased diversion and use probation intake staff to arrange and monitor this.

CASE SCHEDULING

The Juvenile Court Zoo

There are still courts that require everybody to be in court at 8:30 a.m. Parties, witnesses, lawyers, and probation and police officers arrive and then wait. A case is called, and everyone else waits. Another case is called, and so on. At 11:30 a.m., some people are informed their cases have been continued to another day for one reason or another. This is not the way to win friends for the juvenile court. Family members lose wages, the public pays added costs for private appointed counsel, many people waste time.

The better way is careful judicial calendar management. Some cases can be set for 8:30 a.m., others for 10 a.m., and still others for 1:00 p.m. How many cases of what type and at what processing stage can be handled in each short block of time can and should be determined and taken into account when cases are scheduled. Also, courts should assess the length of time cases in their waiting rooms wait until their hearing (known as "wait time"), and take steps to improve efficiency.

Continuances Delay Case Flow

Many courts are far too casual about continuing scheduled hearings. Some courts allow staff members to grant continuances, but better practice requires the approval of a judicial officer. Continuances may be granted because a party or witness fails or is unable to appear, a police officer has not been notified, an attorney is unprepared, a psychological evaluation or a drug evaluation or a gun and bullet assessment is incomplete, a placement plan is delayed, a judge is diverted by other matters, and so on.

Continuances are costly. The meters are running. Lots of people are inconvenienced. Court clerks have to redo various paper work. A juvenile's anxiety is not assuaged. One expert suggests a continuance rate of 15%-20% should be the maximum allowable from the first appearance onward. Courts should record and measure their continuance rate, keeping track of who requests a continuance; why; the type of hearing; the number of requests; and the percentage granted or denied. With this information, an enlightened court can initiate and monitor improvements.

MANAGING FORMAL COURT PROCESSING

Speed Should Not Compromise Fairness

While speed is important, a process may be too speedy. There are courts that reportedly combine a detention hearing with a plea hearing, adjudication, and disposition. This is too much, too quickly. It also probably excludes defense lawyers or co-opts them from zealously representing their clients.

Other courts combine pleas at arraignment with dispositions. In these cases, the predisposition study is conducted early by intake or probation staff (a procedure that should be permitted only with the informed consent of the juvenile). It also may be done on the spot at a court hearing and be based essentially on offense and prior record, or it may be waived. Combining adjudication and disposition, one after the other on the same day, is the most expeditious process a court can use. It is legal and widely used, and holds numerous benefits; however, not all courts accept this as a standard procedure, and it can compromise much.

True Bifurcation of Disposition and Adjudication Has Many Benefits

Separating plea or adjudication from a disposition on a later date is the ideal due process model. While it takes more time to reach closure, it affords an opportunity to investigate and prepare a full predisposition report (PDR) that should enable better-informed dispositions. It allows for a psychological evaluation to be conducted in appropriate cases.

True bifurcation addresses the legal argument that a PDR should not be initiated before guilt is officially admitted or established. It avoids invading the privacy of a juvenile whose charge is withdrawn or not proven.

Bifurcated hearings should not overly delay case flow. Courts that practice true bifurcation must assess the impact of the practice on case flow. These courts should assess whether more cases can or should be diverted or handled informally. Prosecutors and defenders should be encouraged to weigh cases carefully and, early on, deal out the numerous cases which face predictable sanctions. Experienced prosecutors and defenders know it is far more efficient to dispose of cases at a front-end hearing rather than after two or three hearings.

When hearings are bifurcated, a time line of three weeks to disposition is ideal, giving probation investigators time to prepare and file their reports. When a longer time line may be necessary, this should not exceed four weeks.

Overuse of Psychological Evaluations May Delay Dispositions

Numerous courts fail to target the purposes of an evaluation and thus encourage testing that is not needed, resulting in reports that are too long and that take too much time to complete. Psychologists, private or court-based, should comply with reasonable but short time lines for conducting evaluations.

POST-DISPOSITIONAL MATTERS

Managing Probation Services and Violations

Another matter that affects case flow management in those court systems where an intake officer or PDR investigator prepares the PDR is how speedily a new probationer has a first face-to-face contact with the field probation officer. In many courts, there is a gap of several weeks. Ideally, however, this meeting should take place the day of disposition or within a few days of it.

Technical violations of probation conditions regularly abound. Should these children be returned to court routinely? No. Should they be returned to court selectively? Yes. With what degree of selectivity? Significant. Prompt attention to violations is important. In keeping with judicially approved policy, but without judicial hearing, probation officers (POs) should have authority to intensify supervision, add electronic monitoring, impose community service hours that were ordered but suspended, expand urinalysis requirements, add additional program requirements, or schedule administrative hearings to be held by supervisors. In short, POs should be able to adjust conditions of probation quickly or to take other actions so long as they do not deprive the youth of freedom.

Setting Restitution Hearings

In some courts the practice at the disposition hearing is to reserve restitution to allow probation or the prosecutor to obtain victim claim documentation. Ideally, this should be done prior to the disposition hearing so that restitution can be set at that time. Otherwise, the court should set a specific time and date for this hearing. Another alternative is to allow the victim and juvenile to agree in writing on the sum to be paid and to submit this agreement to the court to be entered as a court order. This ensures that victims receive restitution and that juveniles are held accountable.

Expediting Dispositional Placements

Slowdowns frequently occur in placing detained juveniles into residential care. This, in turn, may further detention center overcrowding. Expedited protocols should be developed and followed to locate and move youth quickly into appropriate placements. This includes using a variety of non-residential services. The conventional wisdom is that each jurisdiction should have available a continuum of services of varying intensities and program emphases. Day reporting centers, day treatment, electronic monitoring combined with wraparound services, culturally competent and specific services, intensive supervision, tracking, and more can substitute for 24-hour placements for many youth.

Courts that are authorized to sentence youth to pretrial detention centers do not need to assign the maximum allowable time period. Though a statute may authorize 30 or 45 days, why not use 10—or authorize a review team to evaluate placements after 15 days and advise the court to suspend or continue the sentence?

Curbing Commitment Wait Time

Court commitments to the state youth agency lead to same-day transfers in some jurisdictions but month-long waits in others. Where transfer is delayed, with its attendant impact on the pretrial detention center population, there should be intensive analysis of each step in the process. Is the judicial commitment order prepared the same day as the hearing or a week later? Is the order faxed to the state agency the day it is ordered or mailed a week later? Is the state's approval of placement mailed or faxed? Is it directed to the official who can arrange transport that day or to another official whose subsequent transfer of the approval to the official who can take action takes another day or two? A day here and a day there and you are talking real time.

Data, Data, Data: The Importance of Collecting Information

If smaller courts lack data gathering capability on case processing time, they should seek assistance from their state court administrative offices to obtain these numbers. Other courts should clock these times and gather and review these data at least annually. Police, probation intake personnel , prosecutors, probation PDR writers, and field supervisors should develop their own time line data as well. Systematic or sample data can tell them much.

The courts are central to case processing. They need to take the leadership in promoting data gathering system-wide and in using the data to identify obstacles to be addressed to achieve more efficient case flow. Case flow management goes on forever, but active cases should not.

Chapter 22

Thoughts on Improving Juvenile Court Dispositions

WHO DO JUDGES LISTEN TO?

The San Diego public defender announced, "We accept the recommendations of the probation officer's social study except for number three. Hector should not be required to live in that group home, which is far away from his high school. He should be allowed to stay with a family who is friends of his family, and remain in his present school district."

The judge disagreed. He ordered placement in a group home, participation in an alcohol/drug program, a 9 p.m. curfew except for attendance at the program, staying "clean" of alcohol and drugs, and additional, standard conditions of probation. The judge continued the matter for a month, and ordered the probation officer to investigate the home of the friends of the family, and report back at the next hearing.

Hector, 17 years and 8 months old and in court for a non-serious reoffense, asked for and was granted permission to speak. He told the judge why it was better for him to live with that family. He could not live with his mother, who was having severe problems with her life and would not let him stay at home. He had monthly income, from his deceased father's Social Security, and could pay for his care with the family. He described the family favorably and convincingly.

The judge shifted his disposition, authorized Hector to move in with the family, and ordered the probation officer (PO) to investigate the home and report back at a hearing rescheduled for two weeks from that date.

Studies show an extremely high correlation between what a predisposition report (PDR) or social study recommends, and what a judge orders. But here, a sensitive judge listened and made a contrary decision, right or wrong. Another judge didn't listen, some years ago, and was reversed for not allowing a boy's parents to address the court at disposition. All they wanted to do was speak about their son (**Matter of Raoul P.**, #11020, First Judicial Dept., New York, May 6, 1966).

Everyone in juvenile justice—particularly the juvenile offender—knows the dispositional hearing is an enormously important decision point. Its architecture and form vary: Probation staff frequently control it, but prosecution and defense counsel negotiations and arguments may dominate. A hearing may take two minutes or 30 minutes. There are hybrid structures and other patterns.

This chapter originally appeared in Juvenile Justice Update, *Vol. 3, No. 3, June/July 1997.*

DISTINCTIONS OF THE JUVENILE COURT DISPOSITIONAL HEARING

The concept of the dispositional (or disposition) hearing has been a distinguishing feature of juvenile versus criminal justice. The distinction has been more than a euphemism, representing a more holistic consideration of resources and strategies that might be employed to reshape a juvenile. The adult court stereotype is of law-trained officials dictating the sentence, with the offender being asked curtly, "Is there anything you'd like to say to the court?" Further, the physical design of many juvenile courtrooms has been structured to curb the fear of an "almighty" jurist, and to invite participatory hearings. There are three dimensions to a disposition: the timing, the nature of the hearing itself, and the nature of judicial orders.

A nationally prominent Minneapolis juvenile court judge in 1974 penned a hyperbolic description of the dispositional hearing.

> This is where it is! This is why there is a juvenile court! This is the Golden Rule at its ultimate: the organized power of society, offering not its revenge on a criminal who has dared to offend it but its massive help to a child who will be a citizen. Help for tomorrow, not punishment for yesterday. This is the epitome![1]

Today's application of Judge Arthur's Golden Rule has punitive as well as helpful intent. In some courts the application is done artistically and in others it is done mechanistically.

IS THERE HELP TODAY?

Common juvenile code provisions authorize probation, restitution and community service, substance abuse treatment, residential care, state commitment, and more.

Colorado, one of several states that has legislated juvenile code euphemisms out of its laws, now uses the statutory term "sentencing hearing" to describe this part of the juvenile process. A 1996 Colorado report belies Judge Arthur's promise of "massive help." If there is to be any help at all there, it must come from other than juvenile POs, whose average caseloads were officially reported at 110 cases (and adult caseloads at 160 cases)!

Some San Diego juveniles will get some help, along with surveillance, for a while. In San Diego, intensive supervision POs have average caseloads of 39 juveniles, and the "Aftercare & Project 8%" caseloads averaged just 17 juveniles per officer as of April 1, 1996. Project 8% targets offenders who, unless there is successful intervention, will account for a vastly disproportionate amount of repeat offenses. However, 2,127 San Diego juveniles were on "banked" caseloads (California's term) assigned to a total of just four officers, i.e., 532 juveniles per PO! Due to banked caseloads, California counties now keep their money in the bank.

ORDERS BEYOND THE BASICS

Contemporary juvenile codes have added many potential judicial orders to the dispositional grab bag. Michigan, for example, authorizes fines and court costs, as well as orders against parents to refrain from conduct the court determined has caused or tended to cause the youth's offenses.

Florida judges may revoke or suspend a juvenile's driving license. I don't like this open-ended provision, though judges do. I would prefer to restrict curtailment of driving privileges to offenses that are automobile-related. The judge may also order a juvenile and his/her parents to perform community service, which may or may not enhance the juvenile-parent relationship, and might not be upheld as constitutional.

New Mexico, more appropriately, does not give the judge the authority to order parents to perform community service, but does approve requiring parents to submit to counseling, participate in any probation or treatment program ordered by the court, and pay for the cost of a juvenile's out-of-home care based on their financial ability.

Dispositions to Secure Facilities

Some statutes allow a disposition to a local secure pretrial detention center, a practice that detention administrators tend to loathe. Virginia approves this not just for the usual 30-day period, but for a period of up to six months.

Florida, like California and other states, restricts the length of commitment to a state youth agency; commitment may not exceed the time an adult may serve for the same offense. This is a good principle, and it attempts to end indeterminate sentencing, based on equal protection tenets. But a number of appellate courts have upheld laws that provide that a juvenile might serve more time than an adult. The courts' rationale was that the purpose of state institutionalization of juveniles is rehabilitation and not punishment, a justification that many juveniles might find difficult to accept. (See, e.g., **State v. Rice**, 655 P. 2d 1145 (Wash. 1982); **Maricopa Cty Juv. Action**, 621 P. 2d 298 (Ct. App. Ariz. 1980).)

The New Sweep of Juvenile Court Dispositions

Of course, there are the recent hard-line statutes, such as in Texas, where the legislature allows juvenile court judges to sentence a juvenile to a combined term in juvenile and adult facilities which now can extend to 40 years! New Mexico juvenile court judges can apply criminal sentences to youthful offenders convicted of several categories of very serious or chronic felony offenses. Montana modeled its "Extended Jurisdiction Prosecution" Act after a similar Act in Minnesota, and blends a juvenile disposition with a stayed adult sentence. On violation, the adult sentence is executed.

SHOULD INITIATING THE PDR BE DEFERRED UNTIL AFTER ADJUDICATION?

Historically and today, a significant number of juvenile courts hold the predisposition report hearing immediately following the entry of a plea of admission. Prior to the hearing, typically at the intake juncture, there has been an informal admission by the juvenile, and parental or attorney approval to proceed to the PDR.

Value of Early Hearings

There are two pluses to holding combined, early hearings:

1. The time involved from when the sanction is administered and the juvenile becomes aware of it until the intervention is initiated is telescoped.

2. The court's calendar is expedited and the backlog of cases is reduced.

Problems of Early Hearings

Arguments against the early hearing are usually made by defense counsel and probation managers. Defense lawyers can make a strong due process argument that no PDR investigation should be initiated until after there has been a formal finding of a violation of law. To do otherwise, they argue, would result in knowledge by schools and others of the juvenile's alleged offense, when the case may be dismissed or go unproven.

Some probation managers prefer the time separation between hearings. Performing a PDR is time wasted when there is no adjudication. But the time frame they like—four to six weeks from adjudication to dispositional hearing in order to complete PDR reports for the hearing—is difficult to justify as a general practice, whether for detained or non-detained juveniles.

STATUTORY TIME SPANS TO DISPOSITION

Many state laws now prescribe case processing timelines. Typically the statutes require speedier processing for detained juveniles, both to adjudication and to disposition. California law e.g., provides that for detained youths, an adjudicatory hearing must take place within 15 court days of the detention hearing, and a disposition within 10 court days of the adjudication. For non-detained youth, adjudication must take place within 30 calendar days of the filing of the petition, and disposition within 30 calendar days following adjudication. California PDR investigators, then, can fast-track studies of detained juveniles, and slow-track the others. It would be preferable, of course, if they would fast-track all investigations.

Another time-related issue is how soon the report must be filed prior to the dispositional hearing. Good attorneys want to get the report ahead of time so they can confirm a report's findings and recommendations, and investigate alternative proposals. State laws may require filing the report three to five days prior to the hearing, but often reports come to the court the morning of the hearing, in accordance with local practice.

POs don't like to show the PDR to the juvenile or his or her family. They grudgingly accept defense counsel's obtaining a copy of the report. They are like doctors who will tell you the highlights of your illness, but become almost apoplectic when you demand the written report about your body. But virtue lies in full sharing, and in preparing PDRs that can be shared.

Probation managers would be wise to collect sample data on how long it takes from the notification to prepare a PDR to the date the PDR is filed, for both detained and non-detained juveniles. It would also make sense to collect data on the average amount of time required by POs to do PDRs. Probation managers should conduct a systematic review, in concert with judges, prosecutors, and defense attorneys, of the validity and practicability of the present format and content of the PDR, and evaluate whether a shorter form report will be appropriate for some case types.

THE NATURE OF THE DISPOSITIONAL HEARING

Who Attends the Hearing

Typically, statutes do not specify who must attend the dispositional hearing, other than a judicial officer, the juvenile, and the parents. There are courts where no probation officer attends the hearing unless officially requested, but in most courts the PO who prepared the report, or a PO who represents report preparers, attends all dispositions. I have seen prosecutors and defense attorneys always present, and in other cases, never present.

An active PO presence is vital to this hearing. I like to see lots of people present and participating in these hearings. I want the judge, always, to engage the juvenile and the family in the problems and their remediation. I like to see other family members there, and ministers, and school officials, and community center directors, and substance abuse counselors, and more.

Whose Hearing Is This?

Too often the attorneys and PO monopolize the judge with their "mumbo-jumbo" and shorthand language. The people whose freedom and custody are at stake should understand everything that is said, and all that takes place. This is a hearing and it should be inclusive. Sufficient time should be allowed to enable a real hearing, and it is incumbent upon the judge to create a comfortable ambiance.

It is certainly all right for the judge to tell the juvenile that he or she did wrong, and that consequences must follow. It is not all right for the judge to ask, ask again, and keep asking an inexpressive youth why he or she committed the act. And, it is all right for the judge to spell out several alternative sanctions and remediations, and to ask the youth which are more appropriate and why, or whether the youth can suggest another direction.

Most courts still move cases into the courtroom one at a time. This privacy allows the judge to make the most of the hearing. However, in other courts, full engagement of participants in the case being deliberated is handicapped because half of the morning docket remains sitting behind the bar.

THE NATURE OF DISPOSITIONAL ORDERS

National data show probation in juvenile cases to be the most common disposition (56%). Another 12% of dispositions involve such requirements as restitution, community service, fines, or entry into a treatment or counseling program with "minimal continuing supervision by probation staff." Further, probation department involvement is inherent in many of the 28% of dispositions that result in out-of-home residential placements, except for placements that involve commitments to the state youth agency. The final 4% of dispositions are described as cases "dismissed or the youth was otherwise released."[2]

We know that the services administered by a juvenile probation department vary widely. Some are confined to PDR investigations and reports, field supervision, and intake decision making, although even this role has been eliminated or reduced in states that have placed prosecutors in the front-end determination of whether a law enforcement referral should result in a petition. The nature and extent of programs administered by probation, the right arm of the court, affects the direction judges may take at disposition.

Some are responsible for the detention facility (Tucson), home detention/supervision (Kalamazoo, MI), all-day school/work (Grand Rapids, MI), small group homes (Fairfax, VA), large group facilities (Houston), a boot camp (Cleveland), probation camps or ranches (California), the juvenile parole function (North Carolina), and other program interventions.

Dispositions to Residential Programs

A disposition may be to an out-of-home—sometimes out-of-state—institutional program. During August 1996, 70 San Diego juveniles were in placement at the Arizona Boys Ranch, at an annual cost for each youth of $44,796. Another 13 youths were in residence at the Visionquest program in Arizona.

Juvenile court judges in Los Angeles rely enormously on the 18 camps operated by the probation agency. During 1995, an army of 5,388 juveniles was dispatched to those sites, 41% of all dispositions. Another 814 (6%) were committed to the California Youth Authority (CYA), and 1,348 (10%) were ordered into a "suitable placement." Thus, the total of Los Angeles out-of-home placements far exceeded the national average.

Los Angeles out-of-home placements exceeded those in San Francisco, also. San Francisco's one camp facility, Log Cabin Ranch, located 40 miles southwest of the city, received 96 boys (7%) in 1995. Another 181 delinquent youth (13%) went into different out-of-home placements. The CYA received 26 San Franciscans. Los Angeles camp placements average 23 weeks; the San Francisco expectation is a year's stay.

Rural America Also Needs an Array of Resources

All of this might not mean much to juvenile justice professionals in rural America or in low resource areas, but it can and should. What every juvenile court needs is an array of community-based services to draw on, from low intensity to high intensity, and residential programs when needed. We want to curb our state commitments by filling in the space between almost nothing and the end of the line.

Every juvenile court is part of a state court system, and every juvenile probation agency or community correctional program has some connection to a state entity. A youth who is not able to be handled in the community will be handled at the state level. So the state has an interest in what even locally funded probation and community corrections can and cannot do. Many states assist local programming with funding or resources, but states may have to be educated on this issue. Your state should do this and your juvenile court should have the array of options it needs.

EXCERPTS FROM DISPOSITIONAL HEARINGS

In conclusion, the following are notes I recorded while watching two dispositional hearings, along with a third judge's description of one of his more memorable hearings. These demonstrate the incongruities in juvenile disposition hearings.

An Atlanta judge, in 1983, on reviewing a boy she had placed into the detention center for a short sentence:

> *Judge: What did you learn from the two books you read?*
>
> *Boy: I learned all about O.J. Simpson and what a great football player he was and what a great man he is.*
>
> *Judge (smiling): Did the books say anything about staying out of trouble? Being honest? Working hard?*
>
> *Boy: They taught me how to be good.*
>
> *Judge: Did you learn you could have a good time without getting into trouble?*
>
> *Boy: Yes, ma'am.*
>
> *Judge: All right young man. That's fine. You will now go onto probation.*

A Miami judge mulled a staff recommendation that he place a boy at the Dade Marine Institute, a residential program with an emphasis on marine education and sea experiences. The public defender opposed the plan.

> *Judge (to boy): Are you interested in boats and snorkels?*
>
> *Boy: No, I bake doughnuts.*
>
> *Public Defender: He has worked three years at Dunkin' Donuts.*
>
> *Judge (to boy, spoofing): Can you dunk doughnuts with a snorkel?*
>
> *Judge (to boy, serious): I'm sending you to the Marine Institute.*

A Salt Lake City judge recounts:

> *I was working on this kid to get him anxious when outside the courtroom there were voices calling out, 'Kick him! Kill him!' This kid's eyes kept getting bigger and bigger! As the hearing ended, I went outside. There was my colleague, Judge L., and the county attorney chasing after a mouse!*

Endnotes

[1] Arthur, L. G. & Gauger, W. A. (1974). *Disposition hearings: The heartbeat of the juvenile court*. Reno, NV: National Council of Juvenile Court Judges, p. ix.

[2] Butts, J. (1996). *Offenders in juvenile court, 1993*. Washington, DC: Office of Juvenile Justice and Delinquency Prevention.

Part 4

Community Intervention Programs

What everyone wants is to have intervention with juvenile offenders succeed so that these youths move ahead into constructive lives. Everyone knows that there are failures. Everyone might not know there are many successes.

MAJOR PROBLEM REQUIRES MAJOR COMMUNITY RESOURCES

The public expects too much of juvenile courts. The public is not aware of the problems numerous court juveniles present. The public tends not to see the human faces and life experiences presented by some who enter the court's doorway. Court juveniles' problems include broken families, dysfunctional families, drug addicted parents, serious neglect by parents, violent victimization, violence within the family and other violence witnessed in life, sexual abuse, severe psychological problems, crime-ridden neighborhoods, grinding poverty, school failure and intelligence inferiority complex, gang membership, drug and alcohol use, low self esteem, sexual promiscuity, prostitution, and much more—and many of them in combination. Some juveniles who come to the juvenile delinquency doorway of the court present only a fraction of these problems. But all juveniles who enter this doorway have been apprehended for one or more offenses, from mild to middle range to severe.

Juvenile courts labor hard to increase successes. But they cannot do the job by themselves. The courts must and do turn to community agencies to help these youth: family counseling services, agencies that provide parenting or anger management classes, job placing agencies, mental health services and practitioners, drug and alcohol evaluation and treatment resources, the Boys and Girls Clubs and neighborhood community centers, Big Brothers and Big Sisters or other mentoring organizations, school guidance counselors, group homes, residential treatment facilities, and more. The courts turn to the parents and to relatives and ask for their help. In turn the parents and relatives ask the probation officer to help their youth.

But the conclusion of any professional or community conference that reviews juvenile justice issues is that more resources are needed. However, sufficient, effective resources will never be available.

BROAD RANGE OF PROGRAMMING

The juvenile justice world has not been passive. Much innovation has taken place. There are program developments that hold promise. Many probation departments distinguish between offenders and seek to target their resources and apply differential interventions with different types of youths and youth problems. There is more careful measurement of the risks presented by individual juveniles. There is also better measurement of their needs, along with efforts to arrange to meet these needs. Computers have provided databases that aid court and juvenile justice system operations and enable better record information.

Federal, state, community, and some private dollars have expanded in-community program options. Probation staff training, in-house and at local, state, and national levels, has better clarified what appears to work and what doesn't seem to work, and has transferred what is termed "best practices" to many juvenile justice systems across the land. Demonstration projects have been implemented and evaluated. Research findings have been helpful to understanding and practice.

Failure has been a teacher.

Everyone believes in prevention. Prevention efforts are all over this country, but, of course, there is never enough prevention. Prevention efforts, from school counseling and tutoring to good foster parents to recreational and youth development activities and to job skills training and much more strengthen youth capacities and positive preparation for adulthood. But approximately 1.2 million juveniles charged with a delinquent offense are referred for handling by juvenile courts annually, and because individual juveniles may be involved in more than one case in a year, the annual estimated number of juveniles' cases referred to these courts approximates 1.8 million.[1]

Part 4 focuses on services to juveniles retained in the community, while Part 5 will center on juveniles committed to state institutions who normally proceed to an aftercare or parole experience. However, the dividing line between community-level and state-level services is not an absolute. Programs such as boot camps and those for sex offenders may serve either non-committed or committed youth, depending upon the jurisdiction. Private residential treatment centers for significantly emotionally disturbed youth, not elaborated on in this section, may receive juveniles directly from a court or following a court commitment to the state where, after evaluation, the state may place the youth in this type of facility based on a state-residential facility contract.

Probation is the starting point for looking at community-level programs for adjudicated offenders. Some departments provide only basic probation services but tap external community agencies to expand on these offerings. Other probation agencies provide more programs under their own umbrella or administration.

A narrative of the unusually expansive program offerings of one juvenile probation department is described below. This is followed by descriptive examples of other community-level programs for court juveniles.

FAIRFAX COUNTY, VIRGINIA, JUVENILE AND DOMESTIC RELATIONS DISTRICT COURT

The Fairfax County Juvenile and Domestic Relations District Court in Fairfax, Virginia, a populous (900,000-plus inhabitants) and continuously growing county that appends Washington, DC, receives and services juvenile as well as certain adult cases such as non-support and domestic violence-related matters. It is not a family court per se, as it lacks jurisdiction over divorce. Its FY 1999 report describes vast juvenile services administered by this court agency. Other court and probation departments need to find many of these resources under other agencies' umbrellas, a fact that often slows and complicates referrals of court youths to these external organizations. Court programs include:

- *Psychological Services*—Essentially evaluations.

- *Diagnostic Team*—Court and community agency professionals review difficult cases, usually juveniles who have failed to respond to community-level treatment, and report recommendations to the judge.

- *Family Counseling Program*—Two eight-hour seminars are offered four times a year to families experiencing problems with a child's behavior and other family relationship concerns.

- *Juvenile Traffic School*—This court, unlike most juvenile courts, is the basic court for traffic offenders up to age 18. It handled 5,406 traffic complaints in FY 1999 while delinquency complaints totaled 5,097.

- *Citizen Volunteer Services*—Volunteers serve as probation and parole aides, aides at residential facilities, interviewers, community service supervisors, restitution aides, and special activities leaders.

- *Special Placement Services*—Assessment and Planning Teams seek to ensure that out-of-home placement is essential and then focus resources on the least restrictive placement when removal is necessary. Placement coordinators provide casework services to placed youths and provide aftercare supervision on return to the community.

- *Work Training Program*—Probationers age14 to 18 become trainees at county government and non-profit agencies for 10 to 20 hours a week for up to six months, and are paid for the hours worked.

- *Community Service Project*—Youth are assigned a certain number of hours based on offense seriousness and number of offenses. Work is performed at public and non-profit agencies. Also, court volunteer-supervised "mini" sites operate on weekends for juveniles referred for technical probation violations.

- *Four Alternative Schools*—The court provides the facilities and administrative support, with each school handling eight to 10 students who are on probation supervision. The county public school entity furnishes the teachers, books, and supplies.

- *Girls Probation House*—This is a "family oriented, long-term" treatment facility that serves up to 12 residents 14 to 18 years of age. The five-level program is based on behavior modification; positive peer culture; individual, group, and family counseling sessions; and a bi-weekly parent group. There is a school on the grounds.

- *Boys Probation House*—Two programs are centered here: (1) a 9- to12-month therapeutic program for 16 boys, age 14 to 17, that emphasizes behavior modification; personal responsibility; individual, group, and family counseling; public health education; and the use of local mental health and substance abuse treatment services, and (2) Transitional Living, a 5- to 6-month pre-independent living program for six boys, 17- to 18-years-old, who are required to work full time while pursuing their education and experiencing a curriculum associated with living on their own. Supervision and supportive services are provided to residents for 60 days following program completion.

- *Probation Supervision Services*—These are decentralized at three locations in the county.

- *Juvenile Detention Center*—Traditionally a pre-dispositional holding facility, two 12-bed units were added in 1998 for post-dispositional sentencing and treatment. This increased the overall bed total to 121 beds.

- *Less Secure Shelter*—This non-secure residential facility serves pre-dispositional short-term juveniles and post-dispositional youth placed into the four-month intermediate residential program that seeks to forestall longer-term and more costly residential durations.

- *Supervised Release Services*—Largely a tracking and monitoring program for pre-dispositional juveniles who might otherwise be held in the detention center, this program also includes some youth ordered into its intensive supervision and service provision at the judicial disposition hearing. Staff contact juveniles four times weekly at home, school, or employment, and have at least weekly contact with parents.

Fairfax County juveniles caught in the juvenile justice web are extremely fortunate to live in this county. The court, with financial assistance from the state, works to retain its youth within the county rather than commit them to more costly state facilities away from a youth's familiar surroundings. Indeed, the state of Virginia provided the court with nearly $6 million in FY 1999 to subsidize its array of residential services.

A detention center expansion of 24 beds to receive and work with sentenced juveniles will result in a further decrease in state commitments that appears to have peaked in FY 1996 at 125, then decreased to 103, 105, and 93 during the following three years.

The court does measure and report certain case-flow data that reflect slowness in case movement. For complaints that specify the date of an alleged offense, 39 days elapse from the offense to the date of its handling by intake staff, and there is a 47-day lapse from the date a judge orders a predisposition report to the date the report is completed. However, probation supervision averages 335 days, a duration that is difficult to evaluate without more intensive examination of a variety of relevant factors.

INTENSIVE PROBATION SERVICES PROGRAM IN COOK COUNTY (CHICAGO), ILLINOIS

Intensive probation supervision (IPS) programs are common across the country, though their structure and implementation elements differ. The Cook County juvenile court's program description that follows is drawn from its year 2000 summary of programs and initiatives.

The IPS mission is to provide

comprehensive services and structured supervision to high risk minors within a sound framework of public safety. In partnership with the community and the minor's family, IPS officers promote the opportunities for personal growth and change through expanded services, increased contact and elevated standards of accountability with enhanced expectations of compliance.[2]

IPS probationers are non-violent but high-risk offenders who could otherwise be committed to the state, as well as juveniles diverted from residential placement or on aftercare status following residential placement.

IPS is a team effort; a three-person team of probation officers works with a case-load fixed at 40 juveniles. Case coverage extends over a 14-hour day with 24/7 capacities for emergency services.

The IPS experience begins with home confinement, except for school, counseling sessions, and activities involving direct parental supervision. In time, the confinement requirement is relaxed. All probationers must be engaged in some form of educational program, perform a community service requirement, and earn funds to pay off any restitution requirement. Violations of IPS requirements result in returns to home confinement or an added community service requirement.

A three-person team offers advantages over intensive probation programs that use just one probation officer for this purpose. The 14-hour coverage and activity by staff is attractive. Not all probation departments use probation officers exclusively for this type of program. There are advantages when one team member is an indigenous para-professional who knows the streets and hangouts of these youths and can relate to them in a very knowing way. Finally, while other IPS programs will return a rule violator to the detention center as a sanction, Cook County deliberately avoids this as it seeks to keep a lid on its detention center capacity and has found alternatives to such short-term incapacitation.

ASSOCIATED MARINE INSTITUTES OF FLORIDA AND OTHER STATES

What began in 1969 as a single marine-oriented program for delinquent youth in Ft. Lauderdale, Florida, is now a 48-site program in seven states (Florida, Georgia, Louisiana, New Mexico, South Carolina, Texas, Virginia) and the Cayman Islands. Depending on the particular site, the program uses the ocean, rivers and lakes, and wilderness experiences as a curriculum to challenge juveniles to accomplish adventurous achievements that can lead, following program completion, to abiding by the law.

Typically, a marine institute is a day treatment program, though it is a seven-day-a-week school and treatment program for juvenile law violators 14- to 18-years-old who are referred by a state department of juvenile justice. Typically, the state department underwrites a significant percentage of program costs. Institutes are non-profit entities. The national headquarters for Associated Marine Institutes (AMI) is Tampa. Each institute places two members on the national board.

These institutes emphasize education. They stress that academic success comes first. Like so many juvenile justice programs, they service young people who are far behind in school and basic skill levels and feel a resultant frustration. A primary goal is to improve core academic skills such as reading comprehension, mathematics, and language. AMI uses a student/instructor ratio of seven to one to raise academic proficiency. Some students are later referred for preparation for a GED examination. Some go on to a vocational school or even a college experience.

Academic and vocational education is supplemented at ocean-related institutes with curricula in oceanography, earth sciences, scuba diving, boat handling, maintenance and repair of marine equipment, seamanship, and aquatics, as well as physical education. Students experience boating trips. They contribute work to community environmental projects such as beach restoration, clean-ups, and re-vegetation.

Graduates of this five- to six-month program are placed back into an educational or employment environment. Aftercare is a program component, and provides a support system for the student and family. Post-program recidivism has long been among the lowest of programs funded by the Florida Department of Juvenile Justice.

Adventure-type rehabilitation programs have been on the juvenile justice menu for more than 30 years. The AMI program has been one of the most prominent. Some of its youth receive preparation for a vocational career in a marine industry, and while the sea is an exciting (though also educational) component of its curriculum, AMI has placed more and more stress on its basic educational curriculum as its follow-up assessments reflect that recidivism is directly affected by the level of education its students achieve.

Certain adventure-type programs have involved delinquent youths in conquering difficult physical and, thereby, emotional experiences, Outward Bound programs being among the first. VisionQuest, a well-known program for court youth in several states, headquartered in Arizona, has long stressed physical challenges. Indeed, many state delinquency institutions provide planful adventure experiences into the mountains or the wilderness, as do some local community correctional programs. Adventure experiences for youth appeal to legislators, state funding entities, foundations, charitable contributors, and most juveniles. But AMI and other programs know that it takes more than successful adventure ordeals to mend youth and prepare them well for the future.

CALIFORNIA PROBATION CAMPS

Probation departments in California often administer residential programs known as camps or ranches. One is the 24-bed Sonoma County Probation Camp at Healdsburg, 66 miles north of San Francisco. The program has all the typical individual and family counseling, behavior modification, drug therapy groups, concentration on thinking patterns, and academic programs that characterize residential programs. But it also provides an extremely strong vocational education experience for the 16- to 18-year-old boys committed to the department by the court. The camp should be considered a community correctional stratagem even though it is located away from the communities where these boys have lived. The camp is within the county of their residence.

- The Sonoma camp, established back in 1955, is certified by the state of California to issue competency certificates to graduates that denote employability skills in welding, forklift driving, food services, and landscaping.

- A fully equipped industrial woodworking/metal shop provides the experience in the operation of many hand and power tools and equipment necessary for employment in industry or construction. This can lead to certificates in welding and as a forklift driver.

- The probation department contracts with the California parks department and numerous county departments to produce and sell a range of wood and metal products. These include picnic tables, campsite toilets and food lockers, picnic camp stoves, redwood signs, and bus stop benches.

- Those enrolled in the food service program do all the cooking and baking required to feed camp residents. They plan menus, order food for the camp, and prepare and serve the food. Catering skills are initiated here, too. Employability skills competency certificates are issued in food services.

- There is a modern greenhouse where maintenance and operation are taught to program enrollees. Fresh vegetables are provided to the camp. Produce from planted gardens and fruit trees supplement the camp's food budget. Graduates are certificated in landscaping.

- There is a camp commitment to enable and require all restitution-owing residents to earn at least $50 each month toward this obligation. The camp makes earning opportunities available during a juvenile's unscheduled time. It guarantees a victim compensation fund will be available to compensate residents' work and transfer these earnings to victims entitled to restitution. The $50 a month requirement extends to the camp program's two-month transition phase and the final ninth month community phase.

My visit to this camp was one of the most rewarding days of my professional life. As I stepped out of my car I saw a juvenile operating a forklift to move a large quantity of pre-cut wood planks to a site for use in the next stage of wood product manufacturing. Observing the wood and metal products work emerge into saleable merchandise, under strict product control standards, was immensely satisfying. The tone of the camp was very positive. Young people were being treated as industrial trainees, indeed workers, who were preparing themselves for the world of work. Their work here was to be quality work and would be sold to the public or used to help run the camp. This is not the usual residential program for delinquent youth.

The camp had an advisory board of nearby citizens. One member owned a laser wood products company. He volunteered wood waste products to the camp. These were picked up by the camp's truck, dumped at the camp, and night after night camp residents came to the pile and placed the wood into duffle bags for sale to the public as kindling wood. They earned their restitution money in that way. At other times camp management finds alternative tasks for residents to earn the restitution obligation, such as from compensation derived from producing wood and metal products that are sold to the state parks department.

Ever since this visit, I have been on a campaign to get every residential program for delinquent youth, even state institutions, to guarantee they will find ways for juveniles in residence to earn and pay back what they owe victims. Victims should not have to wait for restitution payments just because a youth is in a residential program.

OTHER COMMUNITY-LEVEL INTERVENTIONS

Day or Evening Reporting Centers

Reporting-center stratagems seek to take over more of a juvenile's life space by requiring his or her appearance at a certain place and certain time. What happens at a center varies from a simple check-in to involvement in group or individualized counseling sessions, a drug abstinence support group, cognitive retraining, or a recreational experience. The Fresno County Day Reporting Center illustrates a comprehensive approach that serves 65 probationers who experience two or more risk factors such as an escalating delinquency pattern, substance abuse, family dysfunction, school problems, and mental health issues. The center provides education, mental health and substance abuse services, life skills and job training, gender specific training, family conferencing, victim-offender mediation, mentoring, intensive supervision/case management, and community integration activities, as well as electronic monitoring during the first 30 days of this experience.[3]

Sex Offender Treatment

Some communities work with these juveniles under extremely tight controls and with extensive sex-offender specific interventions. A specially trained probation officer may service a sex offender caseload exclusively. Sex offense and mental health specialists often collaborate in engaging these juveniles. One juvenile court I have studied reviews juvenile sex offender cases monthly with its consulting psychologist. Parents should be very much a part of the control and treatment approach. Some of these juveniles remain in their own homes under house arrest (except to go to school or work). Removal from home may be prompted when the victim is a young sibling and sufficient controls cannot be erected to monitor this concern.

Some offenders are placed in treatment foster homes or group homes. Neighborhood opposition to such placements is frequent and, as one official has suggested, can be volcanic. There are municipality- and county-enacted ordinances that prohibit more than one sex offender at a time from residing in a foster home or group home. Some courts and communities simply prefer to pass sex-offending juveniles off to a state youth correctional agency. There are private residential facilities that specialize with this type of juvenile, often under contract with the state youth agency or the public child welfare agency. A significant number of these youth are placed in costly out-of-state facilities.

Juvenile courts reduce their political risks in committing sex offenders to the state for placement in either a state or state-designated private facility. But most of these juveniles return to their home communities following a placement, and strong transition and reintegration efforts are needed then. Some statutes mandate that these juveniles register as sex offenders and inform law enforcement of their address and any change of address. This may affect the court's action. One judge told me that at trial he had found a sex offense against a boy not proven while finding other burglary offenses proven. He was not convinced the youth was a true sex offender, consciously wanted to avoid the labeling and registration requirement, and considered it sufficient for the court to take jurisdiction on the other grounds. There are sex offenses and there are sex offenses. Careful examination of the alleged offense and, as fitting, the offender, is necessary.

Boot Camps

Boot camps are operated at local or state levels. They have been enormously attractive to legislators and to many others who believe that adolescent offenders require strict discipline. Boot camp enthusiasm is now waning, however, as noted later in the section on research and evaluations.

Juvenile boot camps, like their adult counterparts, are military-style programs that emphasize military drills, regimentation, physical conditioning, confrontation, discipline, and coping with what might be described as in-your-face measures of provocation by staff. They tend to be 90- to 120-day programs and have an educational component. There is some form of aftercare supervision.

Less well-known are the privately operated boot camps that are not are part of a juvenile justice system. Typically they enroll boys at high costs to parents who are at their wit's end with the behaviors and sometimes informally handled delinquent acts of their sons. The parents hope that military-style discipline will return their youngsters to better-regulated living. But one such youngster was returned dead in 2001. He had been enrolled in a five-week, privately operated, unregulated camp located forty miles from Phoenix. He had collapsed in 111-degree heat having been made to march or stand in the sun for possibly five hours. Camp regimen included forced marches, wearing heavy uniforms in triple digit temperatures, strong discipline, and a daily diet sometimes limited to an apple, a carrot, and a bowl of beans. The camp director was charged with murder and a camp sergeant was charged with child abuse for reportedly "spanking, stomping, beating and whipping more than 14 children." Also, a 16-year-old boy died at the privately run Arizona Boys Ranch in 1998.[4]

Boot camps administered or contracted by state youth agencies have also experienced youth deaths, as in South Dakota, and have resulted in both closures and lawsuits.[5]

RESEARCH AND EVALUATIONS

Philadelphia Longitudinal Study

While many juveniles brought into the juvenile justice system return with another offense, there has long been recognition that a comparatively small number of juveniles commit a disproportionate amount of juvenile crime. Some of this recognition occurred with the notable longitudinal study of the police records of 9,945 boys, all of whom were born in Philadelphia in 1945 and lived in that city at least from their 10th to their 18th birthdays.[6] The study revealed that 3,475 boys (35% of the birth cohort) had one or more recorded police contacts, but 1,613 boys (46%) were one-time offenders only. Further, 1,235 boys (36% of all offenders) recorded more than one but less than five offenses, while 650 (53%) of second offenders did not commit a third offense. However, 627 boys (18% of all offenders or 6% of the birth cohort) were apprehended five or more times and this group was responsible for 52% of the total of 10,214 delinquent acts committed.

The authors proposed that since substantial numbers of offenders desist from reoffending, the limited resources of the juvenile justice system might most efficiently target third-time offenders. Beyond the third offense there was a leveling off of desistance probability.[7] Further, a subsequent Philadelphia cohort study that compared a 1958 birth cohort with the 1945 birth cohort found 23% of those who offended had five or more offenses and committed 61% of the offenses.[8]

Another longitudinal study, this one in Racine, Wisconsin, and published in 1982, provided quite similar findings to the Philadelphia examination. There was a hard-core group of chronic offenders, about 5% of the birth cohort, who, after a fourth police contact had an 80% probability of continuing arrests. The author also urged the juvenile justice system focus its resources on chronic offenders, expand dispositional alternatives, and better integrate these youth back into society.[9]

"What Works" Studies

More recent studies take a different tack. They contend they can early on identify a future chronic offender. They urge that the system not wait until repeated offenses have occurred with identified juveniles. Instead, there should be heavy investments of services for these designated juveniles at the earliest stage of processing. This approach holds confidence in the ability of selected interventions to thwart ongoing delinquencies, which reflects the more recent "what works" contention rather than the nothing much works concern of years earlier.

One such approach is termed the "8% Solution." During the late 1980s the probation department in Orange County, California, tracked two groups of first-time offenders for three years and found 8% of juveniles were arrested at least four times within a three-year period and were responsible for 55% of repeat cases. The factors shown to place these offenders at risk were an offense at an early age and a multiple-problem profile that included significant problems within the family, problems at school, drug and alcohol abuse, and behaviors such as gang involvement, running away, and stealing. A demonstration program was initiated in 1994 to assemble and apply a wide range of interventions with identified youth and their families. Preliminary research conclusions have found chronic recidivism can be reduced.[10]

A meta-analysis of 117 studies of intervention with non-institutionalized juveniles had great trouble declaring what works, as rigorous, acceptable studies were quite few. The interventions that appeared to work were interpersonal skills training, individual counseling, "behavioral programs," multiple services, and restitution. What didn't work were such efforts as group counseling, family counseling, reduced probation caseloads, and wilderness programs. Researchers now suggest the question should be: What works for whom and under what circumstances? Major research with delinquency in Rochester, Pittsburgh, and Denver also entered findings that a relatively small number of juveniles were chronic offenders.[11]

Sherman and his colleagues, in a report to the U.S. Congress that assessed federal funding efforts with crime prevention and research, stressed the importance of the more holistic approaches to delinquency control. The report found that community-based alternative sanctions tend to be ineffective unless they maintain attachments to treatment programs and services. Cited as ineffectual were such interventions as intensive probation supervision, home confinement, urine testing, community residential programs, and wilderness programs when they lacked these attachments. Urine testing, however, when combined with drug treatment was found promising. Presumably, intensive supervision without treatment interventions would be ineffective. The Drug Abuse Resistance Education (DARE) programs that use police officers to educate school children about drugs and the value of drug abstinence were found ineffective at preventing substance abuse.[12]

Blueprint Programs

The Center for the Study and Prevention of Violence at the University of Colorado has to date approved and promulgated "Blueprints" on 11 programs that meet strict criteria for program success. Blueprint programs, screened from more than 500 reports, have been found to reduce violent adolescent crime, aggressive delinquency, substance abuse, pre-delinquent aggression, or conduct disorders. These programs meet rigorous field tests of effectiveness with (1) deterrent effect when using a strong research design, (2) sustained effects, and (3) multiple-site replication, though not all were specific to delinquent youth. This research interest was in the pursuit of a public health approach that has an emphasis on the prevention of disease or injury rather than focusing exclusively on rehabilitation effectiveness with delinquent youth. The Blueprints series is a valuable guide to communities that seek to prevent significant problems.[13] The 11 programs are:

- *Prenatal and Infancy Home Visitation*—by nurses from the prenatal period to two years after birth;

- *Incredible Years Series*—parent, teacher, and child programs that provide a range of benefits;

- *Promoting Alternative Thinking Strategies*—teacher-led multi-year self-management, social, and information skills related to drug use in middle school;

- *Bullying Prevention Program*—a school-based initiative;

- *Big Brothers/Big Sisters of America*—mentoring programs for disadvantaged youth from single-parent households;

- *Life Skills Training*—a three-year life and social resistance skills training program that targets cigarette, alcohol, and marijuana use;

- *Midwestern Prevention Project*—a five-year multi-strategy program to curb cigarette, alcohol, and marijuana use that begins in middle school;

- *Functional Family Therapy*—a family treatment model applied to problem youth and their families to change their communication and problem-solving patterns;

- *Multisystemic Therapy*—intensive, comprehensive targeting of specific factors in a youth's ecology that contribute to antisocial behavior;

- *Multidimensional Treatment Foster Care*—a six- to nine-month treatment foster home experience combined with individualized therapy, and behavioral management training for the youth's family prior to a return home; and

• *Quantum Opportunities Program*—an educational incentives program for disadvantaged high-risk high school age youth.

Less Rigorously Evaluated Assessments

One should look, also, to the claims of success made by individual jurisdictions or programs, compilations that do not meet rigorous methodologies such as comparing an experimental against a control group or multi-site replication success. As an example, the well-programmed juvenile court in Delaware County, Ohio, described in Chapter 33, reports that just 13% of its more difficult cases placed on intensive probation supervision registered a new offense in 2001; just 5% of these probationers committed a felony reoffense. Further, with its supervision of 33 sex offenders, 7 (21%) registered some offense within a year, 3 (9%) of these were felony offenses, and 1 (3%) was a sex reoffense.

Boot Camp Evaluations

Largely, boot camps have been found to be less than productive stratagems. Rearrest of graduates of five Florida juvenile boot camps ran from 64% to 74% over a one-year post-program completion period. Those assigned to a boot camp operated by the juvenile probation department in Los Angeles had rearrests or convictions almost identical to those of the comparison group,[14] and youth assigned to a Michigan wilderness boot camp had higher recidivism rates than similar youth assigned to regular training schools.[15]

Those generally assigned to boot camps are not the most severe offenders, as the camps tend to be alternatives to a deeper-end state facility. One shortcoming frequently cited is inadequate aftercare. Further, there is often a high drop-out rate, which in turn upwardly skews evaluations done of those who do graduate from a boot camp.[16]

Poor camp management is also an issue. Deaths of juveniles in private boot camps were discussed earlier. In another tragic case, a juvenile had been enrolled in a county-operated boot camp in Harris County (Houston), Texas, due to curfew violations of his probation conditions. He hanged himself in an isolation cell after having threatened suicide on several occasions, and having physically harmed himself several times. The isolation cell contained a bed sheet that was used in the hanging. Ironically, agency records reflected that the requisite 15-minute monitoring checks at the isolation cell were falsely recorded up to and for four hours after the body was found. It was routine practice to fill out monitoring reports in advance without having directly monitored an isolated juvenile.[17]

Regretfully, juvenile suicides occur in other types of juvenile justice facilities also, tragedies that may sometimes be related to closures of juvenile psychiatric beds or to imperfect juvenile justice agency care taking.

BALANCED AND RESTORATIVE JUSTICE

Balanced and Restorative Justice (BARJ) was the most positive development to emerge onto the juvenile justice scene during the 1990s and continues to expand today. It had just several advocates to begin with, but today has thousands. It has numerous applications, and though originating in the juvenile justice field is now being adapted into schools, universities,[18] and other settings. Its various objectives can be listed as victim restoration, juvenile accountability, community protection or safety, juvenile competency development, and community participation in helping attain justice system goals. Applications include:

- Restitution;

- Community service;

- Victim-offender mediation;

- Services to victims;

- Victim participation in juvenile justice system proceedings;

- Neighborhood accountability boards; and

- Decentralization of probation services into neighborhoods.

These applications can be multi-dimensional. Agencies, in order to foster restitution payments by juveniles who are unable to obtain employment, have contracted with government and non-profit entities for juvenile work crews to perform "paid community service" that enables pay back to take place. Other agencies solicit job slots from community employers for juveniles to earn restitution money, the employers participating in the goal of victim restoration.

The community can be engaged in arranging and sometimes supervising worksites where juveniles perform their community service.

Focus on Victim and on Juvenile's Role in Community

Performance of community service not only contributes to or helps restore the quality of community life, but also furthers community safety, as the juveniles are not committing additional offenses while at work. Also, the community service experience should enable competency or skill development for the participant, which can take such forms as working with a Habitat for Humanity home building crew or a library assignment where a librarian augments the juvenile's book shelving experience with a weekly book-reading assignment that is followed the next week with a discussion.

Victim-offender mediation typically progresses from (1) expressions by a victim as to the impact of the victimization, (2) to the juvenile's effort to explain how and sometimes why he or she committed the offense, (3) to the youth's expression of regret for the injury or damage, and (4) deliberation about how monetary restitution shall be accomplished. Frequently, the community is involved by serving as volunteer, trained mediators in this format. Infrequently, the restitution agreed upon is for the juvenile to provide direct service in the form of repair of the damage caused to the victim's property. Sometimes a victim will have the offender perform community service at the victim's favorite non-profit agency.

All communities require people and mechanisms to assist victims. Agency professionals augmented by trained citizen volunteers help ameliorate and repair victim injury. Informally, friends and relatives assist victims, of course. At least two probation agencies—in Pittsburgh and Dakota County, Minnesota—maintain crime repair crews that train juvenile probationers to repair damage to victims' homes or stores caused by vandalism, burglary, and other crimes. Numerous justice system agencies now provide victim empathy education for offenders at both community and institutional levels, a stratagem that owes much in its development to California Youth Authority officials.

There is improved, but still inadequate, notification to victims of their right to attend juvenile court hearings and to speak out at dispositional hearings before the judge. Preferably, neighborhood accountability board members should request that a victim participate in their hearings. These board members will assign restitution or community service hours and may mentor a youth who has appeared before the board or arrange a job or community service site.

Decentralized probation services are not always included in a BARJ outline. I prefer this, as it brings probation officers much closer to the communities of the juveniles they work with and enables them to find citizens and neighborhood organizations that can enlarge a juvenile's probation experience and competencies. It can enable a branch probation office to provide after school and weekend structured programs and supervision that furthers rehabilitation as well as public safety.[19]

A Redirection to Community Justice?

Several major BARJ writers and activists urge that probation departments be transformed into departments of community justice and that probation officers be retitled community justice officers, as is happening in Oregon. They suggest that community justice involves building or strengthening the capacity of community groups to prevent and control crime, while probation seeks more simply to change the behavior of offenders. "Community justice advocates promote community-building and problem-solving initiatives to prevent crime by addressing the conditions that cause it." [20]

A standard BARJ approach seeks to have the community assist the justice system in restoring a victim and in seeking to ensure that an offender provides restitution and earns the money to pay the victim. A community justice model builds atop this and goes further. The community is to become a co-producer of justice in planning and agenda setting for how this revised probation office would work. Community justice practitioners would first address victim and community needs while also seeking to reintegrate the offender as a constructive citizen.

An approach such as this may influence the future of the justice system, but the judiciary will have to be satisfied that probationers are not forgotten and are both assisted and controlled in the community by community justice officers.

THE CHAPTERS THAT FOLLOW

This section opens with several chapters that describe probation department developments. One might note that, organizationally, probation offices have evolved from African-American officers serving only African-American youth, and male probation officers serving only male probationers, to a heterogeneity where officers of various ethnic backgrounds serve children of any ethnic background, and male probation officers serve female probationers and female probation officers assist male probationers.

Today, there are numerous African-American and Hispanic chief probation officers who provide leadership to their agencies. Today, there are numerous African-American and Hispanic agency managers who provide leadership in state and local executive-branch agencies that administer the probation function and other juvenile justice programs.

Chapter 23 discusses a juvenile court reformation in Atlanta that directed probation officers back to the more purposeful function of serving delinquent youth directly, moved staff members to become more accountable, and focused the work of these officers on community safety, juvenile accountability, and competency development.

Chapter 24 focuses on the department in Pittsburgh, which moved significant numbers of probation officers into middle and high schools, a development assessed favorably by the court as it continues to expand the number of relocated staff members, and one that is also much appreciated by school officials.

The probation department in Nashville, reviewed in Chapter 25, has placed staff members in pubic housing projects, which has broadened officers' functions to working with neighboring youngsters who are not on probation status and in providing services to others who walk into the office seeking some form of assistance.

Chapter 26 looks at Dakota County, Minnesota, one of the earliest settings to conceptualize and apply BARJ principles and among the first to back up family group conferencing into police stations and schools. Chapter 27, which urges a stronger use of restitution and community work service requirements, follows this.

The next three chapters also focus on juveniles' restoration of victims and the community. The Madison, Wisconsin, description in Chapter 28 illustrates the use of a private non-profit agency that furthers both restitution payments and constructive community service experiences, and the Montana program described in Chapter 29 stresses the benefits of community service performed with a work crew model. A Denver program that can be categorized as expanded day treatment is presented in Chapter 30, one that otherwise might have been named Day Treatment/Night Watch. Youth Passages has done tight monitoring of its mid-serious participants' whereabouts during non-program time. A special school and community work service have been integral to the program, and participants have been provided opportunities to earn money and pay a restitution obligation.

Chapters 31 and 32 focus on interagency collaboration programs in Santa Cruz, California, and Boulder, Colorado. These are accomplished efforts that have acted on the recognition that certain delinquent youth are especially complex human beings and not just normal youngsters acting out their excessive energies or temporarily absent superegos. Their approaches require absolute commitments from the top people in the different agencies and disciplines that make up these concerted interventions. And, of course, dependable and adequate funding streams are necessary. But good programs like these appear to be investments that save money in the long run.

Chapter 33, a description of the juvenile court in Delaware County, Ohio, which is next door to the state capital in Columbus, completes this section. The court has a remarkable record for maintaining juveniles in the community. It does not have to contend with the multitude of severe delinquency offenses that characterize many large cities. But it averts more significant offenses by quite excellent, diverse, and accountable programming.

Endnotes

[1] Snyder, H. N. & Sickmund, M. (1999). *Juvenile offenders and victims: 1999 national report.* Washington, DC: Office of Juvenile Justice and Delinquency Prevention, p. 144.

[2] Juvenile Probation and Court Services Department, Circuit Court of Cook County (2000). *Summary of juvenile probation and court services programs and initiatives 2000.* Chicago: Author, p. 18.

[3] Annual Report FY 1999-2000. Fresno, CA: Fresno County Probation Department, p. 67.

[4] Blackwood, A. (2001, July 6). Death spotlights youth boot camps. Associated Press (wire); Blackwood, A. (2002, February 16). Boot camp head nabbed in teen death. Associated Press (wire).

[5] Abusive practices in South Dakota juvenile institutions curtailed by litigation (2001). *Juvenile Justice Update,* 7(2), 3-6; Maryland closes juvenile boot camps after abuses are uncovered (2000). *Juvenile Justice Update,* 6(1), 1-2, 16.

[6] Wolfgang, M. E. et al. (1972). *Delinquency in a birth cohort.* Chicago, University of Chicago Press.

[7] Id.

[8] Wolfgang M. E. et al. (1982). The 1945 and 1958 birth cohorts: A comparison of the prevalence, incidence, and severity of delinquent behavior. Presentation to Harvard University, February 11-12, 1982 [Mimeo]).

[9] Shannon, L. W. (1982). *Assessing the relationship of adult criminal careers to juvenile careers: A summary.* Washington, DC: Government Printing Office.

[10] Schumacher, M. & Kurz, G. A. (1999). *The 8% solution.* Laurel, MD: American Correctional Association.

[11] Lipsey, M. W. & Wilson, D. B. (1998). Effective intervention for serious juvenile offenders: A synthesis of research. In R. Loeber & D. P. Farrington (Eds.), *Serious & violent juvenile offenders: Risk factors and successful interventions.* Thousand Oaks, CA: Sage.

[12] Sherman, L. W. et al. (1997). *Preventing crime: What works, what doesn't, what's promising.* Washington, DC: Department of Justice, Office of Justice Programs.

[13] Elliott, D. S. (Series Ed.), (1998). *Blueprints for violence prevention.* Boulder, CO: Center for the Study and Prevention of Violence, Institute of Behavioral Science, University of Colorado at Boulder.

[14] Zhang, S. X. (2002). *Evaluation of the Los Angeles County juvenile drug treatment boot camp.* Washington, DC: National Institute of Justice.

[15] Deschenes, E. P. et al. (1995). *The Nokomis challenge program evaluation.* Santa Monica, CA: Rand Corporation.

[16] Bourque, B. B. et al. (1996*). Boot camps for juvenile offenders: An implementation evaluation of three demonstration programs.* Washington, DC: National Institute of Justice, Research in Brief*;* Bourque, B. B. et al. (1996). *A National survey of aftercare provisions for boot camp graduates.* Washington, DC: National Institute of Justice.

[17] Smith v. Blue, 67 F. Supp. 2d 686 (S.D. Tex. 1999).

[18] The Boulder (Colorado) Daily Camera reported on February 14, 2002, that the University of Colorado would provide a "restorative justice program" with 12 students rather than suspending them because of a hazing incident that sent two sorority members to a hospital emergency room. A facilitated conversation will be held "to bring together victims, offenders and members of the community in search for solutions." Sebastian, M. No suspensions from alleged hazing, p. 1A.

[19] See Bazemore. G. & Schiff, M. (Eds.)(2001). *Restorative community justice: Repairing harm and transforming communities.* Cincinnati: Anderson; Umbreit, M. S. (2001). *The handbook of victim offender mediation: An essential guide to practice and research.* San Francisco: Jossey-Bass. See also the 2000 Juvenile Court Annual Report, Allegheny County Juvenile Probation Department, which describes the implementation of numerous BARJ components.

[20] Maloney, D., Bazemore, G. & Hudson, J. (2001). The end of probation and the beginning of community corrections. *Perspectives, the Journal of the American Probation and Parole Association,* 25(3), 23-30, 25.

Chapter 23

Transformation:
A New Start for Juvenile
Probation in Atlanta

Some juvenile probation departments move forward with the times. They apply new intervention techniques, new staff deployment techniques, new management techniques, new community involvement techniques. Others do what they have always done and essentially seek only to maintain conformity by juvenile probationers and conformity with long-applied practices.

The Probation Department of the Fulton County Juvenile Court in Atlanta, Georgia, belonged to the traditional, second category, until recently. I have reviewed this court on several occasions over the past 30 years. I conducted an extensive evaluation of the court's organization and case flow in 1971-72.[1] Along with former Nashville Juvenile Court Judge Andy Shookhoff, I conducted a second comprehensive assessment in 1999. At that time, the court requested a general assessment both of the court and its probation division, which it thought lacked direction and accountability. Following both of those assessments, recommendations for change were made. In addition to the two formal assessments, I met with court staff members periodically during the interim. Also, I interviewed and observed then Judge Romae Powell for two weeks during 1983-84 in order to prepare a chapter about her for a book I was writing on five juvenile court judges.[2]

I returned again in March 2001 to find that more progressive change and modernization had taken place during the 18 months following the 1999 assessment than I had otherwise seen over the preceding three decades. While this court and its probation arm still have a distance to go, they have undertaken significant reforms that have resulted in significant accomplishments.

LOOKING BACK AT THE COURT

Probation Is a Function of the Judicial Branch

The Fulton County Juvenile Court is, as it was in 1971-72, a judge-dominated court that includes probation as a judicial branch function. The judges appoint probation officers from an approved list screened by the county personnel office. Probation leadership has long followed judicial direction or, often, lack of judicial direction.

This chapter originally appeared in Juvenile Justice Update, *Vol. 7, No. 4, August/September 2001.*

Traditionally, it had an intake unit, an investigations section that prepared cases for court hearings, and field supervision officers who had offices in the courthouse or a downtown county building.

Probation has exercised much of the pretrial prosecutorial role. This organization reflected the "weak prosecutor" court system that grew out of the pre-**Gault** era, when the court consisted of the juvenile court judge and the probation officer. Although prosecutors are now part of the system, their role has been limited to handling trials that had to take place.

Probation's Intake Unit, Not Prosecutor, Decided Whether a Police Referral Goes Into the System

Until recently, probation investigators, not assistant district attorneys, interviewed victims and witnesses, examined the evidence and weighed its strength, prepared and filed petitions, subpoenaed witnesses, calendared cases, and arranged for the presence of all necessary persons at a hearing. Twenty-two probation staff comprised the investigations unit in 1999, up from a supervisor and five probation officers in 1971-72. When we interviewed prosecutors in 1999, they complained of continuing close to 2,000 trials annually either because probation investigations were incomplete or late, investigators had not accomplished personal service, police witnesses failed to appear, or assistant district attorneys lacked sufficient timely information to either proceed to trial or enter into an informed plea bargain.

Probation Caseloads Unevenly Distributed

Probation officers monitored the probationary status of both delinquents and status offenders. Although many urban juvenile courts focus fundamentally on more serious delinquency and child abuse/neglect matters, the Fulton County Juvenile Court maintains an extensive focus on status offenders, termed "unruly" in Georgia. During 1999, nine probation officers supervised this specialized workload of 211 to 236 unruly youth, averaging a caseload of 24.

Meanwhile just 16 probation officers served approximately 1,475 juveniles on probation for delinquency violations, a caseload average of 92, although some caseloads were as high as 163 and 173. Caseloads included youth who should have been discharged because (1) their maximum two-year term had expired without a violation, (2) they had been adjudicated but no disposition had occurred within two years, and (3) restitution had been reserved and two years had elapsed with no dollar amount ever ordered.

One senior probation official commented that many juveniles were not seen by their probation officers for months at a time. Someone else said it was common practice for probation officers only to "put out fires." Staff turnover, however, was low, perhaps in response to impressive salaries that begin at $41,000. There is limited staff diversity—just one Hispanic and a few white officers complement the African-American staff.

Probation Staff Serve Child Protection Role

With respect to deprived children, six probation officers filled the essentially clerical role of arranging for service of process or publication of legal papers, copying and distributing court materials to the child protection agency and the various attorneys, and handling other case processing tasks preliminary to a hearing.

RECOMMENDATIONS FOR CHANGE

Following our 1999 evaluation, we made numerous recommendations for change. These included:

- Adoption of the principles of Balanced and Restorative Justice (BARJ) and implementation of approaches and programs that further community safety, victim and community restoration, juvenile accountability and competency development, and active community collaboration in attaining goals;

- Development of BARJ-related probation goals in a presumptive one-year probation experience;

- Development and application of a risk/needs assessment for probationers to permit the assignment of youth to different intensity levels of supervision;

- Shifting of probation staff to neighborhood-based sites to enable the delivery of services to youth in or close to their neighborhoods;

- Transfer of the probation officer investigation function to the office of the district attorney;

- Transfer of probation officer clerical functions in deprived child cases to court clerical and child protection agency staff;

- Development of a detention risk-screening instrument; and

- Merger of the court program development office into the probation department.

RESPONSE TO RECOMMENDATIONS

Report Serves as Catalyst for Change

According to Chief Judge Sanford J. Jones, our report was a catalyst for many changes that followed the 1999 visit and served as a source document for those who brought about these changes. But the perspectives and leadership of Judge Jones have been fundamental to the progressive developments noted in this chapter. The court's new vision statement includes a commitment "to restoration of victims and communities." The probation division's new mission is "to promote public safety and restoration of victims by providing effective supervision and guidance and facilitating treatment to youths and families in partnership with the community." What follows is a discussion of what I saw when I returned to the court this year.

New Chief Probation Officer Spearheads Change

To begin with, the court accepted the recommendation to adopt BARJ principles. It soon brought in a new chief probation officer (CPO), Victor G. Brown, a regional juvenile parole director for the Ohio Department of Youth Services who had implemented BARJ in two juvenile parole regions and had served as a BARJ trainer in several states. He carefully coordinated an array of inclusionary approaches to help staff members face up to a new direction.

BARJ Principles Incorporated Into Organization and Operations

First, Brown organized a working committee of probation supervisors, probation officers, and development staff. A BARJ strategic plan and guidelines were developed using group processes. Other committees and subcommittees were formed to develop BARJ in relation to field probation officer deployment. Staff members were trained to design and develop case management plans. A risk/needs assessment instrument was introduced and staff members were also trained to use it. A Blue Ribbon Panel/Community Advisory Group that consists of more than 100 public and private organizations and individual neighborhood representatives has advised the court on improving its services to families and children.

Probation Officers and Clients Both Accountable Under BARJ

Probation officers are now expected to report regularly on (1) what each probationer has done in the past month to accomplish specific components of the BARJ elements of his or her probation plan, and (2) what the probation officer has done in the past month to facilitate probationers' accomplishments of specific BARJ elements.

Not all field supervision staff like the BARJ model with its different expectations of juveniles, probation staff, and community. While this direction was a natural for Victor Brown, it wasn't for all of the staff he inherited. "I'm an accountability guy," says Brown, "and therefore I'm not a popular guy." Staff members in courts such as this have long expressed grievances to judges directly, and Brown has certainly been the target of complaints.

The probation division's BARJ redirection, however, is very compatible with the recommendation that the probation experience "consist of a series of enumerated goals, falling into categories of community safety, juvenile accountability, and competency development tasks to be performed."

Probation Services Move to Neighborhoods

Our recommendation that services move to neighborhoods is underway. Designated field staff are to work four days each week at one of several county annex locations; other field staff are to spend two days each week at one of five sites, such as the Butler Street YMCA and the Berdine Neighborhood Center, which have signed agreements with the division. A day reporting center is being established at a Boys and Girls Club. Plus, a probation officer is to work either one evening per week or on a Saturday.

Probation Caseloads Have Been Sharply Reduced

The first step in reducing probation caseloads was the development of a Youth Level of Service Inventory (YLSI) to help classify probationers for supervision intensity. A University of Cincinnati professor worked with staff to develop this, a process Brown had used in Ohio. Three levels of supervision were projected: low intensity aimed at interventions of two to four months; medium intensity aimed at six to eight months; and high intensity for the highest-risk youth that is guidelined at nine to 12 months of supervision.

By March 2001, unruly youth and delinquency caseloads had been integrated so that probation officers carried a mix of both. With unruly youth having more needs than risks, their presumptive supervision would likely result in two to four months' probation only, with serious efforts to link these juveniles with external community agencies a high priority.

This, along with a "big-time clean out" of the cases overdue for termination and the significant expansion of the probation officer complement produced when probation officers who had been doing "prosecutorial" and "court clerk" functions were reassigned, has reduced field probation officer caseloads to just 45 juveniles. These officers, as before, prepare pre-disposition reports.

Probation's Prosecution Investigation Function Facing Elimination

Both in 1971-72 and again in 1999, I recommended removing prosecutorial investigation and other functions from probation supervision. The chief judge recently approved and ordered the reorganization and by March, 2001, it had finally taken place. Sixteen investigators were reassigned to intake or field probation units, to present cases at judicial hearings, or to take program development roles. Four others were reassigned to work directly under the prosecutor and another two were reassigned to work directly under the public defender. The court is funding these six positions on a temporary basis, but the positions are expected to coninue with the court as the district attorney and public defender acquire funds to pay these salaries from their own budgets. Chief Judge Jones reports everyone is very satisfied with the new arrangement.

Probation Officers Also Removed From Clerical Role in Deprived Child Cases

When I visited the court in 1999, probation officers still scheduled court hearings and issued subpoenas in deprived child cases. By March 2001, three of these six officers had been reassigned to standard probation functions. The other three are targeted for reassignment as soon as court clerk and child protection agency staffing capability can be expanded to absorb these functions. Another significant step in making probation officers into probation officers, then, is well underway.

Performance Standards Aim at Eliminating "Put Out Fires" Approach

Along with these changes have come new probation division performance standards. These should ensure that probation officers do not only put out fires. A new quality assurance officer will reinforce these standards. Some staff members have found these new directions too difficult. They have been assisted in transferring to different positions within county government. The CPO seeks to motivate himself and his staff by what he terms a "higher goal." "I want to do more than BARJ. I want to show that within four years we will operate at such a high level of standards that a national body, the American Correctional Association, will provide us with accreditation and certification."

Implementation of Detention-Risk Screening Instrument

The Georgia Department of Juvenile Justice (DJJ) operates the pre-trial detention center that serves Fulton County. Since our 1999 study, DJJ has developed a detention-risk screening instrument, which is administered around-the-clock by probation intake officers. DJJ has also implemented an electronic monitoring option as well as tracking services for home-detained juveniles.

Despite these improvements, there is still a need for data gathering on the reported law enforcement practice of transporting large numbers of children arrested for minor offenses to the often distant detention center. Many of these juveniles, predictably, will not be admitted because the modesty of their offense, prior record, and risk data. Nonetheless, intake officers at the center must then secure parental transportation to get these youths home. These are youths who have often been arrested for playground fights, minor shoplifting, curfew violations, giving a false name to an officer, or jumping over a fare gate at a regional transportation station.

MERGED PROGRAM DEVELOPMENT OFFICE FACILITATES POSITIVE CHANGE

New Programs Aid Delinquents and Their Victims

The court has now merged its program development office into the probation department to improve coordination of program options and to facilitate enrollment of probationers in an array of program options. For example, one new program provides

Saturday work crews so that probationers can meet their work requirement over a six-week period, and so that those who owe restitution can reimburse victims from a fund set aside that converts their work hours into dollar payments to victims. Work crew members participate in a cognitive behavior program two evenings a week. Some older youth meet a third evening for employment skills training. Further, the court has successfully facilitated a community effort to bring multi-systemic therapy to court juvenile and families.

Resource Manual Aids Probation Officers

A new resource manual helps probation officers access community agency programs. This project's next phase is to group community agencies by geographical district to allow district-based officers to more readily tap these resources.

Community Organizations See Court in Action

The "A Day in Court" program brings Atlanta-area foundations and organizations, community leaders, and elected officials to the juvenile court for presentations on court processes and concerns, and provides the opportunity to observe court proceedings. The court has been designated by the Council of Juvenile Court Judges of Georgia as a model court to develop best practices with deprived child case handling.

COURT EXERCISES WIDE LEADERSHIP

Judge Nina R. Hickson convened and led a Coalition to Address Girls in Prostitution that succeeded in increasing the criminal law sanction for pimping and pandering of children from a misdemeanor to a felony and authorizes forfeiture procedures. Observation and data showed a growing number of girls, ages 11 to 14, were seduced by adults into prostitution. The Coalition stimulated greater protection and prosecution efforts by police and increased treatment resources provided by community agencies.

In addition to the reforms outlined above, the Fulton County Juvenile Court has "cleaned up" court case backlogs. It has modernized case file management and introduced a significantly improved information technology system that is used both internally and externally. The court and DJJ share data electronically, and the court has provided leadership on a plan to share information about families known to juvenile courts in 28 or more Georgia counties to facilitate disposition planning. Staff are also involved with county government in planning for a new juvenile court facility scheduled for completion in November 2002. A strengthened court administration is evident. (The court's 2000 Annual Report, Constructing Justice, is available at *http://www. co.fulton.ga.us/juvenilecourt/juvenilecourt/html*.)

CONCLUSION

I infrequently get the opportunity to return to a court after conducting a study to review implementation of study findings. It is gratifying to see major progress and the now self-generated momentum to accomplish the vision and mission of Fulton County's court and probation division.

Author's Note

The materials that follow are drawn from an updating report prepared by Victor G. Brown, Chief Probation officer, Juvenile Court of Fulton County (Atlanta). The ongoing progress of this revitalized judicial branch probation agency is evident.

New Intervention Strategies

The court has put in place a pre-adjudication/diversion initiative as an early intervention pilot program. These alternatives to adjudication emphasize restorative justice and community-based programs and are handled in three ways:

1. *Informal conference:* Minor offenses and first-time offenses/offenders are classified as low level and, in general, not in need of ongoing services. But if it is determined that services are needed, a referral is made to our program development department.

2. *Mediation:* Misdemeanor offenses received as complaints involving physical or verbal fights with no injuries, property disputes such as trespassing, small damage to property, and theft are referred for mediation. Unresolved matters are assigned to the probable cause calendar.

3. *Probable cause hearings:* When probable cause has been established for certain misdemeanors and less serious felonies, a judge will continue the matter for 90 days in order to monitor the youth's adjustment during the interim.

Blue Ribbon Panel Recommendation

The Blue Ribbon Panel/Community Advisory Group continues to meet twice a year to review the level of services provided by the court. The following panel recommendations were implemented:

1. Multi-Systemic Therapy (MST) is a functional family therapy. Fulton County has been allotted 15 slots in this intensive three- to six-month family intervention program.

2. The juvenile court's mental health unit has established a service with direct Medicaid billings for the services rendered to youth and their families.

3. The court is building on partnerships with the community in obtaining grants in an effort to establish a family drug court and a juvenile drug court.

DAI and the Use of Court's Resources

Detention decisions are based on Detention Assessment Instrument (DAI) scores. The scores also help determine appropriate resource referrals. For example, the Bakers Ferry Emergency Shelter Center only accepts children with medium-range DAI scores. The scores help determine releases from detention when overcrowding occurs. Georgia Department of Juvenile Justice (DJJ) Detention Alternative Services provides the court with a range of detention alternatives for both pre- and post-adjudicated youth. Medium-range scores (8-11 on a scale of 12 or more) can lead a pre-adjudicated juvenile into such alternative resources as an emergency shelter, wraparound in-home services, house-bound detention, electronic monitoring, and Southwest Key Tracking Plus. Post-adjudicated youths with 8-plus scores can be referred to a short-term treatment such as MST and Tracking Plus.

The tracking services program may be utilized as an alternative to detention, as a progressive sanction step, or as an alternative to returning to a higher level of restriction in programming. The program is guided by a principle of risk control and is based on the premise that high-risk youths can be safely and effectively managed in the community after their behavior has been stabilized.

YLSI/Reduced Recidivism

The court now defines as recidivism "any youth returning to court within one year on an equal or greater offense." Its new research and evaluation unit tracked 500 Youth Level of Service Inventory (YLSI)-measured juveniles against their recidivism data. Errors were found in key areas of the YLSI summary information sheet that decreased the reliability and validity of these data. The form has now been redesigned and a new YLSI recidivism comparison is underway. The goal is a validated YLSI that reliably determines the level of intervention need.

Accountability Through Graduated Sanctions

The frequency of violations of probation and/or court orders and the seriousness of these violations vary considerably. The development and use of the YLSI has helped classify probationers for supervision intensity. Application of graduated sanctions offers a continuum of steps that probation officers can use to respond to violations. This approach applies the lowest level of sanction appropriate for the violation(s). Graduated sanctions provide consequences.

Tables 23-1, 23-2, and 23-3 provide examples of each class of violations and the recommended sanctions. These sanctions are progressive in nature, and are to be applied consistently as soon as possible after the violation occurs.

Table 23-1
Class I Minor Status Violations

Violations	Recommended Sanctions
Curfew violation (occasionally)	Parent/child conference
AWOL from home (for few hours to overnight before returning home)	Verbal reprimand
Being somewhere other than where given permission to be	Stricter curfew
Negative attitude and lack of cooperation with parents and/or probation officer	Restriction of important privilege
Use of alcohol	Increase assignment of household task
Failure to keep appointments with probation officer, medical, or agency	Increased contact and/or appointments with probation officer
Failure to attend school or expulsion for nonviolent behavior	Assignment of written essay
Disrespect toward authority figure	Youth to report to office rather than usual meeting place
Misdemeanor traffic offense	Monitored house arrest for weekend and/or weeknight
Use/possession of tobacco	Monitored house arrest for weekend and/or weeknight
Associating with undesirable/improper person	Monitored house arrest for weekend and/or weeknight
Failure to take prescribed medication	Monitored house arrest for weekend and/or weeknight

Probation Staff Reassignments

Probation officers, like their clients, are to be held accountable under BARJ. Staff members have been reassigned to such areas as quality assurance, research and program evaluation, staff development/training, mediation, and victim services. Others now handle specialized caseloads, e.g., one with girls who are victims of prostitution.

Decentralizing Probation

To maintain closer contact with youth and families, the county has been subdivided into six areas based on zip codes. Field-based probation officers are now equipped with a laptop and a cellular phone with a radio. Court-based officers handle all pre- to post-adjudicated hearings but are not assigned ongoing cases. Field-based probation officers are responsible for violations of supervision/probation, statutorily designated felonies, and any hearing with recommendations for out-of-home placement or detention.

Table 23-2
Class II- Major Status Violations/Misdemeanor Offense

Violations	Recommended Sanctions
AWOL from placement more than 24 hours (overnight)	All sanctions for class I offenses may be recommended
Use of alcohol and other drugs, and/or including one or more positive screens.	House arrest
Failure to attend court-ordered program	Submitting to drug screen
Chronic failure to obey the statutory laws governing minors in the state of Georgia	Referral to substance abuse counseling/program treatment
Out-of-state AWOL (more than 20 hrs)	Community service
Single misdemeanor against property/person Failure to appear for an office conference or staffing to address a violation	VOP/VOS/affidavit/violation of TR's Court-ordered participation in programming
Chronic failure to keep (3 or more) appointments with PO or agency	Court-ordered detention for weekend or overnight
Violating curfew/frequently/daily	Electronic surveillance monitoring
Failure to pay fees, fines, or restitution	Placement of youth in treatment program
Failure to complete community service hours	Place out of home for specific period
Felony/multiple/misdemeanor, DUI/traffic	Extension of probation period Short-term youth development center program Trial release, 30, 60, 90-day Non-final DJJ DJJ – stayed Final commitment DJJ

Table 23-3
Class III – Misdemeanor/Felony Offenses

Violations	Recommended Sanctions
Single/multiple misdemeanor against a person/property	All sanctions for Class I and Class II offenses may be recommended
Felony(ies)	Commitment/DJJ

Engagements with the Community

A BARJ principle focuses on active community collaboration in attaining goals. In April, 2002, the chief probation officer initiated the first interagency cross training between DJJ, the Department of Family and Children Services (DFACS), and the juvenile court. Future training for line staff and case managers is in process.

A partnership was developed between the court and Atlanta Public Schools to examine in-school suspension and behavioral therapy as a potential model to pilot in the upcoming school year. The goal of this program is to reduce the number of complaints and provide treatment in the school setting to youth with repeat discipline problems.

Endnotes

[1] Rubin, H.T. (1972). *Three juvenile courts: A comparative study.* Denver, CO: Institute for Court Management.

[2] Rubin, H.T. (1985). *Behind the black robes: Juvenile court judges and the court.* Beverly Hills, CA: Sage.

Chapter 24

School-Based Probation Officers in Pittsburgh: A New and Different School-Juvenile Court Partnership

Since 1990, Lehigh County, Pennsylvania, has been providing school-based probation services to youth on the juvenile court caseload. The success of the program led to its duplication across Pennsylvania. This chapter looks at the implementation of these services in Pittsburgh.

JUVENILE COURT INVOLVEMENT WITH PUBLIC SCHOOL SYSTEMS NOT NEW

Courts have long reinforced educational requirements and social conformity to them by youth, thus supporting school system managers and public policy. Illinois legislation, in 1883 and 1889, authorized truant officers to "arrest children of school-going age, who habitually haunt public places, and have no lawful occupation, and also truant children who absent themselves from school without leave...."[1] Truant officers, known also as attendance agents, actively prowled the streets and public places, and regularly brought youths to court attention both before and after the first juvenile court was established in Chicago in 1899.

The Illinois legislature that created the nation's first juvenile court authorized the position of probation officer but denied funding for that position. Schools and the police filled this gap in funding by assigning their own staff to the Chicago court. The schools supplied 21 truant officers who were currently in their employ, and donated private funds financed the employment of six probation officers.

In its earliest years, more than 50% of Chicago's juvenile court cases were for truancy and other non-criminal offenses such as incorrigibility, vagrancy, "immorality," and "disorderly behavior." The first annual report of the court's chief probation officer said: "Truancy seems to be at the foundation of most children's delinquency; they stay out of school, idle away their time, find bad company in their neighborhood, and then commit some petty offense."[2]

This chapter originally appeared in Juvenile Justice Update, *Vol. 5, No. 5, October/November 1999.*

As in Chicago, the Boston juvenile court also handled truancy matters, but by 1968, school agents filed truancy complaints "only when it's impossible ... when you try everything and get nowhere." [3] Typically before a truancy case was filed, the probation officer would lecture youths. Robert Emerson wrote of listening to a warning scenario given to two boys, accompanied by their parents, for causing a disturbance within a school and for skipping school: "Would you like me to bring you into court? Have the judge send you away to training school? ... You're going to go to school, and when you're in school you're going to sit in your seat, and you're not going to move." [4]

LEGISLATIVE CHANGES ALTER COURT AND LAW ENFORCEMENT OFFICER INVOLVEMENT

Juvenile courts often impose sanctions for misbehavior, assaults, and other offenses taking place on school grounds. For example, the Utah courts backstopped school concerns over cigarette-smoking students long before smoking was recognized as a public health problem. The juvenile code restructuring of the 1960s – 1970s, however, separated status offenses from the definition of delinquency and sharply constrained the powers courts could exercise with status offenders which, in turn, led to diminished court interest in school-related problems. In the years that followed, courts wanted to focus their resources on more significant law violators. Urban courts, in particular, wanted schools to handle their own truancy and lesser law violation problems. Nonetheless, school attendance has remained a universal condition of probation. Probation officers cajole their caseloads to go to school. And when they don't, they can be "busted."

On the other hand, schools in some communities have specifically sought to involve law enforcement officers. About 30 years ago, amid great controversy, law enforcement officers were invited into Phoenix, Arizona, area schools to assert a preventive presence. Schools in other communities also began inviting the police into their schools. Police presence has never been without detractors; some school officials, along with other citizens, distrust police in schools and protested to boards of education. In recent years, particularly with the rash of school violence, other students, parents, and teachers feel more comfortable with a police officer greeting incoming students and walking hallways. Courts and schools have also linked more closely, too, on drug policy, and attempts to create and maintain drug-free schools.

PENNSYLVANIA HAS MORE THAN 150 PROBATION OFFICERS IN SCHOOLS

Pennsylvania is now leading the way in terms of placing juvenile probation officers (POs) in its schools. Far from merely providing a part-time office where a PO can meet with his probationers, in these schools a PO is berthed full-time. The PO's primary role is to provide the probationers who attend this school with daily intensive supervision and more. The school-based model allows the POs to maintain close contact with the juveniles under their supervision, verify their attendance, and monitor their academic progress and general behavior. School-based POs often attend assemblies, athletic events, and other school functions, bringing them in contact with the student body at large. Supporters of school-based probation believe that it provides better results than traditional probation supervision, while also enabling the POs to provide services to other at-risk students and to generally improve the school environment.

Pennsylvania is a leader, also, in the implementation of balanced and restorative justice (BARJ). There, probation agencies have altered their vision statements and strategic plans to expressly describe BARJ precepts that have been embodied in the juvenile code. School-based probation officers help fulfill the balancing criterion of allocating resources to the community and engaging the community in the juvenile justice system.

The state's school-based approach also includes tighter monitoring of juveniles released from residential or institutional placements. Local POs, then, are responsible for youth on probation and youth on parole or aftercare. Both sets of juveniles have to attend school and both demonstrate numerous behavioral problems, sometimes severe in nature. A PO in the school might prevent or otherwise handle these school incidents.

The concept has caught on. Today, more than 150 POs in Pennsylvania call a school their office. The program is present in 50 of Pennsylvania's 67 counties, and state and county dollars, initially augmented with federal money, fund the program.

TWO MODELS FOR SCHOOL-BASED PROBATION OFFICERS

Lehigh County Model Assigns a Probationer to Two POs

The school-based PO develops case plans and monitors daily behaviors. The other PO attends court hearings with the youth and handles all aspects of case processing. This dual case management model allows the school-based POs to spend more time in the school setting.

Allegheny County (Pittsburgh), Model Uses One PO to Handle Both Roles

Under this single case management model, school-based POs are responsible for all activities involving their clients. Pittsburgh's complement of school-based POs has jumped from three to nine to 18, then to 21 and 26 (at the time of my site visit). Another six were being hired for fall 1999, to bring the number of schools with full-time POs to 26. A team of two POs will serve a school that has a high incidence of probationers. School bases include middle schools and high schools. The remainder of this chapter focuses on this Alleghany County model.

PITTSBURGH SCHOOLS, FACING VIOLENCE, ADD SCHOOL-BASED PROBATION OFFICERS AS A TOOL

Schools in Pittsburgh, like those in many communities, have experienced violence. One *Pittsburgh Tribune-Review* description reported hallway and classroom stab-

bings, students carrying loaded guns, gang fights, brick and stone throwing, a choking, assaults and beatings, and robberies. Victims and other juveniles feared going to
school. There were regular complaints from neighborhoods adjacent to one school of
school youths breaking into homes and businesses, and of gang violence. The problems are real (though media reports typically ignore many of the good things that are
happening in the schools).

City schools use a range of approaches to prevent, quell, or deal with these problems. Pittsburgh schools employ their own police department. They have school
social workers and mental health staffers. Now POs have been added to the mix. The
PO serves as a positive incentive and control agent for probationers, the PO's primary
function, and is also visible in the hallways as students change classes and maintains
a presence at an array of school and after-school functions. The PO is a school disciplinarian only for those on the probation/parole caseload, but is perceived as someone
who helps keeps things under control so that students can be students.

POs Develop Probationers' Case Plans and Pertinent Special Conditions of Probation

The PO formulates and implements a case plan for each probationer. Conditions
are structured into a BARJ format that specifies what the probationer must do to further community protection, accountability, and competency development.
Probationers check in with the PO each morning and receive a form that teachers
complete, verifying classroom attendance and commenting on classroom performance. When a PO attends morning court hearings, these forms are provided to the
probationer either through use of a folder containing these forms that is pinned to the
office door or directly from a school social worker or security officer. The completed form is turned in and reviewed with the PO at school's end.

A daily supervision contact with probationers is a central task, and is not limited
to check-in and check-out. Probationers drop in or are called in throughout the day
for counseling, to discuss family-related concerns, to reinforce juvenile accountability for school accomplishments and court-imposed conditions, or to receive
encouragement to participate in extracurricular activities.

The PO holds family conferences on both PO and family initiative, sometimes at
the family home. POs engage juveniles and families with the services of other community agencies. The PO will place a probationer suspended by a school on home
detention, seek court approval to apply an electric monitor, or request the court to
order other graduated sanctions.

School-Based POs Do Intake Screenings at School for Subsequent Offenses Committed on School Grounds

Allegheny County is the only program in the state that provides intake screening
at a school by the school-based PO to determine whether a delinquent offense committed on school grounds or on the school bus will be handled informally or not and
whether admission to the detention center will be authorized or not. An intake conference, with parents present, is held as speedily as parents can arrange to come to
the school. If the offense is severe and the need for secure detention clear, however,

the arresting police officer will transport the juvenile to detention, the PO will authorize a petition, and the PO and parents will meet at the detention hearing.

Lesser reoffenses and technical violations that are adjusted at an intake conference generally result in the addition of community service hours to the juvenile's existing requirements, along with other tailored add-ons. A school official is another signatory to an adjustment agreement. When the Pittsburgh project received the Court-Operated Program of the Year Award in 1996 from the Pennsylvania Juvenile Court Judges' Commission, this on-site intake received special commendation.

POs Serve as Group Leaders

Some POs run probationer group meetings, sometimes in conjunction with a school social worker or mental health worker. Groups have met on anger management, "thinking errors," and drug and alcohol education. POs, with strong support from their central office, lead schoolwide groups also. One has been a cheerleader coach. Another is a volleyball coach. One coaches a school's basketball team. A fourth developed an after-school exercise program. Others have served as advisors to the school newspaper and audiovisual club.

Each PO serves on a school's "Student Assistance Team," a multi-disciplinary group that evaluates at-risk children and those with special needs, and recommends a course of action. A recommendation may involve student counseling by the PO, though the student is not a probationer. A PO may also see other non-probationers whose parents seek such conferencing. Some POs make juvenile justice system presentations to regular classes. Some choose to observe their probationers in lunchrooms and classrooms.

RESULTS INDICATE PROGRAM MEETS GOALS

The Pittsburgh project seeks to increase the probability that probationers will function successfully in the school environment and reduce their delinquent behavior. Program objectives aim at increased school attendance, reduced tardiness, higher graduation rates, better grade averages, fewer disciplinary referrals and suspensions, and lower rates of reoffense and violation of probation conditions. Additional objectives seek to decrease commitments to institutions and to highly intensive and costly day treatment programs.

Pittsburgh has reported a one-year reduction of 22% in residential placements and 7% in day treatment programs. Other Pittsburgh outcome measures are anecdotal. Probation and school officials report positive experiences in the main, though some school officials have expressed disappointment that the POs cannot always be on-site (because they have to be away from the school to attend court hearings). Both sets of officials indicate the program has increased attendance and reduced the number of students who get into trouble, small or large. On-site, direct PO management of probationer rule violations is particularly well regarded.

Lehigh County data for the first operational year found success:

- Detention/suspension – down 4.0%

- Tardiness–down 9.5%

- Absenteeism–down 15.0%

- Improvements in grades–up 4.1%

- Dropouts–down 29.0%

A University of Pennsylvania assessment of the statewide program[5] found it highly rated by juveniles, school administrators, and probation officers. Researchers compared 75 randomly selected school-based probationers with 75 non-school-based probationers matched by age, race, gender, crime, and county of origin. School-based probationers were significantly less likely to be charged with a serious offense during the 18-month study period but more likely to receive charges that reflected closer supervision—technical probation violations and status offenses.

School-based probationers had 40% fewer placements and less than half the number of days in placement than the control group experienced. The researchers estimated that cost savings derived from reduced placement rates resulted in an average saving of $6,665 for each case assigned to school-based probation. The program was deemed cost effective. The researchers called for a prospective experimental study to confirm these preliminary findings.[6]

Pennsylvania officials are not waiting for a more definitive study. They have locked-in to this approach and visualize it becoming a prototype for collaboration with other service delivery entities.

FOUR CONCERNS

A complimentary article that focused on Pennsylvania school-based PO programs, published by the National Center for Juvenile Justice, raised four concerns.[7] These questions and explanations follow, blending in responses from program officials. My comments conclude the chapter.

Q: Is the resource allocation appropriate? School-based POs carry caseloads of 25-35, while other PO caseloads are in the 55-75 range. This has morale and service delivery ramifications.

A: While school-based POs work more intensively with individual juveniles than a regularly assigned PO who is not in the school setting, the nature of the probationers on both workloads is similar. Since the school-based workload is not comprised of higher-risk probationers, the justification for the difference in caseload is that the more intensive intervention of the school-based function strengthens the capability to prevent reoffenses. Further, facilitating probationers' school achievement helps probationers avoid failures in school and of their probation. Additionally, at-risk non-probationers receive prevention assistance.

It took a few years for regular POs to adjust to their colleagues' lower caseloads. The school-based task is now seen as a difficult PO job that involves large amounts of face-to-face counseling. Senior staff who want more counseling contacts with juveniles are applying for these positions.

Quite possibly the living is easier in the summer when school is out, and school-based POs carry their lighter workloads in the same fashion as other POs carry their workloads year-round. In summer, for example, the school-based PO does not need to allocate time for daily contacts with school officials. Contacts with juveniles and families can be arranged without having to fit them into the hours of the school schedule. At present, the Pittsburgh court is reviewing the issue of disproportionate caseload numbers.

Q: Are the privacy rights of students compromised? The use of school-based POs obviously breaches traditional confidentiality constraints. Probation status carries a stigma. Other students and the faculty know who is on probation. This raises the possibility that probationers may be isolated or overly disciplined because of their known status as probationers.

A: The counter argument is that the PO is a positive buffer to negative stigma. The PO constructively represents juvenile misbehavior to other students and faculty and can be an advocate. Also, the PO can be somewhat of a prize. One PO stated: "Most of my kids, as soon as I walk into the classroom, [call out] 'There's my probation officer.'" Another argument is that school officials often know who is on probation and pass this information on anyway. Additionally, probationers often tell other students they are on probation, and the other students pass this on. This raises the question as to whether the breach of confidentiality as to status is real or perceived.

Q: Does the program expand the juvenile court net? Does a school base create a net-widening effect? That is, does the PO become a case finder who expands referrals to juvenile court? Do school officials send minor troublemakers to a PO who then sends them on to court? Do POs, because of their presence at school and school activities, see more and consequently exercise authority over more school misbehaviors—and send more youth to court in order to demonstrate to the school system they are not too "pro-kid"?

A: Maybe. Maybe not. But this should not be a result. Data from the University of Pennsylvania assessment do not suggest a net-widening effect. The characteristics of juveniles on school-based probation were very similar to those of juveniles assigned to traditional forms of probation in the same counties in terms of gender (over 80% of probationers were males), race (about 65% white, 25% African American, and 10% Hispanic), and current offense (property offenses such as theft and burglary were the most common offenses, followed by person offenses such as simple assault). However, school-based juveniles were younger on average than comparison group juveniles.

Q: Is the school-based PO fulfilling a role that should be handled by school personnel? In short, whose job is this? Schools have police officers or security guards present or on call. They have administrative officials with disciplinary authority. These officials are supposed to prevent or handle problems that arise. Will they relinquish their own responsibilities and turn to the PO to take over almost all problems related to probationers? Will they also ask POs to be disciplinarians for non-probationers? And since when does probation have a prevention function?

A: The response is that Pennsylvania POs are to perceive their primary role as working with a select group of youth—probationers—but cooperatively with and not to the exclusion of other school personnel. While school personnel may want and expect a broader role for POs on the side of a law enforcement function, this is not the school-based PO precept. Their state level operations manual, prepared in collaboration with school officials, describes 36 do's and don'ts for drawing this line. Overall they want to do what they do with their kids, and help the school out only on a more general basis. First things first. And if this involves some prevention, that's good also. Pennsylvania has made a strong commitment to risk-focused delinquency prevention that is very compatible with the school-based probation model.

COMMENTS

More penetrating, more extensive evaluation of school-based PO programs should be done. More measures of outcome should be obtained. Nonetheless, there is no clear reason why this informally well-rated approach should stand still. It makes sense. It is politically popular, with the governor weighing in to secure funding in FY 1999 for significant expansion. Programs go where the dollars are, and right now they are going into this school-based approach.

We have long talked of juvenile courts becoming accountable. This is an example of one way this is happening. The court is no longer a distant bureaucratic vehicle that confounds everyone and impresses few. The court is involved in the day-to-day action and is in partnership with the most vital of enterprises, the education of young people. Further, the school-based PO is in a unique position to smooth a previously institutionalized youth's transition back to school, a largely ignored but serious problem across the country.

School is one of the most important domains in the lives of juveniles. Academic failure and truancy are risk factors for involvement in juvenile delinquency and other problem behaviors. Positive bonding to school increases the likelihood that adolescents will avoid problems which might lead to the revocation of their probation status and possibly residential placement.

Decentralized probation services and broader PO role definitions have not yet come of age, but they, like community policing, are a promising phenomenon that ought to be encouraged.

Author's Note

James Rieland, Administrator, Juvenile Section, Court of Common Pleas for Allegheny County, Pittsburgh, prepared the following update information in mid-2002.

Pennsylvania now has more than 200 Probation Officers in schools.

During the 2001/2002 school year, the Pittsburgh program was further expanded to 39 school-based probation officers. The program operates in 18 of the 43 school districts in Allegheny County. The Pennsylvania Juvenile Court Judges' Commission has contracted with the National Center for Juvenile Justice to evaluate school-based probation in Pennsylvania. The study will be piloted in Allegheny County during the 2001/2002 school year and will be expanded statewide in 2002/2003.

The school-based program continues to thrive in Allegheny County, with many additional schools added to the original group of schools.

Endnotes

[1] Platt, A. (1977). *The child savers, 2d ed.* Chicago: University of Chicago Press, pp. 127–128.

[2] Id, p. 140.

[3] Emerson, R. M. (1969). *Judging delinquents: Context and process in juvenile court.* Chicago: Aldine, p. 53.

[4] Ibid.

[5] Metzger, D. S. & Tobin-Fiore, D. (1997). *School-based probation in Pennsylvania.* Philadelphia: University of Pennsylvania.

[6] Id.

[7] Griffin, P. (1999). *Juvenile probation in the schools.* Pittsburgh: National Center for Juvenile Justice.

Chapter 25

A New Probation Opry in Nashville: Decentralization Strikes a Positive Chord

Lots of juvenile probation departments rent space for district branch offices where sometimes five or six or more probation officers (POs) have their desks and telephones. From this base, the POs conduct interviews and prepare reports, go out into the neighborhoods to counsel and monitor juvenile probationers, meet with families, and consult with schools and other community agencies.

Decentralized service provision has been urged by national standards setting organizations. "Probation services should be based . . . where offenders reside and near other community services. Staff serving probationers should be removed from courthouses and . . . [services] should be provided in the evening hours and on weekends without the usual rigid adherence to the recognized work week."[1]

On a recent visit to Davidson County (Nashville), Tennessee, I discovered a juvenile probation department that is far more decentralized than those located elsewhere. More than half of the 27 POs are located, one or two to an office, in different public housing projects. These "offices" are in former family apartment dwellings. The three intensive supervision POs have offices together in one public housing apartment and share this space with the chief probation officer (CPO) who prefers this site to a courthouse location. Other POs are based in community centers, schools, mental health centers, and the Girls and Boys Club.

PEER SUPERVISION OF AND BY PROBATION OFFICERS

Skilled juvenile probation supervisors across the country who enjoy country music and would love to live and work in Nashville will look in vain for a job announcement for a supervisory position there. Supervisors, who elsewhere guide and oversee six to eight POs, are not used in this department.

The reason is not budgetary, but instead stems from a management philosophy. This approach is known here as Continuous Quality Improvement (CQI). CQI is an adaptation of Total Quality Management (TQM), which is also referred to as the Deming process, after the name of the original conceptualizer. This orientation opposes traditional hierarchical management. According to it, supervisory officials squelch the initiative and effectiveness of line workers. Instead, POs in Nashville supervise each other. The CPO refers to this as a "self-directed work team."

This chapter originally appeared in Juvenile Justice Update, *Vol. 3, No. 2, April/May 1997.*

Seven to eight POs, based in different but reasonably contiguous parts of the county, form such a work team. Each of the three district teams meets weekly. Monica, a school-based PO, says POs get more creative solutions when they discuss their individual cases with their peers than they would if they were to approach a supervisor to gain a supervisory "OK" for what they will do. Teams keep minutes and rotate the four positions (leader, facilitator, time keeper, and recorder) that help make meetings more effective. Monica adds that team meetings reduce the isolation occasioned by decentralization. In her words, "I love it."

The teams assign new probation cases to the individual PO located closest to a youth's home. When a violation of a probation condition occurs, the assigned PO must discuss the different actions that might be taken with another team member, or the full team. Team members must approve a PO's recommendation for any early termination from probation. In addition, the district attorney must sign off on early termination for a felony offense probationer prior to its submission to the court. Case consultations are regular agenda items at team meetings. POs accept a dual purpose for their work:

- A "normal" purpose—to effectively manage probation cases; and

- An unusual purpose—to work aggressively to strengthen the neighborhoods where probationers live.

PROBATION OFFICERS AS AGENTS OF PREVENTION

Nashville caseloads are moderate, averaging 30 probationers. There is no intake or predisposition report role for the probation department. These reports are prepared by a different governmental entity, but only when there is a perceived risk of out-of-home placement. Nashville may well be the only mid-size juvenile probation shop in the country that does not employ a secretary!

The work of Nashville POs is not restricted to their caseloads of adjudicated probationers. They will work with any child of any age who may need some help. They will work with any family that may need nurture or assistance. They work actively with neighborhood organizations in efforts to improve the neighborhood environment and resident welfare. This is old fashioned social work. It is prevention. It is neighborhood oriented. It is door-open, community-related probation.

Monica, the school-based PO, says that the teachers and the school attendance officer contact her to counsel troublesome kids who are not on probation, and that complaining parents are advised by school personnel to bring problems with their juveniles to her. She works a four-day week, 10 hours a day.

Monica showed us a brochure she prepared to advertise the South Nashville Awareness Program (SNAP), her venture to inform the community that she is there to help children, youths, and families. Brochures are being mailed as well as distributed at a supermarket, shopping mall stores, and PTA meetings. As the community buys in to the program, she plans to recruit mentors to work with the youth she sees. She arranges community service work placements at an area food bank, a recycling center, and at juveniles' own churches. She also attends meetings of the neighborhood association.

Mary, a housing project-based PO, states she knows everyone in the neighborhood and everyone knows her. She schedules her own hours, works one Saturday morning a month, and works late one day a week. The Saturday is given over to collaborating with her probationers on community service work such as at a food shelf for the homeless, or to dropping off fliers announcing a housing association meeting. She adds: "I love my job because I don't know from day to day when or whether I will be a PO, a doctor, a lawyer, a police officer, a fingernail painter, a barber, a cook, or what."

Community-based probation, Nashville style, operates in tandem with community policing, which is also occurring in Nashville. Community policing is decentralized: It is knowing the neighborhood and the neighbors; it is working with neighborhood organizations to further their efforts at crime prevention, youth development, and neighborhood development. As with community-based probation officers, some police are based in public housing. Police "apartment offices" may be immediately next door to probation apartment offices. And community police can be seen bicycling through public housing neighborhoods.

THE PO AS NEIGHBOR: ESTABLISHING AN OFFICE

POs had to find their own neighborhood offices (consistent with the TQM approach that those working on the line have a better sense of where to locate than a department's administration has). Cultivating the support of a housing project's resident association and management were entry points to assisting neighbors in need and to working with the association on community betterment efforts.

In locating offices, POs were not to offer to pay rent. Since they would provide a valuable community service, a donation of office space was the way an understanding and appreciative organization could indicate its support of the program. In return for the office space, POs would provide in-kind services to the agency that housed them, such as helping with staff training or arranging for juveniles to perform community service work.

Wendy, a PO who shares an apartment office with Mary, hustled donations to set up a children's playroom in the apartment for all children of the neighborhood. She gathered rugs, toys, dolls, small bicycles, and school supplies. Also, she underwent training in order to open an adult literacy and tutoring program in the project. Wendy and Mary also run a monthly cooking class for seven- to 12-year-olds and have arranged for a social work student to initiate a sex education class in the apartment. A PO at another site has set up a pregnancy prevention program for young males.

Some offices maintain food banks and clothing banks. Creative staff have arranged for regular free deliveries from supermarkets, for garage sale sponsors to donate clothing that has not been sold, and for a dry cleaner to donate clothing that has not been claimed. Neighborhood residents come in for food and clothing, and for reinforcement of their educational pursuits and problem-solving abilities. POs, as helpers, facilitate jobs, effectuate referrals to health and human services agencies, run interference for neighbors who have problems with public utilities and retailers, and do plain crisis intervention within or across families.

PROBATION DEPARTMENT OPERATES A TRUANCY REDUCTION PROGRAM

Taking Advantage of a HUD Grant

The money was there. The grant fit well with how the probation agency defined itself. So the department entered into a contract with the Metropolitan Development and Housing Agency, the pass-through entity for U.S. Housing and Urban Development (HUD) drug reduction funding, to conduct truancy reduction programs at three housing projects.

A PO at each of the three sites carries a half-probation, half-truancy reduction workload. Two to three probation aides, neighborhood residents who each work 15 hours a week, complete each of the three teams. There are several components to this program:

- Neighborhood elementary and middle schools fax in or call in the names of absent or tardy children. An aide goes immediately to the apartment and area of residence looking for the youngster or information about him/her. The objective is to get the child back to school, and the PO or an aide will provide cajoling, conflict resolution, and transportation assistance as needed.

- The project works daily with suspended students, bringing in college students from Tennessee State University as tutors, and a graduate social work student as a family counselor.

- Teacher-parent-youth-PO (or probation aide) conferences are held in the project office. Wherever possible, parents are enrolled in an adjacent adult literacy program.

- During summer 1996, probation aides taught kids "Hooked on Phonics." A PO ran a book club for older youths and got businesses to contribute $50 to each juvenile who completed an assigned number of books. Staff help youths obtain summer jobs.

- Programs have conducted parenting classes, provided drug and alcohol prevention education, taken field trips to city events and sites, and provided mentoring.

Truancy Reduction in a Crack Environment

What POs are doing to hold kids in school, help parents get back to their educations, and strengthen families and neighborhoods sounds and is good, but it competes with the terrible poverty and dim futures of those who live here.

Getting kids to school and keeping them there is a forever problem. POs know that numerous probationers are breaking the court's condition, which mandates school attendance. They carry truants back to school, rather than to court, however. They know that if the kids are in school, "they are less likely to commit a real delinquency."

Kelly, a truancy reduction PO, suggests that 90% of the kids who have significant truancy absences have drug problems in their homes, more generally with a parent(s), less often with the youth him/herself.

Five crack "drops" operate openly within a block or two of a program office. Others nearby are pointed out by Charles Ward, the truancy reduction program director and former long-term PO, as we drive by what is called "Dodge City" because of its shoot outs, and a few blocks later, "Crack Alley." Various clusters of four or five older youths/young adults tend spaces by dumpsters and driveways as drivers come by and make their purchases. Yet we had just left the program office, which was immediately next door to the neighborhood police office!

Charles spots and stops five ex-probationers as we drive along. They appear to be 19- to 21-years-old. "How're you doing?" "I'm staying clean Mr. Ward." (One, obviously, did not look clean, but Charles ignored this). "Are you working?" If the answer is no, Charles Ward gives very specific instructions as to where this person should go to seek a job and whom he should see. Charles Ward knows on a day-to-day basis which contractors and government agencies are hiring low- or semi-skilled people.

"Charles," I said, "you're not a PO anymore. How come you still do street counseling, and particularly with adults?" "This is still part of my job," he replies.

DECENTRALIZATION OF PROBATION MANAGEMENT AND COURT MANAGEMENT

Substituted here for the more customarily used top-down probation management, which is normally augmented by a management team of managers, is the "Quality Improvement Council," another adaptation from the Deming CQI model. The Council is comprised of two POs from each of the three teams, and the CPO. The Council decides how the department's work is to get done. It decides department policies, the general parameters of the PO function, the PO fit with department procedures, and the flow of cases from the court to probation and back again to the court. It has produced a Probation Procedures Manual.

The final notch up for CQI is the "Senior Leadership Team" of the juvenile court itself. The team, originated in 1991, meets twice monthly at the home of one of its seven members. This group sets the overall direction for the juvenile court, its organization, its coordination with programs it is responsible for, such as probation and the community service work program, its coordination with external agencies, its financial management, and the grants and appropriations it seeks and uses to further court system goals.

This team is comprised of the judge; the delinquency, child abuse and neglect, and child support referees; the CPO; the administrator for grants and training; and the administrator for finance. In truth, the team has an eighth member: A Nashville management consultant has been a key ingredient of the entire CQI approach, involved in every important strategic decision made by the senior leadership team since 1991. And he is a volunteer. This volunteer consultant has done well in his field and has an enormously strong commitment to give back to his community—through the juvenile court.

CONCLUSION

Decentralized probation services in Nashville aren't perfect, but they are very interesting. The POs are in the heartland, and they are intervening as well as preventing. They know what life is really like for their kids and the tough odds faced by so many young people today. They more easily avoid moralistic judgments on their probationers' minor rule breaking. They more readily feel they must be a larger part of the solution.

Research evaluation has not been built into what Nashville is attempting. There are no data that can prove the efficacy of what is happening there. But there is a consistency within the probation fabric, and a positive rather than a threat-based orientation that should make probationers feel better about themselves. There is an energetic reaching out to the community to seek a co-ownership of responsibility for delinquency reduction and prevention.

The approach, of course, has its critics. They have trouble puzzling out why the use of authority, within a department tied so closely to an authority-laden court, de-emphasizes authority. They don't see POs much around the courthouse and wonder how well probationers are being served—and where the probation staff's buck stops.

Still, it is refreshing to observe the implementation of such philosophical and programmatic assumptions as "probation officers can be catalysts for change," "most disputes are better handled through mediation in the communities in which they arise," and "staff must work flexible hours; being on the job from 8 a.m. to 4:30 p.m., Monday through Friday, will not work with the concept that probation is most effective when delivered from the neighborhood in which the probationers reside."

Author's Note

Jim Wells, former chief probation officer for this court but currently a supervisor, has prepared the following updating commentary:

Most of what was published in 1997 is true today. However, a new juvenile court judge took office in 1998 with a new administrative and judicial staff. Changes in regard to community-based probation have taken place:

- *More probation officers in school-based offices:* Of the 26 probation officers in the field, 12 are now based in schools, 10 in public housing, and four in community centers. Some of this shift is due to the preference of the administration and part is due to the demolition of two public housing developments that had provided offices for probation officers.

- *Self-directed work teams have been abolished in favor of a typical management hierarchy:* Prior to 1998 the chief probation officer led a division without subordinate supervisors and was advised by a committee of line POs. Although the administration invites suggestions from line staff, most policy and process changes are now driven from the top down.

- *Intensive probation has changed:* Prior to 1998 the three intensive probation staffers shared an office and worked as a unit. Today there is one intensive probation officer assigned to each geographic team.

- *Prevention/truancy reduction changes:* The work continues although not quite as much as before. Truancy reduction programs remain in operation but there has been some shifting due to the aforementioned demolitions.

- *Balanced and Restorative Justice Approach (BARJ):* The emergence of BARJ as an organizational philosophy has not been continued. Victim-offender meetings do continue to take place.

Endnote

[1] National Advisory Commission on Criminal Justice Standards and Goals. (1973). *Corrections. Standard 10.2 and commentary.* Washington, DC: Government Printing Office.

Chapter 26

Dakota County, Minnesota: Repairing Harm and Holding Juveniles Accountable

Restorative justice, at least as a term, has begun to come into our vocabulary and our consciousness. More juvenile justice professionals are now asking: What is this concept? What are its foundations? Would it replace what we do now? Would it only complement what we do now? What does it look like in practice? This chapter discusses what restorative justice looks like in Dakota County, Minnesota.

Professor Gordon Bazemore, of Florida Atlantic University, is heavily engaged in both the development of the ideology of restorative justice and the applications of its principles at juvenile court sites.[1] He believes the most important fact about crime is that it harms people and communities. Accordingly, justice should focus on repairing this harm. Restorative justice also urges that juvenile courts:

- Expand the role of crime victims in the juvenile justice process;

- Give balanced attention to victims, offenders, and the community as clients or "customers";

- Give balanced attention to basic community needs to sanction crime, reintegrate offenders, and increase public safety.

Accountability is placed primarily on the offender to "make it right" with victims and the community. But accountability extends to social agencies and the community, too. Juvenile justice agencies have a responsibility to support the offender in the effort to make it right. The community, according to Bazemore, has a critical obligation to support and guide juvenile justice's efforts to serve victims and offenders. In doing so, it enhances its own safety. Juvenile justice administrators should balance the allocation of resources to meet the needs of the three client groups.[2]

THE DAKOTA COUNTY RESTORATIVE JUSTICE MISSION

Mission Statement Recognizes Restorative Justice

Dakota County, immediately south of the Twin Cities, has a very rapidly growing population which currently is about 330,000. Few non-Minnesotans recognize the names of its county seat, Hastings, or its larger communities of Apple Valley,

This chapter originally appeared in Juvenile Justice Update, *Vol. 3, No. 4, August/September 1997.*

Burnsville, and Lakeville. But this county's Community Corrections Department (CCD) recognizes restorative justice and is actively implementing its precepts across a significant spectrum of interventions, in concert with the juvenile court. Dakota County is a site for the Balanced and Restorative Justice Project (BARJ), which Bazemore heads.

Numerous probation departments have mission statements. But it is doubtful that many rival the mission of this CCD:

We are committed to preventing crime and repairing harm caused by crime. We promote:

- *Public safety and crime prevention in the community;*

- *Accountability and opportunity for positive change of the offender;*

- *Justice for the victim;*

- *Respectful treatment for all involved.*

Juvenile probation and adult probation services are among CCD's numerous program components. While CCD serves, and its mission statement applies to, both juvenile and adult law violators, this chapter focuses primarily on juvenile justice implementation.

Crime Repair Crew

Both juvenile and adult probationers have been involved, though separately, in an unusual program here that repairs damage caused by lawbreakers. The Crime Repair Crew, initiated in 1995, is a resource for citizens who have property that has been damaged from criminal activity. Law enforcement personnel, on responding to a crime scene, provide victims with information about the Crime Repair Crew. The victim contacts the program directly to arrange a schedule for repairs. The program serves all victims: private citizens, businesses, and government and non-profit organizations. A van that transports offender-workers has the words " Crime Repair Crew" painted on its sides.

The response time can be speedy, as juvenile or adult work service crews are in place each day. Windows can be replaced, doors repaired, graffiti removed, additional vandalism damage corrected, and other restorations accomplished.

The juvenile work crew supervisor likes what he sees reflected in the faces of the youths he takes to repair the damage: offenders being offended by what other offenders have done to people and community.

Family Group Conferencing

Another program innovation, Family Group Conferencing (FGC), is on the cutting edge and likely to be widely replicated. This concept is native to the Maori tribes of New Zealand. It involves convening an extended family and significant others, and asking them to take on responsibilities in assisting their adult or child relatives who need care or help. Legislation in New Zealand has applied the concept nationwide. The approach has many similarities to the Navajo Peacemaker Courts in the southwestern United States (See Chapter 43). FGC is now being utilized with dependent, neglected, and abused children in Grand Rapids, Michigan; San Jose, California; and several Oregon communities.[3]

The New Zealand approach and an Australian counterpart are also used to divert lesser delinquency cases to an extended family group. Dakota County has modified and implemented this FGC model. The group consists of the offender, the offender's family and friends, along with the victim, the victim's family, and support people. Participation is voluntary. The FGC diversion strategy is a healing and reintegration strategy. It is expressive therapy for the victim, and accountability therapy for the offender. The restitution amount is one bottom-line consideration. Payment is made at the conference or according to an accepted and monitored plan. In the Minnesota approach, cookies, refreshments, and informal small talk complete the conference.

Steve Strachan, a Lakeville police officer, has done seven FGCs. He does these within seven to 10 days of the offense because "the quicker, the better." One was even held the same day as the offense. In addition to a restitution payment arrangement, the 16-year-old girl agreed to 60 hours of community work service and a written apology. This triad of sanctions is common to FGC, though the juvenile chooses the work site and the parents monitor the work. The juvenile and parents meet again with Strachan 30 days after the conference to report on progress toward completion of the requirements.

He has held FGCs in cases involving assaults, vandalism, property damage, and threats to teachers. The county prosecutor has defined the offense criteria for which FGC may be used. Strachan participated in FGC training with an Australian consultant. Strachan states FGC meetings are to be punitive, emotional, and not touchy-feely. It is, he says, "in your face justice." His role is to facilitate, not to impose.

Dakota County CCD spearheaded and coordinates the legislatively funded two-year FGC demonstration project, which is underway in all seven counties of the judicial district that includes Dakota County. There are eight sites, four at police departments, three school-based, and one within a prosecutor's office. Reportedly, Lakeville police otherwise do very little diversion. For Lakeville juveniles and victims who participate in an FGC, there is no several-month wait for a court hearing, and no 60-mile round trip to the county courthouse.

PROSECUTOR DIVERSION USES RESTORATIVE JUSTICE FUNDAMENTALS

Dakota County Diverts Hundreds of Cases

The office of the county attorney diverts several hundred cases of first-time offenders annually. All must pay restitution if there is victim loss or damage. If they are 13-years-old or older, they perform community work service and CCD will assist in arranging community work service sites. The number of hours each is assigned is based on a grid or matrix that takes into account age and offense seriousness. The minimum that can be assigned is 15 hours, the maximum is 35 hours.

Education Component

All diverted juveniles and their parents must attend an educational class conducted by a nearby family services agency. The class focuses on several areas, including restoration of community values, respect for others, and healthy decision making.

Success Rate

Only an estimated 5% of juveniles fail to complete their requirements and are then prosecuted. Diversion works in the vast majority of cases.

JUDICIAL SYSTEM PRACTICES

Dispositions Include Restorative Justice Programs

Most arraignments, or first hearings, in Dakota County result in a case resolution, with adjudications and dispositions occurring at that time. Dispositions have common elements: restitution, community work service hours, an apology letter, probation. Judicial orders may require residential placement; urinalysis; psychological or psychosexual evaluation; gun safety classes; START, a CCD intensive assessment and intervention program for medium- to high-risk probationers; or New Chance, CCD's six-day-a-week, 12-hour-a-day institutional alternative.

Victim Restitution Fund

An unusual disposition is also used here—a payment to the Victim Restitution Fund. This is ordered regularly when there is no victim injury or loss. Intake investigations may recommend 15 hours of community work service or a $75 donation to this fund; 20 hours or a $100 donation; 30 hours or a $150 donation. Presumably, the choice of work hours or a money payment (and many do choose to pay) allows this procedure to be titled a donation. An hour of work is valued at $5 for this purpose. In 1996, $23,275 was collected from this source. This fund in turn subsidizes payments to victims which follow from work done by other juveniles enrolled in what is called the Youth RePay Program.

Youth RePay Program

People who work with juvenile restitution know that to have a high restitution order to restitution payment ratio one cannot depend only on juveniles finding their own jobs. Rather, one needs to have a program, funded by contracts or public grants or private funds, that allows juveniles to perform work, generally in a work crew, with all or most of the funded moneys paid over to victims.

Here, RePay work crews perform the work tasks that enable the program to repay victims of the juveniles who do this work—juveniles who otherwise would lack a job or other ability to repay. Five dollars goes to the victim for each hour's RePay work. In 1996, victims were repaid $34,763 by this program alone.

Earlier, CCD had a contract with the county government for RePay to pick up recyclable materials from government office buildings. The Victim Restitution Fund was created to hold and disburse this money; it now receives and disburses the donations paid in by juveniles pursuant to court order.

CCD is currently laying the groundwork for an "entrepreneurial revenue producing offender work project" that would support victim payments following juveniles' work with RePay. CCD has gone to the community to ask for paid work opportunities for juveniles. The community, CCD contends, has a very real stake in facilitating and ensuring that victims are paid back and that harms are repaired.

RePay also provides community service jobs for juveniles who have work hours to perform, but no restitution obligation. RePay honors the Balanced Approach to Probation tenet of competency development. Its customary approach is to find work tasks that are educational or skill developing. Juvenile workers have framed a garage at a YMCA camp, built a wall and painted 15 rooms at a homeless shelter, served a meal to 250 homeless people at a day center where the homeless offered a prayer of thanks to the youths, planted trees, repaired "mailbox baseball" damage to a string of mailboxes as a project of the Crime Repair Crew, painted trash cans at a park, and built a staircase at a public golf course.

The accountability tenet is prominent here, also. The probation officer is notified when there is a no-show. No hours are credited when there is poor work performance or smoking at the setting. Conversely, juveniles who have done especially good work are rewarded by the removal of a few hours from the total otherwise required.

While the existing information system does not aggregate overall court restitution payment totals, the total amount ordered in 1996, $119,411, is available. This represents an average order of $204 per juvenile. A recent study of a sample of Dakota County juveniles found that the order-to-payment ratio exceeded 80%. Further, the county attorney's separate diversion program and family group conferences result in additional restitution dollars paid to victims.

Victim/Offender Meetings

A Dakota County probation officer first brought victims and offenders into dialogue in 1980. Now 95-100 VOM meetings take place each year. Here, VOM stands for victim-offender meetings, rather than victim-offender mediation. The term "mediation" is not used out of concern that victims may interpret "mediation" to mean they will have to give up something if they engage in a VOM. The term "reconciliation" is avoided for similar reasons.

Most VOMs are facilitated by volunteer facilitators who, in other settings, would be referred to as mediators. Facilitators are recruited from the community, receive 24 hours of training, and then assist an experienced facilitator at several VOMs before taking on a VOM assignment alone. A significant number of CCD staff have received similar training and apprenticeship, and conduct VOMs as well.

VOMs are a spin off from CCD's Victim Restoration Program. This program is a discrete staff unit which contacts victims to:

- Ascertain whether there will be a restitution claim and what the amount will be;

- Obtain documentation of the claim and verify its accuracy;

- Request any specific recommendations for the court, such as an order that the juvenile have no further contact with the victim; and

- Explore interest in participating in the VOM program.

VOM is used only when there is a restitution claim. When there is victim approval to schedule a VOM, the judge, following adjudication, will delegate the determination of the restitution amount to the VOM.

One facilitator says that, whenever possible, she will visit the victim at the victim's home to discuss VOM as well as firm up the victim's participation and the meeting time. She will also telephone the juvenile and, when possible, meet with the juvenile prior to the VOM.

This same facilitator, an attorney who also does civil case mediation, was recruited through the state association of mediators. She has held VOM meetings at her office, a library, a branch CCD office, and at a fire station (in an arson case which involved setting a grass fire).

Unusual Victim Leads a VOM to Extraordinary Result

Darrel Bussler is a professor of education at Mankato State University in Minnesota. He was also a victim of severe vandalism by two juvenile offenders. He returned to his home one evening to find his house strewn with broken glass and his stereo, computer screen, and antique bedroom mirror smashed. The vandals destroyed picture frames, dishes, and light fixtures. They even drenched his bed linens with lemon juice. The vandalism damage was estimated at $16,000.

Bussler was an eager participant in VOM. He wanted to meet his neighbors who had caused the damage. His juvenile neighbors acknowledged they had not been good neighbors. The boys agreed to, and over time did, pay the $800 insurance deductible for which he was out of pocket. The VOM process was positive and productive, but not enough for him. Bussler suggested to me, "when love is not practiced, all we have left is law."

He wanted to help create a neighborhood where people knew and could trust one another. He proposed a neighborhood dinner at his home. And as the *St. Paul Pioneer Press* described the event, the two boys hand-delivered the invitations to neighbors' homes. Bussler bought the food. The boys cooked the chili and helped set up the fruit and dessert. Thirty neighbors met each other, the boys, and Bussler. Later, a block club was formed and a block party held.[4]

A few months ago, Bussler convened officials of his South St. Paul community—the school superintendent, police chief, church representatives, and others—and a CCD restorative justice specialist, to consider implementation of his belief that it takes a community to raise a child and that hatred should not be met with hatred.

OTHER RESTORATIVE JUSTICE PROGRAMS

Probation Service Center

The Probation Service Center is the CCD approach to providing limited intervention to low-risk probationers. CCD's staffing pattern disallows more intensive intervention with this group. Juveniles come to anywhere from three to six monthly large-group educational sessions, which cover such topics as how to find a job, losing your driver's license for driving while drinking, and how to get along better with your parents.

When the conditions of probation have been completed, the youth is discharged. Common restorative justice conditions used with this group are restitution, community work service, an apology letter, payment to the Victim Restitution Fund, and VOM. Other conditions may include a chemical dependency evaluation, or attendance at gun or fire safety classes.

Intensive Day Treatment/Institutional Alternative Program

New Chance is the CCD's intensive day treatment/institutional alternative program. Three days a month, New Chance juveniles perform community work service. Work that restores or betters the community advances the goals of both accountability and treatment. Included in the New Chance program is an extensive victim empathy curriculum. Some sessions provide victims with an opportunity to describe the multi-dimensional impacts of the crimes they have suffered; this allows juveniles to register the personalized perception of harms they and others have caused.

The Balanced Approach in Practice

In Dakota County there is remarkable consistency in applying BARJ principles and elements to procedures and programs across the spectrum. And this consistency is no accident. A deliberate intent to apply these principles is apparent, for example, in the CCD guide for preparing recommendations for a predisposition report. The guide specifically spells out how to develop a disposition that meets the desired goals:

- *For accountability,* options include restitution, VOMs or apology, no contact with victim, cognitive group to increase victim empathy, and community work service.

- *For community protection,* options include electronic monitoring, urinalysis, risk-of-reoffense assessment to justify a higher level of supervision, and a cognitive group to work on antisocial attitudes.

- *For competency development,* options include a cognitive group, life skills, family counseling, special school program, GED, independent living skills, anger management training, and community work service.

CONCLUSION

Dakota County isn't perfect. Its case processing time—from police delivery of reports, to prosecutor petitioning decision and petition preparation, to scheduled court hearings, to the date a VOM occurs—all need to be shortened. Victims want, and usually need, their payments promptly. Juvenile accountability and the delivery of rehabilitative interventions are, likewise, best done speedily. And community involvement should be organized early.

CCD might have moved earlier to line up new contracts for its RePay work crews—a course it is now actively embarked upon. The information system needs to be enhanced to provide better restitution data reports. But an extremely promising restorative justice model is being synthesized here. CCD director, Mark Carey, stresses that the justice system "must be more responsive to the real and immediate human needs of the principal players—the victim, offender, and community." There is considerable evidence this is happening.

Darrel Bussler wrote a poem, "Reflection," as he thought about the splintered mirror which had been a family heirloom:

Take a look at this piece. What do you see? A broken mirror: That's easy to see.
Take a look at this piece. What do you see? Our culture? That may well be.
Take a look at this piece. What will we do? Will our actions reflect what we need to renew?

Endnotes

[1] Bazemore, G. (1995). Beyond punishment and treatment: A restorative model for juvenile justice. *Juvenile Justice Update, 1*(3), 1-2, 10-15.

[2] Bazemore, G. (1997). What is restorative justice? (Unpublished manuscript).

[3] Wachtel, T. (1995). Family group conferencing: Restorative justice in practice, *Juvenile Justice Update, 1*(4), 1-2, 13-14.

[4] Harvey, K., One victim's "wakeup call" produces a reconciliation. *St. Paul Pioneer Press*, October 29, 1995, p. 11A.

Chapter 27

Let's Do More With Monetary Restitution and Community Work Service

RESTITUTION

Utah's state juvenile court administrator told me a year or so ago that if he had to give up either juvenile probation or the state's monetary restitution/community service program, he'd give up probation. While chief probation officers (CPOs) in that state likely would disagree with John MacNamara, Mac was recognizing the creative work, meaningful juvenile-adult collaboration and relationships at the worksite, juvenile job satisfaction, and the contributions that well-planned tasks were making to community life and environmental preservation in that state. Earlier, Utah's juvenile court system had been farsighted. It had worked out a deal with the legislature so that a significant percentage of income from fines levied on drug violations, juvenile traffic violations, and status offenses like curfew and tobacco possession (yes), would go into a restitution pot. Appropriated monies were used to achieve victim payments through "paid" community service, i.e., probationers and those ordered into community correctional programs were paid to do community service tasks, but 100% of the payments were transferred over to compensate victims. This is how Utah, in 1991, achieved what is probably the nation's highest statewide collection rate, 84%, of monetary restitution ordered. Can any of you top that rate in your local jurisdiction?

Dade County (Miami), Florida, certainly can't. Judge Bruce Levy, senior delinquency judge in the juvenile court there, told me in September, 1994, that, "I order monetary restitution in every case of victim loss or damage. But as far as I can tell, very little is paid in. Moreover, there is no enforcement. No one is ever brought back before me for non-payment."

My own observation is that lots of juvenile courts have no program (the key concept is program) to facilitate juvenile repayment to victims. Older youth who live in suburban communities can get jobs, or their parents may advance payment on their child's behalf. Big city courts will either enter a dollar-amount order but expect no or little payment, or ignore the victim and require only "unpaid" community service as a payback strategy.

This chapter examines several issues in the monetary restitution and community service arena, and offers certain guiding principles that, as implemented, might raise your kids' batting averages in fulfilling judicial orders and both reduce your frustration and increase your satisfaction with how this is done. (Andy Klein, chief probation offi-

This chapter originally appeared in Community Corrections Report, *Vol. 1, No. 2, December/January 1994.*

cer of the district court in Quincy, Massachusetts, where citizen and community pay-back sanctions were born in 1975, says we should term it community work service, since the public likes to think that such a punishment indeed involves work.) Descriptions of productive program models conclude this chapter.

Right off the bat let me say that monetary restitution is our prime goal. Community service hours, unless they result in compensating victims through a funding device, do not make the victim whole. But, you will ask, how in creation can I expect young probationers who live in desolate slums with 70% unemployment to earn and pay back? Many can't, unless you develop an earning program.

COMMON PROBLEMS IN RESTITUTION AND COMMUNITY WORK SERVICE ADMINISTRATION

First, let's list examples of some of the deficits in current restitution and community service administration:

- A juvenile court diverts 25% of referred delinquency cases. Referrals and informal counseling are standard with diversion agreements; monetary restitution and community service are never included since the "system" believes those options can be used only with formally petitioned juveniles.

- Judge A orders repayment in whatever amount the victim claims, even if the victim throws in the kitchen sink, or even if a 12-year-old will never be able to earn $1,000.

- Probation Department B ignores hundreds or perhaps thousands of unpaid restitution orders in "successfully" terminating probation for those who have complied with all other probation conditions (this goes for non-performed community service hours, as well).

- Judge C, in his biennial speech to the Optimist Club, brags of the $12,500 paid back to victims through his court. But he can't answer a question as to whether this might constitute 10%, 50%, or what percent of the annual amount ordered since his information system doesn't aggregate these data.

- Judge D's court does capture useful aggregate data, but annual data show the number of service hours she ordered averages 30, while her colleague, Judge E, averages 110 hours. The staff and kids are disgruntled about this disparity, but the CPO is reluctant to ask the judges to change their individualized approach to sanctions (would any reader support sanctioning the CPO for this?).

- State youth agencies have failed to follow Texas's lead in arranging legislation that authorizes a youth, on aftercare (parole) status, to satisfy a reoffense penalty by victim payback or community service hours in lieu of an institutional return.

- Joe Probationer owes $200 monetary restitution. He reoffends, and Judge F places Joe in a private residential setting and orders another $175 of restitution. Joe's probation officer (PO) lets the facility and its program take over Joe's life, and fails to require that the facility arrange for Joe to work, earn, and pay back. Six months later, another reoffense lands Joe with the state youth agency; the victim will never see a cent, and no one will ever call her and acknowledge the system's unaccountability.

PRINCIPLES FOR SOLID RESTITUTION PROGRAMS

You or I could add other shortcomings and make a much lengthier list, but instead, let's turn to certain principles, and then to some examples of solid achievements. A starting point is the designation of the agency that holds primary responsibility for implementing the local program. This may surprise some of you, but this agency in Madison, Wisconsin, Charleston, South Carolina, Denver, Colorado, and in a substantial number of other cities is a private non-profit agency and not the probation department or another public entity (county and/or state and, sometimes United Way funds subsidize these private shops). Designate a restitution/community service coordinator when this is a probation department function. Now, I'll pick up with monetary restitution.

- *You need a reliable system for speedy notification of victims* concerning the filing of victim claims, a simplified process for filing, and encouragement to file. ("Last year we collected and reimbursed $9,375 and we will do everything possible to see that payment is made to you.")

- *Monetary restitution (and community service, also) should be used fully at the intake diversion stage.* If the law does not authorize this, a court rule can. Paid jobs should be made available to these youths. Victims should not be ignored when we do well by a kid and allow him or her to avoid a formal record.

- *An official should review claims with the juvenile and parent(s),* and otherwise ascertain that a claim is valid and the amount requested is fair. The recommendation to the judge of a restitution amount should be based on typical statutory and case-decision provisions that juveniles should pay back to the extent of their ability to earn or obtain funds in the reasonable future. Here's where a jobs and earning scheme fits in. When you have jobs going for kids, they can earn and the order can be set higher. Without job possibilities, the recommended amount and the judge's order should be set lower.

- *Only the judge (or referee, master, commissioner) can order the dollar amount.* It is unconstitutional for the judicial hearing officer to delegate the dollar amount to a PO or other official. What does pass muster, however, is for the judge to delegate to the PO, for the PO to obtain written approval from the juvenile/parent as to the amount, and for the judge to then enter and ratify this amount as an order.

- *In negotiating plea bargains, the prosecutor or PO should require that monetary restitution be ordered for the charges that are thrown out.* If not, payment cannot be ordered for the dismissed counts, and some victims are left out.

- *You've got to have a scheme for kids to earn restitution.* At least five states (Iowa, North Carolina, Ohio, Utah, and Wisconsin) award funds to local courts or delinquency programs that can be used to pay kids to work. Federally financed summer youth jobs programs are a resource. Schools, local governmental agencies including parks, McDonalds, K-Marts, and Dairy Queens all can be influenced to set aside a rotating job slot for use by restitution-owing juveniles. Or you can contract with a nursing home or recycling center for ongoing jobs to be done. Often, 10- and 11-year-olds will not be able to do paid work tasks. If you can do it, obtain donations so that younger juveniles can do paid community service tasks to earn payback moneys.

- *You've got to enforce defaults when youth demonstrate little ambition to achieve compliance.* The number of defaults can be reduced if, at the time of the order or agreement, absolutely clear messages are provided that the requirement must be fulfilled, and is to be completed within a stated time period. Defaults are reduced, too, if the amount of the order is reasonable and can be accomplished. Close monitoring of the payment schedule, an early discussion of payment failure, and a prompt design of additional earning efforts are further aids. When necessary, formal review before a judge can be advantageous to a youth's motivation.

- *Disbursement to victims should be speedy.* This is not always the case. Check this out at your agency. Some payment agencies will wait until the full amount has been repaid before disbursing a victim's check, even though this may take a year and several hundred dollars are sitting in the account.

- *There should be a good set of written policies and procedures* that have been ratified by the judiciary and key juvenile justice agencies.

PRINCIPLES FOR COMMUNITY WORK SERVICE PROGRAMS

Let's move to community service principles where some of the above rules, such as judges setting the number of hours, the handling of defaults, and written policies and procedures also apply. The two basic work approaches used are: (1) placements of individual juveniles in non-profit or governmental agency settings, and (2) work crews supervised by staff members, often part-time staff members, of the primary organization that administers the community service program. Preferably, you should have both approaches available.

- *Have a system-approved grid or matrix of the number of hours to be recommended and assigned based on differential offense severity, prior offense record, and age.* Limited flexibility can be built into this—for example, 24 to 32 hours for a particular category so that aggravating or mitigating factors can be taken into account. The purpose of the matrix is to further consistency among POs with their recommendations, and among judges with their orders. Proportionality in sanctions is another product. Get the work hours completed in no more than three months. Avoid ordering a very large number of hours to be performed, unless this is part of a multi-pronged program with harder-core youth designed to keep them off the streets except when they are involved with different phases of a comprehensive program.

- *The competency development feature of the Balanced and Restorative Justice Model should be prominent.* Make sure the work activity is productive, and there are opportunities for skill building, for positive interactions with adult role models, and for publicly demonstrating competent and constructive behavior. A youth, on completion of the work, should have greater competencies than before and be more responsible to the community than before.

- *Obtain adequate insurance.* You need an appropriate form of insuring (1) juveniles as to injuries they may incur at work, (2) people or property in the community as to injuries that juveniles may cause at work, and (3) staff against negligent practices. Hundreds of programs have very satisfactorily worked out insurance coverage. In Pennsylvania, e.g., a statewide coalition purchasing arrangement has one company insuring all programs. In some communities, juveniles pay a modest fee or work several hours extra to defray insurance costs. Injury claims have been scant across the country.

- *Establish a policy as to which juveniles, due to their particular offense types or personal characteristics, cannot be placed in particular job settings.* And another policy should regulate the kind of offense information that can be shared with a worksite prior to a juvenile's job placement.

- *Court the press.* Obtain publication of photos and stories of juveniles at work (photos from the back only, unless juveniles/parents sign a frontal or name identification consent). Public respect for juvenile justice will escalate with this, so, do it again and again.

POSITIVE OUTCOMES

Research findings, overall, are quite positive. Juveniles who pay back or work their hours show less recidivism (4% to 12% less) than those who don't receive these requirements. Also, many of you have heard of and some of you possess victim-offender mediation (or reconciliation) programs. This is an especially bright spot in our array of program offerings. Bringing victims (at their option) and offenders together with a trained mediator eliminates facelessness, furthers human connectedness, facilitates agreements on disputed payback amounts, personalizes accountability, and enhances a juvenile's reintegration back into the community. Research findings indicate a higher likelihood of victim payback when victims and offenders meet each other in a mediation process.

Now, for some program examples that have turned me on and which, I hope, will move you from good intentions to positive actions:

- The *Erie, Pennsylvania, program,* where the juvenile probation department's non-profit affiliate, Erie Earn-It Janitorial Services, Inc., has a $60,000 or so contract to clean up the courthouse each late afternoon and to perform janitorial services at a public library and social services agency. Probationers placed in community-based residential programs (including the final, community release stage of a drug treatment facility) also flow into and participate in this work effort. Youths retain 25% of earnings while 75% is transferred to victims.

- *Two programs of the Denver Area Youth Services (DAYS) non-profit agency* in Denver, where I've been on the board for about 20 years: (1) *The Rent-A-Teen*

Program: Work contracts—as with the U.S. Department of Housing and Urban Development, to shovel snow, cut grass, and do certain property maintenance for unoccupied homes that have been repossessed—brought in $60,000 in FY 1993; $36,000 of this was retained by the 128 working youths who averaged 16 years of age and worked an average of two months, while an additional $14,000 was paid back to victims. No participants reoffended during the year; all were high impact offenders. (2) *The Denver Work Adjustment Program (DWAP)*: Colorado law authorizes, and Denver Juvenile Court judges use, this authority to make dispositions of up to 45 days—sometimes a brace of weekend sentences—at the very overcrowded and so-called pretrial detention center. For many such sentenced juveniles, DWAP provides heavily programmed weekends at home, taking responsibility from 7:00 p.m. Friday evenings until 5:00 p.m. Sundays. The program consists of eight hours of community service work each Saturday and Sunday; house arrest otherwise; and active, nightly home detention monitoring on Friday and Saturday nights. FY 1993 participants totaled 326 juveniles who performed 9,528 work hours.

- *Lucas County Juvenile Court (Toledo, Ohio)* uses about $90,000 of its state subsidy program money to pay restitution-owing juveniles to perform community service work for repayment to victims. Juveniles retain 10% of payment. Work crews are used. A particularly nice feature is that juveniles placed at Circle C group home and Timberville Boys' Ranch, 20 and 30 miles away from Toledo respectively, perform their work at their residential settings, have these work hours certified and, thus, pay back victims without logistical nightmares.

- *The Sonoma County Probation Camp (Healdsburg, California)* has a written rule that each juvenile ordered to pay restitution, fines, or court costs must earn $50 a month for payment during the seven to eight months' average placement. Moreover, the camp's administration guarantees on-site earning opportunities. At the time of my visit, juveniles—on their own time—placed kiln-dried walnut wood scraps into a duffel bag for sale to the public as kindling wood. Other earning projects have been to make concrete foundation blocks, engineer's stakes that are sold to lumber yards for resale, cattle guards, and metal crossing signs.

- Briefer vignettes include *Madison, Wisconsin,* juveniles unloading newspapers from trash-collection trucks and reloading these onto a larger truck bound each night for a Chicago recycling plant; the court services agency in *Waterloo, Iowa's* contracts with the city for juveniles to cut grass and clean latrines in the parks, and other contracts to paint nursing homes; contracts with the U.S. Forest Service, as held by the private Partners agency in *Grand Junction, Colorado,* for restitution-owing youths to clear and maintain hiking trails; the High Intensive Treatment Supervision (HITS) program of the *Superior Court, Washington, DC,* for drug sellers and violent offenders that features 120 work service hours along with mandatory victim-offender mediation (staff act out the victim role when a victim chooses not to participate), tri-weekly urinalysis samples, intensive supervision, tracking, family groups, probation peer groups, education programming, and more.

Restitution and community service are the best sanctioning options that have come down the pike since the juvenile court was born in Chicago in 1899. If you don't agree, take a hard look at your effort's deficiencies and design a strategic plan to overcome obstacles and reach the Promised Land. If you do agree, tell your community all about what you and the kids have done to further juvenile accountability and competency development, and to improve community safety.

Chapter 28

Youth Restitution Program: Achieving Juvenile Accountability in Madison, Wisconsin

PROGRAM HAS 94% SUCCESSFUL COMPLETION RATE

Juvenile court judges and probation officers believe restitution and community service are important dimensions of juvenile accountability. They also believe that court orders should be honored. But they often despair as court-involved youth frequently fail to fulfill these court ordered obligations. While restitution and community service programs fall short in many communities, there are some very good programs that focus on these issues. One such program is Madison, Wisconsin's private non-profit Youth Restitution Program (YRP), which has admirably assisted the court, court staff, and court youth in meeting these requirements since 1978.

I first examined YRP in 1985. When I returned a few months ago, I found YRP was no longer a stand-alone program, but had become affiliated with a larger non-profit entity, Community Adolescent Programs, Inc. (CAP). Court youth who have been referred to YRP may, if they wish, also enroll in and benefit from participation in other CAP components. YRP itself is very successful, with its good staff-client ratio, cultivation of constructive job experiences, clarity of policies and procedures, data information base, communication with victims, and public relations. Its strong track record has resulted in continuous local funding and recognition of it as an accountable, integral component of this juvenile justice system. The YRP-CAP non-profit structure provides a programmatic flexibility that is less constraining than a public probation agency administration might experience.

YRP operates in Madison, the capital of Wisconsin, and the county seat for Dane County, with its population of approximately 400,000. The juvenile court administers pretrial facilities such as a detention center, a shelter home, and home detention. The county Human Services Department (HSD) administers the probation function; that agency's court-related staff members are called social workers, not probation officers.

The office of the district attorney makes all filing decisions. Nearly 50% of the court's 1998 caseload was enrolled in the YRP for community service (280), financial restitution (206), or a combination of both (54). YRP handled an additional 233 juveniles, enrolled during 1997, in its 1998 program. YRP juveniles performed 11,387

This chapter originally appeared in Juvenile Justice Update, *Vol. 5, No. 3, June/July 1999.*

community service hours in 1998 and paid victims $74,145. The average community service order was 40 hours and the average restitution order was $296. YRP could boast a 94% ratio of successful completion of court ordered requirements!

Community service hours are determined by formula. YRP designed a grid early on, approved by the court, to promote consistency in the assignment of community service hours. A first offense is assigned 10-30 hours, 30-50 hours, or 70-100 hours, depending on the particular violation, age, treatment needs, and attitude of the offender. A second offense rates 30-50 hours, 40-60 hours, or 90-125 hours. A third or subsequent offense is given 40-60 hours, 50-70 hours, or 120-150 hours. While the YRP guideline states, "staff have found that the maximum impact of a community service disposition is achieved in the 40-60 hour range," YRP accepts clients with smaller and larger numbers of assigned hours. In addition, a statute prohibits the assignment of more than 40 hours to a youth under age 14.

STATUTE COMBINES "REASONABLE PAYMENT" WITH "ABILITY TO PAY"

The Wisconsin statute takes a pragmatic, balanced approach to setting the amount of restitution. The court is to set a "reasonable" payment and find the juvenile "financially able to pay." As a result, many Wisconsin victims do not receive full restoration, and this is unfortunate. This is in contrast to certain other states where juvenile courts are compelled by law to order whatever amount a victim can document, regardless of the juvenile's ability to pay. Many victims in those states do not receive full restoration either, however, because juveniles often have a limited ability to pay. And fewer juveniles in those states get the satisfaction of fulfilling the requirement of what has been ordered.

YRP Discourages Combining Community Service With Restitution

YRP is pragmatic about its program and tells the court what it can and will do. YRP guidelines discourage combination orders of community service and restitution, as "it is extremely difficult to assist juveniles to do community service work and find a paying job at the same time." YRP recommends limiting combination orders to those where the monetary restitution amount is less than $50. It will accept youth age 16 and older with a restitution order up to $1,000 per offense, youth under age 16 with an order of up to $500 per offense, and youth under age 14 with a requirement that does not exceed $250.

YRP Facilitates Restitution Earnings by Younger Clients

Juvenile courts have long been bedeviled with restitution shortcomings that surround victim damage claims caused by children age 10 to 13. If parents can restore the loss, payment is accepted with the admonishment that their children should do additional home-related tasks to accomplish a form of parental reimbursement. Very often the court will be realistic and substitute a community-service-hours requirement for restitution, knowing the youth will not be able to find a job to earn the requisite sum.

Unfortunately, this leaves the victim without any direct reimbursement.

The Dane County program bridges this gap. Its service delivery contract with the county includes a sum of $15,000 that is used to subsidize community service work by younger youth not able to get paying jobs; 100% of the wages from subsidized community service goes to victim payment. The fund can also be accessed by older youths who, because of heavy schedules, cannot find regular jobs. These youths can be assigned to weekend work crews to earn, and consequently pay, restitution.

YRP Processes Formal and Informal Referrals

The Dane County YRP referral process, with formally petitioned cases, is initiated immediately following the court's entry of a community service or restitution disposition. The juvenile is directed to report to a courthouse office to receive a packet of YRP information. There, the social worker or lawyer for the juvenile facilitates a phone call to YRP and an initial youth-YRP telephone conference. YRP intake appointments are scheduled for one to two weeks after the phone contact, unless classified as low-need based on the content of this call. Court social workers also referred 69 informal diversion cases to YRP during 1998. These referrals all involved restitution and flowed into regular YRP screening procedures, classification, and program counselor assistance, as indicated.

YRP REFERRALS ARE CLASSIFIED AS HIGH-NEED OR LOW-NEED

The program specialist conducts an initial intake conference at YRP offices, located several miles from the courthouse. The interview explores the juvenile's job prospects, work experiences, skills and interests, "ideal" and other high-interest jobs, school schedule and other commitments, and transportation availability. Under certain circumstances, the program specialist can accomplish initial classifications based only on phone call referrals, for example, when juveniles:

- Indicate they have a job and will send in copies of regular pay stubs and restitution money orders or checks;

- State they expect to be able to find a job; or

- Indicate that a community service site can be arranged and reports sent in from the site to validate job attendance.

All youths age 15 and older and "employable" who owe restitution are given two to three weeks to find employment on their own. This approach reflects the agency's belief in furthering self-reliance rather than dependence. These clients are tentatively classed as low need. They are expected to turn in copies of four job applications each week. Low-need juveniles are expected to find their own job or payment source, or community service site. Low-need juveniles require minimum counselor involvement unless they have difficulty fulfilling their requirements. Instead, the program specialist retains the low-need juveniles as a caseload, which may average 140 juveniles. She contacts them by phone every two weeks to check on their progress. Perhaps 75% of referrals are first evaluated as low-need. If performance is unsuccessful, an intake conference is scheduled and, most likely, a program counselor is then assigned to the youth. If low-need cases are unsuccessful, they are reclassified as high-need cases and a program counselor will take them on weekly job searches. Juveniles classified as high-need are seen as requiring staff help in finding a job to earn restitution or in determining a community service work site.

Program Counselors Play Important Roles With High-Need Cases

The program counselor takes a very active role assisting in high-need cases. The counselor will arrange for juvenile work permits and will visit potential employment sites with clients. The counselor's introduction goes something like this: "I'm a job coach from Community Adolescent Programs where we help kids get jobs and develop good work habits." The juvenile's law violation record is not shared. Jobs are found at fast food and other restaurants, supermarkets, and large retail establishments. According to one counselor, "If a youth is employable, we can get him a job." After a youth is employed, a counselor may continue to visit the juvenile at the job site and talk with the employer and youth regarding job performance.

When community service is required, the counselor offers choices of sites to the youth: individual placements with non-profits, governmental entities, or YRP work crews. Counselors, whose caseloads average 25 to 30 youth, visit these work sites weekly. They are responsible for particular geographical locations and work with youth who reside in those areas of the county.

Counselors Facilitate Collecting Restitution Payments

Typically, in cases involving high-need juveniles, YRP enters a contract with the youth at an office interview that spells out what the youth must do and what the agency will do. If restitution has not been paid in full up front, the agreement requires the youth to reroute at least 50% of each private sector pay check to the victim. Program counselors know when their clients get paid. They visit youths on payday, or as soon after, as possible. Many of these visits occur at the juvenile's home. They examine pay-check stubs and collect at least 50% of pay, often in cash. (While many public-agency restitution programs prohibit staff from accepting cash, CAP is protected by an agency bond, and YRP allows it.) Low-need juveniles bring family checks, money orders, or cash to the program specialist who monitors their case.

YRP Forwards Restitution to Victims and Informs Them of Case Status

YRP transmits all restitution payments to victims, a function more generally filled by a court clerk or public agency. It does not charge for the administration of the restitution bookkeeping-payment system. Payments received one month are dispatched to victims late in the next, unless the amount is less than $20. The agency is developing a protocol to expedite these payments.

YRP emphasizes communications with victims, something frequently neglected in other communities. It gives victims information about case status as well as restitution status. Letters are individualized, such as:

Dear Mrs…: The juvenile, case #…, responsible for paying you $273.05 in restitution, with an outstanding balance of $127.97, is no longer receiving YRP program services due to having been sent to a correctional facility. The juvenile court has been informed of the youth's status. If you are dissatisfied with this outcome, I strongly suggest you consider filing a civil suit in a small claims court. Parents may be held liable up to $5,000 for damages, plus reasonable attorney fees and court costs. Contact the Dane County Small Claims Court at (608)… for information regarding pursuing a civil claim.

Another example is:

Dear Mr…: Enclosed is a payment from a youth, case number…. The youth was ordered to pay $613.62 in restitution to you. Outstanding balance: $94.28. Payment amount: $50.00. New balance: $44.28. You can expect the next payment in approximately eight weeks. Please notify us regarding any change in address. If you have questions call me at (608)…

STRONG INTER-ORGANIZATIONAL COMMUNICATIONS GIVE YRP CREDIBILITY

YRP is candid with juveniles, their families, victims, employers, courts, and other juvenile justice system participants. It keeps each group informed of the juveniles' progress and deficits. It develops rules and enforces them. Juveniles and their families, on signing agreements, are told what behavior can lead to a return to court, for example: failure to notify a job-site supervisor or counselor when unable to work; failure to make weekly restitution payments when employed in the private sector; failure to work all assigned hours; involvement in illegal activity; or inappropriate, non-compliant behavior at the job site. With these rules in mind, staff work hard to retain youngsters who are having difficulty meeting goals.

Program counselors, on their weekly visits to community service job sites, meet with the youths and work supervisors, and review the supervisor's completed checklist evaluation with both parties. If there are difficulties, they attempt to iron them out. A juvenile fired from a community service job site for work performance deficits may be placed, following counseling, at a second site. A second firing, however, may be grounds for a return to court. In any event, the court social worker, the assistant district attorney, the attorney for the youth, and the juvenile and the parents all receive notices of significant non-compliance. If the social worker arranges a court hearing, the YRP counselor is present and reports to the judge on the youth, YRP's efforts, and its assessment.

COMMUNITY WORK EXPERIENCES ARE VARIED

Juveniles work off their community service hours at different individual placement sites such as the Madison Civic Center (MCC) or as part of a YRP work crew. MCC offers a unique experience for youth, in large part because of a remarkable maintenance supervisor, Mark Weyers. I first met Mark when I assessed YRP in 1985. During that visit as well as my recent visit, I was struck by Mark's special interest in working with court youth in a personal, constructive, and honest way. I was also impressed, on both visits, with the useful jobs that juveniles performed: major theater cleaning, room/event set up and take down, snow removal, graffiti removal from outside walls, and assisting MCC mechanics. During one recent summer, two work crew teams reupholstered 2,200 seat cushions in the MCC theater.

MCC rules and expectations are made very clear up front in interviews with the youth who participate and are similar to those for full-time employees. Mark conducts 90% of these interviews and explains the nature of the work and the responsibility. While no juvenile offender is rejected, Mark wants offense disclosure. "But," according to Mark, "we treat them as people, not as somebody who got in trouble." The juveniles do not perform tasks that staff members do not perform. They punch time cards. "You can be early; you can't be late. If you are late three times, you are fired." They are treated with respect. "There are no dumb questions. If you don't go to school, you can't work, but you, not your parents, must still call in." At work, juveniles are assigned $2,000 walkie-talkie radios for use during their work. "Radios are to be used only when you: (1) are lost; (2) done with work; (3) don't know how to do something; or (4) break something." They are given keys to the building. If they abuse these trusts, they lose them.

I was impressed, then and now, with Mark's practice of providing job references for youths who had successful work experiences at the MCC. Mark describes the youths as volunteers who have been helpful to this civic enterprise. In the past 19 years, more than 750 juveniles have experienced an MCC work opportunity. Three of these juveniles, when old enough, applied and were hired for staff positions.

YRP work crews provide another work experience that is particularly useful for youths under 16 who are unable to arrange their own community service sites, and for younger juveniles who owe restitution but cannot find paying jobs. Work crews pay youths for their services, but 100% of earnings is transferred to victims. During 1998, 87 work crews were deployed, 24 of them in rural parts of the county. In all, 424 youths participated, racking up a total of 2,061 hours. A work crew experience averaged five hours. Specifications for suspension or firing and work crew rules, as with all CAP programs, are made clear to participants: "No visitors, bring a sack lunch, no walkmen or radios."

YRP relies heavily on part-time crew leaders who are paid $8 per hour. The agency's work crew coordinator leads about five crews each year, while also arranging work sites, coordinating the paid and volunteer part-time leader program, and obtaining community sponsorship of work sites. YRP-CAP emphasizes community participation in the work of the juvenile justice system. It locates citizen organizations that can use help with community clean-up, fix-up, and maintenance projects, thus blending the efforts of agency youth with community adults and youth. Volunteer crew leaders are recruited from the University of Wisconsin student body.

CONSTRUCTION COMPANY PROVIDES JOBS TO PAY RESTITUTION

YRP has a contract with a home construction company that pays juveniles who owe restitution to clear away building materials that are no longer needed from construction sites. This began as a pilot project in 1998, with the company providing eight days of work. The 1999 contract triples that, pays for a work crew supervisor, and pays participating juveniles the $5.15 minimum wage for their work. One hundred percent of the payment is returned to victims. YRP is intensifying other efforts to contract for youthful services and expedite payments to victims.

A FINAL WORD

YRP, now part of CAP, began with a mission of facilitating restitution and community service by court youth. After 20 years, it is still fulfilling that mission with the objective of high-level, accountable performance by youth and staff.

Author's Note

Dean C. Bossenbroek, Youth Restitution Program Coordinator, prepared the update that follows.

Between 1998 and the spring of 2000, it became apparent that YRP would need to expand work team operations in order to meet the needs of increasing numbers of clients. This was especially true for younger kids, as the average age of youth coming through the program continued to decrease.

In May 2000, CAP received funding from a Juvenile Accountability Incentive Block Grant (JAIBG) in order to form an anti-graffiti initiative, which came to be known as Community Restoration Crews (CRC). This allowed CAP to hire a full-time work supervisor, purchase graffiti removal equipment, and acquire a van to transport clients to and from work sites.

The impact on overall work team numbers was palpable immediately. Table 28.1 cites some statistics from 1999, 2000, and 2001. The 1999 figures represent the highest output for work teams up to that point. The 2000 numbers reflect six months of regular work teams, plus six months of the initial CRC operations. The 2001 work team/CRC stats illustrate CRC's most productive year by far.

Without the expansion of work teams, many YRP clients would be in a difficult position when it came to actually fulfilling their community service obligations. Individual job site supervisors are reluctant to accept grade school and middle school kids into their places of business. This is understandable when one considers the amount of time and energy it requires to train an able and willing adult volunteer versus the effort it would take to supervise a young person who possesses minimal job skills.

Table 28.1
CRC Work Team Experience

	1999	2000	2001
# of work teams	89	152	235
# of clients	435	700	1,143
# of client hours	2,018	3,224	5,564

Like most human service agencies, CAP has been facing a budgetary crisis for the past year, with no relief in sight. CAP has chosen to not replace staff as people move on; cost-cutting measures are a constant topic of debate; and the existing staff has been asked to take on larger caseloads.

Personnel-wise in 1998, YRP consisted of a director, one program specialist, and five counselors. YRP dealt with a total of 773 clients that year, which translated to an average of 30 clients per counselor at any given time. The contrast to the current team make-up is stark: a director who splits time between four different programs (five up until February 2002), a coordinator with a full caseload, and three counselors. Caseload sizes have exploded during the last 12 months to an average of 75 clients per counselor. In 2001, YRP provided services for 857 clients.

YRP's goal is to shrink these workloads to 40 by July 2002. However, this will involve arbitrary decisions and creative semantics, which will likely result in a reduction in the quality of services rendered. Many incoming clients will automatically be placed on some sort of wait list, which is something YRP historically prided itself in avoiding.

One intriguing part of the current crisis is the fact that in 2001, YRP maintained a 94% success rate. That figure represents the percentage of clients who complete their court-ordered obligations in full. On paper this is impressive (the YRP contract with Dane County Juvenile Court mandates an 85% success rate), but it doesn't reflect the watered down version of counselor-client interaction. Counselors used to perform intake at the client's home, visit clients at jobsites, maintain a line of communication with job site supervisors, and generally deliver services of very high quality. In our present state, counselors spend the bulk of their time on the phone, entering data on the computer, and are largely anchored to a desk.

Chapter 29

Work Crews Working: Montana Project Uses Community Service to Build Skills

COMMUNITY SERVICE THROUGH WORK CREWS, NOT INDIVIDUAL PLACEMENTS

Across the country, juvenile court-imposed community service has served to make thousands of juvenile offenders accountable to their communities for crimes they have committed. In many communities, juveniles are placed individually at any one of an array of non-profit or government agency work settings. But in Montana, juvenile courts in four Montana locations assign youths to the CorpsLINK program, a project of the Montana Conservation Corps. CorpsLINK relies exclusively on a model in which youth ordered to do community service are assigned to a work crew.

CorpsLINK provides more than just an opportunity to fulfill a court-ordered work obligation. Its program design is carefully constructed to increase participants' competencies, teamwork skills, and leadership capabilities. The program also wants to help them enhance their feelings of self-worth. Further, it blends work with mentoring. The mentoring relationship is also carefully designed.

CORPSLINK: AN AMERICORPS PROJECT

CorpsLINK uses AmeriCorps members as work crew leaders and mentors to its young participants. AmeriCorps is a division of the U.S. Corporation for National Service. AmeriCorps participants are assigned to community projects across the country, including the Montana Conservation Corps. Montanans may enlist in the Conservation Corps and, in turn, be enrolled in AmeriCorps.

Annually, about 50 AmeriCorps personnel serve in the Montana Conservation Corps for the full 10-month, 1,700-hour AmeriCorps assignment that begins every February. Usually eight to 10 of these members become CorpsLINK leaders assigned to work with court juveniles. In addition, another 80 or so persons enroll each May for a six-month, 900-hour assignment with the Conservation Corps/AmeriCorps.

This chapter originally appeared in Juvenile Justice Update, *Vol. 8, No. 2, April/May 2002.*

Usually another eight take assignment to the juvenile court project, thus enabling the Corps to increase its number of summer work crews. CorpsLINK's general practice is to assign four to five juveniles to one crew leader/mentor.

CORPSLINK'S PARENT ORGANIZATION

The Montana Conservation Corps, a statewide non-profit agency that accepts into its regular program only young people 17-years-old and older, is the parent organization of CorpsLINK. CorpsLINK was founded in 1994 to work with a younger group—juvenile court youths aged 11 through 17. Like its parent organization, CorpsLINK espouses principles of hard work, teamwork, self-worth enhancement, and leadership development.

In a recent year, the Conservation Corps partnered with more than 250 public and private natural resource and human service agencies to:

- Improve or construct 88 parks;

- Construct 54 miles of fence to protect wildlife habitats;

- Construct or restore 608 miles of trails;

- Build or improve 12 community gardens;

- Preserve 13 historic structures;

- Restore four miles of stream habitat;

- Repair 38 homes of senior citizens; and

- Improve 164 public community buildings.

Conservation Corps workers undertake projects in a wide range of settings in towns, cities, forests, and mountains. In return, they are paid a modest living allowance during their enlistment. Graduates have shown marked success in gaining employment in a state with a youth unemployment rate of 16% and a poverty rate for young people of 18%. They credit the technical and interpersonal skills gained during the Conservation Corps experience as greatly enhancing their abilities both to find and to keep jobs. According to an external evaluation, graduates show a 93% employment level.

CORPSLINK'S OPERATION

Juvenile Work Requirements Average 40 Hours

At the local juvenile court level, youths in CorpsLINK perform community service work after school, on Saturdays, and from two to five days a week during the summer. Court-directed community service requirements average 40 hours, but sometimes exceed 100 hours and, in one case, required 258 hours.

Probation Departments Help Fund Four Programs

The program originally served six juvenile courts, but state-level funding cutbacks that followed CorpsLINK's first fully funded four-year grant period reduced the number of courts served to four. In all four, the probation departments are able to contribute funds to the program. The program has served 798 youths statewide over the past three years.

Participation Increases in Summer

CorpsLINK initially places two AmeriCorps members in each community but supplements their ranks by from one to three members in the summer when juveniles often receive lengthier work requirements and can work on weekdays.

The initial state grant included significant funds for CorpsLINK to arrange for partially "paid community service," a program that provides monetary restitution to victims as a consequence of the juvenile's work performance. Budget cuts have now reduced the amount of money available for this purpose.

Self Enhancement Through Work

Among the key benefits of CorpsLINK are training and skill development. Each workday begins with a safety talk where youth learn to assess work sites for hazards and develop safety as a basic part of their work. Also on a daily basis, AmeriCorps leaders teach conflict resolution and communication skills. Team building initiatives are conducted frequently and used as a tool for teaching other skills.

According to staff members, assigned juveniles often have had very limited participation in sports and other activities that provide team-based experiences. But even the simple act of getting a crew set up for a day of work requires communication, compromise, and cooperation. Corps juveniles learn they each have different strengths and weaknesses, and learn to work cooperatively in order to take advantage of their various strengths while compensating for weaknesses.

To expand discovery of self-worth, the program stresses pushing the limits of participating juveniles, both physically and mentally. "Whether it is working a 10-hour day in inclement weather or simply dealing with an irritating crew member, we encourage juveniles to expand their perceived limits." The program considers that successes achieved on a daily basis allow Corps juveniles to discover their many positive qualities.

Leadership opportunities are provided when youths fill work positions such as the "tool swamper" (the person responsible for making sure crew tools are clean, safe, put away, and inventoried); the "vehicle swamper" (responsible for the daily safety check of the passenger van used in transporting the crew to and from the worksite and making sure it is clean and maintained); historian; or public relations representative.

Example 29.1 illustrates a CorpLINK success.

Example 29.1
Ronnie: A CorpsLINK Success Story

An AmeriCorps mentor wrote as a journal entry:

It seems destined that one of my greatest challenges will be Ronnie [not his real name]: 53 community service hours; major truancy problem; about to be transferred to Spring Creek [a school for conduct disordered kids]; uninvolved, angry (abusive?) father; mother who throws her hands in the air too easily, relinquishing control and responsibility for her son's behavior. The probation officer is fed up with Ronnie and ready to get punitive. Ronnie is very non-communicative ... he is the most intimidating of the kids because he seems so intransigent.

Ronnie had completed only two hours of assigned community service work over several months when he was referred to CorpsLINK. The AmeriCorps mentor continued:

I understood the officer's frustration when I met Ronnie ... he was sullen, gave monosyllabic responses and would look at neither of us virtually the entire time. Then, Ronnie came to our first project at the Salvation Army Thrift Shop on February 22. Over the course of the day I was surprised to observe he had a sense of humor, worked fairly consistently, and seemed to get on fine with the other kids. He complained little if at all.

By this Friday, April 5, Ronnie will have completed all of his community service hours in unprecedented time and without complaint. I often refer to him as the "bright star" of our projects. Sponsors have singled out his work and his attitude for praise. He has proven to be extremely good-natured, considerate and helpful. He is also a success story because he seems to truly grasp the service ethic of our program.

He acted on our crucial ideas ... to get work done and to improve the lives of people ... both directly and through helping other service providers. And he has had perfect attendance at school. In mentoring sessions we discuss work, school, whether he has called his probation officer this week, and personal issues: how he feels his father hates him and his mother covers for him, his close relationship with his older sister, what he might do after high school, and whether friends get into trouble. Ronnie shares his feelings and goals and setbacks. And his probation officer now calls CorpsLINK "God's gift to this kid."

CORPSLINK'S LINKS WITH BALANCED AND RESTORATIVE JUSTICE

Competency development, a core component of the balanced approach to probation, is a prominent part of the CorpsLINK approach. It is linked with a second principle, juvenile accountability, which in this context is the work the youth is assigned to help restore or improve the quality of life of the community, an indirect victim of the offender.

CorpsLINK, consistent with Balanced and Restorative Justice (BARJ) principles, involves the community to aid the justice system's effort to obtain accountability. In Montana, a large citizen volunteer component adds to the mentorship effort provided by the AmeriCorps members. For example, retired carpenters assist the Senior Home Repair project and provide technical help while teaching Corps juveniles carpentry skills; other volunteers help Corps juveniles learn gardening skills in the Community Gardens project. The mentoring is technical and personal, but takes place at the work site and does not follow the youth when the project is completed.

Skilled staff or citizen members of the organization where work is performed also provide technical advice to participants. This technical advice is needed to ensure each project is completed correctly. These partners, such as the Yellowstone River Parks Association, are also required to provide an educational component that allows Corps juveniles to acquire new skills and gain a better understanding of project work.

CORPSLINK WORK IN THE BILLINGS AREA

The accomplishments of program participants are significant. Among the projects completed by CorpsLINK during one six-month span in and adjacent to Billings, one of Montana's largest cities, are the following:

- Rehabilitated trails along the Yellowstone River, by restoring bridges displaced due to flooding and building new walking bridges, laying down gravel and woodchips on trails to prevent erosion, and removing fallen logs and brush;

- With other community volunteers, constructed Habitat for Humanity housing by hanging sheet rock, applying vinyl siding, insulating basements and windows, constructing interior walls and closets, and measuring, cutting, and nailing up exterior siding;

- Improved Lake Elmo Park by sanding and painting more than 30 picnic tables and the lifeguard station, varnishing a handicapped-accessible fishing dock, constructing a drainage ditch, planting trees, constructing a 1,600 foot split-rail cedar fence to allow for re-vegetation, and improving trails;

- Helped the Montana Rescue Mission prepare and serve food to a homeless population, cleaned the interior and shelved donated food, and distributed fliers for a concert to benefit the shelter; and

- Assisted city employees with installation of an irrigation system in Pioneer Park and cut away brush and trees at Riverfront Park to permit paving of parking lots.

Joy Mariska, Chief Juvenile Probation Officer in Billings, adds several other accomplishments to the list—creating paths at the local zoo by collecting and chipping Christmas trees and placing the chips along zoo pathways, and developing displays at an education-conservation center. She applauds the competency development quality of the program. Typically, second- and third-time lesser offenders are directed to CorpsLINK. She is "generally pleased" with the program, sees it as a valuable complement to the court's purposes, and generally finds CorpsLINK staff able to become high quality workers and increasingly skilled in dealing with adolescents and adolescence.

PROBLEMS AND PROSPECTS.

Steve Nelsen, former director of the Conservation Corps, notes both problems and prospects for the CorpsLINK program in Montana. Its problems? One has been funding limitations that have not allowed the program to have a fulltime professional staff person working with the program at each site. Another has been the relative inexperience of the AmeriCorps personnel at the outset of their appointment. He indicates they become quite effective over the course of their 10- to 12-month assignment, but then depart. The agency then must begin anew to train and supervise the well-motivated but unskilled replacements.

Its prospects? He remains "convinced the AmeriCorps model has applicability in the juvenile justice setting, but probably needs to be a larger program in Montana to make it cost effective and have the professional guidance we have not been able to fully provide."

A FINAL WORD

Obtaining AmeriCorps personnel to conduct a carefully executed community service program is a desirable but not problem-free approach that can be undertaken by juvenile justice agencies. However, these agencies should consider applying for AmeriCorps personnel. Competency-developing community service programs need to be on the juvenile court plate and the work crew model is an attractive approach. The small work crew approach illustrated here offers far stronger rehabilitative and personalized benefits than does, for example, a weekend work crew of 20 or more juveniles that uses just one or two staff supervisors.

Juvenile justice agencies, of course, can employ their own work crew leaders. And some employ college students part-time for this purpose. Yet a carefully orchestrated, well-conceptualized small work crew model provides superior benefits and merits replication. This can be done in any state or community, and not only in Montana.

Chapter 30

Youth Passages: Enriched Community-Based Intervention With High-Risk, Mid-Range Offenders

This chapter describes a program model, Youth Passages, that first opened its doors in November 1994. The Denver, Colorado-based program is operated by the private, non-profit Denver Area Youth Services (DAYS), an agency that administers numerous programs that serve delinquent youths and abused and neglected children. Youth Passages was to play an important role in reducing detention center overcrowding.

SENTENCE-TO-DETENTION STATUTES ADD TO DETENTION CENTER OVERPOPULATION

I have long thought that sentence-to-detention statutes arose in conjunction with deinstitutionalization of status offenders. As states embraced the U.S. Juvenile Justice and Delinquency Prevention Act and legislated outright or near-total bans on status offender detention, space was created in detention centers. A sentence-to-detention authorization could fill that space while giving judges an additional dispositional resource.

Approximately 15 years ago, Colorado authorized a sentence (or disposition) to detention. Colorado was not alone. About 15 states allow the juvenile court judge, at disposition, to order a stint in the local pretrial detention center. In Colorado, juveniles may serve up to 45 days. Following this stay, the juvenile returns to probation status. Locking up a juvenile for up to 45 days can send a very clear message to a new or repeat offender. And Denver judges sent that message. In time, the state-operated detention center became very full.

About eight years ago, DAYS contracted with the state to reduce the center's population on weekends. Its Work Adjustment Program took juveniles out of the center for the weekend, substituted eight-hour community service assignments on both Saturdays and Sundays, sent trackers to the juveniles' homes a couple of times each night, and returned the youths to the center after the weekend. That helped the overcrowding a bit, but not enough.

This chapter originally appeared in Community Corrections Report, *Vol. 3, No. 1, November/December 1995.*

NEW "GET TOUGH" LAWS FURTHER INCREASE OVERCROWDING

During the last few years, Denver experienced extensive juvenile shootings and killings that culminated in emergency juvenile-related legislation. Among other "get tough" provisions, new laws banned juvenile possession of guns and mandated pretrial detention following specified violent or gun offenses. Further, misdemeanor concealed weapon charges required a disposition of at least five days in the detention center. Drug-selling juveniles were among the regulars who were held in detention.

These laws caused the center's population to grow. Although its capacity was rated as 64 to 78, it came to house as many as 200 residents.

FEDERAL CLASS ACTION SUIT CLAIMS STATE VIOLATED PLAINTIFFS' CONSTITUTIONAL RIGHTS

A class action lawsuit was filed in the U.S. District Court on December 9, 1994. **E.R., A.W., et al., v. McDonnell, et al.**, Civ. No. 94-N-2816 (D. Colo. 1994). The case, which was filed as a federal civil rights action, claimed that conditions and practices at the detention center denied residents certain constitutional protections, including due process, equal protection, the right to privacy, free speech and association, and access to the courts and counsel. The American Civil Liberties Union of Colorado and the Youth Law Center, San Francisco, represented the plaintiff class. Overcrowding was but one of the issues targeted in the complaint.

The State's Response

Prior to the filing, the state announced it would fund additional detention beds at another to-be-announced Denver-area site. It is now nearly a year later and no location decision has been made. In addition, the state said it would award significant monies to private entities to (1) prevent initial detentions through screening, assessment, and the use of detention alternatives; and (2) provide a community-based alternative sentencing option to a sentence-to-detention. DAYS was awarded the second program option for its Youth Passages proposal.

The Federal Court Consent Decree

On September 1, 1995, the court approved a consent decree that had been agreed to by all parties. Its primary provision stated that no more than 78 juveniles shall be confined in the detention center, and that this maximum must be achieved within 90 days.

There were 46 other provisions, covering such matters as adherence to detention screening criteria, a classification system to meet individual needs of confined youths, staffing ratios of child care workers to residents during both waking and sleeping hours, a requirement that each resident must be provided a bed off the floor, expansions of physical and mental health care, monitoring at least every four minutes of youths on suicide status, and curbs and procedures regarding the use of seclusion rooms, attorney communications, staff training, and educational provisions for residents.

DEMOGRAPHICS OF YOUTH PASSAGES PROGRAM PARTICIPANTS

Youth Passages serves 24 to 30 juveniles at a time. The youths range from 13 to 16 years old, with an average age of 14.5 years. Boys outnumber girls six to one. Program participants are characteristically repeat offenders who have committed such offenses as assault with a deadly weapon, handgun possession, drug trafficking, burglary, aggravated motor vehicle theft, robbery, criminal trespass, and technical violations of a probation condition. Gang activity is prevalent in many of the participants' backgrounds. Several juveniles have committed domestic assault on a parent or other family member. Only 10 of the first 85 participants in the program resided with both natural parents. As people in our field say, these kids come from dysfunctional families.

Most of the program's participants, 64%, are Hispanic. The African-American juvenile complement is 20%. Caucasian youth total 8%, and there are small numbers of Native-Americans, Asian-Americans, and "mixed race" juveniles. The staff is heavily Hispanic.

Due to court control rather than agency control of intake, some juveniles enter the Youth Passages program who otherwise might be rejected. Those with serious drug addictions are one example. An agreement to exclude 17-year-olds is seen as helpful to participant cohesiveness.

YOUTH PASSAGES PROGRAM IN OPERATION

Duration of Program

The intensive program component lasts for 45 to 90 days. After 45 days, a judge reviews a juvenile's adjustment and determines whether continued participation should be ordered. Currently, there is state interest in restricting program participation to just 45 days. Such a time frame would reduce the center's overpopulation problem, and parallel the maximum detention sentence duration. However, DAYS' administration is convinced that the minimum time in the program should be 90 days, although six months would be preferable.

Individualized Treatment Plans, Case Managers

The program calls for an individualized treatment plan that encompasses family needs. Case managers carry 10 cases each, though they, like most program staff, execute additional functions. They provide individual and group counseling. They drive the vans transporting the juveniles to and from the program each day. They coordinate and supervise the community service work. They file weekly progress reports with the probation officers. Case managers also assist the juveniles for three months after completion of the intensive program and facilitate the youth's reenrollment in regular school.

The program has recently added a transition counselor to assist graduates with reintegration into school and compliance with court rules. The program has its own substance abuse counselor. This is greatly preferred to the slow referral process to external drug treatment resources. This counselor makes assessments, and provides treatment to present and past program participants and their families.

In addition to the other program features described in this chapter, Youth Passages can take advantage of other DAYS programs. For instance, DAYS' foundation-funded teen pregnancy prevention project meets with participants through individual counseling and sex education classes, and juveniles owing restitution can be employed immediately in a DAYS' Rent-a-Teen or summer youth employment program. DAYS also makes available pregnancy counseling and employment services.

Program Strategies

The program strategies include:

- *Schooling:* The program operates its own school. Class size is limited to 10. Ten computer stations are available; CD-Rom materials are used one to three hours weekly, and there are more than 70 educational discs. Culturally diverse materials are used to teach core academics, cognitive skills, and life skills. Most juveniles come to the program with an active dislike of their prior school experience, as well as grade level deficits of two to three years. Many just "can't sit still."

- *Community service:* Seventy-five hours of community service are required at such places as the Blind Association, Denver Housing Authority, and public schools. Snow removal, painting homes for senior citizens, and graffiti removal are tasks that might be performed at various settings. The hours are served as follows: at least two hours a day, four days a week. New participants also perform eight community service hours on Saturdays. Case managers arrange and supervise this work, in addition to their other duties. Accountability and competency development are clear goals.

- *Family participation:* There is individual and group counseling of parents, and a 12-session parenting class. Work is also done with siblings. The family counselor attends the initial court hearing when a juvenile is directed to the program, immediately acquainting the family with Youth Passages, and smoothing the same-day or next-day transition into the program. Parents, with their juveniles, must attend at least one family-enhancement activity each month. Staff is convinced that the more the family is involved, the more the youth progresses. Parents' transportation and child care expenses are partially reimbursed by a DAYS token participation incentive.

- *Tight monitoring of non-program time:* Juveniles are on home detention status, except as permission to leave home has been approved. Each new youth wears an electronic monitor. Monitors can be removed upon completion of major treatment plan requirements, but are re-attached following a rule violation. The program funds the necessary telephone tie-in with the monitor if the family lacks a telephone. "Human supervision," in the form of two full-time and two weekend trackers, is seen as more important than the monitors. Initial, random twice-a-night knocks on the door yield, with program advancement, to one knock and two phone calls, and then to just two phone contacts. The goal of the tracking is to engage the youth in talking about progress and problems, rather than "catching" the youth on a technical violation.

- *Experiential Learning:* Fridays are excursion days, described in program materials as "experiential learning." Among other things, there have been ropes courses, horseback riding, wilderness hiking, trips to the state women's prison and the Denver International Airport, a state-capitol tour and meetings with Hispanic and African-American legislators, a guided visit to the art museum, and career exploration visits to local businesses.

PROGRAM RULES

Structural Rules and Rewards

The program has a very structured program of rules, levels, and rewards. The rules ban alcohol, drugs, smoking, weapons, gang dress or activities, new tattoos, obscenities, radios and head-phones, pornography, and disrespect.

The program requires 100% attendance and participation; no program violation; increasing amounts of community service hours performed; book reports; no negative urine tests; participation in drug/substance abuse treatment, if appropriate; successful completion of specified life skills classes such as conflict resolution, anger management, sex education, and gang and HIV/AIDS awareness; active family involvement; and compliance with the free time/home detention schedule.

The program provides a "youth of the week" award and milestone advancements on individual treatment plans.

The program's rewards consist of stipends and clothing purchase awards. The former consist of monies that are distributed 50% to restitution obligations, and the balance—or the entirety if there is no restitution requirement—for personal items, from movies to eye examinations to candy. Parents or the case manager must escort a juvenile to purchase clothing and must submit receipts.

Three Rules Violations Mean Expulsion From the Program

Juveniles are terminated from the program if they violate three rules. Terminated youth cannot re-enter the program, and are returned to court for a different determination. A meeting with the juvenile, parent(s), probation officer, and Youth Passages staff occurs quickly following each violation, to pinpoint opportunities and penalties.

PROGRAM EVALUATION

Current available data evaluate the effectiveness of the program. The data show that 63% of program participants successfully complete the program. Eighty-five percent of unsuccessful terminations are due to the three-rule violation provision and the remaining 15% are due to a new offense being committed.

Through August 25, 1995, 26% of the program graduates had failed to either adhere to the court's drug control guidelines or report to a probation officer. Only one had perpetrated a crime, committing a domestic violence offense. Most of the violations occurred within the first 30 days after graduation. One graduate was later shot to death in a neighborhood dispute.

OUTLOOK FOR THE FUTURE SUCCESS OF YOUTH PASSAGES

I have been a board member of DAYS for more than 20 years. It has long been wedded to making monetary restitution and community service integral to its work with court youth. Youth Passages does fulfill the three goals of the balanced approach to probation, namely: (1) protecting public safety by overseeing much of a child's life space; (2) achieving juvenile accountability by actively facilitating restitution paybacks and community restoration through community service; and (3) promoting competency development by making skill advancement a fundamental component of the work juveniles perform.[1]

Authorizing judges to sentence to detention for 45 days has not worked in Colorado. Dispositions to a range of residential and non-residential programs is the better approach. The state of Colorado has now awarded DAYS major monies to reduce overpopulation in Adams County, adjacent to Denver. DAYS is now working two projects there, both "detention prevention" and a program to get detained juveniles out of that center earlier.

Youth Passages is promising, but intensive work with high-risk juveniles invariably results in only moderate success. One aspect of this program could be improved, however. To improve the program's effectiveness, I would recommend that those who break program rules three times should not be dispatched to state institutions by the court, and that additional graded punishments, controls, and interventions should be ordered.

Author's Note:

Youth Passages' doors closed on June 30, 2002, when state funds were shifted to a less intensive intervention project that could involve a greater number of juveniles. Youth Passages, during its final several years, suffered reduced Division of Youth Corrections' funding that eliminated both its substance abuse component and its durable, multi-dimensional involvement with family members, components seen as integral to the program. It had been able to expand its day school curriculum through educational department funding, and was offering more education and less treatment. It had maintained its extensive community work service requirement.

Youth Passages estimates it has been able to curb the detention center population by an average of 20 youths per day. It served 131 court juveniles during its final year, all but four of them minority youngsters. Although Colorado is no longer using the program, it is a model other jurisdictions might well consider.

Endnote

[1] Bazemore, G. (1995). Beyond punishment and treatment: A restorative model for juvenile justice, *Juvenile Justice Update, 1*(3), 1-2, 10-15.

Chapter 31

How Santa Cruz County's GROW Program Uses Interdisciplinary Teams to Curb Out-of-Home Placements

Every day in the juvenile court world, judges and collaborative staff search out residential settings for delinquent juveniles. They have decided these juveniles are incapable of rehabilitation in their homes and neighborhood settings, and that 24-hour care in a group home or residential facility offers the best prospect for positive growth and an end to law violations.

The placement decision includes an assessment that currently available in-home services are insufficient to protect public safety. Reliable outcome data regarding juveniles earlier placed in these facilities are invariably missing from the evaluation. Often only anecdotal references to successes with juveniles are cited. Further, the "system" generally manifests only limited interest in the program's dollar cost to the public. The court's budget is not responsible for the program's cost, so the judge does not search as diligently for a more intensive in-home intervention effort. County, state, and federal governments put up large, indeed huge, expenditures daily to underwrite out-of-home placement care.

CALIFORNIA LOOKS AT COSTS OF CARE

California, in the mid 1960s, did a painful examination of a different cost-of-care budget—that for its state-level youth authority and correctional department. As a result, California fashioned what likely was the first approach to providing state funds to enrich local juvenile and adult intervention services, provided that more offenders were handled locally. The money carrot motivated an expanded use of community correctional alternatives. Minnesota, Kansas, Pennsylvania, and recently Ohio, are other states which today offer carrots for channeling only more serious juvenile offenders to state-level institutions.

Group homes and residential care or treatment facilities have proliferated over the past several decades, helping fill (perhaps overfill) the space between regular or even

This chapter originally appeared in Juvenile Justice Update, *Vol. 4, No. 3, June/July 1998.*

intensive probation and state institutional confinement. Some programs specialize in substance abusing or sex offending youth; some emphasize a mental health milieu and therapies; some provide rigorous adventure challenges. These programs, traditionally sponsored by non-profit or governmental organizations, are increasingly the province of for-profit corporations. Multi-state operations, both non-profit and for-profit, are increasingly common. Enormous sums of taxpayer moneys go out to these entities. Bed space does not come cheap.

California initiated another effort, in 1984, which focuses on providing a comprehensive interagency "system of care" for seriously emotionally disturbed youth, including seriously emotionally disturbed delinquent youth. Objectives include avoiding costly psychiatric facilities, group homes, and foster care expenditures; emphasizing the use of least restrictive alternatives; reducing rearrests of court youths; and ensuring school attendance and benefits for special education students. First demonstrated successfully in Ventura County, more than 30 counties are now engaged in this program. Santa Cruz County enrolled in the program in 1989.

THE SYSTEM OF CARE MODEL

The "system of care" approach aims to redirect funds to a less costly, more comprehensive, and better service-integrated effort with high-risk children and youth in their own homes and communities. The systems change model promotes teamwork among mental health, juvenile justice, and social services agencies, as well as schools, and has a strong family focus. It combines six essential characteristics:

1. A clear definition of the target population;

2. Simple, clear, and measurable goals and objectives related to the target population;

3. Interagency coalition building;

4. Integrated, collaborative delivery of a wide range of services;

5. Incorporation of cultural competency to understand and respect the values and traditions of the diverse families to be served; and

6. Both internal (county) and external (university) evaluation of child/adolescent and systems' outcomes.

SANTA CRUZ COUNTY PROJECT GETS RESULTS AND SAVES MONEY

Santa Cruz County has a current population which approaches 250,000. In the five years (1983-1988) prior to launching "system of care," it averaged 104 group home placements per year. Over the eight following years (1989-1997), it averaged 67 group home placements per year, although placements increased during the eighth year to an average of 90 youth, and this in turn triggered a new probation-mental health team approach that will be described shortly.

The county's eight-year report on a host of measurable objectives found positive results with clinicians' ratings of child/youth level of functioning, parent or caregiver evaluations of child/youth social competence and problem behaviors, youth self reports of competence and problems, and family and youth ratings of satisfaction with services provided. More than 5,000 evaluations were conducted.

Prior to 1989, Santa Cruz County spent more than the California per capita average for group home expenditures. After implementation of the system of care, the county has continuously spent less than the state's per capita average. Indeed, University of California evaluators calculated eight-year cumulative county savings of just under $11 million, or average annual savings of $1,360,302. The county's annual project budget was $723,000.

The university also found reduced use of state hospitals and group homes, better school attendance and academic achievement for special education students, and significant reductions in rearrests for youth in the juvenile justice system.

KEEPING KIDS IN THE COMMUNITY THROUGH GROW

Santa Cruz County increased its focus on juveniles who manifested both serious delinquency and emotional problems in April 1997 with a family preservation program named GROW, an attractive acronym for a strained title, Graduated Return to Opportunities Within Families and Community. This expanded effort aims to:

- Keep seriously at-risk juveniles at home (about 90% of workload); or

- If juveniles are placed (about 10% of workload), return them home more quickly than has been the norm.

The latter component uses GROW staff to "patch-in" intensive services during the placement and continue an intensive service delivery following return home. Project staff estimate 50% of program-enrolled juveniles are serious drug (i.e., heroin, cocaine, amphetamines) users, and perhaps 35%-40% are hard-core addicted youth. Many, particularly in South County, have gang affiliations.

JUVENILE JUSTICE–MENTAL HEALTH COLLABORATION PROMOTES SUCCESS

GROW is co-directed by a probation department supervisor and a senior mental health professional. The GROW staff consists of three teams of a probation officer and two mental health workers. Each team serves 15 juveniles.

The intense collaboration and integrated services provision by and between probation and mental health is unusual in this country. It has been keenly influenced in California by mental health departments' redefinition of "seriously emotionally disturbed" to include "conduct-disordered" youth. Conduct-disordered juveniles, long seen by mental health agencies as outside their target populations, are abundantly represented in juvenile justice system populations.

Treating Youth in the Community: GROWth Without Walls

When a juvenile remains in the community, GROW takes over the youth's life. Parents are important program partners. So are the several day treatment schools which juveniles attend, and which welcome—and specialize in educating and treating—youth with substance abuse and mental health problems. Five hours a day, five days a week, court juveniles are "walled into" these day settings.

GROW is a highly structured three-level program, which begins with confinement to home (friends are not allowed in) except for school, counseling, program activities, jobs, or when accompanied by a parent. GROW staff meet at least three times a week with the youth. They have weekly interactions with the family to facilitate effective parenthood and the execution of parental responsibilities to the child and the court. Individualized plans are developed which strengthen protective factors and seek to avoid risk factors.

Drug treatment groups led by a clinical staff specialist occupy many youth four or five evenings a week. Project staff run a rock-climbing group, a chess group (where behavioral-cognitive work is done), and community service projects, all designed to provide healthy alternatives and build competencies. Further, an employment developer arranges vocational internships or placements and provides ongoing support. The University of California at Santa Cruz also enhances GROW's services through an internship class offered by GROW staff at the university; student interns provide program enrichment activities and serve as mentors and tutors.

Monitoring Compliance and Handling Violations and Reoffenses

Electronic monitoring is not used as part of the GROW program; instead, human services contact is the emphasis. Probation officers and mental health workers join in recreation, informal counseling, job and mentor searches, family crisis assistance, and school monitoring interventions. Probation officers are the specialists who enforce probation conditions, i.e., drug testing, curfews, and house arrest compliance. Mental health staff do more mental health.

As juveniles progress, they are allowed more unsupervised time. When there is a technical violation, and there are many, probation officers intensify family case conferencing and approaches to enhance parental supervision. Of course, there are reoffenses. Whenever possible, these are handled within the community, and with as brief a detention center stay as can have meaning and be instructive. Examples 31.1 and 31.2 highlight two case reports.

GROW Relies on Integration of Interagency Services

Judith Cox, the Santa Cruz County juvenile probation director, states that fundamental integration of interagency services is critical to the success of GROW, or even to gains with temporary failure cases. She adds this often means probation departments have to "give way," or share some of their power in terms of case management. But while sharing responsibility, "we look upon ourselves as the primary case managers, and ultimately we have the final decision-making power over case management decisions."

Example 31.1
A Success Story

Background: Jonathan is 15. Placed in a group home following an adjudication for assault with a deadly weapon, petty theft, and public drunkenness, he was referred to GROW after he ran from the placement and had been AWOL for six weeks. The run followed his physical attacks on other residents and staff.

Jonathan's father died when he was two years old. His relationship with his mother is described as volatile. School records indicate numerous behavioral problems, suspensions, and an expulsion.

Strengths: Jonathan's strengths included (1) a stepfather, separated from the mother, who wanted Jonathan to live with him and who had a sincere desire to help; (2) a mother-stepfather agreement to follow a step-by-step plan devised with their input and to work together with staff; and (3) a commitment by Jonathan to do all he could to avoid another placement or state commitment, and to attend a treatment-based school, all counseling appointments, and an anger management group.

Weaknesses: Identified weaknesses, which became target areas for intervention, consisted of school behavior problems, physical and verbal aggression toward teachers and peers, an inability to control anger, and substance use. Another concern was the problem relationship he had with his mother.

GROW Changes Jonathan's Environment: Jonathan entered GROW and left the detention center to live with his stepfather. He enrolled in a designated day treatment school with its classroom for the "seriously emotionally disturbed," small teacher-student ratio, and on-site provision of intensive mental health services. With one exception, his subsequent problems were minor compared with his previous precarious position. When he refused to follow directions at school, he threatened a campus guard. He was immediately apprehended by his probation officer and removed to the detention facility. There, he, his stepfather, mother, and GROW staff reviewed Jonathan's need to speak to and discuss his concerns and frustrations instead of exploding outward. Additional ground rules were set and Jonathan returned to stepfather's home and school.

Stepfather-mother communication problems were addressed at this and subsequent family sessions, including their different standards and rules for Jonathan's conduct while in their respective care. Staff worked with them on using consistent guidelines. Jonathan, when visiting his mother, would contact the stepfather for permission to participate in activities that were outside the usual, and the stepfather would carry a pager so he could be reached immediately to discuss the requests.

Jonathan's case summary observes that he is succeeding in learning to control his anger by adapting coping skills taught at a weekly anger management group, and is communicating more with his support team. When under stress, he has "resorted to problem-solving rather than acting out against himself and the community. He has taken advantage of the special classroom and begun to flourish academically. He is respected by staff and peers, and has become a role model for other students. He has not reoffended, physically assaulted anyone, nor harmed himself. His prognosis for continued progress is excellent."

OUT-OF-HOME PLACEMENT ALSO RELIES ON COLLABORATION; FOCUSES ON RETURN TO IN-COMMUNITY CARE

In 1989, an earlier probation-mental health partnership opened a locked, short-term residential treatment facility, Redwoods, on the grounds of the juvenile court/probation complex. Redwoods houses 18 adjudicated delinquents who enter the program under a court order and have significant mental health concerns. Conduct disorder is the most frequent diagnostic category; violence manifestations have been common. Average duration of stay is just 4.5 months.

Example 31.2
A Failure

Background. Federico, a 13-year-old, did not make it at home. While his mother worked at night, he was running drugs for older employers and waving potential buyers down as they passed by in their cars. He was arrested several times after midnight and under the influence of drugs. He was a gang member and very much beyond the control of his mother. School truancies were common and school adjustment problems significant. Federico's three older brothers had extensive criminal records; one was serving time in prison. His mother was raising three younger half-siblings as a single parent.

GROW moved Federico to his father's home in a nearby town. The father and his new wife had two young children. The father was a successfully recovering alcoholic, and his wife was a full-time parent and housekeeper. They lived away from high drug and gang areas, and had a well-organized home and apparent stability.

Strengths: Federico wanted to live with his father, who wanted to work with him and take him to 12-Step meetings. Another strength was his enrollment in a school that emphasized drug and alcohol recovery within a community school context. His stepmother could supervise him after school, and both parents were home at night.

Federico Opts for Peer Environment: The plan failed. Federico stayed drug free for a while, and did reasonably well at school. But he wouldn't help with family chores or conform to family rules. He defied judicial bans on visiting his old peer group, told his parents conflicting and dishonest tales of where he was and who he was with, and spent weekend nights along the railroad tracks with his old gang, crack, marijuana, and alcohol.

Family conferencing continuously tried to work on parental communication and collaboration with project staff. But while the parents signed pledges to advise staff of negatives and problems, they never called these in or shared shortcomings without probing by staff.

Federico was picked up on still another unlicensed return to his old haunts, wearing gang colors and throwing gang signs from a low-rider car with his buddies. He was ordered into a placement with walls. His probation officer claims GROW was not a futile effort and that Federico and his parents had made gains. He posits they will be better able to cope with each other and Federico when Federico leaves the group home, and termed this a "successful failure."

Treating Delinquents In, Not Out-of-County

The 36 or so juveniles who experience Redwoods annually add to Santa Cruz's out-of-home placement numbers, but:

- Their stays are significantly briefer than the 10-12 months that was the earlier norm in group homes and other treatment facilities; and

- They are now housed and assisted within the county.

The presence of a local facility makes possible the weekly conjoint juvenile-family treatment sessions and allows families to participate regularly in multi-family groups. Fewer offender placements 200-300 miles away means greater efficiency for the specialist placement probation officer whose job it is to arrange placements and visit placed juveniles each month.

The basic Redwoods program is run by mental health staff, but probation staff consult regularly with treatment staff and juvenile residents. Following release, juveniles participate in a quite intense one-year aftercare program which significantly reduces the cost and length of residential stay. Three full-time therapists and a probation officer constitute the aftercare staff. The probation officer splits her time between aftercare juveniles and the 18 juveniles in Redwoods. Outcome data reflect 90% of successful dischargees return home, and that rearrests are substantially reduced.

Out-of-Home Placements Must Be Strongly Justified

Probation and mental health supervisory personnel make up the new Pre-Placement Screening Committee which reviews all cases for which probation staff plan to recommend that the court order out-of-home placement. Of the initial 69 cases reviewed, 25 were court-ordered into a placement, 24 into GROW or other less restrictive alternatives, and 20 were placed at Redwoods. Santa Cruz County is not the first program to use a pre-placement review process, but its approach may be different and its alternatives richer.

The different approach is that the county adopted a priority to curb placements and their accompanying costs. Another influence is a probation department policy to constrain pre-judicial detention stays, as well as dispositions (or sentences), to the juvenile detention center, which are authorized by statute in California and at least a dozen other states.

The approach is reinforced further, and very strongly, by the 1997-initiated practice of the California Youth Authority (CYA) to charge counties for delinquent juveniles committed to state care.

A county is now charged $1,800 per year ($150 per month) for a juvenile committed to the CYA. However, the charge is increased by 50%, 75%, or 100% of the annual expense of care cost of $35,400 if the juvenile is committed for a less serious offense. Rapists and armed robbers warrant the minimum charge; a commitment offense of grand theft, first or second degree burglary, or concealed firearms jumps the county's ante enormously.

CONCLUSION

GROW is promising as both an institutional alternative and a shortened institutional stay program. And GROW is still growing. There are plans to buttress juveniles' unscheduled out-of-school time with still more activities. Certainly multiple agency service integration is an accomplishment. Other communities should actively consider GROWing.

Author's Note

Judith Cox, now Chief Probation Officer, Probation Department, Santa Cruz County, California, prepared the commentary that follows.

In 2001, the University of California-San Francisco Child Services Research Group published the California Children's System of Care 2001 Evaluation Report,[1] funded by the California Department of Mental Health. The report presents findings from 39 California counties that were funded to implement the System of Care (SOC) Model prior to the 1997/98 Fiscal Year. Data is current through January 2001. Evaluators, led by Dr. Abram Rosenblatt, collected data regarding four important SOC performance criteria: (1) to insure that the target population is being served as intended; (2) to reduce reliance on restrictive levels of care; (3) to improve educational performance of target population youth in school settings; and (4) to reduce the likelihood of re-arrests for youth who are involved in the juvenile justice system. As one of the original four California counties implementing SOC, Santa Cruz County continues to demonstrate impressive outcomes.

Nationwide, it remains true that increasing numbers of children are separated from their original families and raised in a variety of residential placement or institutional facilities. The cost of residential care in California is approximately $25,000 for a six-month group home stay. And yet there is very limited evidence for the effectiveness of residential care. According to the Child Services Research Group's report, there are extensive concerns regarding not only the costs of these placements, but also the risks associated with residential care including the failure to learn behaviors needed in the community, the probability of trauma associated with separation from family, difficulty in reentering the family, victimization by staff and other residents, and learning of antisocial behavior from other disturbed children.

SANTA CRUZ PROGRAMMING STILL WORKS

Santa Cruz continues to demonstrate a pattern of maintaining per capita group home placements and expenditures rates both below the state level and below historical trends in the county. Overall, $3 in California resources (state and county) was saved for every $1 in state SOC funds invested in Santa Cruz and two other original SOC implementation counties (Riverside and San Mateo) since 1989. In Santa Cruz, the cost savings associated with SOC implementation has been diverted, in part, to community-based services as well as prevention services in high risk communities.

Recidivism outcomes remain impressive. Through December 2001, 328 youth have been served in the Santa Cruz GROW Family Preservation Program without compromising public safety (97% of program participants did not commit a new felony while on the program.) These youth are chronic offenders with high needs who, prior to GROW implementation, would have been in out-of-home placement.

CHANGES AND ENHANCEMENTS TO SANTA CRUZ SERVICES

Several changes have occurred in the Santa Cruz community-based continuum of services for high-risk offenders. In 1999 the Probation Department received a grant from the California Board of Corrections which funds two site-based day treatment centers at both ends of the county, known as the PARK Program. The project is a research-based, experimental design, which compares outcomes (school performance, clinical measures, recidivism, and completion of court-ordered probation terms) in the GROW Family Preservation Program with the new site-based PARK Program. Youth are randomly assigned to either GROW or PARK after the court has found them eligible for "Placement Prevention Services." Following completion of the four-year study, the county will publish results that should indicate whether a site-based program has better outcomes than a non-site based program with a target population of youthful offenders who would have otherwise been in residential placement.

As the PARK Program became operational, the Probation Department noticed that the census dropped at the county-operated residential program (Redwoods). Although a 10-year study of Redwoods outcomes (recidivism, school performance, clinical measures) had always been very positive, there was some decline in positive results. Probation, mental health, and drug and alcohol administrators realized that the top 10% of chronic offenders were frequently cycling through GROW, PARK, Redwoods, and the juvenile detention facility due to drug abuse problems. The county interagency team decided to respond to this need and redesign Redwoods. The purpose of the new program is to intervene at the point of failure in GROW and/or PARK by providing a short-term residential stay during which reassessment, stabilization, skill building, and transitional planning can occur. The program goal is to intervene in the relapse cycle, provide motivational interviewing and behavioral cognitive work while a new case plan is developed. This plan then accompanies the youth back to the GROW or PARK program along with a new commitment from the family which is arrived at through a series of family conferences. There is, therefore, an attempt to return the youthful offender to home and community with a new set of skills rather than escalating the minor to long-term residential care.

Finally, in March, 2001, the Probation Department was selected by the Robert Wood Johnson Foundation as one of 11 sites nationwide to implement the foundation's Reclaiming Futures Initiative[2] to coordinate and utilize drug abuse and alcohol services more effectively and to expand the integrated SOC to address the high rate of recidivism among substance abusing, chronic offenders. The Department is looking forward to an opportunity to add to the body of knowledge on this important topic.

Endnotes

---

[1] For the full report online, see *http://saawww.ucsf.edu/csrgweb/*.

[2] More information on Reclaiming Futures is available online at *www.reclaimingfutures.org*.

Chapter 32

IMPACTing Detention and Commitment: Multi-Agency Collaboration Serves Juveniles With Multi-System Needs in Boulder County, Colorado

SERVING MULTI-NEED YOUTH

Project IMPACT, Integrated Managed Partnership for Adolescent Community Treatment, was implemented to address what many juvenile justice systems across the country experience—a substantial percentage of middle and deep-end juveniles who are clients of two, three, or even more agencies, to wit, the court, probation, substance abuse services, the public child welfare agency, medical care entities, psychiatric facilities, and other community-level resources. IMPACT is a Boulder County, Colorado, interagency collaborative aimed at integrating multiple systems, blending their funding, and sharing financial risks to match clients' needs with those interventions best tailored to meet those needs.

IMPACT's goals are clear:

1. To improve the quality and continuum of services provided to children, adolescents, and families;

2. To decrease out-of-home and out-of-community placements; and

3. When safe and appropriate, to reduce residential lengths of stay.

Severe or repetitive juvenile offenders are a prominent IMPACT focus. But IMPACT is equally concerned with non-delinquent youth, such as abused and neglected children who are either facing or already in placement, youth manifesting severe mental health problems, and youth with significant alcohol or drug abuse. IMPACT juveniles often wrap across these categories and IMPACT wraps services around these youths.

This chapter originally appeared in Juvenile Justice Update, *Vol. 8, No. 1, February/March 2002.*

"YOUR KID IS OUR KID": SHARING RESPONSIBILITY TO IMPROVE SERVICES AND CUT COSTS

The wraparound service delivery collaboration was created in Boulder and other communities to bring different agencies to the table. An aim was to improve service delivery when several agencies were active. The approach sought to cut through obstacles to cooperation such as the perception that "he's your kid, not ours," or funding strictures that allowed agencies to reject cases for different reasons. Long waiting lists for services posed other problems. Often, work with delinquent youth required the court or probation department to get assistance or funding for placements from the public child welfare agency. It was this agency that prompted the development of IMPACT in Boulder County.

Colorado's costs for its state child welfare system had escalated from $40 million in 1992 to $140 million by 1997. That year the legislature authorized the state Department of Social Services (DSS) to find and approve three counties that had interest in reducing out-of-home placement costs (20% of which were borne by a county), to develop pilot programs. Further, managed care concepts had appeared, and legislators wanted approaches that would be cost effective while providing services as good or better than those that existed. The incentive to counties to participate: A pilot county that expended less than a capped allocation could use the unexpended funds to provide expanded services to targeted children and, as feasible, expand services to additional children.

Saving money was not the only motivator. In neighboring Kansas, child welfare services had been turned over to private management. The state DSS wanted to keep the same thing from happening in Colorado. Pilot programs were seen as an opportunity to move managed care concepts forward without moving to a for-profit managed care entity. Boulder County became a pilot location, motivated by a belief that it could improve its quality and continuum of services and broaden its collaboration with key agencies to form a more integrated cross-system of service delivery. It developed IMPACT and has achieved both objectives.

ACTIVE COMMITMENT OF AGENCY EXECUTIVES CRUCIAL TO SUCCESS

The chief executives of key agencies, not their representatives, manage IMPACT. They meet weekly, set policy, and review practice. The chief judge of the Boulder court system, the chief probation officer, the directors of the community corrections agency, the child welfare agency, the mental health center, and the health department, along with the lead juvenile district attorney and the regional director of the state Division of Juvenile Corrections comprise this governing board.

As a group, these executives have the authority to override individual agency decisions in specific cases that are referred to IMPACT. The only exception to this decisional authority occurs when a case requires judicial determination. Then IMPACT can make a recommendation to the judge about services for a youth, but the judge has the final say as to what is ordered.

Such active top-level commitment is rare in projects that provide wraparound services. But agency chief executive commitment translates into the commitment of resources. Further, this commitment devolves to line staff, who see collaboration blessed on high, and who then institutionalize collaborative practices even with non-IMPACT cases.

POOLED FUNDING MAKES SERVICE DECISIONS POSSIBLE

IMPACT goes further than just sharing decisions across agency lines. It shares funds as well. IMPACT is entrusted with funds that key agencies transfer from their budgets to support treatment decisions. This pool combines county DSS out-of-home placement funds, state Division of Youth Corrections (DYC) funds for use by the county for state detention and commitment beds, and DYC money available to fund services as alternatives to the use of these beds. The community mental health center pools its funds that otherwise cover hospitalizations, in-home therapeutic and wraparound services, services needed by detained juveniles, day treatment programs, and the interagency sex offender/containment team. The county health department, the probation department, and the county community corrections agency contribute additional funding. The annual pool currently averages $13 million.

With these funds, IMPACT purchases inpatient mental health treatment, detention and commitment beds, residential treatment programs, and foster home beds. It also buys outpatient mental health, substance abuse, probation, and community corrections services. It does this within the framework of providing case planning across systems without cost shifting or system shifting. When pooled money, as capped by contributing agencies' state-level entities, is underspent, IMPACT can use these funds to enrich its program offerings. At the same time, all agency partners jointly share the risk of any cost overages that occur in out-of-home care and work together to determine how any unspent funds that are realized will be spent. So far, there have not been any overages. IMPACT has always underspent and, thereby, realized the monetary bonus.

Not all administrative functions are shared. The mental health center serves as the fiscal agent for IMPACT. DSS manages all out-of-home placements for the partners, and the mental health center manages all inpatient and community-based mental health service use, though it still pays for inpatient care in coordination with the IMPACT program.

IMPACT OPENS DOOR TO SERVICE

The precept upon which IMPACT operates is that youths any agency works with are Boulder County youths, "our" youths. Enriching local services to keep a youth at or near home is viewed as superior to removing the youth from the community. It does not matter what agency door youths walk through. The goal is to see to it that they get the services they need regardless of funding streams. IMPACT has a single point of entry—case planning based on need. Therefore, referrals can come from anywhere. Any door is the right door.

A juvenile may come to IMPACT through the juvenile court door, but the juvenile's problems may be primarily mental health related, or the youth may need DSS family stabilization services or, if that fails, foster care. Or a DSS youth may become enmeshed in the juvenile court but need inpatient drug or alcohol treatment. Or an outpatient mental health case may involve serious school problems requiring multi-agency assistance. In such a case, the school district would participate regularly in IMPACT oversight. Example 32.1 provides case studies for several IMPACT youths.

ORGANIZING FOR IMPACT

Below the executive, policy-setting level, multi-agency community evaluation teams and placement review teams continuously staff new and ongoing cases. The community evaluation team reviews and addresses high-risk youth in the community—those living at home or returning to the community following a placement. The placement review team reviews and provides interagency collaboration for children or youth going into placement—foster home, residential treatment, psychiatric hospital, or correctional setting. The teams arrange for service provision, review a youth's progress or regression, and evaluate the need for additional or substituted services. An unwritten goal of these teams, but one that is kept very much in mind, is to reduce the use and thereby the cost of out-of-home placements.

IMPACT employs a director and a utilization review staff of intensive case managers who are funded from the central pool. Case managers who work with the community evaluation team implement the case plan developed for each youth by a specially impaneled interagency group. Case managers who work with the placement review team monitor treatment within the placement and work to ensure that designated treatment goals are pursued, that treatment is proceeding appropriately, and that enriched post-placement services are in place to enable the youth to return to the community as soon as possible. This team and state foster care reviewers perform joint foster care reviews.

The combined emphasis is to supplement and deepen services in order to avert placements and to abbreviate the out-of-home placements that are necessary.

IMPACT ON DELINQUENT YOUTH

Boulder County is, overall, a socio-economically privileged community of approximately 260,000 persons located just north of Denver. But it is not a Denver suburb. Rather, the county and its flagship city of Boulder have their own center and integrity. While it has various pockets of poverty, it has no severe inner city concentrations of poverty. It has a reasonably high number of juvenile offenses that range from modest to very serious.

State DYC data indicate that juveniles committed to its care from Boulder County have one of the highest delinquency profiles for adjudicated youth in the state. With the exception of a heinous first-time offender, juveniles from Boulder who are committed to DYC have typically received extensive community services and are committed only when local options have been exhausted.

Example 32.1
Case Studies: The IMPACT Placement Review Team at Work

The following are examples of how the IMPACT placement review team responds to cases before it. Names have been changed to protect the children involved.

Sexual Assault Considered by Placement Team

Sixteen-and-one-half-year-old Mario was in detention for violating his probation by sexually assaulting another boy at a treatment facility where he had been placed following an earlier sexual offense. The facility reported that Mario was "unable to keep his hands off other juveniles." Placement team members questioned Mario's medication treatment and decided that a consultation with the facility's physician was needed. They decided to ask the court to return Mario to the facility. Probation staff were to counsel Mario that his time in detention had been a sanction and that other offenses would bring other sanctions. Probation staff were to return Mario to the facility and become the facility's authoritative partner in working with Mario's mother who had "always been his out." They were also to collaborate with the facility to provide respite for facility staff when Mario's behaviors merited additional detention time. Mario's public defender participated in the discussion and did not object to the plan.

Assault by Psychiatric Patient Calls for New Look at Services

Susan, a nearly 17-year-old patient at a psychiatric facility, was in secure detention after being charged with felony assault with a deadly weapon—a ballpoint pen—on a hospital staff member. During the past three and a half years, Susan had been in and out of a group home and a treatment center. She had also assaulted staff at one of these facilities. She also had two prior hospitalizations and a suicide attempt. She had run away from previous facilities. She had been diagnosed with bipolar disorder with psychotic features. This was not her first time before the placement review team.

The assistant district attorney agreed to contact her counterpart in the nearby county, send a letter that incorporated the case history, and ask that the assault with a deadly weapon charge be dropped. Susan would stay in detention until placement could be arranged at a residential program where she had done reasonably well in the past. DSS, responsible for placement costs, stated its belief that the program had an opening. The facility had an on-grounds school, an advantage for Susan as she had problems with school. The facility also had a "hook up" with the state vocational rehabilitation agency, which would be useful later for transitioning Susan to independent living.

Youth Gets New Direction

Joe was a 17-year-old youth with a long history of Department of Social Services involvement. Abandoned by his mother, the only parent he had known, Joe had lived in a succession of foster homes where his experiences were complicated by his diagnosed mental health and mood disorder problems. Following three adjudications for drug offenses and property crimes, a new drug offense brought him to an IMPACT review for a recommendation to the court on whether commitment was indicated. IMPACT team members saw Joe as a threat to himself and to others, but thought the best strategy was to hold Joe accountable for his offense and transition him to independent living.

The court then entered a disposition to the BEST program's Wilderness Work Camp for a short placement. Instead of a traditional release to probation supervision, Joe then received intensive supervision from a BEST officer. This involved daily contacts, drop-in visits at his school, substance abuse treatment, employment assistance, and a highly individualized and supervised case management plan. Effectuating his educational and employment plan as part of an independent living experience, Joe has now gone 12 months without a new arrest. He is, at present, better grounded in the community than confinement in a secure correctional facility would have allowed. Thanks to IMPACT.

Reducing Detention

Boulder County's community corrections agency, largely locally funded, is a significant force in the county's efforts to retain its youth within the community. The agency entered into a unique contract with the state DYC to receive a monetary bonus if the county used less than an assigned quota of state detention center and state institutional daily costs. Overuse would require county payment to the state. It has not overused.

Although Boulder County maintains its own small short-term detention facility at the rear of the courthouse, detention centers are a state responsibility. Other beds are available at a state detention center about 40 miles away and can be used for longer-term pretrial holds and for secure detention sentences, as authorized by law, for up to 45 days.

The county community corrections contract was absorbed into IMPACT. Under it, IMPACT receives $133 per bed day for below quota detention usage. Boulder "saved" approximately $500,000 in 2000—money that was reallocated locally to further service provision and reinforce the county's ability to curb state detention and institutional bed use.

Transfer of State Parole Function Serves Youth

One final county-state agreement is noteworthy. DYC now provides funds to the county to hire its own parole/aftercare officers—typically a state function in Colorado. Two such officers, officially attached to the probation department for fiscal and authority reasons, provide more aggressive, more intensive aftercare services to Boulder County juveniles who are released from correctional institutions than is believed to be available elsewhere in the state. This staffing, along with the wide array of interventions available to these juveniles on aftercare, allows the state DYC to release committed juveniles earlier than otherwise would be done.

IMPACT Alternatives to Incapacitation

IMPACT and other delinquent youth in Boulder can be assisted with an extremely wide array of service alternatives not normally available in judicial districts that are substantially larger. IMPACT's collaboration success has fostered the development of many other alternatives. Some of these are discussed below.

- *BEST, Boulder Enhanced Supervision Team*, furnishes intensive supervision services to shorten pretrial detention time, to substitute for a detention sentence, or to reduce the duration of a detention sentence. A BEST assessment leads to an individualized treatment plan and interventions that include case management, electronic monitoring, direct support, development of cognitive and life skills, personal empowerment, and individual and group counseling. BEST taps into other programs offered by community corrections, such as the Wilderness Work Camp, rock climbing and rappelling, backpacking and camping, and basic snowboarding and mountaineering techniques.

- *The Wilderness Work Camp* is an explicit substitute for a sentence to secure detention. The Work Camp provides a 10-day outdoor highly structured and regimented work environment in a mountain setting.

- *JAWS, Juvenile Alternative Work Sentence*, provides community service work crew opportunities as an incapacitation alternative. Judges sentence juveniles to varying numbers of JAWS hours based on the severity of their offenses. This is a community-based day program that emphasizes developing competency skills and learning to deal with "real-life" situations as they occur in the work place.

- *ITOP, Intensive Teen Outpatient Program*, administered by the county health department, is a substance abuse treatment program that requires a youth to participate in three group sessions weekly for 10 weeks. One weekly group session involves family members. After the first 10 weeks, groups meet only once a week but continue for the next 42 weeks.

- *The Mental Health Assessment and Intervention for Detained Youth Program* provides mental health services to youth held in the state detention center. It seeks to stabilize these juveniles psychiatrically and expedite their return to the community and a continuum of outpatient mental health services or to a non-correctional placement. The program collaborates closely with community correctional staff who are working with the same youths. Note: The state does not provide this kind of mental health services for detained juveniles.

- *FOCUS, Female Opportunity for Creating Unlimited Success*, is a sentencing alternative to serving time in a locked detention facility and is for girls only. It consists of 10 weeks of intensive supervision by a BEST officer, participation twice a week in an eight-week female-specific curriculum, and biweekly group community service at agencies that provide services to females.

- *Boulder Prep* is a charter school that serves court youths, essentially those who have been suspended, expelled, or are otherwise disconnected from regular school.

- *Intensive probation supervision*, administered by the probation department, serves 30 higher-risk juveniles.

Importance of Transportation Services

Transportation officers who transport juveniles from the state detention center to court and back are hired with state incentive funds. These officers are available to transport youth on a daily basis while the sheriff's office could do so only twice a week. The result is that detention hearings can be held daily, not just twice weekly. And youth are detained for shorter periods, so Boulder pays for fewer detention beds. These transport officers can also take detained juveniles to outpatient medical or psychosexual evaluators and, thus, expedite examinations and, thereby, court processing.

CONCLUSION: IMPACT WORKS

State DYC numbers affirm the effect of IMPACT. Boulder County's use of state detention space is substantially less than statewide rates and its use of commitment beds is just 40% of the statewide rate or those of neighboring counties. Its rate of new commitments is even lower.[1] Since its inception, the county has never exceeded its pre-determined bed quota.

IMPACT methods have resulted in reduced detentions and commitments for delinquents, reduced out-of-home placements of abused and neglected children, and reduced psychiatric hospitalizations of children with serious mental health needs.[2] These reductions are by-products of IMPACT's ability to keep increased numbers of young people in their own families and kinship environments or in nearby non-state facilities. IMPACT has reinvested the cost savings that result from these reductions in wraparound community-based programs.

Boulder's IMPACT collaborative has achieved numerous goals. This has taken much hard work and various paradigm shifts. But this county better owns its own youth and families and is providing much more comprehensive service to those at risk and with high needs.

Endnotes

[1] Omni Institute Presentation. (2000, October). The Senate Bill 94 Incentives: 18 Point Model, 2000 Senate Bill 94 Conference, Vail, Colorado.

[2] "Project IMPACT Report," 2001, p. 13-14.

Chapter 33

Zero Commitments to the State: The Commitment to Community-Based Intervention in Delaware County, Ohio

DELAWARE COUNTY, OHIO, COMMITTED TO CURBING COMMITMENTS

Juvenile courts have long been premised on the concept that, whenever possible, delinquent juveniles should be retained in their own homes. An extension of one's own home is one's community. Retaining juveniles in their own communities, whenever possible, is the complementary strategy when retention in one's own home is not possible. While placement away from home and community is sometimes necessary, some juvenile courts find this more necessary than others.

But how many juvenile courts that serve populations of 110,000 persons can match the following accomplishments of the juvenile court in Delaware County, Ohio, during 1999:

- No youths were committed to the state;

- None of the 50 youths adjudicated for felonies who were served by the intensive supervision probation program committed new felonies;

- None of the 24 juvenile sex offenders served in the community committed new sex offenses;

- New felony adjudications decreased by 28%;

- Nine fewer youths were placed out-of-home than in 1998 (59% less than in 1989).

Further, no youths were committed to the state during the first six months of year 2000.

This chapter originally appeared in Juvenile Justice Update, *Vol. 6, No. 5, October/November 2000.*

The Delaware County juvenile court is not a permissive court. It is no stranger to sanctions. The court holds itself accountable for the accountability of juveniles. Parents are held accountable as well, and are involved in any resolution effort. The court is structured and staffed so that youths are quickly engaged in program options that go a long way toward addressing their problems while protecting public safety—a win-win situation.

TWO DECADES OF PHENOMENAL GROWTH

Delaware County begins about 15 miles from downtown Columbus, Ohio. It has experienced phenomenal growth over the past two decades that has brought a significant increase in urban social problems to an historically rural community. From a small court that, in 1979, served about 300 juvenile referrals a year with basic judicial and probation services, the court has grown to a complex organization that handles more than 2,600 referrals annually through a set of interconnected departments and services that provide quite comprehensive screening, assessment, supervision, accountability, and treatment. Nonetheless, it does not confront the number of severe offenses that more urban courts experience.

Court Incorporates Rehabilitative Outlook of Earlier Era

In some ways this court is a throwback to earlier juvenile court days. Its pronouncements stress rehabilitation and avoid reference to punishment. There is lengthy continuity in the court's leadership with a judge who has served 22 years and a court administrator/director of court services who has served 17 years. The court is the central developer of program services to meet the needs of youths and the community; it administers a wide range of services that in today's world are far more often provided by the executive branch and private agencies than by the court. The court's intake department controls decision making at the front end, determining diversion, informal handling, or formal filing decisions. A part-time prosecuting attorney enters court only for contested or high-profile cases. Typically, neither prosecutor nor defense counsel attends detention hearings.

Modern Concepts of TQM and Balanced Approach Prevail

Despite its adherence to rehabilitation ideals, this is a very modern court that uses contemporary management approaches and advanced treatment modalities. A Total Quality Management (TQM) approach, for example, considers court clients as customers and routinely surveys their satisfaction with court procedures and the extent to which staff treat them with respect. The court has a five-year strategic plan in place that "allows increasingly clear and more measurable goals and objectives." The court adheres to the Balanced Approach in developing "comprehensive and holistic services that address the needs of both community and young offenders." It is involved in outreach to the community. Finally, there is a strong commitment to staff development, and staff members are involved in organizational planning.

COMMITMENT TO REDUCING COMMITMENTS

The question has to be asked: Isn't anyone upset about Delaware County's zero commitment rate? The response from Stuart Berry, the court administrator, is that law enforcement has a preference in selected cases for the banishment of chronic trouble-makers from the community; however, staff members are able to sit down with the police, explain the various intervention strategies that are being used along with the positive results that have been obtained and, thus, sufficiently contain the criticism to prevent harm to the court's efforts.

Further, the court has erected numerous interventions for handling its more serious offenders: electronic monitoring; non-electronic home monitoring; a juvenile drug court; a juvenile sex offender group and sex offender court (modeled after a drug court with weekly review hearings and tight monitoring); intensive probation joined with an intensive probation court; an in-home intensive family therapy program; out-of-home placements, including a group home; wraparound services to avoid placements or expedite return from placements; expansive community service; a twice weekly boot camp; and "military-style probation" that serves a small number of older youths in a last ditch effort to avoid commitment.

The court is acutely aware of research showing a high reoffense rate following juvenile incarceration. Its premise, accordingly, is that "not only is keeping youths in the community more humane and likely to enhance life skills/coping abilities, but it makes our community safer." The court's success in curbing recidivism reinforces its contention that it is best to provide necessary services and maintain and monitor juveniles in their own communities—at home, in foster care, and in local placements.

ONE COURT/ONE JUDGE MAKES A DIFFERENCE

Judge's Philosophy Drives Court

The court's stature and support are aided by the long-term judicial presence of Judge Thomas E. Louden, who maintains a clear and consistent philosophy that

every adult and juvenile is to be recognized as an important person in our community. The family is to be preserved ... people can and do change. When confinement for purposes of safety is not needed, there is overwhelming evidence that proves the concept of punishment and confinement alone to be ineffective and also very expensive.

According to Judge Louden

[t]here is an urgent and critical need for us to develop greater clarity as a community with our priorities. We must commit to immediate and effective identification of the needs of children and parents, and to the services which will accomplish the changes needed.[1]

Success Requires Services

According to its vision statement, "[t]he Delaware County Juvenile Court strives to set standards for justice and encourage the development of a safe and healthy community through the creation of partnerships and the delivery of quality services." Few courts overtly advertise they want to set standards. This court aims high, but knows it cannot walk alone. The court knows that intensive collaboration with community agencies is fundamental. While it administers an impressive number of direct services, it is a full collaborator with the schools, social service, mental health, and other community agencies. The result is a rich availability of court services, which have been aggressively sought and provided. This array of community-based services melded with humanistic ideology and a skilled administration makes this court stand out. There is a coherent whole between judicial philosophy and court practice.

Clear Operating Principles Stress Maintaining Youth Locally

The Delaware County court begins with clear operating principles that guide its juvenile court:

- Utilizing informal strategies to handle the vast majority of referrals which do not require court intervention to succeed;

- Minimally intervening with less serious offenders who can respond to a combination of basic supervision and family assistance services;

- Extensively dealing with the most serious offenders to ensure the greatest likelihood of community protection and youth habilitation;

- Reserving the majority of resources for "extraordinary kids" who require extraordinary supervision and treatment;

- Maintaining youths in their homes and/or community whenever possible, since this is where youths must learn to be successful; and

- Investing in community partnerships as the only viable way to succeed with youths and families.

COURT'S JURISDICTION EXTENDS BEYOND TYPICAL AREAS GIVEN TO JUVENILE COURTS

The Delaware County court is more than a juvenile court that is centered only on delinquency, child abuse/neglect/dependency, and status offenses. Its jurisdiction includes typical probate court areas such as administration of decedents' estates, guardianships for the protection of minors and incompetent persons, and mental illness proceedings. It covers adoptions, and it has jurisdiction over traffic offenses committed by minors. Further, it is responsible for paternity complaints, child support, and custody and visitation matters in cases where parents have not filed for divorce. Judge Louden and two magistrates serve as the court's judicial officers. Between them, they conducted 6,432 hearings in 1999.

This is not a family court. It does not have jurisdiction over domestic violence matters, civil or criminal cases, nor responsibility for divorce and divorce-related matters. It does, however, have a focus on the family and understands that assisting a family is integral to assisting a youth.

INTAKE: THE POINT OF DIVERSION OR ENTRY

Intake Allows for Diversion and Minimal Intervention for Low-Risk Offenders

In Delaware County, intake is a court function. The intake department, the single entry point for delinquency and status offense referrals, handles 55% of referrals informally. Its mission is to ensure that repeat offenders are detected and low-risk offenders are handled quickly with minimal resources. It uses warning letters, but provides more options and supervision than other courts may provide with cases that are "shortstopped."

Next Step Is Informal Intervention Involving Periodic Reporting to Intake Counselor or School Liaison

It is significant that there are no probation officers in this court, only probation counselors, and compliance is monitored with the conditions of informal probation. Youths placed on informal probation generally score low on the prediction scale that is used. This suggests that they will respond well to minimal supervision. During 1999, only 14% of juveniles handled informally later had their cases formalized or returned on a subsequent charge.

Some Formally Filed Cases "Held Open," Permitting Charges to Be Dismissed

"Held Open" is the next intake category. These cases are formally filed, the facts that surround the complaint are established, but no adjudication is made. The court then orders the juvenile to complete particular requirements within a specific time frame, e.g., 90 days. One intake staff member generally monitors the large number of "Held Open" cases by phone, and successful juveniles return to court and have their charges dismissed.

Adjudication Can Result in Return to Intake Monitoring

Another set of decisions leads to legal adjudication by the court, but with a return to monitoring by an intake staff member. Court requirements and staff monitoring may continue for two years. These cases are not dismissed. Because intake probation officers are involved, field probation staff are not engaged with these juveniles. Accordingly, field probation officers are able to devote their efforts to higher-risk juveniles. During 1999, only 8% of Hold Open or Adjudication juveniles returned to the court system with a new charge.

PROBATION DEPARTMENT PROGRAMMING

Treatment Probation

The probation department offers programs to court-involved youths. A program provided to most new formal probationers is the Treatment Probation Program, essentially a case management approach that calls on different court programs, community agencies, schools, and families to hold youths accountable to their victims and provide services that support rehabilitation. Four probation staffers arrange and coordinate the provision of services to approximately 300 youths annually. Their active case loads, however, average just 30 juveniles. These relatively low case loads are achieved because of the case planning system through which specific goals are set; since the juveniles frequently attain these goals, the youths are terminated from probation.

The program draws on court-administered or court-sponsored programs such as four different community work service programs, drug/alcohol assessment and treatment, the brief boot camp, a domestic violence group, university student mentors, a recreation program targeted for court-involved youths, a school suspension alternative program, a widely used tutoring program, and court monitors who focus on community protection by helping assure that youths are where they are supposed to be. Treatment Probation draws on a range of community-sponsored services, as well.

Family Advocate Program

The probation department's Family Advocate Program uses trained paraprofessionals to apply a behavioral systems approach known as Functional Family Therapy with probationers' families in their own homes. It is targeted at families that resist traditional mental health services despite their children's law violations and their significant family difficulties. These families have transportation shortcomings, childcare dilemmas, chronic illnesses or handicaps, family dysfunctions, financial barriers, and other issues that cause resistance to seeking or using outside help. So help comes to the home.

The advocate programs focus on family patterns, not the youth. There is a regular advocate program and an intensive advocate program, which involves meeting with a family at least twice a week. The therapeutic focus is on identifying and modifying chronic maladaptive patterns within a family. Relabeling of family members' statements and directing attention to family dynamics, rather than focusing on the youth as the problem, are of primary importance in this process. A purpose is to improve the ability of family members to see how their behaviors influence other family members' perceptions and behaviors, including law violations. The approach seeks enhanced family communication, reduced family abuse and domestic violence, decreased substance abuse, and improved school and job outcomes. The program served 39 families in 1999.

Juvenile Sex Offenders Program

The Juvenile Sex Offender Treatment Program retains sex offenders in the community under tight supervision and with heavy doses of treatment intervention. All are maintained in the intensive probation supervision category, but there is much more. Many are electronically monitored. Many, along with their families, are provided wraparound services. Several juvenile sex offenders are on independent living status where they are supervised around the clock by court workers who accompany them to and from school. Some have alarms installed on a door where they live; an unscheduled opening rings the alarm directly into the sheriff's office. In one form or another all offenders are under supervision or control 24 hours a day, seven days a week. They also reappear weekly before a judge or magistrate.

Individualized therapy is provided by the local mental health center, and a twice-weekly cognitive restructuring group activity is a joint court-mental health center service. The treatment aims to significantly alter an offender's thinking, improve problem solving approaches, and further coping mechanisms in order to substantially change the youth's behavior. A male and a female probation counselor, both trained in sex offender dynamics, run a group in concert with a male and female sex-offender specific mental health therapist. The Tuesday group works on cognitive behavior, thinking errors, offense cycles, identification of feelings, sex education, healthy relationships, and victimization concern. The Thursday group includes parents and significant support people. Here, offender dynamics are discussed within the context of the family. Parent education is seen as essential for the sustained progress of an offender.

The results of this control and intervention program are very positive. Twenty-four sex offenders were enrolled in the program in 1999; 14 of the 24 were in their second year. No participant committed a new sex offense. The great majority are retained in their own homes. A small number are removed to community placements. Four were successfully terminated from probation; one was unsuccessfully terminated at age 21. It is not unusual for a juvenile sex offender who has been removed from home to be returned successfully even though home is the site where the offender subjected a sibling to a sex offense.

Wraparound Services

Wraparound services are individualized to keep children in their homes and communities. The probation department's wraparound services are focused on providing whatever it takes to keep young persons with complex needs in their homes and communities and avoid residential or other out-of-home placement. This program surrounds court youths with people rather than walls. But it is used, as well, to enrich the reintegration into community of those who do need to be placed. It involves an individualized plan that is "needs driven" rather than service driven, and is family centered rather than child centered. Parents are an integral part of the team and are to have "ownership" of the plan.

Need-related services include such things as school companions who help youths get to school, avoid inappropriate school behaviors, and enhance learning. Home companions can provide supervision and help with behavior management and activities of daily living. The program is supported by the flexible use of existing dollars. Wraparound Services assisted 28 families in 1999.

FOCUS ON FAMILY INVOLVEMENT AND FAMILY SUPPORT

Families Integral to Success

The Delaware County court views families as integral to successful juvenile treatment. As a result, it works to strengthen families and increase parenting skills; it makes parents members of intervention teams and reorients families to recognize that, with lots of support, their sons and daughters can remain in their care without significant disruption to family or community safety.

Family Members Subject to Dispositional Orders

Court dispositional orders increasingly direct parents, and not just youths, to perform certain requirements that aim to expand the likelihood of the youth's success. A probation department program called Positive Activities engages parents with their children in recreational, entertainment, and community work service experiences. Another program presents an education/discussion series on active parenting, which serves parents in the community, and not just those of juvenile offenders. The probation department also provides parent resource centers in the two court waiting rooms that offer extensive information about referral sources for a variety of parenting issues.

DETENTIONS AND PLACEMENTS

In maintaining a zero commitment level, the Delaware County juvenile court occasionally relies, as a sanction, on the short-term detention of youths at the detention center that serves it along with five other counties. Further, in 1999, it placed 41 juveniles in out-of-home placements, 34 of them in local foster care settings. With all of these placements, staff work closely with the family during and after a residential stay.

VICTIM SERVICES AN IMPORTANT COURT SERVICE

Characteristically, victim services are sponsored by a district attorney's office or by law enforcement. In Delaware County, however, court staff directly serve victims of juvenile offenders. Victims are provided information and support, referrals to community resources, restitution, victim-offender mediation, and advocacy for the victim with the justice system. During 1999, the court's mediator conducted 105 victim-offender meetings, and was able to mediate, as well, school truancy concerns that involved youth, parents, and teachers.

An interesting practice is to offer victims a home visit by staff who can assist them with preparation of a victim impact statement and documentation of loss or damage. Staff also recently reviewed and revised restitution documentation forms to make them more user friendly, a process that other juvenile courts should pursue. In addition, the court also obtained a grant to "pay" juveniles who owe restitution to perform "paid community service," with payments then transferred over to victims.

FUNDING NEEDED TO IMPLEMENT THE VISION

Money is necessary to the implementation of the court's vision. The Delaware County court proactively explains its accomplishments and needs to county and state governments as it seeks funds. It also looks for federal grants as well as funds from private sources. Its 1999 budget totaled $2,249,000, and this will expand with significant new grant funding in 2000. The court even collects $58,000 from user fees it charges for electronic monitoring, urinalysis, detention costs, group programs, and out-of-home placements. It also gets some state funds because it avoids sending juveniles to costly state facilities, but significantly less than high-commitment Ohio courts receive.

DELAWARE COUNTY COURT HAS CHARACTERISTICS OF A MODEL

The vision statement, mission statement, philosophy statement, and long-range organization goals of the Delaware County juvenile court portray a progressive organization with a humanistic determination. No court system is perfect, but this one has characteristics of a model. It has the juvenile court spirit.

It hews to what it proclaims: providing the least restrictive intervention, concentrating the greatest resources on those having the most extraordinary needs, being a partner in the development of community responsibility, keeping youths in their own community whenever possible, honoring the entire family as a necessary part of any solution, and believing that the potential for positive change exists in all people.

Author's Note

Steven W. Hanson, the court's program director, prepared this update of the Delaware County Juvenile Court.

Judge Louden has now served 24 years on the bench. Stuart Berry has been the court administrator for 18 years. The court no longer has a boot camp program (but does provide a physical training program). The following statistics update program information provided in the main body of the chapter. In 2001:

- 2,770 referrals were made to the juvenile court;

- Two youths were committed to the state;

- Fewer than 5% of felony-level youths on intensive supervision probation committed a new felony offense;

- One of 33 juvenile sex offenders served in the community committed a new sex offense; 18 of the 33 were in their second year of the program; seven were successfully terminated from probation, two were unsuccessfully terminated;

- 28 of 33 juvenile sex offenders were treated solely in the community;

- New felony adjudication rates fell for the seventh straight year;

- Seven fewer youth were placed out-of-home than in 2000 (down 90 since 1995);

- Long-term residential placements were down 80% from 1990;

- Over 80% of the 42 out-of-home placements were in local foster homes;

- The intake department handled 65% of referrals informally; only 9% of informally handled youth committed new offenses;

- 5.5% of Held Open adjudicated youth were returned to the court system for a new charge;

- Four treatment probation counselors provided services for 282 youths (average caseload, 25-30);

- The family advocate program served 63 families (up 17% from 2000);

- Wraparound and non-traditional services served 49 families in 2001;

- Positive activities served over 500 youth;

- The mediator conducted 74 victim-offender meetings and 33 school truancy mediations;

- The budget totaled $3.1 million;

- $40,000 was collected in user fees.

The vision statement was amended to state:

The Delaware County Juvenile Court strives to uphold standards for justice and encourage the development of a safe and healthy community through partnerships and the delivery of quality services.

Endnote

[1] Delaware County Juvenile Court (1999). *Annual Report*, p. 4.

Part 5

Beyond the Community: State Institutions and Aftercare

INTRODUCTION

It is always good policy to have a continuum of programs provided to delinquent youth at the community level. It is best practice to reserve state institutions for those who are serious or repetitive offenders and who have failed at the community level or whose seriousness of offense and risk level for significant reoffending appear to require a deep-end placement.

Best policy and practice are not always the norm. Too often a court sends a less severe offender off to the state. Too often the state agency lacks effective procedures or sufficient funding flexibility to reject an admission and instead reroute this juvenile back into the right community placement or program. Too often commitment institutions are overcrowded, poorly programmed, and insufficiently staffed by well-trained personnel. There has long been a crisis in the management of many state institutions. There have long been incidents of juvenile maltreatment in state facilities. Juvenile assaults on staff occur, some of them avoidable. Isolation of juveniles for disciplinary rule violations is relied on too frequently in a number of settings. Juvenile suicides do take place.

State institutions are needed. Numerous state facilities appear to do a good job with their clientele. The work of thousands of committed, caring staff is praiseworthy. It is difficult, nonetheless, to avoid commentary on deficiencies in the quality of care provided.

Juveniles in some states are admitted to state institutions immediately or within a day or two of the judicial commitment hearing. Other states may be extremely slow, retaining these youths in the local or regional secure detention center until their admission. An Alabama lawsuit, **S. S. A Minor v. Wood**, CA 01-M-224 N (N.D. Ala. 2001) challenged this wait time as denying substantive due process since, instead of beginning a treatment-rehabilitation program, youths received only schooling at the secure center. The suit alleged that one boy could not enter a state facility for more than four months post-commitment and therefore could receive no residential credit toward his mandated stay of a one-year minimum. Others waited two to three months. Situations like this call for improved collaboration between the three branches of government.

There are victories for some who reach the door of the state. Some juveniles "put it together" during their institutional experience. Some benefit from cognitive-behavioral programs that reorient one's thinking patterns and behaviors. Some benefit from group counseling sessions or anger management classes or the positive peer culture approach that marks a number of institutions. Some benefit from industrial training that provides preliminary job skills. Some just benefit from "time out."[1]

A study of 15 youths nominated as having successfully completed post-institutional aftercare listed the benefits they reported from their prior residency: The structure, a regular schedule, the presence of a positive behavioral program that allowed them to earn privileges, the availability of specific interventions such as a GED program with its potential to earn a high school diploma, assigned jobs, targeted discussion groups, and development of a positive connection with an adult in the facility.[2]

The role and responsibility of the director of a state juvenile correctional agency and of institutional directors is, to use a favorite term of young people today, awesome. It is ever changing. State legislation regarding delinquent juveniles changes. State legislative funding practices change. New judges apply different values that change prior judicial dispositional practices. The governor or state super-agency executive who appoints a director leaves office. A private non-profit agency that contracts with the state to work with particular types of juveniles is purchased by a private for-profit entity. Important regional directors or other key staff leave their positions and the quality of their replacements is less promising. Or a lawsuit that complains of deficient practices is threatened or filed. The state juvenile correctional director may essentially take care of what is given him or her or may take a more activist stance seeking change. Either approach is fraught with difficulty.

MODELS OF JUVENILE COURT-STATE JUVENILE CORRECTIONAL AGENCY BOUNDARIES

Aside from variable state practices in funding or providing certain community-level care to probationers, there seem to be three structural approaches to the court-state agency relationship. These have been termed legislative management, judicial management, and administrative management.[3]

Legislative Management

A state legislative body may mandate a particular type of sentence for a particular juvenile offender. Colorado law, for example, authorizes a juvenile court to sentence an "aggravated juvenile offender" to the state youth agency for a period of at least three but not more than five years, or at least three years and not more than seven years, depending upon the particular aggravated offense. Offense requirements are the top two felonies, a crime of violence, or a particularized sexual offense. The state agency may petition the court to transfer the juvenile, after his or her 18th birthday, to the department of adult corrections by certifying the juvenile is not benefiting from the state youth agency program.

This provision illustrates how the legislative branch controls the flexibility both of the court and of its own executive agency. Aggravated juvenile offenders cannot be released early into community settings even if their rehabilitation has progressed sizably and a full control net is created to surround their community placement.

Other provisions of the Colorado Children's Code constrain residential or institutional stays. There are categories of (1) mandatory sentence, (2) repeat, and (3) violent juvenile offenders for whom a one-year minimum commitment is required unless the court finds an alternative commitment of less than one year is appropriate. Only the judge can curtail the one-year minimum state institutional stay

State youth agency and institutional directors prefer greater flexibility in managing juveniles committed to their care. Some judges may prefer strictures imposed by legislation with more serious offenders since these requirements reduce a judge's political risks that could arise from using an alternative judicial sanction that is followed by a reoffense.

Colorado law otherwise provides that a commitment to the department shall be for a determinate period of up to two years rather than until the offender's 21st birthday, that the state youth agency may petition the court to extend a commitment for up to an additional two years, and that any post-commitment parole experience shall have a one-year minimum and two-year maximum term.[4]

Judicial Management

The Pennsylvania "strong judge" approach exemplifies the judicial management model. Legislation empowers judges with the fundamental authority to choose dispositional options best suited both to protect the public interest and the child's treatment, supervision, rehabilitation, and welfare. Among these options is commitment to an institution, youth development center (a secure, locked facility), forestry camp, or other facility under the direction or supervision of the court or other public authority and approved by the state department of public welfare. Allegheny County Juvenile Court (Pittsburgh) judges place more than 400 juveniles annually in 68 local and regional non-secure residential settings operated by 37 different agencies, all licensed by the state.

The law does guide these judges to impose the minimum amount of confinement consistent with public protection and the rehabilitation needs of the child. The law allows, however, for a commitment up to four years. Nonetheless the sentence may not exceed the duration of time an adult could serve for the same offense.

There are no statutory categories that compel or presume judicial sentences to state care. Judicial empowerment is heightened by an unusual provision that directs Pennsylvania judges to review each commitment every six months and mandates a judicial disposition review hearing at least every nine months. Also, the judge must be notified if an institution wishes to transfer a juvenile to a more secure or less secure facility, with a full hearing required in the former case.

Judges, on committing a juvenile to a state-operated facility such as a youth development center or forestry camp, designate the particular facility for commitment. This is a very different provision than the requirement in numerous states that a judge commit centrally to the state youth agency, with the agency then determining the destination of the juvenile. Pennsylvania judges have retained a very strong role among the triad of the three branches of government.[5]

Administrative Management

Massachusetts is the archetypal example of a strong-executive/weak-judge approach. Judges, fundamentally, make a disposition either to probation status or to the state department of youth services. The state agency is responsible for all institutional and non-residential services across the state. It has a dedicated commitment to contracting more than 60% of its total budget to purchasing services from private vendors. The state code provides a broad-brush mission to the youth agency to build self-respect and self-reliance for juveniles and qualify them for good citizenship and employment. The law allows the agency great latitude in deciding those programs most fitting for different youths.

The former director of the Massachusetts agency clearly prefers this model as "most consistent with a well-managed correctional system." This is because:

1. Administrative policies can change as offenders and program needs change, without a need to obtain legislative approval;

2. The agency can classify and place offenders in programs best suited to meet their needs rather than being directed by a judge as to where and how long a juvenile shall be handled; and

3. A centralized authority can most effectively monitor the quality of private provider programs and ensure the provision and enforcement of state directed program standards.

The range and depth of department managed and contracted programs are impressive, far more than in other states with relatively equal population and delinquency rates which follow one of the other models.

As readers will recall, Massachusetts, during 1970-1972, became the first state to "deinstitutionalize" juvenile offenders when the department closed down a series of secure institutions and returned vast numbers of residents to their communities and to supervision and treatment by private youth agencies.[6] Utah, along with numerous other states, closed facilities or sought to sharply replace institutional commitment with a commitment to community-level services. However, deinstitutionalization lost its cutting edge beginning in the early 1980s as violent juvenile crime magnified and the media and political sectors urged lengthy banishments from the community. Nonetheless, the merit of implementing a continuum of services using a broad provision of community-level interventions has survived the years that have followed. The Massachusetts department maintains its approach as a strong administrative management youth agency model.

Pros and Cons of the Three Models

There is the omnipresent threesome of the legislature, judiciary, and executive agency in every state, so the open question relates to the relative role and responsibility of each branch. The Colorado judiciary and the state's division of youth corrections should not be pleased, overall, with the controls placed on their informed discretion by the legislature. The Pennsylvania state agency just might be pleased to have the judiciary take responsibility for court youth and spare it more responsibilities. Massachusetts's judges have not always appreciated the state's department of youth services and have sparred with the department from time to time. Yet professionals in all three systems get used to the alignment in their state and are not, overall, displeased with their particular balance except when legislators want to unilaterally change laws, when judges complain publicly of state agency deficiencies, or when state agency directors fail to get sufficient budgets to carry out or extend their functions.

On a personal note, I retain the view I developed as a state legislator in the early 1960s when I served as prime sponsor of a measure that directed centralized commitments to the new state youth agency of Colorado. My belief then, which remained my preference through my tenure as a Denver juvenile court judge 1965-1971 and continues today, is that when the judiciary must call upon the state's resources, it should turn over authority to the state with at most a recommendation regarding the type of facility where a youth should be placed. I don't care for the subsequent Colorado legislative prescriptions or the apparent excessive judicial authority of Pennsylvania judges. I would worry about such a dependence as Massachusetts judges have on the state department, particularly if substandard administration, substandard programming, bureaucratic organization or decision making were to take place.

But I do like the Pennsylvania judges' review authority after six- and nine-month institutional stays. I would note parenthetically that that state's juvenile courts administer the parole function as well as the probation function, and that judicial review can therefore better take into consideration the court's capacity to provide competent aftercare. I also like very much the great depth and diversity of community programming in Massachusetts. A judge there can most likely keep a juvenile in a local setting upon commitment to the state as the department has long stressed local program purchases and, following assessment, will keep most youths near their homes.

Judges like to have discretion with case dispositions. Pennsylvania judges retain the greatest discretion in these three states. State youth agencies like to have discretion with case management and their use of different facilities, programs, and durations of stay. This is maximized in Massachusetts. Colorado lawmakers exercised their discretion to curb judicial discretion with case handling of several offender types.

And, of course, legislative actions in all but a few states have sharply curbed the juvenile system's jurisdiction and discretion by removing myriad juveniles into criminal courts.

Political liaison must and does occur in all three models. Colorado's youth agency director continuously courts the judiciary and the legislature. Pennsylvania's judges, through their mechanism of an effective state Juvenile Court Judges Commission, work actively with legislative and executive agency leadership. The director of the Massachusetts department also proactively reaches out to the courts and legislature.

SPECIAL NEED POPULATIONS AT THE STATE LEVEL

The Idaho Department of Juvenile Corrections reported in 2000:

Authorities estimate that 20 to 30 percent of committed youth are placed in residential settings based on bed space rather than assessed risk. Consequently, a juvenile scored as a relatively low risk may, in fact, be placed in a higher security setting because it is available. In institutional settings, the Department's responsibility is to provide a safe environment for residents and staff. Other areas of facility operation include security, order, programming, health and mental health and justice.

A growing portion of offenders placed in state custody are juveniles with special needs, and the Department has begun to develop programs to meet the needs of these offenders. The special needs population includes girls, offenders with mental health needs, sex offenders, offenders with substance abuse issues, and older offenders.

The number of minorities in state custody is disproportionate to the state minority populations. Training on cultural awareness and sensitivity is ongoing at the institutions.[7]

Girls in Juvenile Justice

The greater presence of girls involved in juvenile court proceedings all the way to state juvenile facilities is noteworthy. Specialized programming for girls has followed this development and moved more clearly onto the juvenile justice agenda.

The increased numbers of girls in the system are apparent, but the reasons for the increase are less clear. The number of female juvenile offenders referred to juvenile courts grew by 83% between 1988 and 1997, while the case rate, a better measure, revealed a 62% increase in the rate of offending per 1,000 girls. For 1997, male offenders were held in pretrial detention in 20% of all male cases, and female offenders in 15% of female cases. Following screening, 60% of boys' cases and 47% of girls' cases were petitioned. Sixty percent of girls received probation status and 22% were placed out of their homes.[8]

Very few girls under age 18 are subjects of criminal court case handling. The proportion of serious offenses committed by girls appears to remain rather small. Girls show very large increases, however, in arrests for curfew violation and loitering, for substance abuse violations, and for simple assault. There has been a lesser increase in aggravated assault and weapons offenses for girls.[9]

One report notes that,

> Some experts have found that this growth [in female referrals] is due in part not to a significant increase in violent behavior but to the re-labeling of girls' family conflicts as violent offenses, the changes in police practices regarding domestic violence and aggressive behavior, the gender bias in the processing of misdemeanor cases, and, perhaps, a fundamental systemic failure to understand the unique development issues facing girls of today.[9]

Even with FY 1999 deep-end commitments to the Texas Youth Commission, 19% of female admissions were reported to be for unlawful use of motor vehicle, 8% for theft, 11% for drug offenses, 14% for burglary, 23% for assault or aggravated assault, and 8% for robbery or aggravated robbery among other adjudications.

Girls in juvenile justice facilities are reported to have suffered a high frequency of sexual abuse and physical abuse, to have significant histories with the mental health and foster care systems, and often to be unable to return to their own homes following a residential stay.

Girls' handling or treatment at state level institutions needs to be different from boys. The range of treatment methods and subject areas needs to be conceptualized within the framework of the roles that girls and women fulfill or are provided in this society. The informed view is that girls' programs will cost more than boys', require smaller living units, and necessitate a higher staff to resident ratio and level of staff training. Medical costs are likely to be higher due to teen pregnancies, the percentage of girls testing positive for HIV infection, and a greater presence of psychological and physical illness concerns.[10] Idealized care and treatment and idealized aftercare integration programs, as with boys, are lacking.

Intervention efforts that are cited among the best practices include the continuum of care for girls' programs of the Alternative Rehabilitation Communities, Harrisburg, Pennsylvania; the specialized girls on probation program of the Pulaski County Juvenile Court Probation Department, Little Rock, Arkansas; the Girls' Initiative of the

Division of Prevention and Intervention, Florida Department of Juvenile Justice, Tallahassee; and the Southern Oaks Girls School of the Division of Juvenile Corrections, Wisconsin Department of Corrections, Madison.[11] Yet there has been only extremely limited research that evaluates program effectiveness with institutionalized girls.

Mental Health and Substance Abuse Treatment Concerns

There is consensus that institutionalized juvenile offenders have a substantially greater mental health disorder prevalence than youth in the general population. The former rate is believed to be at least 20%; the latter rate from 9%-13%.[12] Treatment resource availability is very limited for both groups, particularly for those held in delinquency institutions.

There is recognition that significant numbers of juveniles who enter the juvenile justice system could have been better served by the mental health system of services. There is further consensus that numerous delinquent juveniles could have avoided state-level incarceration had communities put together multi-agency wraparound services for multi-system youth such as the Boulder, Colorado, program and Wraparound Milwaukee.

A California Youth Authority assessment of mental health and treatment needs of 4,672 juveniles entering its reception centers during a 30-month period described these findings in 2000:

- Forty-four percent of males and 59% of females had scores indicating some need for mental health services while 16% of males and 18% of females reported combinations of emotional problems that suggested the potential need for intensive mental health services.

- About 7 out of 10 males and females reported substance abuse problems.

- Thirty-seven percent of males and 50% of females had elevated scores in both mental health and substance abuse.[13]

The report recommended initial screening for mental health problems at reception centers to be followed by clinical evaluations of those who might pose a danger to self or others in order to determine those with serious mental health problems and those with more transient emotional distress.

California's recommended procedure is useful, though full implementation is lacking. Those who might be termed the seriously emotionally disturbed and show clinically significant symptoms of depression, anxiety, and other major problems need prioritization and specialized help now. The larger group, those with a mental health disorder that meets a standard classification such as conduct disorder or substance abuse, need day-to-day programming that is specific to these problems and addresses cognitive skills and positive life approaches. A continuum of services is necessary to facilitate successful transition to community following whatever treatment and assistance is provided within the institution.

A report on the specialized treatment programs of the Texas Youth Commission (TYC) reflects the treatment shortcomings of many states. That year TYC reported that just 34% of the "emotionally disturbed" juveniles in its care received specialized treatment. Further, just 34% of sexual offenders and 38% of chemically dependent juveniles in its care received specialized treatment. The commission states: "Unfortunately a lack of correctional resources prevents TYC from providing specialized treatment to all juveniles with specialized needs. TYC's assessment and placement process is designed to ensure that those youth who will benefit the most do receive specialized treatment." Juveniles with major psychiatric symptoms are placed in the single TYC stabilization facility or transferred to a state hospital. Upwards of 40% of new residents are assessed as having mental health problems.[14]

A necessary approach in assisting institutional residents with alcohol and drug problems requires staff training and certification in providing state-of-the-art treatment with these youth. The state alcohol and substance abuse agency is a necessary partner in facilitating this training and in helping to make these services available at institutional and community levels. Indeed, effective work with juveniles with substance abuse and mental health needs requires the fullest collaboration of juvenile justice, mental health, and substance abuse agencies. Some of this is beginning to occur or increase, though significant implementation is very much into the future.[15]

The numerous youth who present co-occurring disorders, both mental health and substance abuse problems, present institutional directors with particular challenges. There are sizable barriers to successful treatment even when there is a provision of staff members with skills in both arenas, barriers that are within the individual youth and with the system of care.

Juveniles often do not seek or want treatment, may manifest what is called "oppositional response patterns," may perceive treatment as a stigma and resist treatment, or have trouble with program controls placed on them in the facility and when they return to community.

System of care barriers include staffing changes that hamper treatment continuity, release to the community without a reliable continuing treatment scheme, absence of community services that will work for youths with co-occurring disorders, and community agency waiting lists.

CIVIL RIGHTS OF INSTITUTIONALIZED PERSONS ACT

Few readers will have heard of the federal Civil Rights of Institutionalized Persons Act (CRIPA) unless they hold prominent positions in states that have been investigated by the Civil Rights Division of the U.S. Department of Justice for failing to protect the constitutional rights of their juvenile correctional institution residents. The investigations may lead to lawsuits that are usually settled by formal agreements and then followed by the monitoring of settlement conditions. Georgia, Kentucky (13 facilities), New Jersey, Puerto Rico (20 facilities), and now Louisiana are important examples of states that have settled suits that have led to significant improvements in institutional care. Juveniles, under CRIPA, must be provided reasonable safety and adequate medical and mental health care. They are entitled to reasonable rehabilitative treatment.

A CRIPA lawsuit, when significant violations are found, can be averted by the federal approval of a state plan to improve conditions. Unlike private lawsuits that are brought on behalf of juveniles, no money damages are sought or awarded.

State officials are often wary and anxious about both CRIPA and private lawsuits. Farsighted administrators view most such efforts as positive and as benefiting the progressive advocacy they have expressed. These suits often become the vehicle for achieving progress. Both types of actions have been filed in states such as Georgia and Louisiana. Governors and legislators take note of these actions and often, though sometimes belatedly, accept well-documented complaints and allocate improvement funds that previously had been low priority despite the suffering that juveniles had experienced. The CRIPA case example that follows focuses on stratagems to improve mental health services in the juvenile justice system.

Case Example

Orlando Martinez became commissioner of the Georgia Department of Juvenile Justice (DJJ) in 1999 with directives from the governor to deal with a CRIPA suit as well as the overcrowding in institutions and the regional pretrial detention centers DJJ administered He received approval to move the department onto a rehabilitation course. One important dimension was improving mental health services. He lists pertinent elements of the federal Letter of Findings such as:

- A DJJ priority had been youth at risk of suicide or self-harm, but few systems were in place for the early screening and detection of more prevalent, chronic, or non-acute problems.

- Clinical evaluation and care management review systems were non-existent for youth with high mental health needs. The principal implementers of those mental health policies and procedures that did exist were direct-care staff who had only limited mental health and behavior management training.

- What clinical resources existed were consumed by those in crisis situations to the detriment of other youth in need of mental health services.

- There was no unifying treatment philosophy or planning among the different service providers such as counselors, teachers, medical staff, and others.

- There was a failure to recognize co-morbidity in that a large percentage of youth experienced both mental health and substance abuse problems.[16]

DJJ had neither an administrative structure nor administrative staff for mental-health services, had only scant professional staff available in its facilities, and possessed only limited data documenting the mental health needs of DJJ youth. But once a federal-state Memorandum of Agreement took effect, DJJ began staffing a central Office of Mental Health to include a director of mental health, a director of substance abuse, two assistant directors, a quality assurance coordinator, an administrative psychiatrist, and a consulting psychiatrist. Typical staffing at institutions was improved to include a clinical director, master's level social service providers, psychometric specialists, a mental health nurse, a consulting psychiatrist, substance abuse counselors, and sex offender clinicians. Regional detention center mental health staffing was enriched, as well. A data sample of committed youth found 66% had a prior history of substance abuse and 66% had experienced some form of mental health intervention, with a co-morbidity rate of 45%.

Several years later DJJ integrated all mental health, substance abuse, and specialized behavioral treatment programs including those for sex offenders and low functioning youth, into an Office of Behavioral Health Services in recognition of the need to coordinate, not separate, delivery of various services and to provide multi-disciplinary treatment, A battery of organizational and procedural protocols were established to guideline services from community to institutional levels.

But Commissioner Martinez notes that the need for mental health services continues to far exceed resources, that inadequacies in staffing, training, and program implementation remain, that information system data are still insufficient, and that mental health services at the community level need to be strengthened substantially in order to remove the role DJJ has been forced to take on, as the mental health system for delinquent children.[17]

What Is Required for Reform?

Substantial reform, when pressured by a CRIPA investigation or lawsuit, tends to require significant implementation time, substantial money, capable and committed department leadership, federal court oversight, and rigorous monitoring by an independent master appointed by the court. Often there are pitfalls along the way. The Georgia CRIPA suit dates back to 1997. Implementation of the agreement continues at this writing, even with enlightened DJJ administration. It can slide back at any time.

Noteworthy here from a mental health perspective was the July 1, 2001, integration of mental health services with the other specialized evaluation and treatment needs. Recognition of the co-morbidity factor is critical; mental health services, when delivered, often must be linked with other specialized intervention methods.

PRIVATE LAWSUITS

CRIPA is not the only form of externally applied pressure for improved juvenile justice services. Private law suits including class action suits on behalf of a class of institutionalized delinquent youth have been instrumental in forcing progress in numerous states. They may seek not only improvements in medical or mental health care but, also, to control restraints that are used and disciplinary methods used or abused, resident maltreatment by staff members or other residents, and the correction of failures to provide educational services for youth with a range of disabilities. Successful private lawsuits may result in orders of substantial attorney fees and reimbursements for the costs of expert witnesses and suit-related expenses. Legal defense costs that state and local governments incur in defending a suit can be very expensive, as well.

A suit against the South Dakota training school that included provisions for improving mental health services reached settlement in December 2000. **Christina A. v. Bloomberg,** No. 00-4036 (S.D. 2000).

A CRIPA suit against four Louisiana juvenile institutions accompanied by a private Juvenile Justice Project of Louisiana suit against the juvenile facility at Tallulah, described in Chapter 35, finally reached agreement in 2000. The federal court approved a 103-page settlement that had major provisions to improve mental, medical, and dental health care, and compelled restraints on the use of force, of mechanical constraints, and isolation. What apparently broke the litigation-settlement logjam was the insertion of the School of Medicine of Louisiana State University as the contract provider of mental and medical health care. **Williams v. McKeithen**, Civ.No. 71-98-B (M.D.La.).

A major suit, pending at this writing, **Stevens v. Harper**, No. Civ. S-01-0675 DFL-PAN-P (E.D. Cal.), was initiated in early 2002 against the California Youth Authority, charging cruel and inhumane conditions, gross absence of mental health care, educational provision deficiencies, failures to protect residents from physical or sexual violence by guards and by other residents, and much more.

PERFORMANCE STANDARDS

The Council of Juvenile Correctional Administrators has been developing performance-based standards for juvenile delinquency facilities across the country that include guidelines for the provision of mental health and substance abuse services, as well. Juvenile correctional programs will be able to measure their services against these standards and work to improve conditions of confinement. Obviously, development of standards is one objective. Measurement of current practices and resources against these standards is another. States, far too often, have far to go to provide the institutional care residents need to obtain rehabilitation and productive living. One stratagem that can lead to advances in the quality of institutional care is state appointment of an ombudsman for incarcerated juveniles to monitor conditions, advocate for improvements, and expose and reduce unlawful deficiencies.[18]

BOOT CAMPS AT THE STATE LEVEL

Boot camps still have strong advocates though these facilities, at both state and local levels, are being shut down or scaled back. Physical abuse of juvenile inmates has been one reason. Excessive physical regimens are another, as the one that resulted in the death of a 14-year-old girl at the South Dakota state-operated girls camp in July 1999. High recidivism rates along with conclusions of harmfulness and ineffectuality have contributed to this drop in use.

Maryland's governor, following high-visibility reports of routine and brutal beatings of residents, shut down that state's three boot camps in late 1999 and dismissed five top juvenile justice officials. A four-part series by the *Baltimore Sun* preceded and spurred this action. Assaults on juveniles that were witnessed over a five-month period by a reporter and photographer revealed guards kicking, punching, and slamming juveniles to the ground. A Baltimore judge took testimony from Baltimore boot camp juveniles and then ordered all 26 youth moved from the camp to other facilities or sent home. Other Maryland juvenile courts followed this action. The facilities were converted to other residential programs.[19] Subsequently, the state of Maryland agreed to pay more than $4 million to settle lawsuits surrounding three closed boot camps. Former residents received monetary payments and a fund was set up, in addition, to assist with their tuition to colleges and trade schools.[20]

Colorado, Arizona, and North and South Dakota have closed their camps while Florida and California have scaled back these enterprises. Georgia has transformed its boot camp facilities into short-term treatment programs. Boot camps, at least for now, seem to have been an idea whose time has come and gone.

PRIVATIZATION

Juvenile justice, at the local level, has forever used private non-profit agencies to assist rehabilitation efforts with delinquent and status offense youth. The program services may be boys' and girls' clubs, family counseling agencies, hospital clinics, residential treatment programs, etc. Non-profit residential programs have tended to be relatively small in scale and implement reasonably good standards of care and treatment. But what is new in the past 15 years or so is a resort to for-profit organizations that provide care for juvenile justice youth.

There are giant providers, essentially residential treatment providers whose stock is sold on a national stock exchange. There are smaller, local-area providers that provide a half dozen or so program services. Some programs meet high standards and fulfill a useful need. Some have massive shortcomings and abusive practices.

Of course, more than a few state-run operations have been very deficient in operational quality and their residents have been neglected and abused. Previously called training schools, there was the adage they neither trained nor schooled. But these operations are responsible to government, executive and legislative bodies, and citizen advocates have a place to turn with complaints and urgings. State facilities have some accountability to the judges who commit juveniles to their care.

The "private shops" worry professionals in this field. They are a threat to public programs and institutional budgets. A high-up decision might be made to move a private management into a hitherto state operated facility. Or a private company might get a state contract to open a new facility when promising second-level state employees had hoped to move up and earn upper level management positions in the new facility.

There is big money in juvenile justice facility contracts, millions and millions of dollars. Some of these dollars go to large corporations that do aggressive bidding, and have marketing staff and development people who design and map out next-stage and long-term acquisitions or new construction sites. They can use slick advertising measures and may hire well-thought-of retiring state officials or former legislators as marketing liaisons to bring them business. They may operate adult prisons and Immigration and Naturalization Service facilities, as well. One vast operator of adult prisons bought out a very large Pennsylvania non-profit juvenile treatment entity. Correctional corporations now operate numerous secure and non-secure juvenile facilities. We hear such corporate names as Cornell Abraxas, Res-Care Inc., Correctional Services Corporation, Corrections Corporation of America, and Wackenhut Corrections Corporation. They operate differently from government.

Some private facilities have had abject records, e.g., Louisiana's Tallulah facility, described in Chapter 35. Another example: a Nevada secure facility where the private operator, Youth Services International (YSI), pulled out of its contract to run Summit View Youth Correctional Center following a roof-top riot with a police stand-off; newspapers reported of massive operational shortcomings. The *Las Vegas Sun* reported there had been extensive program deficiencies, numerous suicide attempts, drugs brought into the facility, women staff having sex with residents, physical abuse of residents, numerous escapes, 80% staff turnover in a short time period, and five administrators over a 16-month period.[21] Among other examples is the federal grand jury award of $3,000,000 to a juvenile assaulted and improperly punished in a Corrections Corporation of America facility in South Carolina.[22]

I prefer public and non-profit management of these programs. Public institutions, like public schools, have to serve all; non-profit and for-profit programs can stake out a particular turf. There can be niches where private programs, non-profit or for-profit, can do it better. They can unload poor-performing employees more readily and can shift program directions more speedily to meet particular or changing needs of young people. While not above politics, their organizations appear less political internally and less dependent on broader political winds. Measuring performance is more natural for them. Newer to this experience and with fewer regulations to conform to than state facilities, they can be more flexible and less bureaucratic.

That said, there are severe deficiencies with for-profit corporations, which must provide dividends to shareholders, the profits drawn from economies of operation. This may mean less food on residents' tables, serious education and medical service provision abbreviations as occurred in Louisiana, and low education levels of custodial staff as illustrated by the YSI Nevada minimum requirement of only a high school degree and a very limited training provision to become an institutional youth worker. Health insurance and pension benefits are skimpier as compared with state benefits. The bottom line of profit for shareholders and the shortcuts that are taken to facilitate this bottom line are of great concern.

When government is not the program operator, it must set forth contractual stipulations that are extremely specific relating to what private contractors must do to ensure high program quality, and then very actively monitor the fulfillment of these requirements.

AFTERCARE OR REENTRY

Parole, now often referred to as aftercare or reentry, has long been a neglected service, quite possibly because it is at the very back end of the system, distant from the power decision making center of the court, and tagging on following the power budget center of state institutional care. All of those on aftercare status need the best kind of help to accomplish successful reentry. More of the right kind of help is needed.

Notable concerns regarding aftercare include the following:

1. There is a lack of coordination between institutional treatment staff and aftercare agents.

2. Post-institutional release plans may be cursory.

3. Supervision and/or monitoring may be scant.

The transition from regimented institutional life to the vastly different, far less structured status of aftercare, is no easy path. Those who have studied this transition urge that aftercare planning begin within several weeks of the onset of institutional life, that back-in-the community aftercare resources become known to the resident during the institutional stay and be experienced on a testing basis even during and particularly toward the end of the stay, and that rather intensive community-level resources be in place for released juveniles who have been assessed as at high risk of a new offense. A detailed program of "reintegration" with the community is critical.[23]

Aftercare lacks the status of the juvenile probation enterprise. It is, normally, a division of a state level organization whose budget and direction are preempted by its management of state institutions. Its staffing has often been relatively sparse and its functions too limited (to monitoring and controlling institutional releasees). But helping all aftercare juveniles put their lives back together is a vital function. They need assistance with their self-perceptions and with how family members, friends, and others view them. They will need help with employment and housing and some will need some funds to tide them over until they can receive a paycheck.

Many aftercare juveniles will fail to fulfill a condition of parole, such as a drug test. Some, too many, will commit another violation of law. The parole agent may handle some violations informally, with others brought before administrative hearings held by an executive agency hearing officer or judicial hearings in a juvenile court. Not all violations or reoffenses need to result in a return to an institution. Just as protocols of adult and juvenile drug courts recognize there will be relapses and that a graduated community-level sanction can usefully be applied with a relapse, so should a similar accountability and community-level sanction be applied with technical and minor offense violations by aftercare youth.

Ohio, among other states, keeps track of recidivism among institutional releasees. Acknowledging that Ohio seeks only deeper-end juveniles for its institutional populations, it reports that 21% of the 665 youths released or discharged during the third quarter of 1999 recidivated within three months and 43% of this universe recidivated within six months.[24]

Aftercare deficiencies are a concern of many in this field including those who are particularly interested in curbing minority overrepresentation in juvenile justice. A four-county Oregon approach, the Minority Youth Transition Program (MYTP), holds promise: Minority aftercare juveniles have two staff members assigned to assist their reentry, one the regular parole officer and the other a transition specialist who is a member of a minority group. The parole officer maintains the official responsibility for the juveniles while the transition specialist is the principal staff member who works intensively with them and their families and is the primary communication link between them, the community, the contracted-for services, and the parole officer. The aftercare plan, developed by the two staff persons while the juveniles are institutionalized, is (1) individualized, (2) culturally specific, (3) gender specific, and (4) language appropriate.

MYTP's contracted services include, e.g., mental health, drug and alcohol, mentors, family support, anger management, grief counseling, gang intervention, education assistance, and employment readiness training. The transition specialist is available to youths and their families "24/7" and provides intensive monitoring, support, and treatment services coordination over a five-month period to a 12- to 15-person caseload. The specialist provides the parole officer with a monthly log of each juvenile's activities and reports any breaches of parole conditions for handling by the parole officer.[25]

Research on the effectiveness of intensive supervision parole programs does not yet permit sound conclusions except to state that successful juveniles require treatment services to address their needs. It is unclear "whether increased surveillance in the community adds anything to the impact of treatment and rehabilitation." [26]

There is now a new interest in strengthening reentry. High recidivism rates of state institutional graduates are prompting more investment in aftercare. There is recognition that a serious reoffense while on aftercare likely destines one for adult court handling. More professionals recognize that more must be done to enfold these juveniles into mental health, drug treatment, education, job skills training, and community participation roles than has been done in the past, and to open day and evening reporting and treatment centers geared to these juveniles. These are our young people and we need to care more about their care and their futures.

THE CHAPTERS THAT FOLLOW

Chapter 34 reports on a Colorado institution for female delinquents, Teen Quest. It was operated by a non-profit entity and is representative of the new wave of gender specific programming. A new 40-bed facility opened on this campus in 2002, operated by a different private entity.

Chapter 35 on Tallulah, a Louisiana institution for boys, subject of two law suits and possibly on the brink of closure, describes what has been an intractable juvenile institution, at first privately constructed and operated, whose only benefit appears to have been for its institutional investors.

More hopeful developments in Georgia are described in Chapter 36—a major, multi-faceted overhaul that fits the definition of the progressive conventional wisdom in moving to emphasize community-level resources. Chapter 37 reports on RECLAIM Ohio, which symbolizes an advanced form of state subsidy for local juvenile court program expansion that can result in a reduction in state commitments. The Georgia approach administers or arranges state-funded programming to enrich juvenile probation services at the local level. The Ohio approach provides state monies to a local court to purchase or otherwise expand community-level program services.

This section closes with Chapter 38's description and analysis of post-institutional aftercare, a neglected arena of juvenile justice programming that is beginning to receive attention at long last.

Endnotes

[1] Justice Policy Institute (1999). *100 Years of the children's court: Giving kids a chance to make a better choice.* San Francisco: Justice Policy Institute. This work profiles 25 individuals who experienced the juvenile and sometimes the adult justice system and went on to lead highly successful lives, e.g., a judge, a large-city district attorney, a prominent author, a U.S. senator, an Olympic gold medallist, and a federal delinquency official.

[2] Todis, B. et al. (2001). Overcoming the odds: Qualitative examination of resilience among formerly incarcerated adolescents. *Exceptional Children, 68,* 119-139.

[3] Loughran, E. J. & Guarino-Ghezzi, S. (1995). A state perspective. In B. Glick & A. P. Goldstein (Eds.), *Managing delinquency programs that work* (pp. 25-51). Laurel, MD: American Correctional Association.

[4] Colo. Rev. Stat. §§19-2-516, 19-2-601, 19-2-908, 19-2-909, and 19-2-921.

[5] 42 Pa. Cons. Stat. Ann. §§6352 and 6353.

[6] Miller, J. G. (1991). *Last one over the wall: The Massachusetts experiment in closing reform schools.* Columbus: Ohio State University Press.

[7] Idaho Department of Juvenile Corrections, Juvenile Justice Commission (2000). *3-year plan 2000-2002.* Boise, ID: Idaho Department of Juvenile Corrections, COC-8.

[8] Puzzanchera, C. et al. (2000). *Juvenile Court Statistics 1997.* Washington, DC: Office of Juvenile Justice and Delinquency Prevention.

[9] American Bar Association and National Bar Association (2001). *Justice by gender: The lack of appropriate prevention, diversion and treatment alternatives for girls in the justice system.* Washington, DC: Author, p. 3.

[10] Albrecht, L. (1995). Facility programming for female delinquents. In B. Glick & A. P. Goldstein (Eds.), note 3 supra.

[11] Greene, Peters & Associates (2000). *Guiding principles for promising female programming: An inventory of best practices.* Washington, DC: Office of Juvenile Justice and Delinquency Prevention.

[12] Cocozza, J. J. & Skowyra, K. (2000*).* Youth with mental health disorders: Issues and emerging responses. *Juvenile Justice VII.* Also Underwood, L. A. et al. (2001). Integrating juvenile correctional and community health approaches: A promising program for juveniles with mental health disorders. *Juvenile Correctional Mental Health Report, 1*(3) 33-34, 42, 46-47.

[13] Haapanen, R. & Ingram, W. (2000). *California Youth Authority mental health and substance abuse treatment needs assessment.* Sacramento: California Youth Authority.

[14] Wheeler-Cox, T. (1999). *An overview of the Texas Youth Commission's specialized treatment programs.* Austin, TX: Criminal Justice Policy Council.

[15] Coccozza & Skowyra (2000), note 12 supra.

[16] Martinez, O. L. (2001). Building a juvenile correctional mental health system. *Juvenile Correctional Mental Health Report, 1*(6), 81-82, 88, 91-92, 94.

[17] Id.

[18] Puritz, P. et al. (1998). *Beyond the walls: Improving conditions of confinement for youth in custody.* Washington, DC: Office of Juvenile Justice and Delinquency Prevention.

[19] Richisson, T. (1999, December 12). Glendening suspends juvenile boot camps. *Baltimore Sun,* p. 1A.

[20] Gately, G. (2002, August 9). Maryland boot camp settlement. *The New York Times,* p. A13.

[21] Smith, K. (2001, September 4). Operator of privatized youth prison calls it quits. *Las Vegas Sun,* p. 1B.

[22] Hines, L. (2000, December 16). Jury finds prison firm abused boy. *The State, Columbia, SC,* p. B1.

[23] Altschuler, D. M. & Armstrong, T. L. (1998). Recent developments in juvenile aftercare: Assessment findings and promising programs. In A. R. Roberts (Ed.), *Juvenile justice.* Chicago: Nelson-Hall.

[24] Ohio Department of Youth Services (2000): *A report on DYS performance measures.* Columbus: Author.

[25] Presentation of Lonnie Jackson, Oregon Youth Authority, to Office of Juvenile Justice and Delinquency Prevention Conference, Washington, DC, December 12, 2000.

[26] MacKenzie, D. L. et al. (1999). *Reintegration, supervised release, and intensive aftercare.* Office of Juvenile Justice and Delinquency Prevention Bulletin, 20.

Chapter 34

Teen Quest: Female-Specific Program Services for Colorado's Delinquent Girls

Three decades ago, 70 to 80 girls were housed at Colorado's Mountview School for Girls near Denver. In time, deinstitutionalization of status offenders cleared most of the girls from the campus. Today, it is just the Mountview School, and its campus is multifunctional. It has six pretrial detention "pods" and one short-term treatment cottage for boys. For girls, it hosts one pretrial detention "pod" and Teen Quest. Teen Quest, the subject of this chapter, is a 20-bed secure facility located on these fenced-in grounds. It has been operated since late 1994 by a private non-profit agency, Denver Area Youth Services (DAYS). (I have been a member of the DAYS board of directors for more than 20 years.)

TEEN QUEST RESIDENTS HAVE TROUBLED SOCIAL AND PSYCHOLOGICAL HISTORIES

Teen Quest's seven-page program description avoids reference to the offenses committed by its residents. While it promotes its many programs that serve girls, it soft-pedals the number of residents who have been sexually abused. It notes, however, that "many have been involved in incidents of physical, sexual, and emotional abuse," which are victimization factors generally recognized as prominent in the pathway to offense commission by girls. The document states, further, that a majority of residents present significant substance abuse issues, have chronic runaway behaviors, and/or have failed in out of home placements. The focus is on the behavioral problems and deficits these young women present that occasion high-risk and failure-related conduct, not on the conduct that brought them to the facility.

This focus on the underlying issues that cause antisocial behavior is evident in conversations with staff. Staff talk treatment. A senior counselor stressed the need to address girls' underlying issues, in contrast to the far greater concern in boys' programs with the nature and severity of an offense and the youth's law violation record. During my recent visit to Teen Quest, the sole reference to a youth's crime came from the facility director who talked of carrying the treatment responsibility for two residents convicted of homicide.

This chapter originally appeared in Juvenile Justice Update, *Vol. 6, No. 3, June/July 2000.*

Girls Committed for a Variety of Offenses

Assault (29%) heads the list of offenses for which 67 girls were committed to the state by juvenile court judges over a recent 30-month period. Assault refers to an assault against a family member or another person. Theft (20%) and motor vehicle theft (18%), the latter more generally initiated by male companions, were second and third ranking offenses, followed by property offenses (7%), substance abuse/possession (7%), and homicide (4%). The remaining 13% of females were committed for such miscellaneous offenses as arson, menacing, weapon possession, forgery, and intimidating a witness.

Offense Profile Mirrors NCCD Study of California Females

On the surface, the offenses of Teen Quest residents appear consistent with findings of a National Council on Crime & Delinquency 1998 study[1] of pre-institutional female delinquents in California. There, "a majority of the girls' more serious charges fell into the assault category. A close reading of the case files of girls charged with assault revealed that most of these charges were the result of non-serious, mutual combat situations with parents. In many cases, the aggression was initiated by the adults." The NCCD study pointed out:

> The small number of girls arrested for the most serious offenses—robbery, homicide, and weapons offenses—reportedly committed these crimes almost exclusively within the context of their relationships with codefendants. These relationships fell into two distinct categories: dependent or equal. The first group included girls who were following the lead of male offenders (often adults) who were typically the primary perpetrators of the crime. The second group included girls functioning in female-only groups or mixed-gender groups (including gangs) as equal partners in the commission of their offenses. Finally, the availability of weapons and an increased willingness to use them appeared to be factors in girls' involvement with serious and violent crime.[2]

Demographic Picture of Teen Quest Residents

Most Teen Quest residents have been Caucasian (46%). These numbers, however, have been balanced by a combination of Latinas (26%) and African-Americans (20%). Residents have also included Native Americans (6%) and those with Asian Pacific Island heritage (2%). Girls range in age from 14 to 20, but most are under 18.

Teen Quest residents have a multitude of treatment needs. Among the many problems presented are post-traumatic stress disorder (100%), substance abuse (80%), psychiatric disorders (67%), sexual abuse (64%), eating disorders (50%), self-harm and self-mutilation (47%), and motherhood (14%). Residents' "psychiatric disorders" are characterized as conduct disorder, major depression, attention deficit hyperactivity disorder, bipolar disorder, identity disorder, and oppositional defiant disorder. These behavior problems manifest themselves in poor impulse control, poor concentration, poor communication skills, poor anger expression, physical aggression, property destruction, inhibited social skills, distorted thinking, uninhibited sexual activity, low tolerance for frustration, inhibited ability to delay gratification, and, of course, low self-esteem.

MULTIFACETED, THREE-PART TREATMENT APPROACH

The Teen Quest approach to treatment helps residents acquire insight into their pasts while they develop skills to function independently in society. The treatment approach stresses strengths and strength building and applies a triad of theoretical bases.

Focus on Accountability

First, from a cognitive behavioral standpoint, residents focus on their own accountability for their (mis)behaviors. Instead of allowing girls to play a "blame game," attributing what they have done wrong to others, they must face themselves and acknowledge responsibility for their own actions or omissions. This includes, as a worst case scenario, filing criminal charges against residents over 18-years-old for assaulting staff members or for property destruction. Nonetheless, this is a treatment facility. I noticed on the facility's "room-to-room board" that for one resident, it was "OK for Teddy Bear," and for another, "OK for angel in room."

Recognizing Factors That Trigger Relapse

A second approach, a "relapse model" approach, teaches a "relapse cycle." There are triggers to one's behavior. Girls are asked, what was the trigger that led you to attack another person? Accept drug use? Revert to drug use? Agree to an ambiguous sexual experience? Blot out what your teacher is teaching? Complicate the Teen Quest community program? The therapeutic intent of the program is to help residents understand and come to grips with what their heads are or are not telling them, and to enable them to move beyond their feelings of failure and prevent future relapses. They may be asked or required to "journal" the cycle and the trigger. Journaling or not, the goal is to have residents return to staff members and communicate what triggered a relapse, and then suggest how to handle the trigger in the future.

Gender-Specific Programing

The third and permeating approach is female-specific programming. By design, the entire staff is female, and there is an intense focus on counseling. Each girl meets weekly with a professional counselor. For all, there are myriad day-to-day brief sessions with staff members and teachers—all oriented to the fact this is a girls' facility, that girls have been given certain roles by society, its institutions, their families, and others, and that girls need to obtain power to control their lives and succeed as women. There is a wide concentration of group activities facilitated by staff and external group leaders that take on numerous concrete issue areas that focus on or incorporate the female dimension. There is relatively little unprogrammed time. Among the areas that are addressed are the following:

- *Parenting Education:* Objectives are to learn birth control options, their cost, effectiveness, and side effects; to understand the signs and stages of pregnancy, labor, and delivery, and the importance of health care and nutrition; to learn the stages of child development, child safety and health care, discipline options and when they are appropriate, and "making memories."

- *Gender Issues in the Media:* Objectives are to assist residents in critically analyzing how the media portrays women in today's society; to provide opportunities for girls to make connections between messages conveyed by the media and the behavior they exhibit; to discuss issues related to relationships, racial and social stereotypes, sexuality, difficult choices, gangs, and other adolescent concerns.

- *Current Events Group:* This group aims to inform and educate residents about current events that may have an effect on their lives; to promote societal awareness and critical thinking; and to encourage dialogue about messages young women receive from society.

- *Close Relationships Group:* The objectives for this group include addressing the significance and dynamics of relationships, teaching interpersonal skills to begin and maintain healthy relationships, recognizing that the task of adolescence is to define oneself and find ways to make attachments to others, and developing communication skills and conflict resolution tools to be used in close relationships.

An array of other facilitated discussion groups covers issues pertinent to putting one's life together better and succeeding with life's choices and achievements. These include:

- *Domestic Violence:* In this group, girls identify and define the cycle of violence. Discussions challenge myths about violence and promote self-esteem while identifying the characteristics of healthy relationships.

- *Victim Empathy:* Girls learn to identify and relate to victims and to develop an awareness of the effects crime has on its victims. In the process, girls learn the value of understanding another person's point of view as an element of making better decisions and improving relationships.

- *Peace Curriculum:* This group provides an opportunity for girls to reflect on past life experiences, identify lessons learned, and plan for the future. It also teaches functional life skills through role playing, reflective writings, and discussion.

- *Survivor's Group:* The objective of this group is to address issues of sexual abuse by focusing on personal safety, self-image, and family dynamics and relationships.

- *Pro-Active Communication Group:* This group seeks to improve the Teen Quest environment and quality of life by teaching pro-active communication and conflict resolution skills, effective anger expression skills, social skills, and the difference between assertive and aggressive presentations. It helps girls

Exhibit 34-1
Observing an Art Therapy Group at Teen Quest

I watched 10 girls in their art therapy group. One said, "This helps me express my feelings even if we don't talk about our feelings. We are not judged or criticized here. Therefore we are the experts with our art. No matter the art, it is the best art!" She spoke of the butterfly she was painting. She likes butterflies, as they develop from caterpillars and later emerge into freedom. "Also, they are pretty."

Others spoke as they painted, drew, made masks, or worked in clay, about having fun in art therapy, of having a time for "peacefulness," or of "bonding with your peers here." One spoke of liking mask making, of painting the inside of the mask—"which is how we see ourselves," and of painting the outside of the mask—"which is how others see us."

As the clock wound down, the therapist asked what the residents would share with others. An 18-year-old young woman, in residence for only two months, described the several-level clay cross she had made. In the middle was her boyfriend's name. She had painted the piece with black, for "our love," blue, for "our happiness," and yellow, for the "five years we've been together." She then told me, in an aside, that she would rather be held in a women's jail where she wouldn't have all these classes and groups.

The girl who painted the butterfly then held up a lock and key she had made of clay. She told the group she is locked up both inside and at Teen Quest, but she holds the key to follow the butterfly into freedom.

develop an empathetic understanding of the correlation between their own victimization and their treatment of others. It addresses the importance of resolving disputes in an appropriate manner, and it discusses issues involving the transition of residents to their homes or community environments.

Other Activities Include School and Family Counseling

Of course, Teen Quest operates an approved school as well as a GED program. Counseling services are provided to individual family groups, as families are able to come to the facility. Some participate in a facilitated multi-family group that addresses family relationships and communication. Residents participate in both a weekly substance abuse education group and in individual and group substance abuse treatment. Teen Quest celebrates Women's History Month, International Women's Day, and Women's Equality Day, along with Cinco de Mayo and African-American, Native-American, and Asian-American History Months. There is also dance therapy and art therapy (see Exhibit 34.1).

PROGRAM INCLUDES FOCUS ON HEALTH AND FITNESS

Healthy Diets an Important Focus

A female-oriented educational curriculum is being tested at Teen Quest that addresses nutrition and aims at the promotion of healthier diets and bodies. There is emphasis on foods that are valuable and those that should be avoided, calorie considerations, and smaller portion size (some girls "purge" after overeating). One result is that the institutional cafeteria now serves smaller portions in the girls' dining room. Within the residence, snacks are mostly fruits or cheese and crackers. From time to time, groups of eight girls do menu planning and meal preparation.

Exercise Is Essential

Teen Quest has a physical fitness curriculum that incorporates calisthenics and stretching. Residents go to the gym daily for volleyball and other large muscle exercise. The instructor works to develop motivation and team-building skills; she sees many as having some depression that holds them back.

TEEN QUEST PROGRAM CHALLENGES

Job Skills Training an Area of Weakness

Job training is not yet a strong suit of Teen Quest. Girls can learn basic computer skills. There is a new culinary arts curriculum for older girls who have completed their GEDs; this is taught at the Mountview kitchen. Finally, employment readiness training is given during the last 30 days of a girl's stay as part of a transitional curriculum. But that is largely it. The treatment curriculum preempts a vocational training curriculum.

Public-Private Collaboration Generates Concerns About Admissions, Aftercare, and Staff Turnover

A public-private collaboration such as exists between the Colorado Department of Youth Corrections (CDYC) and DAYS, which operates Teen Quest under contract to CDYC, can pose problems and complications. For example, CDYC tells Teen Quest which girls are to be admitted. Teen Quest has no intake control over admissions. Further, it is very difficult for Teen Quest to return a girl who doesn't fit the program to alternate CDYC programming.

Likewise, there are certain issues with aftercare. Residents are in placement an average of nine months. When Teen Quest determines a girl has successfully completed the program, it initiates a 30-day transition component. When the girl is released, the state takes over her care and supervision. As a result, Teen Quest generally learns only anecdotally and not systematically how its graduates are adjusting or where they are living. Teen Quest does not operate a continuum of services that its clients need, from secure facility to group home to independent living, all accompanied by an array of program supports. Teen Quest is very aware that return to the community without strong supports is likely to mean failure, despite gains made during a residential stay. While CDYC provides or arranges for community-related aftercare, Teen Quest staff think the resident-staff-program termination of contact is too abrupt and requires more self-reliance than graduates can handle suitably.

A further concern stems from staff salary levels that DAYS is able to provide in light of its contract sum limitations. On too many occasions, Teen Quest has trained promising staff members only to lose them at a later date to a different CDYC program that pays a higher salary. The Teen Quest program suffers as competent staff members depart and their replacements undertake on-the-job training.

PROGRAM ASSESSMENT AND EVALUATION ARE NEXT STEPS

In the past decade, society discovered the delinquent girl, and gender-specific programming was introduced still more recently. Research into the nature of girls' needs and the effectiveness of particular program interventions is at an early stage in this nation.[3] Teen Quest believes in its program, but has no valid measure of its effectiveness. At the moment, there is a modest assessment underway at Teen Quest of the impact of its grant-funded health and fitness training. A more rigorous evaluation of Teen Quest's young women and its program and treatment modalities is on the drawing board. This will look at ways to better determine the specific needs of young women in concert with an assessment of the services and supports required for meeting these needs and attaining successful community readjustment.

DESIGNING FEMALE-SPECIFIC PROGRAMMING TO AVOID INSTITUTIONALIZATION

Colorado's overall population continues to climb, and the judicial demand for intensive treatment services for girls in a secure setting continues to expand. Delinquent girls are handled in several settings less intensive than Teen Quest. Some of the girls in these programs are awaiting an open slot at Teen Quest. The state wants a larger facility for delinquent girls. It plans to build a new structure to double the size of the Teen Quest population, to be completed on the Mountview grounds by 2002.

Yet Colorado, and probably most other states, should look at secure facilities as a last resort. There are examples where a juvenile probation agency redesigned how it worked with its female probationers, retrained its staff, reviewed the specialized needs of these probationers, and created female-specific interventions. In Baltimore, e.g., community agencies assisted with this mission, which is much broader than a probation agency can accomplish unilaterally. As a result of this effort, commitments of females from Baltimore to state institutions have dropped dramatically.[4] With a viable program in place, there is no need to recommend commitment for most property offenses, simple assaults, or runaways. Despite occasional media highlights of a gun-related or dramatic crime, most girls' offenses, in Baltimore, Colorado, or elsewhere, are not severe.

CONCLUSION

It is reassuring to have a Teen Quest-like program in one's state. But it is wise policy, practice, and economics to reduce the need for such placements by providing better female-oriented treatment for girls in their own communities.

Author's Note

A different private entity will assume management of the new 40-bed Colorado delinquent girls' facility that opened during the summer of 2002. The updating information that follows was prepared by Laura Shipman-Hamblin, Program Director, Teen Quest, shortly prior to the termination of its program responsibility.

The Teen Quest program has continued to provide important treatment and educational services to young women from around the state since the original report in this chapter was prepared in early 2000.

As many mental health professionals will attest, the juvenile population is ever changing. To keep up with the changes and provide appropriate treatment services to its clients, Teen Quest reduced the number of resident beds from 20 to 12 in the fall of 2000. This change allowed us to provide treatment that was more intensive.

Teen Quest has made every effort to stay on the cutting edge of gender and culturally specific services. Demographic information was continually gathered and assessed. The most recent figures indicate that from July 1, 2001, through June 30, 2002, Teen Quest served a total of 27 residents: 48% Anglo; 30% Hispanic; 15% Bi-Racial; 4% African American; 4% Native American.

Teen Quest has continually evaluated its groups in order to offer activities that are interactive and fun for its clients, while ensuring they are either skill-based or psychoeducational in nature. Some of the familiar groups have been: Life Skills, Parenting Education, Substance Abuse Treatment and Relapse Prevention, Self-Soothing Skills, Gender Issues in the Media, Domestic Violence Group, Victim Empathy Group, Sexual Abuse Survivor's Group, and Proactive Communication Group. Despite the discontinuation of funding for the Health and Fitness Project, Teen Quest continued to strongly emphasize skill acquisition through participation in team sports, opportunities for daily recreation, and the promotion of exercise as a way of life.

Other group activities have included: Equine Therapy, Girls' Enriched Treatment and Transition, Art Therapy, Music Therapy, Independent Living Skills, Effective Communication, Girl Scouts, Grief and Loss, and a Dance Group.

In addition to the comprehensive treatment services provided, Teen Quest has offered an approved education program that focused on multicultural and gender specific monthly themes. Frequently, outside speakers and organizations were invited to the facility to do presentations in order to supplement and enhance the curriculum.

Endnotes

[1] Acoca, L. & Dedel, K. (1998) *No place to hide: Understanding and meeting the needs of girls in the California juvenile justice system*. San Francisco: National Council on Crime and Delinquency.

[2] Acoca, L. (1999). Investing in girls: A 21st century strategy. *Juvenile Justice, 6*, 3-13, at pp. 7-8.

[3] Id.

[4] Daniel, M. D. (2000). The female intervention team. *Juvenile Offender Solutions, 4*, 16-21.

Chapter 35

Tallulah: Lessons From Louisiana

There was a well-known Broadway actress in the 1940s and 1950s named Tallulah Bankhead. A small town in Northeastern Louisiana named Tallulah (1990 population, 8,526) is also becoming very well known because of its operation, since 1994, of a private for-profit secure delinquency facility called the Tallulah Correctional Center for Youth (TCCY). The similarity is in name only. Tallulah Bankhead, who addressed most people as "darling" (which, in her husky Southern drawl sounded like "daaahlin'") achieved recognition as brilliant, glamorous, talented, and indomitable. TCCY is far less than a brilliant or talented program. TCCY, currently the subject of a class-action suit brought by the non-profit Juvenile Justice Project of Louisiana (JJPL) and another suit brought by the U.S. Department of Justice (DOJ) against TCCY and three state-operated secure juvenile facilities, is anything but a "daaahlin'" to the institution's residents.

TCCY consists of two interrelated physical locations. One, with a capacity for 360 youth, houses both boot camp and non-boot camp participants in nine dormitory-style open housing units, each holding approximately 40 beds (double-bunked) per unit. The second structure, with a capacity for 320 youth, is a maximum-security cellblock facility. Each of its four cellblocks is divided into four sections and each section has 20 individual cells. Tall fences and concertina or razor wire surround both locations.

NEW YORK TIMES TEES OFF ON TALLULAH

Brutality and Neglect Define Conditions

A *New York Times* story on July 15, 1998, carried this headline: "Profits at Juvenile Prisons Earned at a Chilling Cost." Fox Butterfield, who often looks hard and well at delinquency concerns for the *Times*, led off the report, suggesting that TCCY "is so rife with brutality, cronyism and neglect that many legal experts say it is the worst in the nation." He continued, "[I]nmates ... regularly appear at the infirmary with black eyes, broken noses or jaws or perforated eardrums from beatings by the poorly paid, poorly trained guards or from fights with other boys."[1] Butterfield went on to enumerate such other problems as meager meals, scarce clothing, few certified teachers, only an hour a day of education on some days, no books until recently, scant mental health services, excessive use of isolation, and stifling barracks.

This chapter originally appeared in Juvenile Justice Update, *Vol. 5, No. 4, August/September 1999.*

Financial Dealings Raise Concerns

According to Butterfield's *Times* article, a Tallulah businessman, whose father was a state senator, "just happened" to win a no-bid contract to operate the juvenile facility. It also "just happened" that the company he formed included two close friends of the governor, neither of whom had correctional experience. It also "just happened" that the state paid an annual fee of $24,448 per youth, and that 29% of payments, according to Butterfield, went to pay off construction loans. The 29% payment ratio contrasts to an average 7% rate paid elsewhere, wrote Butterfield, citing the belief of the president of the National Juvenile Detention Association.

FEDERAL COURT ACTIONS ENSUE

The JJPL class action suit against the Tallulah center was filed on July 9, 1998, in the U.S. District Court in Monroe (98-886-B-M1) the closest federal court to the facility. Shortly thereafter, it was moved to the federal court in Baton Rouge, which has had jurisdiction over the operations of Louisiana prisons since 1971, and had incorporated juvenile facilities within this purview. The court froze intake at TCCY on July 27, 1998. Previously, in late 1994, the judge had declared a state of emergency at TCCY; this was subsequently rescinded. The court also had issued a series of orders increasing TCCY's population cap from 560 to 620. Both JJPL and DOJ suits are pending before this court while negotiations are going on. The negotiations, aimed at a consent decree and a raft of improvements in care, have been extensive, but at this writing, remain unresolved.

Brian B. and other youths at Tallulah are plaintiffs in the JJPL suit. Defendants include: state officials who run the corrections, health, and education departments; the Tallulah facility superintendent; the private corporation, Trans-American Development Association (Trans-American), which owns and first operated the facility; and the Tallulah mayor and local school officials. The United States of America is plaintiff in the DOJ suit (No. 98-947-B-1) filed November 5, 1998. Defendants are: the governor of Louisiana; the state director of corrections; the wardens of the four facilities; and Trans-American. A second article by Butterfield, on November 6, 1998, the day after the DOJ suit was filed, reported,

> Louisiana has repeatedly insisted that it has tried to make changes in the four juvenile prisons and that the Federal investigators have exaggerated the troubles. The owners of Tallulah have also complained that the improvements demanded by the Justice Department would be so expensive it would put them out of business.[2]

Tallulah Residents Complain of Serious Deficiencies

Among many points of importance and interest in this case is that the underage juveniles sued through their "next friend," Shannon Robshaw, Executive Director of the Mental Health Association of Louisiana (MHA), and asked that she be appointed guardian ad litem. (The MHA works to end the violence and abuse in secure facilities, obtain adequate treatment and protections in these facilities, increase the use of community-based programs as alternatives to incarceration, and increase the number of youths receiving prevention and aftercare services. The MHA has voiced deep concern over the reported gross deficiencies in mental health services provided residents.) While there is, as yet, no ruling on this "next friend" request, Robshaw is present at, and participates in, the negotiations.

Brian B., age 16, the first-named plaintiff, has been incarcerated since 1995. He complained of "use of excessive force by staff, punitive and abusive use of mace by staff, excessive heat in living area, and inadequate access to the courts." The second named plaintiff, Christopher C., also 16, incarcerated since September 1996, added other complaints: "inadequate video monitoring of use of excessive force by staff, inadequate mental health treatment, denial of eye examination, lack of basic sanitation, inadequate educational program, inadequate rehabilitative programming, inadequate access to family, and denial of vocational training."

The complaints of the remaining 10 named plaintiffs include arbitrary and excessive isolation; denial of special education; verbal abuse and racial epithets by staff; arbitrary disciplinary practices; abuse and demeaning practices; lack of privacy in dormitories; failure to report abuse due to fear of retaliation; failure to investigate reports of abuse; failure to protect from harm; inappropriate use of mechanical restraints; inadequate medical care; inadequate nutrition; insufficient food and foreign objects in food; inadequate recreation; and inadequate dental care.

Incidents of Excessive Force, Punitive Isolation, and Abusive Demeaning Practices Alleged

The complaints provide further details and specifics. For example, as to claims that the staff used excessive force and unreasonable bodily restraint, the complaint contains detailed allegations of punching and choking, intimidating or rewarding juveniles for not reporting excessive force to the administration, use of insufficient and insufficiently trained staff to investigate complaints, regular and unnecessary staff use of mace or pepper spray as threats and punishments for juveniles, and the use of shackles and handcuffs.

The nature of the arbitrary and punitive use of isolation and discipline includes regularly placing juveniles in isolation for 22 to 23 hours a day for weeks and sometimes months at a time; the lack of professional regulation and monitoring of isolation time; the failure to provide education, recreation, and rehabilitative treatment to those isolated; and both the arbitrary use of chemical and mechanical restraints as well as extensive isolation for those with mental health disorders who may have trouble complying with routine institutional rules and practices.

Enumerated abusive and demeaning practices include forcing youth to stand *en masse* outside in the blazing sun, requiring youth to keep their foreheads on a desk for hours at a time, "hiring" some juveniles to beat or harass others, and staff engaging in sexual relations with juveniles.

The complaint alleges violations of the First, Fourth, Fifth, Sixth, Eighth, and Fourteenth Amendments, violations of the Individuals with Disabilities Education Act, the Americans with Disabilities Act, and also violations of certain provisions of Louisiana's state law and constitution.

Moolah for Tallulah

Butterfield notes, "One of the poorest areas in a poor state, Tallulah wanted jobs, and like other struggling cities across the country it saw the nation's prison-building spree as its best hope."[3] Yes, Tallulah residents went to work for TCCY. The JJPL suit sets out an unusual arrangement between the state, the city of Tallulah, and Trans-American. In February 1994, the director of the state Department of Public Safety and Corrections entered into a cooperative agreement with the city. The city would construct or cause construction of the TCCY facility. In return, the state would maintain a population there of not less than 686 juveniles and would pay the city an average per diem rate per youth. The mayor then entered into a management services agreement with Trans-American by which the corporation agreed to pay the city $150,000 annually to provide all routine health care, including dental and mental health care, for TCCY residents. Trans-American entered into a management services agreement with GRW Corporation to manage the facility, but shortly thereafter GRW was released from this agreement. On July 23, 1998, less than two weeks after the JJPL filing, the state took over operation of TCCY, sending in an acting warden and 35 corrections officers. Later, in mid-December, Trans-American, with state approval, subcontracted TCCY operations and management to Correctional Services Corporation, a for-profit company with Florida headquarters, thus ending the state takeover.

DOJ INVESTIGATES FOUR SECURE FACILITIES INCLUDING TALLULAH AND FINDS LIFE-THREATENING CONDITIONS

DOJ began its investigation of Louisiana facilities in 1996 following notification to the governor. DOJ used "expert consultants" in the fields of juvenile justice, education, medical and mental health, and abuse prevention. Initially each of four facilities (in Jetson, Bridge City, Swanson, and Tallulah) was toured on three occasions. Investigators interviewed several hundred juveniles as well as institutional administrators and staff. They examined facility and state documents, along with juveniles' records. The gravity of the investigation's findings of "systemic life-threatening staff abuse and juvenile-on-juvenile violence" prompted two emergency letters to the governor. A June 18, 1997, follow-up communication to the governor noted that the state agency director had established a Project Zero Tolerance initiative with a goal of eliminating institutional violence. The letter commented on the director's "strong commitment" to this goal, observed that important progress had been made, but emphasized the need to achieve much more.

The investigation resulted in identifying an array of violations of the U.S. Constitution and statutes. The investigation found approximately 1,700 adjudicated delinquents at the four facilities. The Jetson Center held 470 males and 150 females; the Bridge City facility held 180 males described as young and vulnerable; the Swanson Center held 396 males; the Tallulah Center then held 536 males. About one-third of the 1,700 were identified as needing special education. Of the juveniles, 83% were African-American. Fewer than 25% of those confined in 1996 had committed violent crimes. Page after page of the report documents staff abuses, program shortcomings, and unconstitutional conditions that occurred after Project Zero Tolerance was launched.

No Mental Health Care in a Mentally Unhealthy Facility

According to the June 18, 1997, DOJ letter to the governor:

The most egregious deficiencies in mental health care were noted at Tallulah, where juveniles with extensive psychiatric histories who self-mutilate and/or threaten suicide have never been referred to a psychiatrist. Tallulah employs no psychiatrist and provides no mental health care to its many youth with serious mental illness. At most, counselors who are not trained in mental health care and not supervised by mental health professions speak to juveniles.

Gross deficiencies in managing and monitoring psychotropic medications were reported. Mental health assessments and counseling were found "severely deficient" at all four facilities. At Tallulah, 56 juveniles were identified by the facility as being mentally retarded, but most of these juveniles were not provided any special program.

DOJ Proposes Minimum Remedial Measures

As required under the federal Civil Rights of Institutionalized Persons Act (CRIPA), 42 U.S.C. §1997 et seq., DOJ must allow a state an opportunity to take remedial measures. A letter to the governor listed 14 needed measures. The recommended measures regularly used the terms "adequate" and "ensure," as in: "Adequately" protect juveniles from staff abuse and juvenile-on-juvenile violence. Employ sufficient, trained, independent investigators to "ensure" all incidents of violence, use of force, or serious injury are "adequately" investigated. "Ensure" that juveniles are classified and housed "adequately" to protect them from harm. "Ensure" that restraints and isolation are used only when a youth presents a clear and present danger. Provide "adequate" mental health care, medical care, dental services, general education, special education, and vocational programs. Provide "adequate" access to telephone, mail, and visitation, and to courts.

Following serious negotiation attempts and dissatisfaction with the state's progress as to the remedial measures, the DOJ brought suit to enjoin the four institutions from continuing the acts, practices, and omissions it had complained of. This unusual, drastic federal action is difficult to harmonize with a Louisiana Department of Public Safety and Corrections report stating that all four facilities have received American Correctional Association accreditation.

JJPL's suit against TCCY sought similar remedies with even greater specificity. It urged at the boot camp location, for example, physical changes in dormitories to provide privacy in showers and when using toilets. It sought temperature control in the dormitories, control of vermin, milk at each meal and the availability of fresh fruit and vegetables on a regular basis, as well as the appointment of a special officer to protect the rights of residents while the action was pending.

LOUISIANA CONFINEMENT: LONG SENTENCES IN SECURE FACILITIES

In Louisiana, the maximum jurisdictional age for delinquency is the day before one's 17th birthday. A 1993 legislative measure required that a juvenile adjudicated for one of six violent crimes must remain in a secure environment until age 21. A state agency report, dated March 31, 1999, lists a total secure custody population of 1,973 juveniles, with 63 residents ages 10-13 years, and 385 ages 18-20 years. Twenty-five percent had a scheduled length of sentence of four years of more. According to the same report, another 839 delinquent youth were held in non-secure care, and 4,996 were under non-custodial supervision (informal adjustment, probation, or parole). The ratio of white youth is significantly greater in the first two groups than in the secure custody group.

To deal with overcrowding, a 1997 measure authorized transfer of adjudicated delinquents 17 years of age or more from juvenile facilities to adult prisons, although the newly imprisoned youth had not been allowed such adult court constitutional protections as the right to a jury trial. This measure was voided by the Louisiana Supreme Court in March 1998, **In re C. B., R. B., T. C., R. C., S. C., et al.,** 708 So. 2d 391 (La. 1998), and, as a result, 66 juveniles were transferred back to secure juvenile institutions. As of February 1, 1999, state juvenile institutions housed 145 long-term sentenced juveniles ranging in age from 15 to 21, with an average age of 20 years. They had been sentenced for an average of 4.7 years for first degree murder (2), second degree murder (7), aggravated rape (21), and armed robbery (115). Their lengthy sentences and older ages complicate juvenile institutional management and reinforce the need for only top-flight administration, programming, services, and staffing.

The MHA, in a fact sheet concerning the state agency, reports the following. The state agency spent more than $92 million in FY'98 to house and rehabilitate juveniles, an 80% increase from four years earlier. Over 92% of this budget is spent on secure care. Almost 75% of juveniles in secure care are committed for non-violent offenses. Over 70% of juveniles placed in secure care go on to commit further crimes. Less than a third of youth with serious mental/emotional disorders receive treatment. The MHA works actively with key stakeholders, legislators, public interest lawyers, and local and national media to highlight its concerns and seek effective reforms.

OBSERVATIONS ON THE PRESENT: PROBLEMS ABOUND

Both JJPL and DOJ report that certain improvements in care have been accomplished, some stimulated by their investigations and suits. Both also report that vastly more is necessary. If the case comes to trial, the federal judge will rule on the matter. More likely though, in time, a consent decree will be fashioned that spells out the remedial measures the state will take and how implementation will be monitored.

My own reaction to what is happening is that there must be much fire underlying this smoke. There must be terrible problems. Why? The institutions are far too large, regardless of how they may be carved into decentralized units. A new institution should not be located in a remote, rural corner of a state regardless of the fact that it is easier to get poor rural areas to accept it because of the promise of jobs. There is a growing national consensus as to the imperative of effective and adequate mental health services for institutional residents. These services, like comprehensive medical and dental care, are just not as available in sparsely populated areas.

The Three Branches Must Communicate and Collaborate

Backlash from the seduction of privatization is evident here. Backlash from the politicization of juvenile justice programming is also evident. It is difficult for state youth and correctional agency officials to do their best professional job when back room political favoritism undercuts systematic, objective judgment. There is need, pretty much everywhere, for a mechanism that regularly brings representatives of the three branches of government to the table together to exchange data and research collaboratively, in the interest of fashioning the soundest approaches to justice system policy and practice. The legislative and executive branches would be better served by increasing the availability of mental health services so that youth with emotional problems could use these services instead of entering the necessarily open doors of the justice system. Judges who seek to do the right thing, not the political thing, need support as they select non-institutional dispositions. So do officials who receive juveniles to classify them for non-institutional rather than institutional placement, and to determine release dates, aftercare plans, and preparations.

Secure Care Shouldn't Dominate the Treatment Continuum

There is need in Louisiana, and in other states and communities, for a significantly wider band of community correctional alternatives to secure institutionalization. One must give credence to the views reported above that numerous institutionalized youth can be handled effectively, and at less cost, in community places or placements. Also, a broader continuum of care enables a system to safely release incarcerated juveniles at an earlier date. They then have a good place to go or a good intervention or training program that meets their needs as well as the public safety needs.

One cannot isolate for-profit operations as the sole black sheep, though everything seems wrong about the Tallulah enterprise. The three state-operated facilities appear to present extreme failures and shortcomings as well. How else can these problems be addressed? There needs to be a lawyer ombudsman in juvenile institutions, private and public, whose job is to consult with and represent residents who have important complaints to present. Judges, prosecutors, and everyone else should regularly visit these institutions. They should know what is happening there, and whether, indeed, these are rehabilitation facilities. There must be active, skillful, candid, responsible, critical, and constructive monitoring of these programs. Well-founded population caps are vital. Well-founded staffing ratios are vital. But these measures, if in place, are only the beginning. Nonetheless, it is far better to invest in good programming than in lawyers. The state, its contractors and subcontractors, like juveniles, must become accountable.

While the problems associated with juvenile institutionalization in Louisiana must be considered severe, practitioners across the country—from judges to prosecutors to probation officers and more—should take hard looks at their own state facilities, take nothing for granted, and have a well-founded assurance that youthful residents, whose commitments they have precipitated, are well treated at the end of the line. They should examine, too, their own community-level continuum of care provisions, so that institutionalization can be reserved for those who require this more drastic intervention.

Author's Note

Some of the information that follows was provided to me by David Utter, Director, Juvenile Justice Project of Louisiana, and lead attorney for the plaintiffs in the Tallulah suit; his report is supplemented by other accounts relating to juvenile incarceration in that state including an article by Fred Cohen.[4]

In federal court, in August 2000, four lawsuits related to deficiencies with juvenile incarceration reached settlement. The settlement will expire on January 21, 2003, unless it is extended, which David Utter states is necessary as "so many problems remain."

The agreement was stimulated by a proposal for the Louisiana State University School of Medicine to provide medical, mental health, and dental care at the four facilities, and to accept responsibility for the training of institutional guards and other personnel. Utter's comment, in June 2002, was that he would give the medical school a B grade regarding its provision of medical, mental health, and dental services, but a D grade in regard to its training obligation. He states "guards remain trained in the adult correctional model and, therefore, are quick to use force, continue to verbally and emotionally abuse residents, and are not trained for the high level needs that children have."

The Cohen article notes that the 103-page settlement has extensive features: It defines serious mental illness, limits the use of force whenever possible with juveniles with mental illness, notes that a juvenile's housing assignment shall consider his or her mental health history and not be based solely on security issues, severely restricts the use of mechanical restraints, conditions the use of isolation with a clinical assessment within three hours and treatment as needed, determines the number and nature of mental health staff at a facility that is to screen and assess new and ongoing residents' mental health needs and for another institution that will maintain a 32-bed mental health unit, directs an extensive pattern and staffing for the training component, allows for internal and external monitoring of conditions and an evaluation, and extends in limited fashion to assistance with reentry to community. Cohen notes that fulfilling the conditions of the settlement will not be a cakewalk, though "if the written promises are realized Louisiana will, indeed, come from well off the pace to challenge the leaders in the field." [5]

Utter and his colleagues have continued their reform efforts following settlement. They actively monitor the conditions, care, and life experiences of residents in the four facilities in use. They brought a suit in the Juvenile Court for Orleans Parish where a judge, in December 2001, found conditions at the Tallulah facility violated a resident's constitutional and statutory rights. (**In re S. D.**, 2002-0672 (La. App. 4th Cir. 11/6/02); 2002 LEXIS 3473.) The 17-year-old juvenile had his jaw broken by a guard, although there was "no allegation and no evidence that he posed any danger to himself or others." The court found the state's own abuse investigation had suppressed important evidence, and, further, 140 juveniles had been injured at Tallulah during May 2001, seven seriously and with 18 youth suffering fractures and injuries requiring sutures. However, this decision, a trial court decision, does not govern other judges though it has continuously been brought to public and stakeholder attention.

The Juvenile Justice Project helped stimulate a Jazz Funeral coordinated by parents whose youngsters were incarcerated. Child advocates, grassroots' activists, juvenile justice system officials, and a swing marching band joined the procession as parents demanded system accountability, system reform, and the closing of Tallulah.

The Project sought, unsuccessfully, to have the legislature de-fund the Tallulah institution and in turn apply its budgeted money to improve and expand community-level programs and a continuum of care for juvenile offenders. The bill died in committee but attracted serious attention.

Meanwhile, the state operates Tallulah and the other three juvenile institutions. The Tallulah Correctional Center for Youth has been renamed the Swanson Correctional Center for Youth-Madison Parish. A fifth juvenile facility at Jena, inoperative for some years and privately constructed and owned by a national for-profit correctional firm, remains empty. Utter notes that juvenile courts now send fewer juveniles to state institutions, although community correctional programming remains very limited.

But there is hope: I have received additional information from a state court system representative, that an official Juvenile Justice Commission, assisted by a 43-member advisory board, is looking hard at the entire juvenile justice system, and is very conscious the system is broken and that more than incremental changes are needed. National groups are now currently active in the state, as well—The Annie E. Casey Foundation, the Child Welfare League of America, the American Bar Association's Juvenile Justice Center, and the National Conference of State Legislatures.

Endnotes

[1] Butterfield, F. (1998, July 15). Profits at juvenile prisons earned at a chilling cost. *The New York Times*, A1; A14, at p. A14.

[2] Butterfield, F. (1998, November 6). U.S. suing Louisiana on prison ills. *The New York Times*, p. A14.

[3] Butterfield, F. note 1 supra, p. A14

[4] Cohen, F. (2001). Louisiana juvenile justice settlement: The mental health provisions. *Juvenile Correctional Mental Health Report, 1*(2), 17, 22-24.

[5] Id. p. 22.

Chapter 36

Georgia Department of Juvenile Justice Moves Forward by Moving Back to the Community

FEDERAL INVESTIGATION LEADS TO REFORM IN GEORGIA

Revamping juvenile corrections sometimes happens with the federal government providing the tail wind. While the federal government does not often step into this arena, it did so recently in Georgia, pursuant to the U.S. Civil Rights of Institutionalized Persons Act (CRIPA), because something was very wrong with juvenile institutional care.

In 1998, after a year-long federal investigation, Georgia's governor signed on to a 59-page Memorandum of Agreement (MOA). The federal complaint and the MOA were filed in the U. S. District Court in Atlanta and can be dismissed if Georgia achieves "substantial compliance" with the MOA requirements. As a result of the MOA, the Georgia Department of Juvenile Justice (DJJ) is now engaged in very substantial restructuring. By changing judicial and probation officer decision-making and redirecting detained and delinquent youth into a broader array of community-based options that it is creating or facilitating, the DJJ seeks to stanch the flow of juveniles into what have been overcrowded pretrial detention centers and state institutions. It is also in the process of significantly improving conditions of confinement in its facilities. This article looks at what DJJ is doing in Georgia. Perhaps other states can benefit from Georgia's experience and initiate positive changes without the stimulus of a federal investigation.

PROFILE OF GEORGIA'S DJJ

The Georgia DJJ maintains 22 regional youth detention centers (RYDCs) across the state, one of them privately operated. Their total bed capacity is 1,050. On October 10, 2000, they held 1,192 juveniles. These juveniles are confined pending juvenile court adjudication, disposition, and post-disposition placement in a state-level or alternate facility.

This chapter originally appeared in Juvenile Justice Update, *Vol. 6, No. 6, December/January 2001.*

DJJ administers all or a portion of juvenile probation services in 149 of Georgia's 159 counties. Juvenile courts administer probation in Fulton County (Atlanta), suburban Atlanta counties, and other larger jurisdictions.

DJJ operates 10 youth development campuses (YDCs), four of them privately administered. Two facilities are exclusively programmed for long-term youth, four are exclusively short-term programs, and the remaining four are a combination. Within DJJ there are a total of 1,200 long-term beds and 890 short-term beds. On October 10, 2000, the YDCs supervised 1,109 long-term and 782 short-term juveniles.

DJJ operates five multiservice centers, five group homes, and seven wilderness programs, and it also purchases private residential and non-residential treatment services for youth committed to its custody. Overall, it serves more than 59,000 youth annually, including those it supervises in post-institutional aftercare.

DJJ employs more than 3,500 persons. This past decade its budget quadrupled from $70 million to $284 million. Georgia is among the 10 most populous states in the nation, the seventh fastest growing, and the fastest growing state in the Southeast. Projections anticipate very large growth in populations of youth in the 10- to17-year-old bracket. There will be striking expansions in young Hispanic and African-American male populations, historically disadvantaged groups that experience above-average poverty and disproportionate representation in the juvenile justice system.

Under these circumstances, DJJ cannot afford to and will not do business as usual. It will not proliferate more large state institutions. It wants to reserve institutional care for the highest risk and most severely offending youth, do a much improved job with these juveniles, and arrange a wide array of community correctional and institutional alternatives for other offenders.

Staff Enhanced to Meet MOA Requirements

The MOA required the addition of 128 juvenile corrections officers, the basic institutional line staff. This increase, to expand staff capabilities with the third shift at RYDCs and YDCs, was to be completed by May 1, 1999. While many people have been hired and have completed their pre-job training, the staff has an annual 25% turnover rate. As a result there has only been a net gain of 74 additional positions. To address this, DJJ successfully obtained a significant salary boost for these officers.

The MOA required other staff additions of psychologists, psychiatrists, registered nurses, nurse practitioners, physician assistants, and dentists, 35 special education teachers, and 44 counselors. The legislature approved salary increases for probation and parole specialists, and regular and special education teachers in order to make the positions competitive with the market.

Office of Quality Assurance Created

To provide auditing capacity and to monitor compliance with DJJ policies, an Office of Quality Assurance was created; its director was hired from outside DJJ. Among other objectives, this office is to assure that educational, medical, and mental health programs required by the MOA are provided. Within this office, a director of investigations is to be employed, again from outside DJJ. Under this director, qualified investigators are to be employed and trained to protect residents from abuse. Procedures have been spelled out to enable juveniles to report abuse and be better protected from retaliation. Twenty-five line staff members are to be employed to accomplish the purposes of the office.

RESTRUCTURING INSTITUTIONAL CARE IS GOAL

DJJ closed down its 130 bed Lorenzo Benn YDC on June 30, 2000. It will close its largest institution, the Wrightsville YDC with 475 beds, on July 1, 2001. (This former adult prison will be returned to the Department of Corrections.) There is also active consideration of returning the 349 bed Eastman YDC to the Department of Corrections. As a facility closes, juveniles are transferred to other YDCs or to alternative residential or community care. Staff are offered other positions in DJJ.

Orlando L. Martinez, the Commissioner of DJJ since May 6, 1999, believes strongly that institutional design is extremely important to the potential for juvenile rehabilitation. Facilities should be rehabilitation-friendly. As a result, large and/or outmoded facilities will be replaced by smaller, more functional campus- or community-based facilities.

On October 3, 2000, a new Sumter YDC, designed by a Georgia architect with experience in creating state-of-the-art juvenile campuses, was opened. A nationally recognized California architect, in close consultation with detention services staff from all levels and regions as well as with state office staff, has designed a prototype RYDC at Gainesville. Now under construction, this prototype will be the model for another new RYDC in Crisp County and for others in the future. DJJ has obtained funding approval to replace its Augusta, Macon, and Rome RYDCs.

DJJ's short-term programs have received youth dispatched to their care for placements of up to 90-days. Prior to Commissioner Martinez's tenure, these short-term programs had been boot camps. In May 2000, the Commissioner terminated boot camp activities and substituted other short-term programming features. He was dissuaded from boot camps by published research that showed various negative results. In announcing the closure of these programs, Martinez stated DJJ would no longer operate facilities whose primary components include "hazing or in your face tactics at intake, required drill and ceremony, detail assignments as punishments, group discipline, or military exercise." Military-type uniforms also would no longer be worn. Revamped short-term residential programs, however, would retain "a highly structured and disciplined environment," but have been recast with such programming as education, including vocational education, cognitive retraining and life skills training, specialized treatment for drug and alcohol problems, and recreation.

THE DETENTION NEXUS: DEVELOPING A DETENTION STRATEGY

Annie E. Casey Foundation Supports Alternatives to Detention

The U.S. Department of Justice and the Georgia DJJ are very much in sync in seeking to curb the use of secure detention and in expediting release from secure detention when it is used. Although DJJ is moving actively on several fronts to accomplish this goal, creating and using detention alternatives statewide is not readily accomplished. In moving toward this goal, DJJ has secured the expansive assistance of the Annie E.

Casey Foundation, whose Juvenile Detention Alternatives Initiative has successfully instituted detention control strategies and technologies in such cities as Chicago, Portland, and Sacramento.

Risk Assessment Instrument Developed to Guide Decisions

DJJ was required to develop a risk instrument to guide and standardize intake detention decisions. The goal is:

1. To detain those whose risk factors make secure detention necessary and to release those whose risk levels allow for non-secure handling; and

2. To identify status offenders, locked up in the past despite federal bans, and reroute them to other resources or to their own homes.

The resulting Detention Assessment Instrument has been designed, implemented, and is now being validated on a statewide basis. Consequently, probation officers or DJJ officials responsible for detention screening should be able to make better detention decisions.

Detention Alternatives Created

The MOA required implementation of a continuum of alternatives to detention and the provision of at least 380 additional alternative placement slots for youth who otherwise would have been confined in a RYDC. The DJJ continuum includes: assessment, conditional release to home, tracking, behavior aides (who accompany a youth to school, attend classes with the youth, and help assure a youth's compliance with school rules), in-home wrap-around services, placement in private family homes, non-secure placements, and staff-secure emergency shelters. Not all of these alternatives, however, are available across the state. Tracking, now available in 21 counties, is a program that provides very intensive monitoring and surveillance of juveniles who remain at home pending court action. Southwest Key, a Texas nonprofit that operates tracking programs in five states, Puerto Rico, and now Georgia, holds the contract to provide this detention alternative. Instead of detention, tracking provides a youth with a minimum of five face-to-face contacts each day, seven days a week, with staff accessible 24 hours a day for crisis intervention. A tracking team, comprised of paraprofessional and professional staff, serves an average of just seven youths. Individual case plans and family counseling and development are among the components provided with tracking.

Detention Expediters Reduce Length of Detention

Replicated from the Annie E. Casey Foundation experience, 14 case expediters are now in place. Their goal is to reduce the average length of stay in a RYDC. They seek to accelerate the release of youth who are validly detained initially, but who, following further assessment, are perceived as suitable for transfer to a nonsecure alternative setting. DJJ will pay for psychological assessments and family assessments with these pre-adjudicative youth. It will also provide electronic monitoring as a detention alternative.

Accelerating judicial dispositions and placements of detention-confined juveniles is a further goal of an expediter. If a court dispositional hearing is typically set 28 days from adjudication, can the report be prepared and the disposition determined in 21 days instead? Can, as happens in some Georgia juvenile courts, a detained juvenile's adjudication be entered at the detention hearing, resulting in less overall confinement time between detention admission and judicial disposition?

Retention in Detention until a YDC Slot Opens

RYDCs hold youth pending appropriate placement for disposition. I conducted a juvenile court study in a suburban Atlanta county in late August 2000. On a visit to the nearby RYDC, I asked the following questions:

Q: What is your capacity?

A: Fifty, but three months ago we held 95.

Q: How long are youth held here pending placement following a judicial disposition to a 90-day short-term facility?

A: This averages about 32 days, but some have waited as long as 40 days. We would like the judges to give good-time credit for this wait time, so, for example, a juvenile would serve 32 days fewer than the 90 days.

Q: How long are youth held here pending placement after a judicial disposition to a long-term commitment that can last as long as two years?

A: Perhaps 70 days to get into a YDC, 20-40 days to get into a group home, or 90 days to get into a special residential program.

FEDERAL MONITOR QUESTIONS CLOSING OF YDCS

In August 2000, a report filed by the federal monitor questioned the approach DJJ is taking, i.e., shutting down YDC facilities when RYDCs are crowded or overcrowded, in part due to retaining juveniles in detention until a YDC placement or community residential placement opens. The monitor was not satisfied DJJ had deployed a sufficient array of options to curb RYDC or YDC numbers and had concerns regarding the "relatively high rate of use of force incidents."

The Commissioner took exception to the claims that (1) there was insufficient progress in reducing RYDC and YDC populations, and (2) the rate of serious incidents, including use of force by guards, and youth-on-youth or youth-on-staff assaults, had increased as a result of this lack of progress. His reply noted the promulgation of a master plan and the reduction in RYDC populations compared to the prior year (5% in April, 4% in May, and 10% in June).

The Commissioner contended that DJJ was in substantial compliance with MOA provisions and with the time lines that were written into many of its 142 requirements. He cited preliminary data that revealed expediters had a significant impact on reducing RYDC length of stay in the districts where they worked and that other detention reduction measures were in place. But the Commissioner accepted certain other critical findings in the monitor's report and stated DJJ would be diligent in correcting them. DJJ received noncompliance or partial compliance ratings, for example, on its efforts to improve various education and special education shortcomings, to provide certain mental health services, and to remedy space needs at RYDCs.

THE ATLANTA JOURNAL-CONSTITUTION

The Atlanta Journal-Constitution, Atlanta's leading newspaper, stated in an August 11, 2000 editorial:

> The flaws highlighted by a new federal report on Georgia's system are not the fault of Juvenile Justice Commissioner Orlando Martinez. The neglect and underfunding that have led to dangerous overcrowding in most of the state's 32 youth detention centers and repeated incidents of abuse are the result of an indifferent governor and Legislature.
>
> * * *
>
> The governor and lawmakers can ignore these jailed youngsters because the voting public dismisses them as thugs and believes that their time behind bars should be horrific. The reality is that many of these youths have committed minor offenses and would not be incarcerated if not for their race and poverty.
>
> * * *
>
> Martinez can only do so much if there is no political will to make real improvements and to help kids through community-based programs rather than locking them away. Dumping kids in detention centers for minor crimes—where they serve alongside more serious offenders—simply prepares them for the adult prison system.[1]

COMMISSIONER SEEKS FRESH START

Commissioner Carries Progressive Credentials

Commissioner Orlando L. Martinez directed the Colorado counterpart of the Georgia DJJ for 17 years. Long associated with a progressive, humanistic philosophy that seeks to reserve scarce state-level resources for the most serious offenders and maximizes the use of less costly, closer-to-family community programming for others, Martinez has instructed legislators on how to get more bang for the buck by supporting less costly, nonresidential programs. He has worked with state juvenile systems to apply a rational, research-based, continuum of care programming. For years, he has served as federal court monitor for the Commonwealth of Puerto Rico and, even now, continues to monitor its juvenile justice system. As *The Atlanta Journal-Constitution* said, Martinez is "recognized nationally as a leader in juvenile justice reform." When he took office in Georgia he described the day as an opportunity for himself and DJJ staff to make a fresh start. He knew well the immensity of the task before him. Georgia sought him out because of his reputation as a reformer. Now will it provide him with the money needed to implement needed reforms?

Fresh Start Focuses on Three Critical Areas

Martinez described the fresh start DJJ needs in simple terms as "focusing on three critical areas within the Department: public safety, accountability of juveniles and staff, and helping the youths we serve develop critical life competency skills. A fresh start means ensuring that we have quality staff, well thought-out buildings and programs, and meet professional standards." He added that "a fresh start also means working real hard to get out from under our federal umbrella, and once we have accomplished these feats we will have systematically forged fresh starts for the youths we serve as well."[2]

Orlando L. Martinez is fond of saying the best way to predict a young person's future is to help create it. He particularly wants to build strong vocational training into his longer-term institutions, eliminate harmful staff and institutional conditions, enable judges to place juveniles into non-DJJ institutions and programs at DJJ expense, and gain support for Georgia to deal strategically with current and projected facts of delinquency life.

GEORGIA ARREST AND DISPOSITIONAL PATTERNS STUDIED

An Atlanta research group commissioned by DJJ pulled immense data together in its September 2000 report, "Projecting Confined Juvenile Populations in Georgia." Major findings include:

- *Serious Crime Down, Non-Serious Arrests Up:* Since 1995, juvenile arrests for violent offenses are down 27%. Since 1990, arrests for Part II non-serious offenses have soared 200%. Today, nearly three out of four juvenile arrests are for a Part II offense, driven by drug possession (a 178% increase, with the increased rate for females nearly twice that of males), public order, alcohol, and certain status offenses.

- *Detention Admissions Doubled Since 1990, But RYDCs House Increasingly Less Serious Offenders:* Probation violations, public order, property, and status offenses account for 81% of admissions.

- *At State Level, Just 30% of Admissions to 90-Day Programs Are Felony Offenders Compared with 45% of Admissions in 1995:* One of three admissions is for a probation or aftercare violation. Long-term program admissions included 35% property offenses, 25% violent offenses, and 10% sex offenses. Admissions to short- and long-term facilities increased 124% from 1995 to 2000, with growth most prominent in the 90-day programs.

THE ROAD AHEAD

Juvenile crime rate reductions will not last forever and the Georgia youth population will grow over time. The challenge is daunting, but the direction quite clear. Improved classification systems are required at all levels, and these are being developed. Officialdom and the public need to understand or at least accept that annoying but less serious misbehaviors should be handled without secure confinement. The array of community-based options needs to be increased sizably, including expanded intensive

probation supervision, substance abuse treatment programs, and gender-specific programs for girls. Of course, secure confinement facilities, RYDCs and YDCs, are
important for public safety, juvenile accountability, and juvenile competency development, but they need to be used effectively and appropriately.

The balancing act requires redirecting unnecessary pretrial confinements, and eliminating or at least reducing the wait time in RYDCs for those who must be committed
to short- or long-term YDCs. It requires more money. It also requires patience, but
patience should not mean that DJJ is given a free ride on the journey. It, like the juveniles it works with, must be held accountable for any lack of progress or deviation from
course.

Georgia's DJJ shows evidence of coherent direction, something that can be attributed
to its eloquent, relationship-building commissioner. But juvenile justice systems are
used to working the way they now work. Law enforcement is tuned to its arrest accomplishments, if not to informal arrest quotas. Georgia schools have been turning to
juvenile courts to handle large numbers of modest behavioral disruptions for a long
time. Juvenile courts want and need business. Judges and juvenile probation officers
want places to put kids. Legislators tend to favor reducing taxes or funding interest
group-lobbied and vote-getting projects. Governors prefer a noncontroversial, undis-
rupted juvenile justice administration with problems covered over and not publicized.
Meanwhile, the media hunts out controversy and is available to highlight complaints
about the course reform takes. In short, the road to reform poses numerous roadblocks,
but it is the high way and the only way.

Author's Note

The updating report that follows, prepared in late July 2002, should make all
readers and practitioners feel good about what is being accomplished in Georgia.
This is illustrative of some of the very best of contemporary American juvenile justice. Here is a farsighted vision that is far better than 20/20. And it is happening.

THE 100-YEAR PLAN

by Orlando L. Martinez
Commissioner, Georgia Department of Juvenile Justice

Confucius wrote a proverb that says:

If your plan is for a year, plant rice

If your plan is for 10 years, plant trees

If your plan is for 100 years, educate or grow children.

Since a year and a half ago, when the original *Juvenile Justice Update* article about
this agency's movement back to the community appeared, we have been in the process
of developing and implementing the 100-year plan. That is not to say that our plan
should take 100 years to complete. On the contrary, our hope is that 100 years from

now treatment of juvenile offenders in our state will be such that every child in our system will be better after they've left. I know that the work we have completed over the last 18 months is a positive step forward.

As this agency has moved forward in carrying out its legal mandate, we have not been interested in maintaining the status quo. Rather, we continue our commitment to making Georgia a better place in which to live. The principal vehicle for us in ensuring public safety for our great state is to equip our students to handle the challenges of life upon their return to the community. This means helping them to acquire life competency skills and teaching them to be accountable for the choices they make.

The "move forward of this agency by moving back into the community" begins with the basic belief that the foundation of the juvenile justice system is the early prevention and intervention that can occur in the community. This can only take place with interagency cooperation among a wide variety of state and local agencies in partnership with community, private, and religious groups that offer services to troubled youth and their families.

Over the last 18 months we have prepared ourselves for this forward movement by focusing on several major initiatives:

- Regionalization and results-based management;

- Integrated classification;

- Detention reform;

- Female-focused programs;

- Master plan;

- Juvenile tracking system; and

- Workforce enhancement.

Regionalization and Results-Based Management

Children in the juvenile justice system are best served if they are placed in programs that are close to home. The proximity to their family and legal, religious, and community resources allows maximum support of these youth while in our system and facilitates their transition back home.

To implement this concept, five new regions and 13 districts were established. District and regional plans were developed to advance the work of this new management structure. The plans are designed to take into account the peculiar nature of each neighborhood and to develop and implement a continuum of care that places youth in the least restrictive setting that meets the needs of each youth. Localized support to address the issues of juvenile delinquency will follow.

As of this writing, all members of this new organization have been hired and local plans are being reviewed and implemented. Additionally, accountability plans have been developed for each region that will be used as a guide to monitor performance and to shepherd the process.

Integrated Classification

With the assistance of outside consultants and extensive staff involvement, the DJJ has pulled together a streamlined format to determine the needs, risks, and best placement for youth we serve. This new comprehensive system will be based on the use of service plans, strengths and weaknesses graphs, typology to identify patterns of behavior and automated social summaries. The four main modules include medical, education, behavioral health, and security data.

The cornerstone of the process is a Comprehensive Risk and Needs Assessment (CRN) that is based on current research and literature on juvenile delinquency causation and child developmental theory.

Detention Reform

The most telling sign of our advances in managing our detention population is that, over the last 12 months, we have been either at or below capacity. This is in contrast to years of operating well above our housing limits.

Progress has been achieved principally as the result of:

- Development and implementation of a detention assessment instrument to bring greater consistency and objectivity to decisions regarding the utilization of secure detention beds;

- Development and implementation of alternatives to secure detention; and

- Creation of Case Expediter positions to ensure that cases move through the detention and court processes as efficiently as possible.

Female-Focused Programs

Most juvenile justice agencies are guilty of not distinguishing the differing needs of girls and boys. No accommodations are made for the differences in physical, psychological, and emotional development between the genders.

To move forward with matching children based upon their risks and needs, this agency had to acknowledge two points. First, without interventions, our female population is expected to outpace, percentage-wise, that of the male population. Second, we had to acknowledge that taking our male programs and "painting them pink" was an insufficient response to the need for gender specific programming.

An initial Gender Specific Conference was held and resulted in intensive discussion between the agency and judicial staffs. A second annual Summit on Girls is planned for the fall of 2002 and is being sponsored by this agency and the Georgia Women's Legislative Caucus (GWLC). [Editor's note: This conference, attended by almost 300 persons, was held as scheduled.] The inclusion of the GWLC facilitates greater legislative understanding of female offender issues specifically, and juvenile justice issues generally. Additionally, it builds a natural advocacy base for children in our system.

Master Plan

A Service Development Plan has been drafted and is being used as the basis for requesting funding for programs. This plan looked at the various physical resources of the department, including both short- and long-term institutions, and compared their capability with the projected needs of the agency.

As a result, a number of new facilities have been recommended either as replacement or new institutions. The following priorities were used as a basis for the development of this plan:

- Youth will be diverted to the least restrictive environments.

- Facilities necessary to meet the needs of youth requiring the most restrictive environment will be constructed by DJJ and will be placed in the communities that contribute the youth to the juvenile justice system.

- These facilities will be located so as to encourage inter-agency interaction and collaboration.

- Older/larger existing facilities will be down-sized or eliminated.

- Program opportunities for youth not requiring restrictive environments will be provided in the community through contract providers.

- Sufficient space will be provided for multi-disciplinary activity to occur.

- Long-term assets currently in operation will be given priority for any renovations/modifications needed to ensure appropriate long-term functioning.

Juvenile Tracking System

The DJJ completed the base application to provide shared records for staff with a need to access information about the agency's clients. This application has been developed, tested and deployed. Shared accessibility, in its largest terms, means accessing information as it relates to:

- Demographic data on clients;

- Case notes;

- Legal information, including offense, adjudication, disposition data;

- Placement information, regardless if a private or state provider;

- Institutional information including intake, release, and housing histories;

- Detention assessment instrument scores; and

- Assessment and classification data.

Integrating client information will improve record keeping by enhanced accuracy and record keeping.

Workforce Enhancement

A crucial element of any reform is having quality staff who are well trained, well managed and appropriately compensated. Three significant improvements have occurred in this arena: implementation of a new Discipline Without Punishment (DWP) Program, implementation of a new performance evaluation instrument, and development of a video-based test for the testing of our juvenile correctional officers.

Conclusion

A Chinese proverb says, "A journey of a thousand miles begins with a single step." With the multiple steps this agency has taken, the journey has long begun. The Georgia Department of Juvenile Justice is following the right path for success. Plans have been prepared and implemented. Although our journey is far from an end, the advances we are making are bringing us closer to our destination.

Endnotes

[1] Unsigned editorial (2000, August 11). Fix state's broken, biased system of juvenile justice. *The Atlanta Constitution*, p. A-22.

[2] Quoted in *Directions* (a publication of the Georgia Department of Juvenile Justice), VII(4), June 1999, p. 1.

Chapter 37

RECLAIM Ohio: Funding Formula Bolsters Development of Community-Based Alternatives While Reducing Commitments to the State

FUNDING FOR JUVENILE SERVICES MIGRATES TO THE STATE

Historically, states paid for the confinement of youth committed to them for institutionalization while local governments paid for the services provided to juveniles retained in the community. Providing institutional care for delinquent youth has always constituted the most expensive dispositional alternative, short of very specialized private institutional placement. Nonetheless, commitment often became the judicial disposition of choice, a decision influenced by the fact that the cost was not borne locally. An assumption in more recent years was that only those most in need of removal from the community should become state property. But for years states have received many "virgins" along with the more sophisticated and the many "in-betweens"—suggesting the importance of the role that funding plays in the dispositional determination.

In many jurisdictions, the historical equation was modified over time. State funds came more into play at the local level, often replacing or supplementing local funding for probation services and secure pretrial detention. Frequently, with changes in funding, the administration of these services was transferred from local judges to a state executive agency—though state funding of judicially administered probation remains in quite a few states. These changes have occurred for many reasons. One is that the state often is seen as having a superior tax and revenue base and, therefore, as best able to provide a uniform, suitable quality of services statewide.

STATES STRIVE TO GAIN CONTROL OVER COMMITMENTS

Over 40 years ago, California gained some measure of control over admissions into its institutions through legislation that allowed the Youth Authority to return some

This chapter originally appeared in Juvenile Justice Update, *Vol. 7, No. 6, December/January 2002.*

youths to the community without an institutional stay. Secure care was to be reserved for those who required it, and the Youth Authority could control its expenditures.

In other jurisdictions, state juvenile correctional departments have limited judicial prerogatives in other ways. Generally, they have controlled the release dates of committed youth, thereby determining the length of stay. They usually determine which facility a youth goes to, allowing a judge to recommend a facility but making their own decisions.

Some states still authorize mandatory sentences for certain, more serious offenders. The state must accept these youth for the mandatory institutional period. In other instances, parole officials and/or judges may be responsible for approving releases from state custody, or may return a youth to the state for violation of parole.

California Tries Financial Incentives to Encourage Local Treatment

As early as 1965, California sought to provide financial incentives to local courts to treat juveniles locally rather than commit them to the state. Local communities that reduced their commitments below that of an established base year could receive up to $4,000 for each reduction in number below the base. This probation subsidy act, in a state where local probation departments often administered ranches and camps, lowered the commitment rate in many counties.

There was a down side, however. Some counties frequently retained even significant reoffenders in local facilities, particularly juvenile detention centers, in order to claim the subsidy. Yet the subsidy money was insufficient to allow employment of the additional staff needed to supervise these youths. Further, law enforcement incurred extra costs handling these "retreads," and the subsidy money did not cover their extra costs. As a result, California modified its act to seek a more just balance.

California was not alone in seeking to control commitments through funding formulas. This chapter looks at the efforts of another state, Ohio, to reclaim control of its institutional population and cost.

Ohio's Serious Overcrowding Forces Hard Look at Commitment Practices.

A decade ago, Ohio Department of Youth Services (DYS) officials took a serious look at their state institutions. In 1991, the heavily overcrowded institutions operated at 150% of capacity. In 1992 the problem was worse, with some facilities operating at 85% over capacity. They were housing more youths than any state except California. The overcrowding caused safety and security problems, hampered the recruitment and retention of qualified personnel, seriously harmed treatment efforts, and prompted premature releases of youthful offenders.

When they looked at the juveniles committed to their institutions, DYS officials knew they were getting too many first-time, nonviolent offenders who could be better served in their local communities. Officials surveyed the overcrowding, stared at their budget, and decided to review the funding incentive experience in the handful of states that provided subsidies to local communities to treat juveniles locally. The resulting legislation maintained state responsibility for the cost of any commitment to DYS. A county's failure to reduce its number of state commitments, however, would lead to the loss of subsidy funds that could otherwise allow for more expansive local programming.

PILOT PROGRAMS INITIATE RECLAIM

RECLAIM, short for Reasoned and Equitable Community and Local Alternatives to the Incarceration of Minors, was initiated as a pilot project in 1994 in nine counties of varying populations. Its goals were to empower local judges with more options and alternatives for juvenile offenders, and to improve DYS's ability to treat offenders. RECLAIM sought to encourage juvenile courts to develop or purchase a larger range of community-based services. The resulting reduction in commitments to DYS would allow the department to do a better job with its fewer residents.

In Ohio, juvenile probation is a county judicial branch entity. The nine counties involved in the pilot project reduced commitments to the state by 43% compared with their anticipated projections based on commitment rates from the three previous years. Meanwhile, non-participating counties increased their commitments. RECLAIM was implemented statewide a year later.[1]

RECLAIM's early success in accomplishing its objectives led to its designation in 1996 as a leading innovative governmental program by the Kennedy School of Government at Harvard. A Ford Foundation grant followed, which enabled the establishment of a RECLAIM Academy for juvenile correctional leaders to come to Ohio to learn the principles of RECLAIM and its possible applications in their states.

Basic Funding Formula Derived From Crime Rates

Ohio's 88 counties receive a yearly allocation from DYS that is distributed monthly. To determine the allocation, DYS averages the number of felony adjudications statewide and by each county over the previous four years. The percentage of adjudicated felony delinquents who come from a particular county determines the percentage of the pool that county receives. For example, if a county averages 10% of Ohio's felony delinquents, that county will receive 10% of the state pool.

Public Safety Commitments Charged to the State

DYS charges each county 75% of its daily costs for every day a county juvenile is a DYS resident. But there is an exception for "public safety beds." There is no charge for beds occupied by youth committed for a category one or two felony. These most serious felonies include all homicides and attempts, rape or felonious sexual penetration, aggravated arson, kidnapping, and the use of a gun in the commission of a crime.[2]

While some felony one and two commitments could and may be handled locally through expanded intervention intensity, DYS was pragmatic in establishing public safety beds. It bought political support and avoided negative flak by not charging for these offenders. County allocations were immunized, not crippled, when a judge decided such an offender required secure confinement. Further, if a juvenile commits an offense within a DYS facility which results in either a lengthened institutional stay or a new charge and disposition by a juvenile court, the county is not charged for the increased length of stay.

Counties Charged Less for Local Placements

A different reimbursement scheme applies when a court places a youth in a state-funded but locally operated community corrections facility (CCF). Then the county is charged 50%, rather than 75%, of daily costs of care. Obviously, the stratagem is to keep these juveniles closer to home and family and out of state care.

Counties that commit more juveniles to DYS or to a CCF than their allotted funds allow are not debited against the next year's allotments. Instead, a state contingency fund absorbs those extra costs. Therefore, judges can still commit or place without fear of direct fiscal penalty; rather, by exhausting their allocations their counties will not have the money that otherwise could subsidize community interventions. Counties that "under-commit," then, retain the money that remains unexpended in their accounts and apply this to increase their community-based continuum of services. Ohio juvenile courts receive their own local funding that provides for probation and certain other services. Accordingly, RECLAIM furnishes a judicial system incentive to curb commitments and claim subsidy money for use in expanding the services provided by county funds.

Counties that account for less than 0.1% of all felony adjudications in the state are not debited for any commitment. These counties receive little subsidy, presumably lack the capacity to provide significant community alternatives, and likely send few juveniles to the state.

RECLAIM Funds Designated for Alternative Services

RECLAIM funds may be used for alternative programs such as day treatment, alternative schools, intensive probation, electronic monitoring, drug testing and treatment, wraparound services, and residential treatment. The funds can be used to develop prevention and diversion programs for unruly (status offense) youths, or to serve juvenile traffic offenders or youths at risk of becoming delinquent. RECLAIM funds, however, cannot be used for construction or building renovation, or to supplant local funding for existing programs.

While RECLAIM provides funds for alternative community programs, DYS encourages county use of risk and needs assessment instruments to help them determine whether a youth could be better served in the community than institutionalized.

EVALUATING RECLAIM

Program Appeals to Broad Political Spectrum

Articles that describe and evaluate RECLAIM cite its appeal to both more liberal and more conservative viewpoints. Its support of community-based intervention for nonviolent juveniles and its potential for improved institutional rehabilitation with fewer DYS residents fall along the liberal continuum. Its retention of substantial local control over funds, its allowance for penalty-free dispositional determinations by judges, and its public safety bed provision appeal to the more conservative continuum.

Research Shows Decline in State Institution Population

A statewide evaluation was conducted by academically based researchers and published in 1998.[3] One finding was that the average daily population of state institutions in 1996 declined by 6% since 1992 and was 13% lower than original DYS projections even though local felony adjudications increased from 1994 to 1996.

Since that study was completed, admissions have continued to decline. In FY1996, there were 3,228 admissions. There were 2,923 in 1997; 2,757 in 1998; 2,569 in 1999; 2,548 in 2000; and 2,447 in 2001. The objective of reducing commitments and recommitments is working.

Community Interventions Found Effective

The statewide evaluation found that successful terminations from community based programs had increased by 10% since the pilot period. Overall 91% of RECLAIM youths were not admitted to a state institution or CCF upon termination of local program intervention or during a three-month follow-up period.

Larger urban counties continued to commit the majority of youths to DYS and ended up receiving the smallest proportion of dollars to use locally. DYS needed to do much more work with these counties to get them to "buy in" better. The evaluation urged such an effort, and DYS reports it has made ongoing efforts to reach out to larger counties.

County Officials Initially Lukewarm to RECLAIM

According to the evaluation, numerous county officials remained "tentative at best" in their level of satisfaction with RECLAIM, although they supported the goal of increasing community-based alternatives. Local officials were dissatisfied with the institutional programming committed youths received at DYS and urged more substance abuse, mental health, and sex offender treatment, as well as enhanced educational programs.

DYS officials indicated that changes had occurred in the types and numbers of sentenced youths they received, but evaluators suggested a reevaluation of programming to meet the needs of the more uniformly serious offenders committed to these institutions. Since the evaluation, as population numbers have dropped, DYS is concentrating on program improvement.

The evaluation found that, according to the counties, the four most favorable RECLAIM aspects were: (1) having more options available in the court; (2) having flexibility to tailor programs to youths in their communities; (3) having more money available; and (4) the community-based focus of the program.

Assessment Instruments Were Underused

Risk, needs, and other assessment instruments, encouraged by DYS for local use to help determine whether to keep and serve a youth in the community rather than in an institution, were being applied in less than half of the state's 88 counties. The evaluators found that the most important criteria for determining whether to use a community program disposition were the amount of harm or injury suffered by the victim, whether a weapon was involved, the type of felony committed, whether the youth had a prior DYS commitment, and whether a local program was available to meet the youth's needs.

Uncertainty of Funding Amounts Troubles Courts

Local courts expressed concern with the amount of paperwork required by RECLAIM and the day-to-day uncertainty of how much money would be available for alternative programming that existed because of the way the program operated. Some questioned the equitability of the funding formula and the amount of money their counties received. They questioned how a county could develop and sustain new programs if it received limited funds. Additionally, there was uncertainty about the ongoing level of funding.

FINE-TUNING THE FUNDING FORMULA

As the funding formula now stands, some counties with smaller populations receive significantly larger subsidies than counties with greater populations because the more populous counties register proportionately more commitments. A county that sends very few youngsters to the state may receive significantly less money than a county that commits significantly more juveniles, even though the first county has a larger population. Further, because the number of felony adjudications is used as the measuring stick for funding allotments, there may be a financial incentive for a court to file and adjudicate more felonies. Conversely, there may be a financial incentive to discourage reducing felonies to misdemeanors.

Geno Natalucci-Persichetti, DYS Director, states the formula has been scrutinized over the years by joint task forces of court and DYS personnel, along with national experts. It has worked overall, he indicates, because it is fair for the vast majority of counties, and no one has yet been able to effectively frame a formula that captures every county's special issues. "But we will continue to find ways of improving the process," he adds.

CONCLUSION

RECLAIM Ohio represents a smart approach to balancing local and state resources. It tackles the historic concern that has allowed local courts to commit juveniles without local cost, and changes the state's paradigm from victim to active player in local practices. It helps further the juvenile code precept that directs juvenile courts to retain youths in their own homes and own communities when possible and practical. This is a major plus.

A state subsidy approach can be arbitrary and the administrators bureaucratic. This appears not to be the case in Ohio, and it need not be in other states. Subsidy approaches, however, need ongoing evaluation and adjustment.

Substantially reduced commitments are an impressive hallmark. Non-subsidy states should take a hard look at their local-state interface and actively consider reclaiming this balance.

Endnotes

[1] Latessa, E. J., Applegate, B. K., & Moon, M. M. (1996). *Final evaluation of the RECLAIM Ohio pilot project*. Cincinnati, OH: University of Cincinnati; Moon, M. M., Applegate, B. K., & Latessa, E. J. (1997). RECLAIM Ohio: A politically viable alternative to treating youthful felony offenders. *Crime & Delinquency, 43*, 438-456.

[2] Latessa, E. J., Turner, M. G., Moon, M. M. & Applegate, B. K. (1998). *A statewide evaluation of the RECLAIM Ohio initiative*. Columbus, OH: Department of Youth Services.

[3] Id.

Chapter 38

Taking More Care With Juvenile Aftercare

Juvenile parole, or aftercare, always has been the stepchild of the juvenile justice system. It is not now, nor has it ever been, where the power lies, where the dollars go, or a fashionable subject for practitioner, researcher, or academic writing. To compound this lack, the public still does not seem to understand the difference between parole (a/k/a aftercare) and probation.

For some years, juvenile probation and community corrections have balanced rehabilitative intervention and in-the-community control strategies. Juvenile parole is beginning to do the same, but it is only the start of what is needed.

It needs to be recognized today that aftercare no longer occurs only after release from a traditional state-level secure institution. In some jurisdictions, juveniles may be committed by the court or rerouted by the state to local or regional secure or non-secure settings from which aftercare status is later initiated. Further, the term "aftercare" is now seen by some leaders as a misleading term. Institutional programming should be organically interrelated with what is to follow. The return-to-community experience should begin immediately after departure from the community.

LACK OF JUVENILE AFTERCARE DESCRIBED IN THE PRESIDENT'S CRIME COMMISSION REPORT OF 1967

The 1967 report of the President's Commission on Law Enforcement and Administration of Justice noted that juvenile aftercare was the least developed aspect of corrections and less adequate than its adult counterpart. The report found (1) it was not uncommon for 250 adolescents to be assigned to two or three aftercare counselors who were located at one central location that could be hundreds of miles from the communities where the juveniles were to be under supervision, (2) the average state cost per juvenile was $320 a year, and (3) the state agency that administered delinquency institutions most commonly administered juvenile aftercare as well, but there was a potpourri of administrative structures.

The report criticized the fact that in nine states the committing judge had to approve all or some releases from the training school. It supported the position of juvenile corrections administrators who contended that the training school director or state youth agency administration should make the release decision.

This chapter originally appeared in Community Corrections Report, *Vol. 3, No. 4, May/June 1996.*

TWO SETS OF NATIONAL STANDARDS ISSUED IN 1980

Two prominent sets of national juvenile justice standards were issued in 1980, the Institute of Judicial Administration-American Bar Association (IJA-ABA) Standards (Standard 4.2.C.) and the National Advisory Committee for Juvenile Justice and Delinquency Prevention (NAC) Standards (Standards 3.181 and 3.182). Neither of these sets of guidelines has been widely adopted, although other sentencing revisions have impacted aftercare.

The IJA-ABA Standards

The IJA-ABA standards held a deep distrust of institutional release decision-making. They also came down strongly for determinate sentencing. Accordingly, the standards categorized five classes of offenses, and specified different maximum durations for the five types of dispositions a judge could make (lengthier for the more serious) and how much of these time spans could be spent in secure and non-secure facilities or on "conditional freedom" (essentially probation or aftercare). Only the judge could reduce the timeline of a disposition; aftercare could take place only when the judge at disposition had ordered confinement for a specified period of time, along with a follow-on order of conditional freedom for a specified period of time, and so long as the total span did not exceed the maximum term permissible as a custodial sanction for the offense.

NAC Standards

The NAC report paralleled IJA-ABA, except that it did not recommend a particular set of offense-related maximum terms. Instead, it called on the states to enact their own categories and gave judges the authority to use those parameters to determine the length of disposition, within the maximum, the degree of restraint, and the type of program. The judge's determination was to be made on the basis of a review of the seriousness of the offense and the offender's prior record and age. The judge also could designate aftercare, or what NAC termed "community supervision," as part of the commitment order.

EXAMPLES OF STATES' INSTITUTIONAL RELEASE MECHANISMS

States vary in their approaches to the decision for institutional release. The following list provides examples of some of these approaches.

1. *The state youth agency or youth services division of a state department of corrections makes the decision.* However, in Virginia, judicial approval for early release is required where judicial commitment of a "serious offender" is for the specified six to 12 months minimum. (See also the discussion of Ohio's early release requirements later in this chapter.)

2. *The state youth agency makes the decision based on officially promulgated institutional release guidelines.* For example, Minnesota has fashioned a presumptive determinate sentence. Soon after institutional admission, a minimum-stay release date is set, based heavily on offense severity and prior record. Later, this date may be affirmed or deferred, depending upon the juvenile's progress on an agreed upon treatment plan.

3. *The state youth agency makes the decision with the approval of the court.* For example, the Florida Department of Juvenile Justice (DJJ) must inform the committing court of its wish to discharge a juvenile from institutional confinement or other DJJ commitment program. The court has 10 days to accept or reject the proposal; judicial inaction authorizes release. Coincidentally, Florida law requires that a juvenile not serve a lengthier term than an adult convicted of a similar offense.

4. *A state juvenile parole board makes the decision.* This is the situation in California, Colorado, New Hampshire, New Mexico, South Carolina, and Utah (combined juvenile-adult paroling authorities occur in three other jurisdictions). New Mexico has a three-person board. Although state judges must receive 30 days notice of board consideration and may express a view, the board is the final arbiter. Board members must interview a juvenile prior to authorizing parole and provide juveniles with written statements of reasons for denying parole.

   Colorado's seven-person board conducted 430 parole hearings, 70 violation hearings, and 33 discharge from parole hearings in 1994. The hearings are held weekly at one site, and monthly at two other locations. Most hearings are held by two-person panels. The full board considers appeals from the panels, cases where panel members disagree, paroles of "aggravated and violent offenders," and early discharges from parole.

5. *The court may exercise this authority.* In Pennsylvania, the juvenile court judges, by law, review commitments every six months. Judges in some states may enter a review date upon commitment and then revoke the commitment at the review hearing.

Ohio: Role of Juvenile Aftercare in a State With Indeterminate Sentencing

While every state determines its own juvenile statutes, it is educative to look at how Ohio, a state with indeterminate sentencing, handles its juvenile offenders. Aftercare programming has a prominent role in early release decisions.

The Ohio Department of Youth Services (DYS) in 1995 served 2,800 youths on aftercare and 2,200 juveniles in its institutions, residential treatment centers, and contracted facilities.[1] State law mandates indeterminate sentencing until 21 years of age, as well as several minimum sentence provisions. Committed lesser felony offenders must be institutionalized at least six months, and more serious felony offenders at least 12 months (no misdemeanants may be committed), unless the judge approves an early release. Judicially approved early releases constitute 45% of institutional releases. DYS is the sole release authority for juveniles who are not released early.

Early release judicial decision making can be affected by the extent of available aftercare programming. Early release is less likely if the DYS submits a post-institutional treatment plan for a significant offender that contains minimal aftercare programming. A significant proposal increases the odds for early release.

Colorado: Aftercare Programming Also Affects Parole Decision in State With Determinate Sentencing

An example of a determinate sentence is Colorado's basic two-year maximum. Here, available programming can affect the decision of the Colorado juvenile parole board. Reportedly, one broadly-based aftercare program, recently made available in a particular district, has shortened institutional time by two months.

DELIVERY OF AFTERCARE PROGRAMS

To provide a means for offering an earlier release date, when appropriate, states should beef up aftercare services to better assist aftercare juveniles and improve public safety.

Aftercare commonly is criticized because (1) there is a lack of coordination between institutional treatment staff and aftercare agents, (2) post-institutional release plans may be cursory, and (3) supervision and/or monitoring may be scant. High failure rates after release have caused enough concern to prompt greater interest in enhancing aftercare services.

The gurus of juvenile aftercare, David Altschuler and Troy Armstrong, not only urge prudent resource allocation, but also that aftercare services intervene intensively only with higher risk juveniles.[2] This concept fits well with the recurrent finding that a small percentage of juvenile offenders commit a very high percentage of serious juvenile crime. This group is recidivist prone, and states will need to develop additional intermediate sanctions for use when these parolees commit lesser offenses or technical violations.

Altschuler and Armstrong attribute their initial formulation of intensive aftercare to the intensive adult and juvenile probation supervision movement of the 1980s, which calibrated frequency of contact with risk level.[3] But more is involved as they strive to concentrate a coordinated array of efforts on deep-end juveniles who return to crime-ridden neighborhoods. The new stance involves resource brokerage and advocacy rather than an aftercare agent's direct delivery of all services. Contracts with private agencies and individual service providers, including paraprofessionals, the involvement of noncorrectional public agencies, and the engagement of citizen volunteers are part of the new stance. The aftercare agent, as case manager, assures continuity of services and ongoing communications between all involved entities.

Other tools of this trade are risk and needs assessments, validated in some states for their ability to identify youth most likely to commit a reoffense, and high-tech monitoring of behavior. The mix of surveillance and programming/service provision incorporates positive incentives and graduated consequences.

Coordination of Institutionalization With Early Post-Release Planning

Coordination of institutionalization with early post-release planning is vital. A well conceived, multifaceted assessment that also covers vocational training needs for older youths must be programmed to feed into release plan development. There should be regular case manager-institutionalized juvenile engagements that accelerate one to two months prior to release. Community agencies and individuals who will be involved in aftercare also should be committed to bridging the release process.

Improved or expanded aftercare services are being applied now in a growing number of communities:

- *Colorado:* Colorado, one of the Altschuler-Armstrong demonstration sites in the Office of Juvenile Justice and Delinquency Prevention-sponsored national initiative, has instituted several programs.

    —Selected high-risk juveniles were placed in a particular cottage for specialized intervention during their institutional stay.

    —Day centers, operated by private contractors, were opened in two Denver locations. Supervision levels are used. Maximum supervision level juveniles experience 12 hours daily of school, cognitive skill training, drug/alcohol education/rehab, pre-employment orientation, tracking, and more.

    —In some rural communities, an individual local, part-time private contractor provides aftercare services. This is in lieu of having a single state agent make a monthly sweep across mountain passes to check on a small number of widely scattered parolees.

- *Nevada:* The program initiated residential placement of juveniles from Las Vegas at a pre-release center much closer to many of their homes than the state institution, which improved pre-release contact opportunities with case managers, community agencies, and families.

- *New Mexico:* Juvenile parole agents in the Albuquerque region participate in bimonthly staffings at the various institutions. They perform an early release assessment that includes a home study and development of a care plan. They provide post-release supervision and reassessments of plans of care.

A Community-Institutional Connection in Virginia

Norfolk, Virginia, is another pilot site in the OJJDP initiative. Project-eligible juveniles are age 16 or older and incarcerated at the Beaumont Juvenile Correctional Center. There is almost immediate post-commitment participation of a local youth-serving agency's Community Assessment Team (CAT), which is comprised of Norfolk social services and public health departments, public schools, mental health and substance abuse services, juvenile services bureau, and an interagency consortium. Within two weeks of commitment, the CAT develops a recommended plan aimed at the juvenile's ultimate reintegration into the community. The proposed plan is adapted and refined by correctional center and intensive parole staff in consultation with the juvenile, the family, and pertinent agencies. At least monthly meetings are held by the intensive parole counselor with an individual family and groups of families while the juvenile is incarcerated. The first phase of the release plan is the shift of the juvenile to a community-based group home, which implements school, job training, employment, other community plan elements, CAT involvement, and high-intensity parole officer contact. The group home stay lasts 15-60 days prior to return to the family or alternative residence.

REOFFENSES AND TECHNICAL VIOLATIONS

A significant number of reoffenses and technical violations of parole conditions should be expected. Reoffenses sometimes are handled by a juvenile court, and technical violations (e.g., "dirty" urine, curfew breaches, truancy, etc.) dealt with administratively by the state agency. Lesser reoffenders and violators need not necessarily be reincarcerated. Instead, graduated sanctions (in addition to positive reinforcements that encourage no or fewer reoffenses/violations) should be available.

We are beginning to put new emphasis on juvenile aftercare. We should expand this development.

Endnotes

[1] Ohio Department of Youth Services (1996). *Annual report*. Columbus: Author.

[2] Altschuler, D. M. & Armstrong, T. L. (1994). *Juvenile aftercare for high-risk juveniles*. Washington, DC: Office of Juvenile Justice and Delinquency Prevention.

[3] Altschuler, D. M. & Armstrong, T. L. (1995). Managing aftercare services for delinquents. In B. Glick & A. P. Goldstein (Eds.), *Managing delinquency programs that work*. Laurel, MD: American Correctional Association.

Part 6

The Juvenile Court of the Future

Once seen as one of the greatest inventions in jurisprudence, the juvenile court more recently has been seen as the problem, rather than the solution, in the handling of delinquent juveniles. There has been a series of calls for the abolition of the juvenile court, but also numerous defenses of this institution. Virtually every state has, however, curtailed juvenile court handling of allegedly more serious offenders and offenses, though juvenile court defenders counter that transferring many of these juveniles to criminal court handling is excessive and counterproductive.

At this writing, violent juvenile crime, the trigger that prompted legislative rewrites placing more juveniles into criminal courts, has receded. Also at this time, since the states have rewritten their codes to disallow juvenile court proceedings for certain offenses committed by certain juveniles above a certain age, calls to abolish this court, or the lesser call to structurally remove more juveniles from juvenile court handling, are less common and less strident.

Crystal-balling is always a hazardous exercise. But I venture to predict that juvenile courts will survive, basically retain their present responsibilities and authority, but shape more into family courts that combine juvenile cases with an array of domestic relations and family-related matters.

Some juveniles do terrible things, and their highly publicized individual acts or another violent juvenile crime wave could prompt a new call to transfer still more juveniles to criminal court handling, though recent policy changes have not left much of a pool that might be deemed better handled in criminal proceedings. Another call for abolition is not likely, though foolish, politically propelled, ill-informed stratagems are not strangers to policy formation. Criminal courts should not like to have to deal with lots of younger offenders, and the juvenile court appears reasonably safe to do more and more with its presently lessened workload. One danger, though not now mentioned, is that other states might follow the change made a few years ago by New Hampshire and Wisconsin and lower their maximum jurisdictional age from the 18th birthday to, instead, the 17th birthday, thus casting all their 17-year-olds into criminal proceedings.

Juvenile court jurisdiction over child abuse and neglect proceedings has never been seriously threatened with transfer to another court, only with a series of calls to reform and improve case handling. The court has made progress with this very difficult workload in recent years, matters that should be expected to be maintained within a juvenile or family court structure.

A REVIEW OF THE CALL TO ABOLISH JUVENILE COURTS

Court Changes in Response to Justice System Stakeholders' Complaints

Juvenile courts, during the 1950s and 1960s were the subject of complaints by police agencies for coddling juvenile offenders. From a different vantage point, attorneys began to complain in the 1960s about the fundamental absence of legal protections accorded youthful defendants, and progressive advocates for children added strenuous concerns over the quality and product of juvenile institutions and other juvenile court sanctioning that failed effective rehabilitation accomplishment.

The due process concerns were accepted and honored by the U.S. Supreme Court in **Kent v. United States**, 383 U.S. 541 (1966), **In re Gault**, 387 U.S. 1 (1967), **In re Winship**, 397 U.S. 358 (1970) and **Breed v. Jones**, 421 U.S. 519 (1975), thus draping a constitutional blanket across juvenile defendants. Legislatures then proceeded, some more quickly than others, to substantially revamp their simplified *parens patriae* juvenile codes, enacted in an earlier time and climate, to fold in Supreme Court mandates and other legalization procedures. They needed to deal with, as well, the U.S. Juvenile Justice and Delinquency Prevention Act of 1974,[1] which severely restricted secure pre-adjudicatory detention of status offenders and prohibited state incarceration of these juveniles in institutions housing delinquent offenders.

Meanwhile, national legal and criminal justice entities stepped into action to propose reforms for the juvenile court. They proposed an array of national standards that emphasized due process safeguards together with prosecutor and defense attorney prominence, proportionality in sanctions and determinate sentences, improved programs for delinquent youth, curbing if not repealing the status offense jurisdiction, and joining the juvenile court into a new family court entity. Judicial branch administration of probation and detention services was to be yielded to executive branch administration.[2]

Rise of the Academic Abolitionists

A convergence of implemented changes and additional progressively based proposals led more people to ask the question: why retain a juvenile court that now must relinquish its informality, integrate law and lawyers, and closely resemble a criminal court? But now the detractors were not law and order advocates but critical academics. They were to publish a series of calls for abolition, not reform, of the juvenile court.

Calls for abolition became prominent in 1977 and 1978. This advocacy was not prompted by the violent crime wave that was to follow shortly after. Abolitionist arguments stressed, in general, that the juvenile court is no longer able to be what it used to be, will not be able to adhere carefully to legal protocol due to its interest in rehabilitation, and will not be able to effectuate rehabilitation within a context of a legal regimen. Criminal courts, it was contended, provide more extensive legal safeguards and would better protect juveniles' rights. Little was said as to what criminal courts would accomplish with the minds and salvageability of juvenile offenders.

One abolitionist proposed criminal court handling of serious and chronic offenders, but suggested that lesser offenders and status offenders be turned over to community agencies and informal arbitration services.[3] Another favored complete criminal court transfer, while contending that adult misdemeanor courts, the lowest ranking court in the hierarchy of courts and one that would receive myriad lesser juvenile offenders, could be improved to better handle these youths.[4] A law review article contended that the juvenile court's jurisdiction over delinquency was now obsolete, but that the court should be retained to protect abused, neglected, and "emotionally disturbed" children.[5]

Still another critic preferred an adult system that openly acknowledges punishment as a purpose and could arrange the provision of age-segregated facilities for juvenile offenders. Further, judicial system jurisdiction over status offenders should be eliminated.[6] The court's most persistent abolitionist has suggested that criminal courts provide a "youth discount"—i.e., shorter sentences because of youthful age—as a mitigating factor in sentencing. He believes juvenile courts provide neither therapy nor justice, are just second-class criminal courts, and that juveniles should, at the least, receive full legal safeguards.[7]

Countering the Abolitionist Argument

I have long urged retention, and progressive reforms to fortify the juvenile court's legal regimen and rehabilitation capabilities. I continue to advocate for a strengthened juvenile court that can merge with a domestic relations court when there is interest and feasibility in a state or local court system.

My ongoing arguments are that abolitionists falsely idealize criminal court proceedings and ignore their substantial deficiencies such as processing delays; too few judges; prosecutor overcharging, with its subsequent reliance on plea and sentence bargaining; excessive public defender workloads; insufficient diversion and sentencing alternatives; far less well staffed probation departments; overcrowded jails; and, at the end of the line, gigantic and unsafe penitentiaries.

Further, abolitionists fundamentally ignore the massive deficiencies associated with misdemeanor courts that would handle, with still less finesse and sizably fewer rehabilitative options, a vast quantity of juvenile offenders. Here, defendants are seen more as numbers than as individuals, provision of counsel to indigents may be scant, prosecutors' use of diversion is unusual and they lack time to screen for legal sufficiency, probation agencies are the weakest of any court system, and the misdemeanor court judiciary is not always trained in the law.

Abolitionists may have valid arguments about juvenile court imperfections, but they pale in contrast to the weaknesses and dangers of the abolitionists' alternative, the criminal court and justice system handling of juveniles.

Juvenile courts have done substantial restructuring and continue to expand the variety of their interventions. These courts can and do innovate. Overall, the judges do listen to complaints that are expressed and suggestions that might improve their process and outcomes.

Abolitionists have been silent about what court should absorb the juvenile court's abuse, neglect, and dependency case load if the juvenile court were abolished. Delinquency proceedings and abuse and neglect proceedings were side by side in the early juvenile courts, and that co-location remains current today. A growing number of juvenile courts arrange to have the judge who has heard a child's delinquency proceeding hear the case of a sibling who is brought to court on an abuse, neglect, and dependency petition, and vice versa. This type of judicial case coordination can most easily be accomplished when these two case types are located in the same forum.

REORGANIZING THE COURTS

Major restructuring of America's trial courts has been going on for more than three decades in numerous states. There has been a clear trend to unify trial courts and provide either a single- or double-level organization of all trial courts. With exceptions, both juvenile and domestic relations courts are included within an upper trial court. State judicial system leadership, in assessing future directions, increasingly proposes a family court organization that combines in some form these two workloads. There is no suggestion for juvenile court abolition per se. Either the court is left alone or combined into a family court. Consideration of the commonality of juvenile court cases with the case types of several other court branches is discussed in the following paragraphs.

Alternative Jurisdictional Combinations

Juvenile delinquency, being a violation of a criminal statute applicable to adults also, does fit well with the jurisprudential knowledge of a criminal court judge who needs to know the law of substantive crimes and criminal proceedings. But criminal courts have not distinguished themselves, historically or currently, in handling young offenders, and the prospect of their handling offenders as young as age 10 is frightening.[8]

Child abuse and neglect proceedings are civil proceedings that might advantageously be joined with the case types handled in domestic relations courts. Children are impacted by these family-related matters and there is significant common ground. There, parents may be undergoing a divorce or require a determination of visitation provisions. Or a parent may be petitioning for a restraining order that seeks to prevent a domestic violence assault or may have filed a petition seeking an order of child support. Domestic relations cases of all types are voluminous and amount to nearly 5,200,000 case filings annually.[9]

Also, one can make an argument for combining abuse and neglect proceedings with a probate court whose workload includes protective conservatorship and guardianship proceedings in behalf of certain children, and handicapped or disabled adults and the elderly.

Status offenses do not have a logical fit in any other court, but would fall best within a domestic relations division.

Combining juvenile and domestic relations courts into a family court is generally seen as the best fit if restructuring is to occur. Family courts are being created with increasing frequency. They are organized in different formats. There is now a trend in this direction. This development should be expected to expand to more state and local court systems.

The Juvenile Delinquency Court Prospect

Before launching into a presentation on family courts that will interrelate with but in no way abolish juvenile court proceedings, one should first review how juvenile courts, wherever they are located, might improve their accomplishments in the future.

First, there is nothing wrong with retaining juvenile courts as they are now organized. They do not have to meld into a family court. A proficient union could have benefits to children and families, but there are numerous difficulties associated with large-scale court unification, and anticipated benefits are often idealized and may only be very partially realized.

There are goal-setting national standards for juvenile justice, many good intervention practices being applied, increased awareness of what should be done, and much know how in the juvenile court world. There are well functioning juvenile courts but some are mired in leadership vacuums and bureaucratic morasses. In 2001 I facilitated a national conclave of juvenile justice organizations that outlined the following impressive agenda for improving the court's delinquency work:

- Develop Resource Guidelines, akin to those promulgated and found very beneficial for juvenile court handling of child abuse, neglect, and dependency matters;

- Obtain federal legislation and at least four years of federal appropriations to initiate a state-by-state juvenile justice system assessment, improvement plan design, and plan implementation similar to the scheme that has brought about substantial improvements in this court's handling of child abuse, neglect, and dependency matters;

- Facilitate state supreme court mandates that all juvenile courts within each state meet national standards;

- Eliminate minority overrepresentation and disproportionate minority confinement throughout the system;

- Arrange for every local juvenile court to have a planning entity chaired by the lead juvenile court judge;

- Improve local court management information systems;

- Encourage career juvenile court judges, public defenders, district attorneys, and probation officers;

- Facilitate expansive defense counsel representation;

- Obtain mandated case process time standards in all states for (1) detained and (2) non-detained juveniles, including timelines for prosecutor petitioning;

- Improve case management using classification, interagency collaboration, case planning, and case processing time standards;

- Enhance diversion and intake practices by obtaining more extensive front-end information about each juvenile and having available a wide menu of court alternatives that meet individual juveniles' needs;

- Make intake screening service available 24/7;

- Accomplish probation staff workloads that enable effective probation services;

- Infuse probation conditions with incentives for coming off probation ahead of time based on early accomplishment of targeted conditions;

- Expand research;

- Expand programs found effective by research;

- Expand training;

- Enable on-site training and technical assistance at several standard-setting host juvenile courts;

- Facilitate expanded accreditation of juvenile justice resources;

- Expand community correctional alternatives;

- Obtain effective mental health interventions with youth and their families;

- Obtain comprehensive family treatment services;

- Increase gender-specific programming;

- Expand victim participation in the court process and victim-offender mediation;

- Expand the use of performance measures.

This long-range agenda includes important directions that can more fully actualize the court's promise. Funding is important for much of this. Funding, particularly federal but also state, has facilitated court and rehabilitative effort improvements in recent decades.

Note: this work group rejected three wonderfully idealistic proposals:

1. That all states have a maximum jurisdictional age of 18;

2. That the intake process rescind or strongly curb the authority of prosecutors; and

3. That all juveniles charged with an offense be heard initially in a juvenile court, allowing for juvenile court judge, not prosecutor, waiver to a criminal court.

Also rejected was an alternative to the third proposal, to require particularized prosecutor guidelines that determine what cases shall be handled in a criminal court or in a juvenile court. (This might someday—but don't hold your breath—be forced onto an unwilling and powerful political force, the prosecutors of America, by appellate courts.)

When one reads of grisly homicides by 16-year-olds followed by adult court sentences of 60 years or of life without parole, one knows that juvenile courts will not, without a redemption revolution or a fundamental absence of gun crimes, obtain primary authority over all youth under age 18.

The Abused, Neglected, and Dependent Child Court Prospect

Judges, child welfare agency staff, attorneys who practice in this arena, court administrators, data personnel, legislators, CASA staff, and others have significantly improved their collaboration in working toward a common goal of protecting the health and safety of abused, neglected, and dependent children. A federal-state collaboration titled the "Court Improvement Project," has done just that.

Nonetheless, while one can review the published reports of the 20 jurisdictions that have been engaged in the National Council of Juvenile and Family Court Judges' Model Courts Project [10] and have progressed substantially, one should not infer from this limited array that significant progress has come near to universalization. Some courts have moved forward, but many court/child protection agency efforts still function with too little judge time or judicial appreciation of this critical workload, lengthy waits in deficient and overcrowded court waiting rooms, broken down child welfare agencies, gross lacks of services for parents, poorly paid lawyers, legal representation based on excessive compromise, ultra-low foster parent stipends, too many children who have gotten worse and even been injured in protected care, insufficient services and subsidy assistance for those who adopt special needs children, and many more shortcomings.

There is now significant know-how, and countless knowledgeable and dedicated professionals and foster parents work in this field. There is considerable training and the promulgation of best practices. But the task of this court and of the child welfare agencies that serve these children is immense and immensely difficult. Too many state child welfare agencies have been the subject of federal court litigation.

Clearly it is best for this responsibility to remain in the juvenile court, or in a reconstructed juvenile-family court, as should the delinquency jurisdiction and any status offense cases.

The Family Court Prospect: The Future

Ten years from now many juvenile courts, in terms of court structure, will stand just as they stand now. But the excitement today, as to judicial system structural change, is with conceptualizing and implementing some form of a family court that would integrate juvenile and domestic relations courts and, possibly, criminal cases that involve family members.

Many Definitions of "Family Court." My definition of the jurisdiction of a family court is one that at a minimum combines juvenile delinquency and child abuse, neglect, and dependency as well as adoption proceedings, together with domestic relations matters that are divorce related, and similar custody, support, and visitation matters that concern non-married relationships, as well as the issuance of domestic violence protection orders. I would add in criminal cases that involve family members, though this is more arguable.

The term family court means different things in different states. South Carolina family courts and all statewide family courts in other states do include the delinquency jurisdiction. The recently organized San Francisco family court added in the abuse and neglect jurisdiction but not the delinquency jurisdiction. A family court in one Mississippi district has meant the juvenile court with the addition of the paternity and support jurisdiction. The statewide family court of New York, originated by statute in 1962, has to this day failed to include divorce. The Jefferson County (Louisville), Kentucky, family court excludes delinquency jurisdiction except if a juvenile offense is against another family member.

There are other variations and inclusions. The family court of Hawaii hears mental illness commitment proceedings. The statewide Delaware family court exercises jurisdiction over adult intra-family misdemeanors. The family court in Bend, Oregon, described in Chapter 41, hears adult crimes that an adult family member in a bundled family case commits against a stranger, and will even hear a civil contract suit that involves a member of this family. During its recent first year of operation, the family court in LaCrosse, Wisconsin, included intra-family criminal child abuse cases. It then broadened out during its second year to hear other crimes between family members.

There are name differences as well: family division, family court, unified family court, integrated family court, and community family court.

One Family/One Judge Case Handling. Whatever the court's name today there is significant recognition among policymakers that we should implement a more unified handling of a family's legal problems. Quite possibly data on the ultra-common break up of U.S. marriages has influenced both recognition of this need and decisions to finally go forward with this effort. Quite possibly the vast and growing numbers of family-related cases that impact the judicial system led to reexamination by judicial leaders. Quite possibly the judicial system task forces that worked on the question, "What should the court system in our state look like in the future?" were influenced to think outside the box. What must have helped was the broadening use and communication of a simple code term, "one family/one judge." (Some court-based officials refer to this as one judge/one family. I prefer to standardize this term as one family/one judge. The family should come first.)

In fact, however, one family/one judge is an easy phrase representing a difficult task to accomplish in a large or moderate size court system. First, judges frequently rotate assignments annually between a family court, a criminal court, a civil court, and sometimes a probate court. Rotation, obviously, threatens one family/one judge continuity. While the family remains a family court case, rarely does a family follow "their judge" to the judge's new assignment. Instead, a new family court judge hears the family's next matter.

Other case scheduling realities intrude into one family/one judge continuity. Judges retire. Judges go on vacation. Judges become ill. Further, family courts often use other judicial officers, such as a magistrates, commissioners, masters, referees, or hearing officers, to help with the workload of hearings and cases. These officials may hear a delinquency case detention hearing and then pass on the case to the judge. They may hold the abuse, neglect, and dependency case temporary custody hearing and possibly the next appearance but then move the case to the judge. They may hear temporary custody and support hearings in divorce but a judge will hear a contested property settlement that involves the parties. All this breaks the continuity of a judicial officer.

Several courts, such as one in the Seattle suburb of Kent, accordingly structure a one family/one judge/one magistrate team approach, selecting one of several magistrates, the one who has heard the most preliminary matters with a family, as the particular magistrate to be matched with a particular judge with this family.[11] When a non-judge has heard part of a case, the case can remain the judge's case, as when the judge enters the final orders and then two months later another family case scenario needs judicial attention.

The question needs to be asked whether, in knowing a multi-case family well, the judge may know the family too well and be unable to approach a new hearing fairly and impartially. There are variable answers to this question such as: (1) a judge may contend that it is judicial professionalism to not be swayed by having this information; (2) a judge may indicate that prior case knowledge will enable a better informed and wiser judgment; (3) a judge may openly review and discuss the prior case experience with the parties and attorneys and ask if they now have any question about the judge's ability to render a fair judgement in this matter, expecting a negative reply; (4) an attorney may ask the judge to recuse himself/herself and have another judge hear the matter; (5) a judge may spontaneously recuse himself/herself as a Bend, Oregon, judge does prior to a termination of parental rights proceeding, as is described in Chapter 41.

Several Family Court Approaches. The original family court concept was, quite simply, to place juvenile and divorce and child custody and support matters in one court or court division. That would be its workload. Judges appointed, elected, or assigned there would hear only these family case types. Parties, litigants, victims and witnesses, lawyers, social workers, and probation officers would know which part of the courthouse they should locate. Early multi-judge family courts gave no or little thought of coordinating the cases of different family members before one judge. Judge *A* heard divorces and Judge *B* heard juvenile matters. The first family court began in Rhode Island in 1961, where a judicial specialist in a single type of case was the prevailing practice for at least three decades.

Family courts were initially conceptualized before domestic violence became a statutory, procedural, and court-related safety concern, but this case type, at least its non-criminal dimension, can fit well into the design.

Influential national standards for a family court, published in 1980, promulgated the concept of a one family/one judge design, recommended that probation and social service agencies also seek to maximize single staff member responsibility for an entire family, and included jurisdiction over intra-family criminal offenses in the jurisdictional mix.[12]

As computerized databases became common in courthouses. court records could be organized so that, for example, a judge, in holding a delinquency dispositional hearing, could be provided a page that listed the youth's prior offenses, with court hearing dates and dispositions. The technology now exists to allow a judge to have speedy access to record information on cases that involve other family members and become informed of the court's history with the larger family unit. The technology is now present for referencing one family member's family court case type with another family member's case in order to allow scheduling of the new case before the judge who heard the prior case, even though one case might be, for example, a domestic violence protection order and the other one involve child abuse. The technology can enable a one family/one judge scheduling approach to the degree the court is able to implement this design. Judge *A* can still be the divorce judge but having granted the divorce, can hear the son's delinquency case two years later. Or Judge *B*, having earlier heard the case of child abuse, can be scheduled a few months later to hear the mother's petition for a protection order against her live-in lover.

There may be legitimate reasons some courts will seek only a partial one family/one judge orientation. They may decide that there is little reason for a routine five-minute divorce proceeding to require rescheduling this divorce judge with future family matters. Or a court may determine a judge is far more interested in and able with one type of case such as delinquency, and that it is better for this judge to focus on a largely unilateral workload. A court system may have structural obstacles, as with one large court that has its juvenile and family-related cases heard at five different court locations. A court may find that a one-year rotation works best for the entire court's judiciary and thereby curb and sharply limit one family/one judge scheduling. One family court's view was that a family court may include so many different case types that its judges prefer to hear only one or two types of cases, feeling more competent as judges, thereby, than with hearing all the different case types. There will be other reasons.

A second family court structure, illustrated in Chapter 41, selects a limited number of multi-case families for "bundling" as family court cases. These judges do not rotate, so they retain their cases permanently. They hear a general court workload along with

20 to 25 bundled cases that, over time, has increased to 50 such cases. That court and others influenced by it, e.g., in Jackson County, Oregon, do not need to undergo restructuring into a family court division of their general trial court. Instead, they select only particular cases that appear to need one judge while other family-related cases are heard regularly.

This approach, to avoid the creation of a differently organized family court/division and instead maintain the current court structure while selecting a subset of cases, the more difficult family-related cases, for particularized handling, is an attractive one. Other organizational approaches will be constructed as this development expands.

Information Coordination, Judicial Case Coordination, and Social Intervention Case Coordination. The original family court concept was to place various family case types into one court or court division. The next generation development, regardless of structure, seeks to coordinate a family's case matters before one judge. Several levels of coordination are exemplified in the Bend, Oregon, approach.

1. *Information coordination:* The case is not yet a family court case. Rather, any judge scheduled to hear a new court case can be provided information about other cases involving family members for use with the new case disposition.

2. *Judicial case coordination:* Where there is sufficient multi-case or multi-family problem information that a clerical assistant believes may constitute a suitable family court case, case records are bundled and, on acceptance by a judge, become a case or cases to receive judicial case coordination. The judge will handle and coordinate various current and prospective cases involving family members.

3. *Social intervention case coordination:* Multi-case and multi-problem families often have at least several agencies or organizations that seek to help them solve their problems. There may be a child welfare agency, a probation department, a public assistance entity, a housing service, a job service, an alcohol or drug treatment agency, a family counseling organization, and others. A family case coordinator may gather the family, the attorneys, and these various agencies together and oversee the construction of a multi-agency treatment plan as to who will do what and when, in order to obtain needed services. The family treatment plan is then periodically reviewed with the judge.

Other Family Court Examples. There is now substantial experimentation in developing and refining family court approaches. The Jackson County (Medford), Oregon, circuit court is a particularly interesting one. In late 1998 it began an "integrated family court" to provide comprehensive and coordinated services for families with abused and neglected children. A 27-person Family Law Advisory Committee held continuous meetings with court officials in the design of this approach. Three years later the court added a family drug court that targeted families that were affected by chronic substance abuse and had either abused and neglected children or delinquent children.

These two courts had numerous common elements including a one family/one judge case assignment system, a focus on children, frequent judge and family hearings, heavy family engagement with human services systems, frequent domestic violence, and extensive substance abuse. These two courts used common outcome measures. The court system is currently at work determining how it can it combine these two courts into one, while not reducing effectiveness but rather seeking to increase it. Human service agencies are actively consulted in this redesign. The combined court is to be known as a "community family court."

Keep in mind that coordination and combination approaches to improve court effectiveness with multi-problem/case families did not exist at this court five years ago. Courts like this continue to seek better solutions.

A Colorado Example and Its Evaluation. In late 2000 the district court in Adams County (Brighton), Colorado, initiated judicial case coordination of a limited number of families, no more than 30 during its first year. This was a one family/one judge/one magistrate team combined with expanded court-social service case handling integration. Like the court in Bend, Oregon, which influenced its structure, it included almost any type of court matter that involved a family member, including crimes, though it limited the crimes committed by a family member to misdemeanors.

An assessment compared the handling of its first 27 cases with 28 similar cases handled by other judges and magistrates. Findings from this limited evaluation found family court handling:

- Increased the number of matters dealt with at hearings but did not reduce the number of hearings;

- Moved different types of cases more quickly to resolution (though there were no differences with child dependency cases which were required to move speedily in whatever court handled them);

- More likely ordered counseling or mental health services;

- Meant cases were far less likely to have orders of overlapping services entered (54% of cases handled traditionally had a substance abuse assessment, treatment, or testing order mentioned in two or more court orders); and

- Led, according to involved professionals, to greater awareness of family needs and the prospect for providing improved family services.

This experimental court, during its second year, added felonies to its case eligibility criteria except for the highest, the class 1 and 2 felonies. It increased its number of bundled cases and currently bundles "all appropriate cases." The court's chief judge, and no longer the juvenile court judge, has taken on this judicial responsibility.[13]

A Wisconsin Example and Its Evaluation. La Crosse County, Wisconsin, initiated a unified family court approach with multi-case/multi-problem families that emphasized mediated child protection conferencing as a non-adversarial method to obtain resolution of abuse and neglect cases, known in Wisconsin as child in need of protection or services (CHIPS). CHIPS cases were the common denominator in this unified family court whose cases also included family members' criminal child abuse charges, frequent substance abuse histories, extensive family violence, and heavy engagement with justice and social service agencies.

Classical mediation was not used. Rather, no agreement could be approved by the mediator and submitted for judicial ratification "that did not protect the safety of the child and put the child on the road to permanency." The single judge responsible for all of a family's bundled cases ordered mediation at the first court appearance unless the CHIPS case was not seen appropriate for conferencing.

A limited evaluation examined the results of 37 mediated cases. Agreements were reached in 32 cases. Ten of 14 cases that had criminal case components also reached agreement as a result of the mediation. Mediated CHIPS case resolutions were not more speedily accomplished than those resolved without mediation. Successfully mediated criminal child abuse cases were substantially expedited by comparison, which thereby allowed non-criminal matters to be resolved more quickly.

Mediated conferencing was found to have enabled a more concerted focus on the best interests of the children, an improved treatment plan design, increased parent understanding of the judicial process and social service system objectives and methods, allowed for a safe forum for children to confront parents, and expanded coordination and cooperation among professional representatives.[14]

Affirmation of the Family Court. It appears that nearly every state has at least one family court in place now, and more than one family court structure or approach in many states. A few years ago Michigan became, by my count, the eighth statewide-family-court state. It merged its probate court, which included its juvenile court, into its circuit court, its general trial court, and directed that family courts become the norm since juvenile and domestic relations jurisdictions were now located in the same court structure. The process of implementation remains quite incomplete three years after enactment, however.

During 2002 the California Judicial Council announced that funds were now available for all courts in the state to request planning grants to develop forms of "unified courts for families." These "unified courts," following the six-month planning period, would implement their plans, and six courts would be selected to become mentor courts to provide technical assistance to other courts and to undergo their own extensive evaluation. Thirty-two courts were approved for planning grants.

One can cite a half dozen or more such courts in Kentucky, several in Indiana and Alabama, and extensive redesigns into family courts in Florida. For nearly 10 years Nevada has had family courts in its two largest counties and Missouri has had several, one serving the Kansas City area. It is happening.

SHOULD CRIMINAL OFFENSES BE HANDLED IN A FAMILY COURT?

Some courts will say no, we have enough to handle and integrate without a family's criminal cases, and criminal cases can involve jury trials, will involve scheduling issues with a different set of attorneys and probation officers, and we don't want to do that here. Another court may say yes, we can't deal with the family without including criminal cases, and due to our holistic approach numerous criminal cases will more readily be settled without a trial. Apparently, more family courts do not hear these matters than hear them. This will be an important issue to observe in the future. I would encourage inclusion, as the Hawaii family court has done for many years.

THE CHAPTERS THAT FOLLOW

Bottom line, various forms of a family court appear to be the court of the future, approaches that recognize children are part of a family and that families' needs require a coordinated address.

The three chapters in this Part provide a logical transition. Chapter 39 discusses whether juvenile courts should become family courts, recognizing merit in both types of court structures and pointing out issues and concerns related to a redesign into a family court. Chapter 40, on the future of the juvenile court, presents rationales in support of retention of the juvenile court. Chapter 41 illustrates an exciting approach to a family court that provides judicial case coordination along with coordinated social service intervention. This was accomplished without court restructuring, which is invariably stressful, requires extensive planning, and involves numerous personnel concerns. This is a practical approach that seeks to do a more concentrated effort with a selected, limited workload of more difficult family situations.

Endnotes

[1] Pub. L. No. 93-415, 93rd Cong. 1974.

[2] See Flicker, B. D. (1977). *Standards for juvenile justice: A summary and analysis* [Institute of Judicial Administration-American Bar Association Juvenile Justice Standards Project]. Cambridge, MA: Ballinger.

[3] Fox, S.J. (1977). Abolishing the juvenile court. *Harvard Law School Bulletin, 28,* 22, 26.

[4] McCarthy, F. B. (1977, April). Should juvenile delinquency be abolished? *Crime & Delinquency, 23*(2), 196-203.

[5] Wizner, S. & Keller, M. F. (1977, November). The penal model of juvenile justice: Is juvenile court delinquency jurisdiction obsolete? *New York University Law Review, 52*(5), 1120-1135.

[6] Guggenheim, M. (1978, June). A call to abolish the juvenile justice system. *Children's Rights Reporter II,* 7-19. New York: American Civil Liberties Foundation. See my critique of abolitionists in Rubin, H.T. (1979). Retain the juvenile court: Legislative developments, reform directions, and the call for abolition. *Crime & Delinquency, 25,* 281-298.

[7] Feld, B.C. (1990). The punitive juvenile court and the quality of procedural justice: Disjunctions between rhetoric and reality. *Crime & Delinquency, 36,* 443-466; Feld, B.C. (1999). *Bad kids: Race and the transformation of the juvenile court.* New York: Oxford University Press.

[8] Rubin, H.T. (1972). Now to make the criminal courts more like the juvenile courts. *Santa Clara Lawyer, 13,* 104-120.

[9] Ostrom, B. J., Kauder, N. B., & LaFountain, R. C. (2001). *Examining the work of state courts: A national perspective from the court statistics project.* Williamsburg, VA: National Center for State Courts.

[10] Bailey, C.L. et al. (2001). *Status report 2000: Child Victims Act model courts project.* Reno, NV: National Council of Juvenile and Family Court Judges.

[11] Flango, C. R., Flango, V. E., & Rubin, H.T. (1999). *How are courts coordinating family cases?* Williamsburg, VA: National Center for State Courts.

[12] Institute for Judicial Administration-American Bar Association (1980). *Juvenile justice standards relating to court organization and administration, Standard 1.1.* Cambridge, MA: Ballinger.

[13] Evaluation of the Adams County Courts' One Family/One Judge Program (17th Judicial District, Colorado) [available online: www.courts.state.co.us].

[14] Martin, J. & Weller, S. (2001). *Evaluation of unified family court: Seventh Judicial District of Wisconsin.* Denver: Center for Public Policy Studies.

Chapter 39

Should Juvenile Courts Become Family Courts?

WHAT IS A FAMILY COURT?

Simply put, a family court seeks to place all, or mostly all, child- and family-related legal actions into the same court or court division. In effect, this means that juvenile courts are merged with domestic relations courts. Other family-related matters that are heard in still other courts or court divisions would also be moved to the family court.

I have set up certain jurisdictional criteria for a family court. At a minimum, such courts should integrate delinquency, abuse and neglect, divorce or custody-related, and civil domestic violence matters under a statewide or local family court umbrella. Using these criteria, there currently are seven family court states.

Rhode Island initiated the nation's first statewide family court in 1961. The Hawaii legislature enacted the second family court in 1966. The U.S. Congress established the third family court, for the District of Columbia, in 1970. Delaware became the fourth, in 1971. South Carolina became the fifth, in 1976. New Jersey became the sixth, in 1984. Vermont became the seventh, in 1990.

Virginia keeps "threatening" to become the eighth, but has not yet delivered. It piloted "experimental family courts" in 10 rural and urban courts in 1990-1991, and the legislature later authorized a single trial court with comprehensive jurisdiction over child- and family-related legal issues. This reorganization has not been funded nor implemented.

Nevada and Missouri recently legislated family courts in two and six counties, respectively, but not statewide. They are not counted.

HAWAII FAMILY COURT HAS THE BROADEST JURISDICTION

Hawaii has the most all-encompassing family court system. Its jurisdiction includes delinquency, status offenses, abuse and neglect, termination of parental rights, adoptions, guardianships of children and adults, divorce (dissolution), paternity and child support, other custody matters, criminal actions among family members such as misdemeanors between spouses and felonies by parents against children, civil protection orders in domestic violence cases, child and adult mental illness commitment procedures, and adult abuse cases.

Some family courts lack jurisdiction over intra-family criminal offenses (South Carolina), or mental illness procedures (Delaware). South Carolina family courts may hear child, but not adult, mental illness procedures. Delaware family courts may hear intra-family misdemeanor crimes, but not felonies.

This chapter originally appeared in Community Corrections Report, *Vol. 2, No. 2, September/October 1995.*

Some courts that are titled family courts fail to meet the definitional criteria described above. California divorce courts are called family courts, but do not consider juvenile delinquency or abuse or neglect cases. New York created a family court in 1962, but failed to include divorce in its jurisdiction. Long-established family courts in Gulfport, Mississippi, and East Baton Rouge, Louisiana, also lack divorce jurisdiction. A new family court in Louisville, Kentucky, lacks delinquency jurisdiction.

SEPARATE ENTITIES OR DIVISIONS OF THE GENERAL TRIAL COURT

Family courts may be structured as separate entities that manage themselves and are not connected to any other trial court. Judges of these courts are appointed or elected to preside only in this court and only for this workload. Rhode Island, Delaware, and South Carolina fit this model.

Family courts also may be structured as divisions of the general trial court. Judges are assigned for a limited term, and may be renewed, or reassigned to other divisions of the court, such as criminal or civil divisions. Examples of this type of system include Hawaii, the District of Columbia, and New Jersey.

Vermont uses a hybrid structure. A separate family court was enacted and is administered by a family court clerk, but it does not have permanently assigned judges. Instead, judges from the district and superior courts are assigned on a rotational basis. Interestingly, two "assistant judges," laypersons who have received special training in deciding factual questions, hear matters along with a family court judge. However, the professional judge alone determines questions of law, or mixed questions of law and fact.

All national court standards recommend that the general (top) trial court include a family division, and that its jurisdiction consist of delinquency, abuse and neglect, divorce, and more.[1]

Some reformers prefer a separate family court structure, arguing that this would assure the election or appointment of specialist long-term judges who, presumably, are particularly interested in this work. However, experience in Hawaii, the District of Columbia, and New Jersey, has shown that the creation of a family division often results in extended judicial assignments, frequently for many years.

The term "family court" will be used in the following discussion to refer to any kind of a family court or family division, except where there is a particular reason to distinguish the organizational structure.

VIEWING FAMILY COURTS

Some people in our field see a family court as the greatest innovation since the juvenile court. Others believe gains would be modest, could be obtained in other ways, and would not be worth the pain of a major court restructuring effort. The chief judge of the family court in Honolulu has written that:

A well-organized and unified family court will provide a prompt and fair resolution of the unique legal problems of children and families. In doing so it will: a) help save lives, b) reduce emotional turmoil, c) promote family harmony as much as possible, d) enhance efficiency and effectiveness. It is an idea that will truly "count for the future." It will build in a commitment to therapeutic justice based on the very work you do. [2]

However, a California State Senate Task Force report on the potential benefits of a family court found that "the problems of families involved in multiple courts and receiving conflicting orders ... does not occur in a sufficient number of cases to warrant a total restructuring of the Superior Court." The report added that the problems created by the severe lack of resources in the different courts serving children and families and with the attendant services are so great that they overshadow all other issues, including consideration of the creation of a family court.[3]

Arguments for Establishing a Family Court

The following arguments have been used to support the family court concept:

- Everyone will know where to go. A family's case will be heard in one place.

- Judges will be assigned to this court who want to be assigned there. They will have keen interest in this workload.

- The same judge will be scheduled to hear a wide range of family-related matters (the one family/one judge approach to calendaring), thus providing continuity, and curbing the currently fragmented approach to judicial hearings.

- The possibility of two or more judges entering conflicting orders regarding the same family member(s) will be substantially reduced.

- There will be a judiciary that is better informed of earlier or concurrent court cases that involve different family members.

- The specialized judiciary will facilitate improved and better-coordinated social service agency handling of different family members.

- Hostility between parties will be reduced. The court will make available dispute resolution methods that reduce hostility, address underlying problems, and promote communication and cooperation.

- The chief judge will become the community's lead spokesperson on child- and family-related concerns, needed legal reforms, and improved or increased resources to serve court clientele.

Colorado Rejects a Family Court

While these arguments are persuasive, they "underwhelmed" a legislatively directed Colorado examination of whether that state should undertake a family court.

A 1994 report of the Colorado Administrative Office of the Courts affirmed the present court structure as "adequate" to resolve child- and family-related issues, but recommended a number of approaches to enhance case handling within the present structure.[4] The report rejected the "therapeutic justice" objective advanced by Hawaii's chief family court judge. It recognized that "a variety of services are needed to assist children and families in crisis," but resolved, "it is the function of the courts to decide cases rather than to provide services to meet the social and economic needs of children and families. Unfortunately, those needs exist before issues arise which require judicial resolution."

The report also rejected the one family/one judge precept. There was concern about a judge's overfamiliarity with a family and prejudgment of a matter prior to its hearing. A related concern was judicial access to other court records on the family. The report stated that:

> A judge may not simply obtain all court files and reports about all family members and utilize that information in a decision-making process without giving all participants a full and fair opportunity to respond to negative inferences that might be drawn.

The report's recommendations focused on such matters as: expediting case processing, piloting intensive family preservation services for high-risk juvenile offenders and their families, cooperation with the state child welfare agency to pilot test mediation in child abuse and neglect cases, expanding assistance to *pro se* litigants in domestic relations matters, broadened training for judicial system officials, and a request for legislation to authorize the consolidation in one court of two or more child- or family-related cases that have been filed in two or more counties.

While I disagree with the conclusions of this Colorado report, I do not trumpet family courts as a panacea. Still, family courts allow judges to address family issues more comprehensively. Court clients do, indeed, need social service interventions, and one judge can obtain coordinated service delivery more easily than two or three. A one family/one judge approach to calendaring would be appreciated by most families. Overfamiliarity can be handled by a court rule that simplifies a party's request for a replacement judge. A judge's access to other records that involve a family can be handled readily, as well. Attorneys can receive copies of court records, and comment on them as the judge reviews these records at a hearing. A court rule can prohibit judicial review of family records until the judge, for example, has adjudicated a delinquency petition. However, the judge should know, at this disposition, whether a father is delinquent with child support payments, or a mother obtained a restraining order last week to kick an assaultive partner out of the house, and so on.

HAS THIS FAMILY BEEN TO COURT BEFORE?

Research that several colleagues and I conducted recently sheds light on the frequency of families who experience multiple court cases. We looked at 1,152 case records in Jersey City, New Jersey; Fairfax, Virginia; and Salt Lake City, Utah. The records dealt with families involved with child abuse and neglect, or delinquency, or divorce when a family had children.

Forty-one percent of all case files showed one or more references to other court cases involving the same family during the prior five years. Sixty-four percent of abuse and neglect families had at least one other case, as did 48% of delinquency families. Interestingly, only 16% of divorcing families had such recent court involvement.

Another aspect of the research obtained responses from 195 court or court-related officials across the country. We asked, for example, how important is it to know whether family members are currently, or were previously, involved in related court cases. Seventy-one percent responded it was very important, and another 27% stated it was important to know about other current cases, while 62% found it very important and 34% reported it was important to know about earlier court cases. We concluded that these and other findings supported the need for improved court information and case coordination, and that the data were supportive of a family court direction.[5]

SPECIAL CONCERNS REGARDING CREATION OF A FAMILY COURT

The creation of a family court involves the merger of several high-volume, multi-appearance, and often "multi-problem" cases. Delinquency, abuse and neglect, divorce, paternity and child support, and domestic violence proceedings return repeatedly to the court. Juvenile court intake screening practices should be coordinated with other family court cases involving the family (e.g., issues of paternity or child support). Participation by probation officers, social workers, mediators, mental health specialists, and lawyers is essential. Hearing time can be quite long.

Family court creation involves large tasks and, likely, large-scale resistance and high-scale anxiety, if not trauma. Just ask the Nevada court administrator who called and said, "The legislature just mandated a family court for us. I don't know where to start. What do I do?" It does seem wise to pilot a family court at a few sites, and evaluate its advantages and problems before considering statewide change. Further, holding off on a decision to absorb intra-family criminal offenses can reduce merger problems and allow for a better, future decision on this issue.

Judicial burnout is another consideration for judges of a family court, perhaps even more than for judges of a juvenile court. Long hearings often involve personal conflict, emotion, frustration, and, sometimes, danger. Shootings have occurred in these courtrooms. Judges remove their addresses from the telephone directory, or switch to unlisted telephone numbers.

The family court in Hawaii tries to reduce burnout by rotating judges annually into one of four subdivisions: (1) delinquency and abuse and neglect, (2) domestic relations, (3) criminal, and (4) special, a "catch all" category that includes domestic violence protection orders, adult abuse, guardianships, mental illness, and adoptions. The domestic relations subdivision is viewed as the most difficult assignment. During an annual assignment there, judges can be reassigned each three months, for "R and R," to another subdivision for two weeks. But this rotation model hampers implementation of a one family/one judge calendar.

REORGANIZATION MUST BE MEANINGFUL

A family court in name is not a real family court when reorganization simply places the primary child- and family-related jurisdictions in one place. One statewide family court, for example, has the different judges hearing either delinquency or abuse and neglect or domestic relations matters. No effort is made to schedule a judge with a family member's case that is of a different case type or to provide information about the other case to the judge.

WILL A FAMILY COURT CHANGE A PROBATION DEPARTMENT?

For a long time, juvenile court judges have tapped probation staff to do tasks that are not associated with delinquent youths. The tasks have included adoption studies when no licensed agency is involved; child custody investigations when two unwed parents complain about each other's parenting; custody evaluations with divorcing parties when the divorce court judge has leaned on the juvenile court judge to borrow staff; and assessing maturity with underage marriage applicants or abortion applicants who require judicial approvals.

Some domestic relations courts employ their own divorce counselors, child custody evaluators, or mediators. They, of course, are not probation officials. Conceivably, a family court merger could replace a probation department with a court services department, and a more diversified staff could provide more diversified services. Yet I saw no broadened offerings by the juvenile probation agencies that were tied into the two family courts I researched this past year. Admittedly, the judicial branch administered neither agency.

However, a Virginia probation administrator, whose agency serves the juvenile and domestic relations court that has no jurisdiction over divorce, described certain domestic relations functions her probation officers were performing regularly: mediation of custody, visitation, and support matters with child support enforcement and domestic violence cases; marital, partners, and family counseling with domestic violence and intra-family criminal offense matters; child custody evaluations, including interstate cases; case screening and petition preparation assistance with applicants for a domestic violence protection order; and preparation of consent agreements or recommendations for a child support order. She concluded: "The domestic relations part of what we do has increased, so that more than 50% of probation's work now is domestic relations. And we have had no increase in staff!"

Might this happen if your jurisdiction turns to a family court? And how might this affect your juvenile workloads?

Author's Note

Sizably increased implementation of family courts has taken place since this chapter was originally written. Reportedly, all but two states have launched one or more family courts. Michigan has become the eighth statewide family court jurisdiction. California is accomplishing a reversal of an earlier position. During 2002, 32 superior courts were funded to develop plans for family courts. Colorado initiated a family court in Adams County, contiguous to Denver, in 2000. This was an adaptation of the family court in Bend, Oregon (see Chapter 41).

Judge Michael Town informed me in July 2002 that the Hawaii family court maintains its broad jurisdiction. He reports that very few intra-family felony or adult abuse charges are filed, but that approximately 2,000 domestic violence matters are brought to the court annually. A division of the probation department provides services exclusively to domestic violence cases. Three judges are assigned these matters, one hearing protection order requests and two hearing domestic violence misdemeanors that may include jury trials.

Endnotes

[1] See Institute for Judicial Administration-American Bar Association Juvenile Justice Standards Project (1980). *Court organization and administration, Standard 1.1.* Cambridge, MA: Ballinger; Office of Juvenile Justice and Delinquency Prevention (1980). *Standards for the administration of juvenile justice, Standard 3.121.* Washington, DC: Author.

[2] Town, M. A. (1994) *The unified family court.* (Unpublished manuscript.)

[3] Senate Task Force on Family Relations Courts, Sacramento, CA 1990.

[4] Colorado Administrative Office of the Courts, *Report to the Legislature.* December 23, 1994.

[5] Rubin, H. T. & Flango, V. E. (1992). *Court coordination of family cases.* Williamsburg, VA: National Center for State Courts.

Chapter 40

The Future of the Juvenile Court

Foes of the juvenile court system seek to abolish it. They believe the juvenile court should have no future. In taking this position, the abolitionists focus solely on the court's involvement with delinquents and ignore its role with abused and neglected children.

I would like to take this opportunity to review and revise my previous writings on the future of juvenile court jurisdiction. The present structure and jurisdiction of the juvenile court should be retained, but its current workload should be blended with a range of domestic relations cases to create a family court. Currently, juvenile courts are a more proper setting for delinquents than are adult courts.

A BACKWARD GLANCE AT THE FUTURE

In 1968, while I was a Denver juvenile court judge, the Joint Commission on Correctional Manpower and Training asked me to prepare a consultant's paper on the future of the juvenile court.[1] I was instructed to project this court's future for the next 20 years. However I concluded that, at best, I could look ahead just five years.

I offered those projections at a time of optimism about juvenile justice. We had had the Constitution-affirming decisions in **Kent v. United States**, 383 U.S. 54 (1966), and **In re Gault,** 387 U.S. 1 (1967), and the progressive report and call to action of President Johnson's Crime Commission. We were in the midst of a meaningful assault on—though not truly a war on—poverty. For the first time we had heard the word "empowerment." Victory after victory had been won in the struggle for civil rights. New gains also were also being won on behalf of women and Native Americans. The protests against the American invasion of Viet Nam were in high gear.

In Colorado, a new and very liberal Children's Code, of which I had been the primary architect, had been enacted the year before. And so I made the following projections:

- The most significant movement to alter the jurisdiction of the juvenile court should be the movement away from stigmatizing youngsters as delinquents because they have committed an offense that is illegal only for children. Discretionary intake will permit children in need of supervision to be dealt with through non-judicial means.

- Effective use of discretionary intake procedures will have the effect of reducing significantly the number of cases of minor misdeeds now appearing every year

This chapter originally appeared in Juvenile Justice Update, *Vol. 2, No. 4, August/September 1996.*

before the juvenile courts. The juvenile court of the future may be seeing mainly cases of children alleged to have committed serious offenses, those who have continually repeated minor misbehaviors, and those for whom past attempts at informal dispositions have failed.

- No significant change seems apt to occur in the near future to alter the present [minimum or maximum] age limitations on jurisdiction. Some states, however, have lowered the age at which the juvenile court has concurrent jurisdiction with the criminal court in felony cases. This will undoubtedly result in more transfers of children to criminal court.

- The courts are not a primary prevention agency. All children need a family, a school, health care, social and recreational opportunities; but not all children need a juvenile court. Juvenile courts prevent delinquency by preventing recidivism. Juvenile courts can assist in the prevention of initial delinquency by communicating their research and experiential knowledge to the public in general, to private groups, to governmental institutions, and to social agencies.

- It is incumbent upon the court to make known the rules and regulations regarding detention or non-detention, which will be followed in its particular jurisdiction. As all agencies within the community become accustomed to the fact that the majority of cases will not be detained, agencies will cease to use the detention facility as a convenient shelf on which to store their more troublesome clients pending court action.

- Probable increases in the number of trials and hearings will eventually require the services of more judges. And more of a judge's time will be spent in the courtroom and in legal research. No longer is a judge likely to have time for hiring and supervising the probation staff or for developing and administering the rehabilitation programs provided by the court.

Even in 1968, some police advocated the abolition of the juvenile court, arguing, "Since juveniles now have the rights of adults, they should be treated like adults."

SUPPORT FOR A FAMILY COURT

In 1977-1978, those who proposed abolishing the juvenile courts were generally liberal academics who believed the court's rehabilitation ethos posed irresolvable conflicts with due process of law.[2] I wrote and had published in 1979 an article rejecting these calls to abolish the juvenile court.[3] Instead, I urged the pursuit of many reforms set forth in the Institute of Judicial Administration-American Bar Association Juvenile Justice Standards. One standard I had prepared as a reporter for this project recommended implementing a family court—"to restructure the juvenile court into a family court division of the general trial court ... it presents a reasonable organization of jurisdiction, and could lessen the current fragmentation of issues related to the family [because of] their distribution among different courts and different judges."

A FORWARD GLANCE AT THE FUTURE

Over the last 20 years, there has been a significant increase in hard-line and harder-line juvenile court sanctioning authority and application. In the last five years there have been substantial increases in the criminalization of juveniles. Juveniles are using guns instead of knives, and knives instead of fists. Drug sales and drug use overwhelm our present prevention, control, and treatment efforts. Guns and gangs and drugs have become endemic to our society, and now cross over from cities into suburban areas and rural communities. Prison construction and operating costs dwarf most other state expenditures. The efficacy of the juvenile court is frequently the subject of debate, but few seriously challenge the cost effectiveness of a criminal court sentence of imprisonment.

Now we are in a period of great juvenile justice pessimism. There is a more diverse group of juvenile court abolitionists. They contend, with considerable support, that defense representation of juveniles is often sporadic and ineffective, and they suggest that defining adolescence solely by age fails to recognize the development, maturation, and experience that characterize American teenagers today.[4]

So what should be projected for the juvenile court for the next five years? I do not foresee, nor do I want to see, the end of the juvenile court as the primary home for delinquent offenses. It is easy to predict that juvenile courts will see fewer violent juveniles, fewer juveniles who have been labeled very serious or very chronic offenders, or older offenders. Already we have begun to see several states authorize "blended sentences," where a juvenile court judge issues a combined sentence to both juvenile and adult institutions. More states are sure to enact similar legislation.

EVOLVING TWO-TIER APPROACH TO DELINQUENCY

Most Serious Cases

The smaller, top tier consists of those cases that will be handled once or twice in a juvenile court, a criminal court, or with blended sentences. The juvenile court's job is to (1) minimize the criminalization of juveniles, (2) obtain community programming that will have a positive impact for them, and (3) seek care for them in specialized juvenile facilities when they are sentenced as adults.

More Typical Cases

The larger, lower tier will consist mostly of the juvenile court cases we know today. For many, we will use home detention, diversion, restitution and/or community service at both the diversion and disposition points, levels of probation intensity, and more of the multi-faceted "take-over-their-life-space" approaches we have learned to do well in many communities. Although residential placements will remain, an emphasis will be placed on educational rehabilitation, job training, and juvenile employment.

SHORTCOMINGS OF THE CRIMINAL COURT SUPPORT RETAINING THE JUVENILE COURT

Those who advocate the abolition of the juvenile court do not present a clear blueprint for alternative court handling of this workload, except to recommend placement of all juvenile offenders in a criminal court, and then encourage a more lenient sentence there. But which criminal court? The assumption is that the felony court is the appropriate place. It is touted as having "pristine due process," a right to a jury trial, and able defense attorneys. However, the glorification of criminal court legal protections is bereft of evaluations of actual safeguards and accomplishments. Reports on rehabilitation efficacy there are also absent.

Abolitionists immodestly use selective research evaluations that are critical of juvenile court procedural justice and rehabilitation accomplishments, but do not submit counterpart criminal justice research evaluations that show that the adult system works better and is, therefore, the best. Their arguments should be based on hard data rather than ideological assumptions and their advocacy would be better founded *when and if* they submit consistent research evaluations that find:

- Adult felony defense attorneys represent their clients more effectively than attorneys do in juvenile courts.

- Adult misdemeanor defense attorneys represent their clients more effectively than attorneys do in juvenile courts.

- Adult misdemeanants have a higher rate of defense counsel representation than do delinquent juveniles.

- Jury trials in (1) felony courts and (2) misdemeanor courts free more innocent defendants than do juvenile court trials.

- Adult community corrections curbs reoffending better than the array of community-based juvenile services accomplishes.

- Prisons and jails better protect society than do juvenile institutions.

Typical Felony Court Shortcomings

In the absence of this information, there are many reasons to question the effectiveness of the adult courts based upon the treatment of juveniles who are currently handled there. For the felony courts there is a disproportionate use of waivers with minority youth. Countless waived juveniles are parked in overcrowded, dangerous local jails—and they are held much longer than are juveniles retained as juveniles and held in juvenile detention centers. Overwhelmed judicial dockets may allow trial only after six months of waiting or lead to plea bargains that avoid lengthy jury trials.

Further, staggering workloads slant public defender advocacy away from the exercise of the trial or jury trial right. Their burdened investigative staffs do not match prosecutor investigative capabilities. Also, presentence investigations by adult probation officers are often too cursory to look closely at more than the obvious resources. Finally, lengthier sentences of incarceration are likely, many to facilities under court order because of unconstitutional conditions and where little treatment is available.

Typical Misdemeanor Court Shortcomings

Another criminal court will also process juveniles—the misdemeanor court. Juveniles commit many misdemeanors, sometimes three or four for each felony. The characteristics of misdemeanor courts, which have been described as "sausage factories," often include:

- The absence of a screening mechanism that could frequently result in diversion or informal handling of lesser offenses;

- A three-minute hearing or a 10-minute trial;

- Novice defense counsel;

- Instant sentencing without a presentence investigation;

- Probation without supervision but for a monthly fee;

- Use of the same local jail that holds those accused of felonies, which are used for pretrial holding and for sentences up to a year. (Many of these facilities are under federal court order.)

Certainly the existing juvenile system does not answer all of the deficiencies cited above. Every juvenile court has insufficiencies, but most have something damned good to offer many juvenile offenders. And most have at least someone who cares about kids—a detention center youth worker, a probation officer, or a judge or referee, for example.

WHAT THE PAST 28 YEARS HAVE—AND HAVE NOT—ACCOMPLISHED

Now, I'd like to use my 1968 views as a springboard from which we can look both backward and forward.

Use of Term "Delinquent"

We did accomplish reserving the term "delinquent" for law-violating juveniles only. Today, large numbers of juvenile courts almost never formally process a status offender. There are courts that really like this workload, however, and numerous rural courts take it on because no one else will. So long as we can keep the federal Juvenile Justice and Delinquency Prevention Act (JJDPA) on the books in close to its current form, the present status of status offenders is likely to continue. We appropriately have very limited authority with status offenders, and they rank low on the scale of importance when compared with delinquent and abused and neglected children.

Discretionary Intake

The use of discretion has grown, but much discretion has been transferred from intake officers to prosecutors. Prosecutors have moved up front in many states to influence or control the intake decision. Balances have been struck between intake officers and prosecutors who often (though not always) work well together; and prosecutors do not want to bring first-time lesser offenders to court either. Look for more states to grant either first-level or a form of second-level screening responsibility to the prosecutor.

Transfer of Juveniles to Adult Courts

It is now significantly easier to transfer juveniles to adult court. In addition to judicial waiver, many states have increased the circumstances under which a prosecutor can initiate prosecution in adult court. And legislatures have carved out numerous exceptions to the jurisdiction of the juvenile court, creating legislative waivers. This trend has not abated.

Role in Prevention

It remains true that juvenile courts are not primary, or even secondary prevention agencies. But I wish they would take on a new role, that of working with community organizations to prevent delinquency. In effect, they could apply the probation department analog to community policing. Judicial leadership would be very valuable here.

Detention and Detention Alternatives

Happily, detention alternatives, screening criteria, and detention risk screening instruments are in place in many communities. Unfortunately, guns, gangs, drugs, slow moving courts, and waiting lists at "the state" burden available detention space. Although we should seek to rely on fewer rather than more detention beds, poor detention system and juvenile justice system management continue to lead to significant overcrowding and, ultimately, to lawsuits.

Case-Flow Management

Slow case processing times haunt many juvenile courts. This may be caused more by poor case management than by an insufficient number of judges. Many juvenile courts have paid scant attention to managing the court's case flow. Further, the more burdensome workload expansion of these judges consists mainly of abuse and neglect cases. More states have shifted probation and detention to executive agencies, and this development is likely to continue.

More Family Courts

There are more family courts today, and there should be and will be even more tomorrow. The change is motivated by the following factors: (1) handling different family-related case types in different courts results in further fragmentation of already fragmented families and, sometimes, in conflicting orders; (2) abused and neglected children may be involved with three different courts: juvenile, domestic relations, and criminal; (3) vast increases in the array of domestic relations matters (e.g., domestic violence and paternity/support) suggest the merits of a more coordinated court focus;

(4) social services intervention should become better coordinated, using one rather than several judges; and (5) computers can be programmed to enable family-oriented judicial scheduling and family case tracking.

FUTURE OF CHILD ABUSE AND NEGLECT CASES

The primary forum for child abuse and neglect cases has been the juvenile (or family) court. The juvenile court seeks to protect the child by providing protective orders to enable the child to remain in his or her own home or an approved alternative placement. The juvenile court aims at reunification of the family or an alternative permanent placement for the child.

In 1980, the federal government enacted P. L. 96-272, which interposed court monitoring on the intervention by child welfare agencies.[5] The law sought fewer removals from families, speedier returns to families, or other permanent plans. The effort brought some gains. In some communities there were fewer instances of governmental neglect substituting for parental neglect. In others, the law was ignored or rendered ineffective.

However, parental drug addiction, babies born to addicted mothers, worsening poverty for many families, increased reporting of child sexual abuse, and other negative indicators have overwhelmed children's agencies and the courts.

Each state's public child welfare system is required to implement federal guidelines that focus on family preservation and family support.[6] Family preservation refers to the early insertion of intensive, reasonably comprehensive services that aim at avoiding removal of the child. Fewer removals mean fewer court hearings. Family support refers to the provision of a variety of assisting mechanisms aimed at stabilizing a family, before or after removal. This should result in greater reunification of families and fewer court reviews or permanency planning hearings. This is all very positive.

Additionally, the states have begun a second federal initiative, an assessment of judicial system handling of these cases, together with the design and implementation of improvement plans.[7] The courts and public child welfare agencies are the collaborative centerpieces of this initiative. Both entities need each other. Both have had myriad shortcomings. Never before has there been a systematic examination of what is needed to make both operations work better. We can anticipate a string of gains from these initiatives: fewer children will be removed from their homes; fewer children will drift indefinitely in temporary foster care; for those families unable to benefit from more intensive services, the courts will move far more rapidly to consider termination of parental rights and pursue adoption or another long-term plan; the goal of a finding a permanent home for a child within 12 months of removal will be accepted; and there will be more adoptions by foster parents, hopefully assisted by ongoing adoption subsidy funds.

The juvenile court will hold more and quicker hearings to review parental and children's adjustments. We will not create orphanages. We will accept that a one family/one judge court calendar assignment will enable enhanced judicial administration of the care of these children. Since some of these children have a delinquent sibling, look for the same judge to hear both case types, to deal with both siblings.

This all will be done in a juvenile or family court. Abused and neglected children, as well as delinquent youth, have a better future in this court.

Author's Note

This chapter was adapted from a presentation I made to the Symposium on Juvenile Justice at the Crossroads, sponsored by the Delaware Center for Justice, Wilmington, Delaware, October 5, 1995.

I increasingly embrace the values of a well-functioning family court and recognize that there are different models of court design, some of only limited redesign that can improve judicial system coordination of family-related cases. I retain my caveat that family courts are not for every jurisdiction, in recognition that their idealized accomplishment will be difficult to obtain; I am also aware that some actual family court implementation schemes, as in Miami, Florida, and Prince George's County, Maryland, were discarded some years ago as unsuccessful. Nonetheless, family courts in various formats are being developed in more court locations and are providing energy to judicial system deliberations that seek approaches to: Can't our court do a better job with families?

Endnotes

[1] Rubin, H. T. & Smith, J. F. (1968). *The future of the juvenile court: Implications for correctional manpower and training.* Washington, DC: Joint Commission on Correctional Manpower and Training.

[2] Fox, S. J. (1977). Abolishing the juvenile court. *Harvard Law School Bulletin, 28,* 22-26; Guggenheim, M. (1978). A call to abolish the juvenile justice system. *Children's Rights Reporter, 2,* 7-19; McCarthy, F. B. (1977). Should juvenile delinquency be abolished? *Crime & Delinquency, 23,* 196-203.

[3] Rubin, H. T. (1979). Retain the juvenile court? Legislative developments, reform directions, and the call for abolition. *Crime & Delinquency, 25,* 281-298.

[4] Feld, B. C. (1992). Criminalizing the juvenile court: A research agenda for the 1990s. In I. M. Schwartz (Ed.) *Juvenile justice and public policy.* New York: Lexington Books; Ainsworth, J. E. (1991). Re-imagining childhood and reconstructing the legal order: The case for abolishing the juvenile court. *North Carolina Law Review, 69.* 1083-1133.

[5] U.S. Congress. 1980. The Adoption Assistance and Child Welfare Act. P.L. 96-272.

[6] U.S.C., §670 et seq. (1989).

[7] U. S. Congress. 1993. Omnibus Budget Reconciliation Act. P.L. 103-66.

Chapter 41

Getting Serious About the Coordination of Family-Related Cases: Family Court Operation in Bend, Oregon

NATIONAL DISCUSSION IN 1970S PRECEDES DEVELOPMENT OF FAMILY COURT MODELS

Beginning in the 1970s, various national judicial groups discussed two proposed models that would allow state and local courts to handle family-related cases in one setting. One, known as the Rhode Island, Delaware, South Carolina model, called for a separate family court that was independent of the general trial court. The other, then referred to as the District of Columbia or Hawaii model (subsequently, New Jersey was to fit into this category), created a family division within the general trial court. The latter model became the dominant one insofar as it was uniformly adopted in national standards that emerged from the discussions of these various groups.

Family Court as a Division of the General Trial Court Seen as More Efficient

The family court as a division of the general trial court division approach was supported by those who favored having a unified trial court (or at most a bi-level court system) in any community. This one-court approach was considered better because it would allow for greater efficiencies than would the addition of a separate trial court, and it would be more likely to receive consistent attention and direction from the chief judge and court administrator. This approach was also favored because of a preference for judges who hear family-related cases to be generalists, able to sit on any bench. When assigned to the family division, generalist judges would bring a broad knowledge of law and legal practice. Their rotation into this specialized setting would be for one to three years.

But many communities today complain about excessive rotation of the generalist judge into a family or domestic relations or juvenile division. Some complain that no judge, or at least no highly competent judge, wants to serve in such a setting. But in a number of jurisdictions, highly capable judges do rotate into this division, like the work, become committed to it, and stay in the division for five or 10 years or even longer, making important contributions to that court and community.

This chapter originally appeared in Juvenile Justice Update, *Vol. 6, No. 1, February/March 2000.*

Separate Family Court Would Allow Expertise of "Specialist" Judges

Those who favored a separate family court argued that it would attract judges with a special inclination and sensitivity to family matters. These specialist judges would serve the family court throughout their term of office, bringing greater expertise in specialized law and greater knowledge of community resources to their work. This position was rejected by standards drafters.

Courts Often Follow One Case/One Judge Model

Although multiple problems—legal, social, health, economic, and other—beset many of the families involved in juvenile and family court proceedings, usually each legal case of each family member is addressed unilaterally. It is one case/one judge. When probation is involved, it is one juvenile/one probation officer (PO). Neither the judge nor the PO takes on the several or more cases that involve family members nor the several members of that family who need assistance. Neither the judge nor the PO seeks to coordinate the different services needed by or provided to the youth and to the parent(s) by different agencies. The general practice around the country often promotes segmented court and human services interventions.

Thus, while the goal of the family court (i.e., the centering of juvenile and domestic matters in one place) is to provide sensitized jurists who would look beyond the immediate matter that brought a family member to court to the multiple problems that often beset the family, in general, those states or local jurisdictions that initiated family courts have not done much more than centralize a number of case types in one place. Significant efforts are underway in some communities, however, to do a serious job of coordinating interrelated case handling. This chapter looks at one such community, Bend, Oregon, and examines how it is addressing family matters.

BEND JUDGES SEEK REAL COORDINATION IN FAMILY COURT

The Circuit Court in Deschutes County (Bend), Oregon, located in central Oregon (population: 104,000), is now recognized as having developed a cutting edge approach to the coordination of cases of family members and the delivery of needed services to them. There is a long history of interagency coordination here, but the court's active entry into the coordination scene officially began in November 1995.[1] At that time, the four circuit court judges decided to carve out a partial workload of families with multiple problems for specialized handling. This was the pilot family court in Oregon. Oregon's law allows its judicial circuits to propose a scheme for a family court to the Chief Justice of the Supreme Court for possible approval. Numerous circuits have made proposals, and several have now been initiated, but no statute centers juvenile and family case types all in one place.

Bend's "Family" Judges Are Circuit Court Judges

The judges who handle "family" cases in Bend are circuit court judges, not true family court judges. They hear all the types of cases that are common to general jurisdiction trial courts, i.e., civil, criminal, probate, juvenile/family, and more. Within this spectrum, each judge carves out a specialized caseload of up to 25-30 families. The same judge handles all matters concerning each member of these families. A family's judge will hear a father's drug charge, a mother's theft charge, and a son's driving violation. This judge may also hear an involuntary mental health commitment proceeding or legal matter concerning the need for a guardianship or conservatorship. Even a contract dispute that involves a family member is part of this judge's turf with a family. It truly is a one family/one judge model. It has happened, for example, that a family court judge has called up a family member's fine, imposed in the city court, and converted it to accomplishable community service hours, so that a father's driver's license could be reinstated.

Involved Families Get Integrated Treatment Plans Coordinated by the Family Court Advocate

There is more. This is a one family/one judge/one treatment plan. To ensure this happens, an added court staff member, the family court advocate, coordinates the various interventions that are needed once a family has been designated a family court case. Some interventions are in place at the time a family is designated for special family treatment. Others are added following the designation.

To become a "family" case, the judge must accept it as such and the family must agree to the designation. Immediate family members who are not involved in a court proceeding are included in the definition of family. In so doing, the family agrees to waive the confidentiality of prior and current agency intervention reports. The advocate then arranges a family-screening team meeting composed of administrative personnel and line staff of agencies that are presently involved, along with administrative staff from additional agencies that the family may need. Lawyers for family members attend as well. The focus of this meeting is assessment. What services or assistance does this family and its individual members need to bring themselves into constructive, stabilized functioning?

Graduates Share Their Experience

How does this work in practice from the perspective of the family members who are involved? In late 1998, a husband and wife described to me and several colleagues the nature of their problems and the services they received:

Husband: I was first brought to a court in 1991.

Wife: I have been in court since 1993.

Husband and Wife: We now like having one judge.

Husband: I've been getting services, not just punishment.

Wife: I've had drug and probation violations.

Husband: I've had drug and probation violations and an assault on my wife charge.

Wife: I was violent to him, too.

Husband: I've taken a 20-week course for batterers.

Wife: We've both been sober for 11 months, and we have few arguments now.
I've had weekly counseling in mental health and have been part of a woman's group. We've had a family therapist.
We have my seven-year-old son in our home. He was not from this marriage. My son has attention deficit disorder (ADD) and is getting into a special day treatment school. At regular school he was kicking the teacher and the kids, was stealing, and took a knife to school. He is taking medications, has taken an anger management class, but he needs more. The first time we met with the treatment team we thought we'd be told we were bad parents, and we expected they would take my son away from us. But it was O.K., and then we began looking forward to the meetings.
My husband has ADD, too. And we had some domestic violence in front of my son.

Husband: We were ready for help. We love each other, but we couldn't live with each other. Driving under the influence and drug possession got me into family court. My wife had been off probation a year when I asked her to join me in family court. If she hadn't, our marriage would have ended.

Family Court Advocate: They're graduates, now, but we're still assisting their son.

Wife: I have dyslexia, too. We don't have many friends. Our old friends had all been drug users, and we no longer see them. We only have our parents, so it's good to be able to call agency staff and talk.

Wife: My seven-year-old son is before our judge tomorrow as a dependent child, but for some violent stuff. I hope he throws the book at him.

Husband: I work nights and my wife works days.

Wife: But for family court and the treatment team, we wouldn't be here today telling you we're doing quite well.

Husband: It doesn't work with everyone, but it sure helped us.

GOAL IS DEVELOPMENT OF TREATMENT PLAN

The screening team may determine that necessary services are being provided and that the advocate should just monitor current service provisions and family members' progress or regress. Or it may determine that additional services and programs appear necessary and ask the advocate to obtain these and assemble a treatment team of service providers. The advocate sets up meetings, obtains and facilitates a treatment plan, submits the plan to the court, and brings the family, its attorneys, and the agencies back to court periodically for judicial review of the plan and family developments. While each agency may have its own treatment plan, the coordinator brings these together into one combined, multi-faceted treatment plan. The family featured in this article had seven treatment team meetings before "graduating."
The invocation of a treatment team leads to the single, multi-agency treatment

plan that the court advocate develops. This is an easy-to-read plan that identifies the needs of individual family members, the assistance either currently provided or needed from specified agencies, the time line for obtaining additional interventions and accomplishing tasks, along with projected completion dates. The plan specifies what family members, agencies, and the court advocate will do, and by when.

The gamut of a family treatment plan may run to housing and clothing needs, emergency financial assistance, job assistance, arrangements for medical insurance, specific medical, dental and psychological services, educational assessments, assistance with addiction and domestic violence issues, treatment for batterers, securing a CASA for a child—even securing free hair styling for a family member preparing for a job search—and much more. These are multi-problem families. Typically, there are additional legal matters that arise during a case. But a family's judge is no stranger, and the judge wants, if at all possible, to see that a family and its members make it. Because the problems and needs of family members, individually and collectively, are severe, there is, typically, no linear progression.

An estimated 5%-10% of families, bundled for one judge, reject going beyond judicial-based case coordination. Further, a screening team recommends a treatment team in only one-third to one-half of cases. In other cases recommendations are not made because: (1) current interagency efforts are working suitably; (2) the family is opposed to other interventions; and/or (3) the family is taking care of its problems reasonably well.

SELECTING CASES FOR "FAMILY" COURT PROCESSING

Some families become family court cases subject to judicial coordination alone. Others, with judicial approval, become family court cases subject to coordination by both a judge and the court advocate. The single prerequisite for selection is the presence of children. But the court is highly selective. It knows it cannot give special consideration to all families, nor are all families likely to benefit from such consideration.

Clerk Searches Databases for Likely Families

A senior clerk allocates perhaps half her time to identifying appropriate families. She does a name search of the court's database and the state judicial information network with each new delinquency or abuse and neglect case that is filed. Others, including police, school officials, judges, court referees, or neighbors, may contact this clerk and suggest that a family needs special handling, thus prompting a search. A search is no easy task as the clerk must look for the names of all members of a family, and the computer databases are not preprogrammed for family tracking. The procedure is imperfect and depends on the clerk's skills and memory acuteness, making the search more an art than a science.

Clerks Look for Particular Kinds of Cases

When searching for family cases, the clerk looks for active or recent court stalking orders, misdemeanor or felony cases, family abuse restraining orders, or active divorce cases. When there is a criteria-based "hit," the clerk pulls and assembles all prior and concurrent family case files, prepares a synopsis of the family's record, "bundles" (Oregon term) these materials, and presents them to a judge. The judge is likely to be the one who has had the most contact with family members to date or the one with the fewest number of family court-designated cases. With few exceptions, the judge agrees with the designation and accepts the case. The family will then remain a judge's family court case even if the family refuses to lift its confidentiality privilege or if the screening team does not perceive a need to invoke a treatment team.

The clerk's involvement with an active family court case continues. Each day she searches for any new matter that involves a family member in all bundled family court cases. She reviews the daily printout of all new and continuing county cases, as well as the jail list. When she finds a new hit, she assigns the new matter to the present family court judge.[2]

Active agency involvement is essential to success. The judge handles all legal matters—pretrial, plea, adjudication, disposition or sentence, and review hearings for each case involving a family member. The judge reviews reports and presentations by the community justice (corrections) agency, children's services, mental health services, and other agencies concerning what the family must or needs to do and what community human services are needed and doing. These are user-friendly courts for the agencies and they participate actively in the development of this coordinated court-community agency collaboration. The judge may even incorporate the interagency treatment plan into a judicial order. The agencies find that such orders strengthen a family's cooperation and participation with their service providers. For example, a judge's order of probation may require compliance with the child protection agency's service plan, such as attending anger management or parenting classes, entering drug or alcohol treatment, or having no contact with the child. A victim of domestic violence, also involved with other court proceedings, may be compelled to participate in very extensive victim counseling, with the judge hoping this will enable the victim to decide not to live with this or another abuser.

JUDGES MAY CONDUCT SIMULTANEOUS PROCEEDINGS ON RELATED SUBJECT MATTER

Role of Advocates Expands

According to Chief Judge Stephen N. Tiktin, community lawyers have accepted the precepts of family court handling and bought into the notion that an adversarial perspective should be held in abeyance and that interest in winning a case should come second to an interest in longer-term solutions and assisting a family. As a result, attorneys began to collaborate more with each other, started going to family meetings at child protective services agencies, sat in on screening team and treatment team meetings, and became very constructive agents at court reviews.

Attorneys' Trust of Family Court's Purposes Leads to Interesting Blended Proceedings

Because the attorneys trust what the court is doing, judges have latitude to streamline cases. For example, one judge conducted two trials at the same time: one charged an adult with the criminal abuse of a child; the other focused on whether the child was an abused or neglected child in need of the court's protection. The first was a jury trial, using criminal rules of evidence and a beyond-reasonable-doubt standard of proof. The other was a non-jury trial, using civil rules of evidence and a preponderance-of-evidence standard of proof. Another "two for one" hearing involved a change of custody stemming from a prior divorce proceeding held in concert with a child abuse proceeding.

In the first example described above, the cases involved not only one judge but also one prosecutor, since in Oregon the same county attorney's office handles both criminal and child protection proceedings. When the jury left the courtroom for its deliberations, additional evidence was put on to complete the civil trial. And the child only had to testify once.

SYSTEM OFFERS FLEXIBILITY WITHIN THE ONE FAMILY/ONE JUDGE CONCEPT

At least one judge in Bend places limits on how far she will carry a family's proceedings. If she has heard an abuse and neglect case and followed it through the permanency planning hearing to find a prominently demonstrated parental inability to work constructively toward reunification with the child, she advises the county attorney to file a motion to terminate parental rights. She then transfers the case to another judge, as she questions whether she can be fair and impartial at the termination hearing. Nonetheless, she will schedule and hold a settlement conference with the parent. Many of these conferences result in a parent voluntarily relinquishing parental rights, thus obviating the need for a second judge to conduct the trial.

A FINAL COMMENT

The court in Bend is selective and realistic. It applies its specialized focus to a limited number of cases, letting others receive the usual handling (though, predictably, the judges will apply certain lessons from the selected cases to their handling of non-selected cases). For selected cases, there is family accountability, judicial economy, compatible orders, and frequently improved outcomes. The role of the advocate is critical to court accomplishments. Agency collaboration with the court and other agencies is pivotal. Judicial leadership with interagency coordination is quite unique, requires significant adjustment both by the court and the agencies, and should become less unique as approaches like this are adopted and adapted in other courts.

Author's Note:

Ernie Mazorol, Circuit Court Administrator in Bend, submitted the following update to this chapter.

Only two things have changed:

1. Each of the four judges now has roughly 50 families and we pick up about two new families per week.

2. When a family is accepted into family court, we now set a short orientation meeting without the assigned judge present. Family members and counsel must attend the orientation. Other parties are notified (district attorney, attorney general, etc.) and may attend if they desire. The orientation is in a courtroom and the court advocate discusses family court procedure, with an emphasis on coordination of services. We seek to obtain the confidentiality waiver at this session since counsel is present. This way we can get services coordinated sooner if the family qualifies. We also schedule the first appearance date before the parties leave. We started the orientation last fall and have not had any problems.

Just a few other comments:

- We acquired a new circuit court judge (effective July 1, 2003). We are not sure what type of cases the new judge will be assigned but the four circuit court judges have reaffirmed their desire to maintain, at least for themselves, the one family/one judge/one treatment plan model.

- We had planned to start a family drug court with existing family members, among the four circuit court judges. I acquired a new position, similar to the court advocate, to coordinate services, participate in agency staffings, and conduct home visits. Unfortunately, the budget is in a downward cycle in Oregon. We have an $846 million shortfall, and it's expected to grow this summer. I've cut roughly 6.55% and cannot start this new program until things change. In Oregon, I don't expect to see a turnaround until 2004 or 2005. On the bright side, the staff and judges in the existing family court are intact, functioning well, and still highly committed.

Endnotes

[1] Titkin, S.N. & Mazorol, E.J. III (1997). Family court coordination of human services, Deschutes County, Oregon. *Family and Conciliation Courts Review*, *35*, 342-350.

[2] Flango, C.R., Flango, V.E. & Rubin, H.T. (1999). *How are courts coordinating family cases?* Williamsburg, VA: National Center for State Courts.

Part 7

Juvenile Justice in Other Worlds

The primary focus of this book is juvenile justice in U.S. state jurisdictions. However, trends and developments in other jurisdictions are of interest to juvenile justice professionals. This Part opens a window on juvenile justice as practiced in American tribal courts and in other nations.

JUVENILE JUSTICE IN INDIAN COUNTRY

Young people are a fast growing population in many tribal settings. There are reports of gang activities and more serious offenses occurring on reservations.[1] But very limited tribal resources are allocated to and available for juvenile rehabilitative purposes. Tribal court systems overall provide limited judicial time for juvenile delinquency concerns. Some juveniles are held in terrible tribal jail facilities; others are detained in grossly inadequate tribal juvenile facilities. There may be probation officers, who in turn may split their time between juvenile and adult offenders. More intensive interventions are essentially absent. There is also need for an improved law enforcement capability.

There are now a growing number of tribal juvenile drug courts where the focus is more on alcohol use, banned on many reservations, than on illegal substance use. There is access to a few federal residential alcohol/drug treatment facilities. Recent federal delinquency prevention and intervention grants have been directed to a comparatively small though increasing number of tribes. The grants fund programs that aim to innovate sentencing circles to handle school problems, reduce school dropout rates, delay the onset of alcohol or drug use, enable certain mental health services or provide family counseling, increase diversion and probation services or initiate home detention, operate a teen court, expand community service and restitution programs, foster mentoring, or develop vocational skills and employment opportunities, among other projects. Program efforts are to be implemented within the context of tribal traditions, customs, and values.

Limitations on the Exercise of Tribal Court Jurisdiction

Tribal court handling of juvenile offenders is limited to misdemeanor offenses and punishments; a congressional enactment in 1885 removed tribal court jurisdiction over felony offenses and allocated these to the federal courts. A 1953 Congressional Act, Public Law 280, in turn, directed concurrent jurisdiction, state or tribal, for offenses that occurred in Indian Country in six states (Alaska, California, Minnesota, Nebraska,

Oregon, and Wisconsin), though this action abrogated tribal-federal treaty provisions.[2] Ten additional state governments, largely in western United States, have assumed at least some jurisdiction on tribal lands since the enactment.

Tribal governments in Public Law 280 states often assumed they need not or should not substitute their own court actions because state juvenile courts were asserting jurisdiction over tribal youth apprehended on reservation lands. But a recent example by the Bad River Tribe of Lake Superior Chippewa Indians in Wisconsin reverses this direction; they have developed a tribal juvenile code and initiated diversion and formal processing of the tribe's juveniles, all with the support of the local sheriff, who clearly preferred tribal handling of these matters. The tribe is now able to insert traditional and cultural means of bringing about healing and harmony in its offending youth, while strengthening family structures its way.[3]

Federal courts often lack interest in handling many lesser felony offenses allegedly committed by tribal juveniles or adults. The federal system frequently declines to proceed, but may delay notification to the tribe if, indeed, it provides notification at all. Tribal courts may proceed on a misdemeanor offense that may be related to the felony. This does not always happen, and more than a few felony offenders are not proceeded against in either forum. What is needed is informed communication and written agreements between tribal and federal officials that can improve collaboration. Also needed are expanded tribal resources, so that the federal system may knowingly decline its jurisdiction when a tribal court can and will access such resources as a residential program that provides both custody and treatment, and also has the advantage of being on or close to the reservation.

One annual report on juveniles, not exclusively Native American juveniles, who had been referred to the federal criminal justice system, reported that 468 youth had been referred but that federal prosecutors had rejected taking further action on 229 (49%) juveniles. Federal judicial officers adjudicated 122 of those petitioned, and certain others were referred for prosecution as adults. All together, 45 juveniles were ordered confined in delinquency facilities, 27 of them Native American. On confinement, the Federal Bureau of Prisons tends to contract with state juvenile correctional systems for residential beds and programs.[4]

Native American juveniles who live on reservations but offend off reservation are handled by state juvenile court systems. "Urban Indians" who live off-reservation and offend are handled, as well, by state juvenile court systems.

Tribal courts do hear status offenses, as well as child abuse, neglect, and dependency cases.

Navajo Nation juvenile court data for the 12-month period that ended September 30, 2001, list 288 public intoxication counts, another 130 disorderly conduct counts (some, likely, related to the alcohol counts), 137 charges of marijuana, 201 of assault/battery, and 120 criminal damage charges among the 1,773 delinquency charges brought to court that year. Navajo Nation courts also handled 106 petitions of beyond parental control, 94 for truancy, and 252 curfew violations. The Nation's courts reviewed 543 juvenile traffic citations, as well. These data, like those of some contemporary U.S. courts, count all the charges that police present, although counting juveniles and their one most serious charge is the better measure.

Juvenile incident reports filed with the court of the Yakama Nation, Washington State, commonly list less serious delinquent offenses such as disturbing the peace, vandalism, malicious mischief, assaults, and thefts, Liquor violations are listed, along with status offenses such as runaway.

Full Faith and Credit or Comity

An important concern for tribal courts, as they strive for greater acceptance in the family of courts, is the reluctance of the state judicial and executive system to accept and grant full faith and credit or comity to tribal court orders. The procedure should be the same as one state's recognition of another state's judgments. The U.S. Constitution directs in Article IV, Section 1, that "full faith and credit shall be given in each State to the public Acts, Records, and Judicial Proceedings of every other State." Thus, a state court decision in Alabama shall be given full faith and credit if one litigant brings action against the other litigant following the latter's relocation to Georgia. The case does not need to be re-litigated.

States such as Arizona, Michigan, Washington, and Wisconsin have authorized full faith and credit or comity with tribal court decrees when, for example, a tribal court files official notice with the state court office that it will, in turn, recognize state court orders.

Chapter 11 of this book describes the New Mexico Children's Code of 1993 and the work of the New Mexico Council on Crime and Delinquency in organizing drafting groups and support for this legislation. The law had provisions that are progressive as to juvenile court system authority and other provisions that furthered Native American youths' cultural ties when handled by a state court or state institution. The New Mexico Council took on another legislative effort in facilitating a 1999 full faith and credit statute in that state.

Accordingly, an off-reservation-dwelling Native American youth who offends on-reservation and is placed on probation by a tribal court is to have the decree accepted by the state court judge without any need to adjudicate a state court petition. Further, "An Indian child residing on or off a reservation, as a citizen of this state, shall have the same right to services that are available to other children of the state pursuant to Intergovernmental Agreements." [5] A tribal court order, then, that directs access to a state juvenile facility or resource, shall be approved once there is intergovernmental agreement to the nature and extent of tribal, state, and federal funding that shall be applied. The 19 pueblos and three tribes within New Mexico are to be able to access services that are available to non-Indian delinquent youth once these agreements are accomplished. Yet their accomplishment will require time and commitment; none have been signed onto during the three years that followed enactment. As James W. Zion, former Solicitor to the Navajo Nation Supreme Court noted to me in regard to the New Mexico statute, "It's all very nice to have progressive-looking legislation, but without implementation, it still doesn't work. Navajo Nation judges are still left to do with what they've got, and that's not much."

Commentary

The several worlds of Indian youth severely complicate their maturation. The poverty that surrounds so many contributes to their violations of standards set by their elders. Their prolonged isolation from the opportunities of mainstream America adds to their depressions and substance abuse. Tribal sovereignty over their own affairs, pledged by earlier U.S. governments, has been continuously abridged, and provision after provision of treaty promises have been broken. Uncle Sam has been a bad uncle.

However, there are notable accomplishments by large, indeed very large, numbers of Native Americans—vastly more than is recognized by the wider community. And the institutions and organizations of individual tribes, intertribal entities, and Native American associations are often remarkable.

The Native American community is now both reservation- and urban-based. More reservation youth should be retained in or linked back into a tribal court system granted greater powers. Also, the model of the U.S. Indian Child Welfare Act,[6] which mandates state juvenile court connections to tribal governments when an abused or neglected child with tribal roots enters a state juvenile court, could profitably be extended to young urban Indians charged with state delinquency offenses. Many could benefit from a transfer to the jurisdiction of their tribal court. At the least, they are in need of culturally sensitive and enriched handling when they are a part of a state juvenile justice system.

Native Americans have painfully learned not to expect much from federal and state governments. Regretfully we should not expect, either, that small federal government initiatives, however touted, would do much to equalize opportunity or justice for Native Americans.

Juvenile Justice in the United Kingdom

Juvenile justice across Great Britain is far more uniform than is evident, state-by-state, across the United States. Laws in the United Kingdom are approved by a national parliament, not by various state legislatures. All U.K. juvenile courts are known as youth courts, while juvenile courts in the U.S. are known by different names in different states. There is one national jurisdictional age, 10 through 17 years, though "grave" crimes committed by juveniles, as defined in national law, are handled by "crown courts." There is a national probation service.

Another major difference with the U.S. is that in the U.K. volunteer citizen magistrates serve as youth court judges, a historic practice that is not without its contemporary critics. Law-trained clerks provide counsel to magistrates as legal and procedural issues arise.

The legal rights movement in the U.S., which officially began in 1967, significantly influenced juvenile justice in the U.K. Law and lawyers were then built into its proceedings. There was strong interest in the "4 Ds" of that progressive American era—diversion, decriminalization, due process, and deinstitutionalization. The U.K. parliament enacted the Children and Young Persons Act of 1969, which went so far as to eliminate delinquency proceedings for offenders under age 14, instead allowing these cases to proceed only under "care and protection," the child neglect and dependency label, and a provision borrowed from European nations rather than the U.S. Delinquency proceedings could occur only with 14- to 17-year-old offenders, and as a prerequisite a mandated police-social services conference had first to consider whether or not court proceedings were necessary. Significant curbs and duration of stay limitations were placed on institutionalization. However, this interesting model became more paper than practice, as "ideological differences between the political parties caused key sections of the Act to remain unimplemented.[7]

More recently, as a small number of extremely violent crimes committed by young persons received enormous media attention, U.K. political candidates and office holders made juvenile justice a campaign issue, not unlike the American experience. Beginning with the Criminal Justice Act of 1991, harder-line enactments came into law and practice. The age of criminal responsibility, i.e., when one might be treated as an adult, was dropped to 10. Criminal sanctions for minors were expanded. Juvenile system custodial sentences were authorized for longer periods and for younger children.

However, there are other similarities to the U.S. experience along a more positive vein. Youth offender panels, somewhat akin to our neighborhood accountability boards, are in place to hear juveniles who do not require a "custodial sentence." The lay magistrates make these referrals following entry of a guilty plea. Panel members preferably include a magistrate, a police officer, a member of a "youth offender team," and community panelists who have interest in or expertise with young people. Victims are encouraged to attend, and to participate in a victim-offender meeting, as well.

Also, the Crime and Disorder Act of 1998 expanded juvenile justice system use of "reparations," or what we know as restitution.

> By allowing the offender to undertake some form of practical reparation activity which will benefit the victim (if the victim so wishes it), it is hoped that the victim will gain a greater insight into the reasons for the offence, and will therefore be able more easily to come to terms with the offence, and put it behind them. Reparation to the victim will also help the offender to realize the distress and inconvenience that his or her actions have caused, accept responsibility for those actions, and have the opportunity to make some amends either directly to the victim, or to the community as a whole. [Act section 2.3]

There is a reference to "3 Rs"—restoration, responsibility, and reintegration. The professional literature speaks of community service, cognitive training, electronic monitoring, concerns regarding disproportionate minority confinement, case processing delays, pilot projects, and appellate court reviews of trial court decisions. There is a new thrust on offense prevention. There is considerable research and evaluation of intervention effectiveness.

It is *dé jà vu* when the chair of the national magistrates committee reports that, "Research has shown that the public has little confidence in the Youth Court. I think that is largely because they know little of what we do." [8] The magistrates recommended:

- Improved efforts to engage the defendant with early procedural explanations and at sentencing;

- Hearings, if practicable, with all participants on the same or almost the same plane or level as the magistrates;

- Family members able to sit with the juvenile and the attorney;

- Victims to have the opportunity to attend hearings; information as to the outcome of proceedings to be provided victims;

- The general public may be allowed to attend;

- With magistrate approval, there may be relinquishment of confidentiality of a persistent or serious juvenile's name, address, and photos. [9]

JUVENILE JUSTICE IN NEW ZEALAND

New Zealand originated family group conferencing, used with delinquency matters and cases that concern abused, neglected, and dependent children. This enlightened form of case handling has crossed the ocean to the U.S., though it is used far less frequently here with delinquency matters than the latter type of case.

Family group conferencing was placed into New Zealand law in 1989. A delinquency charge, other than murder and manslaughter or when an offense is denied, must first go to a conference. Many delinquency charges go no further. Conference outcomes may be reviewed by the youth court and a different outcome pronounced. A youth court judge, also, will refer to conference following a trial when a youth has pleaded not guilty but the charge is proven. A youth court judge may refer a youth to an adult court for sentence when charged with a serious offense.

But only about 20% of juveniles even go so far as to a conference. Police are directed to release juvenile offenders with a street warning whenever possible. When not possible, a specialized police Youth Aid Section makes further investigation and, in meetings with offenders and their parents, may divert the case by requiring an apology to a victim, may impose an additional sanction such as community service, or may refer the offender to a conference.

New Zealand conferencing actually was initiated well before 1989; the dominant indigenous Maori tribe of this country had long invoked a broad band of people to consider offenders, their offenses, and their needs. The family, extended family, and community, including the victim and victim support people, would meet to take up the unlawful activity or transgression and work toward a consensus on what should be done to repair the harm and the offender. Different participants would take on different tasks or assignments in working toward resolution of the problem behavior.

Today's official replication invites to a conference professional agency personnel who may be working with the family or juveniles, any lawyer or advocate working with the youth, and a police officer who serves as the "prosecutor." The conference manager is an employee of the department of social welfare. The conference process involves a police officer's narration of the offense, the victim or a spokesperson for the victim describing the impact of the offense, the youth's discussion of the offense and reasons for offending and for prior offending, and preliminary group consideration of options for making good the damage. The family then holds its own private meeting to discuss what plans and recommendations it will propose and steps that should be taken to prevent reoffending. Plans often include an apology, restitution, community service, counseling, and participation in a designated program. A final discussion adopts a plan for submission to the court. One study found that two-thirds of conferences take more than an hour and 10% take more than two hours. There has been strong victim and juvenile/family approval of conferencing.[10]

However, a recent horrific murder by a New Zealand juvenile is prompting official review of how young people, or at least certain young people, are being handled by justice system procedures. Meanwhile, increasing numbers of youth, some as young as 11 or 12, are being charged with money-oriented crimes inspired by their alcohol and drug use.

JUVENILE JUSTICE IN BRAZIL

One massive concern in Brazil is the presence of at least several million—in one report, 7 million—homeless children and youth who live on the streets, particularly in the metropolitan areas of Rio de Janeiro and São Paolo. Reportedly they beg from the public, steal from tourists, inhale glue, and dig into garbage cans for food. Some, or many, abuse drugs and experience early sex, sometimes in exchange for money. A disproportionate number, as compared to the general youth population, are HIV-positive.

Human Rights Watch has documented numerous homicides of these children that are commonly attributed to police officers, on or off duty, or to adults acting with the acquiescence or collusion of police officers. The most frequent victims are reported to be black or dark-skinned adolescent boys. Those who commit the killings are not brought to justice.[11]

Numerous reports document tortures, severe physical abuse, and inhumane conditions at police stations, in various juvenile detention facilities, and in prisons where juveniles may be held and may even share cells with adult offenders. Amnesty International reported in late 2001 that at least 1,000 beatings by prison guards had occurred during the preceding year in the nation's juvenile detention system, again with no charges brought under the nation's anti-torture laws.[12]

Amnesty International in 2000 described a São Paolo detention facility that housed 1,648 juvenile offenders and suspected offenders in an overall complex designed for 364 persons. In one unit 300 boys, held in a space designed for 62 youths, had access to just eight showers and six toilets, and were sleeping on "filthy mattresses on concrete floors." The majority had no access to education, exercise, or work. Boys rioted in August 1999, 69 of them being injured by a police riot squad. Two months later fellow inmates killed four boys. Sexual abuse of younger youth takes place.[13]

Another Amnesty International study[14] found that children who are picked up and questioned by police are frequently beaten, their legal rights often ignored, and their parents not informed of their whereabouts. They may be held longer than the 24 hours in police custody that the law allows, are sometimes held in cells with adults, may be held for 45 days without a juvenile court hearing, and may have been arrested for activities that are not against the law. Human Rights Watch has documented[15] a systemic failure to guarantee legal representation and fair hearings. Custodial sentences entered by judges, to be used only as a last resort, are "overused" by some courts and often place juveniles in facilities seen as filthy and degrading where there are very low staffing levels and, as with pretrial facilities, inadequate medical care.

Brazilian children's rights and human rights organizations have entered similar findings and complaints: of 950 adolescents held in units that are in fact prisons; of 700 residents subjected to torture or physical aggression at several detention facilities, and of transfers to adult prisons without regard to age or seriousness of offense criteria. These reports refer to beatings, and what is described as inhuman and degrading treatment.[16]

Advocacy organizations point to Brazil's enactment of a Children and Adolescents' Statute that establishes fundamental rights for those apprehended, including provisions that detention is to be used only as a last resort and only for the shortest period of time. These organizations complain that the failure to apply statutory provisions is the root problem of the detention center crises. Injunctions were issued by several lower courts that declared these facilities in violation of Brazilian law and ordered their closure. The São Paolo Supreme Court reversed these injunctions.[17]

Public prosecutors as well as police officials investigate reports of physical abuse and torture of detainees. Yet these practices continue.

Brazilian non-governmental organizations and interested international human rights organizations regularly point Brazilian governmental entities to the standards set forth in the Convention on the Rights of the Child, adopted by the United Nations General Assembly in 1989, and ratified by Brazil and every country in the world except the United States and Somalia. They highlight the UN Rules and Guidelines on Juvenile Justice. They ask that the juvenile justice resolutions of the UN Commission on Human Rights be implemented. These organizations continue their monitoring and advocacy efforts but are finding little progress in protecting the rights, the bodies, the minds, and the futures of so many young people.[18]

JUVENILE JUSTICE IN JAPAN

The family court of Japan had borrowed the *parens patriae* orientation of American juvenile courts when it was founded in 1949. It maintained this approach in rather exemplary fashion until April 1, 2001, when statutory changes curbed its rehabilitative license and transferred greater authority to criminal courts in the handling of serious or violent juvenile offenders.

These changes came after this country with a normally low juvenile crime rate had been rocked by a rash of horrific and highly publicized homicides committed by juveniles during 2000. Most notable was the crime by a 14-year-old who first killed and then cut off the head of an 11-year-old, leaving the head outside the school gate. The 14-year-old also had killed another school child, and had left a note to the police that threatened other killings. Elsewhere in the country a 15-year-old schoolboy stabbed three members of a neighboring family to death, a 17-year-old beat his mother to death with a baseball bat, and another 17-year-old hijacked a bus, held its 26 passengers hostage for six hours, and meanwhile stabbed a woman passenger to death. Other juvenile homicides also occurred.[19]

The Japanese family court has had initial jurisdiction over youths who committed offenses up to the day of their 20th birthdays. This age maximum has not been reduced. What was changed in 2001 was the age of criminal responsibility. Previously, family courts had had exclusive jurisdiction over every juvenile offender under age 16. Accordingly, for example, juvenile murderers under age 16 had to be handled exclusively in family court. That is now changed. The court's exclusive authority is now limited to those under age 14. Further, victims of juvenile crime now are entitled to learn of juveniles' dispositions and to make statements to the court that can influence a judicial disposition. By law, victims are no longer to be left in the dark.[20]

The long-term broad acceptance of a rehabilitative premise by the Japanese people now appears to have been shaken. Numerous news reports had relayed accounts of institutionalizations of under one year for juveniles who had committed homicide. The family court's punitive authority was deemed too modest for violent juveniles. It can continue to rely on psychological assessments of wrongdoing, on humanistic counseling, and on educational and vocational instruction in training schools for nonviolent juvenile offenders. Still, the Japanese family court has strong advocates who believe juvenile facilities, not prisons, offer the best hope for a violent juvenile offender's future.[21] Year 2001 amendments were the first changes made to the initial law that took effect in 1949.

Policy makers had long seen the family court as a central site for resolving family-related problems and had recognized that concerns such as delinquent acts, if not related to family problems, needed to involve the family in working toward resolution. The court's jurisdiction encompasses child abuse, neglect, and dependency, as well as status offenders, who are known as "pre-delinquent juveniles." It holds jurisdiction over juvenile traffic offenses and divorce and divorce-related matters, including child custody and child support. Prosecutors are not allowed into this court. They will enter into the criminal investigation of an older juvenile offender when a family court judge directs initiation of criminal proceedings.

Defense attorneys, as such, are not recognized here either. The law has not wanted adversarial proceedings; the family court has not believed controversy improves a child's social development. The court does provide a representative for the juvenile who is to advise the court on the most promising treatment for a youth. The court relies frequently on an elaborate multi-disciplinary evaluation of a juvenile that uses medical, psychological, educational, and other assessments.[22]

Larceny has been the most common juvenile crime in Japan, followed by embezzlement and "bodily injury." Dismissal following hearing is the most common disposition. An order of probation is the second most frequent action taken. Commitment to a juvenile training school is the next most frequent disposition. Training schools are known for their rather rigorous schedules of classwork, exercise, group discussions, counseling, and reflective meditation. Though a sanction, it is to be perceived more as a rehabilitation opportunity.

The Japanese society and culture have undergone very significant change since 1949. Single parent families are more common. There are some violent gangs, as well as other congregations of youth who defy traditional behaviors. The Japanese mafia is long established and among its illegal activities brokers various illegal drugs to juveniles and adults. A government report to the United Nations states that far more juveniles are arrested for the abuse of paint thinner than marijuana or other substances. There is juvenile prostitution. And more juvenile violent crime has been reported.[23]

JUVENILE JUSTICE IN KENYA

Kenya's government seeks to do the right thing legislatively, but falls terribly short on suitable implementation of its promises and standards. Kenya enacted a Children's Bill that took effect March 1, 2002, which conforms to the principles enunciated in the U.N. Convention on the Rights of the Child, and other progressive international documents. It has appointed 43 magistrates to hear children's matters, and created a family division of its High Court to centralize judicial consideration of child-related and divorce-related jurisdictions. The Children's Act provides that all children have a right to a free education, but Kenya is unable to meet this measure.[24]

Kenya and its citizenry must cope with a brutal HIV/AIDS problem. Reportedly, HIV/AIDS has orphaned perhaps a million children, and left many others in deep poverty and unable to turn to their extended families who have also suffered deaths and crippling illness. Many children have left school to seek employment. Many have become street children, who do not attend school or otherwise prepare educationally to obtain vocational skills.

The number of street children nationwide has been estimated at 250,000, with 30% of them congregating in Nairobi, the nation's capital and a significant economic and cultural center. In turn, street children comprise an estimated 80% of juveniles who are brought to juvenile courts. Many are charged with law violations such as theft, drug trafficking, assault, trespass, or property damage. Child prostitution is reported to be a significant problem.[25]

Numerous Kenyan non-governmental organizations, churches, and child advocacy groups, work to improve the welfare of the nation's people and its children. Numerous international organizations and governmental programs of other nations, such as the Netherlands and Canada, are at work to assist with these efforts.

Watchdog groups such as Human Rights Watch and Amnesty International, point out shortcomings in the care of young people. They have reported police brutalities against street children; children locked in police cells for weeks without going to court; children held in adult jails sleeping on bare floors "with vermin-infested blankets in rooms pervaded by the stench of overflowing toilets"; children commingled with adults in adult jails; a juvenile "remand" home designed for 80 children but housing 360 children, which lacked running water and was without programs; street children committed for years to juvenile correctional institutions though found "in need of protection or discipline" in summary proceedings and without legal representation.[26]

Though the juvenile code speaks to rehabilitation and education, not to punishment, and avoids terms like conviction and sentence, it is the administration of the law, the resource shortcomings, and the numerical overflows that weaken the law's good intentions. Many children brought to court under the "in need of protection or discipline" label, a category that encompasses neglected children as well as status offenders, end up in facilities that serve delinquent youth.

Prosecutions are performed by police officers, a practice I observed in Massachusetts 30 years ago and one that occurred in other U.S. states, as well, in our early juvenile court history. Defense representation is rare.

Overall, serious crime occurs infrequently. Offenses are seen as related to poverty. Kenyans are seen as tolerant toward children.[27] The juvenile justice system wants to do well by its children. But as with perhaps all nations, Kenya's youth do not always conform to positive norms of behavior, rehabilitative resources are insufficient or below desirable standards, and the "system" may do as much harm as good.

THE CHAPTERS THAT FOLLOW

Chapter 42 describes my findings from visits to tribal juvenile courts in New Mexico. Approaches to the handling of young offenders and to youth development in Indian Country are reported, and several suggestions are made for the transfer of tribal methods to state juvenile justice systems. Chapter 43 discusses a later visitation to Navajo tribal courts, expanding on Peacemaking, the Navajo's traditional way of addressing and resolving disputes. Finally, Chapter 44 examines the context of a first juvenile court unveiling in the nation of El Salvador. Here, as in countries like Brazil and undoubtedly others, juveniles are crammed into detention facilities, adjudications follow only after prolonged waits, and there is far too little assistance provided before or at the end of the tunnel.

Endnotes

[1] Conway, M. K. (1998). *Gangs on Indian reservations.* Washington, DC: Federal Bureau of Investigation.

[2] Goldberg, C. (1999). Public Law 280 and the problem of "lawlessness" in California Indian Country. In T. R. Johnson (Ed.), *Contemporary native American political issues* (197-225). Walnut Creek, CA: Altamire Press.

[3] National Tribal Justice Resource Center (2001, Summer): *BJA grantee focus: Bad River Tribe of Lake Superior Chippewa Indians.* Boulder, CO: National Tribal Justice Resource Center, *11*(1), 8-9.

[4] Scalia, J. (1997). *Juvenile delinquents in the federal criminal justice system.* Washington, DC: Bureau of Justice Statistics, U.S. Department of Justice.

[5] NM Stat Ann §32A-1-8 (E).

[6] Polashuk, S. S. (1996). Expanding tribal court jurisdiction over native American juvenile delinquents. *Southern California Law Review, 69,* 1191-1231.

[7] Morris, A., Giller, H., Szwed, E. & Geach, H. (1980). *Justice for children.* London: MacMillan, p. 16.

[8] Kilpatrick, A. (2001). *The Youth Court 2001.* London: Home Office, Lord Chancellor's Department. at p. 2.

[9] Lord Chancellor's Department. (2001). *The Youth Court 2001.* London: Home Office.

[10] Morris, A. & Maxwell, G. (1998). Restorative justice in New Zealand: Family group conferences as a case study. *Western Criminology Review 1*(1), [Online] 1-16; Umbreit, M. S. (2000). *Family group counseling: Implications for crime victims.* Washington, DC: US Department of Justice, Office for Victims of Crime.

[11] Human Rights Watch (1994 and 2001). *Children's rights reports on Brazil:* New York: Author.

[12] Amnesty International (2001). Prison guards responsible for at least 1,000 beatings in Brazilian juvenile facilities over past year. Washington, DC: Author.

[13] Amnesty International (2000). *Annual report, Brazil.* London: Author.

[14] Amnesty International (1999). *No one here sleeps safely: Human rights violations against juvenile detainees in Brazil.* London: Author.

[15] Human Rights Watch, note 11 supra.

[16] Justica Global (2002) *Physical abuse and torture in juvenile detention centers in São Paulo.* São Paulo: Author.

[17] Id.

[18] Rodley, R. (2001). *Report of the United Nations special rapporteur on torture in Brazil.* Geneva: United Nations.

[19] BBC World Service (2001, February 24). Japanese juvenile justice.

[20] BBC World Service (2002, January 7). Japan cracks down on youth crime.

[21] Id.; Kakuchi, S. (2000, September 15). Delinquent Japan: Government seeks harsher penalties for young criminals. Inter Press Services.

[22] Japan Criminal Policy Society (2001). *Outline of the juvenile justice system.* Author.

[23] Ministry of Foreign Affairs of Japan (1996). *Report to the United Nations on the Convention on the Rights of the Child.* Author.

[24] United Nations Human Rights System (2002). *Reports to treaty bodies—Kenya.* New York: Author.

[25] Human Rights Watch (2002). *In the shadow of death: HIV/AIDS and children's rights in Kenya.* New York: Author.

[26] Human Rights Watch (1997). *Kenya street kids*. New York: Author; Human Rights Watch (1999). *Children's rights—Kenya*. New York: Author.

[27] Skelton, A. (1999). *Juvenile justice In Kenya*. Bellville, South Africa: Article 40, Children's Rights Project of the Community Law Centre, University of the Western Cape.

Chapter 42

Visiting Native American Juvenile Justice

There is substantial interest in how Native Americans relate to this world. Their oneness with nature and its preservation has been a guidepost for contemporary environmental activists. Their ceremonies and spiritual qualities continue to find adaptation and replication by various groups that are searching for improved meaning for their lives, and even by a prominent multi-state juvenile rehabilitation organization, VisionQuest.

The long-ago forceful, almost obliterative, relocation of Indians to reservations and to second- or-third class citizenship still prompts widespread empathy and anger. Now, the number of tribes entering the gaming and casino industry coupled with the capacity for economic development that goes along with this is bringing myriad visitors to Indian Country.

My role as director (and now consultant) for the Tribal Courts and State Courts: The Prevention and Resolution of Jurisdictional Disputes Project of the National Center for State Courts (1988-94), and from other Native American-related consultancy opportunities, including a Spring 1994 role in Native Rights Advocates' juvenile justice planning study with the 19 pueblos and three tribes in New Mexico, has given me certain information and insights in these matters that I would like to pass on.

OVERVIEW OF THE TRIBAL JUSTICE SYSTEM

Approximately 250 of the 545 federally recognized tribes have established trial courts. There is a significant growth of tribal or intertribal appellate courts, although there are still tribes that provide only for an appeal to an elected tribal council that has authority to overturn a judge or terminate a judge's employment. Many tribal judges are not attorneys, although more tribes are appointing lawyer-judges. Many judges serve only part-time. At some pueblos, the governor or a lieutenant governor also will serve as judge.

New Mexico pueblos (only a few exceed a population of 5,000 persons) often lack written, tribal council-approved juvenile codes. Instead, their judges look to their state juvenile code, the Navajo code,[1] the Zuni code,[2] or model codes promulgated earlier by the National Indian Justice Center or the Indian Law Center at the University of New Mexico. Often, a single probation officer serves both juvenile and adult probationers. Some pueblos do not have a probation officer.

Tribal or pueblo court jurisdiction over juveniles is narrowed by two important limitations. One is that the Major Crimes Act (enacted by the Congress in 1885) grants the U.S. prosecutor and the federal courts primary jurisdiction for felony-level offens-

This chapter originally appeared in Community Corrections Report, *Vol. 1, No. 7, September/October 1994.*

es committed by juveniles or adults in Indian Country.[3] The second concerns the many tribal/pueblo juveniles who either attend senior high or middle school off-reservation or who are "urban Indians" who live in town. If these youth are apprehended in town, they are processed by state juvenile courts. Accordingly, Indian courts largely handle juvenile misdemeanor and status offenses that take place on tribal lands.

Tribal court data concerning juvenile offenses/offenders is often limited. Nevertheless, the data tend to show that the most frequent offenses referred to these courts are assault or assault and battery; theft; damage to property; alcohol intoxication, use, or possession; curfew violation; truancy; and driving either without a license or carelessly. The presence of gangs (more often wannabes) is mentioned by quite a few pueblos, particularly those near Albuquerque.

DETENTION PROCEDURES FOR INDIAN JUVENILES

At the front end of the system are the tribal police, who tend to return offending juveniles to their parent(s) or extended family if they can be located. Otherwise, these juveniles are retained in a "holding cell," without sight and sound separation from adult prisoners, in the reservation jail pending a family member's arrival. Juveniles may be held overnight and longer in regular jail cells.

At present, there is only one Native American-operated juveniles-only detention center in New Mexico. It is a 14-bed regional Navajo facility. The facility serves Navajo youth from New Mexico and from tribal lands nearby in Arizona, and includes juveniles who serve time there as a disposition. It was clear to me, on a visit to the facility in May 1994 that this facility was absolutely incapable of passing any accreditation examination.

Some pueblo governments purchase pretrial or post-dispositional space in local government juvenile detention centers, such as one now operated by the Corrections Corporation of America in Santa Fe County. The $90-$100 per day charge for care mitigates its use, however. Several pueblos have approached the U.S. Bureau of Indian Affairs (BIA), which controls funds that might be used for jails/detention centers, to request money to build a new jail that could separately house juveniles. More hope may be found in a new state statute that has begun to send funds to various regions of the state for the development of regional service plans for juvenile detention and its alternatives, as well as institutional alternatives. The statute includes tribal/pueblo participation.

EXAMPLES OF HOW NATIVE AMERICAN COMMUNITIES HANDLE JUVENILE MATTERS

The Isleta Pueblo

The chief judge of Isleta Pueblo (population 3,948) will meet at night in chambers with the parents and child, sometimes for as long as four hours, talking on-and-off in the native language. The essence of the discussion is that the parents should steep their youth in the traditional culture (e.g., teach their child their unwritten language), strengthen Indian identity (e.g., ceremonial dancing, participate with elders in the *kiva*, and learn of customs), and discourage participation in U.S.-style experiences. This approach illustrates the historic, informal, traditional judicial system model. Some Isleta examples follow:

- Community service is used, supervised by the probation officer.

- A girl was sanctioned by being placed under house arrest. She could not use the telephone, but she could watch television. Police, the probation officer, and a tribal social worker monitored her presence at home.

- An assistant lawyer-judge, a Native American woman who was a member of another pueblo, sentenced a boy to five days in jail. The boy was taken home each morning for a shower and breakfast, then returned to jail until the next morning. Other meals were sent in by the family or obtained from the senior center.

Navajo Peacemaker Courts

Traditional methods are used to "promote peace and harmony" and "integrate the Navajo desire to bring to peace all matters of dispute." The best-known approach to traditional informal resolution is the peacemaker court, which may be conducted at a home, a chapter house, or a courtroom.

Meeting and talking with tribal elders is a time-honored tradition, especially regarding domestic and property disputes and misbehaving children. In 1991, federal funding expanded this approach by allotting funds for the specific purpose of seeking delinquency/status offense referrals.

With this program, a peacemaker court may be invoked prior to any juvenile justice system involvement, e.g., by parents concerned about their child's behavior. Alternatively, it may be invoked by (1) law enforcement or a prosecutor after an alleged offense and before a petition, (2) officials post-petition but prior to adjudication, or (3) the judge as a requirement of the formal court disposition.

Peacemakers in this context receive 16 hours of training followed by observation of an established peacemaker in action, and then are sworn in by a judge. (It is interesting to note that not all peacemakers are elders; there is a 24-year-old peacemaker.) Several staff members do referral screening, coordinate services provided by agencies, and offer counseling if this is preferred to external services.

The usual three-meeting sequence observes the following pattern:

1. *First Meeting.* In addition to the peacemaker, the first meeting may include the youth, extended family, peers, victim, a medicine man, and representatives from social service agencies. The discussion focuses on (a) how the youth, parents, and agencies can help resolve issues and concerns, and (b) designing a plan of action. Restitution and strengthened communication are emphasized. Healing is to begin.

2. *Second Meeting.* This is held about three months later and includes all phase-one participants. The meeting emphasizes the extent to which objectives set out in the plan are being met, and proposes other directions that might be useful.

3. *Third Meeting.* Several months later an evaluation/exit conference is held. Again, all participants are to be present.

For more on Peacemaking, see Chapter 43.

Other Pueblo and Tribal Approaches

Avoidance of the courts occurs elsewhere in Indian Country. A number of pueblos use historic routes to handle child and domestic concerns. For example, it is customary for the parties to meet with family or clan elders who "stood up" for the parents at their marriage, or with the adults who "sponsored" a child at birth. Following this (or in place of it), mediation can be requested of a "sheriff," who has been designated by a tribal government to assist families. Other traditional measures of working with young people, now in use or under active consideration, are of interest:

- In 1993, juveniles and elders reconstructed an ancestral ceremonial house at the Jemez Pueblo. The elders discussed customs and traditions while working with the youths. Adobe bricks were made from mud and straw, rocks were obtained from the hills, no modern tools were used, and the pueblo archaeologist provided guidance.

- An alternative school at the Gila River Indian Community, near Phoenix, uses a farm/garden project as an important component of vocational training. Vegetables, fruits, and flowers are grown and marketed at roadside stands and through other channels. Also, parents and elders come to the school to share their knowledge, teach the language and the history of the community, and teach flute making and other crafts. The program yields funds that enable restitution payback.

- A Mescalero Apache (Southern New Mexico) scheme combines the 4-H activity of raising horses with juvenile/adult planning to participate in three annual rodeos. One of the program's goals is restoring traditional Native American youths' horsemanship skills.

- A Navajo project takes girls to meet with the Ramah, New Mexico, Navajo Weavers Association, a cooperative of traditional women elders, to hear presentations on Navajo women's holistic nurturing practices and become familiar with weaving methods.

- Tesuque Pueblo youth development programs have different activities. One program involves planting pumpkins and then selling them through farmers' markets to earn money. A second project asks juveniles to draw a map of the reservation, locate and write in the names of historic sites in both the native language and English, and then walk to the sites. Learning the pueblo's history from elders and youth workers is another aspect of the program. Also, youth participate with others in the monthly pueblo cleanup.

- The community service program at the Zuni Pueblo has offending juveniles chopping wood for the elderly, helping to construct a traditional oven, assisting with meals at the senior center, cleaning up schools, and performing clerical work at community agencies. There is also a First Offenders Program that provides educational instruction related to what behaviors are legal and illegal, informs about substance abuse, and cultivates cultural identification. Two older juveniles were banished from the reservation—a traditional and severe sanction—until certain conditions had been met.

- The Sandia Pueblo uses an elder as a volunteer probation officer.

- The Laguna Pueblo would like to use elders or Native American university students in volunteer roles as it observed that numerous boys referred to court did not have fathers living at home.

- The Four Corners Regional Adolescent Treatment Center at Shiprock, New Mexico, provides a 90-day treatment program for chemical dependency for Native American youth 12-19 years. An estimated 85 percent of residents enter for alcohol-related problems. The program combines a Western therapeutic approach with Indian cultural activities that promote self-identity and "self harmony." These activities include sweat lodges, talking circles, "cultural wellness" conferencing, and traditional arts and crafts classes.

RESULTS OF A NEW MEXICO STUDY OF MINORITIES

A study of New Mexico's juvenile justice system came up with the following findings:

- Based on the 1990 census, Native American youth, both on- and off-reservation, represented 12% of all youth in the state.

- Native American youth represented 10% of juveniles committed to secure state facilities in FY 1991 and 6% in FY 1992.

- For calendar year 1992, Native American youth represented 8% of all youth held in state-related secure pretrial detention facilities.[4]

The data are difficult to assess without more detail, but it is likely that even if the study's authors added in the limited tribal/pueblo use of secure facilities for on-reservation offenders and the limited federal court secure holding and sanctioning of juveniles prosecuted for major crimes, Native American youth would remain somewhat under-represented in the secure holding picture.

HOW WE CAN APPLY NATIVE AMERICAN APPROACHES TO U.S. JUVENILE JUSTICE SYSTEMS

1. State juvenile/family courts could expand mediation efforts (both with diversion and following disposition) with delinquent youth, and have trained, volunteer elders from the youths' communities conduct these sessions. Victims, community agencies involved with the child or family, and even the juveniles' peers should attend. Pay back to a victim (or community) should be a part of the mediation menu.

2. Community service assignments can have intergenerational dimensions that involve youth with adults and seniors. There can be components of a shared culture as well as the communication of personal and community histories. Juveniles can assist with neighborhood cleanups and certain construction/reconstruction tasks. Cooperative youth workers can facilitate neighborhood mapping and site visitations.

3. Farm/garden work can become "paid" community service where juveniles can earn money with which to pay back their victims from the sale of their harvest. Alternatively, youth can be assigned to work side-by-side with adults or seniors in meaningful ways.

4. Work with families can be expanded. Very often, we focus on the juvenile offender and include the parents in only a limited way. The family, in the Native American culture, is seen as integral to juvenile rehabilitation.

5. We know that many minority youth are involved in the juvenile justice system. Strengthening cultural ties should become a more important ingredient of our rehabilitative intervention. The probation officer's predisposition report should outline a plan that provides for a youth's increased knowledge of his/her roots and enriched cultural embrace. The youth's self identity is vital in a larger world where conflicting values and influences abound. Implementation of the plan should be monitored by judicial or supervisory review.

Endnotes

[1] The Navajo Nation is the largest tribe in the United States. Its court system is viewed as the most sophisticated in Indian Country.

[2] The Zuni reservation is the second most populous in New Mexico.

[3] For adults, tribal court sentencing authority is limited to a one-year jail sentence and/or a $5,000 fine.

[4] Engstrom, D. & Larsen, C. (1994). *A draft report to the governor's committee on juvenile justice on minority over-representation in the juvenile justice system*. Las Vegas, NM: New Mexico Highlands University.

Chapter 43

Peacemaking: From Conflict to Harmony in the Navajo Tradition

INTRODUCTION: A LOOK AT DELINQUENCY IN THE NAVAJO NATION

Between October 1, 1998, and September 30, 1999, 1,616 delinquent charges were filed against youth in the Navajo Nation, and another 581 charges, filed during the prior year, were carried over and acted on during the same time span. Navajo courts, like some state juvenile courts, count charges that are filed rather than individual juveniles who are filed on. Assault/battery and public intoxication are the two most common charges filed, with approximately twice as many as the third most common offense, disorderly conduct, and the fourth, damage to property. Marijuana possession or use is the fifth ranking offense.

Gangs have also arrived. The Crips, Homies, Cobras, and other gang entities have shown a presence in the Nation, probably introduced by returning youths who had lived off-reservation and experienced the alienation of urban neighborhoods. Between 1995 and 1997, the problem was most acute, with drive-by shootings and organized violence. Carjackings, drug trafficking, and considerable graffiti also have been part of the gang presence.

This chapter examines how juvenile crime is addressed within the Navajo Nation and how the Nation is incorporating traditional ways like Peacemaking into its juvenile justice services. But to get there, a description of the overall legal structure within which tribal courts operate is needed. I conducted three evaluations of this tribal court system in recent years

THE NAVAJO NATION AND ITS COURTS

The Navajo Nation has the largest land base and second largest population of America's 554 Native American nations. Located in Arizona, New Mexico, and Utah, it consists of 25,000 square miles and is larger than nine U.S. states. Its population of approximately 250,000 comprises more than 11% of the total Native American population. Nearly one-half of its population is under age 21, and at least 47% of its families live below the poverty level.

This chapter originally appeared in Juvenile Justice Update, *Vol. 7, No. 1, February/March 2001.*

The Navajo Nation operates what is generally regarded as the finest of tribal court systems. It has nine trial court locations in seven judicial districts. The Supreme Court is located in the capital of the Nation, Window Rock, Arizona. There are 14 trial district court judges and three Supreme Court Justices. Just three jurists are law trained. The Navajo Nation bar examination is not limited to law school graduates, and licensed non-lawyers practice daily in these courts.

The Navajo Nation Tribal Code directs that Navajo Nation common law and tribal statutes enacted by the Navajo Nation Council are the laws of preference for court actions. Otherwise, federal law, if applicable, is used. Lastly, state law may be applied.

Source of Navajo Nation Common Law

Navajo common law consists of the traditional ways of the Navajo people, and these are regularly argued in the Nation's courts. This common law is found in books and articles on Navajo culture and in Navajo Nation Supreme Court opinions that are published in the *Navajo Reporter* and the *Indian Law Reporter*. Navajo elders and teachers of Navajo culture are other sources of the common law as are Navajo ceremonies, stories of creation, and oral history tales. Stories set out certain facts, have a conclusion, and apply a principle to the given case, thus forming a foundation for indigenous or common law. Indigenous law is built on the solidarity of reciprocal relationships.

The Navajo word for law is *beehaz'aanni*, which means something fundamental, something that is absolute and has existed from the beginning of time. Navajos say that "life comes from *beehaz'aanni*, because it is the essence of life." The foundations of life derive from the songs and prayers of its people.

Chief Justice Robert Yazzie describes the vision of the Nation's courts: "It is not to punish, boss people around, have courts seen as powerful people who tell others how to live their lives, or courts being distant and alien from the people. It is a vision of courts as partners in the process of making it possible for Navajos to live freely as Navajos."[1]

Qualities of the Common Law

The Chief Justice indicates that common law must consider norms, which are values and shared feelings about the way to do things. He comments:

> Sometimes the Navajo say, "Do things in a good way." As Indians, we know what it means to do things in a good way. Therefore, the People's shared feelings fill in that broad term of "law" to give it meaning. We must also consider moral values in the definition of law. Too often, people reject the word morality because of its religious overtones. It means something more. It is shared feelings about the right path. To complete the definition of law, the traditional Indian institutions must be included: family, clan, ceremonial bodies or societies, and even people dealing with each other.[2]

He provides an example cited in an anthropologist's writings. A man stole a woman's blanket and jewelry at a dance so he could sell them and buy wine. The woman suspected him and confronted him the next day. He immediately admitted what he had done and gave the woman enough sheep to make up for the loss. The man had replied honestly, and offered *nalyee*, or restitution. Chief Justice Yazzie comments that these two people were applying norms, values, moral principles, and emotions in addressing each other in a "good way," as this is a shared value.

Tribal Courts Reflect Cultural Values With American Overlays

The American concept of crime, imposed by the U.S. government on the Nation in 1892, along with the American judicial system's procedural and substantive values of technical rules and "win-lose" outcomes, was at variance with how Navajos perceive wrongdoing. Navajos believe in judging an action, not the actor, and in correcting future actions through reparative and restorative approaches.

In 1959, the Navajo Nation established its own court system and began enacting statutory laws. On the surface, writes James W. Zion, Solicitor to the Court of the Nation, Navajo courts and codes reflect American court procedures and statutes and look very familiar to lawyers. But Navajo judges do not appear to apply all the rules they have adopted. They apply their own cultural values since they consider the law as "plastic" and designed to meet the circumstances of the case. Zion adds that the Navajo judicial approach relies on, or seeks to rebuild, the consensual relationships that emerged from families and clans. It prefers to find agreement and resolution of a dispute.[3]

This has led to a practice and preference for using common law in Supreme Court opinions and to the institutionalization of the historic Peacemaking practice of using community leaders and elders to resolve conflicts. Zion adds that "the Navajos accept what they find useful to them and reject what they do not. The Peacemaker Court was founded upon demands that are the product of the persistence of the Navajo culture and the Navajo judges have chosen the correct method of blending Navajo common law into an American-style court system."[4]

PEACEMAKING AS PART OF THE JUDICIAL SYSTEM

Peacemaking embodies the philosophy and principles of Navajo common law and principles of restorative justice. It is used commonly in disputes between neighbors, husbands and wives, and parents and children, and with problems due to alcohol abuse, sexual misconduct, conduct that causes disunity in a family or community, and small business matters. While, at present, it is used infrequently in juvenile delinquency or child dependency/abuse cases, that is beginning to change and an expanded application to these matters is likely.

Peacemaking, organizationally, is a component of the Navajo Nation judicial system. District courts employ Peacemaker liaisons who arrange for Peacemakers to meet with individuals or families, record the findings of the meeting or meetings and, in some cases, monitor implementation of a Peacemaking agreement. But parties do not have to be involved with the court to participate in Peacemaking. Indeed, most Peacemaking cases are initiated without court involvement, as Navajos often prefer to place their cases before a community leader or elder in an informal setting; however, Peacemaking may be used as a diversion from court or as directed by a judge at a judicial disposition.

Healing and Harmony Are Goals

Peacemakers are not studiously neutral, as mediators are supposed to be, but will comment on problems using journey narratives and traditional values; the directions or resolutions they will propose are taken from traditional Navajo wisdom narratives. The emphasis is on healing relationships rather than victim reconciliation, the Western concept of evidence is rejected, the primary focus is on the feelings of the participants, and the goal is solidarity, balance, and harmony in one's relations and within oneself. Peacemaking excludes lawyers and judges, and participation by other professionals is infrequent. Further, an act of violence is perceived as an absence of love and nurturing for that person. Restitution is not seen as fully healing for either victim or offender; rather, a talking out process is also needed to enable authentic healing.

Examples of Peacemaking

A young Navajo woman sued a man for paternity. The man denied the charge, and the judge invoked Peacemaking. The families of the woman and the man participated in the proceeding. The parties stopped the "he is/I'm not" talk. Instead, they talked about what to do about "our" child. The young man had no job and could not pay child support. The woman, who lived in a rural area, relied on firewood for heat and cooking. The families agreed the young man should supply firewood to the woman until he could pay child support. By involving the child's families, the discussion turned from paternity to practical problem solving.

In another case, a man told a Peacemaker that, since his return from military service in Vietnam, he had been troubled, could not sleep, drank too much, and had problems dealing with his family. Navajos see war as an evil that can affect one's spirit. The Peacemaker knew of a Navajo ceremony, used for warriors who return from war. The ceremony cleanses them of the "evil" they have seen and experienced. The ceremony exorcises the evil. Although the veteran said he did not believe in that "traditional stuff," he undertook the ceremony. The Peacemaker met later with the veteran who said he did not know why, but the ceremony had worked. He could now sleep through the night without waking with bad dreams. He felt at peace. In the Navajo perception, a post-traumatic stress disorder is not a disorder, but an evil that must be slain or weakened in ceremonies.

JUVENILE JUSTICE AND THE NAVAJO NATION

The Navajo Children's Code, supplemented by rules of procedure, governs delinquent, status offense, and dependent children. The Code and the rules look very much like state juvenile codes of an earlier era, with all delinquent offenses initiated in the juvenile court and a fallback procedure for transfer to a criminal court if a youth is 16- or 17-years-old.

To understand the nature and extent of delinquency or criminal case processing in Navajo courts today, one must know that, in 1885, the U.S. Congress curbed the sovereign and exclusive authority of Native American tribes to administer their own criminal justice systems. It provided concurrent federal court jurisdiction over "major crimes," or felonies. Further, federal law restricts tribal court sanctioning authority over adults to one year in jail or a fine up to $5,000. Add to this a severe lack of rehabilitative and correctional resources and personnel in Native American country compared with those available to the federal courts. As a result, federal prosecution tends to preempt Navajo prosecution of significant felonies committed by either juveniles or adults on the reservation. It is, therefore, not surprising that Native American youth comprise a disproportionate ratio of juveniles held in the custody of the U.S. Bureau of Prisons, which administers federal youth incarceration.

Service Resources Within the Nation Are Limited

The most secure alternative available to Navajo judicial authorities is the Western Navajo Juvenile Services Center in Tuba City, Arizona. This facility, which opened in 1996, holds 30 to 34 juveniles in its long-term custody program that extends from six to 12 months. Juveniles in this secure facility tend to be 15- to 17-years-old and receive mental health, substance abuse, and social work services, but, as of May 2000, no assistance from a traditional counselor. Regrettably, no formal schooling is provided within its walls.

Public intoxication, juvenile or adult, is viewed as a serious problem in the Nation, with driving under the influence the most frequent adult criminal charge. The Tuba City Center and a second juvenile facility that will open in 2001 in Chinle, are prepared to handle intoxicated juveniles on a short-term detention basis. However, there is current discussion of whether Indian Health Service facilities should accept this responsibility.

LIMITED DETENTION SERVICES

The Nation currently maintains just four to eight secure pretrial detention beds in the Tuba City facility and another 14 beds at a sole function detention center at Tohatchi, New Mexico. The not-yet-operational Chinle facility will blend a small number of detention beds with 36 treatment beds. There have been calls to shut down the Tohatchi facility because it fails to comply with fire, safety, and security standards. It also lacks a school. A construction management company recently estimated it would take $1,125,245 to remedy an array of structural shortcomings and to install a fire sprinkler system, fire/smoke detection equipment, and heat in the male detoxification cell.

When I visited this thinly staffed facility for the third time in May 2000, I talked with a girl who had been held 35 days for inhaling gasoline fumes while she awaited placement in a treatment facility. She was receiving neither schooling nor counseling. Another girl was detained because of several runaway attempts, though status offense children are supposed to be barred from secure detention. A third girl, who said she drank vodka with her boyfriend, was to be released that day.

Probation Services Overwhelmed; Options Limited

Navajo probation officers, who used to have either specialized juvenile or adult caseloads, have had combined caseloads since 1996. Because Navajo jails are under federal court order for overcrowding and other very substantial deficiencies, jail must be used sparingly. As a result, more adults are sentenced to probation, the adult caseload is overwhelming, and juveniles receive insufficient attention.

Probation officers refer juveniles to alcohol and mental health treatment facilities, but resources are slim and not immediately available. They impose a limited amount of community service and restitution. Anderson Jones, a Chinle probation officer, describes the community service approach he uses, which differs from standard state court practice that limits an assignment to a governmental or nonprofit agency. He will assign a juvenile to a "chapter," a unit of local government, that will in turn assign the youth to assist a farm family that raises its own crops for its own use. Anderson comments, "To help your own people is community service."

UTILIZING PEACEMAKING WITH JUVENILES

Anderson Jones is not a Peacemaker, but the mother of a 16-year-old youth he was counseling asked him to participate in the family's Peacemaking meeting. The boy was causing trouble at school, had truancy and curfew violations, and was beyond his family's control. He was not listening to his stepfather. At Peacemaking, Anderson spoke in English and Navajo about four issues: communication, understanding, accepting the stepfather, and the love between the mother and the stepfather and how it affected the boy. Grandparents and the immediate family attended. The single session lasted four hours. Soon after, the case was dismissed, the boy joined an older brother in Chicago, attended a trade school there where he did very well, and moved to Phoenix to take a position. According to Jones, they caught this early. Further, he added, Peacemaking works best when the family is traditional and the juvenile is brought up in traditional ways.

Yaa Da' Ya: OJJDP Funded Program Incorporating Peacemaking

Between 1994 and 1996, OJJDP funded a program in Chinle district called *Yaa Da' Ya*. The program assisted 81 "at risk, troubled and adjudicated youth" and their families in conjunction with a traditional plan of healing. Two counselors provided initial and ongoing assistance; Peacemaking was invoked by and for many families. On average, six family members were involved in each case. The approach was a blend of Western and Navajo resources and methods. *Yaa* is translated as skyward, or upward. *Da' Ya* means to be mobile or move toward. *Yaa Da' Ya* tried to provide opportunity for young Navajos to be mobile and move toward goals set in Navajo life philosophy.

Characteristically in a case, three Peacemaking sessions were held over a year's time, interspersed with staff counseling. The first meeting gathered information about the clan, youth, and family problem issues and history, and developed an individualized treatment plan. A second session several months later reviewed progress and needs. External service providers and school representatives could participate and treatment plans could be modified. A final exit session assessed whether the treatment plan was completed and was effective, and an aftercare plan was designed.

Individualized treatment plans included community service projects, alcohol or drug treatment, peer support groups, mental health services, domestic violence counseling, school activities, probation services, residential treatment, and relatively intensive counseling. Community service could take the form of building sweat lodges for the family, assisting the elderly, or delivering firewood.

The project was found to demonstrate the value of Peacemaking in the lives of juveniles and families where discord was common. Families often were reunited through traditional values, but unlike stand-alone Peacemaking, *Yaa Da' Ya* added ongoing counselors to work with youth and families, to network with agencies to obtain necessary services, to monitor progress and not let treatment efforts fall through the cracks, and to continue to engage the family in treatment plan execution.

Peacemaking Restores Balance

Peacemaking is centered on *Hozho*, a Navajo term that describes balance, perfection, good relations, and peace. It seeks to provide a foundation for the physical, psychological, and spiritual well-being of all participants. It is a participatory effort by all present to talk about and correct an imbalance. Imbalance is displayed by acts of disharmony, and disharmony leads to disputes within one's self and delinquent or other behavior where the "inner being needs help."

What Peacemaking does not do is attempt to place blame or judgment on an individual or family member. Accordingly, participants feel able to be more open. On discovering or accepting the disharmony, guidance is provided to help restore harmony. Respect for self and others is fostered. Relationships are restored to proper order. Along with the Peacemaker, Navajo elders, religious leaders, and medicine men and women are resources to provide traditional counseling, healing ceremonies, sweat lodge ceremonies, and other indigenous forms of treatment that can eliminate an imbalance.

PEACEMAKING INCORPORATES CULTURAL APPROACH TO TREATMENT

The Navajo Nation is in a longstanding struggle to retain its culture and way of life in competition with American materialism, commercialism, consumerism, and an absence of connection between land and spirit. A member of the Navajo Nation's legislative judiciary committee explained to me in May 2000 that Western approaches to treating Navajo youth will fail unless traditional methods are used as well. Peacemaking, medicine men and women, ceremonies, and traditional counselors are needed as help for juveniles to live with their families' values and to understand their people and their culture. "One must walk on two legs. If only the Western approach is used, one falls down as there is but one leg to stand on."

The judiciary committee is now actively considering amending the purpose clause of its Children's Code to urge the application of traditional methods in working with children and youth. This committee, as well as the Judicial Branch of the Nation, wants to expand Peacemaking with both delinquent and dependent/abused children and their families. As always, there is a problem with funding. Some families cannot afford the limited fee Peacemakers charge. And there would need to be increased Judicial Branch staff to coordinate additional Peacemaking.

America's children and families increasingly have informal mediation opportunities with or without court involvement. But they miss something that Navajo tradition can teach its children and families.

Author's Note

The updating information that follows was provided in July 2002 by Ed Martin, Administrator, Navajo Nation Courts, and Marie Collins, Probation Officer, Window Rock District Court of the Navajo Nation.

- The new facility at Chinle is open and serves both to detain juveniles and provide post-dispositional treatment. This allows the Tohatchi facility, which remains open, to be used largely for short-term detentions up to 10 days. Both the Tohatchi and Tuba City facilities continue to lack an on-grounds school. The several detention facilities continue to accept intoxicated juveniles whose parents are unable to provide for them.

- Federal funding has enabled juvenile drug courts to be opened at seven court locations, with a drug court counselor at each site. Alcohol is the primary habit or addiction of drug court juveniles.

- Typically, four probation officers serve each judicial district, carrying a mixed adult-juvenile workload. Marie Collins reports she is currently responsible for 75 adult and 21 juvenile probationers. The preparation of reports for the court is a major focus, which in turn means less direct service to probationers. Home visits are scant. Juveniles age 14 and older who owe restitution may be employed in a summer "Work Force" program to earn payback monies. Community service is used as a disposition from time to time.

- There appears to be no increase in the use of Peacemaking with delinquent juveniles and their families. Limited mental health treatment services may be accessed, and some juveniles are placed in a private treatment facility in Utah.

- A study of reservation gangs is being completed. Impressionistic information is that gang violence is reduced from five or six years ago, but gangs may have spread out more across the reservation. "They are there."

Endnotes

[1] Yazzie, R. (1999) *Judicial branch of the Navajo Nation*. Window Rock: AZ: The Navajo Nation, at p. 1.

[2] Yazzie, R. (1995, Spring). Healing as justice: The American experience. *Justice as Healing*, 1, 1-6, at p. 1; See also Yazzie, R. (1998). The Navajo response to crime. *Justice as Healing, 3,* 1-6.

[3] Zion, J. W. (1985). The Navajo peacemaker court: Deference to the old and accommodation to the new. American Indian Law Review, 11, 89-109.

[4] Id. See also, Zion, J. W. (1998). The dynamics of Navajo peacemaking. *Journal of Contemporary Criminal Justice*, 14, 58-74.

Chapter 44

El Salvador Initiates a Juvenile Court

The United States unveiled its first juvenile court in Chicago in 1899. Once hailed as "the greatest step forward in Anglo-American jurisprudence since the Magna Carta,"[1] the juvenile court is no longer the acclaimed academy award winner for best production or performance. Nonetheless, despite at least 30 years of ongoing assault by the public, it executes a reasonably decent brand of justice that includes positive intervention accomplishments with a significant number of offending youth.

We approach our centennial greatly concerned about whether juvenile courts will reach their second centennial. There are several valid reasons for this concern: (1) we are losing more and more juveniles to adult courts; (2) more of the courts' prerogatives have been taken away by legislative prescriptions mandating what we can or cannot do with particular juveniles, for how long, or under what conditions (not all of this is bad, though these changes diminish the use of our professional capabilities); (3) in a number of states, court reorganization may make the juvenile process subservient to family courts; and (4) some courts assign a criminal court judge to hear the delinquency calendar.

I trust it will be of interest to compare what is happening in our juvenile justice system with what is occurring in El Salvador, the Central American nation that inaugurated its first juvenile court on March 1, 1995.

SOME BACKGROUND ON EL SALVADOR

El Salvador is a small, mostly rural nation of over 5 million people. It may be best known to North Americans for its recent (1979-1992) armed conflict associated with military control of the country; death squad murders of Jesuit priests, nuns, labor unionists, and protesters; and a wholesale exodus to El Norte.

The United Nations finally brokered an accord that resulted in an internationally monitored election in which control was retained by the former ruling party, though minority parties gained representation in the national assembly. Presumably, civilian control of the nation was reasserted. In January 1995, military control of the national police yielded to a new policing organization whose stated mission is traditional law and order protection.

Following the war's end, the United States Agency for International Development took on the job of helping El Salvador accomplish judicial reform. The U.N. and some member nations have assisted with this task. Pre-accord, the judiciary was known for its corruption, obeisance to ruling party directives, acceptance of human rights violations, and lack of independence. Post-accord, there was recognition that preservation of the new democracy was in no small way dependent on the implementation of an honest, professional, coherent, efficient, and effective judicial system.

This chapter originally appeared in Community Correctiions Report, *Vol. 2, No. 4, May/June 1995.*

SLOW JUSTICE: RECENT STATISTICS SHOW 50% OF SALVADORAN DETAINEES TOOK MORE THAN TWO YEARS TO COMPLETE THE JUDICIAL PROCESS

El Salvador does not require speedy trial and disposition. Countless numbers of accused adults, as well as juvenile offenders, have been incarcerated for years awaiting adjudication, sentence, or disposition. For example, during 1993, just 30% of persons charged with crimes completed the judicial process within one year; 20% required from one to two years; 40% required between two and seven years; and 10% required more than seven years. Juvenile offenders are included in these data.[2]

The director of Tonacatepeque, the juvenile facility for 16- to 18-year-old-boys, informed me during my juvenile justice consultation in this country in January 1995, that only 17 of the 146 boys in residence at the time of my site visit were sentenced. The average incarceration time of the 129 inmates awaiting disposition was two-and-a-half years. (More on this institution later.)

This kind of information should give us pause, and then cause us to pay tribute to our own constitutional provisions for speedy trial and habeas corpus, and for our statutes and rules that provide guidelines for case processing times.

Note: A new criminal code, criminal procedure code, and separate criminal sentencing law were expected to be passed into law in April 1995. This chapter focuses on the Minor (i.e., Juvenile) Offender Law. The original act provided for an effective date of October 1, 1994, but the El Salvador National Assembly subsequently pushed it back to March 1, 1995. Prior to the new law, juvenile offenders have been sanctioned by criminal courts, often incarcerated with adults, not provided with counsel, and afforded no, or virtually no, due process protections.

AN ENLIGHTENED NEW "MINOR OFFENDER LAW"

While our state legislatures are busy finding ways to confine youths under 18-years-old in jails and prisons, the Salvadoran law has accomplished a complete reversal of such practices.

The U.N. employed two Italian consultants, both familiar with U.N. conventions concerning children and the law, to draft the law in consultation with a special Salvadoran commission. The product is a refreshing document, like one that might have been enacted nearly a century ago in the United States, but with such contemporary concepts incorporated as due process safeguards, conciliation with victims, and restitution. The law sets forth the following jurisdictional provisions and fundamental principles which can be considered either naive or honorable and idealistic:

- All imposed sanctions shall have an educational purpose.

- Offenses by youth under age 12 may not be brought to the court, but shall be referred to an external youth agency.

- Offenses by youth between 12- and 18-years-old may be heard only by a juvenile court.

- Juveniles are not to be institutionally detained (pre- or post-trial) except by judicial order, and only as an exceptional measure and for the shortest possible period of time.

- Juveniles are presumed innocent, are not to be forced to give testimony, must be provided with counsel from the beginning of an investigation, and shall have fair, private, and speedy trials.

- Juveniles are not to be interned in places intended for adult incarceration.

Until this law, Salvadoran courts were unfamiliar with psychosocial studies, segregated pretrial detention for juveniles, probation, conciliation, monetary restitution, or community service. There were neither juvenile prosecutors nor public defenders. Offenders either were released to their families or remained incarcerated.

The new court system has the following authorizations and appropriations for staff: 12 juvenile court judges are to be appointed by the Supreme Court from among 90 trained lawyer applicants; each of these judges is to be assigned a trained specialist team, consisting of a psychologist, a social worker, and an educator, whose role is to conduct psychosocial studies and perform probation supervision and other functions; the Fiscalia (attorney general's office) is funded for 10 attorneys and 35 law students full-time; and the Procurador General is to assign one defense attorney to each juvenile court and provide three other attorneys to handle appeals.

SALVADORAN JUVENILE JUSTICE SYSTEM'S FRONT-END PROCEDURES

Attorney General Has Bulk of the Power

The law's provisions regarding apprehension, case investigation, diversion, and other pre-court practices are startlingly different from ours. One major difference is that the authority of law enforcement is severely curbed. Juveniles simply cannot be interrogated by the police, and the police are prohibited from keeping records. Another important difference is that the attorney general (i.e., the prosecutor) has a great deal of authority. For example, the attorney general is charged with offense investigation responsibility and authorized to question a juvenile in the presence of defense counsel. Juveniles caught "in flagrante" either by police or by citizens who obtain police custody over them must be turned over to the attorney general within six hours. The attorney general's staff also is authorized to decide whether juveniles will be detained prior to trial. If there is to be a pretrial detention, a detention hearing must be held within 72 hours. For other than in-flagrante referrals, only a judge can decide whether detention may be used. In addition, a "psychosocial study" must be ordered for a detained youth.

Conciliation Proceedings

Except for very serious offenses, if there is sufficient evidence to prove an offense, the attorney general is to offer and conduct conciliation with victims and juveniles. Victim participation is voluntary. Conciliation agreements are to provide monetary restitution to the victim or the repair of damage by the juvenile.

Charges Must Be Filed Within 30 Days

If charges are to be filed, the attorney general must file them within 30 days of the offense. Judges may grant an additional 30 days. The attorney general may determine whether to dismiss non-provable cases.

JUDICIAL PROCEEDINGS

Process

Generally, until the recent overhaul of its legal system, El Salvador's judicial process relied on written briefs filed by lawyers. Now, oral hearings at which attorneys present and cross-examine witnesses and make statements regarding the evidence are provided by the Minor Offender Law as well as other statutes. However, two provisions relating to judicial proceedings, differ from U.S. practice:

1. As the hearing opens, the judge invites the youth to make a statement, and advises the youth that he or she is not required to do so. If a statement is made, both the prosecutor and the defense counsel may question the youth. This process suggests that the juvenile has the burden of proving innocence, rather than having the burden placed on the prosecutor to prove that the offense was committed by the youth.

2. The findings and conclusions of the mandatory psychosocial study are presented even before the lawyers present and cross-examine witnesses. The content of the study is not defined by law, but is likely to be similar to what U.S. juvenile courts generally refer to as a predisposition report.

U.S. legal developments in the late 1960s clarified that a judge must find the evidence sufficient to adjudicate a juvenile before the dispositional stage can be entered into. **In re Corey**, 72 Cal. Rptr. 115 (1968). The Minor Offender Law sets a very prompt 30-day time frame for the completion of judicial proceedings.

Dispositions

The Salvadoran statute authorizes six dispositional alternatives, all of which are to have an educational purpose and be complemented with the family's participation: (1) orientation and family support; (2) admonition; (3) imposition of rules of conduct; (4) community service; (5) probation; and (6) internment or confinement. Apparently, these measures may be combined as the case allows.

BACK END OF THE JUVENILE JUSTICE SYSTEM

The new statute declares that juvenile institutionalization should be "a last recourse," for "as short a duration as possible," and with separation from other inmates over age 18. Such juveniles may "never be held incommunicado, nor placed in isolation, nor subjected to corporal punishment." Professional social, health, and educational services are to be provided, along with information as to the regulations of the facility and the disciplinary measures that might be taken.

Offenders age 12 through 15 may receive a sanction of up to five years. (*Note: While this sounds severe, remember the common clause in our juvenile codes until the late 1960s (still alive in some states today) of institutionalization—or even probation— until one's 21st birthday unless sooner terminated.*) Sixteen- and 17-year-olds may be incarcerated for up to one-half the minimum and maximum terms for like adult offenders, but never to exceed seven years.

There also is provision for an appeal of a juvenile court decision, something that was absent in many of our states until the historic **Gault** decision in 1967. **In re Gault**, 387 U.S. 1 (1967).

AN INNOVATIVE CONCEPT: A DIFFERENT JUDGE OVERSEES THE EXECUTION OF SENTENCES

El Salvador has adopted a really interesting concept in designating a special judge whose job it is to assure that (1) the juvenile court judge's orders are carried out, (2) the juvenile's rights are not violated during post-dispositional intervention, (3) sanctions that do not fulfill their intended objectives or that prove contrary "to the minor's reinsertion into society" are modified, and (4) officials who fail to fulfill their responsibilities under the law or fail to accomplish them within the lawful time are warned and/or sanctioned.

INSTITUTE FOR THE PROTECTION OF MINORS TAKES OVER RESPONSIBILITY FOR EL SALVADOR'S JAILED JUVENILES

On March 1, 1995, the Institute for the Protection of Minors, a governmental entity founded in 1993 to work with abused, neglected, and dependent children and younger delinquents, took over responsibility for Tonacatepeque, the country's juvenile institution, from the prison department. The Institute, which will also be responsible for another 500 jailed juveniles, must accomplish its goals with severely inadequate resources and a strained budget.

Under the prison authority, Tonacatepeque was run very much like a prison— including prison guards armed with guns and batons. The Institute for the Protection of Minors is expected to bring a more humane orientation to this facility. Prior to March 1, 1995, the Institute was to have had a physician examination of each resident and have public health workers check out the water system, the sanitation, and the kitchen. In addition, youth workers will replace the guards.

At the time of my site visit, the boys were housed 10 to a cell. Three teachers taught classes of 20 boys for four hours a day. There were no afternoon classes, and no effort was made to educate the other 86 boys in residence. The "vocational training" room had essentially no artificial light. Limited natural light entered from several holes in the roof. The only apparent recreation area was an open space where several boys were kicking a poor-grade soccer ball. The soccer field on the premises was off limits because several boys had tried to escape from it. Most of the facility's population were either in their cells or just sitting around.

A separate isolation area held 10 boys. Three of them had been confined there since an escape attempt some 41 days earlier. Three others said they had been in isolation for 30 days. One boy talked openly in front of the institutional director of easy access to marijuana and capsule drugs. There was another bank of 20 unoccupied single rooms. "For what purpose are they used?" asked this uninstructed North American. For sex, answered the director of prisons. Girlfriends, and quite possibly prostitutes, are brought in for conjugal visits.

NEW CODE WILL HAVE TO FIGHT TO SUCCEED

One observer suggested that this new juvenile law is better suited to Sweden than El Salvador. There are real concerns that violent acts by juveniles will force legislative review of the code and prompt provisions for harsher handling of certain juvenile class-es. Also, a significant number of Salvadoran-born members of Los Angeles gangs have been deported back to their native country, prompting reports of gang-related drug sell-ing, robberies, and burglaries.

Some members of the ruling party have openly stated that they distrust the code. Reportedly, several justices of El Salvador's Supreme Court, which has administrative responsibility over all courts, also dislike this law. How long the police, with their "de minimus" role, will remain silent regarding their restrictions is a further concern.

Finally, there are weighty problems in merely getting this new entity off the ground. For instance, all officials are "new hires," the court's infrastructure is severely inade-quate, and intervention resources, in short supply in many countries, are barren here. So, we'll hold our collective breath regarding the great step forward in El Salvador. Quite likely, the sponsors of the 1899 Cook County Juvenile Court did the same.

Author's Note

As of 2002, the progressive tenets of the Minor Offender Law, i.e., the Salvadoran juvenile code, remain unscathed. There are no direct filings into a criminal court. The durations of juvenile sentencing are the same. Alternatives to incarceration remain an emphasis. The basic rights of juveniles who are in conflict with the law continue on the books.

The magnitude of the contribution of the United Nations and its Convention on the Rights of the Child to juvenile rights in Latin America must be applauded. The U.N. has stimulated numerous other progressive juvenile codes as well, in Bolivia, Brazil, Costa Rica, the Dominican Republic, and Ecuador.

Good laws are one thing. Combating El Salvador's immense poverty, huge short-comings in academic and vocational educational offerings (one report indicated that 17% of urban children and 34% of rural youth were not attending school, which is mandated through the ninth grade or until age 14, though rural schools often fail to pro-vide this duration of education), joblessness, vast health care deficits, thousands of street children, solvent-sniffing youngsters, extensive juvenile prostitution (one report indicated that at least 44% of prostitutes in three major red light districts of San Salvador were between 13- and 18-years-old), and now juvenile violence and juvenile gangs, is quite another task.

A series of reports (information sources have included a report of the Pan American Health Organization, Sojourner Magazine, Infomundi, Inter-American Development Bank reports, Human Rights Watch, Amnesty International, and El Salvador Human Rights Reports published annually by the U.S. Department of State) indicate the nation has made good progress with judicial system reform, including the creation of an independent judiciary, though inefficiency and corruption among general court judges receives continuing comment. Funds from international private (e.g., Save the Children) and public (e.g., the Inter-American Development Bank) entities, have enabled certain training of juvenile justice system personnel including police officers, delinquency prevention programs, and improvements in the condition of juveniles' confinement. Several detention and rehabilitation centers are to be constructed along with four detoxification clinics. Non-governmental organizations (NGOs) are major providers of intervention with juveniles and families.

Gang membership and violence are viewed as a grave social problem. Salvadorans deported from Los Angeles and their L.A. gangs have had their influence felt as younger youths have formed into San Salvadoran gangs. There are the tattoos, the baggy pants, the boom boxes, and weapons. Drug selling and use are everyday activities. (One study found that marijuana, alcohol, and crack were the favorite drugs of choice, respectively.) Violence is common, and inter-gang rivalries produce numerous deaths among gang members. Territories are marked by graffiti and to trespass into alien territory is to risk one's life. The gangs are known as *maras*.

A positive development, however, has been the creation of "*Homies Unidos*," a group of former active gang members who have given up violence, and who work to assist present gang members and others to prevent or stop violence and to instead train for the job market and pursue constructive life stabilization.

Endnotes

1 Roscoe Pound, cited in National Probation and Parole Association (1957). *Guides for juvenile court judges*. New York: National Probation and Parole Association, p. 127.

2 *La Realidad de la Justicia Salvadorena 1994: Analisis del Censo de Juicios Activos*, Corte Suprema de Justicia, 1994, p. 6.

Postscript

The fundamental focus of this book is the intersection of juvenile delinquency with the juvenile court and juvenile justice system. Juvenile courts, and indeed I, myself, have been on a long journey to best define how this invention and its collaborating agencies and services should assist in the best interests of juveniles and their families, provide for community protection, and accomplish the more recent concept of juvenile accountability.

Many good things have come to pass, and advances continue to be made each day and each year as enhanced knowledge and professionalism are applied to court proceedings and court clientele. Advances are connected to provision of better training prior to and during one's work in this setting, research evaluations that better tell us what might work, the continuing innovation of programs that institute new approaches aimed at improving the human condition of juvenile court youths, law-trained people who seek to ensure that juvenile processing meets the standards of legislation and the Constitution, and the expanded alliance of justice system collaborators who seek to better integrate what they do with the goals and purposes of the court.

As a long-term judicial system participant, activist, observer, and author, I should be entitled to make some parting comments. I will, and they deal with six matters that concern me particularly at this time.

POLICING JUVENILES

The serious violent crime wave, occasioned not only by juveniles, which for now is in an uneasy rest period, led to an outpouring of effort, money, and personnel determined to stop delinquency in its early tracks. More police officers have been put in the field, risking their lives to protect ours, but often busily arresting slight offenders. Arguably, the police are being told to arrest more young people, as this is what is wanted by a fearful society, and there are rewards, personally and for one's department, when arrest numbers are increased.

FBI data for 1999 tell much about the nature of arrests. That year an estimated total of just under 2.5 million arrests of juveniles took place. It should be noted that the definition of juvenile used here includes all young people under age 18, even though 13 states fully deny juvenile court eligibility to those 16- or 17-years-old. There were 103,900 arrests for violent crimes, serious matters, almost 70% of them aggravated assaults, 1,400 for murder and non-negligent manslaughter, 5,000 for forcible rape, and 28,000 for robbery. But the most severe charge in almost half of all arrests, 1,162,400 of them, was larceny-theft, simple assault, drug abuse violation, disorderly conduct, or curfew violation, offenses that do not score high on a seriousness chart. Most of these offenses are nuisance and low-pain irritants that injure victims' health, welfare, or business interests, but not in life-threatening ways. They are offenses that we wish didn't happen but have, and that some wish should not have to involve the police or the court and instead be handled in an informal manner. Also, the larceny-theft category, for some archaic reason, is still considered an Index Crime by the FBI; it includes such matters as shoplifting, theft from a motor vehicle, and bicycle theft.

Should this arrest picture prompt great societal concern and regressive policy changes? No. Add in 165,700 liquor law violations and 21,700 drunkenness apprehensions, 119,500 vandalism offenses, 29,100 receiving or possessing stolen property arrests, and 150,700 runaways and one can then obtain an image of the expansive amount of police activity.

Yes, there were lots of burglars (101,000), some arsonists (9,200), and juveniles driving under the influence (23,000).[1] Fortunately there were not more violent offenders, but the point is that rank and file policing is of less serious matters and that juvenile criminals are normally not so numerous and frightening that law makers in New Hampshire and Wisconsin should have had to drop their top age for juvenile court processing from the 18th to the 17th birthday. Nor should lawmakers in just about all states have had to drop the bar and eased such a broad band of automatic transfers to criminal court handling.

While not a conspiracy theorist, I do suggest an interactive joinder of public expressions—by political people from presidents on down to governors and to prosecutors and police, in part led by sophomoric media accounts and acquiesced in by juvenile court officials—that led to the policy changes that became very politically correct, and also excessive. There is no simple fix, no free lunch, and it is likely society will pay for the failures of this criminalization drive. Enormously lengthy sentences stack the deck for thousands and thousands of juveniles who will cost governmental entities dearly and protect society only as long as they are locked up. This could be your child. It could have been you. Stereotypes that juveniles in the system are essentially all minority youth are indeed no small part the result of differential decision making that turns unfairly against the poor and those of color.

CRIMINALIZATION OF LESS SERIOUS JUVENILE OFFENDERS

There are trends and practices that are distressing to me. Some of this concerns what the juvenile court is becoming. This relates, not coincidentally, to what criminal courts are becoming.

Juvenile courts were born because criminal courts were not appropriate forums for juvenile offenders. With exceptions, criminal courts remain an improper forum for handling juvenile offenders. Again with certain exceptions, it is better to rely on a juvenile court judge's informed determination of whether the juvenile justice system is or is not the better setting for handling a serious or violent offense.

It is surely true that the juvenile system is not the appropriate place for some offenders, for example, a 17-year-old who deliberately murders a stranger. But the sweep of statutory changes that substituted direct legislative and prosecutorial waiver in place of procedurally defined juvenile court judge waiver proceedings has brought too many youths into the criminal court world who could have been handled better in the juvenile court world. Juvenile court critics apparently perceive juvenile court judges as soft-talking hand slappers who cannot prove their combination of accountability and rehabilitation practices is reforming. The critics do not demand proof by criminal court judges and their prison systems that their intervention works. The public does not expect much from imprisonment, only that it takes place, and for many, the longer off the streets the better.

Studies have not shown that handling juveniles in criminal court yields less recidivism when compared one-on-one with like juveniles handled in a juvenile court Studies thus far, as cited earlier, have shown the opposite. Further, juvenile courts overall do things far more quickly, better assure that some sanctioning takes place, and offer a better turnaround prospect because of their intervention efforts.

MINORITY OVERREPRESENTATION AND DISPROPORTIONATE MINORITY CONFINEMENT

Minority overrepresentation is a vital civil rights concern, a moral concern. It should be a grave societal concern. Hopefully it will become a strong political concern. Political forces and biases have driven the darkening of justice, and justice system officials and policy makers up and down the line, usually unknowingly, have been party to injustice.

My comments above on policing and criminalization tie in closely to disproportionate minority confinement (DMC). Where and how the police are deployed and make arrests absolutely impacts DMC. Decisions made at each step along the juvenile justice system have now been widely documented as feeding DMC. Fingers are not to be pointed toward officials as systematically discriminating against minority youth. But minority overrepresentation happens in a systematic way. Unintentionally, white youth are its beneficiary. How American society views black and Hispanic juveniles intrudes on the practices of police and prosecutors, of detention screeners and judges, of probation officials and state juvenile agency officials toward white youth.

Minority confinement is disproportionate to any disproportion of crimes black or Hispanic juveniles may commit. The percentage of black youths in Miami-Dade County, Florida, e.g., approximates 20% of its youth population, but black youths constitute a reported 68% of juveniles in juvenile detention and 74% of those juveniles held in jail as adult defendants. Black youths, waived into adult courts by prosecutors, are locked into jail at 15 times the rate of white youth, and Hispanic youths are at least 50% more likely to be locked into jail than white youth.[2]

A 1999 report from Maryland shows similar findings. Blacks constitute approximately 32% of all youth in the state, but consist of 64% of those in secure pretrial detention facilities and 72% of those in secure juvenile facilities. Here, as often elsewhere, the percentage of white delinquent youth sent to private residential treatment facilities, rather than to secure state institutions, far exceeds these placements for black youth.[3]

Data now emerging on Hispanic overrepresentation show that, like other youth of color, they receive harsher treatment than Caucasian youth charged with the same offense. The process begins with police stops or arrests and continues throughout the system. For example, Hispanic youths have been found to be 13 times more likely to be incarcerated for a drug offense than white youths and will spend twice as long in a secure facility. Anti-gang laws are cited as just one factor seen as resulting in more harsh and unfair consequences.[4] Read the Kentucky data or the Idaho data or the Washington data or the Colorado data or the data from other states and you will find that minorities are disproportionately apprehended and detained, penetrate to adjudication and disposition, are committed to the state, and transferred to criminal courts.

Something has gone wrong with the American dream. Many, far too many, youths with dark skins have their dreams in correctional beds, juvenile and adult. This should make all of us irate. It makes me irate. Let's all intensify our work against this injustice.

JUVENILE COURT HEARINGS

I have long and proactively encouraged defense representation for juveniles at court hearings. Now I need to send a message to the judges of this court as to their conduct of hearings: Too many judges and their law-trained hearing officers appear to largely ignore the juvenile who is the subject of a hearing. Instead, in open court they talk in the main with the attorneys, defense and prosecution, who are present, and verbally active.

Juvenile courts began in courtrooms or judicial chambers where the judge and everyone else at the hearing sat on the same floor level. Later juvenile court hearing rooms had the judicial bench one step up, rather than the loftier three-step-up perch of other courtrooms. The structural design was to enable and facilitate communication between the judge and the youth and family. Judges sought to individualize each juvenile and to make the court experience both personal and impressionable. It was hoped and believed that the youth would incorporate the judicial interest and advice and redirect his or her delinquent ways into acceptable behaviors.

But now the lawyers preempt judicial attention, and the youth often seems to be peripheral to what is going on. Legal professionals have their own language. Some of what is happening may be explained to the youth, but this lacks personalization except, perhaps, for the bottom line of what the judge orders.

Judges experience pressures of workloads, time-line standards, and waiting lists that obstruct placements into desired programs. The lawyers face their own pressures, as do the probation officers who in more courts today are no longer in the foreground but rather are background officials who provide their court reports to the attorneys who then negotiate recommendations and agreements to the court. Nonetheless, there still can be magic in the way a judge involves a juvenile in a hearing. We want a youth to tell others about "my judge," one "who talked with me about my interests and problems, and even talked with me about what actions the court should take to help me stay out of trouble, and asked whether I had other suggestions."

Such personalization can be accomplished. New Zealand family group conferences enable an extensive discussion and dialogue between a panoply of officials and the youth and extended family members. United Kingdom magistrates want to engage the juvenile more extensively, have all participants on the same plane or level, and have family members sit with the juvenile and attorney. Similar approaches would benefit juvenile justice in the U.S. Our judges should not allow the legal repartee to disallow significant judge-juvenile and family interchanges. These interchanges need not lead to a juvenile court therapeutic state.

THE THERAPEUTIC STATE

Early juvenile delinquency theory combined both environmental and psychological causation. The urban immigrant slum environment was seen by opinion makers as prompting law violations and an array of antisocial behaviors. An early popularization of psychology sought to explain deviations from establishment norms as due to internal mental health deficits or unmet emotional needs. Mental health professionals found a nexus between their newly professionalized expertise and the nascent juvenile court movement. The court welcomed their interest in inserting psychological testing and treatment services to combat deviance.

The nation's first mental health clinics were organized in early juvenile courts in Chicago and Boston. Juvenile courts employed psychiatrists to evaluate and even treat delinquent juveniles, and to train probation staff to adapt their methods. These were to become social agency and clinical settings. A former U.S. Supreme Court justice, referring to the court's clinical approach, suggested, in 1968, that "the love and tenderness possessed by the white-coated judge and attendants were not sufficient to untangle the web of subconscious influences that possessed the troubled youngster."[5]

Yet, psychologically oriented methods, in time, had to compete with a counter perspective that since so many poor juveniles come to juvenile court, initiatives should target poverty, job training, and community development in order to combat delinquency causation and control. Economic and sociological causation trumped psychological causation, for a time.

Studies such as the Wolfgang Philadelphia cohort study[6] and Martinson's Nothing Works analysis[7] of intervention cooled off many who exhorted treatment as the solution. The concept of desistance—that if left alone numerous juveniles do not reoffend—influenced many to take a hands-off approach until an offender appeared at the juvenile court doorway for a repetitive or serious offense. There was recognition that psychologically based applications did not appear to work particularly well with impoverished and educationally deficient youths.

More recently, there has been a rush to focus more heavily on juvenile accountability and punishments, controls, and intensive monitoring.

Then came those who claimed some things do work and others who contended that serious and repetitive offenders have characteristics that can be identified following a first and even low-serious offense. They proposed that an array of interventions should be required of these juveniles and families.

There is a renaissance of belief that unmet emotional needs should be addressed in juvenile courts. The assumption is that we know what can shortstop criminal careers and that we can accomplish this. But the research to date does not seem to indicate that we are effective in that many cases. The old legend may still be true today: one-third get better in our care, one-third get worse, and one-third remain unchanged. We should recognize that in trying to help youth make better lives we can, unintentionally, injure those we try to help. What of the right to be held accountable and then be left alone?

We have learned certain things. Judicial case processing should not be antithetical to healthy human processes. But blending elements of therapeutic approaches with control mechanisms leads to lots of failures as well as some successes. Requiring juveniles and family members to do so many "thises" and "thats" leaves little time for life. Being subject to the court's jurisdiction should not need to mean one must relinquish everyday life to what some professionals think should be the way you must conduct every hour of your life.

An Ohio court pioneered a procedure in the 1980s to have a restitution-only involvement with juvenile offenders. Paying back a victim when there was a direct loss or doing community service for the community when there was no direct victim loss was the sole requirement for non-serious offenders. The court funded a community service program. It set aside for restitution-owing juveniles the minimum hourly wage less 10% for administrative costs, the earnings to be transferred to the victim. When a juvenile put in the requisite hours, the deferred petition was dismissed. The youth did not have a judge or a probation officer, only an accountability task to perform. There was no intervention with psyches.[8]

Lots of juveniles can be handled informally or formally, required only to do community service hours or reimburse the victim … and then be gone from the court. Many of these youths will still have lots of educational, family, and emotional hang-ups, but this should not make them, if non-serious or repetitive non-serious offenders, into court cases. A therapeutic state need not descend upon modest offenders.

The concept of goal-oriented probation fits well here. Collaborate with the juvenile in designing behavioral goals such as staying out of trouble, doing one's restitution or community service, passing all or most school subjects, and getting and keeping a job. After six or nine months, if all has gone well, *voilà*. That's it. Then we can apply our energies with more serious offenders both directly and indirectly, by mobilizing community and external agency resources to take over more of the life space of higher-risk juveniles. Of course, we do need a psychological brush, but we should not paint too broadly with it.

Surely some, indeed more than some, court juveniles will need "professional help." But recidivism, even stubborn recidivism when parents cannot control their youth, should not result in an automatic disposition to a costly residential program. Juvenile courts and the justice system do fall into the trap of categorizing poor children as bad and requiring punishment while middle class, white delinquent youth are, instead, deemed in need of treatment

There is money to be made in the residential care of children. There are expansionist providers, particularly for-profit and non-profit entities. Recent national data reflect an increase of 827 youth residing in public placement facilities but an increase of 2,144 youth residing in private placement facilities during one-day counts taking place in 1999 compared with 1997.[9] Other data show that juvenile court out-of-home placements grew from 119,700 youths in 1989 to 163,800 youths in 1998, a 36.8% leap. Placements were defined as residential treatment centers, juvenile correctional centers, foster homes, and group homes. The data do not separate the different growth numbers for the four settings, though my expectation is that residential treatment centers experienced the greatest growth, a growth that would symbolize a construct that residential placement is what a doctor would order.[10]

The therapeutic state advertises it has the remedy for delinquent juveniles, but the promise, often, is greater than the result even as a private facility creams its applications and rejects admissions of juveniles who appear to have only a slight chance for success. Judges get little objective, validated feedback on institutional placement successes or failures, individually or collectively. However, it should not be seen as naïve to suggest that we can do a lot more effective retention of juveniles in their communities, and do this far more cheaply than with residential placements. The judicial quest for out-of-home treatment needs to be modified in part and redirected toward more intensive community non-residential programming.

We do need residential placements, public and private (preferably non-profit private entities). But we need to acknowledge that placements, often politically correct to use, may be overused and that such overuse eats up funds that might be better spent for expanding community-based options.

The renaissance of therapeutic juvenile justice extends to the next concern. The juvenile court's blend of forms of treatment intervention along with its authoritative intervention sets it up as a receptacle to receive juvenile drug users and school truants.

DRUGS, TRUANCIES, AND MINOR SCHOOL OFFENSES

I position myself with many others who conclude the War on Drugs has been ineffectual. It has created an industry of thousands and thousands of personnel employed to rein in substance abuse, and to apprehend, control, and treat abusers. This, too, is a very large moneymaker for the urinalysis firms, construction companies that build juvenile and adult jails, those who manufacture electronic monitors and create software programs for overseeing offender whereabouts, and myriad officialdom. These enterprises visibly support substance abuse policing and judging users, sellers, and distributors. But do users need courts?

Juvenile substance abuse is common throughout much of America. All juveniles placed on probation for a drug offense or for any other offense agree to a requirement not to use illegal substances. Every week countless juvenile probationers nonetheless use an illegal substance. Their probation officers learn about this and either ignore it, bring the juvenile back to court, or threaten court the next time there is a dirty "UA." All this presents a dilemma, if not a game. If the juvenile goes back to court, it may result in a community-service hours sanction, time in detention, compelled drug treatment, or other sentence. Meanwhile, peers, not engaged with the court, smoke their marijuana without worry of a random urinalysis.

Drug courts for delinquent juveniles are now encouraged, and provide the benefit of funds that enable readily obtained treatment services. A national guide to these courts suggests their use with those who (1) have committed nonviolent drug or drug-related offenses, (2) present no danger to the community, and (3) demonstrate moderate to heavy substance use.[11] To avoid this application of the authority-laced therapeutic state, I prefer to deal with these types of juveniles using community resources, not court resources. Why should court be used unless there are other, serious offenses with which to contend?

Relapse is common in drug court cases. A benefit of drug courts is the overt recognition that relapses are common. A relapse results in a court sanction. Another relapse means a stiffer court sanction. Plain drug-using youth are better left alone or steered to community drug treatment programs. A juvenile drug court, instead, should focus its efforts on more serious and repetitive delinquent offenders who have more serious substance abuse problems.

The truancy issue comes down to the symbiosis between a school system that wants to strengthen its hold on children via the court's authority and a court that is willing to open its doorway to help out another youth-serving entity. But, with exceptions, schools have not exhausted existing alternatives or constructed sufficient court alternatives. Here, as well, some truants, when they come to court, will respond to the court's directives and others will not. And the court, for those who fail, must take action in some form to reinforce its authority. So these kids are not only school outcasts but also have a court record and, indeed, often a court sanction. Of course it will be said that "we are only here to help you."

It should be clear that, while an advocate of good programming in juvenile justice, I want to reserve the court for more difficult cases and rely on community agencies for the other violations. And, yes, the judge and probation staff should actively participate in community efforts to expand service provisions to youths and families and increase in lieu of court handling.

One approach used in a small number of communities, known as a community assessment center, is a well-intended effort to obtain help outside the court system, but presents problems in microevaluation and micromanagement of children's welfare by officialdom. A center is to provide "immediate and comprehensive assessments, integrated case management, and a comprehensive and integrated management information system" for youngsters brought in by police officers and other referral sources. This includes truants and lots of others.

I am fond of bias-free risk and needs assessments as used at critical juvenile justice processing stages, but their regularized use at an assessment center gets worrisome. I suggest that referred children will be found to have plenty of needs. To meet these needs, project developers have hoped to have lots of mental health, child welfare, and juvenile justice services to engage these youngsters and retard future juvenile law violations. Good luck. The centers are to "avoid stigmatizing and labeling youth, ensure due process for juvenile offenders, and be careful not to 'widen the net.'" [12] Again, good luck.

While some will benefit from this process and its follow-on services, others will be stigmatized, labeled, experience net widening, and be subjects of a subversion of due process. Here again is the therapeutic state, therapy-oriented professionals merging with social science risk and needs researchers to provide overkill to some who are only curfew violators or school misbehavers.

We always need to keep in mind that the court—yes, even a juvenile court—is a delicate but dangerous instrument. Their juvenile court record may forever harm those who enter its portals, though we believe we have only wanted to help them. Those we hold in detention even for one night know this isn't home, and for some this is an unforgettable trauma of their childhood.

A thoughtful federal court judge, addressing a national gathering of juvenile court judges in 1970, pointedly favored limiting court intervention when he spoke to the issue of status offender handling, an admonition that can apply, as well, to drug use and lesser offenses. He stated,

> The situation is truly ironic. The argument for retaining beyond control and truancy jurisdiction is that juvenile courts have to act in such cases because "if we don't, no one else will." I submit precisely the opposite is the case: because you act, no one else does. Schools and public agencies refer their problem cases to you because you have jurisdiction, because you exercise it, and because you hold out promises that you can provide solutions. [13]

Endnotes

[1] Snyder, H. N. (2001). *Law enforcement and juvenile crime. Juvenile offenders and victims: National report series.* Washington, DC: U.S. Office of Juvenile Justice and Delinquency Prevention, p. 9.

[2] Schiraldi, V. (2002, May 2). Trying youths as adults is unjust. *Miami Herald,* p. 7b.

[3] Feldman, L., Males, M. A., & Schiraldi, V. (2001). *A tale of two jurisdictions: Youth crime and detention rates in Maryland & the District of Columbia.* Washington, DC: Justice Policy Institute.

[4] Villarruel, F. A. & Walker, N. E. (2002). *Dónde está la justicia: Latino youth in the juvenile justice* system. Lansing, MI: Michigan State University. See state-by-state compilation at *www.building blocksforyouth.org*. See also national compilation in Minorities in the Juvenile Justice System, National Report Series (1999). *Juvenile Justice Bulletin,* U.S. Office of Juvenile Justice and Delinquency Prevention; and see Juszkiewicz, J. (2000). *Youth crime/Adult time: Is justice served?* Washington, DC: Pretrial Services Resource Center.

[5] Douglas, Justice W. O. (1968). Juvenile courts and due process of law. *Juvenile Court Judges Journal, 19*(1), 9-15; at p. 11.

[6] Wolfgang, M.E., Figlio, R.M. & Sellin, T. (1972). *Delinquency in a birth cohort.* Chicago: University of Chicago Press.

[7] Martinson, R. (1974, Spring). What works? Questions and answers about prison reform. *Public Interest,* pp. 22-54; Lipton, D., Martinson, R. & Wilks, J. (1975). *The effectiveness of correctional treatment.* New York: Praeger.

[8] Field test of audit format, Lucas County Juvenile Court, Toledo, Ohio, done for Thornton, M., Rubin, H.T., & Henderson, T.A. (1989). *Juvenile restitution management audit.* Washington: DC: Office of Juvenile Justice and Delinquency Prevention.

[9] Sickmund, M. (2002). *Juvenile offenders in residential placement: 1997-1999.* Fact Sheet #07, p. 1. Washington, DC: U.S. Office of Juvenile Justice and Delinquency Prevention

[10] Puzzanchera, C. M. (2002). *Juvenile court placement of adjudicated youth, 1989-98.* Fact Sheet #02, p. 1. Washington, DC: U.S. Office of Juvenile Justice and Delinquency Prevention

[11] Cooper, C. S. (2001). *Juvenile drug court programs.* U.S. Office of Juvenile Justice and Delinquency Prevention, *Juvenile Accountability Incentive Block Grants Program Bulletin. 5,* 1-15.

[12] Oldenettel, D. & Wordes, M. (1999). *Community Assessment Centers.* Fact Sheet #111. Washington, DC:U.S. Office of Juvenile Justice and Delinquency Prevention.

[13] Bazelon, D. L. (1970). Beyond control of the juvenile court. *Juvenile Court Judges Journal, 21*(2), 42-45, 50; at p. 44.

Index

[References are to pages.]

A

ABA, *See* American Bar Association (ABA)

Abuse and neglect cases
California. *See* California
DSS agencies, role of, 4-1–4-2
intervention programs
Kellogg Foundation grants to abuse and neglect intervention programs, 4-5–4-6
Kent County Michigan early intervention model, 4-5
issues confronting judges, 4-2–4-3
juvenile court jurisdiction over, P1-3–P1-4
juvenile delinquency proceedings, similarities with, 5-2
Kellogg Foundation grants to abuse and neglect intervention programs, 4-5–4-6
Kent County (Michigan) early intervention model, 4-5
oversight requirements, juvenile court, 4-3
post-dispositional review hearings, 5-2
predictions for, 40-7
proceedings, reforming. *See* Court Improvement Project (CIP)
processing times for, 5-2–5-3, 5-7
RAFT program, 4-4–4-5
statistics, 4-2
tribal courts, hearings by, P7-2

Accelerated Citation Program, Sacramento (California), 19-3

ACLU. *See* American Civil Liberties Union (ACLU)

Adams County (Brighton, Colorado) family court, P6-11

Adjudication
disposition and, bifurcation of, 21-5
predisposition report (PDR) investigation, initiation of, 22-3–22-4

Admissions decision
authority over, parties with, P3-1
families' perspectives, P3-2
interested parties in, P3-2
juveniles' perspectives, P3-2
management of, P3-6
statutory criteria, P3-3–P3-4
victims' perspectives, P3-2

Adolescent girls. *See also* Females
sexual matters, walk-ins into Denver juvenile court to address, 1-3–1-4

Adolescents, federal officials urging treatment of, 3-4

Adoption
GAO study on, 5-7
increasing rates of, federal funding for, 5-4
opportunities for, increasing, 5-3
permanency hearings expediting opportunities for, 5-3
state actions furthering, 5-5
tax credits for, 5-5
2002, goals for, 5-4

Adoption and Safe Families Act, 5-7

Adoption Assistance and Child Welfare Act of 1980, 4-3

Adult courts, transfer of juveniles to, 40-6

Adult prisons, juveniles in, P2-3–P2-5

African-Americans, overrepresentation of. *See* Minority overrepresentation

Aftercare
Colorado's management of, 38-4
concerns surrounding, P5-13–P-15
criticisms of, 38-4
early post-release planning, coordination of institutionalization with, 38-5
IJA-ABA standard for, 38-2
maximum term lengths, P2-6
NAC standard for, 38-2
national standards for, 38-2
North Carolina juvenile code provisions, 12-7
Ohio Department of Youth Services (DYS) management of, 38-3–38-4
President's Commission on Law Enforcement and Administration of Justice report on, 38-1
probation, distinguished from, 38-1
programs, delivery of, 38-4–38-6
Project IMPACT parole/aftercare officers, 32-6

Aftercare, continued
   reoffenses, handling of, 38-6
   states' institutional release mechanisms, 38-
      2–38-4
   violations, handling of, 38-6
   Virginia Community Assessment Team
      (CAT), 38-5–38-6

Age maximums for juvenile courts, P1-1–P1-2

Aggravated juvenile offender, legislative control
   over sentencing of, P5-2

Alcohol screening as factor in detention decisions, P3-6

Allegheny County (Pittsburgh, Pennsylvania)
   model of school-based probation services,
      24-3–24-9
   case plans developed by probation officers,
      24-4
   concerns, 24-6–24-8
   expansion of, 24-8
   group leaders, probation officers as, 24-5
   intake screenings, 24-4–24-5
   program objectives, 24-5–24-6
   Student Assistance Teams, 24-5
   violence in, 24-3–24-4

Alternative schools as probation add-on, P3-16

Altschuler, David, 38-4

Amenability hearings, P1-2–P1-3

American Bar Association (ABA)
   Institute of Judicial Administration-American
      Bar Association (IJA-ABA)
      Standards, 40-2
      aftercare, for, 38-2
   Juvenile Justice Center, 35-9
   Juvenile Law Center (JLC)/Youth Law
      Center (YLC) collaborative survey on
      defense attorneys, 15-2, 15-4

American Civil Liberties Union (ACLU), 2-3

American Society of Criminology, 3-3

AMI. *See* Associated Marine Institutes (AMI)

Amnesty International, P7-7, P7-10

Annie E. Casey Foundation, P1-6
   Detention Initiative, 9-5, 9-8
   Georgia detention strategy, support for,
      36-3–36-4
   Sacramento (California) detention-control
      initiative, 19-2
   Tallulah Correctional Center for Youth
      (TCCY), 35-9

Appeals of decisions
   defense attorneys, initiation by, P2-10
   Gault, In re, 2-3–2-4

Arizona
   detention issues, 18-7
   judicial authority, delegation of, 18-7
   RAFT program, 4-4–4-5

Armstrong, Troy, 38-4

Arrest rates, P1-3, PS-1–PS-2

Associated Marine Institutes (AMI), P4-5–P4-6

Attendant care network, North Dakota, 17-3–
   17-4

Attorneys
   California. *See* California
   child welfare agencies, for, 5-6
   court-appointed private attorneys, 15-2
   defense attorneys. *See* Defense attorneys
   dual representation in California cases,
      6-4–6-5
   family-retained private attorneys, 15-2
   hearing officer, as, P2-11–P2-12
   juvenile proceedings, role in, 2-8
   North Carolina juvenile code, rights under,
      12-3
   predisposition reports and, P2-10–P2-11
   public defenders, 15-2
   use of, P2-9
   review hearings, representation at, 5-5–5-6
   right to. *See* Counsel, right to
   roles of, P2-9

B

Bail, juveniles right to, P3-4

Balanced and Restorative Justice (BARJ), P1-8,
   P4-12–P4-14, 20-10
   applications of, P4-13
   Dakota County (Minnesota). *See* Dakota
      County (Minnesota) restorative justice
      program
   focus of, 26-1
   Fulton County (Georgia) Juvenile Court
      Probation Department, adoption of
      principles by, 23-4
   Montana CorpsLINK program links with,
      29-4–29-5
   Nashville (Tennessee) reduction program,
      25-7
   Pennsylvania, 24-3
   probation departments, suggestions for, P-14
   victim-offender mediation, P4-13

victims, focus on, P4-13–P-14

BARJ. See Balanced and Restorative Justice (BARJ)

The Beast (Lindsey), 1-6

Bend (Oregon) approach to coordination in family court. *See* Family court

Berlin, Karen, 20-8

BEST. *See* Boulder Enhanced Supervision Team (BEST)

Betts v. Brady, 2-5

Bias, use of risk assessment scales for, 9-5

Blueprint programs, P4-11–P4-12

Blue Ridge Institute for Southern Juvenile Court Judges, 2-1–2-2

Boot camps, P4-9, 3-5
   Delaware County (Ohio) court, 33-3
   evaluations of, P4-12
   physical abuse in, P5-11
   reductions in numbers of, P5-11

Bosenbroek, Dean C., 28-7

Boulder (Colorado) Project IMPACT. *See* Project IMPACT

Boulder Enhanced Supervision Team (BEST), 32-6

Boulder Prep, 32-7

Brazil
   human rights issues, P7-7–P7-8
   juvenile court system, P7-7–P7-8

Breed v. Jones, 14-3–14-4
   due process, P6-2

Brown, Victor G., 23-4, 23-8

Budgets, state, 3-5

Burden of proof
   application of, P2-6
   Winship, In re. See Winship, In re

Bureau of Justice Statistics (BJS) data on juveniles in adult prisons, P2-3–P2-4

C

C. B., R. B., T. C., R. C., S. C., et al., In re, 35-6

CABs. *See* Community accountability boards (CABs)

CACs. *See* Community assessment centers (CACs)

California
   attorneys
      dual representation by attorneys in, 6-4–6-5
      role of, 6-4–6-5
      workload standards for, 6-5
   Beyond the Bench IX Conference, 6-1–6-3
   case filings, reductions in, 6-6, 6-7
   dual representation by attorneys in, 6-4–6-5
   family group conferences, 6-6
   foster care drift
      case management intervention, integration of, 6-2
      child protection and services, assessment of California's, 6-1–6-2
      interagency cooperation, 6-2–6-3
      slow case movement, targeting of, 6-3–6-4
      statistics, 6-1
   Fresno County measures for dealing with truancy, 8-5
   group homes, 31-1–31-2
   institutional placements, financial incentives provided for, 37-2
   judges and attorneys, workload standards for, 6-5
   juvenile justice process
      collaboration to speed up, 6-1–6-4
      interagency cooperation, 6-2–6-3
      paperwork, streamlining, 6-4
      petition reduction measures, 6-6
      scheduling issues, 6-3–6-4
      shortcomings, 6-1–6-4
      slow case movement, targeting of, 6-3–6-4
   minority overrepresentation, Santa Cruz County approach to reduce, 9-3–9-6
   one family/one judge goal, 6-5–6-6
   petition reduction measures, 6-6
   probation camps, P4-6–P4-7
   Sacramento, detention center overcrowding addressed by. *See* Sacramento (California) detention center overcrowding initiative
   Santa Clara County neighborhood accountability boards (NABs), 20-1–20-10
   Santa Cruz. *See* Santa Cruz County (California)
   seriously emotionally disturbed youth, "system of care" for, 31-2, 31-7–31-8
   "system of care" for seriously emotionally disturbed youth, 31-2, 31-7–31-8
   workload standards for judges and attorneys, 6-5

California Youth Authority (CYA), 10-6
  commitments to, 19-9
  dispositions to, 22-6
  juveniles committed to, charges for, 31-7
  mental health assessment findings, P5-7
  private lawsuit against, P5-11

Case flow, juvenile delinquent
  collaboration, requirement for, 21-1
  formal court processing
    disposition and adjudication, bifurcation
      of, 21-5
    fairness, effect of speed on, 21-4–21-5
    hearings, bifurcation of, 21-5
    psychological evaluations, overuse of,
      21-5
  front end
    detention, children in, 21-3
    intake process, 21-3–21-4
    police referrals, 21-2–21-3
    school offenses, 21-2
  management of, P3-13–P3-14, 21-1–21-2,
    40-6
  post-dispositional matters
    commitment wait time, reducing, 21-6
    data collection, 21-7
    dispositional placements, expediting,
      21-6
    probation services and violations, man-
      agement of, 21-5–21-6
    restitution hearings, 21-6
  scheduling
    calendar management, 21-4
    continuances, 21-4

Case law
  Betts v. Brady, 2-5
  Breed v. Jones, P6-2, 14-3–14-4
  C. B., R. B., T. C., R. C., S. C., et al., In re,
    35-6
  Christina A. v. Bloomberg, P5-10
  Corey, In re, 44-4
  E.R., A.W., et al., v. McDonnell, et al., 30-2
  Gault case. See Gault, In re
  Gideon v. Wainwright, 2-5
  Johnson v. Zerbst, 2-5
  Juvenile Action No. 92-J-040, 18-7
  JV-111701 v. Superior Court, 18-6
  Kent v. United States. See Kent v. United
    States
  Laurence T., In re, P3-9
  Maricopa Cty. Juv. Action, 22-3
  Martarella v. Kelley, 2-7

Matter of Raoul P., 22-1
McKeiver v. Pennsylvania, P2-6, 2-7
Powell v. Alabama, 2-5
R.P v. State, 18-5
S. D., In re, 35-8
S. S. A Minor v. Wood, P5-1
Schall v. Martin, P3-4
Servin v. State, P2-10
Stanford v. Kentucky, P2-10
State v. R. F., 18-6
Stevens v. Harper, P5-11
Thompson v. Oklahoma, P2-10
Williams v. McKeithen, P5-11
Winship case. See Winship, In re

Case managers, P3-13–P3-14

Case processing times
  abuse and neglect cases, 5-2–5-3, 5-7
  state variations in, P2-6

Center for the Study and Prevention of
    Violence, 3-3
  Blueprint programs, P4-11–P4-12

The Challenge of Crime in a Free Society, P2-1

Chesterton, G. K., x

Child abuse. *See* Abuse and neglect cases

Child in need of protection or services (CHIPS),
    P1-4
  Wisconsin family court, cases in, P6-11–P6-12

Child in need of supervision (CHINS), 7-1

Child protection agencies, minority overrepre-
    sentation in, P1-7

Children and Young Persons Act of 1969, P7-4

Children's Court of Conciliation, 1-7

Children with special needs. *See* Special needs
    children

"Child saving," P2-1

Child welfare agencies
  attorneys for, 5-6
  shortcomings of, 5-1–5-2

Child welfare cases, minority overrepresentation
    in, P1-7

Child Welfare League of America, 35-9

CHINS. *See* Child in need of supervision
    (CHINS)

CHIPS. *See* Child in need of protection or serv-
    ices (CHIPS)

Christina A. v. Bloomberg, P5-10

Chronic offenders
early identification of, P4-10–P4-11
Philadelphia Longitudinal Study, P4-9–P4-10

Chronic truancy, 8-6

CIP. *See* Court Improvement Project (CIP)

Civil Rights of Institutionalized Persons Act
(CRIPA), P5-8–P5-10
case example, P5-9–P5-10
reform required by, P5-10
remedial measures, right to undertake, 35-5

Cleveland (Ohio) probation officer jailed for
contempt, 18-7–18-8

Clinton, William (President), 3-4

Cognitive retraining programs, P3-16

Collaboration
case flow, requirement for juvenile delinquent, 21-1
Fulton County (Georgia) Juvenile Court
Probation Department, community
with, 23-11–23-12
interagency collaboration programs
Project IMPACT. *See* Project IMPACT
Santa Cruz (California) GROW program.
See Santa Cruz County (California)
juvenile justice process, to speed up, 6-1–6-4

Collins, Marie, 43-8

Colorado
Adams County (Brighton) family court
example, P6-11
aftercare, management of, 38-3–38-4
Boulder County Project IMPACT. *See*
Project IMPACT
Boulder Enhanced Supervision Team
(BEST), 32-6
Children's Code, sentencing guidelines deter-
mined by, P5-2–P5-3
Columbine High School, 7-5
delinquent girls, Teen Quest program for. *See*
Teen Quest
Denver Area Youth Services (DAYS) agency,
30-1
Teen Quest, operation of. *See* Teen Quest
Denver detention center overcrowding,
30-1–30-2
Denver Juvenile Court. *See* Denver Juvenile
Court
E.R., A.W., et al., v. McDonnell, et al., 30-2
family court, rejection of, 39-3–39-4
"get tough" laws, 30-2

juvenile justice system. *See* Denver juvenile
court
Project IMPACT. *See* Project IMPACT
sentence-to-detention statute, 30-1
Teen Quest program. *See* Teen Quest
violation of constitutional rights, class action
for, 30-2
Work Adjustment Program, 30-1
Youth Passages program. See Youth Passages
program

Columbine High School, 7-5, 8-2

Combination prosecutor and defense counsel
joint decision-making dispositional
model, P3-15–P3-16

Combined strong judge-strong probation department dispositional model, P3-15

Community accountability boards (CABs),
10-7

Community Adolescent Programs, Inc. (CAP),
Madison (Wisconsin) Youth Restitution
Program (YRP) affiliation with, 28-1

Community assessment centers (CACs), 7-6,
PS-8

Community Assessment Team (CAT), Virginia,
38-5–38-6

Community-based intervention, Delaware
County (Ohio) program for, 33-1–33-10

Community coordinators in Santa Clara County
(California) neighborhood accountability
boards (NABs), 20-3

Community Corrections Department (CCD),
Dakota County (Minnesota), 26-2

Community hearing panel as diversion strategy,
P3-10–P3-11

Community intervention programs. *See*
Intervention programs

Community prevention interventions prompted
by violent offenses, 7-5–7-6

Community service, PS-6, 3-5
assignment of, 13-3
diversion strategy, as, P3-9
Madison (Wisconsin) Youth Restitution
Program (YRP)
placement sites, 28-5–28-6
restitution combined with, discouragement of, 28-2
Montana CorpsLINK program. *See* Montana
CorpsLINK program

Community service, continued
    North Carolina juvenile code provisions,
        12-6–12-7
    positive outcomes of, 27-5–27-7
    principles for, 27-4–27-5
    probation add-on, as, P3-16
    problems with, 27-2–27-3
    work crews, through. *See* Montana
        CorpsLINK program

The Companionate Marriage (Lindsey), 1-6

Confidentiality, ix, P2-6
    juvenile court records, 8-3

Contempt, probation officer jailed for, 18-7–18-8

Continuous Quality Improvement (CQI)
    approach, Nashville (Tennessee) proba-
    tion department, 25-1, 25-5

Cook County (Chicago, Illinois) intensive
    probation supervision (IPS) program,
    P4-4–P4-5

Corey, In re, 44-4

CorpsLINK program, Montana. *See* Montana
    CorpsLINK program

Council of Juvenile Correctional Administrators,
    performance-based standards for juvenile
    delinquency facilities set by, P5-11

Counsel, right to
    Betts v. Brady, 2-5
    Gault, In re, P2-6, 14-2
    Gideon v. Wainwright, 2-5
    Johnson v. Zerbst, 2-5
    variants in, P2-6
    waiver of, 15-1–15-2

"Count day," school funding based on, 8-2

Court administrators, P3-13–P3-14

Court-appointed private attorneys, 15-2

Court Appointed Special Advocate (CASA), 6-4
    agency, 5-2

Court clerk, importance of, P3-13

Court Improvement Project (CIP), P6-6
    changes instituted, 5-5–5-7
    extension of, 5-7
    findings of, 5-2–5-3, 5-6
    focus of, P1-7
    Iowa Year One CIP report, 5-3
    purpose of, 5-1
    state advisory committees, 5-2

Court orders, violations by status offenders of, 7-2

Courts
    mental health court, Sacramento (California),
        19-10
    truancy, Sacramento (California), 19-10

Cox, Judith, 9-3–9-4, 9-8, 31-7

Crime and Disorder Act of 1998, P7-5

Crime Repair Crew, Dakota County
    (Minnesota), 26-2

Crime victims
    client of court, as, 10-1–10-2
    decision making, role in, 10-5
    expeditious resolution of cases, 10-3
    juvenile court, role in, 10-1–10-7
    notification procedures, 10-2–10-3
    presence in court, 10-2
    restitution practices, efficacy of, 10-6
    Santa Clara County (California) neighbor-
        hood accountability boards (NABs),
        involvement with, 20-4, 20-9
    treatment of, 10-4
    victim impact statements, 10-4–10-5
    waiting areas for, 10-5

Criminal court
    misdemeanor court, shortcomings of, 40-5
    Native Americans, referrals of, P7-2
    shortcomings of, 40-4–40-5
    waivers to. *See* Waivers

Criminalization strategem, P1-3

Criminalized juveniles, PS-2–PS-3
    concerns regarding, P2-2–P2-3, P2-4
    detention options for, 18-2–18-3
    family court, handling in, P6-12

Criminal Justice Act of 1991, P7-5

CRIPA. *See* Civil Rights of Institutionalized
    Persons Act (CRIPA)

Curfew ordinances
    status offender referrals, 7-6

Curfews as detention alternative, P3-3

CYA. *See* California Youth Authority (CYA)

D

DAI. *See* Detention Assessment Instrument
    (DAI)

Dakota County (Minnesota) restorative justice
    program, 26-1–26-8
    Community Corrections Department (CCD),
        26-2
    guide, 26-7

Crime Repair Crew, 26-2

dispositions, elements of, 26-4

diversion of cases by prosecutors, 26-3–26-4

Family Group Conferencing (FGC), 26-2–26-3

intensive day treatment/institutional alternative program, 26-7

mission statement, 26-1–26-2

New Chance program, 26-7

Probation Service Center, 26-6–26-7

victim/offender meetings (VOMs), 26-5–26-6

Victim Restitution Fund, 26-4, 26-5

Youth RePay Program, 26-4–26-5

The Dangerous Life (Lindsey), 1-6

DAYS. *See* Denver Area Youth Services (DAYS) agency

Decision making, role of crime victims in, 10-5

Decline hearings, P1-2–P1-3

Defense attorneys, 15-1–15-6

American Bar Association (ABA)/Juvenile Law Center (JLC)/Youth Law Center (YLC) collaborative survey on, 15-2, 15-4

appeals of decisions, initiation of, P2-10

court-appointed private attorneys, 15-2

Gault, In re, impact of. *See Gault, In re*

influence of, 2-8

presence of, negative effect of, 15-3

public defenders, 15-2

use of, P2-9

role of, P2-9

suggestions from, 15-4–15-5

surveys of, 15-1–15-2

vigorous defenses by, 15-6

Dejailing,

North Dakota efforts at, 17-3–17-4

juveniles, 17-1–17-2

Delaware County (Ohio)

community-based intervention program. *See* Delaware County (Ohio) court

truancy, measures for dealing with, 8-4

Delaware County (Ohio) court

accomplishments, 33-1

commitments, reductions in, 33-3

community-based intervention program, 33-1–33-10

detentions, 33-8

dispositional orders, family members subject to, 33-8

Family Advocate Program, 33-6

family involvement, focus on, 33-7–33-8

Functional Family Therapy, 33-6

funding, 33-8–33-9

intake system, 33-5

interventions utilized, 33-3

jurisdiction, 33-4–33-5

Juvenile Sex Offender Treatment Program, 33-6–33-7

long-term judge, 33-3–33-4

operating principles, 33-4

placements, 33-8

population growth, 33-2

probation department programs

Family Advocate Program, 33-6

Juvenile Sex Offender Treatment Program, 33-6–33-7

Treatment Probation Program, 33-6

Wraparound Services, 33-7

rehabilitation, focus on, 33-2

services provided, 33-3–33-4

statistics, 33-9–33-1

Total Quality Management (TQM) approach, 33-2

Treatment Probation Program, 33-6

victim services, 33-8

vision statement, 33-3–33-4

Wraparound Services, 33-7

Delinquent youth

intensive probation intervention with, 4-4–4-5

referrals of, P3-7–P3-8

two-tier approach to, 40-3

types of, P1-4

use of term, 40-5

Denver Area Youth Services (DAYS) agency, 30-1

Teen Quest, operation of. *See* Teen Quest

Youth Passages, operation of. *See* Youth Passages

Denver Juvenile Court, 1-1–1-7

adults that harm or fail to support children, jurisdiction over, 1-5–1-6

creative dispositions, implementation of, 1-5

criminal court procedures, elimination of, 1-4

doorways into, 1-2–1-3

informal resolutions, 1-2–1-3

non-attorneys in, use of, 1-2–1-3

role of, Lindsey's view of, 1-6

sexual matters

addressing, manner of, 1-3

adolescent girls, walk-ins by, 1-3–1-4

sexual activity as moral failing, 1-4

snitching and ditching, 1-5

Department of Justice (DOJ) suit against
    Tallulah Correctional Center for Youth
    (TCCY), 35-1
Department of Social Services (DSS)
    abuse and neglect cases, role in, 4-1–4-2
    California. *See* California
Dependency, child, P1-3–P1-4, 4-2
    tribal juvenile courts hearings on, P7-2
DER program. *See* Sacramento (California)
    detention center overcrowding initiative
Detention
    alternatives to, P3-2, 9-5–9-6, 40-6
    Arizona case, 18-7
    bail, right to, P3-4
    disposition, as, 19-7
    drug/alcohol screening, P3-6
    Florida case, 18-6–18-7
    legal parameters of, P3-3–P3-4
    mental health assessment, P3-5
    North Carolina juvenile code, under, 12-4
    physical health assessment, P3-5–P3-6
    police officers, requests by, P3-7
    preventive, P3-4
    risk assessment instrument (RAI), P3-3,
        P3-4–P3-5
    Schall v. Martin, P3-4
    sentences, 19-1–19-2
    Supreme Court decision on, P3-4
Detention Assessment Instrument (DAI), 23-9
    See also Risk assessment instrument (RAI)
Detention center officials
    admission authority of, P3-1
    police officers, relationship with, P3-1
Detention centers
    admissions decision. *See* Admissions decision
    alternatives to, P3-2
    criminalized juveniles, management of, 18-3
    factors in use of, P3-1–P3-3
    geographic factors, P3-2–P3-3
    minority overrepresentation, P3-2–P3-3
    Native American-operated, 42-2
    New Mexico, 42-2
    overcrowding, P3-6, 18-3–18-5, 19-1–19-10
        Denver, Colorado, 30-1–30-2
        Ohio, 37-2
    purposes served by, P3-3
    Sacramento (California), overcrowding
        addressed by, 19-2–19-10
Detention Early Resolution (DER) program,
    Sacramento (California), 19-4–19-5

short-form report, 19-5
Detention hearings
    judicial officers, conducted by, 19-1
    prosecutors at, 14-4
    scheduling of, 18-5–18-6
    universalization of, P1-8
    weekend and holiday, 18-5–18-6
Detention intake screening, 19-1
Detention release expediter, Sacramento
    (California)
    database support, 19-4
    staff position, 19-3–19-4
Detention-risk screening instrument, 23-6
Dispositional hearings
    excerpts from, 22-7
    help provided by, 22-2
    judges opinions, 22-1
    juvenile, criminal distinguished from, 22-2
    nature of, 22-5
    orders delivered at, 22-2–22-3
    parties at, 22-5
    prosecutors at, 14-5
    statutory time spans to, 22-4–22-5
Disposition proceedings
    follow ups on, 13-6
    handling of, 13-4
    North Carolina juvenile code, radical
        changes under, 12-5–12-6
Dispositions
    adjudication and, bifurcation of, 21-5
    Dakota County (Minnesota) restorative jus-
        tice program, 26-4
    detentions as, 19-7
    economic influences on, P3-16
    El Salvador, alternatives in, 44-4
    influences on, P3-16
    juvenile blended with adult, 22-3
    models, P3-15–P3-16
    nature of, 22-5–22-6
    residential programs, to, 22-6
    rural areas, in, 22-6
    secure facilities, to, 22-3
    speeding release after, 18-4–18-5
    types of, P3-15, 22-5
Disproportionate minority confinement (DMC),
    9-1. *See also* Minority overrepresentation
    identification of, JJDPA requirement for, 9-
        2–9-3
    statistics on, PS-3–PS-4

Diversion strategies
community hearing panels, P3-10–P3-11
community service, P3-9
Dakota County (Minnesota) restorative
justice program, 26-3–26-4
data on, P3-12
neighborhood accountability boards, Santa
Clara County (California). *See* Santa
Clara County (California) neighborhood
accountability boards (NABs)
peer courts, P3-11
restitution, P3-9
strategies, P3-8–P3-11

DMC. *See* Disproportionate minority confinement (DMC)

Domestic relations courts, combination of
juvenile courts and, P6-4

Drug Abuse Resistance Education (DARE)
program, P4-11

Drug courts, PS-7
Delaware County (Ohio) court, 33-3
family, P2-13
juvenile, P2-13
Sacramento (California), 19-10
tribal. See Tribal juvenile courts

Drug screening as factor in detention decisions,
P3-6

DSS. *See* Department of Social Services (DSS)

Due process
Breed v. Jones, P6-2
Gault, In re, P6-2, 2-2, 2-4, 2-6
Kent v. United States, P6-2
Powell v. Alabama, 2-5
protections for children, states enacting, 2-7
requirement for, 2-2
Winship, In re, P6-2

E

Early case resolution, alleviation of detention
center overcrowding through, 18-4

Edna McConnell Clark Foundation, 4-4

Education, importance of, 8-1–8-2

"8% Solution," P4-10

Electronic monitoring, 3-5
Delaware County (Ohio) court, 33-3
detention alternative, as, P3-3
detention center overcrowding, alleviation of,
18-4

probation add-on, as, P3-16
Sacramento (California), 19-2–19-3

Eligible cases, determination of, P1-1

Elliott, Delbert S., 3-3

El Salvador
attorney general, powers of, 44-3
charges, filing of, 44-4
conciliation proceedings, 44-3
dispositional alternatives, 44-4
education statistics, 44-6
gang membership, 44-7
historical background, 44-1
Homies Unidos, 44-7
Institute for the Protection of Minors,
44-5–44-6
judicial process, time for completion of, 44-2
juvenile justice system
back-end procedures, 44-4–44-5
challenges facing, 44-6
front-end procedures, 44-3–44-4
proceedings, 44-4
Minor Offender Law, 44-2–44-3, 44-4
sentences, designation of judge to oversee,
44-5
Tonacatepeque facility
design of, 44-5–44-6
incarceration time in, 44-2
Institute for the Protection of Minors
responsibility for, 44-5–44-6

Emergency shelters, diversion of female population to, 19-6

Emotionally disturbed youth
statistics on, P5-7
treatment programs, P5-7–P5-8

Equal protection, P3-9–P3-10

E.R., A.W., et al., v. McDonnell, et al., 30-2

Extended Jurisdiction Juvenile Prosecutions Act
(EJJ), P2-5

F

Fairfax County (Virginia) Juvenile and
Domestic Relations Court
programs administered by, P4-2–P4-4

Family court, vii
Adams County (Brighton, Colorado) example, P6-11
affirmation of, P6-12
approaches to, P6-9–P6-10

Family court, continued
   Bend (Oregon) approach to coordination
      circuit court judges, use of, 41-2–41-3
      family court advocate, integrated treat-
         ment plans coordinated by, 41-3
      graduates, sharing of experiences by,
         41-3–41-4
      recent changes to, 41-7–41-8
      selectivity of, 41-7
   bundling cases, P6-9–P6-10
   case handling, one family/one judge, P6-8
   child in need of protection or services
      (CHIPS) Wisconsin family court
      cases, P6-11–P6-12
   Colorado's rejection of, 39-3–39-4
   coordination
      Bend (Oregon) approach. *See subhead*:
         Bend (Oregon) approach to coordi-
         nation
      levels of, P6-10, 39-4–39-5
   creation of
      concerns regarding, 39-5
      increase in, P6-4, 39-6, 40-6–40-7
   criminal offenses in, handling of, P6-12
   criteria for, jurisdictional, 39-1
   definitions of, P6-7–P6-8
   establishment of, arguments for, 39-3
   examples of, P6-10–P6-12
   general trial court, as division of, 39-2, 41-1
   Hawaii, jurisdiction of, 39-1–39-2, 39-6
   information, judicial case, and social inter-
      vention case coordination, P6-10, 39-
      4–39-5
   judicial burnout, 39-5
   La Crosse County (Wisconsin) example,
      P6-11–P6-12
   models for, 41-1–41-2
   multi-problem cases, 39-5
   one case/one judge model, 41-2
   one family/one judge case handling, P6-8, 41-7
   probation department, effect on, 39-6
   rejection of, Colorado's, 39-3
   selecting cases, process for
   databases, clerk search of families in, 41-5
      types of cases, 41-5–41-6
   simultaneous proceedings on related subject
      matter, judge's conducting of, 41-
      6–41-7
   specialist judges, 41-2
   states which have affirmed, P6-12, 39-1
   streamlining of cases, 41-6–41-7
   structuring of, 39-2

   support for, 40-2
   treatment plans, 41-4–41-5

Family drug courts, P2-13

Family group conferencing
   Dakota County (Minnesota), 26-2–26-3
   Santa Clara County program, 6-6
   New Zealand program, P7-6

Family preservation
   attorney representation, 5-5–5-6
   front-end, 4-4
   Homebuilders program, 4-4
   RAFT program, 4-4–4-5
   review hearings, attorney representation at,
      5-5–5-6

Family-retained private attorneys, 15-2

Female Opportunity for Creating Unlimited
   Success (FOCUS), 32-7

Females
   emergency shelters, diversion to, 19-6
   Georgia, female-focused programs in, 36-10
   intervention efforts, P5-6–P5-7
   juvenile justice facilities, statistics on, P5-6
   sexual matters, adolescent walk-ins into
      Denver juvenile court to address,
      1-3–1-4
   Teen Quest. *See* Teen Quest
   treatment of, P5-6

Fingerprinting of juveniles under North Carolina
   juvenile code, 12-3

Florida, detention issues in, 18-6–18-7

FOCUS. *See* Female Opportunity for Creating
   Unlimited Success (FOCUS)

Focus groups, judge-victim, 10-1–10-7

Fortas, Abe, 2-5–2-7

Foster care drift, 4-4, 5-1
   California, in. *See* California

Foster children, expediting permanent residences
   for. *See* Adoption

Foster homes, placement of sex offenders in,
   P4-8

Foster or mentor homes, 3-5

Fourteenth Amendment, 2-5, 2-6

Fresno County (California)
   Day Reporting Center, P4-8
   truancy, measures for dealing with, 8-5

Fulton County (Georgia) Juvenile Court
   Probation Department, 23-1–23-12

"A Day in Court" program, 23-7

Balanced and Restorative Justice (BARJ) principles, adoption of, 23-4

Blue Ribbon Panel recommendation, 23-8–23-9

caseloads
distribution of, 23-2
reduction of, 23-5

chief probation officer, 23-4

child protection, role in, 23-3

clerical role in deprived child cases, removal of probation officers from, 23-6

community, collaboration with, 23-11–23-12

decentralization of probation, 23-10

Detention Assessment Instrument (DAI), 23-9

detention-risk screening instrument, 23-6

graduated sanctions, accountability through, 23-9–23-10, 23-11

historical overview, 23-1–23-3

intake unit, role of, 23-2

leadership exercised by court, 23-7

mission, 23-4

neighborhoods, services in, 23-5

new intervention strategies, 23-8

performance standards, 23-6

probation officers, reporting requirements, 23-4

probation staff reassignments, 23-10

program development office, benefits from merged, 23-6–23-7

prosecution investigation function, elimination of probation's, 23-5

"put out fires" approach, elimination of, 23-6

recommendations for
report, 23-3
response to, 23-3–23-6

resource manual, 23-7

Youth Level of Service Inventory (YLSI), 23-5, 23-9

G

Gang intervention, P3-16

Gangs
El Salvador, in, 44-7
Navajo Nation, in, 43-1

Gault, In re, P1-8, P2-1, P2-2, 2-1–2-8, 14-6, 16-3, 40-1, 44-5
advocates of, 2-1
appeals of, 2-3–2-4
application of *Gault*, 2-4
changes brought by, vii, 7-1
counsel, right to, P2-6, 14-2
defense attorneys use of, 2-8, 15-1, 15-6
due process, requirement for. *See* Due process
effect of, 2-7
facts of, 2-2–2-4
informal hearings held in, 2-2–2-3
judges opposed to, 2-1–2-2
probation officer, questioning by, 2-2
reversal of, U.S. Supreme Court, 2-4
training, research, and litigation arising from, 2-7

Gender-specific correctional programs
Teen Quest. *See* Teen Quest

General Accounting Office (GAO), survey of defense attorneys by, 15-1–15-2

George, Ronald, 6-2

Georgia
arrest and dispositional patterns, study of, 36-7
Department of Juvenile Justice (DJJ), 36-1–36-12
arrest and dispositional patterns, study of, 36-7
Atlanta Journal-Constitution editorial, 36-6
challenges facing, 36-7–36-8
Comprehensive Risk and Needs Assessment (CRN), 36-10
detention reform, 36-10
detention strategy. *See subhead*: detention strategy
female-focused programs, 36-10
fresh start, critical areas for, 36-6–36-7
goal of, 36-3
group homes, 36-2
integrated classification, 36-10
Memorandum of Agreement (MOA) requirements, 36-1, 36-2
multiservice centers, 36-2
Office of Quality Assurance, 36-2–36-3
100-year plan, 36-8–36-9
profile of, 36-1–36-3
regionalization, 36-9
regional youth detention centers (RYDCs), 36-1–36-2, 36-5
residential and non-residential treatment service centers, 36-2
results-based management, 36-9
Service Development Plan, 36-11
tracking system, 36-11–36-12

Georgia, continued
    wilderness programs, 36-2
    youth detention centers (YDCs), 36-2,
        36-5
    detention strategy
        alternatives to detention
            Annie E. Casey Foundation support
                for, 36-3–36-4
            creation of, 36-4
            electronic monitoring as, 36-4
            tracking as, 36-4
        case expediters, 36-4–36-5
        Detention Assessment Instrument, devel-
            opment of, 36-4
        disposition, retention until, 36-5
        electronic monitoring as alternative to
            detention, 36-4
        tracking as alternative to detention, 36-
            4, 36-11–36-12
    Discipline Without Punishment (DWP)
        Program, 36-12
    Fulton County Juvenile Court Probation
        Department. *See* Fulton County
        (Georgia) Juvenile Court Probation
        Department
    regional youth detention centers (RYDCs),
        36-1–36-2
        closing of, federal monitor's questioning
            of, 36-5
    workforce enhancement, 36-12
    youth detention centers (YDCs), 36-2
        closing of, federal monitor's questioning
            of, 36-5–36-6

Gideon v. Wainwright, 2-5

Goal-oriented probation, PS-6

Great Britain. *See* United Kingdom (U.K.)

Group homes, 31-1
    California, in, 31-1–31-2
    Delaware County (Ohio) court, 33-3
    sex offenders, placement of, P4-8

GROW program. *See* Santa Cruz County
    (California)

H

Habitual truancy as status offense, P1-4

Hanson, Steven W., 33-9

Hard to place youth
    Sacramento (California) community place-
        ment coordinators for, 19-7

special needs children. *See* Special needs
    children

Hawaii, jurisdiction of family court in,
    39-1–39-2, 39-6

Hearing officers
    attorney as, P2-11–P2-12
    authorization of, P2-6
    role of, P2-11–P2-12

Hearings
    amenability, P1-2–P1-3
    decline, P1-2–P1-3
    juvenile court, PS-4
    Neighborhood accountability boards (NABs),
        Santa Clara County (California), 20-2
    permanency, 5-3
    rescheduling of, 6-3
    review, 5-5–5-6
    serious Case Review (SCR), 19-8
    transfer, P1-2–P1-3
    waiver, P1-2–P1-3

Homebuilders program, 4-4

Home supervision in Sacramento (California),
    19-2–19-3

House arrest as detention alternative, P3-3

House of Human Welfare, 1-8

Human Rights Watch, P7-7, P7-10

Human trackers, 19-1
    detention alternative, as, P3-3
    probation add-on, as, P3-16

I

IJA-ABA. *See* Institute of Judicial
    Administration-American Bar Association
    (IJA-ABA) Standards

Illinois
    Cook County (Chicago) intensive probation
        supervision (IPS) program, P4-4–P4-5
    Juvenile Court Act of 1899
        abuse/neglect/dependency, defined,
            P1-3–P1-4
        maximum age standards, P1-3–P1-4

Incorrigibility as status offense, P1-4

Indian reservations, tribal court systems on. *See*
    Tribal juvenile courts

Informal hearings, 2-2–2-3

In-home detention, 3-5

In-home intensive family therapy program,
    Delaware County (Ohio) court, 33-3

Institute of Judicial Administration-American Bar Association (IJA-ABA) Standards, 40-2
aftercare, for, 38-2

Institutional placements, 1-1
California, financial incentives to reduce, 37-2
control over, states', 37-1–37-2
funding of, 37-1
juvenile delinquency facilities. See Juvenile delinquency facilities
maximum term lengths, P2-6
private lawsuits, P5-10–P5-11
states, migration of funding to, 37-1

Intake officers, P2-12–P2-13
detention center admission authority, P3-1
New Mexico, authority in, 11-3
North Carolina, 12-1–12-2, 12-4
prosecutors, balance with, 40-6
role of, P2-5–P2-6

Integrated Managed Partnership for Adolescent Community Treatment (IMPACT). See Project IMPACT

Intensive probation court, Delaware County (Ohio), 33-3

Intensive probation supervision (IPS) program
Colorado, 32-7
Cook County (Chicago, Illinois), P4-4–P4-5

Intensive Teen Outpatient Program (ITOP), 32-7

Interagency collaboration programs
Project IMPACT. See Project IMPACT
Santa Cruz (California) GROW program. See Santa Cruz (California)

International Covenant on Civil and Political Rights, P2-10

International juvenile court systems, P7-4–P7-10
El Salvador. See El Salvador

Intervention programs
abuse and neglect cases
Kellogg Foundation grants to abuse and neglect intervention programs, 4-5–4-6
Kent County (Michigan) early intervention model, 4-5
Associated Marine Institutes (AMI), P4-5–P4-6
boot camps, P4-9
California probation camps, P4-6–P4-7
chronic offenders, studies of, P4-9–P4-12
Cook County (Chicago, Illinois) intensive probation supervision (IPS) program, P4-4–P4-5

delinquent youth, intensive probation intervention with, 4-4–4-5
Fairfax County (Virginia) Juvenile and Domestic Relations Court, programs administered by, P4-2–P4-4
females, for, P5-6–P5-7
Fresno County (California) Day Reporting Center, P4-8
Fulton County (Georgia) Juvenile Court Probation Department. See Fulton County (Georgia) Juvenile Court Probation Department
intensive probation intervention with delinquent youth, 4-4–4-5
Outward Bound programs, P4-6
probation programs. See Probation programs
sex offender treatment, P4-8
status offenders, effect of intervention on reduction in delinquency in, 7-4–7-5
truancy, for, 7-6
Truancy Intervention Project (TIP), 8-5
VisionQuest, P4-6, 42-1

Iowa Year One CIP report, 5-3

ITOP. See Intensive Teen Outpatient Program (ITOP)

J

Jailing
congressional ban on, 17-2
data on, 17-5
dejailing of juveniles, 17-1–17-2
rejailing of juveniles, 17-1

Japanese juvenile court system, P7-8–P7-9

JAWS. See Juvenile Alternative Work Sentence (JAWS)

JDCs. See Juvenile detention centers (JDCs)

JJDPA. See Juvenile Justice and Delinquency Prevention Act of 1974 (JJDPA)

JJPL. See Juvenile Justice Project of Louisiana (JJPL)

JLC. See Juvenile Law Center (JLC)

Johnson v. Zerbst, 2-5

Jones, Sanford J., 23-3

Judges
abuse and neglect issues confronting, 4-2–4-3
appointment or election of, P2-7
family court. See Family court
hearing officers other than, authorization of, P2-6

Judges, continued
   influence of, P3-14–P3-15
   on- and off-bench roles of, P2-8–P2-9
   probation officers and, improving working
      relationship between, 16-1–16-4
   roles of, on- and off-bench, P2-8–P2-9
   social workers and probation officers,
      coordination with, 4-1–4-2
   specialist judges, family court, 41-2
   statutes authorizing, P2-6–P2-7
   workload standards, California, 6-5
Judge-victim focus groups, 10-1–10-7
Judicial officers, detention hearings conducted
   by, 19-1
Judicial waivers, 3-2
   "proving up" party with, 3-3
Jury trials, right to, P2-6, 2-7
Justice Policy Institute, P1-6
Juvenile Action No. 92-J-040, 18-7
Juvenile Alternative Work Sentence (JAWS), 32-7
Juvenile and Family Relations Court of Denver,
   1-2
Juvenile codes
   analysis of, P2-5–P2-6
   criminalization features, P2-2–P2-3
   updating and modernizing of, P2-2
Juvenile conference committees, 20-7
Juvenile court proceedings
   California. *See* California
   case processing, time requirement, 18-3
   confidentiality of, P2-6
   defective, 2-6
Juvenile courts
   abolition of, calls for, P6-1, P6-2–P6-3,
      40-1, 40-4
   abuse/neglect/dependency jurisdiction,
      P1-3–P1-4
   age maximums, P1-1–P1-2
   agencies assisting, P4-1
   alternatives to, P3-8–P3-11
   atmosphere created, 13-2–13-3
   benefits of, viii-ix
   Brazilian system, P7-7–P7-8
   case, preparation of, P3-12–P3-13
   case flow, management of. *See* Case flow,
      juvenile delinquent
   caseloads of, P1-5–P1-6
   case managers, P3-13–P3-14
   concerns regarding, 44-1

   confidentiality, ix
   court administrators, P3-13–P3-14
   crime victims in, role for, 10-1–10-7
   current trends, ix-x
   Delaware County (Ohio). *See* Delaware
      County (Ohio) court
   delinquency jurisdiction, P1-2–P1-3
   Denver juvenile court. *See* Denver juvenile
      court
   diversion strategies, P3-8–P3-11
   domestic relations courts, combination of,
      P6-4
   eligible cases, determination of, P1-1
   emotional needs, addressing, PS-5
   environment, judge's management of, P3-
      14–P3-15
   evolution of, vii-viii, P2-1
   Extended Jurisdiction Juvenile Prosecutions
      Act (EJJ), P2-5
   hearings, PS-4
   improving, agenda for, P6-5–P6-6
   intake, P3-7, 40-5–40-6
   issues, ix-x
   Japanese system, P7-8–P7-9
   judges. *See* Judges
   jurisdictional combinations, alternative, P6-4
   Kenyan system, P7-9–P7-10
   limited resources of, 8-7
   New Zealand system, P7-6
   one-judge, benefits of, 13-6–13-7
   oversight requirements, 4-3
   predictions for, 40-1–40-2, 40-3
   problems addressed by, P4-1
   proposals for, P6-4–P6-6
   public child welfare agencies, oversight of,
      5-1
   public expectations of, P4-1
   records, confidentiality of, 8-3
   reforms to, P1-8
   reorganization of, P6-4–P6-12
   retention of, support for, 40-4
   role of, 40-3
   schools
      probation officers in Lehigh County
         (Pennsylvania) model, 24-3
      promotion of involvement with, 8-7, 24-1
      required communication between, 8-3
   separate structure, P2-7–P2-8
   serious crime, response to, 3-4–3-5
   state agency relationship, approaches to
      administrative management, P5-3–P5-4
      advantages and disadvantages of,
         P5-4–P5-5

judicial management, P5-3
    legislative management, P5-2–P5-3
threats to existence of, P6-1
tribal juvenile court approaches, application
    of, 42-5–42-6
truancy, role in solving, 8-1–8-2
unified structure, P2-7
United Kingdom (U.K.) system, P7-4–P7-5
victim impact statements, use of, 10-4–10-5

Juvenile delinquency
   defined, P1-2
   facilities
      admissions to, P5-1
      directors, roles and responsibilities of,
         P5-2
      non-profit management of, P5-13
      performance-based standards for, P5-11
      privatization of, P5-12–P5-13
      Tallulah Correctional Center for Youth
         (TCCY). See Tallulah Correctional
         Center for Youth (TCCY)
      Teen Quest. See Teen Quest
   proceedings
      abuse and neglect proceedings, similarities
         with, 5-2
      case flow. See Case flow, juvenile
         delinquent
      minority overrepresentation in,
         P1-6– P1-7
   system, drawn in for minor offenses, 8-6

Juvenile detention centers (JDCs), 17-1
   conditions in, 17-1
   youths, negative effects on, 17-1

Juvenile detention facilities (JDCs)
   North Dakota, in, 17-3

Juvenile drug courts, P2-13

Juvenile justice agency screener, admission
   authority of, P3-1

Juvenile Justice and Delinquency Prevention
   Act of 1974 (JJDPA), P6-2, 17-1
   adult jail, segregation of juveniles in, 18-2
   amendments to, 17-2
   disproportionate minority confinement
      (DMC), requirement for identification
      of, 9-2–9-3
   jailing, congressional ban on, 17-2
   proposed amendment to, 7-7
   status offenders under, treatment of, P1-4,
      P2-1, 7-2–7-5

Juvenile Justice Center, ABA

Tallulah Correctional Center for Youth (TCCY),
   35-9

Juvenile Justice Project of Louisiana (JJPL) suit
   against Tallulah Correctional Center for
   Youth (TCCY). See Tallulah Correctional
   Center for Youth (TCCY)

Juvenile justice system
   formalization of, P2-1–P2-2
   therapeutic, PS-4–PS-7, PS-8

Juvenile Law Center (JLC)/American Bar
   Association (ABA)/Youth Law Center
   (YLC) collaborative survey on defense
   attorneys, 15-2, 15-4

Juvenile proceedings
   attorneys in, role of, 2-8
   legal actors, role of, P2-2

Juveniles
   adult courts, transfers to, 40-6
   adult prisons, in, P2-3–P2-5
   bail, right to, P3-4
   criminalization of, PS-2–PS-3
   punishment of, 3-1–3-2

Juvenile sex offenders
   North Carolina juvenile code, registration
      under, 12-7
   registration of, P2-6

JV-111701 v. Superior Court, 18-6

K

Kellogg Foundation grants to abuse and neglect
   intervention programs, 4-5–4-6

Kent County (Michigan)
   abuse and neglect cases, early intervention
      model for handling, 4-5
   Day Treatment/Night Watch Program,
      3-6–3-7

Kent County Day Treatment/Night Watch
   Program, 3-6–3-7

Kent v. United States, P1-2, P1-8, P2-11, 40-1
   due process, P6-2
   facts of, 2-5–2-6

Kenyan juvenile court system, P7-9–P7-10

Ku Klux Klan, Lindsey's feud with, 1-7

L

La Crosse County (Wisconsin) family court,
   P6-11–P6-12

Latino Strategic Planning Collaborative, 9-3

Laurence T., In re, P3-9

Law enforcement agencies, referrals of delinquent youth from, P3-7–P3-8

Legislative waivers, 3-2

Lehigh County (Pennsylvania) model of school-based probation services, 24-3

Lewis, Amelia
 award bestowed upon, 2-8
 Gault case, role in, 2-3–2-4

Lindsey, Ben B., 1-1–1-8
 background of, 1-4
 California, record in, 1-7
 controversies surrounding, 1-6
 Denver juvenile court. *See* Denver juvenile court
 file burning by, 1-7
 "kids' judge," as, 1-5
 Ku Klux Klan, feud with, 1-7
 removal from bench, 1-7
 role of juvenile court, view of, 1-6
 sex education, advocate for, 1-6
 sexual matters, addressing of, 1-3–1-4

Liquor law violations, status offender referrals for, 7-6

Louden, Thomas E., 33-3, 33-9

Louisiana
 Juvenile Justice Project of Louisiana (JJPL), P5-10, 35-1
 sentencing guidelines, 35-5–35-6
 Tallulah Correctional Center for Youth (TCCY). *See* Tallulah Correctional Center

M

Madison (Wisconsin) Youth Restitution Program (YRP), 28-1–28-8
 case status, informing victims of, 28-4–28-5
 Community Adolescent Programs, Inc. (CAP), affiliation with, 28-1
 community service
  placement sites, 28-5–28-6
  restitution combined with, discouragement of, 28-2
 community service orders, 28-1–28-2
 completion rate, 28-1–28-2
 construction company, jobs provided at, 28-6–28-7
 credibility, 28-5
 inter-organizational communication, credibility aided through, 28-5

Juvenile Accountability Incentive Block Grant (JAIBG), 28-7
 payments to victims, transmission of, 28-4–28-5
 personnel, 28-8
 program counselors, assignment of, 28-3–28-4
 reasonable payments decided by ability to pay, 28-2–28-3
 referrals
  formal and informal, 28-3
  high- or low-need, 28-3–28-5
 restitution orders, 28-2
 success rate, 28-8
 work teams, expansion of, 28-7
 young clients, subsidizing restitution by, 28-2–28-3

Major Crimes Act, 42-1–42-2

Maricopa Cty Juv. Action, 22-3

Marine institutes, P4-5–P4-6

Martarella v. Kelley, 2-7

Martin, Ed, 43-8

Martinez, Orlando L., 36-3, 36-6
 credentials of, 36-6–36-7

Massachusetts
 juvenile offenders, deinstitutionalization of, P5-4
 strong-executive/weak-judge approach, P5-3–P5-4

Massachusetts Youth Screening Instrument (MAYSI), P3-5

Matter of Raoul P., 22-1

MAYSI. *See* Massachusetts Youth Screening Instrument (MAYSI)

Mazorol, Ernie, 41-7

McKeiver v. Pennsylvania, P2-6, 2-7

Mediators, schools use of, 8-4

Mental health assessment
 California Youth Authority (CYA), findings of, P5-7
 detention decisions, in, P3-5

Mental health clinics, PS-5

Mental health court, Sacramento (California), 19-10

The Mental Health Assessment and Intervention for Detained Youth Program, 32-7

Mentoring as probation add-on, P3-16

Michigan
abuse and neglect cases, early intervention model for handling, 4-5
intervention programs
abuse and neglect cases, early intervention model for handling, 4-5
Kellogg Foundation grants to abuse and neglect intervention programs, 4-5–4-6
juvenile justice law, provisions of, 3-6–3-7
Kellogg Foundation grants to abuse and neglect intervention programs, 4-5–4-6
Kent County Day Treatment/Night Watch Program, 3-6–3-7

Minnesota
blended sentencing reform, P2-5
criminalized juveniles, P2-5
Dakota County restorative justice program. *See* Dakota County (Minnesota) restorative justice program

Minor in need of supervision (MINS), 7-1

Minority overrepresentation, PS-3–PS-4, 9-1–9-9
child welfare cases, P1-7
data on, 9-1–9-2
detention centers, P3-2–P3-3
differential handling of, impact of, 9-2
factors contributing to, 9-4
juvenile delinquency proceedings, P1-6–P1-7
North Carolina juvenile code addressing, 12-6
public perceptions, 9-3
reducing, 9-3, 9-6–9-7
Santa Cruz County (California) approach to reduce, 9-3–9-6, 9-8

Minority Youth Transition Program (MYTP), Oregon, P5-14

Minor Offender Law, El Salvador, 44-2–44-3, 44-4

MINS. *See* Minor in need of supervision (MINS)

Misdemeanor court, shortcomings of, 40-5

Montana Conservation Corps, 29-2

Montana CorpsLINK program, 29-1–29-6
AmeriCorps members, use of, 29-1–29-2
Balanced and Restorative Justice (BARJ), links with, 29-4–29-5
Billings area, projects completed in, 29-5
leadership opportunities, 29-3
mentors and leaders, 29-1–29-2
Montana Conservation Corps, 29-2

operational aspects, 29-2–29-4
problems and prospects, 29-5–29-6
programs funded, 29-3
projects undertaken, 29-2
seasonal participation rates, 29-3
self-enhancement, 29-3
success story, 29-4
work requirements, 29-2

Multiethnic Placement Act, 5-4–5-5

MYTP. *See* Minority Youth Transition Program (MYTP), Oregon

N

NAC. *See* National Advisory Committee for Juvenile Justice and Delinquency Prevention (NAC)

Nashville (Tennessee) probation department, 25-1–25-7
agents of prevention, probation officers as, 25-2–25-3
Continuous Quality Improvement (CQI) approach, 25-1, 25-5
dual purpose of probation officer work, 25-2
neighborhood offices, 25-3
peer supervision of and by probation officers, 25-1–25-2
Quality Improvement Council, 25-5
recent changes to, 25-6–25-7
self-directed work teams, 25-1–25-2, 25-6
Senior Leadership Team, 25-5
truancy reduction program
changes to, 25-6
drug problems, family, 25-4–25-5
HUD grant for, 25-4

National Advisory Committee for Juvenile Justice and Delinquency Prevention (NAC) aftercare standard, 38-2

National Center for Juvenile Justice, 9-2
status offenders, data archive reports on, 7-5

National Center for State Courts (NCSC)
child protection and services, assessment of California's, 6-1–6-2
slow case movement, review of, 6-3–6-4
workload standards, California, 6-5

National Council of Juvenile and Family Court Judges' Model Courts Project, P6-6

National Council on Crime & Delinquency (NCCD) study
Teen Quest, similarities with, 34-2

National District Attorneys Association (NDAA),
    juvenile prosecution standards of
primary duty, 14-1
screening function, 14-3

National Youth Survey, 3-3–3-4

Native Americans
federal criminal justice system, referrals to,
    P7-2
Navajo Nation. *See* Navajo Nation
New Mexico Children's Code of 1993 treat-
    ment of, 11-5, 11-6
study of minorities, New Mexico, 42-5
Tribal Courts and State Courts: The
    Prevention and Resolution of
    Jurisdictional Disputes Project of the
    National Center for State Courts, 42-1
tribal juvenile courts. *See* Tribal juvenile courts

Native Rights Advocates, 42-1

Navajo Nation
Children's Code, 43-4
common law
    qualities of, 43-2–43-3
    source of, 43-2
demographics, 43-1
detention services
    limited options for, 43-5–43-6
    Western Navajo Juvenile Services
        Center, 43-5
gangs in, 43-1
Peacemaking
    balance restored through, 43-7
    courts, 42-3–42-4
    cultural approach to treatment, as,
        43-7–43-8
    examples of, 43-4
    goals of, 43-4
    judicial system, as part of, 43-3
    use of, 43-3, 43-6
    Yaa Da' Ya program, 43-6–43-7
population statistics, 43-1
probation officers, 43-5–43-6
tribal court system
    cultural values, reflection of, 43-3
    current status of, 43-8
    offenses, data on, P7-2
    Peacemaking. *See subhead*: Peacemaking
    structure of, 43-2
    vision of, 43-2
Western Navajo Juvenile Services Center,
    43-5
Yaa Da' Ya program, 43-6–43-7

youth, most common charges filed against,
    43-1

Navajo Nation Tribal Code, 43-2

Navajo peacemaker courts. *See* Navajo Nation

NCCD. *See* National Council on Crime &
    Delinquency (NCCD) study

NDAA. *See* National District Attorneys
    Association (NDAA)

Neglect cases. *See* Abuse and neglect cases

Neighborhood accountability boards (NABs)
Norfolk (Virginia), 20-6, 20-7
Santa Clara County (California). *See* Santa
    Clara County (California) neighbor-
    hood accountability boards (NABs)

New Chance program, 26-7

New Mexico
Children's Code of 1993, P2-4–P2-5,
    11-1–11-6
    Council on Crime and Delinquency,
        drafting by, P7-3, 11-3
    Native Americans, treatment of, 11-5,
        11-6
    prevention and treatment, provision of
        continuum of services stressing,
        11-3–11-5
    sentencing under, 11-6
Council on Crime and Delinquency, 11-6
    Children's Code of 1993, drafting of,
        P7-3, 11-3
criminalized juveniles, P2-4–P2-5
delinquent offender category, 11-2–11-3, 11-6
detention center, Native American-operated,
    42-2
intake probation officer, authority of, 11-3
Isleta Pueblo, handling of juvenile matters
    by, 42-2–42-3
juvenile offenders, categories of
    delinquent offenders, 11-2–11-3, 11-6
    serious youthful offenders, 11-1, 11-6
    youthful offenders, 11-1–11-2, 11-6
minorities, study of, 42-5
Native Americans, treatment of, 11-5, 11-6
Navajo peacemaker courts, 42-3–42-4
offenders, approaches to handling, 42-4–42-5
pueblo jurisdiction, 42-1–42-2
serious youthful offender category, 11-1, 11-6
study of minorities, 42-5
youthful offender category, 11-1–11-2, 11-6

New Zealand
family group conferencing, P7-6

juvenile court system, P7-6

Non-profit corporations, P5-13

Non-secure placements, commitments of juveniles to, 18-5

Norfolk (Virginia) neighborhood accountability boards (NABs), 20-6, 20-7

North Carolina juvenile code, 12-1–12-8
admissions and confessions, protections for, 12-3
aftercare provisions, 12-7
attorneys, rights to, 12-3
commitment
aftercare provisions on, affect of, 12-7
point score resulting in, 12-5
10-year olds, for, 12-6
community disposition, 12-5
court counselors, 12-4
detention
burden on state to prove need for, 12-4
for punishment, 12-4
disposition proceedings, radical changes in, 12-5–12-6
fingerprinting of juveniles, 12-3
intake probation officers, 12-1–12-2, 12-4
intermediate disposition, 12-5
jurisdictional age provisions, 12-2–12-3
juvenile offenders, point system for classifying, 12-5
"least restrictive interference," abandonment of, 12-4
minority overrepresentation, 12-6
Office of Juvenile Justice
minority overrepresentation, 12-6
role of, expansion of, 12-7–12-8
open hearings, 12-7
photographing of juveniles, 12-3
restitution and community service provisions, 12-6–12-7
reverse transfer provisions, 12-2
school notification, requirements for, 12-7
sex offender registries, 12-7
single juvenile justice entity, creation of, 12-1–12-2
status offender jurisdictional age, extension of, 12-3
training schools, commitment to, 12-5–12-6
transfer provisions, 12-2–12-3
undisciplined juveniles, jurisdiction over, 12-3

North Dakota
attendant care network, 17-3–17-4
dejailing effort in, 17-3–17-4
de minimis exceptions, full compliance with, 17-5
juvenile detention facilities (JDCs), 17-3
police lock-ups, juveniles in, 17-4

Notification procedures, crime victim, 10-2–10-3

O

Office of Juvenile Justice, North Carolina
minority overrepresentation, 12-6
role of, expansion of, 12-7–12-8

Office of Juvenile Justice and Delinquency Prevention (OJJDP), 17-1
Yaa Da' Ya program, 43-6–43-7

Ohio
aftercare, management of, 38-3–38-4
community-based intervention, Delaware County program for, 33-1–33-10
Delaware County
community-based intervention program. *See* Delaware County (Ohio) court
truancy, measures for dealing with, 8-4
detention center overcrowding, addressing, 37-2
RECLAIM project. *See* RECLAIM Ohio project

OJJDP. *See* Office of Juvenile Justice and Delinquency Prevention (OJJDP)

Omnibus Revenue Reconciliation Act of 1993, 4-3

One case/one judge model, 41-2

One family/one judge
goal for, 6-5–6-6
model, P6-8, 41-7

Oregon
Bend approach to coordination in family court. *See* Family court
Minority Youth Transition Program (MYTP), P5-14

Out-of-home placements, PS-6
Delaware County (Ohio) court, 33-3, 33-8

Outward Bound programs, P4-6

Overcrowding
curbing, approaches to, 18-3–18-5
detention centers, in. *See* Detention centers

P

Parental rehabilitation, 5-3

Parents, working with, 13-4

PARK Program, Santa Cruz County (California), 31-8–31-9

Parole. *See* Aftercare

PDR. *See* Predisposition report (PDR) investigation

Peacemaker courts, Navajo. *See* Navajo Nation

Peer courts as diversion strategy, P3-11

Pennsylvania
 Allegheny County (Pittsburgh) model of school-based probation services. *See* Allegheny County (Pittsburgh), model of school-based probation services
 Balanced and Restorative Justice (BARJ) principles, implementation of, 24-3
 Lehigh County model of school-based probation services, 24-3
 school-based probation services
  Allegheny County (Pittsburgh) model. *See* Allegheny County (Pittsburgh, Pennsylvania) model of school-based probation services
  Lehigh County model, 24-3
 "strong judge" approach, P5-3

Permanency hearings, 5-3

Permanent placements. *See also* Adoption
 hard to place youth, 5-4–5-5
 special needs children, 5-4–5-5

Person in need of supervision (PINS), 7-1

Petitions, prosecutors, preparation of, 14-4–14-5

Philadelphia Longitudinal Study, P4-9–P4-10

Photographing of juveniles, 12-3

Physical health assessment in detention decisions, P3-5–P3-6

PINS. *See* Person in need of supervision (PINS)

Pittsburgh model of school-based probation services. *See* Allegheny County (Pittsburgh, Pennsylvania) model of school-based probation services

Placements, PS-6
 Delaware County (Ohio) court, 33-3, 33-8
 permanent *See also* Adoption
  hard to place youth, 5-4–5-5
  special needs children, 5-4–5-5

Santa Cruz County (California) GROW program
 in-home placement, 31-4
 out-of-home placement, 31-5–31-7
 Pre-Placement Screening Committee, 31-7

Plea bargaining, role of prosecutors in, 14-5

Police lock-ups, juveniles in, 17-4

Police officers
 admission authority, P3-1
 detention, requests for, P3-7
 detention officials, relationship with, P3-1
 referrals of delinquent youth, P3-7–P3-8
 schools, in, 8-3, 24-2

POs. *See* Probation officers

Post-dispositional review hearings, 5-2

Pound, Roscoe, P1-8, 3-1

Powell v. Alabama, 2-5

Predisposition report (PDR) investigation, 18-2
 adjudication, initiation after, 22-3–22-4
 detention center overcrowding, alleviation of, 18-4
 early hearings, 22-4
 expediting, 18-4
 initiation of, 22-3–22-4

Predisposition reports, P2-10–P2-11

Pregnancy
 Sacramento Birthing Project, 19-6
 walk-ins into Denver juvenile court to address, 1-3–1-4

Pre-institutional facility, detention center as, P3-3

President's Commission on Law Enforcement and Administration of Justice report on aftercare, 38-1

Pretrial detention centers, factors in use of, P3-1–P3-3

Prevention efforts, P4-2, 40-6

Preventive detention, P3-4

Prison system, state budgets and, 3-5

Private for-profit corporations, P5-12
 increase in use of, P3-16
 residential dispositions, P3-16
 Tallulah Correctional Center for Youth (TCCY), operation of. *See* Tallulah Correctional Center for Youth (TCCY)

Private residential facilities, commitment of juveniles to, 18-5

Probation
  aftercare, distinguished from, 38-1
  goal-oriented, PS-6
  intensive supervision, types of, P3-16
  maximum term lengths, P2-6
  school-based
    Allegheny County (Pittsburgh) model.
      See Allegheny County (Pittsburgh,
      Pennsylvania) model of school-
      based probation services
    Lehigh County (Pennsylvania) model,
      24-3
Probation departments
  decentralization of. *See* Nashville
    (Tennessee) probation department
  Delaware County (Ohio) court programs. *See*
    Delaware County (Ohio) court
  family court, effect of, 39-6
  Fulton County (Georgia) Juvenile Court
    Probation Department. *See* Fulton
    County (Georgia) Juvenile Court
    Probation Department
  Nashville (Tennessee). *See* Nashville
    (Tennessee) probation department
  Santa Cruz County (California) GROW pro-
    gram, collaboration between probation
    departments and mental health profes-
    sionals in, 31-3–31-5
Probation officers, P2-2, P2-12–P2-13
  contempt, jailed for, 18-7–18-8
  Gault case, questioning in, 2-2
  judges and, improving working relationship
    between, 16-1–16-4
  primary tasks of, P2-12
  school-based
    Allegheny County (Pittsburgh) model.
      See Allegheny County (Pittsburgh,
      Pennsylvania) model of school-
      based probation services
    Lehigh County (Pennsylvania) model,
      24-3
  social workers and judges, coordination with,
    4-1–4-2
Probation programs, 3-5
  California probation camps, P4-6–P4-7
  Cook County (Chicago, Illinois) intensive
    probation supervision (IPS) program,
    P4-4–P4-5
  intensive probation intervention with delin-
    quent youth, 4-4–4-5
  school-based

Allegheny County (Pittsburgh,
  Pennsylvania) model. *See*
  Allegheny County (Pittsburgh,
  Pennsylvania) model of school-
  based probation services
Lehigh County (Pennsylvania) model,
  24-3
The Problems of the Children and How the
  State of Colorado Cares for Them
  (Lindsey), 1-2
Progressive Era, vii
Project IMPACT, 32-1–32-8
  aftercare officers, 32-6
  alternatives to, 32-6–32-7
  case managers, 32-4
  case studies, 32-5
  categories of juveniles in, 32-1
  delinquent youth, effect on, 32-4–32-6
  detention, reduction in number of youths in,
    32-6
  funding of, 32-3
  goals of, 32-1
  management of, 32-2–32-3
  open door policy, 32-3–32-4
  organizational aspects of, 32-4
  parole/aftercare officers, 32-6
  placement review team, case studies of, 32-5
  pooled funding of, 32-3
  positive effects of, 32-8
  referrals to, 32-3–32-4
  single entry point into, 32-3–32-4
  transportation officers, importance of, 32-7
  wraparound service, 32-1–32-2
Proof, standard of
  application of, P2-6
  Winship, In re. See Winship, In re
Prosecutorial waivers, 3-2
Prosecutors, P2-2, 2-8, 14-1–14-7
  charges, filing of, P3-7
  detention hearings, at, 14-4
  dispositional hearings, at, 14-5
  file a case, decision to, 14-2–14-3
  front-end decision making, 14-3–14-4
  increased role of, 3-4
  National District Attorneys Association
    (NDAA), juvenile prosecution standards
    of
    primary duty, 14-1
    screening function, 14-3
  organizational problems, 14-5–14-6
  other titles for, 14-1

Prosecutors, continued
    petition for court, preparation of, 14-4–14-5
    plea bargaining, 14-5
    role of, P2-5–P2-6, P2-9, 13-5–13-6,
        14-1–14-2
    screening function of, 14-2–14-3
    terms of, 14-1
    working with, tips for, 14-6–14-7
"Proving up" party with judicial waivers, 3-3
Public child welfare agencies
    attorneys for, 5-6
    shortcomings of, 5-1–5-2
Public defenders, 15-2
    use of, P2-9
Punishment of juveniles, 3-1–3-2

R

RAFT program, 4-4–4-5
RAI. *See* Risk assessment instrument (RAI)
Reasonable doubt standard, 2-7
Reasoned and Equitable Community and Local
    Alternatives to the Incarceration of
    Minors (RECLAIM). *See* RECLAIM
    Ohio project
Reclaiming Futures Initiative, 31-9
RECLAIM Ohio project, 37-3–37-7
    alternative services, funds designated for, 37-4
    broad appeal of, 37-4
    community correction facility (CCF), 37-
        3–37-4
    community interventions, effectiveness of,
        37-5
    county officials, reaction of, 37-5
    crime rates, funding formula derived from,
        37-3
    evaluation of
        broad appeal of, 37-4
        community interventions, effectiveness
            of, 37-5
        county officials, reaction of, 37-5
        risk assessment instruments, utilization
            of, 37-5
        state institution population, 37-4–37-5
        uncertainty of funding, 37-6
    funding formula, 37-3, 37-6
    initiation and implementation of, 37-3
    local placements, charges to counties for,
        37-3–37-4
    public safety commitments, handling of, 37-3

        risk assessment instruments, utilization of,
            37-5
        state institution population, declines in,
            37-4–37-5
        subsidy approach, 37-6
        uncertainty of funding, concern of courts
            over, 37-6
Record, avoidance of juvenile, P3-8–P3-9
Reentry, concerns surrounding, P5-13–P5-15
Referrals
    delinquent youth, of, P3-7–P3-8
    Madison (Wisconsin) Youth Restitution
        Program (YRP)
        formal and informal referral, 28-3
        high- or low-need referrals, 28-3–28-5
Rehabilitation programs, 2-7
    parental, 5-3
Rejailing of juveniles, 17-1
    data on, 17-4–17-5
Renewing Arizona's Family Traditions (RAFT).
    See RAFT program
Reno, Janet, 3-4
Reoffense rates, P1-3
Restitution practices, 27-1–27-2, PS-5–PS-6
    crime victims, for, 10-6
    diversion strategy, as, P3-9
    Madison (Wisconsin) Youth Restitution
        Program (YRP). *See* Madison
        (Wisconsin) Youth Restitution
        Program (YRP)
    North Carolina juvenile code provisions,
        12-6–12-7
    positive outcomes of, 27-5–27-7
    principles for, 27-3–27-4
    probation add-on, as, P3-16
    problems with, 27-2–27-3
Restorative justice practices, 10-6–10-7
    impact of, 20-6–20-7
    Santa Clara County (California) neighbor-
        hood accountability boards (NABs).
        See Santa Clara County (California)
        neighborhood accountability boards
        (NABs)
Restorative Justice Program (RJP), Santa Clara
    County (California), 20-8–20-10
Reverse waiver process, P2-3
Review hearings, representation by attorneys at,
    5-5–5-6
The Revolt of Modern Youth (Lindsey), 1-3

Rieland, James, 24-8

Risk assessment instrument (RAI), 18-1, 19-1
court systems, variations across different, P3-5
factors measured by, P3-4–P3-5
Georgia detention strategy, development for, 36-4
invasive, 18-1–18-2
point systems, P3-4–P3-5, 19-1
purpose of, P3-3
required information, 18-2
Sacramento (California), 19-2

Risk assessment scales, use of, 9-5

Roedema, Jack, 3-6–3-7

R. P. v. State, 18-5

Running away as status offense, P1-4

Rural areas, dispositions in, 22-6

S

S. D., In re, 35-8

S. S. A Minor v. Wood, P5-1

Sacramento Birthing Project, 19-6

Sacramento (California) detention center overcrowding initiative, 19-2–19-10
Accelerated Citation Program, 19-3
admission criteria, 19-2
community placement coordinators for hard to place youth, 19-7
detention as disposition, 19-7
Detention Early Resolution (DER) program, 19-4–19-5
short-form report, 19-5
detention release expediter
database support, 19-4
staff position, 19-3–19-4
disposition, detention as, 19-7
drug court, 19-10
efficacy of, 19-7–19-8
electronic monitoring, 19-2–19-3
emergency shelters, diversion of female population to, 19-6
facilities, 19-9
female population, diversion of, 19-6
hard to place youth, 19-7
health and mental health issues of detained youth, 19-10
home supervision, expansion of, 19-2–19-3
judicial hearings, acceleration of, 19-4–19-5
juvenile hall population, 19-7–19-8
Proposition 21, 19-8, 19-9

risk assessment instruments (RAIs), development of, 19-2
Serious Case Review (SCR) hearing, 19-8
transfer cases
criminal court transfers, juvenile court settling, 19-6–19-7
targeting of, improved, 19-6
truancy court, 19-10
youth profile, 19-10

Santa Clara County (California) neighborhood accountability boards (NABs), 20-1–20-10
case study, 20-1–20-2
community coordinators, 20-3
community members, endorsements from, 20-5
components of, 20-7–20-8
county officials, support from, 20-6
expansion of, 20-2–20-4
hearing, 20-2
neighborhood-focused sanctions, 20-4
Probation Community Workers, 20-9
program update, 20-8–20-10
restorative justice
celebrating, 20-4–20-6
major component of, as, 20-2–20-4
priorities, 20-4–20-5
victim involvement, 20-4, 20-9
Victim Services Coordinator Probation Officer, 20-9
youth intervention workers, 20-3–20-4, 20-5, 20-9

Santa Clara County (California) Restorative Justice Program (RJP), 20-8–20-10

Santa Cruz County (California)
GROW program, 31-2–31-9
changes and enhancements to, 31-8–31-9
compliance, monitoring, 31-4
drug treatment groups, 31-4
failed case, example of, 31-6
Family Preservation Program, 31-8
in-home placement, 31-4
interagency services, integration of, 31-4
monetary savings, 31-3
out-of-home placement, 31-5–31-7
positive results, 31-3
Pre-Placement Screening Committee, 31-7
probation department, collaboration between mental health professionals and, 31-3–31-5
recidivism, 31-8

Santa Cruz County (California), continued
    Redwoods program, 31-5–31-7, 31-9
    reoffenses by juveniles, 31-4
    success story, 31-5
    treatment options, 31-4
    violations, 31-4
    minority overrepresentation, approach to
        reduce, 9-3–9-6, 9-8
    PARK Program, 31-8–31-9
    Reclaiming Futures Initiative, 31-9
    truancy, measures for dealing with, 8-4–8-5

Schall v. Martin, P3-4

School-based probation services
    Allegheny County (Pittsburgh, Pennsylvania)
        model. *See* Allegheny County
        (Pittsburgh, Pennsylvania) model of
        school-based probation services
    Lehigh County (Pennsylvania) model, 24-3

School delinquency, reliance on juvenile court
    for solving, 8-1–8-4

Schools
    court-involvement with, promotion of, 8-7,
        24-1
    courts and, required communication between,
        8-3
    mediators, use of, 8-4
    police officers in, 8-3, 24-2
    teachable moments, 8-3–8-4
    truancy. *See* Truancy
    violence in, 8-2–8-3

SCR. *See* Serious Case Review (SCR) hearing

Screening procedures
    detention center overcrowding, alleviation of,
        18-3
    prosecutors, function of, 14-2–14-3

Seals, James H., interview with, 13-1–13-8

Sentence-to-detention statutes, 30-1

Serious Case Review (SCR) hearing, 19-8

Serious crime, juvenile courts' response to,
    3-4–3-5

Seriously emotionally disturbed youth
    California "system of care" for, 31-2, 31-
        7–31-8
    Santa Cruz County (California) GROW pro-
        gram. *See* Santa Cruz County
        (California)

Servin v. State, P2-10

Sex education, Judge Lindsey as advocate for,
    1-6

Sex offender court, Delaware County (Ohio),
    33-3

Sex offenders, juvenile
    foster or group homes, placement in, P4-8
    intervention programs, P4-8
    North Carolina juvenile code, registration
        under, 12-7
    registration of, P2-6

Sexual matters addressed by Lindsey's Denver
    juvenile court, 1-3–1-4

Shipman-Hamblin, Laura, 34-8

Social workers
    abuse and neglect cases, role in, 4-1–4-2
    probation officers and judges, coordination
        with, 4-1–4-2

Sonoma County (California) Probation Camp,
    P4-6–P4-7

Specialist judges, 41-2

Special needs children
    Idaho Department of Juvenile Corrections
        report, P5-5
    permanent placements for, 5-4–5-5

Standard of proof
    application of, P2-6
    Winship, In re. See Winship, In re

Stanford v. Kentucky, P2-10

State budgets, 3-5

State institutions. See Juvenile delinquency
    facilities

State v. R.F., 18-6

Status offenders
    community assessment centers (CACs), 7-6
    court orders, violations of, 7-2
    curfew ordinances, effect of, 7-6
    decriminalization of, 7-1
    delinquency, effect of intervention on reduc-
        tion in, 7-4–7-5
    delinquency sanctions, imposition of, 7-2
    intervention with, effect of, 7-4–7-5
    Juvenile Justice and Delinquency Prevention
        Act of 1974 (JJDPA), treatment under.
        See Juvenile Justice and Delinquency
        Prevention Act of 1974 (JJDPA)
    large urban environment, management in,
        7-3–7-4
    liquor law violations, 7-6
    national statistics, 7-5
    North Carolina juvenile code, extension of
        jurisdictional age under, 12-3

referrals of, 7-2–7-4, 7-5–7-6
secure detention of, P1-4–P1-5, 7-1–7-7
treatment of, changing, 7-1–7-2

Status offenses, P1-4–P1-5
referrals of, 7-2–7-4
tribal courts, hearings by, P7-2

Stevens v. Harper, P5-11

Strong judge dispositional model, P3-15

Strong probation department dispositional
model, P3-15

Strong prosecutor dispositional model, P3-15

Substance abusing youth, PS-7
treatment programs for, P5-8

Supreme Court, United States
Betts v. Brady, 2-5
Gault case, reversal of, 2-4
Johnson v. Zerbst, 2-5
Powell v. Alabama, 2-5

Swanson Correctional Center for Youth-
Madison Parish (Louisiana), 35-9

"System of care" model for seriously emotionally
disturbed youth, 31-2
data on, 31-7–31-8

T

"Taken into custody," P3-8–P3-9

Tallulah Correctional Center for Youth (TCCY),
35-1–35-9
branches of government, requirement for
communication between, 35-7
brutality and neglect at, 35-1
constitutional rights, violations of, 35-3, 35-8
current problems, 35-6
Department of Justice (DOJ) suit against,
35-1, 35-2
facilities, investigations of, 35-4–35-5
life threatening conditions, discovery of,
35-4
remedial measures proposed, 35-5
facilities
DOJ investigations of, 35-4–35-5
types of, 35-1
financial dealings, concerns regarding, 35-2,
35-4
improvements made at, 35-6
Juvenile Justice Project of Louisiana (JJPL)
suit against, P5-10, 35-1
abusive and demeaning practices, 35-3

complaints by residents, 35-2–35-3
defendants, 35-2
excessive force, incidents of, 35-3
financial dealings, 35-4
Mental Health Association (MHA) of
Louisiana, concerns raised by,
35-2–35-3
punitive isolation, incidents of, 35-3
remedial measures proposed, 35-5
life threatening conditions, DOJ discovery of,
35-4
mental health care, DOJ discovery of deficient, 35-5
monitoring of, 35-7
New York Times articles on, 35-1–35-2
remedial measures, DOJ and JJPL proposed,
35-5
renaming of, 35-9
Swanson Correctional Center for Youth-
Madison Parish, renamed to, 35-9

TCCY. *See* Tallulah Correctional Center for
Youth (TCCY)

Teen courts as diversion strategy, P3-11

Teen Quest, 34-1–34-8
admissions, concerns about, 34-6
aftercare, concerns about, 34-6
art therapy group, 34-5
assessment of, 34-7
challenges facing, 34-6–34-7
demographics of residents, 34-2, 34-8
focus of, 34-1
group activities, 34-8
health and fitness, focus on, 34-5–34-6
increase in population, 34-7
job skill training, 34-6
offenses committed by residents
California females, similarities with,
34-2
description of, 34-1
National Council on Crime &
Delinquency (NCCD) study, similarities with, 34-2
types of, 34-2
physical fitness curriculum, 34-6
school and family counseling, 34-5
staff turnover, concerns about, 34-6–34-7
treatment approach
accountability, focus on, 34-3
gender-specific programming, 34-3–34-5
relapse model, 34-3
treatment needs, 34-2–34-3

Tennessee
Nashville probation department. *See*
Nashville (Tennessee) probation
department

Texas Youth Commission (TYC) report on emotionally disturbed youth, P5-7–P5-8

Therapeutic juvenile justice, PS-4–PS-7, PS-8

Thompson v. Oklahoma, P2-10

TIP. *See* Truancy Intervention Project (TIP)

Total Quality Management (TQM) approach of
Delaware County (Ohio) court, 33-2

Town, Michael, 39-6

Tracking delinquent youth as alternative to
detention, 36-4, 36-11–36-12

Training schools
North Carolina juvenile code commitment to,
12-5–12-6
private lawsuit against, P5-10

Transfer hearings, P1-2–P1-3
North Carolina juvenile code, under, 12-2–
12-3
Sacramento (California) detention center
overcrowding initiative, 19-6–19-7

Treatment plans, family court development of,
41-4–41-5

Tribal Courts and State Courts: The Prevention
and Resolution of Jurisdictional Disputes
Project of the National Center for State
Courts, 42-1

Tribal juvenile courts
abuse and neglect cases, hearings of, P7-2
dependency cases, hearings of, P7-2
detention procedures, 42-2
drug courts, P7-1
full faith and credit or comity, granting of,
P7-3
jurisdictional limitations, P7-1–P7-2
Navajo Nation juvenile court. *See* Navajo
Nation
New Mexico, in. *See* New Mexico
offenders, approaches to handling, 42-4–42-5
orders, granting of full faith and credit or
comity to, P7-3
Public Law 280, effect on jurisdictional
powers of, P7-1–P7-2
pueblo jurisdiction, 42-1–42-2
resources of, P7-1

status offenses, hearings of, P7-2
system, overview of, 42-1–42-2
U.S. juvenile courts, application of approaches
to, 42-5–42-6
Yakama Nation juvenile court data, P7-2

Truancy, PS-7
approaches to dealing with, 8-4–8-7
chronic truancy, 8-6
community prevention interventions for, 7-6
court-related special programs, 8-5
crimes committed and, 8-2
Delaware County (Ohio) measures for dealing with, 8-4
detention for, 8-6
Fresno County (California) measures for
dealing with, 8-5
habitual truancy as status offense, P1-4
hearings, costs associated with, 8-5–8-6
Lindsey's interpretation of, 1-2
Nashville (Tennessee) reduction program.
See Nashville (Tennessee) probation
department
Santa Cruz County (California) measures for
dealing with, 8-4–8-5
solving, reliance on juvenile court for, 8-1– 8-2

Truancy court, Sacramento (California), 19-10

Truancy Intervention Project (TIP), 8-5

Tutoring as probation add-on, P3-16

TYC. *See* Texas Youth Commission (TYC)

U

U.K. *See* United Kingdom (U.K.)

Undisciplined juveniles, North Carolina juvenile
code jurisdiction over, 12-3

Unified court systems, P2-7

United Kingdom (U.K.)
Children and Young Persons Act of 1969,
P7-4
juvenile court system, P7-4–P7-5

United Nations Convention on the Rights of the
Child, P2-10, P7-8, P7-9, 44-6

United States Supreme Court. *See* Supreme
Court, United States

Urinalysis, 3-5

U.S. Indian Child Welfare Act, P7-4

Utter, David, 35-8

V

Victim impact panels, 10-6–10-7

Victim impact statements, juvenile court use of, 10-4–10-5

Victim-offender dialogues, 10-6

Victim/offender meetings (VOMs), Dakota County (Minnesota) restorative justice program use of, 26-5–26-6

Victims of crime. See Crime victims

Violence, PS-1, 3-1
  increase in, community prevention interventions prompted by, 7-5–7-6
  National Youth Survey on, 3-3–3-4
  schools, in, 8-2–8-3

Virginia
  aftercare, community-institutional connection for, 38-5–38-6
  Community Assessment Team (CAT), 38-5–38-6
  Fairfax County Juvenile and Domestic Relations Court, programs administered by, P4-2–P4-4

VisionQuest, P4-6, 42-1

W

W. Haywood Burns Institute, P1-6

Waiting areas for crime victims, 10-5

Waiver hearings, P1-2–P1-3

Waivers, 3-1
  criminal court, to, 3-1–3-2
  impact of, 3-3
  judicial, 3-2
  legislative, 3-2
  prosecutorial, 3-2
  reverse, P2-3
  right to counsel, 15-1–15-2

Wells, Jim, 25-6

"What works" studies, P4-10–P4-11

Wilderness Work Camp, 32-7

Williams v. McKeithen, P5-11

Winship, In re
  due process, P6-2
  standard of proof, P1-8, P2-6, 2-7

Wisconsin
  child in need of protection or services (CHIPS), P1-4, P6-11–P6-12
  La Crosse County family court example, P6-11–P6-12
  Madison Youth Restitution Program (YRP). *See* Madison (Wisconsin) Youth Restitution Program (YRP)

Wolfgang Philadelphia cohort study, PS-5

Work crews, community service through. *See* Montana CorpsLINK program

Wraparound services
  Delaware County (Ohio) court, 33-3, 33-7
  project IMPACT, 32-1–32-2

Y

Yaa Da' Ya program, 43-6–43-7

Yakama Nation juvenile court data on offenses, P7-2

Yazzie, Robert, 43-2–43-3

YINS. *See* Youth in need of supervision (YINS)

YLC. *See* Youth Law Center (YLC)

YLSI. *See* Youth Level of Service Inventory (YLSI)

Youth courts as diversion strategy, P3-11

Youth in need of supervision (YINS), 7-1

Youth intervention workers. *See* Santa Clara County (California) neighborhood accountability boards (NABs)

Youth Law Center (YLC), P1-6, 9-1, 9-8
  Juvenile Law Center (JLC)/American Bar Association (ABA)/collaborative survey on defense attorneys, 15-2, 15-4

Youth Level of Service Inventory (YLSI), 23-5, 23-9

Youth Passages program, 30-1–30-6
  case managers, 30-3
  closing of, 30-6
  community service requirement, 30-4
  DAYS programs, utilization of other, 30-4
  duration of, 30-3
  evaluation of, 30-5
  experiential learning, 30-5
  expulsion from program, 30-5
  family participation, 30-4
  future outlook of, 30-6
  individualized treatment plans, 30-3–3-4
  non-program time, monitoring of, 30-4
  operational aspects of, 30-3–30-5
  participants, demographics of, 30-3
  rewards, 30-5

Youth Passages program, continued
  rules, 30-5
  school operated by, 30-4
  strategies, 30-4–30-5
  transitional counselors, 30-3
  violations, 30-5
Youth Restitution Program (YRP). *See* Madison
    (Wisconsin) Youth Restitution Program
    (YRP)
YRP. *See* Madison (Wisconsin) Youth
    Restitution Program (YRP)

Z
Zero tolerance policies, 8-2–8-3
Zion, James W., 43-3